KU-254-774

PERSONALITY THEORIES

An Introduction

EIGHTH EDITION

Barbara Engler
Union County College

WADSWORTH
CENGAGE Learning™

Australia • Brazil • Japan • Korea • Mexico • Singapore • Spain • United Kingdom • United States

LEARNING CENTRE
C. C. SALTASH
CLASS
ACC No.
DATE   CHECKED

WADSWORTH
CENGAGE Learning

Personality Theories: An Introduction, Eighth Edition
Barbara Engler

Executive Publisher: George Hoffman

Senior Sponsoring Editor: Jane Potter

Marketing Manager: Amy Whittaker

Discipline Product Manager: Damaris Curran

Development Editor: Katherine C. Russillo

Project Editor: Aimee Chevrette Bear

Senior Media Producer: Nancy Hiney

Content Manager: Rachel Wimberly

Art and Design Manager: Jill Haber

Cover Design Director: Tony Saizon

Senior Photo Editor: Jennifer Meyer Dare

Senior Composition Buyer: Chuck Dutton

Marketing Assistant: Samantha Abrams

Editorial Assistant: Laura Collins

Cover images: (top left) © Kevin Fitzgerald/Getty Images; (top middle) © Annabelle Breakey/Getty Images; (top right) © ThinkStock/Superstock; (bottom left) © Ryan McVay/Getty Images; (bottom middle) © Dimitri Vervitsiotis/ Getty Images; (bottom right) © Age fotostock/Superstock.

Photo credits appear on page 554, which constitutes an extension of the copyright page.

© 2009 Wadsworth, Cengage Learning

ALL RIGHTS RESERVED. No part of this work covered by the copyright herein may be reproduced, transmitted, stored or used in any form or by any means graphic, electronic, or mechanical, including but not limited to photocopying, recording, scanning, digitizing, taping, Web distribution, information networks, or information storage and retrieval systems, except as permitted under Section 107 or 108 of the 1976 United States Copyright Act, without the prior written permission of the publisher.

For product information and technology assistance, contact us at **Cengage Learning Customer & Sales Support, 1-800-354-9706**

For permission to use material from this text or product, submit all requests online at **www.cengage.com/permissions**
Further permissions questions can be emailed to **permissionrequest@cengage.com**

Library of Congress Control Number: 2008931612

ISBN-13: 978-1-4266-4865-6

ISBN-10: 1-4266-4865-0

Wadsworth
10 Davis Drive
Belmont, CA 94002
USA

Cengage Learning is a leading provider of customized learning solutions with office locations around the globe, including Singapore, the United Kingdom, Australia, Mexico, Brazil, and Japan. Locate your local office at **international.cengage.com/region**

Cengage Learning products are represented in Canada by Nelson Education, Ltd.

To learn more about Wadsworth, visit **www.cengage.com/wadsworth**

Purchase any of our products at your local college store or at our preferred online store **www.ichapters.com**

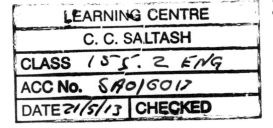
LEARNING CENTRE
C. C. SALTASH
CLASS 155. 2 ENG
ACC No. SA0/6017
DATE 21/5/13 | CHECKED

Printed in the United States of America
3 4 5 6 7 11 10

Learning Centre
C C Saltash

PERSONALITY THEORIES

WITHDRAWN

SA016017

CORNWALL COLLEGE

To my sons, Ted and Bill

BRIEF CONTENTS

CONTENTS

PREFACE

Like its predecessors, the Eighth Edition of *Personality Theories: An Introduction* provides accurate and thorough coverage of personality theories in an easily accessible text enhanced by pedagogical features intended to stimulate critical thinking. In this edition, as in earlier ones, I have worked to achieve these four objectives:

1. *To present a clear and concise picture of the major features of each theory.* I have strived to present the material in an approachable style and, wherever possible, to illustrate theoretical points with concrete examples. I have presented each theory succinctly, to allow for adequate coverage of all the theories. Each chapter focuses on one theory or group of related theories. Brief biographies of the major theorists shed light on how they formed their theories.

2. *To focus on significant ideas and themes that structure the content of the theories.* I regularly compare theories to outline the distinctive characteristics and contributions of each theory and to emphasize significant ideas around which the theories are structured. Because many theories have elaborated on, modified, or refuted psychoanalysis, I have devoted substantial space to Freudian theory, providing the reader with a focal point from which comparisons and contrasts may be made.

3. *To provide criteria to guide the evaluation of each theory.* Many of the theories that influence contemporary thought did not develop from strict scientific methods but instead reflect philosophical assumptions. In addition, the application of a theory to a real-life situation such as psychotherapy is a creative act, demonstrating that a personality theory may function as an art. Therefore, the evaluation of a personality theory is best accomplished when the theory is examined from the viewpoints of philosophy, science, and art and judged according to criteria appropriate to each one. Within each chapter, two features—"Philosophy, Science, and Art" sections and "Philosophical Assumptions" boxes—refer students back to the basic philosophical assumptions introduced in Chapter 1, relating parts back to whole and drawing attention to significant ideas that have generated the structure and content of personality theories. The "Conclusion" at the end of the text wraps up the evaluation discussion.

4. *To present activities, informed by the tenets of each theory, that will stimulate critical thinking.* Effective learning is not a passive process; it requires active participation. The fourth objective is accomplished through "Thinking Critically" boxes, which provide activities that foster critical thinking. This feature, introduced in the Third Edition, has proven to be very popular. Some of the activities are new to the Eighth Edition; others have been carefully reviewed and revised to provide students with a clearer context for the activity. New to the Eighth Edition is the "Personal Experiences" feature, created by Thomas Finn of Bentley College, at the end of each chapter. It consists of questions and activities designed to engage students more directly with the theories and to bridge the gap between the theories and students' lives.

Features of the Book

To help students read with a sense of purpose and review important points quickly, each chapter opens with a list called "Your Goals for This Chapter" and ends with a "Summary," whose items are keyed to each goal. Thus the goals listed at the beginning of the chapter pose questions answered in the numerated summary. Key terms and concepts are boldfaced within the text, and a glossary at the back of the book, and on the student website, provides definitions. The illustration program has been revised to include more figures and tables that help students understand technical concepts and summarize the concepts being presented. "Suggestions for Further Reading" for each chapter have been updated and placed on the website.

"Thinking Critically" activities appear in each chapter. These boxes ask students to revisit material in the chapter and reconsider it or apply it critically. The new "Personal Experiences" feature offers still another opportunity for students to thoughtfully consider the material.

The "Philosophical Assumptions" boxes (with accompanying scale on the inside back cover) give students an opportunity to compare and contrast their own philosophical views with those of the theorist at hand. Actual ratings on the scale are not provided for each theorist, because to do so might foreclose students' thinking and debate about where each theorist stands on the issues. It would invite focus on the "correct" rating of each theorist and undermine the critical thinking, discussion, and support of students' own answers, which are the goals of the activity. A timeline on the inside front cover places the theorists in the context of important historical events that occurred during their lifetimes. A table at the back of the text summarizes the theorists' primary research methods, theoretical orientations, and strengths.

New to the Eighth Edition

My revisions to the book reflect recent developments in the field of personality psychology and feedback that I received from instructors and students who used the previous edition. All content has been updated to reflect the status of current research on each theorist. Throughout, I pay considerable attention to two major emerging interests in personality theorizing: (1) the neurobiological basis of personality and (2) spiritual dimensions of personality that transcend the physical and call for broader methodologies. The text continues to emphasize multicultural, feminist, and postmodern concerns.

Highlights of the changes in the book, by chapter, include the following:

Chapter 2

- Additional material on Freud's background in neurology and belief in the neurological basis of personality.
- Discussion of the light that current neuroscientific research sheds on Freud's theory.

Chapter 3

- Discussion of Jung's pioneering efforts to explore the spiritual and interpersonal facets of personality.

Chapter 4

- Expansion of material on family therapy.

Chapter 5

- Discussion of neuroscientific research that may help us to understand terrorism by identifying neural sources of emotion, behavior, and belief, and to screen for potential aggressive behavior.

Chapter 6

- Revamping of "Thinking Critically: The Life Cycle."
- Expanded coverage of McAdams's theory.
- New: "Thinking Critically: Your Life Story."

Chapter 7

- Clarification of borderline personality disorder.
- New: "Thinking Critically: Families Today."
- Expansion of "Thinking Critically: Disconnections and Connections."
- New section on the neurobiological basis of relationships and relational cultural theory.

Chapter 8

- New opening section on the experimental analysis of behavior, to provide historical background.
- Discussion of Skinner's recognition of the role of biological processes in behavior.
- Inclusion of Arthur Staats and psychological behaviorism.

Chapter 9

- Revision of material on Bandura to focus on the transformation of his theory from an initial exploration of modeling to an agentic perspective and the change in emphasis from the importance of reinforcement to self-regulation.
- New: "Thinking Critically: Moral Disengagement and Reprehensible Behavior."
- New information on contributions of social cognitive theory for helping us develop and use new technologies in positive ways.
- Revamping of "Thinking Critically: Behavioral Signatures."

Part V

- Newly titled "Dispositional and Biological Theories."

Chapter 10

- Revision of "Thinking Critically: The Thematic Apperception Test."

Chapter 11

- Newly titled "Factor Analytic, Genetic, and Evolutionary Theories."
- Exanded coverage of behavioral genetics and evolutionary personality theories.

Chapter 12

- Expanded coverage of the biological and genetic bases of behavior and neurosis.
- Summary of new research on brain functioning.

Chapter 13

- Inclusion of information on the self-determination theory of Deci and Ryan.
- Revision of "Thinking Critically: Friendlier Arguments."
- Expansion of the table "Responses to Emotional Communications" to include consequences.
- New sections on positive psychology and transpersonal psychology.
- New: "Thinking Critically: Should Psychologists Study Spirituality?"

Chapter 14

- New: "Thinking Critically: Cultural Myths and the Media."
- Inclusion of Victor Frankl and his search for meaning.

Chapter 16

- Revision of "Thinking Critically: Using the BASIC-ID."
- New section on Stephen Hayes and mindfulness.

Ancillaries

This text is supported by *Online Study Center*, which encompasses the interactive online products and services integrated with Cengage Learning Psychology programs. *Online Study Center* is available through text-specific student and instructor websites. Many useful materials have been developed to support *Personality Theories* 8/e, emphasizing its role as an integrated teaching and learning experience for instructors and students alike. For more information, visit **college.cengage.com/pic/engler8e.**

For the Instructor

Online Study Center Instructor Website (**college.cengage.com/pic/engler8e**) includes the complete *Instructor's Resource Manual,* PowerPoint presentations, Classroom Response System content (clickers), *Personality Psych in Film* video guide, downloadable PDFs of overhead transparencies, selected art from the textbook, and feedback for the *To Learn More* critical thinking essays.

    Online Instructor's Resource Manual, revised by Andrew Pomerantz, Southern Illinois University, Edwardsville, is available at the *Online Study Center* instructor website at **college .cengage.com/pic/engler8e.** It contains lecture/discussion topics, classroom exercises, and handouts for new and experienced instructors. It is available for your convenience in both Microsoft Word™ and PDF formats. A print version is available upon request. Please consult your sales representative.

    Diploma Testing CD-ROM (powered by Diploma), revised by Andrew Pomerantz, Southern Illinois University, Edwardsville, is a flexible testing program that allows instructors to create, edit, customize, and deliver multiple types of tests via print, network server, or the Web on either Macintosh or Windows™ platforms. The test bank contains approximately 800 questions. Multiple-choice, short-answer, and essay questions are written at the chapter and learning objective levels and are labeled by type—factual or conceptual/applied. The test bank Word files are also included on the CD-ROM for easy reference. A print version is available upon request. Please consult your sales representative.

New! Enhanced PowerPoint Slides and Overhead Transparencies contain comprehensive lecture outlines and images from the textbook. These slides can be displayed in class and/or printed, and PDFs of overhead transparencies are available for your convenience. These are located on the *Online Study Center* instructor website accessible via **college.cengage.com/pic/engler8e.**

New! Classroom Response System (Clickers) content, available on the *Online Study Center* instructor website accessible via **college.cengage.com/pic/engler8e,** allow instructors to perform on-the-spot assessments, deliver quick quizzes, gauge students' understanding of a particular question or concept, conduct anonymous polling for class discussion purposes, and take class rosters easily.

Content for Course Management Software Blackboard® and WebCT® course cartridges are available, allowing instructors to use text-specific material to create an online course on their own campus course management systems. The cartridges feature all of the content described on the instructor and student websites and include *Diploma Testing.*

Personality Psych in Film DVD contains clips from Universal Studio films, illustrating concepts in personality that bring psychology alive for students and demonstrate its relevance to contemporary life and culture. Teaching tips are correlated to specific text chapters and concepts on the *Online Study Center* instructor website, which can be accessed via **college.cengage.com/pic/engler8e.**

For the Student

Online Study Center Student website (**college.cengage.com/pic/engler8e**) helps students prepare for class, study for quizzes and exams, and improve their grades. Resources include an online *Study Guide,* Study Skills material, ACE Practice Tests, flashcards, *To Learn More* Web activities, and *Practice Essays. Suggestions for Further Reading* are now available on the student website. Students who have bought a used textbook can purchase access to the *Online Study Center* website separately.

Online Study Guide offers students twenty multiple-choice questions per chapter to reinforce their reading. It is available for download on the *Online Study Center* student website.

Downloadable eBook Purchase a downloadable PDF version of this textbook directly from our eCommerce site. Please go to **college.cengage.com/pic/engler8e** for further details.

Acknowledgments

I would like to thank the following theorists for reviewing and commenting on the manuscript for the Eighth Edition: Albert Bandura, Amy Banks, Aaron Beck, Nancy J. Chodorow, Paul Costa, Judith Jordan, Otto Kernberg, Arnold Lazarus, Dan McAdams, Robert McCrae, Jean Baker Miller, Walter Mischel, and Robert Plomin.

In addition, I would like to acknowledge two special people whose help began with the Fourth Edition. Yōzan Dirk Mosig, Ph.D., a professor of psychology who has practiced Zen Buddhism for a considerable amount of time, wrote the first draft of the chapter on Zen Buddhism. The original draft that he prepared had to be cut because of space limitations, and Dr. Mosig has offered to answer any questions that readers may have on the material. He can be contacted c/o Psychology Department, University of Nebraska, Kearney, NE 68849. Nancymarie Bride, RN, LPC, a certified clinical mental health counselor in private practice in Westfield, New Jersey, and a close personal friend, gave me a great deal of information, some of which I was able to use verbatim, on Albert Ellis, Aaron Beck, and Arnold Lazarus for the chapter on those theorists.

I would also like to thank my colleagues at Union County College for their continued interest, support, and constructive comments about the text and its revision. I am especially grateful to Sian Chen, reference librarian, who patiently fulfilled my every request for abstracts, articles, information, and interlibrary loans.

The following reviewers thoughtfully evaluated the manuscript or provided prerevision advice:

Paul Bartoli, East Stroudsburg University

Eugenia Cox–Fuenzalida, University of Oklahoma

George-Harold Jennings, Drew University

Eric Miller, Kent State University

D. Cleve Mortimer, University of Central Florida

Clay Peters, Liberty University

Finally, I would like to thank the following people at Houghton Mifflin who assisted in the development and production of the Eighth Edition: Thomas Finn, Development Editor; Kate Russillo, Development Editor; Aimee Chevrette, Project Editor; and Laura Collins, Editorial Assistant.

—B.E.

PERSONALITY THEORIES

Introduction: Evaluating Personality Theories

YOUR GOALS FOR THIS CHAPTER

1. Explain why the term **personality** is difficult to define.
2. Define the term **theory.**
3. Discuss the role of personality theory in psychology.
4. Describe three orientations of personality theorists.
5. Identify some of the basic philosophical issues on which personality theorists differ.
6. Explain how to recognize **philosophical assumptions.**
7. Explain how philosophical assumptions are evaluated.
8. Explain how science has its basis in **philosophy.**
9. Explain the characteristics of **scientific statements.**
10. Explain how scientific statements are evaluated, and describe how scientists decide between rival hypotheses.
11. Describe two techniques used to assess personality and three approaches used in research on personality.
12. Identify three goals of **psychotherapy,** and indicate the criteria of evaluation suitable for each goal.
13. Explain why it is important to distinguish among the different orientations of personality theories.

Defining the word *personality* would be a good way to begin a book that considers various theories of personality. However, writing a definition is not that simple. A complete search for such a definition takes us back to the early history of the human race, back to the time when the first person asked, "Who am I?," thereby reflecting on his or her identity. The different answers that people have given to that question have found expression throughout history in various cultural constructs such as philosophy, religion, art, politics, and science. Each one of us begins the search anew; as children seeking identity, and later as adults reflecting upon our identity, we wonder who we are and join fellow travelers on the road in search of the self.

What Is Personality?

In common speech, the term **personality** usually refers to someone's public image. Thus people say, "Becky has a terrific personality!" or "If only Jeff had a more dynamic personality." This common usage reflects the origin of the word *personality* in the Latin *personae*, which referred to the masks that actors wore in ancient Greek plays. In the Greek theater, there were often more roles in a play than there were actors. Thus actors changed *personae* to let the audience know that they were assuming different roles. The concept of social roles, however, does not include the complications that are involved in the long search to understand the self.

There is little common agreement among personality theorists on the appropriate use of the term *personality* (see Figure 1.1). Gordon Allport described and classified over fifty different definitions. For Allport, personality is something *real* within an individual that leads to characteristic behavior and thought. For Carl Rogers, another personality theorist, the personality or "self" is an organized, consistent pattern of perception of the "I" or "me" that lies at the heart of an individual's experiences. For B. F. Skinner, possibly the most well known American psychologist, the word *personality* was unnecessary. Skinner did not believe that it is necessary or desirable to use a concept such as self or personality to understand human behavior. For Sigmund Freud, the father of contemporary psychoanalysis, personality is largely unconscious, hidden, and unknown.

Each theorist presents us with his or her own understanding of the term *personality*. In part, this helps to explain why there are so many different personality theories. Although such a variety of definitions and theories may be confusing and even disturbing, it does not mean that the theories are not useful. Each offers insight into the question of the self, and each can be helpful to us as we develop our own answers.

What Is a Theory?

Since we are referring to theories of personality, the next question is "What is a theory?" Here you may be pleased to see that there is a more definitive answer. The term *theory* comes from the Greek word *theōria*, which refers to the act of viewing, contemplating, or thinking about something. A **theory** is a set of abstract concepts developed about a group

WHAT IS PERSONALITY?

It is an organized, consistent pattern of perception of the "I" or "me" that lies at the heart of an individual's experiences.

Carl Rogers

It is largely unconscious, hidden, and unknown.

Sigmund Freud

It is an unnecessary construct.

It is something real within an individual that leads to characteristic behavior and thought.

Gordon Allport

B. F. Skinner

FIGURE 1.1 THE MANY VIEWS OF PERSONALITY

"Personality" is not a readily defined concept. Shown here are just some of the views of personality held by different personality theorists. As you proceed through this text and examine the work of individual personality theorists, you will discover many more different views of personality.

of facts or events in order to explain them. A theory of personality, therefore, is an organized system of beliefs that helps us to understand human nature.

Describing a theory as a system of beliefs underscores the fact that a theory is something that we create in the process of viewing and thinking about our world. Theories are not given or necessitated by nature; rather, they are constructed by people in their efforts to understand the world. The same data or experiences can be accounted for in many different ways, and people of all cultures are interested in and have engaged in the scholarly effort to understand themselves, constructing a wide variety of explanations. As we shall see, there are many theories of personality. Historically, a Western focus has dominated the formal discussion of theories of personality, but preliminary efforts are being made to attend to other perspectives, such as Asian and Afrocentric.

The Role of Personality Theory in Psychology

Because personality addresses that important question "Who am I?," you might imagine that personality is the primary emphasis of psychology. In fact, personality is not the dominant concern in contemporary psychology; it is simply one area of specialization.

The question "What is personality?" takes us back to early human history. As psychology found expression in the early philosophies of Plato and Aristotle, it sought to clarify the essence of a human being and explore what it means to be a person.

By the late nineteenth century the scientific revolution had made great strides in comprehending the physical world, and people were eager to apply scientific methods to the study of human beings. Modern-day psychology emerged from a combination of various movements in philosophy and science. In 1879, Wilhelm Wundt (1832–1920) established the first psychological laboratory at the University of Leipzig in Germany to explore the experience of consciousness. By combining careful measurement with *introspective observation,* or self-examination, Wundt sought to reveal the basic elements and structure of the conscious mind.

Wundt was successful in establishing a meticulous, systematic method of study based on the experimental method. However, his emphasis on conscious experience was criticized in the 1920s by John Watson (1878–1958), who came to be known as the father of American behaviorism. Watson pointed out that it is almost impossible to observe mental processes directly. Therefore, he suggested that the psychologist should act as if mental processes do not exist and should concentrate on overt behavior. Although few psychologists today agree with Watson's extreme view, and new brain scanning equipment gives us glimpses of the brain in action, the behaviorist position that Watson generated became the dominant movement in American psychology throughout most of the twentieth century. Watson was succeeded as leader of the movement by B. F. Skinner, who took the behaviorist position to its logical extreme. Because of Skinner's influence, students of psychology rapidly discovered that, for the most part, they were engaged not in the study of the person but in the study of behavior (usually of rats and pigeons). They were encouraged to adopt a rigorous scientific methodology that emphasized *extrospective observation,* or looking outward. B. F. Skinner's theory is discussed in greater detail in the chapter on experimental analysis of behavior.

Today, psychologists are very interested in the mental processes shunned by Watson and Skinner. Indeed, one current trend is toward cognitive psychology, which emphasizes how people receive, process, and react to information from their environment. On the other hand, psychology has retained from the behaviorists an emphasis on rigorous methodology emphasizing extrospective observation.

Not all of the personality theorists that we will consider agree that a rigorous scientific method is the best way to understand personality. In fact, the first theories of personality developed outside the mainstream of academic experimental psychology. While Wundt was at work in his laboratory at Leipzig, Sigmund Freud (1856–1939), who was *not* a psychologist but rather a neurologist and physician in private practice in Vienna, was employing introspection somewhat differently in his treatment of patients who were suffering from emotional problems. Instead of using introspection only to examine present phenomena, Freud also taught his patients to employ it retrospectively to examine past experiences. Thus Freud was able to examine phenomena that could not be elicited in a laboratory. Freud found introspection to be a valuable tool for discovering and exploring unconscious processes. On the basis of his clinical observations, Freud developed a theory of personality discussed in the chapter on psychoanalysis. Freud's method was far different from the experimental laboratory research that characterizes much of psychology today.

Some of Freud's followers became dissatisfied with orthodox psychoanalysis and founded their own schools of thought. Although these theorists were all deeply indebted to Freud, they reacted in varying ways against his theory and developed their own positions. The study of personality became a formal and systematic area of scientific specialization in American psychology in the mid-1930s, and it is most often considered to fit somewhere between social and clinical psychology. Some psychologists have recommended that all research in personality be conducted and evaluated along strict scientific guidelines as defined by mainstream academic psychology. The study of personality is the heir of two different approaches: *academic psychology* and *clinical practice* (see Figure 1.2). These traditions have never fully merged (Boneau, 1992). Examples of each are found in the theories discussed in this book.

It is also helpful to distinguish between **macro theories** of personality, which seek to be global and which emphasize comprehension of the whole person, and **micro theories,** which have resulted from specific research focused on limited aspects of human behavior. Some of the micro studies can be very narrowly focused; for example, one study explores how a specific model of personality might clarify impulsiveness (Whiteside & Lynam, 2001). Courses in personality theories tend to emphasize macro theories, and courses in personality research favor a topical (i.e., micro) approach. In general, but by no means entirely, macro theories are more likely to stem from the tradition of clinical observation, whereas micro theories reflect academic psychology.

A review of the Brief Contents at the beginning of the book will give you a good overview of the theories we will consider, most of which would be considered macro theories. We will begin with the theory of Sigmund Freud and then cover some of his early followers, as well as contemporary theorists who continue the tradition of psychoanalytic thought that Freud initiated. Next we will turn to a group of theorists who emphasize the role of

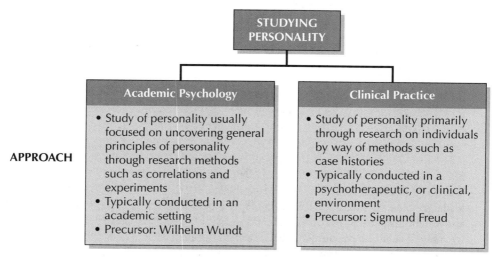

FIGURE 1.2 APPROACHES TO THE STUDY OF PERSONALITY

learning in the development of human behavior. B. F. Skinner is the most recognized among these behavior and learning theorists. We also will look at a number of other approaches to the study of personality. Gordon Allport, for example, is one of several dispositional theorists who emphasize the importance of long-term characteristics in personality. Research in that area today encompasses biology and genetics. We will discuss humanist and existential theories, which stress the tendency of the human personality toward growth, and cognitive theories, which focus on how people process information about themselves and their world. Carl Rogers and Abraham Maslow are two representatives of the humanist approach, and George Kelly and Albert Ellis reflect the cognitive approach. We will round out our presentation of personality theories with recognition of the growing importance of non-Western approaches and an in-depth look at Zen Buddhism. A table at the very back of the book summarizes the theorists discussed here.

The Evaluation of Personality Theory

Personality theorists work out of three complementary orientations: philosophy, science, and art. Theories of personality are not just armchair speculations but belief systems that find expression in ways that are designed to help us understand and improve ourselves and the world. The *art* of personality theory, or its expression in practical application, is much older than the science or even the philosophy behind it. From earliest times, much has been spoken and written about how to live a good life and to understand one another as people have practiced ways of understanding themselves and living together. Before the study of personality became a specialization of academic scientific psychology, questions of personality and the good life were generally included under the broader umbrella of *philosophy.* Even today, many personality theories resemble philosophical investigations rather than scientific studies. As the *science* of personality theory—investigations governed by appropriate rules—has developed, it has provided us with new knowledge, tools, and methods of self-understanding and improvement. Science further demands that scientific theory be empirically validated, or ultimately based on sensory experience. However, the specific mode of study and investigation characteristic of a modern personality scientist arises out of a prior philosophical encounter with the world. Science is an offspring of philosophy and its methods are the fruit of philosophy's labors. The methods of art, science and philosophy are distinguishable but not unrelated; they complement one another and together provide us with a fuller understanding.

Philosophy, science, and art may be seen as three complementary orientations from which personality theorists work. As *philosophers,* personality theorists seek to explore assumptions about what it means to be a person. As *scientists,* they hope to develop a workable set of hypotheses that will help us understand human behavior. As *artists,* they seek to apply what is known about people and behavior to foster a better life. Each activity is conducted according to certain rules with its own criteria for success. The metaphor of games is useful here because even young schoolchildren know that if we want to play a game properly and fairly, we have to understand its rules and follow them. Each activity that personality theorists engage in as philosophers, scientists, and artists may be seen as a distinct game to be conducted according to certain rules with its own methods of play and criteria for success. Just as potential athletes need to become familiar with the rules, equipment, and

Just as potential athletes need to become familiar with the rules, equipment, and scoring of whatever sport they wish to engage in, students of personality theory need to become familiar with the different rules governing personality theories to avoid getting into trouble.

scoring of their sport, so students of personality theory need to become familiar with the rules that govern how these three distinct facets of personality theory—philosophy, science, and art—work. You will have difficulty understanding a personality theorist unless you can identify the particular activity or approach that the theorist is engaged in and know how to evaluate it.

Philosophical Assumptions

No psychologist or personality theorist can avoid being a philosopher of sorts. All sciences, but particularly the "hypercomplex" social sciences (Wilson, 1999), are influenced by philosophy. The very act of theorizing, or thinking about what we see, which all people—not only personality theorists—do, entails making certain **philosophical assumptions** about the world and human nature. These basic philosophical assumptions profoundly influence the way in which we perceive the world and theorize about it.

The term **philosophy** comes from the Greek *philein,* "to love," and *sophia,* "wisdom"; it means the love or pursuit of wisdom. Wisdom denotes not merely knowing about something but knowing what ought to be done and how to do it. As philosophers, we make assumptions and judgments about the good life and how to live it.

Very few of us have complete and articulate philosophies of life, but our thoughts, statements, and theorizing are informed by our philosophical assumptions. In the same sense, very few, if any, of the personality theorists whom we will consider aim at developing complete philosophical pictures of ourselves and the world. Most consider themselves psychologists rather than philosophers. Nevertheless, in their psychologizing they raise philosophical issues and, in doing so, reflect philosophical assumptions.

BASIC PHILOSOPHICAL ASSUMPTIONS

Many of the differences among personality theories can be attributed to fundamental differences in philosophical assumptions. Some of the common issues about which personality theories disagree are described below. Each issue is presented here as a bipolar dimension. Some theorists agree with one or the other extreme. Others are neutral toward the issue or seek a synthesis.

Freedom versus determinism. Some theorists believe that individuals basically have control over their behaviors and understand the motives behind them. Others believe that human behavior is basically determined by internal or external forces over which individuals have little, if any, control.

Heredity versus environment. Theorists differ over whether inherited and inborn characteristics or factors in the environment have the more important influence on human behavior.

Uniqueness versus universality. Some theorists believe that each individual is unique and cannot be compared with others. Others contend that people are basically very similar.

Proactivity versus reactivity. Proactive theories view human beings as acting on their initiative rather than simply reacting. The sources of behavior are perceived as lying within the individual, who does more than just react to stimuli from the outside world.

Optimism versus pessimism. Do significant changes in personality and behavior occur throughout the course of a lifetime? If an individual is motivated, can genuine changes be effected in

Philosophical Assumptions

Where do you stand on these issues? See the Philosophical Assumptions box "Examining Your Own Philosophical Assumptions" on page 11.

personality? Can we help others to change by restructuring their environment? Some personality theories are decidedly more optimistic and hopeful than others concerning these possibilities.

DISTINGUISHING PHILOSOPHICAL ASSUMPTIONS FROM SCIENTIFIC STATEMENTS

Philosophical assumptions may be *explicit* or *implicit*. It is often difficult to identify a person's assumptions when they are implicit, or not stated clearly. You will find it easier to recognize philosophical assumptions if you understand that philosophy frequently posits a distinction between *what is* and *what ought to be*. Philosophical statements suggest that things are not necessarily what they appear to be. *What is* is not necessarily *what should be* or *what really is*. For instance, the fact that many people are aggressive does not necessarily mean that aggression is right or that aggression represents what it means to be human.

Philosophical knowledge is ultimately an **epiphany** (from the Greek *epiphaneia*, which means "appearance" or "manifestation"), or a perception of essential meaning. The "seeing" of philosophy is a special act of knowing, an extraordinary intuition that transcends everyday experience. Philosophical assumptions, therefore, differ from *empirical statements,* which are based on ordinary observation. The statement "All people seek what is good," for example, does not refer to something that can be seen in everyday observation. It refers to some kind of ultimate reality that is perceived in a different way. We say that this statement is based on *epiphanic evidence.*

Scientific statements, too, often refer to things that we cannot see in ordinary observation. Many important constructs in science involve imaginary concepts that cannot be seen. However, even these scientific statements are ultimately, even if indirectly, based on empirical observation, and the methods used to test them differ from the methods of philosophy.

How do scientific statements and philosophical assumptions differ? The difference lies in the nature of the observation that gives rise to the construct and in the way in which it is tested. Scientific statements must be open to falsification; science is required to indicate the conditions under which its statements might be proven incorrect. When an exception is found to a scientific generalization, that generalization must be qualified. In contrast, philosophical assumptions are not tentative hypotheses to be discarded when evidence contradicts them. There is no way to construct an empirical test that would let us falsify a philosophical assumption. If I maintain the philosophy that "all people seek what is good," I will not permit any ordinary observations to disprove the assumption. On the contrary, I can account for all exceptions and seeming contradictions in terms of my assumption itself.

The easiest way to recognize whether specific declarations of a theory function as scientific statements or as philosophical assumptions is to ask what evidence would lead the theorist to change his or her position. If empirical evidence does not lead to a revision of the theory, you can be pretty sure that the declaration functions as a philosophical assumption.

The personality theories described in this book represent philosophical points of view as well as scientific investigations. Some of the theories are explicitly philosophical. In others, the philosophical assumptions are not clearly stated, but they are nevertheless present. Carl Rogers openly acknowledged that his view of the self was philosophical and that his primary differences with other theorists, such as B. F. Skinner, were philosophical ones. Sigmund Freud initially conceived of his work as lacking any philosophy but finally admitted that many of his assumptions functioned philosophically. Because personality theories and our own thoughts involve philosophical assumptions, it is important that we recognize and evaluate them as such.

CRITERIA FOR EVALUATING PHILOSOPHICAL ASSUMPTIONS

Scientific statements are proven false by the process of perceptual observation. In contrast, philosophical assumptions have criteria that are suitable to the epiphanic vision that underlies them, but we cannot set up a crucial test or experiment that will determine whether or not the vision is justified. Philosophical assumptions have their own criteria or tests.

Here are three criteria for evaluating the philosophical assumptions that underlie personality theories. These three criteria add up to a fourth and final criterion: compellingness.

The first criterion is **coherence.** Are the philosophical assumptions of a personality theory clear, logical, and consistent, or are they riddled with contradictions and inconsistencies? A philosophical system may have apparent inconsistencies, perplexing metaphors, or paradoxes and still be coherent, provided that the contradictions are ironed out within the philosophical stance itself so that the final position represents a clear, coherent whole. A person's philosophical system may also be unfinished—that is, open to further growth—but to be coherent, it must have a clearly recognizable, consistent thrust.

The second criterion is **relevance.** To be meaningful, a philosophical assumption must have some bearing on our view of reality. If we do not share the philosophical view of reality, we will have considerable difficulty judging the assumption. In our postmodern world, the criterion of relevance further implies that the assumption is compatible with empirical reality as best we can ascertain it; thus, philosophies are invariably reshaped by scientific discoveries. For example, people's current assumptions regarding the impact of heredity versus environment have been influenced by recent scientific findings in genetics.

The third criterion is **comprehensiveness.** Is the philosophical assumption "deep" enough? In part, this question refers to scope. Does the assumption cover what it intends to cover? Further, the criterion of comprehensiveness asks whether the treatment of the subject is profound or superficial. A philosophical assumption is superficial if it leaves too many questions unanswered or if it refuses to address them.

These three criteria lead to the fourth criterion: **compellingness.** The final and most important question is "Does the assumption and its underlying philosophy convince you?" A philosophical assumption convinces you if it grabs you in such a way that you find the belief inescapable. It is as if you *have* to believe in it. Actually, it is perfectly possible that a philosophical assumption may strike you as being coherent, relevant, and comprehensive, but in spite of those features it does not compel you to believe it. In such a case, the belief does not move you and you cannot "buy" it.

My language here deliberately describes you as passive: "The philosophical assumption grabs you." "You are compelled." This language underscores the fact that philosophical assumptions are not merely subjective opinions that a person has about the world. Rather, they emerge out of a person's encounter with the world. They entail an active meeting of the person and the world that leads to a position about reality that the person finds inescapable.

The way in which philosophers create their views of the world is similar to, although more formal than, the manner in which each one of us comes up with our own view. We may not have thought as much or written about it, but each one of us, upon reflection, can

☀ Philosophical Assumptions

Examining Your Own Philosophical Assumptions

By looking at your own philosophical assumptions, you can better prepare yourself to recognize them in the theories of others. In Table 1.1, each basic issue is presented as a bipolar dimension along which a person's view can be placed according to the degree of agreement with one or the other extreme. You can rate your own views on a scale from 1 to 5. On each issue, if you completely agree with the first statement, rate the issue with a number 1. If you completely agree with the second statement, rate the issue with a number 5. If you only moderately agree with either statement, a number 2 or 4 would best reflect your view. If you are neutral toward the issue or believe that the best position is a synthesis of the two extremes, rate the issue with a number 3.

The first time you go through the items, rate each issue according to your beliefs. The second time, consider each issue in terms of your actions, the way in which you generally behave.

When you have determined where you stand on each of these major issues, a comparison of your positions can help you assess the importance of these issues to your own understanding of personality. Those assumptions that you feel very strongly about and mark with a 1 or a 5 probably play a very important role in your personal philosophy. If you are not strongly committed to any particular issue, that issue is probably not as important in your thinking about personality.

You should note that even experts differ in their responses to the statements in Table 1.1. The different personality theorists that we shall discuss vary markedly in their position on each of these issues. Each adopts the position that appears most commendable or compelling. Throughout the text, you will be asked to return to these assumptions to consider the stance of specific theorists and to see how your attitudes toward certain theorists are related to your own stance on these five dimensions.

probably think of a significant incident or period in our lives when we experienced something that led us to think about ourselves and our world in a different way. For example, after an illness or accident an individual often perceives life as having a new mission or purpose that was not present before. Such experiences constitute the formative insights that shape our lives.

During the second half of the twentieth century, we moved from a modern view of the world to the postmodern view that no one has a monopoly on "Truth" and that knowledge is a matter of perspective. This is not to say that there is no truth or that all perspectives are equally valuable. Most of our reconstructions of the past reveal a deliberate ethnocentric Western view of personhood (Hermans, Kempen, & Van Loon, 1992). Postmodernism raises a special challenge as we move to develop more globally relevant, multiculturally sensitive explanations appropriate for the twenty-first century.

Scientific Statements

As scientists, personality theorists seek to develop a workable set of hypotheses, or tentative assumptions, that will help us understand human behavior. Scientists confirm their hypotheses by testing them according to generally agreed-upon methods. Thus, science, which

TABLE 1.1 SOME BASIC PHILOSOPHICAL ASSUMPTIONS

STRONGLY AGREE	AGREE	IS NEUTRAL OR BELIEVES IN SYNTHESIS OF BOTH VIEWS	AGREE	STRONGLY AGREE
1	2	3	4	5
FREEDOM People basically have control over their own behavior and understand the motives behind their behavior.				DETERMINISM The behavior of people is basically determined by internal or external forces over which they have little, if any, control.
1	2	3	4	5
HEREDITY Inherited and inborn characteristics have the most important influence on a person's behavior.				ENVIRONMENT Factors in the environment have the most important influence on a person's behavior.
1	2	3	4	5
UNIQUENESS Each individual is unique and cannot be compared with others.				UNIVERSALITY People are basically very similar in nature.
1	2	3	4	5
PROACTIVITY Human beings primarily act on their own initiative.				REACTIVITY Human beings primarily react to stimuli from the outside world.
1	2	3	4	5
OPTIMISM Significant changes in personality and behavior can occur throughout the course of a lifetime.				PESSIMISM A person's personality and behavior are essentially stable and unchanging.

comes from the Latin *scire,* "to know," is a group of methods of acquiring knowledge that are based on certain principles.

THE PHILOSOPHICAL BASIS OF SCIENCE

Science has its origins in philosophy, and, as such, it retains elements of its forebears. Thomas Kuhn (1970), a physicist who has studied the history of science, points this out when he reminds us that the observation on which scientific activity is based is not fixed once and for all by the nature of the world and our sensory apparatus but depends on a prior paradigm. A **paradigm** is a model or concept of the world that is shared by the members of a community and that governs their activities. Everyday observation and perception are shaped through education and are subject to change over time. Your view of the world, for example, is very different from that of a person in ancient Greece or a member of an isolated primitive tribe. Indeed, without some sort of paradigm, we could not draw any conclusions from our observations at all.

     Scientific statements, therefore, are statements about the world based on empirical observations arising from currently accepted paradigms, which could also be seen as shared philosophical assumptions. The paradigms are not derived from scientific activity but exist prior to it. For example, the scientific viewpoint that one *should* base conclusions on perceptions that can be shared by others rather than on private, intrinsically unique, perceptions is a value statement that is not mandated by our observations but chosen by the community of scientists as more useful; it is a paradigm.

RECOGNIZING SCIENTIFIC STATEMENTS

The keystone of science is **empirical** observation, and the simplest kinds of statements in science are empirical statements, such as "There is a person in the room." To know whether or not an empirical statement is valid, an individual has to be shown evidence based on sensory data regarding what has been seen, heard, felt, smelled, or tasted.

     Empirical statements may be based on objective data or subjective data. If someone reports, "I see a person," we can interpret the statement in two ways. The person may be saying, "I see a *person*" or "I *see* a person." In the first case, we are referring to the object of experience, or **objective data.** In the second case, we are referring to an experience of seeing, or **subjective data.** Both objective and subjective knowledge refer to empirical data. The difference between them lies in the position of the observer. In objective knowledge, the position is I-it: the self is looking outward on the world as object. In subjective knowledge, the position is I-me: the self is looking inward on its own experience as the object.

     Reports that are concerned with the object of experience, or extrospective data, are relatively simple to verify. We merely indicate the conditions under which the observation may be repeated. If a second observer does not see the reported phenomenon, we suggest that the conditions were not clearly specified—for example, the observer looked for the person in the wrong room. Or we may suspect that the original observer has a distorted sense of perception. Repeated observations of the same phenomenon under specified conditions lead to **consensual validation,** or agreement among observers.

     Reports that are concerned with introspective or subjective phenomena are much more difficult to validate consensually. A certain piece of art may give one person much joy but fail to move someone else. This is because subjective phenomena often occur under complex conditions and are more difficult to describe than objective information. Repeating such subjective observations may require the second observer to undergo extensive training or other experiences in order to duplicate all of the conditions. Undoubtedly, one's joy on seeing a particular piece of art depends not simply on the art itself, but also on one's culture, mood, personal history, and so forth. Considerable effort is needed to duplicate these observations, but it is not impossible (Tart, 1975).

Since reports that are concerned with subjective phenomena are much more difficult to validate, some psychologists have tended to ignore them and invest their efforts in extrospective or objective findings. As we saw, John Watson recommended that inasmuch as our thoughts, feelings, and wishes cannot be directly observed by another person, the psychologist should ignore them and concentrate on overt behaviors. Few psychologists today would agree with this extreme position. Most personality theorists emphasize that we need to be concerned with both subjective and objective data in order to understand behavior.

When a number of different instances of observation coincide, the scientist may make a **generalization.** A **scientific** (or **empirical**) **generalization** is a conclusion that something is true about many or all of the members of a certain class. Suppose I wanted to test the statement "All aggressive people are controlling." The evidence for this statement could be a number of facts about individual members of the class. I could observe this aggressive person, that aggressive person, and other aggressive persons. If all of them are also controlling, I might conclude that all aggressive people are controlling, even though I have not examined each and every aggressive person.

Because it is impossible for me to examine each and every aggressive person who has existed in the past or might exist in the present or future, I can never know for certain that my empirical generalization is true. Indeed, misleading stereotypes are the result of premature and unwise generalizations. As a scientist, the personality theorist must leave empirical generalizations open to possible falsification.

The scientist also uses **definitions,** statements that are true because of the way in which we have agreed to use words. Some words are easy to define clearly and precisely. Other words are harder to define and subject to more disagreement. To resolve this problem, the social scientist frequently tries to develop operational definitions. An **operational definition** specifies which behaviors are included in the concept. "Stress" might be operationally defined in terms of the rate of one's heartbeat and extent of one's perspiration as measured by polygraph apparatuses, which translate such bodily changes into a printed record. It frequently is difficult to reach agreement on suitable operational definitions, and at times an operational definition distorts or even misses the concept it is trying to describe. For example, "stress" can also be defined as a subjective feeling of intense anxiety. The value of operational definitions lies in giving us a common ground of reference.

The most important statements in science are based on scientific constructs. A scientist uses **scientific constructs,** which are imaginary or hypothetical and cannot be seen with the naked eye or even with sophisticated optical equipment, in order to explain what we observe. The building blocks of nature—protons, neutrons, and electrons—remain visibly elusive by direct observation but are indirectly confirmed by their necessary existence in the construct. Today's atomic models require further inference to even smaller unseen particles such as quarks, leptons, and hadrons. The difficulty of not being directly observable does not imply nonexistence; rather it has provided for continual progress toward an understanding of what may be real. Another familiar hypothetical construct is that of IQ or intelligence quotient. IQ is an imaginary construct that is used to explain certain behaviors, namely, one's likelihood for academic success. Many of our concepts in science, in fact almost all of the important ones, cannot be directly seen; we can know them only through their effects.

SOME BASIC SCIENTIFIC CONSTRUCTS

Constructs such as trait, reinforcement, and self have been created in efforts to understand personality scientifically. The concept of **trait** refers to a determining tendency or predisposition to respond in a certain way. Examples of traits are emotional stability and introversion versus extraversion. Allport, Cattell, Eysenck, and the theorists who identified five primary personality factors known as the Big Five make extensive use of trait constructs in their theories. The **self** is another useful construct for understanding personality that is present in many contemporary theories. In Carl Rogers's theory *self* refers to those psychological processes that govern an individual's behavior. In Albert Bandura's theory the self is conceived more narrowly in terms of cognitive structures.

Indeed, some personality theorists conceive of the term *personality* itself as a scientific construct. Thus Cattell (1950) defines personality as "that which permits a prediction of what a person will do in a given situation." For Cattell, personality is an imaginary construct that permits us to explain and predict behavior. The scientific constructs of a personality theory tie together the empirical findings of that theory and suggest new relationships that will hold true under certain conditions.

CRITERIA FOR EVALUATING SCIENTIFIC STATEMENTS

As already pointed out, there is no one method of validating scientific statements. Personality theorists use a variety of techniques, some of which are very complicated, to evaluate their work. We will be looking at a number of these later in this chapter and in subsequent chapters when we discuss the specific assessment and research procedures used by different personality theorists. However, we can make some general comments about evaluating scientific statements.

In order to qualify as scientific, statements must fulfill the criterion of **verifiability:** They must ultimately be based on empirical observation, and the theory behind them has to specify how they can be confirmed or refuted. Even though scientists may build elaborate theories referring to things that they cannot observe directly, they base their theories on perceptions of human sense organs. It is true that I cannot test the statement "John has an IQ of 110" in the same way that I can test the statement "There is a person in the room." I cannot simply look. The statement must be tested indirectly, but the test is still based on empirical observation, such as looking at John's performance on an IQ measuring device. Given the identical conditions, another person could be expected to share the same perceptions and draw the same conclusions. Scientific statements, therefore, are based on *what is* and *what occurs* in our everyday world as it appears to us through our sense organs.

Second, scientific statements must be *open to falsification*. As a scientist, the personality theorist is required to indicate the conditions under which theoretical statements might be proven incorrect. If an exception is found to a scientific statement, that statement is considered to be false or in need of qualification. The generalization "All aggressive people are controlling," for example, is disproven by pointing to an aggressive person who is not controlling or qualified by indicating the conditions under which an aggressive person will not seek to control others. This helps us to understand why a scientist never claims that the information produced by scientific methods is ultimately true. Scientific hypotheses are tentative and need to be discarded when evidence contradicts them. Although scientific methods cannot be said to yield ultimate truth, they do provide a wealth of useful information to assist us in living in the everyday world. It is to our advantage, therefore, to act as if the conclusions from our scientific methods are true. Indeed, the final criterion for evaluating scientific constructs is that of **usefulness** rather than compellingness. Usefulness is the ability to generate information that can assist us in living.

In the process of scientific investigations, the personality theorist frequently develops more than one hypothesis. Each one is examined in turn to rule out those that do not stand up under test conditions. Occasionally, the scientist is left with rival hypotheses. Given that both are sound hypotheses, how does the scientist decide between them? In general, three criteria have been used: compatibility, predictive power, and simplicity. Each of these criteria has advantages and limitations.

Compatibility refers to the agreement of the hypothesis with previously well-established information. This criterion is a sensible one since it is a lot easier for us to accept a new hypothesis if it is consistent with findings in other areas. However, it should not be too rigidly applied. There are times in science when a new idea completely shatters earlier theories, forcing us to revise or reconsider them.

Predictive power refers to the range or scope of the statement. Scientists seek not only to explain the phenomena that we observe but also to predict and anticipate them. The more predictions or consequences that we can infer from a theory, the greater is its range and usefulness in generating new ideas. On the other hand, too strict a reliance on this criterion may lead to the notion that the only value of a theory lies in the amount of research and predictions it generates. Some theories express their heuristic value by integrating and encompassing ideas rather than by generating specific predictions and research projects.

The third criterion for deciding between rival hypotheses is **simplicity,** or parsimony. The preferred theory is the one that adequately accounts for the complexity of material in the simplest way. This criterion comes into play only when rival hypotheses generate *identical* consequences, which is a rare occurrence.

> **Thinking Critically**
>
> How can you evaluate personality theories? See the Thinking Critically box "Evaluating Personality Theories."

We should note that in the West, theories of personality have often developed within the strict limits of a scientific paradigm. Some of the personality theorists that we will cover (such as Jung, Fromm, Horney, Rogers, Maslow, and May), however, have argued that that paradigm frequently fostered *scientism*, or the exclusive reliance on a narrow conception of science, which is inappropriate for understanding human nature. Some of these, most notably Jung and Horney, have suggested that we turn to the East for a more balanced comprehension.

The Art of Personality Theories

If theories of personality have their origin in philosophy and seek to validate their constructs through scientific methods, they also culminate in some form of art or practical application. Personality theories have found application in many ways, and the criteria for evaluating each way are varied. In this section we introduce three applications of personality theory: assessment, research, and psychotherapy.

ASSESSMENT

Assessment is a major area in the application of personality theories to everyday life. **Assessment** refers to evaluation or measurement. You have probably been touched by assessment to

Thinking Critically

Evaluating Personality Theories

As you review the personality theories in this text, you can use the following criteria to determine how successfully each theory functions as a philosophy and as a science.

First you need to determine *which assertions function as philosophical assumptions and which function as scientific statements.* Look at the major tenets of the theory, and determine whether each is based on epiphanic or empirical evidence. Philosophical assumptions are based on a vision of ultimate reality, whereas scientific statements are based on empirical observation.

Then, ask *how well the philosophical assumptions fulfill the criteria of philosophy.* The following criteria can be used to evaluate the assumptions you identify:

Coherence: Is the philosophical position clear, logical, and consistent?

Relevance: Does the theory deal with issues that are important and meaningful to us today?

Comprehensiveness: Does the theory encompass a wide array of phenomena, inclusively covering aspects of the subject it claims to deal with?

Compellingness: Does it convince you?

Then, ask *how well the scientific statements fulfill the criteria of science.* The following criteria can be used to evaluate scientific statements:

Verifiability: Are the statements ultimately based on empirical observation, and does the theory clearly specify how they can be confirmed and refuted?

Compatibility: Does the theory build on, and is it consistent with, other well-established information?

Predictive power: How successful has the theory been in generating new ideas and research?

Simplicity: Does the theory adequately account for the complexity of material in the most economical way?

Usefulness: Does the theory provide useful information to assist us in living in the everyday world?

Note: Some texts present a single list of criteria combining aspects of both philosophy and science (e.g., a good theory should have empirical support, refutability, comprehensiveness, heuristic value [the ability to generate new ideas and research], applied value, and parsimony). This text reflects my conviction that the philosophic and scientific aspects of personality theorizing require different criteria of evaluation.

a greater degree than you realize. In education, for example, assessment is used to measure progress and to evaluate learning disabilities. Psychologists in industries and organizations use assessment to assist in job placement. Prior to deciding on a course of counseling, a clinician needs to assess the individual in order to evaluate the nature of his or her problem.

What makes for a good personality assessment? The most important criterion is **validity,** the quality of measuring what a construct is supposed to measure (Ozer, 1999). This is often a difficult criterion to meet. For example, nearly all psychologists agree that certain intelligence tests are valid measures for predicting school performance. They are not at all certain, however, that these tests are valid measures of that elusive quality "intelligence." In developing assessment techniques appropriate to their concepts, personality theorists need to show how the construct fits within the theory and also show that the assessment situation effectively measures it. A response "false" to the statement "I like most people" is probably more indicative of hostility than the response "true" to the statement "Red is my favorite color."

Reliability, or consistency of scores over time, is also important. A thermometer must register the same degree each time for the same amount of heat in order to be a consistent and useful measuring tool. The measurement of personality, however, is not that simple. A change in measurement may indicate not unreliability of the measure but growth and change in light of other events such as therapy. **Objectivity,** or the avoidance of subjective bias, is also prized in assessment. Objectivity is easier to obtain if responses are clearly delineated. In a true-false test, each response clearly indicates a certain factor. It is more difficult, but nevertheless possible, to develop objective criteria for scoring protracted written or verbal responses. Such criteria provide objectivity in evaluating interviews, written essays, projective techniques, and so forth.

Although it is very difficult to develop and evaluate appropriate assessment techniques, the wise and judicious use of assessment can be invaluable in developing individual and group potential. However, as scientific tools, assessment techniques must remain open to falsification, and our use of them needs to reflect that fact.

The personality theorists discussed in this book have developed specific ways of assessing personality that are informed by and also inform their theories. These procedures range from the interpretation of dreams to statistically sophisticated and elaborately constructed tests. We will discuss each theorist's particular method, but first some general words about two important approaches to assessing personality: psychometric tests and projective tests.

Psychometric Tests

Psychometric tests measure personality characteristics by means of carefully designed questionnaires developed with theoretical and statistical techniques. Psychometric testing had its origin in the psychological laboratories established at the end of the nineteenth century.

One of the most carefully researched questionnaires is the Minnesota Multiphasic Personality Inventory (MMPI), first published in 1942 and most recently revised in 1989. The MMPI is made up of over 550 self-report items or printed statements to which the participant answers "true," "false," or "cannot say." Designed to measure tendencies toward pathology or abnormal behavior, the MMPI is employed as an aid in the diagnosis of psychiatric disorders and is widely used in personality research.

Psychometric measuring devices and techniques have not been used without controversy (Buchanan, 2002). Many individuals view such tests as an invasion of personal privacy and are wary of the use to which the test results may be put.

Projective Tests

Some psychologists, particularly in a clinical setting, also employ projective techniques. The participant is presented with a deliberately ambiguous stimulus. In responding to the stimulus, the participant expresses personal attitudes, values, needs, and feelings. Two of the best-known projective techniques are the Rorschach Inkblot Test and the Thematic Apperception Test (TAT), which are derived, respectively, from the theories of Carl Jung and Henry Murray.

The main advantage of projective techniques is that they disguise the purpose of the assessment. Because the stimuli are ambiguous and the participant is free to respond in any way, it is difficult for the participant to know what would be an appropriate answer and to fake a "correct" response. The difficulty with projective tests is that they are very hard to score in an objective manner that avoids subjective bias and the projection of the scorer.

RESEARCH

Personality theorists also differ widely in the type of research methods that they use. Some follow very strict scientific guidelines in their work. Here the interface between science and application is very clear. Others encourage the use of a wider range of acceptable methodologies, making use of interdisciplinary and eclectic approaches. Indeed, restraints on creative and productive research may occur when the area of personality inquiry is too narrowly demarcated. Three research approaches commonly used by personality theorists are the clinical approach, the psychometric approach, and the experimental approach. It is difficult to be specific about the evaluative criteria here because they vary according to the specific activity and its canons of research.

The Clinical Approach

Many of the personality theories that we will be considering originated in the clinical setting. The clinician conducts research through intensive interviews and observation of the participant. Clinical methods of research may also include the analysis of dreams and/or early memories. A clinician may further structure the observations by asking questions or giving one or more tests. Frequently there is considerable overlap between a theorist's methods of research and methods of assessment.

A primary tool in the clinical approach to personality is the development of a *case history,* a carefully drawn biography of an individual. Sigmund Freud developed psychoanalytic theory largely on the basis of case histories (including his own). Unlike most other research methods, the case history entails studying one individual or a small number of individuals in great depth rather than large numbers of subjects. Freud and Erik Erikson also developed case histories of prominent historical figures such as Michelangelo, Leonardo da Vinci, Martin Luther, and Gandhi.

The Psychometric Approach

The use of mathematical and statistical tools to measure personality characterizes the psychometric approach to research. **Psychometrics** has been faciliated by the growth of new and powerful mathematical techniques for analyzing and synthesizing vast quantities of clinical data. The expansion has been accelerated by the ready availability of inexpensive computer hardware and software programs. The **correlation** is a major statistical tool used by psychometricians.

In a *correlational study,* events or variables are systematically observed as they naturally occur to see the extent to which they covary, or occur together. Events that covary are said to be correlated. Correlations are expressed by a number that ranges from +1.00 to –1.00. The plus or minus sign tells us if the relationship is positive or negative. The numeric value tells us the extent of the relationship. The closer the numbers are to +1.00 or to –1.00, the higher is the frequency with which the two events occur or do not occur together.

It is important to remember that a correlation does not imply that one variable caused the other. For example, there is a high correlation between brown hair and brown eyes. This is not to say that brown hair causes brown eyes but rather that a great many people who have brown hair also have brown eyes. Nevertheless, when two variables have a high correlation, it is reasonable to hypothesize that one caused the other or that a third variable caused both. However, such a hypothesis would have to be subject to further testing. We are not permitted to draw that conclusion simply on the basis of a correlational study. Cattell and Eysenck make considerable use of a sophisticated correlational procedure, *factor analysis,* in developing their theories.

The Experimental Approach

Many psychologists favor an experimental approach because it permits them to infer a cause-and-effect relationship between two factors. In its simplest form, a researcher systematically varies the presence of one factor, the *independent variable,* while keeping all other variables constant. The researcher can then determine whether or not changes in the independent variable have any effect on a particular behavior, the *dependent variable.* If they do, it is assumed that the changes in the independent variable caused the changes in the dependent variable. For example, after students are provided with either positive or negative feedback following their performance on a memory test, they could be given a depression questionnaire to test for a change in mood. The two levels of feedback would serve as the independent variable, and the score on the depression questionnaire would serve as the dependent variable. Experiments can be very complex, with several independent and dependent variables.

The experimental method is considered the most precise method of psychological research. It has the advantage of permitting the experimenter to posit a clear cause-and-effect relationship, but it has limitations. To limit the findings of personality explorations to those that can be demonstrated only within the experimental laboratory would be to circumscribe the study of personality to merely those aspects about the person that can be studied by manipulation. Because of this constraint, many questions about the ultimate meanings, purposes, and goals of human living—questions that traditionally have been and could be included in the study of personality—would be ruled out of inquiry. A wider range of acceptable methodologies is necessary (Henwood & Pidgeon, 1992).

Multiple approaches and methodologies are needed to understand the whole person. In general, the field of personality inquiry is broadening in scope (McCrae, 1996). Since Sarbin (1986) suggested that narrative might be considered a root metaphor for understanding human behavior and experience, the integrative life story has emerged as a significant vehicle for expressing and understanding personality (McAdams, 1993). Narrative thought has emerged as a primary form of cognition and self-understanding that qualitatively varies from abstract proportional or scientific thinking (Mueller & Tingley, 1990) and that further enables us to understand moral development (Greenberg, 1995). In general, the growing openness of personality theorists to more effective methods contrasts with the perpetuation by some other psychologists of a narrow view of science.

The art of **psychotherapy** is the effort to apply the findings of personality theory in ways that will assist individuals and meet human goals. The word *therapy* comes from the Greek *therapeia*, which means "attending" and "healing"; however, psychotherapists are not interested only in healing sick people. They are also interested in understanding "normal" people, learning how they function, and helping them to function more creatively. Although in many respects psychotherapy is the flowering of personality theory, it is also the seed of it, because the desire to help people has fostered and nourished the development of personality theories. The two have gone hand in hand. Many theories of personality cannot be adequately understood without understanding the theory of psychotherapy that led to them.

Goals of Psychotherapy

Joseph Rychlak (1968) points out that psychotherapy has three major motives or goals: the scholarly, the ethical, and the curative.

The *scholarly* motive considers therapy as a means of understanding the self and human nature. Psychoanalysis, for example, was seen by Freud as a tool for discovering truths about human nature. His goal was to help the individual acquire self-understanding and to develop a comprehensive theory of human nature. He developed psychoanalysis as a method of research aimed at these ends.

The *ethical* motive considers therapy a means of helping the individual to change, improve, grow, and better the quality of life. Carl Rogers's work is an example of the ethical motive. His emphasis is on a climate created by the therapist that permits change to occur within the client rather than on cognitive understanding or the manipulation of behavior.

The *curative* motive aims directly at eliminating troublesome symptoms and substituting more suitable behavior. Most behavior therapists, for example, consider that they have been hired to do a job and seek to do it as effectively and quickly as possible. From this point of view, the therapist is responsible for creating changes, removing symptoms, and controlling behavior.

Most people enter therapy with the expectation that they will be cured or helped to improve. In this respect, the curative motive is most consistent with the popular view of psychotherapy. Because of this expectation, many people have difficulty, particularly at the beginning, in undergoing psychoanalysis or other forms of "insight" therapy. If they stay with it, however, their reasons for being in therapy change, and they begin to appreciate the value of the other motives. Obviously, the reasons for entering, continuing in, and practicing psychotherapy are many and mixed. This is why the evaluation of therapy is a difficult issue.

Evaluating Psychotherapy

How does one go about evaluating psychotherapy? What criteria are appropriate? In 1952, Hans Eysenck stunned the therapeutic community with a report on treatment outcomes indicating that various forms of psychotherapy are no more effective than providing a placebo or merely waiting for the condition to get better on its own (cf. Eisner, 2000). Eysenck's report created a flurry of research and comment, as *meta-analyses** of psychotherapy outcome studies were conducted showing that various forms of psychotherapy are consistently beneficial (Landman & Dawes, 1982; Smith & Glass, 1977). Eysenck's criterion for improvement

---

* A meta-analysis is a comprehensive analysis of several studies.

focused on "symptom remission." Eysenck (1994a, 1994b, 1994c) continued to reaffirm his position but acknowledged that the problem is a paradigm conflict in which different criteria are used. Eysenck was an advocate of the behaviorist position. Differences in theory lead to differences in therapy. Symptom remission may be an appropriate criterion for therapies governed by the curative motive but not necessarily for those that are conducted for other purposes.

If the proportion of cures were the only criterion by which psychotherapies were to be judged, psychoanalysis and other insight therapies would have long since disappeared from the scene with the arrival of more efficient and less costly curative techniques. This, however, has not been the case. If one's criterion rests on scholarly grounds, psychoanalysis emerges a clear winner. No other method of therapy has provided us with such a wealth of information about the complexity and depth of the human personality.

In brief, each method of psychotherapy must be evaluated in terms of its own goals and purposes. Behavior therapists, who aim at curing clients, are particularly interested in discovering the proportion of cures associated with various techniques. Ethical theorists, who aim at creating a suitable climate for therapeutic change and life improvement, have stimulated the study of those conditions that foster personality change and their effects. Freudian psychoanalysis asks to be evaluated in terms of its effectiveness as a method of research aimed at understanding human nature. Figure 1.3 summarizes the evaluation of psychotherapy and the other main points of the chapter.

The Challenges of Evaluation

I have suggested that personality theorists may function as philosophers, scientists, and artists. The use of this threefold approach allows us to recognize each activity as it arises and gives us a better idea of how personality theories in general, and specific personality theories, work. It is important to identify the different hats (of philosophy, science, and/or art) that personality theorists are wearing as they make their statements because each activity has its own rules and procedures for establishing information, and each has its own criteria for judging the worth of its findings.

No theory is simply philosophy, science, or art; every theory combines elements of all three. Nor are we trying to establish a model that all personality theories must follow. The fact is there is no one scientific method, philosophical approach, or psychotherapeutic strategy that would serve as an adequate model for all others.

Scientific studies of personality rely on paradigms that can be established only philosophically and that generally culminate in some form of art or practical application. The desire to be scientific reflects itself in an effort to test constructs by validating evidence rather than by relying on the gut-level feeling of illumination that everyday language calls "understanding something" (Perrez, 1991).

Some psychologists have attempted to narrow the possible activity of a personality theorist to one function or interpretation of science, such as an objective experimental methodology, and have ignored the philosophical assumptions on which all scientific work is based. Others have assumed that the compelling character of philosophical assumptions is sufficient to establish their credibility as scientific findings about personality. Either position is unnecessarily limiting. It is important that we distinguish among the different kinds of

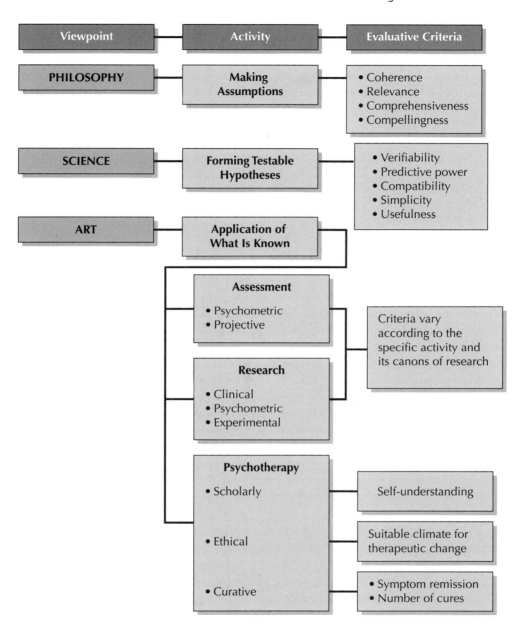

FIGURE 1.3 VIEWPOINTS FOR UNDERSTANDING AND EVALUATING PERSONALITY THEORIES

Shown here are three complementary orientations of personality theorists. Each viewpoint entails different activities that contribute to personality theory, and each activity must be evaluated according to its own criteria.

functions that personality theories entail so that we can recognize them and evaluate them accordingly. Part of the current problem in personality theorizing is that the theorists are not always clear about what hat they are wearing or what activity they are engaged in.

As we discuss the major personality theorists in the following chapters, we will try to clarify the function of philosophy, science, and art in each theory. This should enable you to see how the theories fit into the overall framework of personality theories as philosophy, science, and art. As you will see, there is a wide variety and diversity of personality theories, providing you with a rich selection from which to choose or develop your own theory of personality.

 TO LEARN MORE about personality theories and psychotherapy, and for a list of suggested readings, visit the *Personality Theories* textbook website at **college.cengage.com/pic/engler8e.**

Summary

1. The term **personality** (p. 2) is difficult to define because there is little common agreement on how the term should be used. In everyday speech it usually refers to someone's public image. Different personality theorists present their own definitions of the word based on their theoretical positions.

2. A **theory** (p. 2) is a set of abstract concepts that we make about a group of facts or events in order to explain them.

3. Two traditions inform contemporary theories of personality. One stems from psychological laboratories and academic research. The other stems from psychoanalysis and clinical psychology. The study of personality became a formal and systematic area of specialization in American psychology in the mid-1930s, but the two traditions have never fully merged.

4. Personality theories may function as philosophy, science, and art. As scientists, personality theorists develop hypotheses that help us understand human behavior. As philosophers, they explore what it means to be a person. As artists, they seek to apply what is known about human behavior to make a better life.

5. Some of the basic philosophical issues on which personality theorists differ are **freedom versus determinism** (p. 12), **heredity versus environment** (p. 12), **uniqueness versus universality** (p. 12), **proactivity versus reactivity** (p. 12), and **optimism versus pessimism** (p. 12).

6. **Philosophical assumptions** (p. 8) suggest that things are not necessarily what they appear to be. They are based on a special **epiphanic** (p. 9) vision, which goes beyond the ordinary perception of our sense organs. Philosophical statements tend to be global and do not allow for any exceptions. They often are implicit rather than explicit.

7. Philosophical assumptions are evaluated by criteria appropriate to the special act of knowing that underlies them. The criteria are **coherence** (p. 10), **relevance** (p. 10), and **comprehensiveness** (p. 10), all of which add up to a final criterion, **compellingness** (p. 10).

8. Science has its basis in **philosophy** (p. 12) because the ordinary observation on which science relies depends on a prior **paradigm** (p. 13) that is established philosophically. The values and standards of science also function as philosophical commitments.

9. The simplest kinds of **scientific statements** (p. 13) are **empirical** (p. 13), based directly on observation. The data on which these statements are based may be **objective** (p. 13) or **subjective** (p. 13). When a number of different observations coincide, a scientist may make a **generalization** (p. 14). Scientists also use **operational definitions** (p. 14), which specify the behaviors included in a term, and **scientific constructs** (p. 14), which use imaginary or hypothetical concepts to explain what we observe.

10. Scientists use a variety of techniques to evaluate their work. All of these techniques are ultimately **verifiable** (p. 15)—that is, based on observation, the ordinary perceptions of our sense organs—although some statements can be tested only indirectly. Scientific statements must be open to falsification; a scientist must indicate the conditions under which a statement might be proven false. Scientists do not claim that the information produced by their methods is ultimately true. Scientific statements should be judged for their **usefulness** (p. 16) rather than their truth. When scientists end up with more than one hypothesis, the criteria they use to decide between rival hypotheses are **compatibility** (p. 16), **predictive power** (p. 16), and **simplicity** (p. 16).

11. Personality theories have found application in assessment and research. Two major approaches to assessing personality are psychometric and projective techniques. Three primary research approaches used in personality are the **clinical approach** (p. 19), the **psychometric approach** (p. 19), and the **experimental approach** (p. 20).

12. The three major goals of **psychotherapy** (p. 21) are the **scholarly** (p. 21), **ethical** (p. 21), and **curative** (p. 21) motives. Scholarly therapies should be evaluated on the basis of their contributions to the understanding of the self and human nature. Ethical therapies should be evaluated in terms of the suitability of the climate they create for fostering change and life improvement. Curative therapies should be evaluated on the basis of symptom remission and number of cures.

13. It is important to distinguish among the different orientations of personality theories so that we can recognize each viewpoint and use appropriate methods to evaluate each theory.

Personal Experiences

1. You can begin to evaluate your own personality. First list five qualities that you think may describe and define who you are as a person. Then examine each quality individually. Can you trace a specific quality to something in your environment—to your mother or father, a period or event in your life, and so forth? Or is this quality something that you were just born with? Ultimately you can use yourself as a case study to begin negotiating the balance of nature versus nurture as a determinant of your personality and identity.

2. You use theories in your personal life all the time—theories about the fastest way to get from home to the mall, theories about how to attract and keep a boyfriend or girlfriend, theories about how to get what you want from your parents, theories about how to get an A in this class. Each theory needs evidence to support and legitimate it. Discuss a theory you've come up with in the past year or so, perhaps a theory about love or a theory about how to achieve success after college. What prompted you to come up with this theory,

how have you been testing it, what kinds of evidence have you used, and how is your theory holding up?

3. To better understand theories that you develop in your own life, you need to better understand your own philosophical assumptions. Look at Table 1.1, and answer as honestly as you can where you fall on the scale of each of the criteria. Once you've evaluated your philosophical assumptions, try to determine how they may have impacted the theory you discussed in question 2.

4. Although this text focuses exclusively on theories as they pertain to personality, many of the same principles of evaluation and assessment hold true for all theories. Look at the Thinking Critically box "Evaluating Personality Theories," and use the assessment list provided there to evaluate your theory in question 2. How is your theory measuring up? Is it more a philosophy or a scientific statement? Is there any tweaking you could do to your theory to make it fit into one category or the other?

5. Have you ever undergone psychotherapy? Has someone you've known? What are your personal feelings with regard to such therapy? Do you have a sense of how your friends and family feel about it? Are their opinions positive or negative? What philosophical assumptions underpin your personal beliefs about psychotherapy? What assumptions underpin the beliefs of your loved ones and your community? Can you explain the rationale behind these individual and collective assumptions?

PART ONE

The Psychoanalytic Approach

Of all the giants of intellectual history, Sigmund Freud emerges as an unquestionable and controversial leader in helping us to understand human nature. Many of the other theories that we will study were developed as efforts to elaborate on, modify, substitute for, or refute the concepts of Freud. The systematic study of personality may be said to have begun with Freud's development of psychoanalysis at the end of the nineteenth century. Not only did Freud revolutionize psychology, but his influence has also been felt in all the social sciences, as well as in literature, art, and religion. Salvador Dali's artwork and Alfred Hitchcock's movies are just two of the many areas Freud's work has influenced. Over the years, Freud's ideas have been in and out of favor. But Freud continues to haunt us. We dismiss him at our own peril. Somewhat surprisingly, today's advanced neuroscientific research gives credence to many of Freud's insights and hunches.

CHAPTER 2

Psychoanalysis

▪ Sigmund Freud

YOUR GOALS FOR THIS CHAPTER

1. Describe Freud's early use of the "talking method," and indicate the conclusions Freud drew about **unconscious processes.**

2. Describe Freud's concept of the role of emotions in human life. Explain why **wishes** are repressed and how they may be dealt with when brought back into consciousness.

3. Cite the instructions for **free association,** and explain the premise on which the procedure is based.

4. Indicate the importance of **slips** and dreams, and explain how they are analyzed.

5. Identify the nature of repressed wishes and desires, and explain how Freud's use of the word **libido** and his concept of **drive** led to a new understanding of sexuality.

6. Describe the child's sexual activity, and outline Freud's **psychosexual stages** of development, explaining the important events of each stage.

7. Describe how the effects of the psychosexual stages may be seen in various adult character traits and disorders.

8. Describe the characteristics and functions of the **id, ego,** and **superego.**

9. Explain how the id, ego, and superego are related in adjusted and maladjusted personalities.

10. Explain how the id, ego, and superego are related to conscious and unconscious processes.

11. Distinguish among the three forms of anxiety that Freud described.

12. Describe the function of **defense mechanisms,** and define and give examples of common defense mechanisms.

13. Describe what happens in psychoanalysis.

14. Discuss efforts to test Freudian concepts.

15. Evaluate Freud's theory from the viewpoints of philosophy, science, and art.

The stature and distinguished contributions of Sigmund Freud place him at the forefront of contemporary personality theorists. He is seen both as a heroic figure and as an extremely flawed individual (Breger, 2000; Roth, 1998). For over forty years, Freud meticulously studied dimensions of human nature. Developing the technique of free association, he reached far into the depths of his own unconscious life and that of others. In the process, he created psychoanalysis, a unique method of research for understanding the human individual. He discovered psychological processes such as repression, resistance, transference, and infantile sexuality, many of which are still focused on today. He developed the first comprehensive method of studying and treating neurotic problems. His controversial position in the history of intellectual thought clearly justifies an extended study of his ideas.

Biographical Background

Sigmund Freud was born in 1856 in Freiburg, Moravia (a small town in what became Czechoslovakia), to a Jewish wool merchant and his young wife. Sigmund was born in a caul—that is, a small portion of the fetal sac covered his head at birth. According to folklore, this was a sign that he would be famous. Freud did not practice religion as an adult, but he remained very conscious of his Jewish origin. His mother, twenty-one at the time of her favored first son's birth, was loving and protective. Freud's father, Jacob, was forty-one, almost twice as old as his wife. Jacob was stern and authoritarian, but his son respected him. Only later, through his self-analysis, did Freud realize that his feelings toward his parents were mixed with fear and hate, respect and love.

When Sigmund was eleven months old, a brother, Julius, was born, but he died eight months later. A sister, Anna, arrived when Freud was two and a half. Later, four other sisters and a brother completed the family. When Freud was very young, he was very fond of his nanny and impressed by her religious teachings of Catholicism. Nevertheless, shortly after Anna was born, the nanny was suddenly fired for having stolen from the family. Sigmund was also born an uncle. His father, a widower, had two grown sons by his former marriage, and Freud's elder half brother had a child. Freud and his nephew John, who was one year older than he, were close childhood companions. Freud was to view their early relationship as very significant to his later development. Many have thought that Freud's unusual family constellation set the stage for his later theory of the Oedipus complex.

At the age of four, Sigmund and his family moved to Vienna, where he was to live for almost eighty years. Although he was critical of Vienna, he did not leave the city until it was overwhelmed by Nazis in 1938, the year before he died. In his youth, Freud was a conscientious student. His parents encouraged his studies by giving him special privileges and expecting the other children to make sacrifices on behalf of their older brother. He was the only member of the family who had his own room; he studied by oil lamp while the others had to use candles. A natural student, Freud entered high school a year earlier than normal and stood at the head of the class for most of his days at the Sperl Gymnasium. He was good at languages and was an avid reader, being particularly fond of Shakespeare.

As a child, Freud had dreams of becoming a general or a minister of state, but in reality professional choice was severely restricted for a Jew in Vienna. He thought of becoming a

Sigmund Freud was the founder of psychoanalysis, which emphasizes the importance of unconscious forces.

lawyer but instead began medical studies at the University of Vienna in 1873 and graduated eight years later. His studies there took longer than usual because he took his time with those areas that were of particular interest to him. He never intended to practice medicine, being more interested in physiological research; practical considerations, including occupational barriers to Jewish people and the desire to marry, led him to establish a practice as a clinical neurologist in 1881. While still a student, he made substantial and noteworthy contributions to research, publishing his findings on the nervous system of fish and the testes of the eel. He developed a method of staining cells for microscopic study and as a physician explored the anesthetic properties of cocaine. (cf. Frixione, 2003; Kalb, 2006). Because he initially had no reason to believe that there were dangers connected with cocaine, he was somewhat indiscriminate in using it himself and in recommending it to others. After the addictive character of the drug was discovered, Freud said he suffered "grave reproaches." However, he may have continued to use it. Cocaine claimed many physicians as casualties in the 1880s and 1890s.

Because the private practice on which Freud depended for a living brought him patients suffering from primarily neurotic disorders, his attention became focused on the problem and study of neurosis. *Neurosis* refers to an emotional disturbance, but the disturbance is usually not so severe as to prevent the individual who has it from functioning in normal society. As Freud's goal was a complete theory of humanity, he hoped that his study of neurosis would eventually provide a key to the study of psychological processes in general. He studied in Paris with the French psychiatrist Jean Charcot. On his return from Paris, Freud became influenced by a procedure developed by Joseph Breuer, a Viennese physician and friend, who encouraged his patients to talk freely about their symptoms. Breuer and Freud worked together in writing up some of their cases in *Studies in Hysteria* (1895). Freud's further investigations with Breuer's "talking cure" led to his own development of free association and later psychoanalytic techniques. Eventually they separated, because, according to Freud, Breuer could not agree with Freud's emphasis on the role of sexuality in neurosis.

In 1900 Freud published *The Interpretation of Dreams*. Initially, the book was ignored by all but a few. Nevertheless, Freud's reputation grew, and he began to attract a following. He also encountered a lot of criticism; some even said his work was pornographic. However, he may have exaggerated the degree of intellectual persecution he received. A psychoanalytic society was founded by Freud and his colleagues, and many of Freud's disciples later became noted psychoanalysts: Ernest Jones (his biographer), A. A. Brill, Sandor Ferenczi, and Karl Abraham. Originally, Carl Jung and Alfred Adler were also close associates, but later they left Freud's psychoanalytic movement to develop and stress other ideas.

In 1909, G. Stanley Hall, noted psychologist and president of Clark University in Worcester, Massachusetts, invited Freud and his associate, Carl Jung, to present a series of lectures (cf. Fancher, 2000). It was Freud's first and only visit to the United States. These lectures contained the basic elements of Freud's theory of personality, and their delivery marked the change of psychoanalysis from a small Viennese movement to one of international scope and recognition.

Freud's work, however, was by no means over. He continued to develop and revise his psychoanalytic theory until his death. By the end of his life, psychoanalytic concepts had been applied to and were influencing almost every cultural construct of humanity. Freud's published works fill twenty-four volumes in the *Standard English Edition*. He died in London in 1939 at age eighty-three, after many years of suffering from cancer of the jaw, with what would be called today physician aid in dying. With the long-anticipated release of the Freud archives, scholars are able to shed additional light on this important figure.

The Origins of Psychoanalysis

Sigmund Freud did not complete a perfected system. *An Outline of Psychoanalysis* (1940), which he began in 1938, the year before he died, had as its aim "to bring together the doctrines of psychoanalysis and to state them . . . in the most concise form." But this book was never finished; in fact, much of his work has an unfinished character about it. Ideas appear and are dismissed, only to reappear in a new context. His thought moves in phases, changing and synthesizing what has gone before. The only works that Freud systematically tried to keep up to date were *The Interpretation of Dreams* (first published in 1900) and *Three Essays on Sexuality* (1905). In describing Freud's theories, therefore, it is important to recognize that psychoanalysis represents not a finished theory but rather an ongoing process of discovery about the self.

THE DISCOVERY OF UNCONSCIOUS FORCES

A logical place to begin discussion of the origins of psychoanalysis is Freud's early work with Joseph Breuer. This, in fact, is where Freud began his presentation on the history of psychoanalysis to the American public in his lectures at Clark University. As we have already seen, Freud was deeply influenced by a procedure developed by Breuer, and he frequently credited Breuer with the discovery of the psychoanalytic method. Thus psychoanalysis may be said to begin with the case history of one of Joseph Breuer's patients, who is known in the literature as Anna O. (Freud, 1910).

Anna O. was a twenty-one-year-old, highly intelligent woman. In the course of a two-year illness beginning in 1880, she had developed a number of physical and mental disturbances. Among her symptoms were a paralysis of the right arm and leg, difficulty in vision, nausea, the inability to drink any liquids, and the inability to speak or understand her mother tongue. Further, she was prone to states of absence, an altered state of consciousness in which there may be considerable personality change, and later amnesia or forgetting of events that occurred during that period.

The medical profession of 1880 was quite puzzled by illnesses such as these and diagnosed them as cases of hysteria, an illness in which there were physical symptoms but no physiological basis for the problem. (Today such disorders are less common and are known as *conversion disorders.*) The cause of hysteria was a mystery. Because they could not understand or effectively treat the problem, many doctors tended to view patients suffering from hysteria with suspicion and to be punitive. Some even went so far as to accuse their patients of faking an illness (cf. Huopainen, 2002).

Breuer, however, treated his patients sympathetically. He noticed that during her states of absence, Anna frequently mumbled several words. Once he was able to determine these words, Breuer put her under hypnosis, repeated the words to her, and asked her to verbalize for him any associations that she had to the words. The patient cooperated. She began to tell him stories about herself that seemed to center on one particular event of her life: her father's illness and death.

Before he died, Anna's father had been very sick. She had taken care of him until her own illness prevented her from doing so. After she had related a number of these stories, Anna's symptoms were relieved and eventually disappeared. Anna gratefully called the cure the "talking cure," or referred to it jokingly as "chimney sweeping."

For example, Anna told of a time when she was sitting by her father's bed during his illness and was very worried about him. She was trying to hide her tears so that her father would not see them, when he asked her what time it was. Since she was crying, it was only with difficulty that she could look at her watch and make out the position of the hands on the dial. Recollecting that event and the emotions she had restrained at the time restored her clarity of vision.

Later she recalled another memory. A black snake (common in the area in which she lived) appeared in the room and seemed to go toward her ill father. She tried to drive the

reptile away, but it was as if she could not move her arm. She wanted to call for help, but she could not speak. Recalling these events and the emotions they included relieved her paralysis and restored her knowledge of her native tongue.

Breuer concluded that Anna's symptoms were somehow determined by traumatic or stressful events of the past and that the recollection of these events had a cathartic effect. *Catharsis* refers to emotional release. When Anna recalled the events, she did so with a great deal of emotional intensity. This evidently freed her of the symptom to which the emotion had become attached.

By mid-1882, it appeared that Anna was completely and dramatically cured. In any event, it was said that Breuer was anxious to end the treatment, because Anna's open proclamation of love and strong demands for his services embarrassed him and created domestic problems with his wife. When Breuer announced his wish to end the case, Anna offered a phantom pregnancy as a final symptom.

Best known as the first patient treated by psychoanalysis, Anna O. (Bertha Pappenheim in real life) later became one of the first social workers.

Breuer was very shaken by this turn of events and abruptly dropped the case. He avoided the cathartic method in treating future patients. Although her treatment may not have been as successful as Breuer and Freud asserted (Roth, 1998), Anna, whose real name was probably Bertha Pappenheim, eventually became well known as one of the first social workers, striving to improve the rights and status of children and women (Guttmann, 2001; Swenson, 1994). The entire case would probably have gone unnoticed in medical history had Breuer not mentioned it to some of his coworkers, including the young doctor Sigmund Freud, who was deeply interested.

Some time later, Freud recalled the Anna O. episode and began to use the "talking method" with his own patients. He had some measure of success and, after observing his own explorations with the technique, concluded that at the time of the original traumatic event, the patient had to hold back a strong emotion. Perhaps because of the circumstances that surrounded the event, the patient was unable to express the emotion it evoked in a normal way through thought, word, or deed. The emotion, prevented from escaping normally, had found another outlet and was expressing itself through a neurotic symptom. Until they were recalled under hypnosis, the details of the events and the emotions they involved were not a part of the patient's awareness. Thus the patient was *unconscious* of these memories, but the unconscious memories were influencing the present behavior.

Shortly thereafter, Freud decided to give up hypnosis (cf. Aron, 1996). In part, it was a practical necessity, because not all of his patients could be hypnotized. He assured his patients that eventually they would be able to remember the traumatic events in a normal waking state. Abandoning hypnosis also proved to be an important step in Freud's discovery of resistances. He had found that assisting his patients to remember was a long process. This led him to think that although the patient consciously wanted to remember those events, some force within prevented the patient from becoming aware of them and kept the memories unconscious. Freud labeled this force *resistance.*

Recognizing resistance leads to a dynamic understanding of **unconscious processes,** or forces of which a person is unaware. You may not immediately be able to recall what you did on your last birthday, but with a little effort you probably could remember. Unconscious memories are different. You may recall having been punished as a child but be unable, no matter how hard you try, to remember why you were punished. Such a memory has been rendered unconscious or *repressed.* It can be recalled, if at all, only with considerable difficulty.

What were those ideas or thoughts that would be repressed and rendered unconscious? Freud believed that they were **wishes.** During the traumatic event, a wish had been aroused that went against the person's ego-ideal. Because it is hard for people to accept the fact that they are not what they would like to be, such incompatibility causes pain. If it causes too much pain, the wish is repressed.

Underlying Freud's theory is the concept that events and happenings in our lives evoke strong feelings. These emotions help us to evaluate our world, but in some instances the immediate expression of emotion is inappropriate or even disastrous. Ideally, one acknowledges, accepts, and guides an emotion into constructive, or at least harmless, channels of expression.

A certain amount of **repression,** the blocking of a wish or desire from consciousness, is unavoidable and necessary in order for a civilized society to exist. But the repression is not always successful or constructive. An example Freud gave during his lectures at Clark

University illustrates the problems that repressed ideas can create. Suppose, he suggested, that during the course of his lecture a young man in the back of the room interrupts rudely by laughing, talking, and stamping his feet. Other members of the audience, disturbed by his behavior, forcibly eject the young man from the room and station themselves at the door to make sure that he will not reenter the hall. This unpleasant young fellow, however, bangs on the outside of the door, kicks, screams, and, in short, creates a worse ruckus than he made in the first place. A new solution is required: a compromise. Perhaps the audience will agree to permit the young man back into the lecture hall if he will agree to behave a little bit better.

Freud admitted that his spatial metaphor was somewhat misleading, but it served to illustrate his primary concepts. We eject painful wishes, not permitting them to enter consciousness, but the repressed wishes refuse to behave agreeably. Instead, they are expressed in other ways; they create all sorts of problems, produce neurotic symptoms, and so forth. The need, then, is to restore the wishes to consciousness so that we can deal with them realistically.

THE PSYCHOANALYTIC METHOD OF ASSESSMENT AND RESEARCH

Our initial discussion of the origin of psychoanalysis presented it as being simple only for the purpose of abbreviation. In fact, the process is much more complicated than the original illustrations suggest. Essentially, several opposing forces are at work. First, there is a conscious effort on the part of the patient to remember the forgotten events. Second, there is resistance, which persists in keeping the memories unconscious. Finally, there are the unexpressed emotions that continue to seek expression. If a wish cannot get out on its own identity, it will seek an outlet in a disguised form. By putting on a mask, it will manage to sneak out and find expression in the person's behavior. Although the trauma cannot be immediately remembered, it may express itself in a hidden manner through the memories and thoughts that are recalled. In order to delve behind these masks and discover the repressed ideas, Freud developed two primary procedures: free association and the interpretation of dreams and slips.

Free Association

In **free association,** a patient is asked to verbalize whatever comes to mind, no matter how insignificant, trivial, or even unpleasant the idea, thought, or picture may seem. Free association is based on the premise that no idea is arbitrary and insignificant. Eventually, these ideas will lead back to the original problem. For example, Anna O. did not immediately remember the scene of her father's death, but her arm was paralyzed, her vision clouded, and she was unable to use her native tongue. Then, what she did talk about hinted at the hidden event. The instructions for free association are deceptively simple, but, in fact, they are very hard to follow. What happens when we try to verbalize everything that comes to mind? We may be flooded with thoughts and find it impossible to put them all into words. At other times, we may go blank and discover that nothing comes to mind. Also, the thoughts that do come may be very painful to discuss. These intruding ideas are like ore, however, for the analysis eventually reduces them from their crude state to a valuable metal.

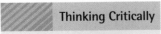

Thinking Critically

What is it like to free-associate? See the Thinking Critically box "Free Association."

Thinking Critically

Free Association

Freud developed free association as an important tool in self-understanding. You can begin to appreciate the value of this tool by trying the following exercise.

Using a tape recorder, choose a time and place where you can be alone and in relative quiet. Assume a relaxed position, and then try to speak into the recorder whatever thoughts come to mind for a period of one half-hour or more. In general, we try to speak logically and develop points in an orderly sequence. Free association requires that we verbalize whatever occurs to us without such order and restriction. You may be surprised, ashamed, and even afraid of the thoughts that emerge. It is difficult to acknowledge hostile and aggressive tendencies, particularly toward those we love. Some of us even have difficulties expressing tender thoughts. Moreover, a petty or trivial thought is often the hardest of all to express. You will be successful if you verbalize and record all of your thoughts, regardless of their significance, importance, pleasantness, or logical order.

When you are finished, put the tape aside. After a reasonable amount of time, perhaps the next day, play the tape back and reflect upon what you have said. Look for patterns and themes. You will be listening to a person who reminds you of yourself in many ways, but in other respects will be unknown. You may discover that you have thoughts and impulses that you did not realize before. They may seem minor, but they will surprise you.

After free association, one *reflects* upon what one has said. In the process, the resistance is analyzed, understood, and weakened so that the wish is able to express itself more directly.

The Interpretation of Dreams and Slips

In the process of free association, particular attention is paid to slips and dreams. **Slips** are bungled acts: a slip of the tongue, a slip of the pen, or a lapse of memory. Many of us dismiss such events as trivial and meaningless, but to Freud slips like these are not without meaning. The Freudian theory assumes that in our psychic life nothing is trifling or lawless; rather, there is a motive for everything.

To understand Freud's view of slips, it is important to distinguish between cause and motive. *Cause* implies the action of a material, impersonal force that brings something about. *Motive* refers to personal agency and implies an emotion or desire operating on the will of a person and leading him or her to act. For Freud, all events are *overdetermined*—that is, they have more than one meaning or explanation. To illustrate: A ball is thrown into the air; after traveling a certain distance, it falls to the ground. A causal explanation of this event would use laws of gravity to account for the ball's fall. A motivational explanation would emphasize that the ball was thrown by someone. This particular ball would not have fallen at this time if someone had not willingly thrown it. Both explanations are correct, and they complement each other. Thus it is not sufficient to argue that we make slips of the tongue because we are tired, although it is true that fatigue may provide the physiological conditions under which a slip may occur. The slip expresses a personal motive as well. Freudian theory is particularly concerned with the explanation in terms of motive.

Here is an example of a slip and its analysis, which Freud reports in *The Psychopathology of Everyday Life* (1901). He recalls how a young student was talking excitedly about the difficulties of his generation and tried to end his comment with a well-known Latin quotation from Virgil but could not finish the line. Freud recognized the quotation and cited it correctly: *"Exoriare aliquis nostris ex ossibus ultor"* ("Let someone arise from my bones as an avenger"). The forgotten word was *aliquis* ("someone"). The student was embarrassed but, remembering the significance that Freud attached to such slips, indicated that he was curious to learn why he had forgotten the word. Freud took up the challenge and asked the student to tell him honestly and without any censorship whatever came to mind when he directed his attention to the word *aliquis*. The first thought that sprang to his mind was the notion of dividing the word as follows: *a* and *liquis*. Next came the words *relics, liquify, fluid.* These associations had little meaning for him, but he continued and thought of Simon of Trent and the accusations of ritual blood sacrifices that had often been brought against the Jewish people. Next he thought of an article that he had read recently entitled "What Saint Augustine Said Concerning Women." The next thought appeared to be totally unconnected, but following the cardinal rule he repeated it anyway. He was thinking of a fine old gentleman whose name was Benedict. At this point, Freud noted that he had referred to a group of saints and church fathers: St. Simon, St. Augustine, and St. Benedict. That comment made the student think of St. Januarius and the miracle of blood. Here, Freud observed that both St. Januarius and St. Augustine had something to do with the calendar and asked the student to refresh his memory about the miracle of blood. The blood of St. Januarius is held in a vial in a church in Naples. On a particular holy day it miraculously liquifies. The people attach a great deal of importance to this miracle and become very upset if it is delayed. Once it was delayed and the general in command of the city took the priest aside and made it clear to him that the miracle had better take place very soon. At this point the student hesitated. The next thought was surely too intimate to pass on and, besides, it had little connection. He had suddenly thought of a lady from whom he might get an awkward piece of news. "Could it be," Freud guessed, "that she missed her period?"

The resolution of the slip was not that difficult. The associations had led the way. The student had mentioned the calendar, the blood that starts to flow on a certain day, the disturbance should that event fail to occur, and the feeling that the miracle must take place. The word *aliquis* and its subsequent allusions to the miracle of St. Januarius revealed a clear concern with a woman's menstrual period. That concern was what was unconsciously occupying the young student when he made the slip. Often a slip is not so obvious and is revealed only after a long chain of associations.

A second area explored by free association is that of dreams (Freud, 1900). For Freud, the dream is the royal road to the unconscious. It is often easy to understand the dreams of young children, because their defenses have not yet masked their motives. They dream very simply of the fulfillment of unsatisfied wishes from the day before. The child who has not received candy desired during the day may dream of an abundance of it at night.

Adult dreams also express unsatisfied wishes, but, because in the adult many of these wishes have become unacceptable to the self-concept, the dream is in disguise. Therefore, Freud distinguishes between the manifest dream and the latent dream. The **manifest dream** is the dream as it is remembered the next morning. Such a dream frequently appears incoherent and nonsensical, the fantasy of a mad person. Nevertheless, it presents some kind of narrative story. The **latent dream** is the meaning or motive underlying the manifest dream.

Analysis seeks to discover the latent meaning that is expressed within the manifest dream. The dream wish, however, has undergone distortion, and its mask must be removed before it will reveal its meaning.

Dreams provide a particular wealth of information because in sleep a person is more relaxed than when awake, and resistance, so to speak, may be caught off guard. The wishes and desires that are forbidden access in normal conscious states have a chance to slip out. Thus, the manifest dream may be described as a disguised fulfillment of repressed wishes.

It is possible, Freud held, to gain some insight into the process that disguises the unconscious dream wishes and converts them into the manifest dream. This process is called *dream work,* and it has many elements. One important element is its use of symbols. Some symbols employed in dreams are unique to the individual dreamer and can be understood only in terms of the individual's particular history and associations. Others are shared by many dreamers. In some instances, symbols have acquired universal meanings; such universal symbols find expression in our myths, legends, and fairy tales, as well as in our dreams (see Bettelheim, 1977).

Freud did not believe that anxiety dreams or nightmares contradicted his concept that dreams fulfill wishes. The meaning of a dream does not lie in its manifest context; thus a dream that provokes anxiety may still serve to fulfill an unconscious wish. The expression of a forbidden wish also causes anxiety or pain to the conscious self, so an anxiety dream may indicate that the disguise was unsuccessful and permitted too clear expression of the forbidden wish.

An example of a dream that Freud analyzed in the course of his self-analysis and reported in *The Interpretation of Dreams* may help to illustrate the procedure of dream analysis. Freud had this dream when he was seven or eight years old and analyzed it some thirty years later. It was a most vivid dream in which his mother, who was sleeping with a particularly calm expression on her face, was carried into the room and laid on the bed by two or three people with birds' beaks.

Freud indicated that as a child he awoke crying from the dream, but he became calm when he saw his mother. In his subsequent analysis of the dream, the tall figures with beaks reminded Freud of illustrations in Philippson's version of the Bible. The birds appeared to be Egyptian deities such as are carved on tombs. Freud's

In his famous dream, Freud saw tall figures with birds' beaks (such as in this statue) carrying his mother, who was sleeping with a calm expression on her face. The analysis of his dream led Freud to the discovery of the Oedipus complex.

grandfather had died shortly before the dream. Before his death, he had gone into a coma and worn a calm expression on his face identical to Freud's mother's expression in the dream. At this level of interpretation, the dream appeared to express a young boy's anxiety over the possible death of his mother. Further analysis led deeper. The name "Philippson" reminded Freud of a neighborhood boy named Philip with whom he used to play as a child. Philip introduced Freud to the slang expression *vögeln,* a rather vulgar German phrase for sexual intercourse. The term originates from the German word *Vogel,* which means "bird." Thus, on a deeper level, Freud had to conclude that the wish expressed in the dream was that of sexual (and therefore forbidden) desires toward his mother. This dream led Freud to the discovery of the Oedipus complex, which will be discussed shortly, and assisted Freud in clarifying the nature of repressed wishes and desires.

The Dynamics and Development of Personality

According to Freud, the nature of our repressed wishes and desires is erotic. This emphasis on sexuality is an aspect of Freud's work that many people find problematic. To understand it requires one to understand how Freud redefined the term *sexuality* and how he used it in his work. Still, Freud's theoretical position on the role of sexuality and his insistence on the human being's sexual nature is threatening to some people.

THE IMPORTANCE OF SEXUALITY

In his early work, Freud viewed sexuality as a bodily process that could be totally understood under a model of tension reduction. The goal of human behavior was simply to reduce the tension created by the accumulation of too much energy and to restore a state of balance. Sexual desires could be compared to a wish to remove an itch. However, as his work developed, Freud began to emphasize the psychological character of mental processes and sexuality. His use of the word **libido** to refer to the emotional and psychic energy derived from the biological drive of sexuality testifies to this shift in his thought.

Freud's desire to emphasize the psychological character of mental processes is also seen in the development of his concept of **drive,** a psychological or mental representation of an inner bodily source of excitement. In his concept of drive, Freud abandoned an earlier attempt to reduce psychological processes to physiological ones and also began to resolve a problem inherited from Cartesian philosophy. The French philosopher René Descartes (1596–1650) had divided all reality into two separate categories: mind and matter. Matter included all material substances, inorganic and animate, including human bodies. These things, Descartes suggested, could be understood under scientific laws. Mind, which included all conscious states (thinking, willing, feeling, and so forth), was a second kind of substance that Descartes believed could not be explained by scientific laws. For the first time in history, a sharp distinction between mind and matter was made the basis of a systematic philosophy. Descartes's philosophy led people in the West to posit the center of the person in the mind rather than in the entire organism. Freud recognized that a comprehensive view of personality must see body and mind as a unity, and his holistic approach began to help repair the Cartesian split. For Freud, a drive is a form of energy that cannot be reduced to either a bodily aspect or a mental one because it combines elements of both.

A drive is characterized by four features: *source,* the bodily stimulus or need; *impetus,* the amount of energy or intensity of the need; *aim,* its goal and purpose (to reduce the excitation); and *object,* the person or object in the environment through which the aim may be satisfied. If Freud had characterized drives simply by source and impetus, he could have continued to think of the sexual drive as just a bodily process. He chose to include also aim and object, which forced him to view sexuality differently and to emphasize its psychological and intentional character. Freud used the German verb *besetzen* (translated as "cathect") to refer to investing libidinal energy in a mental representation of an object that will satisfy a desire; a person cathects an object that he or she wants. The importance of one's sexual life as a bodily process begins to diminish in favor of one's response to it. For this reason, Freud used the term *psychosexuality* to indicate the totality of elements included in the sexual drive. In Freud's view, drives provide a genetic base from which later structures of personality will emerge (Cavell, 1991).

Freud suggested that there are two basic groups of impulsive drives. **Eros** refers to *life impulses* or drives, those forces that maintain life processes and ensure reproduction of the species. The key to these forces is the sexual drive, whose energy force is "libido." **Thanatos,** encompassing *death impulses* or drives, is a biological reality (Badcock, 1992) and the source of aggressiveness, and reflects the ultimate resolution of all of life's tension in death. Although Freud emphasized the importance of the death drive, his discussion of the development of personality centers around the sexual drive.

What is the purpose of sexuality? The traditional answer was reproduction. The medieval theologian Thomas Aquinas (1225–1274) argued in *Summa Theologica* that according to natural law the primary purpose of sexuality was reproduction of the species. Other purposes of sexual activity were secondary and should be submissive to the primary purpose of reproduction.

In the nineteenth-century culture in Vienna, from which Freud's theories emerged, sexual behaviors that did not lead to reproduction, such as homosexuality and masturbation, were disapproved of or regarded as perverse. It is difficult for us today to appreciate the extent to which sexual impulses and desires were then forcibly repressed, especially by the middle and upper classes. The sexual act was generally viewed as beastly and undignified, but it was tolerated as an outlet for a natural shortcoming of men and for purposes of reproduction. Women were supposed to be above sexual impulses, and children were thought incapable of them.

There was considerable anxiety over what were thought to be inappropriate sexual activities and perversions. Rigid taboos were put upon masturbation, and limits were set on the expression of sexuality in adult life. The body's excretory functions were taken care of with embarrassment, and prudery was practiced to fanatical extremes.

At the same time Vienna was undergoing a cultural renaissance in philosophy, music, and literature. The intelligentsia was seeking the realities that lay behind the facade of the decaying Austrian empire. One such reality was sex. To a large extent, Freud shared society's puritan attitude; nevertheless, he also relentlessly searched for the reality behind the mask.

Freud suggested that the primary purpose of sexual behavior is pleasure, opening the door to a host of new ideas. Activities that do not focus on the genitals may be seen as key expressions of sexuality to the extent to which they produce pleasure. The young child, who invariably seeks pleasure in the body, may be seen as having a rich sexual life. Activities such as sucking the thumb, previously seen as separate from sexuality, may be viewed as sexual.

Freud, in effect, turned the traditional concept upside down. This reversal permitted him to account for behaviors that were previously inexplicable, such as sexual variations and infantile sexuality. Freud's redefinition of sexuality was twofold. First, he divorced sex from its previous close restriction to the genitals and reproductive activity. Second, he enlarged the concept of sexuality to include activities such as thumb sucking and sublimation that previously were not thought of as sexual.

In Freudian terms, the child, who actively seeks pleasure from many areas of the body, is **polymorphous perverse**—that is, children's activities differ in many respects from reproductive sexual activity. The sexual activity of children is essentially *autoerotic;* they seek pleasure from their own bodies rather than from the body of another person. They find pleasure in sucking their thumbs, exploring their genitals, and so forth. Only in the course of a long history of development do children progress toward reproductive activities.

THE PSYCHOSEXUAL STAGES OF DEVELOPMENT

Freud (1905) outlined a path that children travel as they progress from autoerotic sexual activity to reproductive activity. In this journey, the libido or sexual drive invests itself in various *erogenous zones* or areas of the body that provide pleasure. Indeed, observations have shown that as children grow they do focus on different areas of the body; this attentional sequence follows the sequence outlined by Freud. He believed that by passing through a series of **psychosexual stages** in which different erogenous zones are important, children move from autoeroticism to reproductive sexuality and develop their adult personalities.

Oral Stage

The first stage is the **oral stage,** which lasts from birth to approximately age one. During this time, the major source of pleasure and potential conflict is the mouth. From it infants receive nourishment, have their closest contact with the mother (in breastfeeding), and discover information about the world. Infants explore new objects with their mouths. The two main types of oral activity, ingestion and biting, are the first examples of character types and traits that may develop later on. Oral activities are also a source of potential conflict because restraints may be placed on them. A mother may seek to discourage thumb sucking or stop her child from biting the breast. Thus the focus of greatest pleasure and conflict for infants is located in the mouth.

Anal Stage

Freud's second psychosexual stage is the **anal stage,** which is expected to occur in the second year of life. At this time, the major source of pleasure and potential conflict is activities involving the anus. Generally, toilet training occurs during this period. Toilet training involves converting an involuntary activity, the elimination of bodily wastes, into a voluntary one. It frequently represents the child's first attempt to regulate instinctual impulses. A clash of wills with the caregiver may develop. Children may obtain pain or pleasure in either retaining or expelling their waste products. These two primary modes of anal expression, retention and expulsion, are further models for possible future character traits. In their efforts to train children, parents may forget that control over the sphincter muscles and elimination is an activity that only the child can perform. As early efforts to discipline children begin, the buttocks are frequently selected as a site on which to inflict pain. Since stimulation

Freud outlined psychosexual stages that children travel as they progress from autoerotic sexual activity to mature reproductive activity. During the oral stage, new objects that the infant meets are typically explored with the mouth.

in the area causes both pleasure and pain, sadistic (pain-inflicting) and/or masochistic (pain-receiving) patterns of behavior may emerge. Subsequent forms of self-control and mastery have their origins in the anal stage.

Phallic Stage

The **phallic stage** of development usually occurs between the ages of three and six. The characteristics of this stage are pleasurable and conflicting feelings associated with the genital organs. The child's interest in the genitals is not with their reproductive function but with their ability to give pleasure in autoerotic activity and their significance as a means of distinguishing between the sexes. At this time, children discover that not all individuals are similarly endowed. They expend considerable energy in examining their genitalia, masturbating, and expressing interest in sexual matters. They are extremely curious, even though their curiosity outstrips their ability to understand sexual matters intellectually. They spin fantasies about the sexual act itself and the birth process, which are frequently inaccurate and misleading. They may believe that a pregnant woman has eaten her baby and that a baby is expelled through the mouth or the anus. Sexual intercourse is frequently viewed as an aggressive act by the father against the mother.

Freud pointed out that for children a fantasy can be as powerful as a literal event in shaping personality, and so in that sense it does not matter whether or not an event really

Thinking Critically

How true are memories recalled in therapy? See the Thinking Critically box "Memories: True or False?"

occurred (cf. Juda, 1991). This point is remarkably consistent with contemporary phenomenological and cognitive points of view, which stress that what is important is not an object or event in itself but rather how it is perceived by an individual. This is not to deny that some children do endure real situations of incest or sexual abuse, or that such situations can have a pervasive negative effect on a child's personality development. Recently Freud has been criticized for abandoning his early "seduction theory," which held that adult neurosis was caused by actual incidents of sexual abuse in childhood, in favor of a theory that saw childhood sexual fantasy and immature cognitive structures as primary contributors to neurosis. Moreover, he has been criticized for suppressing the seduction theory for intellectually dishonest reasons (Masson, 1983) (see also Eissler, 2001; Esterson, 1998; Robinson, 1993; Schimek, 1987). Did ambition or fear of criticism lead Freud to change his theory (e.g., Smith, 2000)? He wrote in a letter that renouncing his earlier position dashed his prospects of becoming a famous physician (Jones, 1953–1957). However, Freud more than anyone else has helped us see that we are often unaware of the motives behind our behavior.

The pleasures of masturbation and the fantasy life of children set the stage for the **Oedipus complex,** which Freud considered one of his greatest discoveries. Freud's concept was suggested by the Greek tragedy of Sophocles in which King Oedipus unwittingly murders his father and marries his mother. A key point is that Oedipus was unaware, or unconscious, of what he was doing. He did not realize that the man whom he met on the road and killed was his own father, nor did he know that the queen whom he later married was his mother. At the same time, he played an active role in bringing about his fate. On discovering the truth, he blinded himself. Within that Greek myth, Freud perceived a symbolic description of the unconscious psychological conflict that each one of us endures. In brief, the myth symbolizes each child's unconscious desire to possess the opposite-sex parent and do away with the same-sex parent.

If the Oedipus complex were to be taken literally, many people would have quickly dismissed Freud's concept as absurd and nonsensical. Incredible as it may seem, Freud suggested that children have incestuous wishes toward the opposite-sex parent and murderous impulses toward the same-sex parent. Do children actually desire to perform sexual intercourse and commit murder? Most preschool-age children have no clearly articulated concept of what sexual intercourse is all about. Furthermore, even if they had the will, they would lack the means to perform the act. Finally, for the preschool-age child, the permanence and reality of death are incomprehensible. As a literal depiction, Freud's concept of the Oedipus complex is clearly absurd.

Nevertheless, by this stage in development, the young boy (to tell his side of the story first) has become very fond of his mother, his primary caregiver. He loves her very much, and he wants to love her as fully as possible. He senses that Mommy and Daddy have a special kind of relationship, which he wants to imitate. He becomes frustrated because he cannot imagine what the relationship is all about or perform it in a similar manner. At the same time, he wants his mother's love in return, but he views love quantitatively as a fixed amount. It is as if his mother's love constitutes an apple. Each kiss or sign of attention that his father receives indicates that a big, juicy chunk has been bitten out of that apple, so that less remains for him. He cannot conceive of love as qualitative or as able to increase to fill a void.

Thinking Critically

Memories: True or False?

Freud's revision of his seduction theory is pertinent to the current debate over "false memories," forgotten childhood events that are remembered in the course of therapy. Loftus (1993) observes that patients often leave therapy with memories of abuse that they did not have on entering therapy. She asks whether the memories reflect actual events or the suggestions of the therapist. Some children do endure real situations of incest or sexual abuse, and such situations can have a pervasive negative effect on a child's personality development. What is an issue, however, is the factualness of memories recovered in therapy—some of which have led to alienation from and even lawsuits against alleged perpetrators. Our memories are not camcorders that record events exactly as they occur. Rather, our memories are reconstructions of the past based on present clues, and they can be altered as data are introduced, discovered, reconceived, or even distorted. The problem, therefore, is that recovered memories, be they positive or negative, may or may not be true.

You can get a clearer idea of how our memories are reconstructions by comparing your recollection of past events with those of your siblings or other family members. You may discover that your version of formative (or not so formative) events in your life is considerably different from how others recall them. Indeed, there may be some key events that you or another family member recalls that others have no memory of whatsoever.

Can you think of past events that you now perceive very differently from before? What led you to change your perception? Perhaps a more important question is, Does your reconstruction play a constructive or destructive role today in your personal development and in your relationships with others?

Viewing love as a quantity, the child perceives his father as a rival who prevents him from obtaining the full love that he desires from his mother. This perception creates wishes and impulses about getting rid of the father, an activity the child is powerless to carry out.

The child's feelings are very intense and conflicting, besides being too difficult for the child to cope with directly on a conscious level. Furthermore, the feelings create guilt because the child's sentiments toward his father are hostile but also affectionate. The child finds it difficult to cope with ambivalent feelings of love and hostility directed toward the same person. His rivalry culminates in **castration anxiety,** which means that he fears physical retaliation from his father, in particular that he will lose his penis.

The Oedipus complex is resolved as follows. First, the son gives up his abortive attempts to possess his mother and begins to identify with his father in terms of sexual gender. In identifying with the same-sex parent, he adopts the moral codes and injunctions of his father. This introjection of the parent's standards of good conduct leads to the development of a social conscience, which assists him in dealing with his forbidden impulses. By identifying with his father, the boy can through his imagination vicariously retain his mother as his love object, because he has incorporated those characteristics of his father that his mother loves. Although he may not have his mother in fact, he can wait until he grows up and then look for a woman who reminds him in some ways of Mom.

The little girl undergoes a similar complex. Freud deliberately did not give it a separate name, because he wished to emphasize the universality of the Oedipal situation. Others, however, have referred to the feminine version as the **Electra complex.** The primary love object for girls is also the mother. Yet girls, on discovering the genitals of the opposite sex, abandon the mother and turn to the father instead, making possible the Oedipal situation in reverse. The disappointment and shame that they feel upon viewing the "superior" penis leads to jealousy of the male, **penis envy,** a sense of inferiority, and a feeling of resentment and hatred toward the mother, who is held responsible for the effected castration. Reluctantly, the girl identifies with her mother, incorporates her values, and optimally makes the transition from her inadequate penis, the clitoris, as her chief erogenous zone, to the vagina. Eventually, her desire for a penis expresses itself in a desire to have a baby boy. Because the female Oedipus complex is secondary, Freud suggests that it is resolved differently from that of the male; thus the woman's ego-ideal (discussed later in the section "The Id, Ego, and Superego") is closer to its emotional origins, and she appears to have less capacity for sublimation. The role that the girl adopts for herself is one that has been outlined for her by her society. Doris Bernstein, however, points out that there really is no parallel story for the girl and that Freud's wish to have one developmental theory blinded him to clear differences (1991).

Latency Period

After the phallic stage, Freud believed that there is a period of comparative sexual calm from the age of about seven to puberty. During the **latency period,** psychic forces develop that inhibit the sexual drive and narrow its direction. Sexual impulses, which are unacceptable in their direct expression, are channeled and elevated into more culturally accepted levels of activity, such as sports, intellectual interests, and peer relations. Freud was relatively silent about the latency period. He did not consider it a genuine psychosexual stage because nothing dramatically new emerges. Today, the latency period as such is questioned by most critics, who suggest it is more correct to observe that children learn to hide their sexuality from disapproving adults.

Genital Stage

With the onset of puberty, the infantile sexual life is transformed into its adult form. The **genital stage** emerges at adolescence when the genital organs mature. There is a rebirth of sexual and aggressive desires, and the sexual drive, which was formerly autoerotic, is redirected to seeking gratification from genuine interaction with others. During the latency period, children prefer the company of same-sex peers; however, in time the object of the sexual drive shifts to members of the opposite sex. According to Freud, the genital stage is the end point of a long journey, from autoerotic sexual activity to the cultural norm of heterosexual activity. Freud believed that mature individuals seek to satisfy their sexual drives primarily through genital, reproductive activity with members of the opposite sex.

Mature people satisfy their needs in socially approved ways. They accommodate themselves to, function within, and seek to uphold the laws, taboos, and standards of their culture. These implications are clearly spelled out for both males and females. The hallmarks of maturity can be summed up in the German expression *lieben und arbeiten,* "to love and to work." The mature person is able to love in a sexually approved way and also to work productively in society.

The Effects of the Psychosexual Stages

The lingering effects of the psychosexual stages are revealed in various adult character types or traits. Freud believed strongly that events in the past can influence the present. If the libido is prevented from obtaining optimal satisfaction during one or more of the stages because it has been unduly frustrated or overindulged, it may become fixated or arrested at that particular stage. This **fixation** creates excessive needs characteristic of an earlier stage. Various adult behaviors that have been ascribed to fixations include smoking, gossiping, overeating, and collecting. The fixated libido expresses itself in adult life according to character types or traits that reflect the earlier level of development. Hence, an orally fixated person is likely to be dependent on and easily influenced by others. At the same time, oral personalities are optimistic and trusting to the point of being gullible. Anal personalities tend to be orderly, miserly, and obstinate. Most people, of course, do not reflect a pure type, but these personality traits and their opposites have their origin in the various psychosexual stages (cf. Caspi, 2000).

All of the sexual activities that Freud considered abnormal are—in his view—at one time normal sexual activities for children. Prototypes of sadistic and masochistic forms of behavior, sexual disorders in which a person obtains pleasure by inflicting pain (sadism) or receiving pain (masochism), are apparent during the toddler years. Voyeurism, obtaining pleasure from seeing sexual organs or sexual acts, is present in the curiosity of the preschool child. Homosexuality, primary attraction to the same sex, is apparent during the latency period and early adolescence when one's primary association is with same-sex peers. Thus Freud believed that sexual deviations may be accounted for in terms of arrested development.

Freud also viewed neurosis as the outcome of an inadequate sexual development, in particular an unsuccessfully resolved Oedipal conflict. Such people are bound to their unhappy past and respond in emotionally immature ways. These unrealistic ways are not helpful to them in the everyday world.

Freud's presentation of the stages of human psychosexual development may appear clumsy, because the gradual change from one stage to another is not as distinct as the outline implies. Therefore, the age references should be seen not as beginning and end points, but rather as focal points, where the stage is at its height. The emergence of the genital stage does not signify the end of the earlier stages; instead, it transforms them. Thus adult behavior is shaped by a complex of earlier conflicts and dynamics. See Figure 2.1.

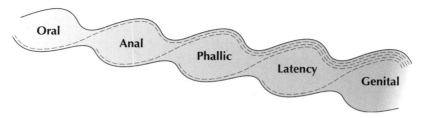

FIGURE 2.1 FREUD'S PSYCHOSEXUAL STAGES

The gradual change from one stage to another is not as distinct as Freud's outline implies. Each stage begins gradually, swells to a climax, and then wanes as the following stage begins to emerge. The dotted lines indicate that remnants of the earlier stages continue into the later ones. The emergence of the genital stage does not signify the end of the earlier stages; instead, it transforms them.

Freud's discussion of the psychosexual stages of personality was set in the framework of nineteenth-century biological determinism (Richards, 1990) and has been soundly criticized for its failure to appreciate deeply enough the influence of social and cultural factors. Nevertheless, empirical child development research argues against outright rejection of Freud's ideas on psychosexual development (Neubauer & Neubauer, 1990; Wilson, 1996). Moreover, Freud's conclusion overturned almost the entire Western tradition of thought concerning humanity. In Freud's theory, human life is subsumed under a sexual model. The way in which people invest their libido determines their future. Freud used sexuality as a model for a person's style of life: Character is built up by responding to one's sexuality; the way in which a person resolves the Oedipus complex is crucial to adult personality; neurosis represents a fixation at an earlier stage of sexual development. The normal or mature individual is one who behaves conventionally, having attained the genital level of sexuality and all its implications. Furthermore, the development of culture and civilization is made possible by sublimated sexuality. Sexuality essentially becomes the model for human understanding.

The Structure of Personality

The familiar Freudian concept of the structure of personality as an id, ego, and superego was a rather late product of Freud's thought. Not until 1923 with the publication of *The Ego and the Id* did his final theory of a threefold structure of personality emerge. In discussing the id, ego, and superego, we must keep in mind that these are not three separate entities with sharply defined boundaries, but rather that they represent a variety of different processes, functions, and dynamics within the person. The psychoanalytic approach to the study of the mind illuminates processes that cognitive and neurological psychologists are studying today from their perspectives. Moreover, in his writings Freud used the German personal pronouns, *das Es, das Ich,* and *das uber-Ich.* Literally translated they mean "the it," "the I," and "the above-I." The Strachey translation into Latin pronouns has made them less personal (Bettelheim, 1982), raising the issue of the desirability of attempting a new translation (Cheshire & Thoma, 1991; Likierman, 1990).

THE ID, EGO, AND SUPEREGO

The **id** is the "core of our being," the oldest and original function of the personality and the basis of the ego and superego. We know little of the id, because it does not present itself to our consciousness in naked form. Therefore, we can describe it only by analogies and by comparing it with the ego. Freud referred to it as a "chaos, a cauldron full of seething excitations." The id includes the instincts and drives that motivate us as well as our genetic inheritance and our reflexes and capacities to respond. It represents our basic drives, needs, and wishes. Further, it is the reservoir of psychic energy that provides the power for all psychological functioning.

The impersonal and uncontrollable character of the id is more readily expressed in the German language than in English. For example, the German idiom for "I am hungry" ("*Es hungert mich*") translates literally as "It hungers me," implying that I am a recipient of actions initiated *in* me, not *by* me.

The id operates according to the pleasure principle and employs primary processes. The **pleasure principle** refers to seeking immediate tension reduction. When libido (psychic energy) builds up, it reaches an uncomfortable level of tension. The id seeks to discharge the tension and return to a more comfortable level of energy. In seeking to avoid painful tension and obtain pleasure, the id takes no precautions but acts immediately in an impulsive, nonrational way. It pays no heed to the consequences of its actions and therefore frequently behaves in a manner that may be harmful to the self or others.

The id seeks to satisfy its needs partly through reflex action. Inborn automatic responses like sneezing, yawning, and blinking are spontaneous and unlearned, and operate without any conscious thought or effort. Many of our reflexes are protective in that they help us to ward off dangers in our environment. Others are adaptive and enable us to adjust to the conditions of our environment. Newborn infants have several reflexes that help to ensure their survival. For instance, they turn their heads toward the source of tactile stimulation. This "rooting reflex" assists them in locating the nipple. Sucking is also an automatic reflex enabling infants to take in nourishment.

The id also seeks to reduce tension through **primary processes,** hallucinating or forming an image of the object that would satisfy its needs. Freud thought that visualizing a forthcoming hamburger or sirloin steak momentarily relieves our hunger pangs; such activity is also called **wish fulfillment.** It is present in newborns, in our dreams, and in the hallucinations of psychotics. Visualizing a bottle or the breast partly pacifies the infant, but it does not satisfy its hunger. Since the primary process does not distinguish between its wish-fulfilling images and real objects in the external world that would satisfy needs, it is not very effective in reducing tension. A second structure must develop if the organism is to survive.

The **ego** ("I") emerges in order to realistically meet the wishes and demands of the id in accordance with the outside world. People who are hungry have to be effective in securing food for themselves from the environment in order to meet their needs and survive. The ego evolves out of the id and acts as an intermediary between the id and the external world. It draws on the id's energy, acquires its structures and functions from the id, and endeavors to serve the id by realistically meeting its demands. Thus the ego is the executor of the personality, curbing the id and maintaining transactions with the external world in the interests of the fuller personality.

Whereas the id obeys the pleasure principle, the ego follows the **reality principle,** satisfying the id's impulses in an appropriate manner in the external world. The ego postpones the discharge of tension until the appropriate object that will satisfy the need has been found. Although the ego does not prevent the satisfaction of the id, it may suspend or redirect the id's wishes in accordance with the demands of reality. The id employs the fantasies and wishes of the primary process; the ego uses realistic thinking characteristic of **secondary processes,** the cognitive and perceptional skills that help an individual distinguish between fact and fantasy. They include the higher intellectual functions of problem solving, which let the ego establish suitable courses of action and test them for their effectiveness. Actually, there is no natural enmity between the ego and the id. The ego is a "faithful servant" of the id and tries to fulfill its needs realistically.

Harbored within the ego as "its innermost core" is the **superego** ("above-I"). Heir to the Oedipus complex, it represents internalized values, ideals, and moral standards. The superego is the last function of the personality to develop and may be seen as an outcome of the interactions with one's parents during the long period of childhood dependency. Rewards and punishments originally placed on us from without become self-administered as we internalize the teachings of our parents and society. As a result of the activity of the super-ego we experience guilt when we disobey acceptable moral standards.

The superego consists of two subsystems: the conscience and the ego-ideal. The **conscience** is the capacity for self-evaluation, criticism, and reproach. It scolds the ego and creates feelings of guilt when moral codes are violated. The **ego-ideal** is an ideal self-image consisting of approved and rewarded behaviors. It is the source of pride and a concept of who we think we should be.

The superego strives for perfection. It seeks moralistic rather than realistic solutions. Practically speaking, the development of the superego is a necessity. The id's demands are too strong, and young children's egos are too weak to prevent them from acting on their impulses. For a period of time, strong introjected moral injunctions—"Thou shalt nots"—are required to curb behavior. But the superego may also be relentless and cruel in its insistence on perfection. Its moralistic demands may resemble those of the id in their intensity, blindness, and irrationality. In its uncompromising manner, the superego may inhibit the needs of the id, rather than permit their ultimate necessary and appropriate satisfaction.

In the well-adjusted adult personality, the ego is the primary executor. It controls and governs both id and superego, mediating between their demands and the external world. In ideal functioning, the ego maintains a balanced, harmonious relationship among the various elements with which it has to deal. Development, though, does not always proceed optimally. The ego frequently ends up harassed by two harsh masters. One demands instant satisfaction and release. The other places rigid prescriptions on that release. Drawing on Plato's analogy, Freud described the ego as a charioteer trying to control two strong horses, each of which is trying to run in the opposite direction from the other.

Freud's final picture of personality is that of a self divided (cf. Brunner, 2002). The specific roles played by the id, ego, and superego are not always clear; they mingle at too many levels. The self is seen to consist of many diverse forces in inevitable conflict. Freud's picture of the person is not optimistic, but it is an attempt to account for the fact that as human beings we are not always able to cope with certain situations.

Although the trifold division of personality appears to be a finished structure, essentially the person is understood as a product of development. The ego and superego have evolved historically in response to specific personal situations. In the case of the superego, that situation is also interpersonal, as it involves other people. It would be wrong to freeze the id, ego, and superego into systems; instead, the personality is created by a dynamic of forces that can be divided against themselves at many levels. Thus, in his mature formulation, Freud holds in tension the biological ground of the self and its historical development.

THE RELATIONSHIP OF THE ID, EGO, AND SUPEREGO TO CONSCIOUSNESS

There is no easy correlation between the words *id, ego,* and *superego* and the qualities of "conscious" and "unconscious." At times, Freud tended to make the easy equation of ego with consciousness and id with unconsciousness. His discoveries, reflected in *The Ego and the Id* (1923), that aspects of the ego and the superego are unconscious, as is the id, forced him to revise his theory. *Conscious* and *unconscious* could be used only as adjectives describing qualities that psychological processes may or may not have.

If one were to diagram Freud's picture of the psyche, perhaps the best image would be Freud's own: an iceberg, nine-tenths of which is submerged under water (see Figure 2.2).

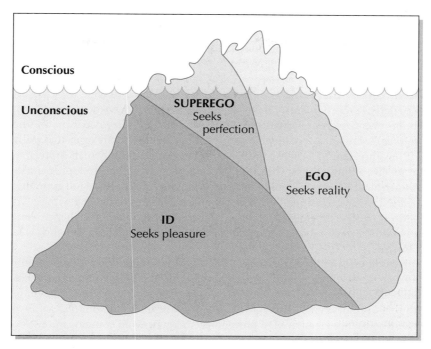

FIGURE 2.2 THE STRUCTURE OF PERSONALITY

Freud used the metaphor of an iceberg to depict the psyche, or personality, in order to emphasize that nine-tenths of it lies submerged in the realm of unconsciousness. Whether unconscious or conscious, the three functions of the personality—id, ego, and superego—interact at many levels as the ego tries to control and moderate the drives of the id and superego.

The surface of the water represents the boundary between conscious and unconscious. Its line intersects, or potentially intersects, all three functions: id, ego, and superego. But any spatial metaphor is ultimately misleading. *Id, ego,* and *superego* are best understood as dynamic functions of personality, whereas *conscious* and *unconscious* are adjectives that describe qualities that these functions may have. The merit of Freud's rejecting his early assumption that consciousness is located in a single center is confirmed by twentieth-century brain-activity monitoring and imaging (Beer, 2003).

The dynamic forces within the self are many. The self is not simply divided against itself by id, ego, and superego but is divided against itself and the world at many levels. Conflict is the keynote of Freud's final understanding of the self. The world, Freud once wrote, is *anake* (the Greek word for "a lack"), too poor to meet all of our needs. As the id's demands increase, the ego becomes overwhelmed with excessive stimulation that it cannot control and becomes flooded with anxiety.

The Ego's Defense Mechanisms

Freud made a distinction among three kinds of anxiety. *Reality anxiety* refers to fear of a real danger in the external world. *Neurotic anxiety* refers to fear that one's inner impulses cannot be controlled. *Moral anxiety* is fear of the retributions of one's own conscience. All have their basis in reality anxiety. In order for an individual to cope with anxiety, the ego develops **defense mechanisms,** procedures that ward off anxiety and prevent our conscious perception of it. Defense mechanisms share two features: They occur on an unconscious level so that we are not aware of what we are doing, and they deny or distort reality so as to make it less threatening. Defense mechanisms are not necessarily maladaptive; indeed, we cannot survive without them. They must be created to assist the developing ego in carrying out its functions. However, should their distortion of reality become too extreme or should they be used to the exclusion of other, more effective means of dealing with reality, defense mechanisms may become maladaptive and destructive, preventing further personal and social growth (cf. Erdelyi, 2001). Some of the more common defense mechanisms follow (see also Table 2.1).

Repression involves blocking a wish or desire from expression so that it cannot be experienced consciously or expressed directly in behavior. It is an involuntary act that prevents us from being aware of many of our own anxiety-producing conflicts or remembering certain traumatic emotional events from our past. The repressed emotion seeks an alternative outlet, and resistance is required to prevent its emergence into consciousness. Nevertheless, once formed, repressions are difficult to eliminate.

Denial entails refusing to acknowledge an unpleasant reality or fact of life. Many people who indulge in substance abuse deny that the alcohol, nicotine, crack, or other substance could ever really hurt them. They may see it affect other people, but they think, "That's not going to happen to me."

Projection refers to the unconscious attribution of an impulse, attitude, or behavior onto someone or something else in the environment. An individual who unconsciously feels hostile toward someone may project the hostility onto the other person. Such a defense reduces anxiety by placing its source in the external world, which makes it seem easier to handle. Further, it permits us to defend ourselves aggressively against our opponent and thereby indirectly express our impulses.

Reaction formation expresses an impulse by its opposite. Hostility, for example, may be replaced by friendship. Frequently, however, the substitution is exaggerated, thereby calling into question the genuineness of the feeling.

In **regression** the person moves backward in time to a stage that was less anxious and had fewer responsibilities. Regression

According to Freud, the defense mechanism of denial allows us to refuse to acknowledge an unpleasant reality or fact of life.

TABLE 2.1 DEFENSE MECHANISMS

MECHANISM	CHARACTERISTIC	EXAMPLE
Repression	Blocking a wish or desire from conscious expression	Being unaware of deep-seated hostilities toward one's parents
Denial	Refusing to accept an unpleasant reality	Refusing to believe that one has AIDS or a terminal cancer
Projection	Attributing an unconscious impulse, attitude, or behavior to another	Blaming another for your act or thinking that someone is out to get you
Reaction formation	Expressing an impulse by its opposite	Treating someone whom you intensely dislike in a friendly manner
Regression	Returning to an earlier form of expressing an impulse	Resuming bedwetting after one has long since stopped
Rationalization	Dealing with an emotion intellectually to avoid emotional concern	Arguing that "Everybody else does it, so I don't have to feel guilty."
Identification	Modeling one's behavior after the behavior of someone else	Imitating one's mother or father
Displacement	Satisfying an impulse with a substitute object	Scapegoating
Sublimation	Rechanneling an impulse into a more socially desirable outlet	Satisfying sexual curiosity by researching sexual behaviors

frequently occurs following a traumatic experience. The child who begins bedwetting again when frightened by the prospect of going to school may be showing signs of regression.

Rationalization involves dealing with an emotion or impulse analytically and intellectually in order to avoid feeling it. As the term implies, it involves faulty reasoning, since the problem remains unresolved on the emotional level. Aesop's fable about the fox who could not reach the grapes and concluded that they were probably sour is a classic example of rationalization.

In **identification** we reduce anxiety by modeling our behavior on that of someone else. By assuming the characteristics of a model who appears more successful in gratifying needs, we can believe that we also possess those attributes. We may also identify with an authority figure who is resented and feared. Such identification may assist us in avoiding punishment. As we have already seen, identification with the same-sex parent plays an important role in development of the superego and subsequent personality.

If an object that would satisfy an impulse of the id is unavailable, we may shift our impulse onto another object. Such substitution is called **displacement.** A child who has been scolded may hit a younger sibling or kick the dog. The substitute object, however, is rarely as satisfying as the original object. Thus displacement does not bring complete satisfaction but leads to a buildup of undischarged tension.

Sublimation rechannels an unacceptable impulse into a more socially desirable outlet. It is a form of displacement that redirects the impulse itself rather than the object. For example, sexual curiosity may be redirected into intellectual research, sexual activity into athletics. Freud suggested that sublimation was crucial to the development of culture and civilization. It is clear from biographical studies that sublimation was a defense commonly used by Freud.

> **Thinking Critically**
>
> Which defense mechanisms do you favor? See the Thinking Critically box "Identifying Defense Mechanisms."

Defense mechanisms, in and of themselves, are not harmful. No one is free of defenses; we need them in order to survive. Although defenses can block personal and social growth if they become predominant, they do protect us from excessive anxiety and frequently represent creative solutions to our problems. Freud developed his concept of defense mechanisms within a western culture and subsequent research on defenses has primarily been conducted in western cultures. However, a comparative study of Americans in the United States and Asian Buddhists living in Thailand showed clear similarities in the use of many defense mecahnisms among the two cultures (Tori & Bilmes, 2002). Research on the development, measurement, and future potential of Freud's concepts of defense mechanisms and ego processes has been summarized by Cooper (1989) and Vaillant (1992a, 1992b) (see also Cramer, 2000).

Psychoanalysis

We have seen that for Freud neurosis emerges from an unsatisfactory or arrested libidinal development, when the realistic satisfaction of erotic needs is denied. The person turns to neurosis as a surrogate satisfaction and creates a partially satisfying world of fantasy. Neurotics have no peculiar psychic content or functioning of their own that is not also found in healthy people. The neurotic is one who falls ill from the same conflicts and complexes with which normal people struggle. There are no clearly defined boundaries between illness and health. The primary question is not "Am I normal or neurotic?" but rather "To what degree is my neurosis debilitating?" Freud himself does not explain pathological and functional behavior by simply separating people into abnormal and normal. His thinking in terms of a continuum has had an impact on how we think about the mentally ill and how we treat patients today. It is also congruent with efforts to encourage the description of psychopathology in terms of dimensions rather than categories (Livesley, Schroeder, Jackson, & Jang, 1994; Millon, 2000b).

TRANSFERENCE

Early in his work, Freud realized that the relationship between patient and physician was important in determining the outcome of the therapy. Nevertheless, it was with considerable embarrassment that he discovered one of his patients had fallen in love with him. We recall that a similar episode with his patient Anna O. had led Dr. Breuer to abandon the cathartic technique. Only after considerable reservations and initial attempts to discourage

Thinking Critically

Identifying Defense Mechanisms

You can familiarize yourself with the various defenses by trying to identify each of the mechanisms in Table 2.1 as you have seen them occur in someone else, and then trying to recognize instances in which you may have used them yourself. It is much easier, of course, to observe defense processes at work in someone else; however, some of the following hints may help you to spot them in yourself.

Have you ever "forgotten" an important event, such as an assigned test or a dentist appointment? You may also recall momentarily forgetting the name of someone you know quite well. Such occasions indicate the tendency we all have to repress. Memory gaps about childhood events, in which you can recall only part of an event but not what preceded or followed, may indicate that the event involved certain traumatic elements that make it hard for you to remember it completely. Have your parents ever told you about an experience that you had as a child but cannot remember? Have you ever found yourself laughing at an inappropriate moment? You may have compensated for an impulse you are ashamed of by reaction formation. Have you ever provided an alibi for something you did or did not do? Could it have been an attempt to rationalize your behavior? Can you recall ever taking out your anger on someone who was helpless, such as a child or pet? Use of scapegoats is a common form of displacement. What kinds of leisure activities, sports, or creative and artistic activities do you enjoy? Through sublimation you may have been able to redirect certain antisocial impulses into socially approved and constructive behaviors. Sublimation is one of the more productive defense mechanisms available to us. In short, we all have and need defenses. Recognizing the use of a defense mechanism is not an occasion for finding fault with ourselves; rather, it is an opportunity for further exploration of our use of defense mechanisms so that they can be employed to foster instead of hinder growth.

---

similar occurrences did Freud begin to appreciate the dynamics of what was happening. He discovered that the feelings that were expressed toward him as a doctor were not directed at him as a person but rather were repetitions of earlier feelings of love and affection that the patient had for significant persons in her life. Thus Freud was forced to recognize the value of the **transference,** a process whereby the patient transfers to the analyst emotional attitudes felt as a child toward important persons. By deliberately cultivating and analyzing the transference, Freud and his patients were able to learn a great deal.

Freud distinguished between *positive transference,* friendly, affectionate feelings toward the physician, and *negative transference,* characterized by the expression of hostile, angry feelings. By studying the transference, Freud learned that his patients were relating to him in the same unsatisfactory and inefficient ways in which they had related to other important people in their lives. However, in the security of analysis, the patient could rework these earlier unsatisfactory relationships through the current relationship to a satisfactory resolution.

It is difficult to know if Freud himself ever fully recognized the implications of the transference, but its cultivation and interpretation have become crucial to the psychoanalytic technique he fathered. Transference offers the patient an opportunity to relive the emotional conflicts and cognitive structures that led to repressions and provides the analyst with a deeper understanding of the patient's characteristic ways of perceiving and reacting. The major point here is that in analysis the patient experiences conflicts under a different set of circumstances. The analyst does not respond to the patient with disapproval or rejection as earlier individuals may have done. Rather, the analyst reacts with insight and understanding, which permits the patient to gain insight into experiences and feelings and allows for change.

Freud's solution is one of *insight,* but the insight that psychoanalysis provides is a special kind of knowing that is not intellectual but existential. It touches the heart as well as the head. The solution lies not in the realm of knowing but in the realm of doing: working through earlier conflicts (cf. Bernstein, 2001). Discovering one's self is not only an intellectual act but also an emotional experience. To use the Socratic expression: "To know is to do." Thus therapy provides a more effective resolution of the situation that provoked the neurosis.

THE ANALYTIC PROCESS

In classical analysis, the patient lies on a couch and the analyst sits behind, out of view. The patient is instructed to verbalize whatever comes to mind regardless of how irrelevant, absurd, or unpleasant it may seem. During free association the patient may make a slip of the tongue or refer to a dream, both of which may be interpreted and utilized to assist the patient to acquire a deeper understanding of the problem.

In the initial phase of analysis, the patient obtains considerable relief just by being able to unburden certain thoughts and feelings to a sympathetic listener. A positive transference is developed, and the patient frequently believes that the analysis has reached a successful conclusion, even though the work of analysis has barely begun. There are as yet undisclosed and conflicting feelings. During the next phase, the analyst gently assists the patient in exploring these emotion-laden areas by pointing out and interpreting the resistance in an effort to weaken the patient's defenses and bring repressed conflicts into the open. The analyst's efforts leave the patient angry, anxious, or depressed; the analyst is now perceived as rejecting and unhelpful. Thoughts of prematurely concluding the analysis may again arise. Eventually the negative transference begins to cohere around specific areas. The patient reconstructs and reexperiences crucial episodes from childhood. The unremediated situation of the past includes not simply insufficiently resolved traumatic events but, more important, inadequately resolved interpersonal relationships and fantasies. The analyst maintains a neutral stance (Thompson, 1996), interpreting the transference and encouraging the patient to reexamine those circumstances in the light of increased maturity. The analyst's stance enables the patient to work through these situations to a more satisfactory conclusion. Last, the analyst assists the patient in converting newly won insights into everyday existence and behavior. This emotional reeducation enables the new insights to become a permanent part of the patient's personality (see Figure 2.3).

In its traditional form, analysis is a protracted and expensive procedure. The patient meets with the analyst for fifty-minute sessions an average of five times a week for a period of several years. This requires a considerable commitment of time, effort, and money. Contemporary analysts have refined the process further, realizing the importance of such issues

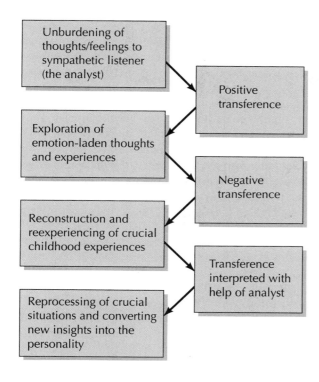

Unburdening of thoughts/feelings to sympathetic listener (the analyst)

Exploration of emotion-laden thoughts and experiences

Reconstruction and reexperiencing of crucial childhood experiences

Reprocessing of crucial situations and converting new insights into the personality

Positive transference

Negative transference

Transference interpreted with help of analyst

FIGURE 2.3 THE ANALYTIC PROCESS

Shown here is a graphic illustration of what happens in psychoanalysis to help move the patient toward a full understanding, reorganization, and basic change of his or her personality structure.

as overcoming resistance, recognizing the danger of countertransference (which proceeds from the analyst to the patient; see Goleman, 1993a; Ornstein, 1993), and working through issues on an emotional level. The goal of psychoanalysis is an ambitious one—a full understanding, reorganization, and basic change of the personality structure. Such goals cannot be accomplished quickly or easily. And, as Freud (1917) once wrote, "A neurotic who has been cured has really become a different person . . . he has become his best self, what he would have been under the most favorable conditions."

Empirical Validation of Psychoanalytic Concepts

Freud's theory generated a great deal of empirical research and attempts to test his concepts. A large body of literature (for example, Fisher & Greenberg, 1977, 1985, 1995; Geisler, 1985; Kline, 1972; Sears, 1943) deals with attempts to test in a laboratory or other setting hypotheses derived from Freud's ideas to see whether they function usefully as science.

As we have seen (in the preceding chapter), many psychologists favor an experimental method because it permits them to infer a cause-and-effect relationship between two factors. Thus, for example, Lloyd Silverman (1976) designed an experiment to test the hypothesis that depression arises from aggressive feelings that have been turned inward against the self. He tried to activate unconscious aggressive wishes to see whether or not they would result in an intensification of depressed feelings. In one session, he showed a group of participants pictures and verbal messages that were designed to elicit unconscious aggressive wishes. The images included pictures such as a fierce man with a knife and the message "Cannibal eats person." In another session, Silverman showed the same group neutral images of people reading or walking. These two sets of images constituted the independent variable. The subjects were exposed to the images for only 4/1000 of a second, so that their perception was assumed to be subliminal. Before and after the sessions, the subjects were asked to rate their feelings. Their self-ratings represented the dependent variable. As expected, the participants reported more depressive feelings after seeing the aggressive images than after seeing the neutral ones. Silverman's experiment, and other efforts to test Freud's theory, have demonstrated much ingenuity and sophistication.

Not all Freudian concepts have held up well under scrutiny. For example, it has become untenable in light of modern research in embryology, biology, and female psychosexual development to view the female as a castrated male whose less-developed superego and negative view of her body are due to penis envy (Small, 1989). Wolberg (1989) suggests that Freud's views on female sexuality are more illuminating about the dilemmas Freud faced when his observations did not fit his theory. Similar comments have been made about some of his case studies (Magid, 1993). Nor has it been substantiated that the male resolves the Oedipus complex by identifying with the father and accepting his superego standards out of fear (cf. Bernstein, 2001; Schultz, 1990). Studies have supported Freud's idea that dreams may express in a disguised or symbolic manner an individual's emotional concerns (Breger, Hunter, & Lane, 1971), but they do not confirm that dreams fulfill unconscious wishes (Fisher & Greenberg, 1995).

> **Thinking Critically**
>
> Did Freud hate women? See the Thinking Critically box "Freud on Women and Women on Freud."

Other Freudian concepts, however, appear to stand up under scrutiny. These include aspects of Freud's oral and anal personality types (Fisher & Greenberg, 1995; Kline, 1972). Studies in both normal and psychiatric populations seem to confirm that psychopathology results from unconscious, conflicting aggressive or sexual wishes. Brain research has supported concepts such as unconscious processes, primary process cognition, conversion disorders, and the conflictual nature of the mind (Ducat, 1985). The concept of repression has been operationally defined as a stronger tendency to forget events identified with unpleasant or fearful associations than with neutral or pleasant events (Davis, 1987; Glucksberg & King, 1967). Defining unconscious as *unable to be verbalized* enables such processes to be subjected to experimental study (Kline, 1987). Experimental testing of these and other psychoanalytically oriented hypotheses indicates their usefulness (Hammer, 1970; Shurcliff, 1968; Silverman, 1976).

It is often difficult to translate Freud's concepts into operational procedures that allow for unequivocal testing. The operational translation of many of Freud's concepts may misinterpret and oversimplify his ideas. The Freudian theory of repression does not simply imply experiences associated with unpleasant thoughts; thus studies on repression and unconscious forces may deal with phenomena that are essentially different from the kind of phenomena that concerned Freud (Kihlstrom, 1999). At this time, there is no direct evidence that will substantiate many of Freud's concepts. Moreover, if the concepts are distorted and minimized, they will not truly represent the constructs in Freud's thought. Freud's own investigations and those of other psychoanalysts hardly allow for replication because they were carried out under conditions of privacy and confidentiality.

Some critics believe that the scientific pretension of psychoanalytic theory rests on very shaky ground (Fingarette, 1963; MacIntyre, 1958). In his assertions of this thesis, Grünbaum (1984, 1993, 2006) concedes that some of Freud's concepts are open to falsification, one of the criteria for evaluating scientific statements, but he contends that clinical data are unacceptable as scientific support; Macmillan (1991, 1997) asserts that Freud made his theory more complex as he sought to cover over the failure of his earlier concepts to account for his observations; and Crews (1996) baldly concludes that "there is literally nothing to be said, scientifically or therapeutically, to the advantage of the entire Freudian system or any of its component dogmas." In response to these critics, Robinson (1993) wrote a sustained rebuttal suggesting that the arguments are biased and the evidence used is ambiguous.

Thinking Critically

Freud on Women and Women on Freud

Most of his patients were women, but Freud usually wrote as if he were dealing only with men, and he used a male paradigm, or model, in his theory. The little he wrote of the development of women has been the subject of considerable criticism and debate. In Freud's theory, women come across as deficient men, lacking a penis and with an immature superego. Freud's view of women reflected the male chauvinistic position of his time.

In his famous dictum "anatomy is destiny," Freud intended to correct Napoleon's earlier motto, "history is destiny," pointing out that history is not the sole component of personality development. In his theory, Freud emphasized the importance of anatomy, in particular one's reproductive organs, as well as history. Research on sexual differences shows that much of Freud's explanation was based on incorrect information. The clitoris, for example, is not an immature penis. The prenatal precursors of the genitals mature into female organs unless the fetus is programmed by genetics to become male. At the same time, research in behavior genetics, gender, and moral development indicates the importance of biology for understanding the individual (also see Neubauer & Neubauer, 1990).

The problem is not that Freud's view of women was determined by anatomy, biological determinism, and cultural restraints, but that his understanding of *all* human development was colored by the same interpretation. His discussion of the psychosexual stages of the male, no less than the female, was permeated with the notion of biological determinism and reflected the bias of the male-dominated culture in which he lived. As Juliet Mitchell (1974) has pointed out, "psychoanalysis is not a recommendation *for* a patriarchal society but an analysis *of* one." The basic beliefs of contemporary psychoanalytic theory are very relevant to the understanding of the psychology of women and gender (Chodorow, 2002). You should note, moreover, that women played a major role in the psychoanalytic movement and that Freud encouraged his daughter Anna and other women to become actively involved.

What do you think? Has Freud been unfairly or appropriately maligned for his discussion of women? To what extent were his concepts a product of his social and cultural milieu? How does your sense of yourself as a man or a woman draw on both the personal experience of your body and the culture to which you belong?

Moreover, he claims that the critics basically distort Freud and ignore his achievements in revolutionizing the way we think about ourselves (cf. Lothane, 2001). Greenberg and Fisher (1995) suggest that although much of Freud's theory defies or fails scientific testing, it has more scientific backing than is commonly recognized.

Shevrin (1995a) has stimulated discussion on the possibility that psychoanalysis is two separate but related sciences: an applied clinical science and a basic science of the mind. And Jacobson (1996) has introduced a series of essays about the relationship between psychoanalysis and science, in which Schwartz (1996) questions why such criticisms of Freud have had such an impact, since they are based on a narrow conception of science. Other critics are very optimistic about achieving a merger of experimental operations and clinical observations in the study of psychoanalytic phenomena. Western (1998) summarizes experimental findings that support the existence of pervasive unconscious influences on emotional responses, social preferences, and habitual behavior. Most psychologists today agree that much of our behavior occurs against our conscious wishes, on an unconscious level (Pervin, 2003).

There are similarities in the approaches of psychoanalytic theory and cognitive psychology. Both draw on a multidisciplinary perspective and seek to discover and describe the mental structures that underlie conscious events. Stein (1997) has brought together efforts by researchers to create a synthesis incorporating the best of the two traditions (cf. Funder, 2001). The work of these researchers and clinicians underscores the importance of collaboration in developing an integration between an interpretive approach that risks dismissing unconscious mechanisms as insignificant narrative devices and a narrow scientific approach that risks missing significant meaning, social context, and interaction among biological and psychological levels.

Freud was initially a neurologist. He often said that psychoanalysis and the biology of the mind needed to be brought together. In an unfinished, unpublished manuscript *Project for a Scientific Psychology* begun in 1895, he started to describe the brain and the mind in a way that anticipates contemporary neuroscience (Tabin, 2006). But without today's technology of brain scanners and monitors of brain electrical activity, Freud hit a stone wall and thus detoured into psychology and talk therapy.

Today, functional MRI technology confirms the existence of unconscious emotional processes. For example, activity is seen in the amygdala, the brain's fear center, as subjects are shown images of frightening faces, paced too quickly for conscious awareness (Etkin et al., 2004). Brain-scanning images of "motivated forgetting" show activity reduced in the hippocampus (which retrieves memories) and increased in the lateral prefrontal cortex (which inhibits reflexive actions), confirming Freud's notion of a mental mechanism at work in repression (Anderson et al., 2004). Attempts to test Freud's theory through such technologies as brain scanning have only begun. Other researchers are studying the neurological circuitry of the mind in conflict, the libido, and the impact of early emotional traumas (Adler, 2006; Guteri, 2002). Some foresee a convergence of psychoanalysis and neuroscience (Edelson, 1986; Kandel, 2006; Power 2000). It is unrealistic to imagine that all of the particulars of Freud's theory will be confirmed by modern technology. However, advanced neuroscientific research gives credence to many of Freud's insights and hunches (cf. Damasio, 2001), and we marginalize him at our own peril. Perhaps it's time to admit him back into mainstream psychology (Bornstein, 2005).

There is a wealth of information in modern psychology that was not available to Freud: the findings of anthropology regarding the cultural nature of humanity, empirical studies of mother-infant interaction and of the competence of infants, the discovery of REM (rapid eye movement) sleep (Winson, 2002), the role of emotions in individual arousal and social communication, the growth of the psychology of sex differences, and studies in cognitive style (Lewis, 1988), as well as the field of psychoanalytic infant research (Wilson, 1996) and neuroscience (Domhoff, 2001). Given the information that was not available to him, the visionary nature of many of Freud's ideas and the fact that his concepts continue to engender such lively research and debate is all the more impressive.

Freud's Theory

Educated in the precise methods of nineteenth-century science, Freud established a reputation as a medical researcher before he developed the theory of psychoanalysis. In his writings he clearly defined and described the scientific enterprise. He asserted that knowledge is based on empirical observation, and he dogmatically maintained that his own theories were so based. His concepts, he claimed, were merely tentative constructs to be discarded if later observation failed to confirm them. He frequently revised his theories because new data had emerged that could not be accounted for by those theories.

Freud made careful observations of his patients in the therapeutic setting and garnered considerable information from the techniques of free association and dream analysis. He made interpretations and viewed the subsequent behavior of his patients as either confirmation or disproof of his hypotheses. And he also conducted his own self-analysis, beginning in 1897 and continuing throughout his life. Data collected through self-analysis may properly be called empirical, since it is based on observation. The fact that the observer is looking in ("introspection") rather than out ("extrospection") does not make the data any less empirical, although information gathered through introspection may be more difficult to test.

Nevertheless, in determining how Freud's theory functions, we have to look not only at the data on which it was initially based but also at the method Freud used to test the data. Although he claimed that he was merely extending scientific knowledge by placing the psychic life of human beings under scientific observation, Freud permitted many of his concepts to function philosophically. We have seen that an important criterion of scientific constructs is the requirement that they be open to falsification; the desire to be scientific reflects itself in an effort to test constructs by validating evidence rather than by simply relying on the compelling character of a philosophical assumption. Freud, however, defined many of his concepts as all-controlling factors in everything we do, think, and are. It is impossible to conceive of any activity in Freud's theory that does not reflect unconscious motives, as well as conscious ones. The doctrine of unconscious processes is thus lifted out of an immediate empirical construct and made applicable to all possible human behavior. Even objections to the concept can be explained in terms of resistance or other unconscious processes. Sexuality is a philosophical concept insofar as Freud asserted that all human behavior can be considered in its light.

And so we see that Freud drew conclusions from careful self-observation and from the observation of his patients in a clinical setting and projected those conclusions into philosophical assumptions. Although Freud invested his theories with an aura of science, in evaluating them he made primary use of philosophical criteria, relying on their compelling power rather than on validating evidence. The kind of knowing on which psychoanalysis is ultimately based is epiphanic, a form of knowing that does not rely on everyday experiences but transcends them.

It is inaccurate to portray Freud as a scientific medical doctor. To do so distorts much of the humanism present in his writings and blunts the challenge of psychoanalysis, which is to know oneself with the constant obligation to change oneself

(Bettelheim, 1982). In evaluating Freud's opus, therefore, it is most appropriate to use the criteria that apply to philosophical positions and ask if his work is coherent, relevant, comprehensive, and compelling.

Which philosophical assumptions did Freud emphasize? See the Philosophical Assumptions box "Examining Freud."

Although Freud changed and revised his theory, in the end it presented a coherent pattern with a clearly recognizable, consistent thrust. To be sure, his theory is not a finished whole. Not only did he continually modify it, but it has been revised, modified, and updated by others working within the Freudian tradition. Freud was frequently unsympathetic to efforts to modify his theory and claimed the ultimate right to declare what should and should not be called psychoanalysis, but he was not unreceptive to changes that reflected the spirit of psychoanalysis as an evolving movement of a particular form of thought and investigation.

MacIntyre (1958) suggested that Freud's theoretical work denoted a "kind of creative untidiness." His thought was characterized by illuminating insights followed by efforts at sterile systematization, yet "he never presents us with a finished structure but with the far more exciting prospect of working through a number of possible ways of talking and thinking." This may be taken as the essential character of Freud's work. He seems to be saying, "You don't have to talk that way"—that personality can be illuminated by a different picture. If you take one image and isolate it, you tend toward being either reductionistic or projectionistic. Thus Freud himself would talk several different ways at once, often flagrantly contradicting himself in order to illumine his subject. Freud depicted a person as simultaneously an economic machine, a personal history, and a case, and as a being who is comprehended totally by sexuality, as well as socially and historically constructed.

For Freud's ideas to be relevant in the twenty-first century, they must be reworked and reformulated in contemporary terms (cf. Chessick, 2000; Gauchet, 2002; Weinberger & Westen, 2001). Many of Freud's arguments, informed by nineteenth-century culture, science, and philosophy, are quite dated. New challenges to the ideas that have undergirded psychoanalysis require that theorists work to broaden the scope and power of psychoanalytic theory (Flax, 1994). Critiques of Freud that focus on the analysis of language and meaning (for example, Ricoeur, 1970) have been helpful in assimilating Freud's work into the greater body of philosophy. Today several of Freud's concepts are seen as foreshadowing current views on the importance of both nature and nurture held by evolutionary biologistic and developmental psychologists (Carver, 1996; Faveret, 2002; Koch, 1991). Freud's theory does not constitute a finished structure; it is an open one capable of continued growth.

The relevance of Freud's theory is evidenced by its impact on the Western world (cf. Loewenberg, 2001). His influence can be seen in the works of Salvador Dali and Alfred Hitchcock, for example. Freud's faults were his virtues in that they enabled him to break through the rational optimism of the Enlightenment and make possible a new view. Most of the particulars may be proven wrong (Adler, 2006), but Freud changed, perhaps irrevocably, humanity's image of itself. Since Aristotle, the essence of humanity had been located in the ability to think. This image found

✳ Philosophical Assumptions

Examining Freud

Many of the differences among personality theories can be attributed to fundamental differences in philosophical assumptions. Which of the basic philosophical issues, described in the introductory chapter and summarized on the inside back cover, seem to be clearly important to Freud in the development of his theory? How, for example, does Freud's emphasis on unconscious factors underlying behavior influence his stance on freedom versus determinism? In his articulation of the psychosexual stages, is his emphasis on heredity, on the environment, or on both? Does his discussion of psychoanalysis lead you to believe that he has an optimistic or pessimistic view concerning the possibility of significant changes in behavior? Does his theory address any other philosophical assumptions? Rate Freud on a scale from 1 to 5 on those philosophical assumptions that you feel his theory applies to most. Compare your ratings of Freud with your own philosophical assumptions. Did your study of Freud lead you to change any of your assumptions? Why or why not?

ultimate expression in Descartes's phrase "I think, therefore I am." In this post-Freudian world, our self-image has changed. We no longer conceive of ourselves as primarily rational animals; rather, we are pleasure-seeking, sexual, and aggressive creatures driven by our emotions. In a sense Freud begins his philosophy with "I love (or crave), therefore I am." For many, the gospel of psychoanalysis is not "good news" because it forces us to consider aspects of ourselves that we would prefer to ignore. Still, it is nearly impossible to deny Freud his influence.

The impact of Freud's accomplishments has been compared with the impact of Copernicus, Darwin, and Einstein. Freud's name is a household word. Errors of the pen or tongue are commonly known as "Freudian slips," and many people cannot make one without wondering what the unconscious reason is. Freud grappled with ideas that were, are, and will continue to be of primary concern to us. Because of that, his theories interest, allure, and excite people.

Freud's aim was to develop a comprehensive theory of humanity. He consistently maintained that his study of neurosis would eventually provide a key to the study of psychological processes in general. Freud's quest for the truth was unrelenting. No question was too small for his consideration; no probe was too trivial; no psychological process was too insignificant for his attention. To look for meaning on the surface was, for him, to settle for appearances and superficiality. Only by risking a plunge into the depths of the unconscious could one discover the truth about oneself and others. Any contradiction or opposition to his theory was to be met by analysis of the resistance, for only through such analysis could true insight emerge.

Some (see, for example, Ellenberger, 1970; Sherman, 1995) have suggested that Freud founded a school comparable to the philosophical schools of ancient Greece and Rome. With the creation of psychoanalysis, Freud developed a movement characterized by its own rules, rituals, and doctrine of membership. As an art,

Freudian psychoanalysis is an excellent example of the scholarly approach to psychotherapy (cf. Magid, 1993). The proliferation of later forms of talk therapy is part of Freud's legacy (Adler, 2006; Kole, 2006).

It is possible that after studying Freud one may agree that his concepts are coherent, relevant, and comprehensive, yet remain uncompelled. Freud would counter that the insight required for a full appreciation of his theory is of a particular kind, one that can be acquired only through the kind of analytic self-investigation that he and his followers practiced. Freud's theory is by no means universally accepted. Indeed, few other positions in the history of philosophical thought have been subject to as much attack, ridicule, criticism, and revisionist study (see, for example, Crews, 1998; Torrey, 1992). In modern science, only the theory of Charles Darwin has been met with equal scorn and resistance. Nevertheless, Freud's picture of personality is one that compels many people. Freud's "core idea" is that life is "essentially conflicted" (Lear, 2005). His picture of the person as beset by anxieties, governed by forces of which we are largely unaware, living in a world marked by external and internal strife, resolving problems by solutions informed by fantasy or reality, is a concept of personality that some people find inescapable. Nevertheless, Freud's work reflects the cultural and social values of Western Europe and North America. The concept of ego is rooted in a culture that cultivates and emphasizes the individual. Such a concept may not be as fundamental to the development of personality in collectivist societies such as Latin America, Africa, and Asia (Landrine & Klonoff, 1992; Markus & Kitayama, 1991). Psychodynamic theories have also been criticized for implying that pathology arises out of deviations from a nuclear patriarchal family model. Empirical evidence indicates that healthy psychological development occurs within other varieties of family structure, such as matriarchal, extended, gay, lesbian, and single-parent families (Hall & Barongan, 2002). Still, Freud's original theory was revolutionary (cf. Kramer, 2006) and formed the basis for much theoretical expansion and current reflection. His later writings on the dynamics and necessary tensions of political life tellingly warn us against our "fundamental urge" to seek premature dogmatic solutions in an era of terrorist behavior (Edmundson, 2006). We can expect that psychoanalytic theory will continue to evolve in the future and will take into account a broadened cultural perspective.

TO LEARN MORE about hypnotherapy, about the status of psychoanalysis today, and about defense mechanisms, and for a list of suggested readings, visit the *Personality Theories* textbook website at **college.cengage.com/pic/engler8e.**

Summary

1. The case of Anna O. may be seen as the beginning of psychoanalysis. Anna O. suffered from a conversion disorder in which her right arm and leg were paralyzed. She had difficulty seeing, was nauseous, and was unable to drink any liquids or to speak and understand her mother tongue. She was also prone to states of absence. Dr. Joseph Breuer hypnotized her and asked her to verbalize associations she might have to words she mumbled during her absences. She began

to tell him stories about her father's illness and death. After she had told a number of these stories, her symptoms went away.

Freud began to use the "talking method" with his own patients, and he concluded that at the time of the original trauma the patient had had to hold back a strong emotion. The patient had forgotten the event and was unconscious or unaware of it. Freud's concept of unconscious processes is a dynamic one in which certain forces repress undesirable thoughts and then actively resist their becoming conscious.

2. An emotion that is prevented from expressing itself normally may be expressed through a neurotic symptom. **Wishes** (p. 33) are repressed because they are at odds with a person's self-concept. Underlying Freud's concept is the idea that emotions that accompany events must ultimately be expressed. If they cannot find direct expression, they will find indirect expressions, such as neurotic symptoms. Ideally, the expression of emotions is nondestructive.

3. Freud developed the technique of **free association** (p. 34) in order to help his patients recover repressed ideas. The patient is asked to verbalize whatever comes to mind no matter how insignificant, trivial, or even unpleasant the idea might be. Later he or she *reflects* upon those associations.

4. Freud considered **slips** (p. 35) and dreams to be the "royal road" to the unconscious. They are analyzed by free-associating to the slip itself or to various elements of the dream. The analysis helps us to distinguish between the **manifest dream** (p. 36) and the **latent dream** (p. 36) that underlies it.

5. The nature of our repressed wishes and desires is sexual. Freud redefined the concept of sexuality as pleasure seeking. In doing so, he reversed many traditional concepts and was able to account for previously unexplained behaviors. As his work developed, he emphasized the psychological aspects of mental processes and sexuality, an emphasis apparent in his use of the terms **drive** (p. 38) and **libido** (p. 38).

6. Freud outlined a set of **psychosexual stages** (p. 40) that children travel as they progress from **autoerotic** (p. 40) sexual activity to mature, reproductive activity. The libido invests itself in various **erogenous zones** (p. 40). During the **oral stage** (p. 40), the major source of pleasure and pain is the mouth. The **anal stage** (p. 40) follows; libidinal energy is focused on the anus and the buttocks. During the **phallic stage** (p. 41) the genital organs become important, and children experience the **Oedipus complex** (p. 42), whose resolution leads to the development of a **superego** (p. 47) and sexual identification. The **latency period** (p. 44) is one of rest, and the **genital stage** (p. 44) begins at puberty when the sexual organs mature and the individual is able to assume the sexual role outlined by his or her culture.

7. The effects of the psychosexual stages can be seen in various adult character traits and disorders. If the libido is unduly frustrated or overindulged at an early stage, it may become **fixated** (p. 45). Many adult behaviors reflect early patterns that are characteristic of the different stages.

8. The **id** (p. 46), **ego** (p. 47), and **superego** (p. 47) represent different structures of the personality. The id is the oldest and original structure. It includes our genetic inheritance, reflexes, and instincts and drives that motivate us. It operates according to the **pleasure principle** (p. 46) and uses **primary processes** (p. 47). The ego develops in order to realistically meet the wishes of the id. It follows the **reality principle** (p. 47) and operates according to **secondary processes** (p. 47). The superego consists of a **conscience** (p. 48) and the **ego-ideal** (p. 48). It strives for perfection.

9. In the mature and well-adjusted personality, the ego is the executor controlling and governing the id and superego and mediating between their demands and the external world. In the maladjusted personality, the id or the superego gains control.

10. There is no easy correlation between the id, ego, and superego and consciousness or unconsciousness. The terms **conscious** (p. 48) and **unconscious** (p. 48) are best seen as adjectives describing qualities that the id, ego, and superego may or may not have.

11. Freud distinguished between reality anxiety, neurotic anxiety, and moral anxiety.

12. In order to protect us against anxiety, the ego develops defense mechanisms that occur on an unconscious level and deny or distort reality so as to make it less threatening. Some of the more common defense mechanisms are repression, denial, projection, reaction formation, regression, rationalization, identification, displacement, and sublimation. Freud believed that by strengthening the ego we can become more aware of our impulses and deal with them more effectively.

13. Freud's psychoanalysis emphasizes the importance of the **transference** (p. 53), in which the patient transfers to the analyst emotional attitudes felt as a child toward significant persons. The patient repeats with the analyst infantile and ineffective ways of relating to other people. The analysis permits the patient to reexperience and rework these relationships to a more satisfactory resolution.

14. Efforts to test Freud's concepts have been made, and the results are mixed. It is difficult to translate many of his concepts into operational procedures that allow for an unequivocal test.

15. Although Freud frequently suggested that his theory functioned as science, he permitted many of his concepts to function philosophically. Thus, in the final analysis, Freud's theory needs to be evaluated as a philosophy, in terms of its coherence, relevance, comprehensiveness, and compellingness.

Personal Experiences

1. When was the last time you suppressed (deliberately held back) a thought or action? What was the nature of the emotion—anger, laughter, aggression, lust? What context were you in, and how did context play a part in your suppression? How did the situation unfold because of your suppression, for better or worse? Would circumstances have unfolded differently had you acted upon your emotions? If so, how? Unlike suppression, repression occurs involuntarily and on an unconscious level so that we do not realize at the time that we are doing it. Freud claimed that suppression and repression are necessary for a civilized society to exist. Does your experience support or refute his claim?

2. Did you ever commit a Freudian slip? If so, what was the context? Do you feel as did Freud that the slip revealed something about your unconscious motives? If so, how? You can use free association to begin to understand your own slips. Simply verbalize whatever comes to mind as you ponder a slip. Later, reflect thoughtfully on your associations, looking for patterns and themes that emerge.

3. Recall the last vivid dream you had or a recurring dream from your childhood. Describe it in as much detail as you can, recounting colors, people, emotions, actions. Why has this

dream remained with you above all others? Do you feel that it relates somehow to your waking life? Taking each element of the dream one by one, you can use free association to begin to interpret your dream. Are you able to identify a dream wish underlying the manifest dream? Do you agree with Freud's theory of dream interpretation? How does your own experience with dreams refute or support Freud's assessment of dreams?

4. How does your own experience relate to the psychosexual stages of development that Freud described? For your earliest years, ask your family members for information about your habits, behaviors, and tendencies. Did you suck your thumb, use a pacifier? For how long? Were you easy to potty-train; how long did your potty training take? What was your temperament like and when? Then use your own recollections to fill in the later years of your childhood. Once you've compiled all the information about yourself, see how it fits into (or doesn't fit into) Freud's theory about psychosexual stages of development. Do any of your past behaviors help inform who you are today?

5. Think of a situation in which you experienced conflict between something you wanted to do but felt you should not do. If you were to dramatize the roles of the id, ego, and super-ego in this conflict, how would you do so? What would each of them be saying to you and urging you to do? Draw a picture of the id, ego, and superego in this conflict. What images come to mind to best express their roles?

PART TWO

The Neopsychoanalytic Approach

Although he always had a group of loyal followers, it was no doubt inevitable that a dynamic figure like Freud would both attract and repel. Some of his original followers became dissatisfied with orthodox psychoanalysis, defected from the movement, and founded their own schools of thought. Carl Jung, Alfred Adler, Karen Horney, and Erich Fromm were all deeply indebted to Freud and psychoanalysis, which provided a major impetus for their work. At the same time, each reacted in varying ways against Freud's psychoanalytic theory and developed his or her own position. In many instances, certain developments in these theories have been identified as valuable elaborations or adjuncts to classical psychoanalysis. Nevertheless, each theorist presented his or her theory as one that could stand by itself, and they all attracted followers who continue today to champion their contributions.

CHAPTER 3

Analytical Psychology

▪ Carl Jung

YOUR GOALS FOR THIS CHAPTER

1. Explain how Jung used the term **psyche.**
2. Explain how Jung's concept of the **libido** differs from Freud's.
3. Compare and contrast Freud's and Jung's concepts of the ego.
4. Identify two basic **attitudes** and four **functions.**
5. Describe the **personal unconscious** and its **complexes.**
6. Explain how Jung's concept of the **collective unconscious** enlarges upon Freud's.
7. Discuss the following **archetypes: persona, shadow, anima** and **animus, self.** Explain the use of active imagination.
8. Discuss what is involved in Jung's concepts of **self-realization** and how it led to today's quest for **spirituality.**
9. Describe some major features of Jungian psychotherapy.
10. Discuss assessment and research in Jung's theory by describing the Myers-Briggs Type Indicator and efforts to explore ethnic identity.
11. Evaluate Jung's theory from the viewpoints of philosophy, science, and art.

Carl Jung is recognized as one of the greatest and most controversial psychological thinkers of the twentieth century. It would be unfair to consider Jung only as a defector from the psychoanalytic movement. He was a mature scholar, with his own developing ideas, before he encountered Freud. Although he was closely associated with Freud for a period of time, he went on to develop an independent school of thought that contrasts markedly with orthodox psychoanalysis. He is indebted to Freud but is a personality theorist in his own right. His concept of the collective unconscious vastly enlarges an aspect of personality that Freud barely explored.

Biographical Background

Carl Gustav Jung was born in 1875 in Switzerland, where he lived all his life. He was the only surviving son of a poor country pastor and scholar of the Reformed church. Jung described his father as conventional and kind, but weak. He respected his father even though he had difficulty communicating with him, especially in matters of religion, which concerned Jung throughout his life. Skeptical of the orthodox faith in which he was reared, he searched relentlessly for adequate answers. This search is reflected in his psychology, with its interest in religion, mythology, and the occult.

His mother was a powerful person. Jung felt that she was a good mother but that she suffered from emotional disturbances. He was later to describe her as possessing two personalities, one kind and loving, the other harsh and aloof.

Jung described his childhood as lonely and his personality as introverted. Two brothers had died in infancy before Jung was born, and his sister was not born until he was nine. The young boy frequently played by himself, inventing games and carving a small companion out of wood to console himself. These long periods of solitude were later to find expression in his self-analysis. His psychology also reflected his predilection for being alone. Maturity for Jung is defined not in terms of interpersonal relations, as it is for Freud, but in terms of integration or balance within the self.

As a child, he had several close contacts and brushes with death, and he also was familiar with illness. When he was a young child his mother had to be hospitalized for several months, leaving him in the care of an elderly aunt and a family maid. During his youth a series of fainting spells caused him to miss over six months of school. The boy enjoyed the freedom from formal studies that his illness afforded him and the opportunity to explore other areas that interested him but were not in the traditional academic curriculum. However, shortly after he overheard his father's anguished comment to a friend, "What will become of the boy if he cannot earn his living?" his health was restored and he returned to school. Speculation continues to this day as to whether Jung suffered from a childhood psychosis. In any event, his life is a testament to the healing power of the psyche, which can motivate a sufferer to extraordinary accomplishments (Winnicott, 1993).

Jung originally wanted to be an archaeologist, but he could only afford to attend the University of Basel, which did not offer courses in that area. Therefore, he chose to study medicine. He was planning to specialize in surgery when he came across a textbook by Krafft-Ebing, a German neurologist (1840–1902), that described psychiatry as invariably

Carl Jung, initially a follower of Freud, later broke with him and developed his own theory of personality, exploring in depth the collective unconscious.

subjective. The description piqued Jung's interest. From early life Jung had recognized within himself a spiritual dimension that he refused to deny or minimize (Masse, 1994); here was a field that might provide the key to some of the dreams, mysteries, and obscure happenings that he had been trying to understand.

His first professional appointment was as an assistant in a mental hospital in Zurich, where he worked with Eugen Bleuler, a well-known psychiatrist who coined the term *schizophrenia.* Later, he became a lecturer at the University of Zurich. He established a private practice and developed a word-association test in order to study emotional reactions.

Jung first met Sigmund Freud in 1907 after having corresponded with him about their mutual interest for a short period. The two men were highly impressed with each other and with each other's work. That meeting began an intense personal and professional relationship. For some time Freud regarded Jung as his heir apparent, and he looked on him with all of the affection that a father has for his son. When the International Psychoanalytic Society was founded, Jung, with Freud's endorsement, became its first president. They traveled together to Clark University, where both had been invited to lecture.

On several occasions when Jung disagreed with Freud, Freud became very upset and in a few instances actually fainted. In 1913, Jung broke away from Freud and his school. Freud described the break as "a great loss," and it was also shattering for Jung, who entered a period of extensive inner disorientation in which he could not read or write and which eventually led to his self-analysis. Many reasons underlay the break with Freud; the most pronounced point of disagreement was Jung's rejection of Freud's emphasis on sexuality. For Freud, all higher intellectual processes and emotionally significant experiences are ultimately substitutes for sexuality and can be understood thereby. For Jung, sexuality itself must be seen as symbolic. Sexuality and the creativity it represents have a mysterious quality and cannot be fully analyzed or completely depicted.

Thereafter, Jung developed his own school of thought, which eventually came to be known as **analytical psychology.** He wrote extensively, and his unique theories were informed by a vast array of concerns, including Eastern religions, mythology, and alchemy. Although such subjects are frequently considered scientifically suspect, Jung felt that they were essential to the psychologist and indispensable in understanding the mysterious forces of the unconscious. Some critics argue that Jung's theories foster racism and that Jung was anti-Semitic and pro-Nazi. These criticisms continue in spite of different sentiments expressed in Jung's correspondence, denials by Jungian psychologists, and assertions that analytical psychology and Nazi ideology are totally incompatible (Gaillard, 1995; Gallard, 1995). Although Jung was troubled at times, he was a sensitive individual with unique and insightful ideas. His emphasis on the importance of a psychology of cultural difference suggests his ideas can make a powerful contribution to those who are concerned about processes of political and social transformation (Samuels, 1992). Jung died in 1961 at the age of eighty-five after a long and fruitful life.

The Nature and Structure of Personality

Whereas Freud described the structure of personality in terms of three forces that are in conflict—id, ego, and superego—Carl Jung conceived of the structure of personality as a complex network of interacting systems that strive toward eventual harmony. The main systems are the ego; the personal unconscious with its complexes; and the collective unconscious and its archetypes (see Table 3.1). Jung also described two primary attitudes toward reality and four basic functions, which together constitute separate but related aspects of the **psyche,** or total personality. Here, *psyche* refers to all psychological processes: thoughts, feelings, sensations, wishes, and so forth. Jung used the terms *psyche* and *psychic,* rather than *mind* and *mental,* to avoid the implications of consciousness in the latter and to emphasize that the psyche embraces both conscious and unconscious processes.

Jung and Freud differed in their approaches to the unconscious. Freud tended to view the unconscious essentially as materials that have been repressed. Jung viewed the unconscious as the source of consciousness and the matrix of new possibilities in life.

PSYCHIC ENERGY

Different theorists often use the same word—for example, *psyche, unconscious, libido,* and *ego*—to define processes and characteristics of human beings that they feel are well rendered by the term. These various uses are not interchangeable and must be understood in the context of each theory as a whole.

For Freud, the motive force of personality is libido, the sexual drive. Jung also used *libido* to refer to psychic energy, but his use should not be confused with Freud's definition. Jung

TABLE 3.1 JUNG'S STRUCTURE OF PERSONALITY

Jung conceived of personality as a complex network of interacting systems that strive toward eventual harmony.

ego one's conscious mind

personal unconscious	**collective unconscious**
• perceptions, thoughts, feelings that are easily retrieved	• universal thought forms or predispositions to respond
• repressed or forgotten individual experiences	• expressed as archetypes
• organized into complexes	

used the term in a more generalized fashion to refer to an undifferentiated life energy (1948). For him, **libido** is an appetite that may refer to sexuality and to other hungers as well. It manifests itself as striving, desiring, and willing. Psychic energy operates according to the principles of equivalence and entropy; it seeks a balance and moves the person forward in a process of self-realization.

Although Jung did not reject an instinctual basis of personality, he criticized Freud's emphasis on sexuality, suggesting that it is ultimately reductive or simplistic, as it reduces any and all activities to sexual ones. For example, Jung argued that the phallus represents *mana* or power as well as sexuality. Jung believed that sexuality itself must be seen as symbolic, having a mysterious quality of otherness that cannot be fully described.

The Ego

For Freud, the ego is ideally the executor of the personality. Although Freud initially thought that the ego is primarily conscious, he later considered that a large portion of the ego is unconscious and beyond conscious control or awareness.

For Jung, the **ego** is one's conscious mind, the part of the psyche that selects perceptions, thoughts, feelings, and memories that may enter consciousness. The ego is responsible for feelings of identity and continuity. It is through the ego that we establish a sense of stability in the way we perceive ourselves. The ego, however, is not the true center of personality for Jung. This runs counter to our everyday point of view. Most of us identify ourselves or our center as that awareness of consciousness that we have of ourselves, but for Jung, as we shall shortly see, the true center of personality lies elsewhere.

The Personal Unconscious and its Complexes

Jung compared the conscious aspect of the psyche to an island that rises from the sea. We notice only the part above water, even though a much greater landmass, the unconscious, lies below (Fordham, 1953). The **personal unconscious** is a land that is not always covered by sea and thus can be reclaimed. Here reside those perceptions, thoughts, feelings, and memories that have been put aside (for consciousness can hold only a few items at a time), and they may be easily retrieved. The personal unconscious also includes those experiences of an individual's life history that have been repressed or forgotten. This is an aspect of the unconscious that, as we have seen, Freud also emphasized. These forgotten experiences are accessible to consciousness even though becoming aware of some of them may be an arduous process.

Experiences in the personal unconscious are grouped into clusters, which Jung calls complexes. A **complex** is an organized group of thoughts, feelings, and memories about a particular concept (Jung, 1934). A complex is said to have a **constellating power,** which means that the complex has the ability to draw new ideas into itself and interpret them. It can be compared to a magnet that attracts related experiences. The more constellating power a complex has, the more powerful the complex may become. Complexes have important implications for our interpersonal relationships, specifically influencing how we react toward others.

A complex may be organized around a particular person or object. One of Jung's examples concerns motherhood (1954). A *mother complex* is the cluster of ideas, feelings, and memories that have arisen from our own particular experiences of having been mothered.

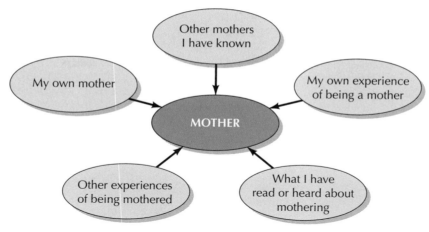

FIGURE 3.1 COMPLEX

A complex is an organized group of thoughts, feelings, and memories about a particular concept. It draws new ideas into itself and interprets them.

This complex also draws into itself other experiences of mothering to which we have been exposed. Each new instance of mothering that we encounter becomes part of our mother complex and is understood and interpreted by it (see Figure 3.1).

A complex, however, may make it difficult for us to disengage ourselves from a situation. Jung described a man who believed that he was suffering from a real cancer, even though he knew that his cancer was imaginary. The complex, Jung wrote, is "a spontaneous growth, originating in that part of the psyche which is not identical with consciousness. It appears to be an autonomous development intruding upon consciousness" (1938). A complex may act like an independent person, behaving independently of our conscious self and intentions.

A complex may be conscious, partly conscious, or unconscious. Certain elements of it may extend into the collective unconscious. Some complexes appear to dominate an entire personality. Napoleon is frequently described as being driven by inner forces to obtain power. Jung's concept of complex may be seen as an effort to overcome the traditional categories of mind versus body and conscious versus unconscious (Brooke, 1991).

THE COLLECTIVE UNCONSCIOUS

Whereas the personal unconscious is unique for each individual, the **collective unconscious** is shared. Jung referred to the collective unconscious as "transpersonal." By this he meant it extends across persons. It consists of certain potentialities that we all share because we are human (1936). Many critics believe that Jung made a unique contribution to depth psychology in his concept of the collective unconscious. Freud's concept of unconscious forces was mostly limited to personal experiences that have been repressed or forgotten. Whereas other dissenters from Freud tended to minimize the power of unconscious forces, Jung placed a greater emphasis on them and stressed the qualities that we share with other people. In coining the term *transpersonal*, Jung preceded and inspired others, such as Maslow, in exploring the spiritual and transpersonal facets of human nature. His term and interest were later picked up by theorists in the movement of transpersonal psychology, which is discussed in the chapter on humanism.

All people, because they are human beings, have certain things in common. All human beings live in groups and develop some form of family life or society in which roles are assigned to various members. These roles may vary from society to society, but they exist in all human groups. All human beings share certain emotions such as joy, grief, or anger. The ways of expressing these emotions may vary, but the emotions themselves are shared. All human beings develop some form of language and symbolization. The particular words may vary, but the concepts and symbols are shared. Thus certain archetypes and symbols reappear again and again from society to society, and they may be seen to have a common meaning.

Jung considered the collective unconscious an empirical concept whose existence can be demonstrated through dreams, mythology, and cross-cultural data. The workings of the collective unconscious are seen in experiences we all have had, such as falling in love with a "perfect other," feeling overwhelmed by a piece of art or music, or being drawn to the sea, and it expresses itself in shared symbols that have universal meaning.

Archetypes

Within the collective unconscious lie archetypes, or primordial images. An **archetype** is a universal thought form or predisposition to respond to the world in certain ways (Jung, 1936). The word *predisposition* is crucial to Jung's concept of the collective unconscious and archetypes. It emphasizes potentialities, for archetypes represent different potential ways in which we may express our humanness. Efforts to deny or destroy archetypes place us at risk of becoming unbalanced or one-sided. Myyra (1992), for example, contends that Western culture's denial of the dreadful facets of the archetypal great mother culminated in a patriarchal society that oppresses women and destroys nature.

Archetypes can never be fully known or described because they never fully enter consciousness. They appear to us in personified or symbolized pictorial form and may penetrate into consciousness by means of myths, dreams, art, ritual, and symptoms. It is helpful for us to get in touch with them because they represent the latent potentiality of the psyche. In doing so, we go beyond developing our individual potentialities and become incorporated in the eternal cosmic process.

Jung wrote, "The archetype is a kind of readiness to produce over and over again the same or similar mythical ideas. Hence it seems as though what is impressed upon the unconscious were exclusively the subjective fantasy—ideas aroused by the physical process. We may therefore assume that the archetypes are recurrent impressions made by subjective reasons" (1954).

Jung described several influential archetypes: the persona, the shadow, the anima and animus, and the self.

PERSONA   The **persona** is the social role that one assumes in society and one's understanding of it. As mentioned in the introductory chapter, the Latin word *personae* refers to the masks that actors wore in ancient Greek plays (*persona* is the singular form). Thus, one's persona is the mask that one wears in order to adjust to the demands of society. Each one of us chooses or is assigned particular roles in our society. The persona represents a compromise between one's true identity and social identity. To neglect the development of a

Jung suggested that coming to know our archetypal shadow will expand the boundaries of ego consciousness and add zest to life.

persona is to run the risk of becoming asocial. On the other hand, one may identify too completely with the persona at the expense of one's true identity and not permit other aspects of one's personality to develop. The persona assigned to a group—for example, to women, African Americans, or persons of Asian descent—may limit and cripple the development of individuals in the group as well as the group itself. Changes in one's social role, such as marriage, unemployment, or retirement, can lead to dissonance.

SHADOW The **shadow** encompasses those *unsocial* thoughts, feelings, and behaviors that we potentially possess and other characteristics that we do not accept. It is the opposite side of the persona, in that it refers to those desires and emotions that are incompatible with our social standards and ideal personality. It could be described as the devil within. Robert Louis Stevenson's story of the highly regarded Dr. Jekyll and his evil counterpart, Mr. Hyde, typifies the persona and the shadow. Jung's choice of the word *shadow* is deliberate and designed to emphasize its necessity. There can be no sun that does not leave a shadow. The shadow cannot be avoided, and one is incomplete without it. Jung agreed with Freud that such base and unsocial impulses may be sublimated and channeled to good ends. The shadow can also be projected onto others. Casting Jews as "shrewd" or African Americans as "impulsive" fosters racial prejudice (Fanon, 1967). Confronting the shadow increases the possibility of widening the boundaries of ego consciousness and of integrating otherness (Connolly, 2003).

To neglect or try to deny the shadow involves us in hypocrisy and deceit. Angels are not suited for existence on earth. Jung suggested a need to come to know our baser side and recognize our animalistic impulses. To do so adds dimension and credibility to personality, as well as increased zest for life.

ANIMA AND ANIMUS Each one of us is assigned a sex gender, male or female, based on our overt sexual characteristics. Yet none of us is purely male or purely female. Each of us has qualities of the opposite sex in terms of biology and also in terms of psychological attitudes and feelings. Thus, the **anima** archetype is the feminine side of the male psyche, and the **animus** archetype is the masculine side of the female psyche. One's anima or animus reflects collective and individual human experiences throughout the ages pertaining to one's opposite sex. It assists us in relating to and understanding the opposite sex. For Jung, there was a distinct difference between the psychology of men and the psychology of women. Jung believed that it was important that one express these opposite-sex characteristics in order to avoid an unbalanced or one-sided personality. If one exhibits only the traits of one's assigned sex, the other traits remain unconscious, undeveloped, and primitive. Those of us who have difficulty in understanding the opposite sex probably are not in tune with our anima or animus.

Jung has usually been considered friendly to women because of his assertion of the need to get in touch with one's opposite-sex archetype. However, his writings have also been criticized for including stereotypes of women, as well as potentially racist comments about other groups such as Jews, blacks, and primitive peoples (cf. Hyman, 1999). Jung stoutly maintained that the psyche of women is different from that of men, and he tended to be rigid in his discussion of those behaviors that would or would not overstep the boundaries of appropriate expression of one's assigned gender role and one's opposite-sex archetype. He warned of the dangers of pushing one's capacity to behave like the opposite sex too far, so that a man loses his masculinity or a woman her femininity.

Jung believed that women's consciousness is characterized by the ability to enter into relationships, whereas men's consciousness is characterized by the ability to engage in rational and analytic thought. The persona, or social mask, differs for men and women because of the various roles that society and culture have assigned to them. The anima and the animus function in ways that compensate for the outer personality and show the qualities that are missing in outward conscious expression. Because psychological development involves integrating one's persona and one's anima or animus, Jung believed it will progress differently for the male and for the female.

A woman may react to her animus in various ways. Traditionally, women have repressed their masculine qualities and striven to fulfill their feminine role. Jung thought this might lead to an imbalance in the personality and unconscious efforts on the part of the animus to intrude upon the woman's life; he pointed out that both the anima and the animus may behave as if they are laws unto themselves and have disruptive influences. Another way to react to the animus is to identify with it (i.e., behave in a masculine fashion), but this usually makes it more difficult for a woman to fulfill her assigned role.

However, a woman's animus need not be thought of as acting in opposition to femininity. In ideal development, the animus will lead a woman to transform her femininity into a renewed form of consciousness that overcomes the traditional dualities. The same would be true of ideal development in the male.

While Jung's theory may be interpreted as sexist, a feminist analysis of his work may be warranted (Romaniello, 1992). His comments about the anima and the animus led to the now very popular concept of an androgynous ideal. *Androgyny* refers to the presence of both masculine and feminine qualities in an individual and the ability to realize both potentialities. Considerable research has been done in the area of androgyny (see, for example, Singer, 1991).

SELF The central archetype in Jung's understanding is that of the self. Jung's use of the term *self* differed from the usual use of the term. The **self** represents the striving for unity of all parts of the personality. It is the organizing principle of the psyche that draws unto itself and harmonizes all the archetypes and their expressions. The self directs an orderly allotment of psychic energy so that different parts of the personality are expressed appropriately. Depending on the occasion and our personal needs, the self allows us to be socially acceptable at work (persona), outrageous at a Halloween party (shadow), emotional at a concert (shadow), and so forth. The self, rather than the ego, is the true midpoint of personality. Thus the center of one's personality is not to be found in rational ego consciousness. For Jung, the true self lies on the boundary between conscious and unconscious, reason and unreason. The development of the self is life's goal, but the self archetype cannot begin to emerge until the other personality systems have been fully developed. Thus it usually does not begin to emerge until one has reached middle age. Jung spoke of the realization of the self as a goal that lies in the future. It is something to be striven for but is rarely achieved.

Jung (1955) believed that the **mandala,** which in Hindu and Buddhist thought is a symbol of the universe, is also a symbol of the self. The mandala is a concentrically arranged figure such as a circle, wheel, or cross, which Jung saw appearing again and again in his patients' dreams and in the artwork of all cultures (see Figure 3.2). It represents the self striving toward wholeness.

Jung described numerous other archetypes of the collective unconscious: birth, death, rebirth, power, magic, the child, the hero, God, the demon, the great mother, and the wise old man. Archetypes find expression in cultural forms. Rock star Madonna draws on the archetype of the great mother, as does the "grandmother" in

> **Thinking Critically**
>
> Where are Jung's archetypes in our culture? See the Thinking Critically box "Archetypes in Cultural Forms."

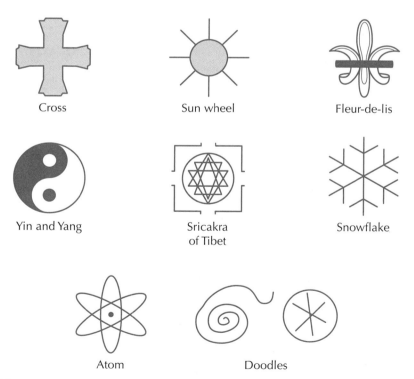

Cross   Sun wheel   Fleur-de-lis

Yin and Yang   Sricakra of Tibet   Snowflake

Atom   Doodles

FIGURE 3.2 MANDALAS

Jung believed that the mandala, a concentrically arranged figure, is a symbol of the self. Mandalas appear in the symbolism of both East and West, in nature, and spontaneously in our doodles.

Thinking Critically

Archetypes in Cultural Forms

Jung believed that there is an indeterminate number of archetypes. Some of the most common ones are listed here:

persona	social role or mask
shadow	the devil within
anima	feminine side of the male psyche
animus	masculine side of the female psyche
self	ultimate unity of the personality
great mother	the ultimate good and bad mother
wise old man	spiritual father
hero	conqueror of enemies and evil forces
trickster	animalistic prankster
child-god	the future
hermaphrodite	unity and wholeness

Can you recognize archetypes in our culture today? Identify three archetypes in each of the following areas: the political arena, your favorite sport, your favorite action movie, and your favorite television show. Why did you make the choices you did? Do you think that everyone would agree with your choices? Why or why not?

Native American folklore and Demeter, goddess of the earth in Greek mythology. Joseph Campbell (1949) has described the many faces of the archetypal hero figure in literature, and James Iaccino (1994) has identified archetypes in horror movies. Religious symbols may also be seen as archetypes: Adam is the first man; Christ and Buddha represent the self.

Freud and the Collective Unconscious

At the deepest levels, Jung believed that our unconscious remains archaic, despite our scientific technology and the development of our rational powers. Freud disclaimed Jung's plea for originality in articulating the collective unconscious, stating that he (Freud) had known all along that the unconscious is collective. And, of course, there are certain archetypal patterns in Freud's understanding of the unconscious. The psychosexual stages involve predispositions toward acting out the human drama in certain ways. The Oedipal situation that we experience is a collective archetypal myth. Symbols in dreams may be unique to the individual, but also shared. Thus a concept of collective unconscious forces is implied in Freud's theory, although certainly not clearly articulated. And whereas Freud emphasized the unique unfolding of unconscious forces in the individual's life history and personal unconscious (it is not enough to know that one has gone through the Oedipal

Archetypes, universal thought forms or predispositions, appear in various cultural forms throughout history. The classic cycle The Lord of the Rings *is full of archetypes. For example, Gandalf is the wise old man, and Frodo is the hero who undertakes an archetypal quest.*

situation—one must fully experience its particular unfolding within one's distinct family constellation), Jung emphasized the shared and collective aspects. As you might imagine, Jung's concept of the collective unconscious is an important and controversial one in personality theorizing, evoking both considerable support and opposition.

PSYCHOLOGICAL TYPES

One of Jung's contributions to the psychology of the conscious psyche is his explanation and description of psychological types, which arise out of various combinations of two basic **attitudes** and four **functions,** or ways of perceiving the environment and orienting experiences.

The Attitudes

Extraversion is an attitude in which the psyche is oriented outward to the objective world. The extravert tends to be more comfortable with the outer world of people and things. **Introversion** is an attitude in which the psyche is oriented inward to the subjective world. The introvert is more comfortable with the inner world of concepts and ideas. These words have become so commonplace that many of us readily identify ourselves as introverted or extraverted. Jung labeled himself an introvert and Freud an extravert. Yet in describing people as introverted or extraverted, Jung dealt primarily with the psychology of consciousness. An individual's habitual conscious attitude is either introverted or extraverted, but the other attitude is also present, although it may be undeveloped and mostly unconscious.

The Functions

Jung's four functions are grouped into opposite pairs. The functions of **sensation** and **intuition** refer to how we gather data and information. The sensor is more comfortable using the five senses and dealing with facts and reality. The intuitor looks for relationships and meanings or possibilities about past or future events. **Thinking** and **feeling** refer to how we come to conclusions or make judgments. The thinker prefers to use logic and impersonal analysis. The feeler is more concerned with personal values, attitudes, and beliefs. Jung suggested that one of these functions tends to be dominant in each individual and its opposite inferior. The other two functions play an auxiliary role. A professor, for example, may have so cultivated intellectual and cognitive powers that the feeling aspect of personality is submerged. Though primitive and undeveloped, feelings may nevertheless invade the professor's life in the form of strange moods, symptoms, or projections.

The two attitudes and four functions combine to form eight psychological types, which are summarized in Table 3.2. Jung cautioned that the types as described rarely occur in a pure form. There is a wide range of variation within each type, and people of a specific type may change (though not to another type) as their personal unconscious and collective unconscious change. No one type is better than another type. Each has its own strengths and weaknesses.

TABLE **3.2** PSYCHOLOGICAL TYPES

Jung's attitudes and functions combine to form eight psychological types. As you read them, note which type resembles you most closely.

EXTRAVERTED TYPES	INTROVERTED TYPES
Thinking: Tend to live according to fixed rules; repress feelings; try to be objective but may be dogmatic in thinking.	*Thinking:* Have a strong need for privacy; tend to be theoretical, intellectual, and somewhat impractical; repress feelings; may have trouble getting along with other people.
Feeling: Tend to be sociable; seek harmony with the world; respect tradition and authority; tend to be emotional; repress thinking.	*Feeling:* Tend to be quiet, thoughtful, and hypersensitive; repress thinking; may appear mysterious and indifferent to others.
Sensing: Seek pleasure and enjoy new sensory experiences; are strongly oriented toward reality; repress intuition.	*Sensing:* Tend to be passive, calm, and artistic; focus on objective sensory events; repress intuition.
Intuition: Are very creative; find new ideas appealing; tend to make decisions based on hunches rather than facts; are in touch with their unconscious wisdom; repress sensing.	*Intuition:* Tend to be mystic dreamers; come up with unusual new ideas; are seldom understood by others; repress sensing. (Jung described himself as an introverted intuitor.)

Self-Realization

Jung did not outline stages in the development of personality, nor did he consider the early childhood years to be the most important ones, as Freud did. Jung suggested, however, that the self is in the process of **self-realization.** The "psychic birth" of an individual does not really occur until adolescence, when the psyche starts to show a definite form and content. Personality development continues throughout life, and the middle years (thirty-five to forty) mark the beginning of major changes.

Although the concept of self-realization was fully described by Jung, it cannot be said to be new with his thought. The origin of the principle takes us back to the Greek philosopher Aristotle (384–322 B.C.). Aristotle held that everything has a **telos,** a purpose or goal, that constitutes its essence and indicates its potentiality. Thus every acorn has the essence of treeness and the potential to become a mighty oak. In the same way, each one of us has the potential to develop into a self—that is, to realize, fulfill, and enhance our maximum human potentialities. This viewpoint is essentially *teleological,* or purposeful. It explains the present in terms of the future with reference to a goal that guides and directs our destiny. Whereas Freud's view was primarily a causal one, comprehending personality in terms of antecedent conditions in the past, Jung maintained that both causality and teleology are necessary for full self-realization.

SYNCHRONICITY

In addition to the principles of causality and teleology, Jung (1960) included a third component that could lead to self-realization: **synchronicity,** a phenomenon in which events are related to one another through simultaneity and meaning. In synchronicity, two events occur either at the same time or close in time (simultaneity), and, though they happen independently, they seem inextricably linked (meaning). We may dream of a friend whom we have not seen in a long time, and the next day we learn that our friend died the night before. Logic tells us that such synchronistic experiences are merely chance or coincidental, but Jung believed that at another level they are very significant; their impact on our lives is equal to that of causality. Jung suggested that such events are related through meaningful simultaneity.

Jung believed that synchronistic events arise from the simultaneous occurrence of two different psychic states. In the external world a situation occurs in the normal chain of causal events; in the internal world an archetype emerges into consciousness. This leads one to conjecture that in some way in the example above the transpersonal collective unconscious was "in touch" with the death before the conscious mind was aware of it.

To illustrate how synchronicity can operate on self-realization, Jung (1960) cited one of his patients, who was experiencing considerable intellectual resistance to therapy. She described a dream in which she was given a golden scarab. At that very moment, Jung heard an insect tapping on the window. He let the bug in, caught it, and, noticing that it was a close insect relative to the sacred Egyptian beetle in her dream, presented it to the patient with the words, "Here is your scarab." The event broke the ice of her resistance and permitted the therapy to move forward. Was the event merely fortuitous, or was it a moment of grace?

Jung believed that synchronicity is involved in phenomena studied by the science of parapsychology, which investigates the perceptions that come to us in ways other than through the normal five senses. He suggested that our skepticism concerning extrasensory perception is without justification and due to an ingrained belief in a constricted sense of cause and effect. Jung also linked synchronicity to *I Ching,* an intuitive traditional Chinese method of grasping a situation and choosing alternatives, in which straws are randomly divided or coins are tossed and the resultant pattern is consulted to divine an answer. Jung believed that using I Ching makes it possible to overcome the limitations of conscious decision making because it grasps a situation as a whole and places its details against a cosmic background.

Jung suggested that the synchronicity factor stipulates the existence of a fourth dimension in addition to space, time, and causality, rendering the classic triad of physics a balanced set of four (see also Storm, 1999). Jung even collaborated with Nobel physicist Wolfgang Pauli in identifying this noncausal side to reality experienced in both physics and the psyche; their collaboration resulted in the publication of a book, *The Interpretation of Nature and the Psyche,* in 1952 (Lindorff, 1995).

INDIVIDUATION AND TRANSCENDENCE

Self-realization involves individuation and transcendence (Jung, 1916, 1939). In **individuation,** the systems of the individual psyche achieve their fullest degree of differentiation, expression, and development. **Transcendence** refers to integration of the diverse systems of the self toward the goal of wholeness and identity with all of humanity. Jung's concepts of individuation and transcendence are difficult for the average Westerner to understand. In Western psychology, we generally think of personality in terms of an individual's uniqueness. People who do not appear to be unique are often said to "lack personality."

For Jung, individuation does not mean individualism in that narrow sense, but rather fulfilling one's own specific nature and realizing one's uniqueness in one's place within the whole. In the process of transcendence, a deeper self or essence emerges to unite a person with all of humanity and the universe at large.

Individuation and transcendence are both ongoing processes. However, the first half of life is often more concerned with the cultivation of consciousness and gender-specific behavior, and the second half of life may be more concerned with coming into closer contact with self and expressing our collective unconscious and oneness with humanity as a whole. Mary Loomis (1991) has made a comparison to a process that Native Americans refer to as the Red Road.

Thus, as the self realizes, a stormy process that may never be fully completed, it perpetually rises to a greater enhancement and realization of itself and humanity. If we view the psyche as a wheel, the hub of which is the archetype of the self, we can suggest that the true self emerges when the opposites coincide (see Figure 3.3). The true person does not consist of the conscious or the unconscious, mind or body, persona or shadow, overt sexual characteristics or complements. The true person consists of all of these. Neurosis results from a one-sided personality development. The coincidence of opposites is the ultimate goal of personality development in the Jungian view. Although both Freud and Jung emphasized the dynamic opposition of portions of the personality, they differed in the implications of this conflict. For Freud, the person is inescapably in conflict; for Jung, the person ultimately seeks harmony. Mansfield and Spiegelman (1991) have employed quantum mechanical models and symbols to deepen our understanding of the coincidence of opposites. Van Eenwyk (1991) has further suggested that chaos theory, which attempts to describe compli-

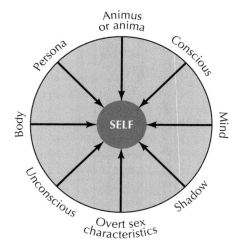

FIGURE 3.3 THE COINCIDENCE OF OPPOSITES

If we view the psyche as a wheel, the hub of which is the archetype of the self, the true self emerges when the opposites coincide. The resulting image is, of course, a mandala.

cated systems formerly outside the range of classical mathematics and physics, illumines Jung's theory.

Believing that the spiritual is an essential requirement of our quest for wholeness, Jung was not fearful of investigating the spiritual. His thoughts foreshadowed a quest for **spirituality** that is evident today—the search for meaning or for a power beyond the self rather than adherence to particular tenets, as in a formal religion. Jung's self archetype is the God within. In his *Answer to Job* (1958), Jung reminds us that we must take responsibility for the transformation of our god-images. Our longing for the spiritual must be satisfied in a loving, life-affirming, and constructive quest for self-understanding that goes beyond the rational and includes the transformative intuition. Otherwise, we will be led to find new gods: perhaps horrific ones, such as alcohol or drugs, codependent relationships, or fanatical devotion and terrorist actions in behalf of our deities. Jung was gravely concerned over the development of weapons of mass destruction. He believed that humankind must assume responsibility for the survival of our earth (Burns, 2006).

Jung was especially interested in exploring the transcendent function of intuition (Cambray, 2006). We are *homo religious,* hardwired to experience spiritual feelings, according to molecular biologist Dean Hamer (2005). The great shortcoming of American mainstream psychology has been its refusal to develop a spiritually infused psychology and to embrace the spiritual essence of the person (Jennings, 1999). Jungian concepts, such as the archetypes and the collective unconscious, can present a structure for embracing spiritual matters and psychic phenomena. The power and strength of the intuition that Jung described in the mid-twentieth century may be receiving confirmation from contemporary findings in quantum physics suggesting the interconnectedness of all things. One could even argue that he anticipated the emergence of the thirst and need for the spiritual evidenced as we have moved into the twenty-first century. Spiritual concepts need to be integrated with our more traditional concept of personality. The field of personality is a natural place to begin to integrate spiritual concepts into the discipline. We need to expand our focus and methodology to provide the means to more fully comprehend and work with the spiritual nature of human beings.

Jungian Psychotherapy

Jung viewed emotional disturbance as a person's attempt to reconcile the contradictory aspects of personality. One side of the psyche, such as the conscious, adaptive, social persona, may be exaggerated at the expense of the darker, unconscious aspects. For Freud a neurosis represents the return of the repressed, but for Jung it is the insistence of the undeveloped part of the personality on being heard and realized. It is difficult to describe Jung's method of psychotherapy specifically because he did not clearly outline his procedures as Freud did.

Further, Jung maintained that no one approach is suitable for everyone. The individual who has had difficulty in accepting the sexual and aggressive urges of life may well require a Freudian interpretation. But for others, or at different stages in development, the Freudian understanding may not be sufficiently comprehensive.

In classical Freudian psychoanalysis, the analyst remains detached and reveals few personal feelings and reactions in order to facilitate the transference. The Jungian analyst is more self-disclosing, foreshadowing Rogerian and other contemporary therapies. Therapy is a "dialectical procedure," a dialogue between doctor and patient, conscious and unconscious. Although the couch may be used to facilitate procedures such as active imagination, for the most part analyst and patient sit facing each other. The Jungian analyst also sees patients far less frequently than the Freudian. The frequency of visits depends on the stage that the patient has reached.

During the early stages of treatment, there is a need for *confession.* Such confession is generally accompanied by emotional release, and Jung viewed it as the aim of the cathartic method originated by Breuer and Freud. But Jung pointed out that emotional release, in itself, is not therapeutic any more than temper tantrums or other emotional outbursts are curative in and of themselves. For Freud, conscious intellectual understanding and insight renders the catharsis effective. Jung emphasized that the presence of the other, the therapist who supports the patient morally and spiritually as well as intellectually, makes the confession curative.

Projection and transference play an important role in Jungian analysis, though Jung added to Freud's concept of transference the recognition that not only significant persons from the patient's past but also archetypal images are projected onto the analyst. Jung also viewed the sexual components of the transference as symbolic efforts by the patient to reach a higher integration of personality. In contrast to Freud, Jung did not think that transference was a necessary precondition for therapy.

Whereas Freud treated dreams as the expression of unconscious wishes, Jung gave them a prospective function as well as a retrospective one. By prospective function Jung meant that the dream represents an effort by the person to prepare for future events. Dreams also have a **compensatory function;** they are efforts to complement the patient's conscious side and to speak for the unconscious.

In interpreting dreams, Jung used the method of **amplification** (1951) rather than the method of free association. In free association, each dream element is the starting place for a chain of associations that may lead far afield from the original element. In amplification, one focuses repeatedly on the element and gives multiple associations to it. The dream is taken exactly as it is with no precise effort to distinguish between manifest and latent contents. The therapist joins the patient in efforts to interpret the dream, adding personal associations and frequently referring to mythology, fairy tales, and the like in order to extend the dream's meaning. Unlike Freud, who tended to deal with dreams singly, Jung concentrated on series of dreams. Analysis of a series of dreams unfolds the inner life of the patient, which is taken as a guide to true-life meanings for the patient.

As a therapist, Jung also valued the use of active imagination as a means of facilitating self-understanding and the use of artistic production by the patient. In *active imagination* a person might be invited to enter a dream scene and explore it further by letting the dream continue to unfold. The conscious can pay attention to the unconscious and help in giving it form, by simply letting things happen. Jung also encouraged his patients to draw, sculpt, paint, or develop some other art form as a means of listening to their inner depths. In all of this, he emphasized obedience to the unfolding inner life as the appropriate, ethical fulfillment of one's humanity.

Assessment and Research in Jung's Theory

Jung's ideas have had a significant but frequently unacknowledged impact on assessment and research in personality. Jung developed the *word-association test,* which provided the first experimental data on unconscious processes and is widely used in current laboratory research and clinical practice. The participant responds to a list of stimulus words designed to elicit emotions. An unusual response, a long pause before responding, the same response to very different words, and other factors may indicate a complex. Jung's word-association test may be termed the forerunner of later projective techniques and attempts to assess personality by techniques such as free association, sentence completion, and psychophysiological monitoring, including the polygraph, or lie detector. Indeed, Jung is credited with identifying at least two thieves through the technique of word association (Ellenberger, 1970).

A Swiss psychiatrist, Hermann Rorschach, developed the Rorschach Inkblot Test, which is heavily influenced by Jungian concepts such as introversion and extraversion. Henry Murray also was deeply influenced by Jung when he developed the Thematic Apperception Test, which is discussed in the chapter on traits and personology.

Jung's typology has also led to the development of assessment and research on psychological type. The Myers-Briggs Type Indicator (MBTI) is one of the most popular tools for nonpsychiatric populations in the area of clinical, counseling, and personality assessment. The instrument, developed primarily by Katherine Briggs and her daughter Isabel Briggs Myers, is designed to implement Jung's theory of type by sorting people into groups on the basis of four separate dichotomies or indices: Extraversion-Introversion (EI), Sensing-Intuition (SN), Thinking-Feeling (TF), and Judgment-Perception (JP). You will recognize the first polarity as the two attitudes identified by Jung and the second and third polarities as the four ego functions. The last polarity indicates a preference for judgment or perception (JP): J's prefer a great deal of structure and closure in their lives, and P's prefer more spontaneity and openness. The J pole refers to the two judging functions (thinking and feeling), and the P pole refers to the two perceiving functions (sensing or intuition). The preference for J or P tells which mode—J (decision making) or P (information gathering)—is shown to the outside world (see Table 3.3).

Given the four dichotomies, sixteen different four-letter types are possible. An ESFJ, for example, is an extravert who is sensing, feeling, and judging. The assessment manual provides descriptions that distinguish each type from the others. One of the distinct advantages of the MBTI is its face validity: Individuals invariably recognize themselves in their types (cf. Furnham, 1990). As in Jung's original typology, no one type is preferred over other types. Each type has its own strengths and weaknesses.

The MBTI generated considerable research; some of the early research was summarized by Myers and McCaulley (1985). Literature reviews on the MBTI conclude that is a reliable and valid measure (Carlson, 1985; Carlyn, 1977; Carskadon, 1979; Murray, 1990) (see also Thompson & Borrello, 1986). It is widely used in business, research, and guidance (Bubenzer, Zimpfer, & Mahrle, 1990). The instrument has been a very successful tool. It helps relate

TABLE 3.3 THE MYERS–BRIGGS TYPE INDICATOR: SAMPLE QUESTIONS

In the Myers-Briggs Type Indicator, forced-choice questions similar to the following sort people into groups on the basis of four polar indices: Extraversion-Introversion (E or I), Sensing-Intuition (S or N), Thinking-Feeling (T or F), and Judgment-Perception (J or P).

1. Given a free evening, I would prefer to
   a. stay home by myself.
   b. go out with other people.

2. In gathering information, I am more interested in
   a. facts.
   b. possibilities.

3. In making a decision, it is more important to me to
   a. come up with a correct answer.
   b. consider the impact of the solution.

4. I prefer to do activities
   a. that have been planned in advance.
   b. on the spur of the moment.

Answers are keyed as follows: 1a: I; 1b: E. 2a: S; 2b: N. 3a: T; 3b: F. 4a: J; 4b: P.

psychological type to various topics, such as risk tolerance, problem solving, information systems design, and conflict management (Gardner & Martinko, 1996). The MBTI is widely used in organizational consulting, career counseling, and job selection, as well as in couples counseling. McCrae and Costa (1989) suggest that the MBTI measures aspects of their five-factor model of personality, described in the chapter on factor analytic theories (see also Saggino, Cooper, & Kline, 2001). Pittenger (2005) recommends caution, and more research needs to be done on whether or not the findings of the MBTI apply across cultures.

Jung's techniques of research and assessment drew upon not only empirical and scientific methods but also nonscientific and mystical approaches. Thus Jung studied a variety of cultures and periods, exploring their myths, symbols, religions, and rituals. He was interested in alchemy and astrology, believing that the "Philosopher's Stone" was not gold transformed from lead but the spiritual realization of the archetypal self through individuation (Bucher, 2004). This "unorthodox blend of opposites" (Schultz, 1990) does not always sit well with more scientifically oriented psychologists who, in spite of the widespread use of the MBTI, tend to ignore Jungian concepts.

Jung referred to ancestral experiences in the collective unconscious as phylogenic or racial memories. He traveled to many places throughout the world to explore the symbols, myths, rituals, and religions of diverse cultures. Although he sought to uncover and emphasize the many universal archetypes shared by cultures, he implied that ethnic groups inherit different variations of the collective unconscious, as well as different physical traits. The exploration of "ethnic unconscious" and its development continues in the study of different groups of our multicultural society (Herron, 1995). Specific research on ethnic identity is discussed in the chapter on ego analytic psychology.

Although Jung's writings have been criticized for including stereotypes and potentially racist comments, his work also generated interest in various ethnic forms of human expression. Jung contributed to the effort to understand oneself as an individual, as a member of an ethnic group, and as a part of humanity as a whole.

| PHILOSOPHY, |
| SCIENCE, |
| *and* ART |

Jung's Theory

Many of Jung's discoveries, like Freud's, took place in the clinical setting. Jung also obtained information from sources outside the treatment room. Observations of other cultures and studies of comparative religion and mythology, symbolism, alchemy, and the occult afforded him a wealth of information. Jung considered these sources secondary but legitimate ones for psychologists seeking to uncover the mysteries of the human psyche. He believed that a comparative method of study, often used in history and anthropology, was a valuable approach in science as well.

Jung did not believe that psychologists should be bound to an experimental, scientific approach. He did believe, however, that conclusions should be based on empirical data. Jung criticized the contemporary scientific atmosphere for limiting its concepts to those of causality, and he emphasized the concept of teleology. After all, he pointed out, the concepts of *cause* and *goal* are not themselves found in nature but are imaginary constructs imposed by scientists. Jung urged scientists to work within a broader scope and conceptual design.

Jung's concepts are particularly difficult to study in the laboratory. As with Freud, it is almost impossible to define many of his terms operationally or to develop a test that would disprove them. Further, Jung's interest in the occult has led many critics to dismiss him as a mystic. Consequently, scientific psychology has until recently largely ignored Jung's analytical psychology, and his position in academia is problematic (Tacey, 1997). Nevertheless, Jung has influenced developments in psychology and other disciplines.

Recasting some of Jung's concepts may help to render them more viable. Empirical studies have not been able to provide evidence that archetypes are inherited (Jones, 2000; Maloney, 1999). Perhaps it would be better to view archetypes as symbolic forms influenced by culture (Pietikainen, 1998), arising from the self-organization of the inherited cognitive and emotional structures of the human brain and mind (Cambray, 2006; Saunders & Skar, 2001).

Jung indicated that he was more interested in discovering facts than in developing a philosophy. Because his concepts were based on empirical data, in the broadest sense of the word he operated as a "scientist." However, his theory falls short of rigorous standards of compatibility, predictive power, and simplicity. Fundamentally, the Jungian quest may be viewed as a philosophical or religious one. Jung explicitly raised philosophical questions and suggested philosophical answers. For example, asserting that questions about human nature should be answered empirically is in itself a philosophical position that distinguishes science from philosophy. For Jung, the power of self-understanding stems from an appropriate philosophy of life. It should not be surprising that although Jung has been largely ignored by experimentally oriented psychologists, theologians have found his work very fruitful. His concept of God's revealing himself through the collective unconscious is particularly attractive to theologians who seek a more relevant articulation of traditional theistic concepts. It is also attractive to many people in the twenty-first century seeking spirituality. Although his theory is complex, it is coherent; its relevance is attested to by the resurgence of interest in it today; and the comprehensive features of his theory are remarkable for their profundity.

Philosophical Assumptions

Which philosophical issues did Jung emphasize? See the Philosophical Assumptions box "Examining Jung."

As an art, Jungian therapy emphasizes a scholarly goal. With the resurgence of interest in Jung, training in Jungian analysis has become available in major American cities.

It has been argued that Jung's visionary powers and deep spirituality have helped many to find an alternative set of values to the barren materialism prevailing in Western society (Stevens, 1994). Bill W. (cofounder of Alcoholics Anonymous) credits Jung with helping him understand the importance of spirituality in recovery from addiction (W., 1988). Jung's emphasis on inborn qualities, the duality of human nature, symbolism, androgyny, and the importance of inner experiences—factors that at one time led psychologists to neglect his work—are now seen as important, if not indispensable, for understanding personality. Indeed, Jung's concept of androgyny formed the basis for the interest in androgyny that developed in the 1970s and has become well incorporated into the gender literature. Jung's interest in the developmental process with his attention to the second half of the human life span has proved valuable to social scientists who are concerned about the needs and growth of our older population (Moraglia, 1994). In particular, Jung helps us deal with the reality of death (Mogenson, 1990).

In this postmodern era, Jung's concepts can further help us understand the place of the self in our talk about different cultures (Thrasher, 1991) and forge a new holistic paradigm (Clarke, 1992). Many of Jung's archetypal images tell an ecological tale of the profound dialogue between the earth and the soul (Noel, 1991) and speak to the contemporary concern of balancing human needs and desires with the ecological needs of the natural world (Yunt, 2001).

Philosophical Assumptions

Examining Jung

Many of the differences among personality theories can be attributed to fundamental differences in philosophical assumptions. Which of the basic philosophical issues, described in the introductory chapter and summarized on the inside back cover, seem to be clearly important to Jung in the development of his theory? How, for example, does Jung's introduction of the collective unconscious influence his stance on freedom versus determinism? How does his description of individuation and transcendence influence his stance on uniqueness versus universality? Does his theory address any other philosophical assumptions? Rate Jung on a scale from 1 to 5 on those philosophical assumptions that you feel his theory applies to most. Compare your ratings of Jung with your own philosophical assumptions. Did your study of Jung lead you to change any of your assumptions? Why or why not?

Drawing upon Jung, Sliker (1992) explores how politics, culture, and ethnicity can be understood. She believes her model can foster discussion for resolving conflicts among various cultures.

Jung's thinking poses a significant challenge to Western thought and psychology, which emphasize an extrospective methodology based on experimentation and causal rather than teleological or other acausal explanations. His ideas are compatible with thinking in the East, and because his goal was to regain balance, Jung believed that a dialectic between Western and non-Western cultures was essential (Bagby, 1995). Jung recognized that "it is not famine, not earthquakes, not microbes, not cancer but man himself who is man's greatest danger" (1976, par. 1358). It is unfortunate that many psychologists in America have been quick to dismiss the concepts of Jung. They merit more serious consideration.

TO LEARN MORE about the Jungian technique of active imagination, about a type of dreaming that is receiving considerable attention today, and about the Myers-Briggs Type Indicator, and for a list of suggested readings, visit the *Personality Theories* textbook website at **college.cengage.com/pic/engler8e.**

Summary

1. Jung uses the term **psyche** (p. 71) to refer to all psychological processes, emphasizing that it embraces both conscious and unconscious processes.

2. For Freud the libido consists of the sexual drive. Jung used **libido** (p. 72) in a more generalized fashion as an undifferentiated energy that moves the person forward.

3. For Freud the ego is the executor of the personality. For Jung the **ego** (p. 72) is one's conscious perception of self.

4. Jung described two basic **attitudes** (**introversion** and **extraversion**) and four **functions** (**sensation, thinking, feeling,** and **intuition**). In each person, one of the attitudes and one of the functions is dominant, and its opposite is weaker. The other two functions play an auxiliary role.

5. The **personal unconscious** (p. 72) includes experiences of an individual's history that have been repressed or forgotten. These are organized into **complexes** (p. 72).

6. Freud's concept of unconscious forces is mostly limited to a personal unconscious; Jung's **collective unconscious** (p. 73) consists of potential ways of being that all humans share.

7. **Archetypes** (p. 74) are universal thought forms of the collective unconscious and predispositions to perceive the world in certain ways. Some widely recognized archetypes are the **persona** (p. 74), the **shadow** (p. 75), the **anima** (p. 75), and the **animus** (p. 75). The **self** (p. 76) is the central archetype and true midpoint of the personality. Active imagination is a method of getting in touch with the archetypes.

8. **Self-realization** (p. 81) is a teleological process of development that involves **individuation** (p. 82) and **transcendence** (p. 82). In the process, the systems of the psyche achieve their fullest degree of differentiation and are then integrated in identity with all of humanity. **Synchronicity** (p. 81) is a phenomenon in which events are related to one another through simultaneity and meaning. Jung's thinking foreshadowed the quest today for **spirituality** (p. 83).

9. In his psychotherapy, Jung sought to reconcile unbalanced aspects of the personality. It is a dialectical procedure and initially entails confession. Jung considered dreams to have a prospective as well as a **compensatory function** (p. 84); in interpreting them, he used the method of **amplification** (p. 84).

10. Jung's word-association test was the forerunner of projective techniques. The MBTI implements Jung's theory of type by sorting people into groups on the basis of four separate dichotomies. It is widely used in a variety of settings.

11. Although his concepts were based on empirical data, Jung raised philosophical questions and suggested philosophical answers. His theory may therefore be seen as largely philosophical.

Personal Experiences

1. Jung's concept of persona refers to the social role one assumes in society and one's understanding of that role. What different personas have you assumed in society? How does social context influence the persona you choose or are forced to take on? Describe your personas around your parents and your friends, around your friends and your lover, around your lover and your professor, and around your professor and your boss at work. Are they different? If so, how? Discuss your personas in three different social contexts, and explain the similarities and differences. Do you feel that your persona in each context is healthy? How much dissonance is there between your social personas and your true self?

2. Jung's discussion of shadow often leads to a discussion of prejudice. Jung believed it is necessary for each individual to confront and understand these darker thoughts and impulses in order to lead a healthy, rich life. With that in mind, try confronting your own prejudices. What prejudices, or prejudgments, influence your view of those who may be different from you? Toward what person or group do you feel you harbor the most prejudice? What factors do you think have contributed to your feelings? Are these factors based on actual personal experiences or on stories you've heard and read? How does each type of evidence validate and invalidate your feelings?

3. As gender lines continue to shift and change, Jung's concept of anima and animus can be helpful in negotiating our roles as men and women. How would Jung's theory account for the increased acceptance and occurrence of female aggression (and male passivity) in the classroom? Take a few minutes to list five different ways in which you can internally identify with or outwardly express your anima (if you're male) or your animus (if you're female). If you're particularly daring, ask your roommate or friends of the same sex to do the same thing, and then compare and contrast lists. Are you seeing more similarities or differences in the responses? Try to explain your findings.

4. Would you classify yourself, in Jungian terms, as an introvert or an extravert? Use Table 3.2 to explore the criteria for both attitudes. After reviewing the criteria and where you fit in, do you feel that you harbor more respect for one attitude than for the other? Put it to the test. Use the same criteria to analyze your closest friends. Do they fit into the same category as you? If they do, why do you think you are attracted to people like your-

self? If they don't, why do you think you are attracted to people *un*like yourself? What about your upbringing or social experience could help inform your feelings?

5. Now that you've studied the theoretical perspectives of both Freud and Jung, whose theories do you feel have more relevance in your life? Which of the two makes the most sense in terms of your personal experiences? Do you find one's concepts easier to apply to the real world? Do you think you could use one's concepts more readily in trying to understand your own thoughts and behavior, your friends and loved ones? Why do you think this is so?

CHAPTER 4

Interpsychic Theories

- **Alfred Adler**
- **Harry Stack Sullivan**

YOUR GOALS FOR THIS CHAPTER

1. Distinguish between an **intrapsychic** and an **interpsychic** emphasis in personality theorizing.

2. Explain what Adler meant by **social interest** and **finalism,** and give examples of **fictional finalism.**

3. Describe how the **goal of superiority** arises from **inferiority feelings** and leads to an individual's **style of life.**

4. Describe how **family constellation** and **family atmosphere** shape personality.

5. Discuss Adler's concept of the **creative self,** and show how it restores consciousness to the center of personality.

6. Describe some of the major features of Adlerian psychotherapy, assessment, and research.

7. Evaluate Adler's theory from the viewpoints of philosophy, science, and art.

8. Describe the following basic concepts in Sullivan's theory: **personality, anxiety, unawareness,** and **security operation.**

9. Define and give examples of **dynamism** and **personification.**

10. Describe Sullivan's six stages of personality development and three **cognitive processes.**

11. Explain how the concept of **participant observation** influences Sullivan's psychotherapy, assessment, and research.

12. Evaluate Sullivan's theory from the viewpoints of philosophy, science, and art.

13. Describe **family therapy.**

The theories of Alfred Adler and Harry Stack Sullivan mark a shift from a stress on **intrapsychic** ("within the psyche") phenomena such as Freud and Jung dealt with to an appreciation of **interpsychic** ("interpersonal") relations. The human person emerges as a social and cultural creature rather than a sexual and biological one.

Alfred Adler chose the term **individual psychology** for his conception of personality because he was interested in investigating the uniqueness of the person. He maintained that the individual was indivisible and must be studied as a whole. Adler's theory holds that understanding a particular individual entails comprehending his or her attitude in relation to the world. According to Adler, we are motivated by social interest, and our primary life problems are social ones.

Adler had a tremendous influence on Harry Stack Sullivan, whose theory, known as **interpersonal psychiatry,** also provides us with insights into how we interact with others. Sullivan believed that the personality of an individual could never be studied in isolation, as we do not exist separately and independently from other persons. He explored the dynamics of interpersonal relationships and their influence on personality development.

Alfred Adler (1870–1937)

BIOGRAPHICAL BACKGROUND

Alfred Adler, second of six children born to a successful merchant, was born in 1870 and reared in a suburb of Vienna. He described his childhood as difficult and unhappy. He suffered from rickets, a deficiency disease of childhood that affects the bones and made him clumsy and awkward. Initially, his parents pampered him, but when his younger brother was born he sensed that his mother transferred her attention to him. He felt dethroned and turned to his father, who favored him and expected great things from him.

When he was three, he saw his younger brother die in the next bed. Twice during his early childhood Adler was run over in the streets. He began to be afraid of death, and his fear was further increased by a bout of pneumonia at the age of four. Later, he traced his interest in becoming a doctor to that near-fatal illness.

At school he was an average student. At one point his teacher suggested that his father take him out of school and apprentice him to a shoemaker. Nevertheless, he rose to a superior position in school, especially in mathematics, which he originally had had the greatest difficulty in mastering. In spite of his physical handicaps, he developed courage, social interest, and a feeling of being accepted in his play with other children. His interest and joy in the company of others remained throughout his life.

His weak physique and feelings of inferiority during childhood were later to find expression in his concepts of organic inferiority and the striving for superiority (cf. Durbin, 2005). His sensitivity about being the second son was reflected in his interest in the family constellation and ordinal position of birth. His efforts to get along with others found expression in his conviction that the human being is a social and cultural animal and in the Adlerian concept of social interest.

Adler studied medicine at the University of Vienna, where Freud had received his medical training. Although he trained as an eye specialist, he became a general practitioner and

With Alfred Adler, the emphasis shifted from intrapsychic to interpsychic phenomena. The human person emerged as a social and cultural creature rather a sexual one.

later established himself as a practicing neurologist and psychiatrist. In 1902 he was invited by Freud to join a group for weekly discussions on psychoanalysis. This group eventually grew into the Vienna Psychoanalytic Society, of which Adler was the first president, and later became the International Psychoanalytic Association.

There are many stories concerning Adler's association with Freud and their subsequent split. Adler was never a student of Freud, nor was he ever psychoanalyzed. He joined the discussions because he was interested in psychoanalysis, but from the beginning he discovered points of disagreement. By 1911 these differences appeared crucial. Adler was invited to state his position to the society, and he did, but his views were denounced, he resigned, and about one-third of the members left with him. The relationship between Adler and Freud has been further clarified by Fiebert (1997).

Adler founded his own group and attracted many followers. He served in the Austrian army during World War I. Afterward he assisted the government in establishing child guidance clinics in Vienna. Although he and Freud both practiced in Vienna during the 1920s and early 1930s, they did not associate with each other.

Adler visited the United States frequently and came here to live in 1935. He continued his private practice, accepted a position as professor of medical psychology at the Long Island College of Medicine, and lectured widely. He died suddenly in 1937 of a heart attack while on a lecture tour in Scotland; he was sixty-seven.

BASIC CONCEPTS

A leading concept of Adler's individual psychology is his emphasis on the importance of human culture and society. Human society is crucial not simply for the development of an individual personality, but also for the orientation of each and every behavior and emotion in a person's life.

Human beings, like all living creatures, are driven by certain innate instincts, drives, or needs, such as the impulses to maintain life and to reproduce. But although much of the behavior of lower animals appears to be regulated by instincts, this is not true of human behavior. Human beings have tamed their instincts and subordinated them to their attitudes toward the environment. At times, human beings deny or disobey their natural instincts because of their social relations. A terrorist, for example, may undergo a suicide mission on behalf of a cause. A young child may refuse food if he believes that such a tactic gives him an advantage in a power struggle with his parents.

Social Interest

This shaping of instinctual expression in terms of one's attitude toward the environment suggests that underlying all other instincts and needs is the innate characteristic of social interest (Adler, 1939). **Social interest** refers to that urge in human nature to adapt oneself to the conditions of the social environment. It expresses itself subjectively in one's consciousness of having something in common with other people and of being one of them. It expresses itself objectively in cooperation with others toward the betterment of human society. While common to all, social interest does not automatically emerge, nor does it invariably find constructive expression. It must be nurtured and cultivated.

Finalism

Adler stressed the fact that the movement of all living things is governed by goals. We cannot think, feel, will, or act, except with the perception of some goal (1927). To try to understand human behavior in terms of external causes is to fail to understand psychic phenomena. If we know a person's goal, we begin to understand in a general way the individual's behavior.

When an individual behaves in a certain way, we naturally ask why. Past efforts to answer that question had emphasized material and mechanical explanations. Freud maintained that it is not enough to look for physiological causes; we must also try to understand the psychological motives underlying behavioral events. However, Freud was misled by the principle of causality into regarding these motives as past and looking to the past for the explanation of all human behavior. Adler emphasized the purposefulness of human behavior by recognizing that the motivational force of every human action is the goal or future orientation of that action. Thus Adler agreed with Jung that teleology is necessary for a full understanding of personality. For Adler, the goal that the individual pursues is the decisive factor, and he called this concept of goal orientation the principle of **finalism** (1930).

Adler suggested that many of our guiding goals are fictions. He did not equate fiction with falseness; rather he indicated that we cannot know whether or not our goals are true or false because there is no way to scientifically test them. *Fiction* comes from the Latin root *fictio*, which means "to invent," "fashion," or "construct." We are unable to have a complete understanding of things as they really are, so we structure our own idea of reality. "Fictions" are an individual's or group's interpretations of the events of the world. We may assume that it is best to tell the truth, that all people are basically good, or that hard work will eventually pay off. In Adlerian vocabulary, such basic concepts are **fictional finalisms.** Adler was indebted to an earlier philosopher, Hans Vaihinger, for his concept of fictional finalisms. Vaihinger suggested that people create fictions or guiding ideas and then behave "as if" their goals were true. If people believe that it is to their best advantage to be honest, they will strive to be so, even though there is no way in which they can ultimately test that belief as a hypothesis.

A fiction may be healthy or unhealthy. Adler maintained that it is inappropriate to judge a fiction as true or false, right or wrong; rather, the goal should be judged according to its usefulness. Belief in a deity and the desire to serve it have proved to be a valuable fiction for many individuals. For others, however, belief in God and the desire to please God have had deleterious effects. Whether or not God really exists is beside the point; the point is that belief in God has a demonstrable effect, positive or negative, on the behavior and life of an individual. Healthy individuals continually examine the effectiveness of their fictions and alter their goals when they are no longer useful. They maintain their fictions in a state of flux in order to meet the demands of reality.

Striving for Superiority

Adler suggested that the psyche has as its primary objective the **goal of superiority.** This is the ultimate fictional finalism for which all human beings strive, and it gives unity and coherence to the personality. Initially, Adler conceived of the primary motivating force as aggression. Later, he identified the primary drive as a "will to power." Then, he refined the concept of a drive toward power and suggested that the essential dynamic of human nature lies in its striving for superiority (1930). Finally, he changed from striving for individual superiority to striving for a superior society.

Adler's concept of the striving for superiority does not entail the everyday meaning of the word *superiority.* He did not mean that we innately seek to surpass one another in rank or position, nor did he mean that we seek to maintain an attitude of exaggerated importance over our peers. Rather, the drive for superiority involves the desire to be competent and effective in whatever one strives to do. The concept is similar to Jung's idea of self-realization. Adler frequently used the term *perfection* as a synonym for the word *superiority.* This term can also be misleading unless we recognize its origin in the Latin *perfectus,* which means "completed" or "made whole."

The striving for superiority may take the form of an exaggerated lust for power. An individual may seek to exercise control over objects and people and to play God. The goal may introduce a hostile tendency into our lives, in which we play games of "dog eat dog." But such expressions of the goal for superiority are abortive and do not reflect its constructive nature.

The striving for superiority is innate and part of the struggle for survival that human beings share with other species in the process of evolution. According to Adler, life is not motivated by the need to reduce tension or restore equilibrium, as Freud tended to think; instead, life is encouraged by the desire to move from below to above, from minus to plus, from inferior to superior. This movement entails adapting oneself to and mastering the environment. The particular ways in which individuals undertake this quest are determined by their culture, their own unique history, and their style of life.

The striving for superiority arises because as human beings we feel inferior. **Inferiority feelings** have their origin in our encounter as infants with the environment. As human infants, unlike other animals, we are born immature, incomplete, and incompetent to satisfy even our basic needs. There is a protracted period during which we are almost totally dependent on other people for our survival. Feelings of inferiority thus reflect a fact of existence. Such feelings are inescapable but also invaluable because they provide the major motivating force that leads to growth. Our efforts and success at growth and development may be seen as attempts to compensate for and overcome our imagined or real inferiorities and weaknesses. Thus feelings of inferiority are not deviant but are the basis for all forms of human accomplishment and improvement in life (Adler, 1927).

The concept of human nature as driven by feelings of inferiority first came to Adler during his practice of general medicine. He observed that many of his patients localized their

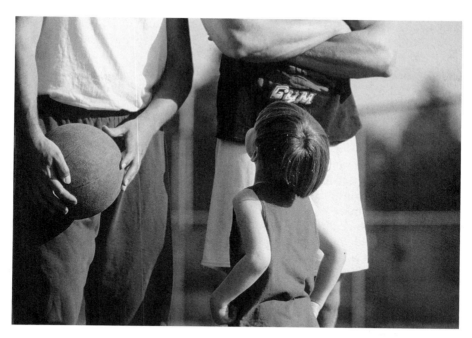

In Adler's theory, inferiority feelings arise because as children we are so much smaller and less competent than adults.

complaints in specific body organs. He hypothesized that in many cases an individual is born with a potentially weak organ that may not respond adequately to external demands (1917). This "organ inferiority" can have profound effects on both the body and the psyche. It may have a harmful effect and lead to neurotic disorders, but it can also be compensated for and lead to optimal achievements. The ancient Greek Demosthenes learned to overcome his stuttering and became a great orator by forcing himself to shout in front of the ocean with pebbles in his mouth. Later, Adler broadened the concept of organ inferiority to include any feelings of inferiority, whether actual or imagined.

In his early writings, Adler termed the compensation for one's inferiorities the **masculine protest.** At the time, he associated inferiority with femininity, but later Adler became an early proponent of women's liberation, recognizing that the alleged inferiority of women was a cultural assignment rather than a biological one.

Adler's views were no doubt fostered by his marriage to Raissa Epstein, a member of the intelligentsia, who expected equality between them and helped him to overcome his earlier concepts. Adler came to appreciate fully the role that culture and society have played in perpetuating male dominance and privilege. He suggested that psychological differences between women and men are the result of cultural attitudes and pointed out the devastating effect of these attitudes on the lives of children. He described how such biases disturb the psychological development of women and have led some to a pervasive dissatisfaction with their role. Adler felt that exaggerated masculinity has a negative impact on men and women alike. He recommended the cultivation of comradeship and education for cooperation between the sexes. His ideas are confirmed today by research on sex roles and the influence of education.

Style of Life

Each individual seeks to cope with the environment and develop superiority in a unique way. This principle is embodied in Adler's concept of the **style of life,** which was a primary theme in his later writings (1929a, 1931). One individual may try to develop competence and superiority through intellectual skills. Another may seek self-perfection by capitalizing on physical strengths. Style of life acts in part as a perceptual filter, influencing the ways in which we view the world. These different life-styles develop early in childhood. Adler suggested that the life-style is pretty clearly established by the time a child is five years old. Thereafter it remains relatively constant. It can be changed, but only through hard work and self-examination.

The style of life results from a combination of two factors: the inner goal orientation of the individual with its particular fictional finalisms and the forces of the environment that assist, impede, or alter the direction of the individual. Each individual's style of life is unique because of the different influences of our inner self and its constructs. Adler suggested that no two individuals, including identical twins, ever had or could have the very same style of life.

Nevertheless, Adler (1927) felt that he could distinguish four primary types of style, three of which he termed "mistaken styles." These include *the ruling type:* aggressive, dominating people who have little social interest or cultural perception; *the getting type:* dependent people who take rather than give; and *the avoiding type:* people who try to escape life's problems and engage in little socially constructive activity. The fourth primary life-style Adler termed *the socially useful type:* people with a great deal of social interest and activity.

Thinking Critically

How has your birth order influenced you? See the Thinking Critically box "Birth Order and Personality."

Among the factors that lead to different life-styles are the ordinal position of birth and different experiences in childhood. Adler did not postulate any stages of development as Freud did, but he emphasized the importance of the atmosphere of the family and the family constellation. **Family constellation** refers to one's position within the family in terms of birth order among siblings and the presence or absence of parents and other caregivers. Adler hypothesized that the personalities of oldest, middle, and youngest children in a family are apt to be quite dissimilar simply by virtue of the different experiences that each child has as that particular member of the family group.

Oldest children tend to be more intelligent, achievement oriented, conforming, and affiliative. They often try to regain the glory that was theirs before they were dethroned by younger siblings. Thus they are frequently oriented toward the past and show a high degree of concern with power, which may express itself as a desire to exercise authority, lead, or protect and help others. Adler described Freud as a "typical eldest son."

The second child may feel the need to accelerate and catch up with the first child. Whereas oldest children often dream of falling from places (dethronement), second children often dream of running to catch things. Second children are apt to be competitive and ambitious and often surpass the firstborn in achievement and motivation. However, they are not as concerned with power. Adler was a second child.

Thinking Critically

Birth Order and Personality

Read through the following lists and check those items that apply to you in comparison with your brothers and sisters. If you are an only child, check those items that apply to you in comparison with your peers.

List A
You tend to

1. be more conforming
2. be less hostile
3. have more motivation
4. be a better student
5. achieve more recognition
6. assume more leadership roles
7. be closer to your parents
8. like nurturing professions
9. consult others when making a decision
10. be less aggressive
11. associate more with others
12. receive high expectations from your parents
13. have similar values to your parents
14. seek help or nurturance from others
15. be more anxious
16. have more worries
    Total _____

List B
You tend to

1. be more aggressive
2. be more democratic
3. be more independent
4. be more popular
5. value parents' opinions less
6. like solitary professions
7. fight, "get into trouble" more
8. be a better mixer
9. like more dangerous activities
10. be less verbal
11. be less likely to seek help from others
12. be less conforming
13. "slide by" more
14. have been brought up less strictly by your parents
15. be more of a "loner"
16. have been given less attention by your parents
    Total _____.

Add up your totals in each list. If you are an only or a firstborn child, the research indicates that more of the items on List A will apply to you. If you are a later-born child (but not the youngest in a large family), more of the items on List B will apply. If you are the youngest child in a large family, your pattern will be closer to that of a firstborn. If you are a middle child, you will show a combination of the characteristics of both lists.

How do your findings compare with the research predictions? Can you think of alternative explanations for some of the birth-order effects? For example, firstborns are exposed to more adult language, which may be a simpler explanation for their tendency to do better in school. Can you think of other factors in your family constellation that have helped to shape your personality? Today, many students live in families other than the traditional nuclear family. They may live with a single parent or have stepparents and step- or half siblings. How might these constellations further influence personality?

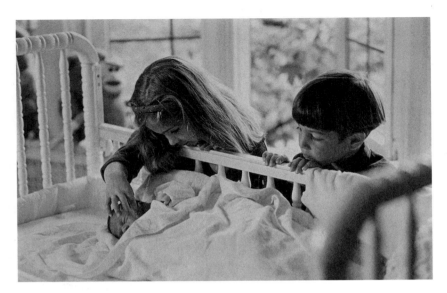

Adler suggested that the personalities of oldest, middle, and youngest children in a family often differ greatly. The firstborn tends to assume a nurturing and leadership role. The last-born child risks remaining the "baby" of the family. The middle child often seems confused as to his or her place in the family.

Last-born children are more sociable and dependent, having been the "baby" of the family. At the same time they may also strive for excellence and superiority in an effort to surpass their older siblings. Adler pointed out that many fairy tales, myths, and legends (for example, the biblical story of Joseph) describe the youngest child as surpassing his or her older rivals. (It was Adler who fully developed the concept of *sibling rivalry,* in which the children within a family compete with one another.) The last-born child who is spoiled and pampered may continue a helpless and dependent style of life into adulthood.

Only children tend to be more like older children in that they enjoy being the center of attention. Because they spend more time in the company of adults, rather than siblings, they tend to mature sooner and to adopt adultlike behaviors earlier in life. However, only children are also the most likely to be pampered. Adler considered pampering the "greatest curse of childhood."

Middle children show a combination of the characteristics of oldest and youngest. If children are spaced several years apart, they have more of the characteristics of only children. The family constellation becomes further complicated when one considers all the additional possibilities, such as the only brother among sisters, twins, and so forth. In recent years a considerable amount of research has been done in the area of birth order and family constellation, some of it finding smaller birth-order effects than Adler would have predicted. One of the interesting findings suggests that longer marriages may occur among partners whose birth orders are complementary. Thus an oldest brother of sisters will probably be happier with a younger sister to a brother than with an only child, because each of them is used to that familial pattern and mode of relating.

The quality of emotional relationships among members of the family reflects the **family atmosphere,** which assists in determining whether or not the child will react actively or passively, constructively or destructively, in the quest toward superiority. Adler thought children who are pampered or neglected are particularly predisposed to a faulty style of life. The pampered child is one who is excessively spoiled, overindulged, and protected from life's inevitable frustrations. Such a child is being deprived of the right to become independent and learn the requirements of living within a social order. Parents who pamper a child make it difficult for the child to develop social feelings and become a useful member of society and culture. The child grows to dislike order and develops a hostile attitude toward it. The neglected child is one who feels unwanted and rejected. Such a child is virtually denied the right to a place in the social order. Rejection arouses resistance in the child, feelings of inferiority, and a tendency to withdraw from the implications of social life. Adler pointed out that child-rearing practices frequently consist of a continuing alternation between indulgence and rejection. The pampered child often demands undue attention and regard, which eventually leads to parental anger and punishment that are often interpreted by the child as rejection. Though few parents actually reject their children, many children feel humiliated and defeated.

Although parental "rejection" is overcome when parents learn alternative ways of handling their children that avoid pampering or neglect, Adler stressed that the individual is fully responsible for the meaning attached to parental behavior and action. Many of us harbor deep feelings of having been rejected by our parents when they actually gave us their best efforts. Thus, in the end, only the person can assume responsibility for his or her style of life.

The Creative Self

Adler considered the concept of **creative self** the climax of his theory (1964). It is the self in its creative aspects that interprets and makes meaningful the experiences of the organism and that searches for experiences to fulfill the person's unique style of life. In other words, the creative self establishes, maintains, and pursues the goals of the individual. Adler's concept of the creative self underscored his belief that human nature is essentially active, creative, and purposeful in shaping its response to the environment.

The concept of the creative self also reinforces Adler's affirmation that individuals make their own personalities from the raw materials of their heredity and environment. In his concept of the creative self, Adler restored consciousness to the center of personality. Adler believed that we are aware of everything we do and that, through self-examination, we can understand why we behaved in a certain way. The forces of which we are unaware are simply unnoticed; they are not buried in a sea of repression.

Adler's position regarding consciousness was in direct contrast to that of Freud. Adler did not deny unconscious forces, but he minimized them by reducing unconsciousness to simple temporary unawareness. He opposed Freud's determinism by emphasizing the vast extent to which people can achieve conscious control over their behavior. People, Adler argued, may become largely aware of their deepest impulses and fictional finalisms, and with conscious intent create their own personalities and life-styles that will achieve their highest goals. In the end, Adler's position was almost the complete opposite of Freud's, which emphasized that our behavior is largely determined by forces of which we are unaware. Freud offered his followers the hope of being able to endure or live without crippling fear of one's unconscious conflicts, but he never offered freedom from them. By restoring consciousness to the center of personality, Adler aroused Freud's anger. To Freud, Adler was encouraging the very illusion that Freud had sought to destroy.

For many people, Adler's optimistic view provides a welcome contrast to the pessimistic and conflict-ridden picture of human nature shown in Freudian psychoanalysis and reinstates hope to the human condition. In his optimism, Adler foreshadowed the theorists to be discussed in the chapter on humanism and existentialism; in his emphasis on the creative self as organizing behavior and emotions, he foreshadowed the cognitive-behavioral theorists.

ADLERIAN PSYCHOTHERAPY

Neuroses, according to Adler (1929b), entail unrealistic life goals or fictional finalisms. Goals are not realistic unless they take into account our capacities, limitations, and social environment. A person who felt extremely inferior or rejected as a child may set goals that are too high and unattainable. A person of average intelligence cannot expect to perform at a consistently outstanding level in academic work. Some individuals adopt goals that are unrealistically low. Having felt defeated and unable to cope with certain situations, such as school, people may seek to avoid situations in which they could develop and perfect those skills that would enable them to perform effectively.

Neurotics also choose inappropriate life-styles as a means of attaining their goals. In their efforts to offset feelings of weakness, neurotics tend to overcompensate. **Compensation** entails making up for or overcoming a weakness. For example, blind people learn to depend more on auditory senses. **Overcompensation** refers to an exaggerated effort to cover up a weakness that entails a denial rather than an acceptance of the real situation (Adler, 1954). The bully who persists in using force may be overcompensating for a difficulty in working cooperatively with others.

Adler's terms *inferiority complex* and *superiority complex,* phrases that have become commonplace in our vocabulary, also describe neurotic patterns. Individuals who feel highly inadequate may be suffering from an **inferiority complex.** In Adlerian terms, there is a gulf between the real person and excessively high life goals. Individuals who exaggerate their own importance may be suffering from a **superiority complex.** In Adlerian terms, such individuals have overcompensated for feelings of weakness. Both complexes originate in a person's responses to real or imagined feelings of inferiority.

Adler suggested that neurotics actually live a **mistaken style of life,** or *life lie.* Neurotics strive for personal aggrandizement. Their style of life belies their actual capacities and strengths. They act "as if" they were weak, "as if" they were doomed to be losers, when in fact they could create a constructive existence for themselves. They capitalize on imagined or real weaknesses and use them as an excuse rather than a challenge to deal constructively with life. They employ **safeguarding tendencies,** compensatory devices that ward off feelings of inferiority in a maladaptive rather than adaptive fashion. To be sure, we all use such protective defense mechanisms at times, but neurotics employ them in an exaggerated manner and degree.

Adlerian therapy aims at restoring the patient's sense of reality, examining and disclosing the errors in goals and life-style, and cultivating social interest. Radical changes occur when an individual adopts new goals (cf. Durbin, 2006). Adler did not establish strict rules or methods for treatment; he believed that the patient's life-style should determine the procedure. On the whole, Adler's approach was somewhat more informal than Freud's. He abandoned the use of the couch, suggested that the patient sit facing the therapist, and reduced the frequency of contact between patient and doctor to once or twice a week.

The first goal of the Adlerian therapist is to establish contact with and win the confidence of the patient (1929b). Such confidence is won by approaching the patient as a peer, thus soliciting cooperation. Whereas Freud viewed the transference as essential to the effectiveness of treatment, Adler suggested that therapy is effective because healthy features of the physician-patient relationship are carried over into the patient's life. Such transference need not have regressive features and is really another name for the cultivation of social interest.

Second, the therapist seeks to disclose the errors in the patient's life-style and provide insight into the present condition. The patient is led gently and gradually to recognize the errors in personal goals, life-style, and attitude toward life.

Adlerian therapy seeks to encourage the patient to face present problems and to develop constructive means of dealing with them. The therapist hopes to instill (or promote) the courage to act "as if" the old limiting fictions and mistaken life-styles weren't true. The therapist who does not make decisions or assume responsibilities for the patient may structure or suggest situations that will assist in cultivating the patient's own skills. Such encouragement enables the patient to become more courageous and to accept new tasks and responsibilities. In this sense, the therapist plays the role of an educator who reeducates the neurotic in the art of constructive living. Additionally, Adler sought to minimize latent feelings of rejection and resentment and to cultivate feelings of social interest and good will. Adler believed that only by subordinating our private gain to public welfare can we attain true superiority. The true and inevitable compensation for all the natural weaknesses of individual human beings is that of social justice for all.

Many of Adler's concepts have been used to develop more effective methods of child rearing and education (Bitter, 1991; Dreikurs & Soltz, 1964). Adler would most definitely encourage prospective parents to engage in parental training, and his work is reflected in such programs (e.g., Dinkmeyer & McKay, 1976). As creative selves, we construct the primary forces that shape our existence: our goals and life-styles. We can change these, should they become inappropriate, through insight into our errors. Through education, Adler believed, our innate and shared concept of social interest and justice could be made to flower and to provide the final and most appropriate form of compensation for our individual weaknesses. However, Adler, who consulted with school systems regularly, felt that schools frequently compound the problem of inferiority feelings through the extensive use of tests that have a built-in mechanism for failure. In order to establish a ceiling, many tests, such as the SAT, include questions that almost no one can answer and that lead to feelings of frustration and failure. Adler was active in child guidance clinics and involved in penal reform. He was attracted to the political movement of socialism, and many hours of his later years were devoted to specifying ways of educating for social justice. Adler "was radically opposed to the kind of therapy which overemphasized independence and egocentricity" (May, 1991).

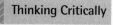

Thinking Critically

Should prospective parents be required to get training? See the Thinking Critically box "A License to Parent?"

Thinking Critically

A License to Parent?

Adler's concepts have been used to develop programs for more effective parenting, such as STEP: systematic training for effective parenting (Dinkmeyer & McKay, 1976). If you were to develop a training program based on Adler's ideas, what would your program entail? STEP focuses on how to raise children in a loving way while also maintaining discipline. It emphasizes how to listen and talk to a child and build self-esteem. Such efforts raise the question of whether specific instruction and education should be required for all prospective parents. Our society requires that its members obtain special training and earn credentials before they are permitted to engage in several significant activities, such as practicing medicine or driving a car. Although parenting is undoubtedly one of the most important jobs that any of us may be called upon to do, almost anyone who is biologically capable of reproducing is permitted in our society to do so without any prerequisites.

Should we require a license for engaging in the activity of parenting? If credentialing procedures were established, what should the prerequisites be (high school education, a certain amount of financial resources, specific courses in parenting)?

Questions such as these are likely to generate strong opinions. Why do they evoke such a reaction? What would be the objections and problems to implementing requirements for parenting? Where do you believe Adler would stand on these issues?

ASSESSMENT AND RESEARCH IN ADLER'S THEORY

Adler's theory, like that of many others, stemmed from clinical observations. Like Freud, Adler paid close attention to patients' nonverbal behavior as well as to what they said. He noted how they stood, walked, sat, or shook hands. He believed that nonverbal communication or behavior is indicative of a person's life-style. Adler himself conducted little systematic empirical research to validate his ideas. Instead, he viewed the importance of these data in terms of their relevance as clinical observations. Adler referred to the study of birth order, early memories, and dreams as the "three entrance gates to mental life"; these three tools constituted Adler's primary techniques of assessment.

Many early researchers attempted to test Adler's birth-order theory. Not all of the research supports Adler's findings, but his theory was valuable in stimulating further research and discussion. Zajonc and Markus (1975) theorized firstborns are more intelligent because the intellectual climate of a family decreases as the number of children increases (see also Zajonc, 2001). Steelman (1985, 1986) countered that educational, occupational, and income levels of the parents could be the primary reason (see also Zajonc, 1986).

Noting the contradictory findings of birth-order research, Sulloway (1996) maintains that methodological problems and an inadequate theoretical perspective have contributed to confusion rather than clarification. He draws on the work of Darwin and evolutionary science to further Adler's interest in birth order and family dynamics. Individual personality differences originate from within the family, as siblings develop strategies to compete for scarce parental resources. Birth order is a crucial factor. Whereas oldest children tend to identify with their parents and authority and to sustain the status quo, younger children tend to rebel (cf. Averett, Argys, & Rees, 2006). Moreover, the repercussions of sibling rivalry extend beyond individual development to society as a whole (see also Michalski & Shackelford, 2002; Rodgers, Cleveland, van den Oord, & Rowe, 2000; Zajonc & Mullally, 1997). Birth-order research continues to generate interest (Leman, 2004; Herrera, Zajonc, Wieczorkowska, & Cichomski, 2003; Mancillas, 2006; Sulloway, 2007) and has expanded to look at sibling dynamics and interrelationships (Kluger, 2006).

Research about life-style is limited, but research in early memories, birth order, and social interest continues. Adler believed that early memories frequently summarized the essential characteristics of one's stance toward life. For example, Adler observed from a study of over one hundred physicians that their first memories often entailed the recollection of an illness or death. In the course of successful therapy, Adler also discovered that patients frequently recall previously overlooked memories that are more consistent with their new life-styles. Reichlin and Niederehe (1980) summarized research confirming Adler's belief that early memories reflect personality traits. New research on memory ties it to the development of language and the ability to shape events into a story, supporting Adler's view that our earliest memories are full of meanings (Goleman, 1993b).

In Adler's theory, dreams are goal oriented rather than reflections of the past. They reveal the mood that we want to feel and suggest how we might deal with a future problem or task. Taking note of the options we choose to follow in our dream life gives us further insight into our style of life (see Lombardi & Elcock, 1997). Research by Greisers, Greenberg, and Harrison (1972) provided evidence that dreaming may assist individuals in dealing with ego-threatening situations, and their analysis may suggest alternative options.

Adler preferred to use clinical observations rather than psychological tests in the assessment of personality (Rattner, 1983). However, a Social Interest Index (SII) and a Social Interest Scale (SIS) have been developed by other psychologists to measure Adler's concept of social interest and to test related hypotheses. Comparisons with other measures show the Social Interest Index to be a valid indicator of social interest (Hjelle, 1991). Measurements of inferiority still need to be developed; most measurements today focus on the self-concept (Dixon & Strano, 1989). Thus Adler's theory has been helpful in generating additional assessment tools.

Adler's Theory

PHILOSOPHY, SCIENCE, *and* ART

Adler's commitment to a philosophical viewpoint is clear in his discussion of fictional finalisms. Human beings, he asserted, are goal-oriented organisms, and all human behavior can be understood in terms of its contribution and adherence to a goal. Difficulties in living result from an inappropriate philosophy and the inappropriate style of life that accompanies it. By recognizing and cultivating the need for social justice, a person fulfills her or his ultimate potential.

Adler added **usefulness** to the criteria for judging philosophical assumptions: A philosophy is useful if it fosters productive living and enhances our lives. In doing so, he followed the pragmatic philosophy of William James (1842–1910), who argued that the meaning of a statement lies in the particular enriching consequences it has for our future experiences and the quality of our lives. Adler's emphasis on the importance of the usefulness of our goals has become very popular among psychologists and personality theorists.

Although Adler emphasized the factors in society that contribute to the shaping of personality, he did not adopt a radical environmentalist position and suggest that personality is *entirely* shaped by society. There are forces within the self, such as the drive for superiority and the creative self, that assist in shaping personality. Thus the individual plays an important, responsible role.

Adler was much more optimistic than Freud about human and societal potentialities. He saw human nature as flexible and changeable. The forward-moving tendency within the self, the drive for superiority, implies that many obstacles to growth are imposed by society rather than by human nature itself. However, through the creative self, human beings largely create their own personalities. Ultimately, Adler envisioned the possibility of creating a better society through the cultivation of our social interest. He stressed the application of personality theory through the art of psychotherapy, believing that through self-understanding and education we can construct a better world.

Critics, however, have found Adler optimistic and naive, suggesting that he may have exaggerated the potentialities of the creative self in being aware of and creating the personality that will best fulfill the individual's goals and the possibilities of change at any point in one's lifetime. Although initially Adler adhered to the notion of determinism, in the end he was a strong advocate of free will. At times, it appears that the creative self is exempt from or able to overcome causal laws, an idea that both Freudians and later behaviorists would have trouble with. Grounding Adler's insights in current neuroscience and quantum mechanical research and expressing them in a philosophy in which both efficient and final causes shape behavior could strengthen them (Smith, 2003).

Philosophical Assumptions

Which philosophical issues did Adler emphasize? See the Philosophical Assumptions box "Examining Adler and Sullivan" on page 116.

Adler's emphasis on the social forces that play a part in shaping personality influenced subsequent social psychoanalytic theorists such as Karen Horney and Erich Fromm. Adler's optimistic constructs also influenced the humanistic school of thought in psychology (see Ansbacher, 1990). Moreover, many of Adler's concepts, particularly that of the creative self, are congruent with the contemporary cognitive emphasis in psychology. Adler has had a tremendous impact in the counseling and education communities (see Hirsch, 2005). Adlerian therapy is finding application in education, school systems, business, and counseling. Adlerian concepts have been used to explore corporate leadership (Miranda, Goodman, & Kern, 1996) and to generate new ways of working with traditional and alternative family constellations (Chandler, 1995). Acceptance of and respect for such variation contributes toward the achievement of Adler's goal of social equality (Chernin & Holdren, 1995).

Mozdzierz and Krauss (1996) point out that research in psychology, anthropology, and evolutionary biology supports Adler's emphasis on the importance of interpersonal relationships. Stasio and Capron (1998) indicate that Adler's construct of social interest is significantly different from other theoretical constructs to warrant continued study. Albert Ellis's system of rational-emotive therapy

(1973), which holds that behaviors are a function of beliefs, draws on Adler's psychology, as does the cognitive social learning theory of Julian Rotter, who studied with Adler in New York City. Thus Adler's ideas and their application have spread, even though they are sometimes not recognized as Adlerian, possibly because Adler does not mesh with America's "intoxication with narcissism and the ego-centered self" (May, 1991).

Adler's concept of social interest is extremely significant cross-culturally. Both Christian and Buddhist concepts of religious maturity include ideas similar to Adler's social interest. Adler tried to bring understanding to a significant part of our heritage as individuals. Adler saw the individual as concerned not only with the self but with the entire world. One of Adler's goals for his individual psychology was to demonstrate that it was "heir to all great movements whose aim is the welfare of mankind" (Weiss-Rosmarin, 1990). Evans and Meredith (1991) ponder whether Adlerian psychology was in advance of its time.

Harry Stack Sullivan (1892–1949)

BIOGRAPHICAL BACKGROUND

Harry Stack Sullivan was born in 1892 in Norwich, New York. He was the only surviving child of Irish Catholic farmers, who had to struggle to provide the basic necessities for their son. A shy, awkward boy, he had difficulty getting along with the other children in the predominantly Protestant Yankee community in which he lived.

Although Sullivan suggested that ethnic and religious differences were the primary contributors to his feelings of isolation as a child, personality difficulties created by his home

life and his own character were probably equally important. Sullivan did not have a close relationship with his father, whom he described as "remarkably taciturn." His mother, a complaining semi-invalid, was the more important figure in his life. Mrs. Sullivan resented the fact that through marriage she, a Stack, from a professional middle-class family, had sunk in social, educational, and economic status. Her son bore the brunt of her laments, tales of earlier family prominence, and unrealistic dreams.

When Sullivan was eight and a half, he developed a close friendship with a thirteen-year-old sexually mature adolescent boy. Although Swick-Perry (1982), Sullivan's biographer, has argued that the relationship was not homosexual, it was viewed as such by

Sullivan believed that the personality of an individual could never be studied in isolation. He explored the dynamics of interpersonal relationships and their influence on personality development.

the townspeople. Sullivan later wrote (1972) that close relationships between a young child and an early-blossoming adolescent of the same sex invariably lead to homosexuality. As an adult, he admitted with regret that he never achieved a heterosexual genital relationship.

Sullivan was valedictorian of his high school class and won a state scholarship to Cornell. Encouraged by one of his teachers, he decided to become a physicist in order to rise above his poverty. At Cornell, however, his grades fell, and in his second year he was suspended for academic failure. During the next six years, Sullivan earned enough money to enter the Chicago College of Medicine and Surgery, an inferior school that he later described as a "diploma mill," suggesting that it granted degrees for payment of tuition rather than academic performance. The school closed in 1917, the same year in which Sullivan received his degree.

The shabby education that Sullivan received had detrimental effects in his later life. He never learned to write well, and he did not have a solid formal training in scientific methodology and research. Nor did Sullivan receive any formal training in psychiatry. Thus there were gaps in his medical knowledge. He was also relatively ignorant of many cultural subjects. Nevertheless, Sullivan worked hard at self-instruction, and his lack of formal education may have freed him from some of the set attitudes and prejudices that a standard education can foster.

Sullivan entered psychiatry at the age of thirty when he was appointed to the staff of Saint Elizabeth's Hospital in Washington, D.C. Here Sullivan developed a working knowledge of psychiatry through his work with disturbed veterans and his attendance at lectures, seminars, and case history presentations. He later suggested that his patients were his primary teachers. In 1923 Sullivan moved to the Sheppard and Enoch Pratt Hospital in Baltimore. His energy and devotion to work and his descriptions of therapeutic techniques brought him to the forefront of American psychiatry. However, his stress on the treatment environment has been deemphasized with the advent of psychopharmacology (Schulz, 2006).

In 1930 Sullivan moved to New York and established a private practice. While in New York he had some three hundred hours of personal psychoanalysis. In 1933 Sullivan assisted in founding the William Alanson White Psychiatric Foundation, named after a neuropsychiatrist who had greatly influenced Sullivan's work. He started the journal *Psychiatry* to publicize his own views.

In his later years Sullivan served as a consultant to the Selective Service Board and to UNESCO. To the end of his life, Sullivan involved himself in the political struggles and social conflicts of the United States. He was one of the first psychoanalysts to pay serious attention to the problems of African Americans in both the South and the North. After Hiroshima, he was quick to recognize the implication: Either world wars or human life must end. He died suddenly in Paris in 1949 while returning from an executive board meeting of the World Federation for Mental Health at which he had been trying to enlist the support of psychiatrists from all over Europe to oppose any further use of nuclear weapons.

BASIC CONCEPTS

Sullivan (1953) defined **personality** as the characteristic ways in which an individual deals with other people. He believed that it was meaningless to think of an individual as an object of psychological study, because an individual develops and exists only in the context of relations with other people. Interpersonal relations constitute the basis of personality.

Indeed, the very term *personality* was only a hypothesis for Sullivan (1964). It was merely an imaginary construct that is used to explain and predict certain behaviors. It would be a mistake, Sullivan suggested, to consider personality as a separate entity apart from the interpersonal situations in which it emerges. Thus Sullivan's definition of personality stresses the empirical components that we can directly observe rather than intrapsychic structures. We can see, hear, and feel that an individual is relating to other people in certain ways, such as in a passive or dominant fashion.

Anxiety and Unawareness

Anxiety is a central concept in Sullivan's theory, as it was for Freud. Sullivan conceived of **anxiety** as any painful feeling or emotion that may arise from organic needs or social insecurity. However, he emphasized the anxiety that arises from social insecurity and thought of anxiety as interpersonal in origin, beginning with the child's empathetic perception of the mother's concerns.

Sullivan also emphasized the empirical character of anxiety, pointing out that it can be described and observed through a subjective description of how one feels or an objective notation of physical appearance and reactions and through physiological changes that are indicative of anxiety.

In our relationships with others, we are to some extent aware of what we are doing and why we are doing it, and to some extent unaware of these things. Sullivan appreciated that an individual may be unconscious or unaware of some of his or her motives and behaviors. The ease with which a person can become aware of his or her interpersonal relationships varies from individual to individual and can be objectively demonstrated by talking with someone and observing that person's actions. Thus the concepts of awareness and unawareness are also empirically based. However, if we are unaware of our interpersonal relationships, we do not experience them and cannot learn from them. An individual who believes that he or she is inept may be aware only of the way in which he or she bungles things but unaware of successful experiences. When we are aware of the pattern of our interpersonal relationships, we can modify and change them.

Security Operations

In order to reduce anxiety and enhance security, we employ security operations of which we are usually unaware (Sullivan, 1953). A **security operation** is an interpersonal device that a person uses to minimize anxiety. These security operations are healthy if they increase our security without jeopardizing our competence in interpersonal relations; they are unhealthy if they provide security at the expense of developing more effective interpersonal skills. Unhealthy security operations merely blunt our anxiety and may lead to other painful emotions and psychiatric illness.

Sullivan's notion of security operations parallels Freud's concept of defense mechanisms. Both are processes of which we are unaware and means by which we reduce anxiety. The primary difference lies in Sullivan's stress on what is observable and interpersonal. Sullivan's emphasis is not on an intrapsychic activity, such as repression, but on the way in which a person may become disassociated from certain aspects of his or her experience of the world. Sullivan pointed out that security operations are processes that we can observe as they arise in the matrix of interpersonal relationships.

Some of the security operations that Sullivan described are sublimation, selective inattention, and "as if" behavior. Sullivan reconceived Freud's mechanism of sublimation to include an emphasis on how we learn to behave in interpersonal situations. *Sublimation* to Sullivan is the expression and discharge of uncomfortable feelings in ways that are interpersonally acceptable, such as releasing anger verbally rather than by hitting or kicking the object of anger. Sullivan also described *selective inattention,* the failure to observe some factor in an interpersonal relationship that might cause anxiety, such as not noticing a spouse's flirtations because those activities threaten one's own self-esteem. Sullivan considered selective inattention a very powerful and potentially dangerous security operation that may blind us to what is going on in our world and make it difficult for us to cope effectively with events. Finally, "as if" behavior means that we act out a false but practical role. A person may act "as if" he or she were stupid to fulfill the expectations of others, when in actuality the person is not stupid. For the mentally disturbed person "as if" may mean acting as normally as possible. As in Adler's theory, the mechanism of "as if" may also have positive consequences. We may convince ourselves that we are competent by behaving consistently in an effective fashion.

Dynamisms

Sullivan maintained that we can observe certain processes in an individual's interpersonal relationships and that these processes can be used to describe the development of the individual's personality. One such process is a **dynamism,** a pattern of energy transformation that characterizes an individual's interpersonal relations (1953). Dynamisms result from experiences with other people. Sullivan's work differs from Freud's in that it replaces a Newtonian mechanical concept of material objects and forces in the universe with a contemporary view of the flow and transformation of energy in the universe. In Freud's theory, forces come out of the id, ego, and superego. When they collide, they create emotional conflict. Sullivan focused on the transformation of energy as it flows between people in relationships. The interpersonal contact between mother and infant, particularly with reference to nursing, begins a flow of energy. The mother nurses the child, and her activities lead the infant to respond in certain ways, such as feeling satisfied and behaving contentedly. This creates a dynamism or pattern of energy characteristic of the interpersonal relationship.

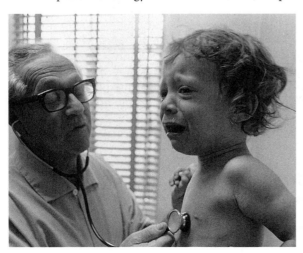

In later childhood and adolescence the dynamisms become more complex. The child who is afraid of strangers illustrates the *dynamism of fear.* The young male who during adolescence seeks sexual relations with young women is expressing the *dynamism of lust.*

One of the more significant dynamisms is that of the self or **self-system.** The self-system is made up of all of the security operations by which an individual defends the self against anxiety and ensures self-

A child who is afraid of doctors is expressing a dynamism of fear.

esteem. It is a self-image constructed on the basis of interpersonal experiences. Sullivan suggests that the concept of self is no more than a response to the interpersonal relationships in which one has been involved. The dynamism arises out of the child's recognition of potentially anxious situations—that is, parental disapproval and rejection, and the child's attempts to avoid them.

Out of the child's experiences with rewards and anxiety, three phases of what will eventually be "me" emerge. The term *good-me self* refers to the content of awareness when one is thoroughly satisfied with oneself. It is based on experiences that were rewarding and is characterized by a lack of anxiety. The *bad-me self* is the self-awareness that is organized around experiences to be avoided because they are anxiety producing. The *not-me self* entails aspects of the self that are regarded as dreadful and that cannot be permitted conscious awareness and acknowledgment. These dynamisms are processes rather than structures, behavior patterns that have come to characterize one's interpersonal relationships. But they can result in a dissociation of the self in which certain experiences literally become cut off from identification with the self.

Personifications

A **personification** is a group of feelings, attitudes, and thoughts that have arisen out of one's interpersonal experiences (Sullivan, 1953). Personifications can relate to the self or to other persons. Personifications of the *good-mother* and the *bad-mother* develop out of satisfying or anxiety-producing experiences with the child's mother. In fairy tales, these personifications find expression as the good fairy and wicked stepmother or witch.

Personifications are seldom accurate; nevertheless, they persist and are influential in shaping our attitudes and actions toward others. Moreover, on a group level, they are the

Sullivan believed that a "chum" relationship is the beginning of genuine human relationships. In healthy preadolescence the relationship may but need not entail overt homosexual genital activity.

basis of *stereotypes,* or prejudgments, which frequently hinder our ability to relate to people of diverse cultures and backgrounds.

Stages of Development

Sullivan (1953) outlined six stages in personality development prior to adulthood: infancy, childhood, the juvenile era, preadolescence, early adolescence, and late adolescence. His stages remind us of Freud's in that they frequently emphasize bodily zones. However, Sullivan thought that the stages themselves were determined socially rather than biologically, and he saw the period of adolescence as crucial, warranting three stages (see Table 4.1).

Cognitive Processes

Sullivan described three **cognitive processes** by which we experience the world and relate to others in the course of personality development. The process that occurs at the lowest level is **prototaxic experience,** which is characteristic of the infant. There is no distinction between the self and the external world. The child directly perceives certain sensations, thoughts, and feelings but does not think about them or draw any conclusions. From masses of undifferentiated sensations, the child gradually distinguishes material objects, people, and him- or herself. This distinction moves the child into the next level.

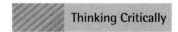

Thinking Critically

Can you demonstrate Sullivan's modes? See the Thinking Critically box "Prototaxic, Parataxic, and Syntaxic Experience."

The **parataxic experience** perceives causal relations between events that happen together. It involves making generalizations about experience on the basis of proximity. The infant whose cry has brought the mother to nurse assumes that his or her crying has produced the milk. Superstitions are examples of parataxic thinking. Random movements or patterns that are reinforced at an inopportune time may be repeated or avoided because they are thought to be the cause of the satisfying or anxiety-producing situation. Parataxic thinking is characteristic of the young child, whose mind

TABLE **4.1** S<small>ULLIVAN'S</small> S<small>TAGES OF</small> D<small>EVELOPMENT</small>

In Sullivan's stages, human personality is shaped by interpersonal relations rather than biology.

STAGE	FOCUS
Infancy	Interpersonal relationships that crystallize around the feeling situation
Childhood	The development of healthy relationships with one's parents
Juvenile era	The need to relate to playmates and same-sex peers
Preadolescence	A chum relationship, the beginning of intimate reciprocal human relationships. Could entail overt homosexual genital activity
Early adolescence	The development of a lust dynamism and a stable heterosexual pattern of sexual satisfaction
Late adolescence	Integration and stabilization of culturally appropriate adult social, vocational, and economic behavior

Thinking Critically

Prototaxic, Parataxic, and Syntaxic Experience

Sullivan depicted three cognitive processes—prototaxic, parataxic, and syntaxic—that occur developmentally, and he showed that we experience the world differently at different levels of development. You can demonstrate Sullivan's modes by conducting the following activities with children.

Dangle your car keys in front of an infant three to six months of age. The child will reach up to grab for them. But if you remove the keys from the child's sight, the child will not look for them. This illustrates prototaxic experience, in which objects that are not present as a sensory experience do not exist.

Swing your keys in front of an infant eight to eleven months of age, and note how the child responds (perhaps by arching the body upward and then falling back or by reaching forward toward the keys). Seek to reinforce and repeat the child's specific response behavior by swinging the keys again. Let a pattern develop: Hold the keys motionless until the child displays that response behavior; then swing the keys. After the pattern is developed, hold the keys still and discontinue swinging them. The child probably will repeat the behavior five or six times more while looking at the keys before stopping. This activity illustrates parataxic experience, in which the child believes that his or her behavior caused the movement of the keys.

Observe the behavior of a child who has just been taught to use the word *please* when requesting something. Young children originally associate their utterances with a general feeling of power and magic. The child may become very upset when the use of the magic word *please* does not immediately invoke the desired response. The child is still at the level of parataxic experience and has yet to learn that words are socially agreed-upon terms that enable individuals to communicate with each other rather than personal magical pronouncements. Such learning enables the child to move into the cognitive level of syntaxic experience.

Sullivan suggests that much of our thinking does not advance beyond the parataxic level. Can you give examples of superstitions that are characteristic of parataxic thinking?

---

is too immature to understand the causal laws of nature. Pervasive fear and the inability to react realistically following a terrorist attack reflect parataxic thinking. Sullivan suggests that much of our thinking does not advance beyond the parataxic level.

The highest level of cognitive activity is that of **syntaxic experience,** which uses symbols and relies on **consensual validation,** or agreement among persons. Syntaxic experience relies upon symbols whose meaning is shared by other people in one's culture, such as the use of language. When a word has been consensually validated, it loses its personal meaning and power, but the validation enables individuals to communicate with one another and provides a common ground for understanding experiences. Syntaxic thought begins to develop in childhood. Ideally as adults our experience is almost completely symbolic and dependent on syntaxic modes of cognition.

PSYCHOTHERAPY, ASSESSMENT, AND RESEARCH

Sullivan viewed psychotherapy as a interpersonal process in which one person assists another in resolving problems of living (1954). He used the concept of participant observation to define the nature of psychiatric inquiry and treatment (1954). In **participant observation,** an observer is also a participant in the event being observed. While observing what is going on, the psychiatrist invariably affects the relationship and alters the other person's behavior. Sullivan suggested that it is absurd to imagine that a psychiatrist could obtain from his or her patient data and/or behaviors that are uninfluenced by the therapist's own behavior in the relationship.

Sullivan, who spent his youth doing manual labor on his father's farm, suggested that psychotherapy is the hardest possible work, requiring continual alertness, honesty, and flexibility. The therapist is emotionally involved in the therapeutic process. He or she may be interested, bored, frustrated, or angry but must continually be aware of his or her reactions, understand them, and keep them at a minimum in order to continue to be an alert observer. Not only is psychotherapy hard work, but it must not be expected to provide the usual satisfactions of ordinary interpersonal relationships. The therapist does not look for friendship, gratitude, or admiration from the patient but aims simply to have the patient understand him- or herself better. The therapist's rewards come from doing a job well and being reasonably paid for it.

A major portion of therapy is spent in examining the two-person relationship that exists between the therapist and the patient. This is one sample of the patient's interpersonal life that is made available for direct study. During therapy, the patient frequently begins to treat the physician as if he or she were someone else. Freud labeled this phenomenon transference. In Sullivan's terms, the patient develops a *parataxic distortion.* A patient who had a harsh, authoritarian father may react to the therapist as if he or she were also harsh and authoritarian. Such parataxic distortion is not unique to therapy. When it occurs in everyday life, however, it simply invites puzzled or angry responses from other people and interferes with effective interpersonal relationships. In therapy, it is an invitation for further exploration and study that can be used to increase the patient's self-awareness of what is happening in his or her interpersonal relationships. Eventually the parataxic distortion must be destroyed so that the patient can work cooperatively with the therapist.

In addition to examining the patient-therapist relationship and dealing with anxiety and security operations, psychotherapy involves exploring the patient's past and current relationships with others. These can be examined to see how they reiterate the processes that have been observed in the present patient-therapist relationship. Sullivan also paid attention to immediate interpersonal crises. These provide a wealth of information, especially if they can be tied to similar crises in the past. Sullivan coined the term *codependent,* used frequently in Al-Anon, an organization for relatives of alcoholics, to characterize behavior of other people that, usually unwittingly, helps to reinforce dependence and other dysfunctional conduct. Sullivan also discussed future interpersonal relationships by asking what the patient thinks his or her relationships with certain people will be like in the future. Sullivan referred to such an exploration of the future as *constructive reverie.* Through constructive reverie the therapeutic process can take into account and deal with the patient's expectations and apprehensions about the future.

Sullivan paid considerable attention to the **interview,** his term for the interpersonal process that occurs between the patient and therapist. He suggested that each individual interview and the course of psychotherapy itself are composed of four parts: the *inception* or beginning, during which the patient introduces the problem; the *reconnaissance,* during which the therapist raises questions in order to develop a case history and tentative hypotheses about the patient; the *detailed inquiry,* in which the therapist tests his or her hypotheses by observing the patient's behavior and responses; and the *termination,* a structured ending during which the therapist summarizes what has been learned and prescribes some kind of action that the patient might take in regard to his or her problem.

Influenced by Sullivan's view that psychotherapy should focus on patient interactions with significant others, Lorna Smith Benjamen (1996) has developed a method of assessing interpersonal styles that is particularly helpful to patients and therapists. Her *structural analysis of social behavior* (SASB) teaches clinicians how to recognize various interpersonal patterns, much as one would recognize a melody in all its variations. Such recognition greatly facilitates the interview process, diagnostic procedures, and treatment interventions.

Sullivan's Theory

PHILOSOPHY, SCIENCE, *and* ART

Sullivan's emphasis on personality characteristics that can be directly observed within the framework of interpersonal relationships leads to a new direction in personality theorizing. Freud and Jung emphasized a philosophical approach to personality; Sullivan's theory veers toward a greater stress on science and empirical validation. Sullivan stopped trying to reckon with unseen mental processes and concentrated on the interpersonal processes that can be verified by observing individuals within their social contexts. With this emphasis on behaviors that can be directly observed, Sullivan points toward the theorists discussed in Part IV on behavior and learning theories and illustrates a scientific approach that is consistent with current American academic psychology.

This is not to say that philosophical assumptions are absent from Sullivan's theory. They are evident in his views on issues such as freedom versus determinism, constitutional versus situational factors, and optimism versus pessimism, as well as in his belief that the personality of an individual can never be studied in isolation. Still, his primary intent was not to present a philosophical view of human nature but to conduct empirical research on personality.

Philosophical Assumptions

What were important philosophical issues for Sullivan? See the Philosophical Assumptions box "Examining Adler and Sullivan."

Thus Sullivan was more aware of the need for validating evidence in personality theorizing than Freud, Jung, and Adler. He emphasized that his theory was grounded in empirical data and observation, and he tried to avoid formulating imaginary concepts that could not be tested.

In his concept of dynamism as energy transformation, Sullivan is in tune with contemporary physics, which since Einstein (1879–1955) and Planck (1858–1947) has viewed the universe in terms of the flow and transformation of energy. Sullivan's vocabulary is also consistent with current information and communication theory, which stresses interpersonal relations.

Although his concepts have a clear empirical reference, they are frequently stated in a vague or ambiguous manner; translating them into operational definitions for

✳ Philosophical Assumptions

Examining Adler and Sullivan

Many of the differences among personality theories can be attributed to fundamental differences in philosophical assumptions. Which of the basic philosophical issues described in the introductory chapter and summarized on the inside back cover seem to be clearly important to Adler and Sullivan in the development of their theories? How, for example, does Adler's concept of the creative self influence his stand on freedom and determinism and proactivity versus reactivity? How does Sullivan's view of personality as a product of social interactions influence his view of heredity versus environment? Do their theories address any other philosophical assumptions? Rate Adler and Sullivan on a scale from 1 to 5 on those philosophical assumptions that you feel their theories apply to most. Compare your ratings of Adler and Sullivan with your own philosophical assumptions. Did your study of Adler and Sullivan lead you to change any of your assumptions? Why or why not?

definitive testing is often difficult. It is hard, for example, to distinguish between dynamisms and personifications. Research on Sullivan's theory has focused primarily on the techniques of interviewing and the therapeutic process.

Sullivan demonstrated sophistication in his grasp of scientific concepts, which was particularly remarkable since he had no formal training in the philosophy of science. His concept of participant observation shows that he knew that a scientific method can never be purely objective because it is always influenced by the observer. He made a significant contribution to psychopathology in his articles on the causes, dynamics, and treatment of schizophrenia. He has been criticized for neglecting narcissism and maintaining a stubbornly optimistic view of human nature (Kafka, 2006).

Sullivan's major contribution has been in the area of art, and in moving away from a drive theory to one emphasizing interpersonal relationships (Cooper & Guynn, 2006). He is best known for his research on the therapeutic process and, in particular, on the techniques of interviewing.

FAMILY THERAPY

Treating psychological problems in the context of the family is a logical outcome of the theories of Adler and Sullivan, even though the practice did not actually take off until the mid-1950s. Today, managed health care and other cultural influences favor the economy of treating the full family or **family therapy** rather than separate individuals.

Family therapists suggest that psychological problems are developed and maintained in the social context of the family. Concurrent with the emphasis of Adler and Sullivan, the focus of treatment shifts from the intrapsychic world of the individual to the interpsychic relations of the family. Rather than explaining dysfunctional behavior in terms of mechanisms within the individual, problems are seen in the perspective of mutually influential interpersonal relations within the family.

Contemporary family therapy that treats psychological problems in the context of the family has its roots in the work of Adler and Sullivan.

Influenced by the study of group dynamics, family therapists emphasize that the *process,* or the way in which ideas are communicated, is just as important as the *content,* or the ideas themselves. Looking at the process can help families improve how they relate to each other and increase their ability to handle the content of their problems. Virginia Satir, a key pioneer in the development of family therapy, described several roles that people play in a family. If one child is the troubled "rebel," another may seek to relieve the stress by assuming the role of a "good child." Such role reciprocity makes it harder to change behavior. Other early proponents include Murray Bowen, who developed *family systems therapy,* which many consider the most thoughtful and complete statement of family therapy (Nichols & Schwartz, 1998), and Carl Whitaker, who would include three generations in his sessions. Whitaker moved family therapy in a postmodern direction by emphasizing that people construct or give meaning to their experiences (Smith, 1998). Sal Minuchin suggests that family and therapist map out a family tree indicating patterns of connection, distance, anger, and so forth among members of the family to clarify relationships, and Jay Haley's *strategic therapy* focuses on short-term targeted efforts to solve a specific problem. Integrative relational psychotherapy (IRP), summarized by Jeffrey Magnavita (1999), combines a rigorous biopsychosocial model of personality with a relational framework to develop a therapy systems theory for patient assessment and treatment planning that can be incorporated into individual couple and family therapy practices. Theodore Millon has encouraged changes in the clinical diagnosis of personality disorders that reflect the importance of interpersonal relations (2000a, 2000b, 2003). Current trends include treating the family rather than prescribing medication, a strategy that increases awareness and decreases the development of more serious disorders (Prosky & Keith, 2003), adding action methods such as role playing

(Wiener & Pels-Roulier, 2005), and empowering family therapy with a feminist perspective, adding sociocultural content (Silverstein & Goodrich, 2003; Prouty-Lyness, 2003).

 TO LEARN MORE about family constellation/birth order, and for a list of suggested readings, visit the *Personality Theories* textbook website at **college.cengage.com/pic/ engler8e.**

Summary

1. The theories of Adler and Sullivan mark a shift from an emphasis on **intrapsychic** (p. 93) phenomena to an emphasis on **interpsychic** (p. 93) phenomena.

2. Adler believed that human beings have an innate urge, a **social interest** (p. 95), to adapt to the conditions of the environment. This urge needs to be cultivated. The principle of **finalism** (p. 95) means that individuals are oriented toward goals that guide their behavior. These **fictional finalisms** (p. 95) cannot be proven and are judged by their **usefulness** (p. 105).

3. The primary objective of the psyche is the **goal of superiority** (p. 96), the desire to be competent and effective in what one does. As young children, we normally feel inferior, and these **inferiority feelings** (p. 96) lead us to seek ways in which we can compensate for our weaknesses. Each individual develops a unique way of striving for superiority that is called a **style of life** (p. 98).

4. The style of life is influenced by factors such as **family constellation** (p. 98), or birth order, **family atmosphere** (p. 101), and the quality of emotional relationships.

5. The **creative self** (p. 101) interprets the experiences of the organism and establishes a person's style of life. Adler maintained that the creative self is essentially conscious; he restored consciousness to the center of personality (in direct opposition to Freud's view).

6. Adlerian therapy aims at restoring the patient's sense of reality, examining and disclosing the errors in goals and style of life, and cultivating social interest. Adler believed that birth order, early memories, and dreams provide the best tools for assessing personality.

7. Adler's theory emphasizes a philosophical point of view rather than an effort to study personality empirically. Adler also made substantial contributions to psychotherapy, education, and child rearing.

8. Sullivan defined **personality** (p. 108) as the characteristic ways in which an individual deals with other people. Sullivan thinks of **anxiety** (p. 109) as interpersonal in origin and observable. Anxiety may lead a person to be unconscious or unaware of his or her motives and to develop **security operations** (p. 109), interpersonal devices that minimize anxiety. Security operations are observable and arise in the course of interpersonal relationships.

9. **Dynamisms** (p. 110) are patterns of energy transformation that characterize an individual's interpersonal relations. The most significant dynamism is the self-system. **Personifications** (p. 111) are groups of feelings, attitudes, and thoughts that have arisen out of one's interpersonal experience. An example is the good mother.

10. Sullivan outlined six stages of personality development. Three of the stages refer to adolescence, which Sullivan saw as crucial. He also outlined three **cognitive processes** (p. 112) that occur developmentally: the **prototaxic** (p. 112), **parataxic** (p. 112), and **syntaxic experiences** (p. 113).

11. Sullivan used the concept of **participant observation** (p. 114) to define the nature of psychiatric inquiry and treatment. Sullivan also outlined four stages of the **interview** (p. 114) process: **inception** (p. 115), **reconnaissance** (p. 115), **detailed inquiry** (p. 115), and **termination** (p. 115).

12. In his emphasis and practice of empirical research and his recognition of participant observation, Sullivan placed a greater emphasis on a scientific approach than did Freud and Jung. His greatest contribution, however, has been in the area of psychotherapy.

13. Adler's and Sullivan's work influenced contemporary **family therapy** (p. 116), which treats psychological problems in the context of the family.

Personal Experiences

1. Adler believed that on a fundamental level we all strive for superiority and that the attempt of each individual to master his or her environment is determined by the individual's unique history, and style of life. Assuming this is true, list three ways in which you've attempted to master your physical and/or social environment. You may go back as far as your childhood or focus on your time in college. Then try to list three ways in which your individual endeavors were shaped by your culture and style of life. How did such factors affect your beliefs about yourself, the goals you were trying to achieve, and the ways in which you went about achieving them?

2. Working from Adler's definition of *inferiority feelings,* list three ways in which you tend to feel inferior to others. Do you, for example, feel inferior in intelligence, wit, athleticism, or attractiveness? Do you think that any of these feelings stem from your experience as a child? If so, how? How do these feelings impact your sense of self today? Do you believe, as Adler did, that such feelings of inferiority are actually healthy and necessary for human accomplishment and improvement? If you didn't believe this before, do you think that you could start believing it now?

3. In this chapter Adler's discussion of *overcompensation* is used to illustrate neurotic behavior. Overcompensation, however, can be applied more broadly as an occasional coping strategy. Describe an instance in which you overcompensated for feelings of inferiority. To get started, try mentally scrolling through various contexts of your life—the sports field, embarrassing moments with friends, new college acquaintances, intimate relationships. Select an example of overcompensation. In what way did you overcompensate—physically, verbally? What would have happened had you not overcompensated but instead acknowledged your feelings of inferiority at that time? Would the situation have been better or worse? Is such masking of your true self sometimes necessary and healthy? Why or why not?

4. Apply Sullivan's notion of security operation to your own life. Sullivan describes three security operations that we all occasionally use: sublimation, selective attention, and "as if." Describe a personal example of each one. Do you find one of the security operations more easily applicable to your life than the others? If you do, explain the reason for your preference. How does it inform your personality and your relationship to friends, family, and people in general?

5. Sullivan felt that the self, or self-system, is constructed primarily from interpersonal relationships and the dynamics that result from them. These interpersonal relationships shape and mold the self throughout a person's life. Using Sullivan's stages of development in Table 4.1, list for each stage of your own life the specific people who you feel were important in shaping your self-system—who you are. Do you think that one stage was more significant than the others? If you do, explain the source of that significance. Were your relationships with friends and family particularly strong or weak at that time? What interpersonal dynamics would lead to constructive or destructive self-systems?

CHAPTER 5

Psychoanalytic Social Psychology

- **Karen Horney**
- **Erich Fromm**

I n nineteenth- and early-twentieth-century Vienna, where a strict Victorian ethos prevailed, many of Freud's patients may well have expressed guilt feelings about their sexual desires. In other societies, however, social and economic factors often seem to play a primary role. Many of the theorists who followed Freud reacted against his emphasis on instincts and the importance of sexuality in personality formation. We have seen a shift away from intrapsychic factors and toward interpsychic and social forces in Alfred Adler's and Harry Stack Sullivan's theories. The shift continues in the theories of Karen Horney and Erich Fromm.

Horney and Fromm emphasized forces in society that influence personality. Horney stressed social forces that operate within the family; Fromm pointed beyond the family toward social factors within society at large. Drawing on their own clinical experience, as well as on cultural, anthropological, and literary evidence, Horney and Fromm showed how Freud's concepts were a product of his social and cultural milieu. In turn, their own theories of personality were informed by the then emerging social sciences of sociology and anthropology, which stressed that personality is primarily a social product. Horney and Fromm remained within the psychoanalytic framework, however, and conceived of themselves as rejuvenating psychoanalytic theory rather than as pioneering new theories. Their theories can be appreciated as part of the historical and social climate in which they emerged. Moreover, many of the concepts they developed underlie contemporary views in psychoanalysis, and the tools they developed remain useful in clinical practice.

Karen Horney (1885–1952)

BIOGRAPHICAL BACKGROUND

Karen Danielson Horney (pronounced "horn-eye") was born in 1885 near Hamburg, Germany, into an upper-middle-class family that was economically and socially secure. Her father was of Norwegian descent and her mother was Dutch. As a child, Horney sometimes traveled with her father, a sea captain. Although she admired her father, he was frequently stern and often critical of her intelligence, interests, and appearance. Because of her father's long absences from home, Horney spent considerably more time with her mother, a younger, dynamic, freethinking woman who greatly influenced her daughter. Karen was devoted to her mother even though at times she felt that her mother favored her older brother. An experience with a kind doctor when she was twelve years old made her want to become a physician. Her adolescent diaries provide clues to her originality and independence in becoming the first to challenge Freud's ideas about women (Quinn, 1994). They also reveal emotional problems of depression, insecurity, and a desperate need for attention and love from men. Mrs. Danielson encouraged her daughter to study medicine at a time when it was difficult and unusual for women to enter that profession (Eckardt, 2005) and in spite of rigid opposition from her husband. It was not the first time that the differences of temperament in Horney's parents led to discord. Eventually they separated, and Horney's mother moved near Freiburg, where her daughter was pursuing her studies at the university. Later, Horney emphasized in her writings the role that a stressful environment plays in nurturing basic

Much of Karen Horney's work was groundbreaking for the emerging field of the psychology of women.

anxiety. Lack of love and encouragement, quarrelsome parents, and other stressful environmental factors lead to feelings of rejection, depression, worthlessness, and hostility. She acknowledged these feelings in herself and worked hard to overcome them.

Horney received her degree in medicine from the University of Berlin. Thereafter she was associated with the Berlin Psychoanalytic Institute. She was analyzed by Karl Abraham and Hans Sachs, loyal disciples of Freud, who were two of the foremost training analysts of the day.

In 1909 she married Oscar Horney, a Berlin lawyer. They had three daughters. As a result of their different interests and her increased involvement in the psychoanalytic movement, they were divorced in 1937. The challenges of being a career woman and a mother, and of dissolving a marriage that was no longer viable, gave her considerable insight into the problems of women. She was one of the first theorists to oppose Freud and to speak directly to the issue of feminine psychology.

Horney spent most of her life in Berlin, but in 1932 she was invited to come to the United States and assume the position of associate director of the Chicago Psychoanalytic Institute. Two years later, she moved to New York City, opened a private practice, and taught at the New York Psychoanalytic Institute. Horney and Erich Fromm had a long liaison, both personal and professional, which provoked feelings of bitterness and desire for revenge when it was over (Hoffman, 1994b).

Coming to America during the Great Depression, Horney began to appreciate more and more the role of environmental factors in neurosis. Her patients were troubled not primarily by sexual problems but with the struggle to keep a job and pay the bills. Economic, educational, occupational, and social pressures seemed to be foremost in inducing neurotic behavior. Eventually her disagreements with the Freudian point of view and the refusal of orthodox psychoanalysis to integrate or even acknowledge her ideas led her to leave the New York Psychoanalytic Society (see also Robb, 2006). In April 1941 she walked out singing "Go Down, Moses." Horney founded the Association for the Advancement of Psychoanalysis and the American Institute of Psychoanalysis and was dean of the Institute until her death, from cancer, in 1952.

Karen Horney concentrated on the neurotic aspects of behavior. She subscribed to much of Freud's work but sought to overcome what she perceived as his limitations by emphasizing social and cultural factors and minimizing biological ones. Her work provides us with a number of fascinating insights and provocative concepts that have received a lot of attention.

BASIC ANXIETY

Horney concurred with Freud that anxiety is the basic human condition. However, she saw anxiety not as inevitable but rather as a result of social forces.

As human beings, our essential challenge is to be able to relate effectively to other people. **Basic anxiety,** an insidiously increasing, all-pervading feeling of being lonely and helpless in a hostile world (Horney, 1945), results from feelings of insecurity in these relations. According to Horney's concept of basic anxiety, the environment as a whole is dreaded because it is seen as unrealistic, dangerous, unappreciative, and unfair. Children are not simply afraid of their own inner impulses or of punishment because of their impulses, as Freud postulated in his concepts of neurotic and moral anxiety; they also feel at times that the environment itself is a threat to their development and innermost wishes. Some parents and caregivers, for example, are unable to meet children's needs. Horney called all of the negative factors in the environment that can provoke insecurity in a child **basic evil.** Some of these conditions might be domination, isolation, overprotection, hostility, indifference, inconsistent behavior, disparagement, parental discord, lack of respect and guidance, or the lack of encouragement and warmth. Such behaviors undermine a child's security and cause feelings of *basic hostility,* which must be repressed for fear of losing the parent's love (Horney, 1937). Children's fears may be objectively unrealistic, but for them they are real. In a hostile environment, children's ability to use their energies and develop self-esteem and reliance is thwarted. Children may be rendered powerless in the face of these encroachments. Their biological dependency and the failure of parents to foster adaptive self-assertive behavior may leave them helpless. Although children may endure a certain amount of frustration and trauma, it is essential for healthy personality development that they feel safe and secure.

Some of the same concerns that occupied Horney led to the formulation of object relations theory (Ingram & Lerner, 1992). Horney's ideas on the importance of early interpersonal relationships are reflected in the writings of Heinz Kohut, whose theory is discussed in the chapter on human relations. Horney suggested (1939) that the emphasis on the Oedipus complex tends to detract from the significance of "early relationships *in their totality.*" This view forecasts Kohut's position that the Oedipus complex is a product of disintegration resulting from parents' failure to respond with pride and empathy to the growth of their children (Quinn, 1994).

NEUROTIC NEEDS OR TRENDS

In the face of basic anxiety, children develop certain defense attitudes or strategies that permit them to cope with the world and afford a certain measure of gratification (Horney, 1937). Many of these strategies continue into adulthood. Specifically, we use them to deal with or minimize feelings of anxiety and to assist us in effectively relating to others. When they become exaggerated or inappropriate, these strivings may be referred to as **neurotic needs or trends.** Neurotic trends are the result of the formative experiences that create basic anxiety. The trends are not instinctual in nature but highly dependent on the individual's formative experiences of being either safe or insecure in the world. The term *neurotic* was discontinued in the fourth edition of the American Psychiatric Association's *Diagnostic and Statistical Manual of Mental Disorders* (DSM-IV, 1994). However, it was commonly used in the first half of the twentieth century to refer to emotional disturbances, particularly those that were not so severe as to prevent the individual from functioning in normal society.

Horney identified ten different neurotic needs or trends (see Table 5.1). For the neurotic, the need is too intense, too unrealistic, too indiscriminate, too anxiety laden. These trends lead to three types of coping strategies or **primary modes of relating** to other people: **moving toward** (compliance), **moving against** (hostility), and **moving away** (detachment). These types of behavior lead, in turn, to three **basic orientations** toward life: the **self-effacing solution,** an appeal to be loved; the **self-expansive solution,** an attempt at mastery; and the **resignation solution,** a desire to be free of others (1950). These orientations are interpersonal in nature, unlike the Freudian and Jungian character types, which are intrapsychic. Research on attachment patterns in infants suggests a distinct similarity between Horney's three basic orientations and young children's behavior.

TABLE 5.1 HORNEY'S TEN NEUROTIC TRENDS

NEUROTIC TRENDS	PRIMARY MODES OF RELATING TO OTHERS	BASIC ORIENTATIONS TOWARD LIFE
1. Exaggerated need for affection and approval 2. Need for a dominant partner	Moving toward (compliance): accepting one's helplessness and becoming compliant	Self-effacing solution: an appeal to be loved
3. Exaggerated need for power	Moving against (hostility): rebelling and resisting others to protect one's self from a threatening environment	Self-expansive solution: a striving for mastery
4. Need to exploit others		
5. Exaggerated need for social recognition or prestige		
6. Exaggerated need for personal admiration		
7. Exaggerated ambition for personal achievement		
8. Need to restrict one's life within narrow boundaries	Moving away (detachment): isolating one's self to avoid involvement with others	Resignation solution: a desire to be free of others
9. Exaggerated need for self-sufficiency and independence		
10. Need for perfection and unassailability		

SOURCE: Based on information in K. Horney, Self-Analysis. *New York: Norton, 1942; K. Horney,* Our Inner Conflicts, *New York: Norton, 1945; and K. Horney,* Neurosis and Human Growth, *New York: Norton, 1950. Used by permission of W. W. Norton & Co.*

Normal or mature individuals resolve their conflicts by integrating and balancing the three orientations, which are present in all human relations. They are able to express each mode at the appropriate time. Neurotics express one mode at the expense of other aspects of their personality. They actively, although unconsciously, repress tendencies to react according to the other orientations. This repression, however, is not successful; the repressed tendencies continue to seek expression and increase the neurotic's anxiety. As the neurotic continues to emphasize one need or mode and overlook the others, a "vicious circle" develops, and the anxiety is never adequately resolved. Thus neurotics transform normal strivings into pathological ones. Table 5.1 summarizes the ten neurotic trends, three modes of relating to others, and three basic orientations toward life.

THE IDEALIZED SELF

Karen Horney (1950) distinguished between the real self and the idealized self. The **real self** represents what we are—those things that are true about us. The **idealized self** represents what we think we should be. We use it as a model to assist us in developing our potential and achieving self-actualization. The dynamic of creating an idealized self in order to facilitate self-realization is universal and characteristic of each of us. An individual who seeks to be a competent doctor posits an ideal of what an effective doctor is like. In the normal individual, the idealized self and the real self largely coincide because the idealized self is based on a realistic assessment of one's abilities and potentials. In the neurotic individual, the real self and the idealized self are discrepant or separated. A doctor who believes that an ideal doctor never loses a patient to death is being unrealistic. This situation can be represented diagrammatically by circles, as is shown in Figure 5.1.

A person is able to recognize and develop only those aspects of the real self that coincide with the idealized self. Thus, as neurosis becomes more severe, an increasing amount of the powers and potentialities of the real self may be rendered unavailable for cultivation. In an extreme neurosis, the individual may completely abandon the real self for the sake of an idealized *glorified self.* Horney referred to this situation as one of **alienation** (or the *devil's pact*). In a state of alienation, a person identifies with the ideal self and thereby loses the true and only source of strength, the real or actual self.

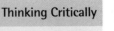

Thinking Critically

How do you "should" on yourself? See the Thinking Critically box "The Tyranny of the Should."

Horney (1950) suggested that neurotics' lives are governed by the **tyranny of the should.** Instead of meeting genuine needs, those individuals create false ones. For example, individuals who have the idea that in order to be good they must never feel jealous may posit an idealized self that does not permit feelings of jealousy. In doing so, they deny the part of the real self that does experience feelings of jealousy, and they become estranged from part of the self.

Horney's concept of the idealized self may be seen as a constructive revision or correction of Freud's concept of the ego-ideal. Freud's concept of the superego includes two aspects: an introjected social conscience and an ego-ideal that is an idealized image consisting of approved and rewarded behaviors. The ego-ideal is the source of pride and provides a concept of who we think we should be. In her elaboration, Horney emphasized social factors that influence the development of an idealized self. Furthermore, Horney viewed the idealized self not as a special agency within the ego but as a special need of the individual to

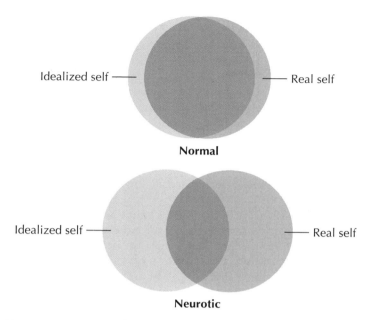

FIGURE 5.1 THE NORMAL SELF AND THE NEUROTIC SELF

Circles are used to represent the real self and idealized self in Horney's theory of personality. In the normal individual, the circles largely coincide. In the neurotic individual, the circles are increasingly distinct.

Thinking Critically

The Tyranny of the Should

Horney believed that much of our lives may be governed by the tyranny of the should. Name some significant "shoulds" that you have devised to safeguard your image of self, such as being a good student or maintaining an ideal weight. Can you identify the origin of your "shoulds"—for example, your parents or your culture? Can you think of different types of "shoulds" that diverse cultures foster? What might happen if you were to give up one of the "shoulds" that is giving you problems?

keep up appearances of perfection. She also pointed out that the need to maintain an unrealistic idealized self does not involve simply repression of "bad" feelings and forces within the self. It also entails repression of valuable and legitimate feelings that are repressed because they might endanger the mask. Carl Rogers, whose theory is discussed in the chapter on humanism, makes a similar distinction between the real self and the self as perceived.

FEMININE PSYCHOLOGY

Karen Horney's interest in feminine psychology—psychological theory that focuses on women's experiences—was stimulated by the fact that certain clinical observations appeared to contradict Freud's theory of the libido. Freud had suggested that penis envy was largely responsible for a woman's development, that women view themselves as castrated males. Horney pointed out that both men and women develop fantasies in their efforts to cope with the Oedipal situation. She also emphasized that many men and boys express jealousy over women's ability to bear and nurse children, a phenomenon that has since been clearly seen in ethnographic accounts from many cultures (Paul, 1992), as well as in clinical settings. Horney termed this phenomenon **womb envy.** Her work suggests that womb envy and penis envy are complements (1967), reflecting the mutual attraction and envy that the sexes have for each other.

Horney believed the essence of sexual life lies in its biological creative powers; a greater role in sexual life belongs to the female because she is the one who is able to bear and nurse children. This superiority is recognized by the male and is the source of intense envy. Womb envy, rather than being openly acknowledged by most males, has often taken subtle and indirect forms, such as the rituals of taboo, isolation, and cleansing that have frequently been associated with menstruation and childbirth, the need to disparage women, accuse them of witchcraft, belittle their achievements, and deny them equal rights. Similar attempts to deal with these feelings have led men to equate the term *feminine* with passiveness and to conceive of activity as the prerogative of the male.

Both men and women have an impulse to be creative and productive. Women can satisfy this need naturally and internally, through becoming pregnant and giving birth, as well as in the external world. Men can satisfy their need only externally, through accomplishments in the external world. Thus Horney suggested that the impressive achievements of men in work or other creative fields may be seen as compensations for their inability to bear children.

The woman's sense of inferiority is not constitutional but acquired. In a patriarchal society, the attitude of the male predominates and successfully convinces women of their supposed inadequacies; it socializes them into a restricted set of role expectations of submissive and loving wife and mother. But these are cultural and social factors that shape development (Eckhardt, 1991, 2005; Symonds, 1991), not biological ones.

During her practice in the 1920s, Karen Horney believed that she was observing a "flight from womanhood." Many women were inhibiting their femininity. Distrusting men and rebuffing their advances, these women wished that they were male and could enjoy the career opportunities and power held by male members of society. This flight from womanhood was due to their experience of real social and cultural disadvantages. Sexual unresponsiveness, Horney pointed out, is not the normal attitude of women. It is the result of cultural factors. Our patriarchal society is not amenable to the unfolding of a woman's individuality (see also Burger & Cosby, 1999; Cyranowski & Anderson, 2000; Westkott, 1996).

Horney's psychology of women, which is almost a direct inversion of Freud's theory, has met with criticism because she maintained that the essence of being a woman lies in motherhood. Nevertheless, her contributions to feminine psychology have been very valuable. Much of Horney's work in feminine psychology and her challenge to male authority laid the foundation for the new psychology of women. (In breaking away from orthodox psychoanalysis, Alfred Adler and Erich Fromm were also especially concerned about female

According to Horney, women can satisfy their creative needs internally or externally, but men can satisfy their creative needs only externally, often through work.

development.) In many ways, Horney was prophetic. As early as the 1920s, she observed that it was men who had written human history and men who had shaped the psychoanalytic movement. Those enterprises reflected male needs and biases. Men, she insisted, should "let women speak, and hear *their* 'interpretations', even 'biases', if you will" (Coles, 1974). Horney as such became the first psychoanalyst who sought to define the feminine self in terms of a woman's own self and not in terms of a woman's relationship with a man (Miccolis, 1996).

Feminine "values of closeness, love, intimacy, and sensitivity to relationships . . . as contrasted with achievement, success, power, mastery, and repression of feelings assigned to men in our culture can be readily understood in Horneyan terms" (Symonds, 1991, p. 301). In her later writings, Horney developed a theory "that was not gender-specific, but applied to all humans. Perhaps, because Horney was a woman who saw the distortion that developed by overlooking women's identity, she was able to encompass a broader spectrum of human behavior." As such, her theory can be very helpful in "illuminating gender issues and the conflicts that women [and men] struggle with" (p. 304).

ASSESSMENT AND RESEARCH IN HORNEY'S THEORY

In her assessment of personality, Karen Horney primarily employed the techniques of free association and dream analysis. She also suggested (1942) that **self-analysis** can assist normal personality development. Significant gains may be made in self-understanding and in reaching freedom from inner restraints that hinder the development of one's best potentialities.

Each one of us engages in self-analysis when we try to account for the motives behind our behaviors. A student who fails a test that she thought was unfair might ask herself whether she had properly prepared for it. An individual who concedes to another might ask himself whether he was convinced that the other person's point of view was superior or was afraid of a possible argument. Such analyses are common in normal living.

Systematic self-analysis differs from occasional self-analysis in degree rather than kind, entailing a serious and protracted effort for self-understanding undertaken on a regular basis. Systematic self-analysis employs the tool of free association, followed by reflection on what one has thought and analysis of the resistance that aims to maintain the status quo. When one obtains insight into one's personality, energies previously engaged in perpetuating neurotic trends are freed and can be used for making constructive changes. When we are cognizant of our feelings and values, we are able to make good decisions and assume responsibility for them. Although self-analysis can never be considered a totally adequate substitute for professional analysis of neurosis, its possible benefits for enhancing individual development merit its use.

Compared with Freudian psychoanalysis, Horney's theory recommends greater interpersonal understanding of a patient's issues. Like Freud, however, Horney felt that tracing the origin of early patterns is critical, as is the analysis of transference.

Van den Daele (1987) has suggested that Horney's theory of personality can be operationally defined and is essentially compatible with the requirements of psychological measurement. Research that fails to support some of Freud's ideas concerning women (Fisher & Greenberg, 1977) can be seen as supportive of Horney's views (Schultz, 1990). Horney's three primary modes are seen as providing an excellent framework for investigating interpersonal patterns in personality disorders (Coolidge, Moor, Yamazaki, Stewart, & Segal, 2001). Research on parenting styles underscores Horney's conviction that parenting patterns have a strong impact on children and that children respond positively to parents who are both affectionate and firm (Baumrind, 1972; Maccoby & Martin, 1983).

Relatively early in the twentieth century, Horney (1937) began to see a trend in America toward **hypercompetitiveness,** a sweeping desire to compete and win in order to keep or heighten beliefs that one is worthy. Ryckman, Hammer, Kaczor, and Gold (1990) developed a Hypercompetitive Attitude Scale to evaluate the soundness of Horney's concept and found empirical backing for it. College men and women scoring higher in hypercompetitiveness had less self-esteem and were not as healthy psychologically as those who scored lower. Moreover, men with higher scores were more macho and thought of women as sexual objects. Kaczor, Ryckman, Thornton, and Kuelnel (1991) forecast and found that hypercompetitive men were more likely to charge rape victims as being responsible for having been raped and to view them as losers in a fierce physical fight for supremacy.

In his analysis of the contribution of Karen Horney to contemporary psychological thought, Paris (1996) suggests that her most important modification of Freud was her emphasis on an individual's current situation rather than on the past. She began by addressing current defenses and inner conflicts. Her mature theory inspired the interpersonal school of psychoanalysis and furnished a model for therapies that focus on the present. Her concept of the tyranny of the should is remarkably consistent with Albert Ellis's concept of "musterbation" and Aaron Beck's idea of cognitive distortions, discussed in the chapter on cognitive-behavioral theories.

ATTACHMENT AND PARENTING RESEARCH

Horney's emphasis on the importance of parenting is reflected in research that has confirmed the significance of attachment and parenting to child outcomes. Early research with baby monkeys who distinctly preferred being fed by and clinging to terry cloth rather than wire surrogate mothers indicated the importance of tactile comfort as well as nourishment in the mother-child relationship (Harlow, 1958). Higher infant mortality rates in orphanages showed the importance of nurturance needs as well as physical needs in a child's ability to "thrive" (Spitz, 1945).

Bowlby (1977, 1988) suggested that seeking interpersonal attachments is a primary goal of development. He developed **attachment theory** as a way of understanding the tendency of people to bond to specific others and to account for the distress that may follow separation and loss. He saw infants as engaging in specific behaviors, such as smiling and gazing, that lead to closeness and a secure bond with a preferred caregiver. In his research on attachment, Bowlby (1969), like Horney, stressed the importance of "felt security," which arises out of parental sensitivity and appropriate response to infant clues of attachment, distress, fatigue, and happiness. Having established a secure base, the child is free to explore physical and social surroundings and develop other appropriate behaviors. This early attachment creates a basic pattern for later relationships with others.

Infants whose caretakers respond sensitively to their needs develop secure attachments. Ainsworth and her colleagues (1978) observed the behavior of caregiver and infants in a "strange situation" in which a child is separated from and then reunited with the mother or primary caregiver after being exposed to a stranger. She identified three styles of infant attachment patterns. *Secure* children seek proximity with their mother but also use her as a "secure base" from which to move and explore. As they grow, such children show greater ego strength, peer competence, and persistence in problem solving than other attachment groups. *Avoidant* children mix proximity seeking with avoidance behavior toward their mother. There is little affective sharing in the mother-child relationship. Such children show less ego strength, peer competence, and freedom in exploring. *Resistant* children alternate proximity seeking with passive or aggressive behavior (hitting or kicking). Such children are wary and appear unable to trust others. They may actively resist exploring the environment and show little ego strength and peer competence.

Feiring (1984) further subdivided Ainsworth's secure infants into two groups, thus creating a fourfold classification: a healthy balanced form of attachment and three unhealthy patterns comparable to Horney's moving toward, moving against, and moving away. Secure children who use the mother as a safe base for further exploration are using a healthy balance of Horney's three modes. Those who cling to the mother are moving toward, and avoidant and resistant children are moving away or against.

Research on attachment, based on behavioral observations of infants, projective stories told by children, and interpersonal narratives told by adults, has yielded "impressive findings" (Weinberger & Westen, 2001), providing a useful framework for understanding adult emotional reactions and patterns of coping. Attachment styles are based on the working models of the self and others that we develop in infancy and childhood. Such styles continue into adulthood and carry with them personality characteristics consistent with the earlier behaviors (Cassidy & Shaver, 1999; Hazen & Shaver, 1987; Mickelson, Kessler, & Shaver, 1997). The links between early childhood attachment and the dynamics of adolescent and adult relationships are becoming clearer (Bartholomew & Horowitz, 1991; Simpson & Rholes, 1998). Securely attached individuals are socially skilled and have low levels of loneliness (DiTommaso, Brannen-McNulty, Ross, & Burgess, 2003). They show greater compassion and altruistic behavior (Mikulincer, Shaver, Gillath, & Nitzberg, 2005). Although attachment styles are generally stable over time, meaningful and predictable changes can occur due to various factors such as changes in perceptions of self and one's interpersonal relationships (Cozzarelli, Karafa, Collins, & Tagler, 2003). Studies indicate that variations in gender differences in romantic attachment across cultures are associated with certain sociocultural indicators: Men and women are more similar in cultures with higher fertility and mortality rates and fewer resources (Schmitt, 2003). Diamond (2001) argues for the integration of psychophysical measures into adult attachment research to help clarify the underlying biological processes. The characteristics of adult attachment patterns match traits identified with biologically determined temperaments, discussed in the chapter on biological traits, suggesting that they arise out of the interaction of one's biology and cultural heritage. Attachment theory is also being studied in terms of interpersonal constructs such as those described in the chapter on human relations (e.g., Gallo, Smith, & Ruiz, 2003). Attachment theory provides a developmental model of depression that integrates both cognitive approaches, discussed in the chapter on cognitive-behavioral theories, and interpersonal approaches (Cyranowski & Bookwala, 2003; Simpson, Rholes, Tran, Wilson, & Campbell, 2003).

Research on parenting has generally relied on Diana Baumrind's concept of **parenting style,** which describes normal variations in parenting by focusing on two important dimensions: parental warmth or support and parental demands or behavioral control (Baumrind, 1971). Classifying parents according to whether they are high or low in warmth and control creates a typology of four parenting styles. *Indulgent* parents are more responsive than demanding. Nontraditional and lenient, they permit the child considerable self-regulation and seek to avoid confrontation. *Authoritarian* parents are high on demands but low on warmth and support. They provide well-ordered, structured environments and expect obedience. *Authoritative* parents are high in both demands and warmth. They provide clear standards and supportive disciplinary measures. They encourage children to be assertive, socially responsible, self-regulated, and cooperative. *Uninvolved* parents are low in both warmth and control, providing little emotional support and making few behavioral demands on their children. Most parents of this type fall within the normal range of parenting, but in an extreme form this style could entail rejection and neglect.

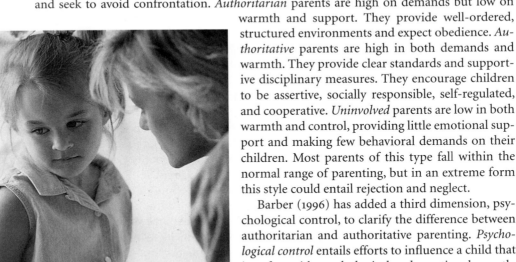

Barber (1996) has added a third dimension, psychological control, to clarify the difference between authoritarian and authoritative parenting. *Psychological control* entails efforts to influence a child that interfere with psychological and emotional growth, such as shaming, inducing guilt, or withdrawing love. Whereas authoritarian and authoritative parents are both high on behavioral control, authori-

Horney believed that children respond positively to parents who are both affectionate and firm.

tarian parents also tend to be high in psychological control, a factor generally low in authoritative parenting.

Consistent with the expectations of Horney's theory, authoritative parenting is seen most reliably as a family variable associated with higher instrumental and social competence and lower levels of problem behavior in childhood and adolescence, whereas uninvolved parenting is associated with poorer performance and higher levels of problem behavior (Baumrind, 1991).

Cross-cultural studies have questioned the assumption that healthy development is most likely to arise within the nuclear family model in which the mother is the primary caregiver. A positive attachment to the mother is not necessarily a mandate for healthy development. Attachment to the father also leads to positive outcomes, as does good care provided by members of an extended family or other caregivers. Single parenting does not necessarily put children at greater risk for psychopathology, nor does parenting within a gay or lesbian family (Hall & Barongan, 2002). Each family alternative has its own advantages and disadvantages, and when the challenges are met constructively, healthy development can and does occur.

It is also important to be aware of differences in cultural perceptions. For example, in Japan parents demonstrate their sensitivity to children's needs by anticipating them, whereas in the United States parents tend to wait for the child to express them and then respond appropriately (Rothbaum, Weisz, Pott, Miyake, & Morelli, 2000). Further, particular parenting styles may be perceived differently in different cultures. Parenting behaviors deemed authoritarian by European Americans were rated more positively by Latino Americans (Sonnek, 1999). Positive effects of authoritative parenting, consistently shown for Caucasians, are not always seen for Asians (Ang & Goh, 2006). Children in different eras and cultures may interpret and respond to the same parenting style differently. In the mid-twentieth century, children in the United States tended to react submissively to authoritarian parents. Today, they are more likely to rebel.

| PHILOSOPHY, |
| SCIENCE, |
| *and* ART |

Horney's Theory

Horney was an astute observer and a talented clinician. She frequently tested, revised, and discarded her theories in the light of new observations. She asserted that certain therapeutic approaches bring forth desired and predictable changes in behavior, changes that can be observed during the course of therapy if not in a rigorous laboratory experiment. She was clearly engaged in scientific activity and believed that her method and therapy must be open to scientific investigation and research.

Philosophical Assumptions

Which philosophical issues seem most important to Horney? See the Philosophical Assumptions box "Examining Horney and Fromm" on page 143.

Horney was not greatly interested in abstract thinking, but her theory does reflect deep philosophical commitments, such as a belief in the process of growth and forward movement (akin to Jung's concept of self-realization) and an optimistic view of human nature, foreshadowing contemporary transpersonal and humanistic psychologies (Morvay, 1999). Toward the end of her life she became interested in Zen Buddhist writings and practices (see DeMartino, 1991; Westkott, 1998).

Horney's concepts of the "tyranny of the shoulds" has led to research on motives for fulfilling obligations (Berg, Janoff-Bulman, & Cotter, 2001). Her theory of three basic neurotic modes, presented in the language of actual clinical experience, lends itself well to operational definition. Studies support the construct validity of her theory and suggest that it can be useful in clarifying both normal personality development (De Robertis, 2006) and pathological personality disorders (Coolidge, Moor, Yamazaki, Stewart, & Segal, 2001; Coolidge, Segal, Benight, & Danielian, 2004; Shorey & Snyder, 2006).

Horney's contributions to the art of psychotherapy have been particularly valuable. Several aspects of her technique are discussed in current Freudian literature as useful additions to psychoanalysis. Clinicians recognize the usefulness of her concepts in the practice of group psychotherapy (Garofalo, 1996; Maiello, 1996).

Horney has been criticized for simply elaborating on concepts that were implied but not clearly expressed in Freud's writings; however, these elaborations contain valuable, original contributions. Horney clarified the ego-ideal; her concept of neurotic trends clarified Freudian defense mechanisms; and she provided significantly more insight into the psychology of women. Moreover, "her disagreements with Freud were profound" (Garrison, 1981), as she emphasized that "everything depended upon the interaction of culture and personality." Her work helped inspire the interpersonal school of psychoanalysis (Paris, 1996) and foreshadowed the work of object relations theorists, who emphasize interpersonal relations (Ingram & Lerner, 1992), and of Heinz Kohut, who identified grandiosity as a major developmental trend. These represent substantial and enduring contributions to psychoanalysis.

Erich Fromm (1900–1980)

BIOGRAPHICAL BACKGROUND

Erich Fromm was born in Frankfurt, Germany, in 1900, the only child of a deeply orthodox Jewish family. At the age of thirteen, he began to study the Talmud, beginning an interest in religious literature and an admiration of the German mystic "Meister" Eckhart (1260?–1327?) that remained throughout his life. In his later years, Fromm did not formally practice religion, but he referred to himself as an "atheistic mystic," and it is clear that his early religious experiences left a distinct mark on his personality and work. The moral and committed tone of his writings has a quality that has been described as reminiscent of the Old Testament prophets.

Fromm wrote little about his early childhood. In his few comments, he described his early family life as tense and acknowledged that his parents were probably neurotic. His mother was "depression-prone," and his father, an independent businessman, "moody" and "overanxious." Fromm was fourteen years old when World War I broke out. He was impressed, almost to the point of being overwhelmed, by the irrationality of human behavior as it showed itself in the brutalities of war. By 1919 he had identified his political attitude as socialist and began to pursue formal studies in sociology and psychology at the University of Heidelberg. He received the Ph.D. in 1922.

For Erich Fromm, one's personality is a compromise between one's inner needs and the demands of society.

Erich Fromm was trained in analysis in Munich and at the Institute of Berlin. He was one of the early *lay analysts;* he had no formal medical training. Many psychoanalysts in America view psychoanalysis as primarily a medical method of treatment for neurotic disorders and therefore consider a medical background indispensable. Freud, however, had argued against medical training as the optimal background for an analyst and had advocated the training of laypeople. He felt that analysis should be viewed as more than simply a method for the treatment of neurosis, and he suggested that it also should be seen as a wide cultural force offering insight into such areas as sociology, philosophy, art, and literature. Fromm's own broad understanding of the social sciences and philosophy was to enrich his understanding of psychoanalytic theory and its applications. At the same time, these interests eventually led to severance from orthodox psychoanalysis and criticism of Freud for his unwillingness to acknowledge the importance of social and economic forces in shaping personality.

In 1933, during the Depression, Fromm came to the United States and worked closely with Karen Horney prior to their rupture. Later he helped found the William Alanson White Institute for Psychiatry, Psychoanalysis, and Psychology in New York and was a trustee and teacher there for many years. He taught at other universities, such as Yale and the New School for Social Research, and maintained an active private practice. In 1949 he was appointed professor of psychiatry at the National University in Mexico. After his retirement in 1965, he continued teaching and consulting activities. He moved in 1976 to Switzerland, where he died of a heart attack in 1980. He was almost eighty years old.

BASIC HUMAN CONDITIONS AND NEEDS

The early 1920s were a time of vibrant excitement in the academic community. Nineteenth-century scholars such as Freud, Comte, Spencer, and Marx had opened the door to the analytical study of human behavior and social institutions. New disciplines of psychology, sociology, and anthropology were emerging, and efforts were being made to build interdisciplinary foundations for understanding social institutions and human behavior. Erich Fromm was particularly impressed with the writings of Freud and Marx, and he attempted a synthesis of their ideas.

He began with the thesis (1941) that *freedom* is a basic human condition that posits a "psychological problem." As the human race has gained more freedom by transcending nature and other animals, people have increasingly experienced feelings of separation and isolation. Thus a major theme of Fromm's writings is the concept of loneliness. To be human is to be isolated and lonely, because one is distinct from nature and others. This sense of isolation and loneliness radically separates human nature from animal nature. The condition of loneliness finds its ultimate expression in the problem of knowing that we are going to die. This knowledge leads to feelings of despair, for most of us find death incomprehensible and unjust—the ultimate expression of our loneliness.

How will human beings respond to the "psychological problem" posed by freedom? Fromm saw two alternatives: They can work with one another in a spirit of love to create a society that will optimally fulfill their needs, or they can "escape from the burden" of freedom into "new dependencies and submission" (1941). Such escape may alleviate feelings of isolation, but it does not creatively meet the needs of humanity or lead to optimum personality development.

Escape Mechanisms

Fromm (1941) identified three common mechanisms of escape from freedom: authoritarianism, destructiveness, and automaton conformity. These mechanisms do not resolve the underlying problem of loneliness; they merely mask it.

Authoritarianism offers escape from the problem of freedom through submitting to a new form of domination. Individuals may permit others to dominate them or may seek to dominate and control the behavior of others. In either case, the root of the tendency comes from an inability to bear the isolation of being an individual self and from an effort to find a solution through *symbiosis,* the union of one's self with another person or with an outside power. A common feature of authoritarianism is the belief that one's life is determined by forces outside one's self, one's interests, or one's wishes, and that the only way to be happy is to submit to those forces.

The teenage years are typically a time of "finding yourself," but the process often entails a period of what Fromm might consider to be "automaton conformity." Notice that these girls not only are dressed in a similar fashion but also have the same impassive expression on their faces.

Destructiveness offers escape from the problem of freedom through the elimination of others and/or the outside world. "The destruction of the world is the last, almost desperate attempt to save myself from being crushed by it" (1941). Fromm believed that signs of destructiveness are pervasive in the world, although this escape mechanism is frequently rationalized or masked as love, duty, conscience, or patriotism.

The majority of individuals seek to escape the problem of freedom through **automaton conformity.** They cease to be themselves and adopt the type of personality proffered by the culture in which they live. Like a chameleon that changes its color to blend in with its surroundings, they become indistinguishable from the millions of other conforming automatons in their world. Such individuals may no longer feel alone and anxious, but they pay a high price: "the loss of the self."

Fromm perceived similarities between his mechanisms of escape and Karen Horney's neurotic trends. The differences between them are that Horney's emphasis was on anxiety, whereas Fromm's was on isolation. Also, Horney's neurotic trends are the force behind individual neurosis, whereas the mechanisms of escape are forces within normal people.

The mechanisms of escape do not offer satisfactory solutions. They do not lead to happiness and positive freedom. By relating spontaneously to love and to work and by genuinely expressing our emotional, sensual, and intellectual abilities, however, we can become one again with other human beings, nature, and ourselves without forgoing the independence and integrity of our individual selves.

Basic Needs

According to Fromm, the human condition of freedom gives rise to five basic needs (1955): **relatedness, transcendence, rootedness, sense of identity,** and a **frame of orientation and object of devotion.** Later, Fromm (1973) added a sixth need, **excitation and stimulation** (see Table 5.2). These needs must be met in order for a person to develop fully. Our primary drive is toward the affirmation of life, but unless we can structure our lives in such a way that our basic needs are fulfilled constructively, we either die or become insane.

Human beings create society to fulfill these basic needs, which arise independently of the development of any particular culture. But the type of society and culture that humans

TABLE 5.2 BASIC NEEDS

Beyond the basic drive toward the affirmation of life, Fromm identified basic needs that must be met in order for a person to develop fully (based on Fromm, 1955, 1973)

Relatedness	Relating to other people and loving productively
Transcendence	Rising above the animal level of creatureliness and becoming active creators
Rootedness	Feeling that we belong
Sense of identity	Becoming aware of ourselves as separate and unique individuals
Frame of orientation and object of devotion	Having a stable and consistent frame of reference to organize perceptions and make sense of our environment
Excitation and stimulation	Actively striving for a goal rather than simply responding

create structures and limits the way in which the basic needs may be fulfilled. For example, in a capitalistic society, acquiring money is a means of establishing a sense of identity. In an authoritarian society, identifying with the leader or state provides a sense of identity. Thus the individual develops a final personality as a compromise between his or her inner needs and the demands of the society.

CHARACTER ORIENTATIONS

A person's character is determined in large measure by the culture and its objectives; thus it is possible to speak of social character types or qualities that are frequently shared by the people of a particular culture. Fromm identified five character orientations that are common in Western societies (1947): **receptive, exploitative, hoarding, marketing,** and **productive** (see Table 5.3). The primary difference between Fromm's theory of character types and orientations and that of Freud is that whereas Freud envisioned the fixation of libido in certain body zones as the basis for future character types, Fromm set the fundamental basis of character in the different ways in which a person deals with basic human conditions.

The traits that arise from each of Fromm's character orientations have both positive and negative qualities, but on the whole Fromm saw the first four types as largely unproductive. A person may exhibit a combination of types. The first three types are reminiscent of Freud's oral and anal character types, and parallels can be drawn between Freud's and Fromm's typologies. It is in his discussion of the marketing orientation that Fromm is generally thought to have made a significant contribution and developed a new character orientation. The concept of supply and demand, which judges an article of commerce in terms of its exchange worth rather than its use, is the underlying value. Marketing personalities experience themselves as commodities on the market. They may be described as opportunistic chameleons, changing their colors and values as they perceive the forces of the market to change.

TABLE 5.3 CHARACTER ORIENTATIONS

Fromm identified five character orientations common in Western societies.

Receptive	Receptive personalities believe that the only way they can obtain something they want is to receive it from an outside source; they react passively, waiting to be loved.
Exploitative	Exploitative personalities take the things they want by force or cunning; they exploit others for their own ends.
Hoarding	Hoarding personalities hoard and save what they already have; they surround themselves with a wall and are miserly in their relations to others.
Marketing	Marketing personalities experience themselves as commodities on the market; they may be described as opportunistic chameleons, changing their colors and values as they perceive the forces of the market to change.
Productive	Productive personalities value themselves and others for who they are; they relate to the world by accurately perceiving it and by enriching it through their own creative powers.

Fromm's description of the productive orientation tries to go beyond Freud's definition of the genital stage and describes an ideal of humanistic development and moral stance that characterizes the normal, mature, healthy personality. These individuals value themselves and others for who they are. In using their powers productively, they relate to the world by accurately perceiving it and by enriching it through their own creative powers.

Such people use humanistic, rather than authoritarian, ethics (Fromm, 1947). Whereas **authoritarian ethics** have their source in a conscience that is rooted outside the individual, **humanistic ethics** represent true virtue in the sense of the unfolding of a person's powers in accordance with the law of one's own human nature and the assumption of full responsibility for one's existence.

Fromm (1964, 1973) also distinguished between **biophilous character** orientations that seek to live life and a **necrophilous character,** which is attracted to what is dead and decaying and seeks to destroy life. Fromm suggested that Adolf Hitler was a classic example of the necrophilous character. The biophilous character is largely synonymous with the productive orientation. The desire to destroy emerges when life forces are frustrated.

Fromm believed that malignant forms of aggression can be substantially reduced when socioeconomic conditions that favor the fulfillment of human needs and potential are developed in a particular society. Productive, biophilous people comprehend the world through love, which enables them to break down the walls that separate people. Productive love, Fromm asserted, is an art. We can master its theory and practice only if we make love a matter of ultimate concern. Productive love is the true creative answer to human loneliness; symbiotic relationships are immature or pseudo forms of love.

It was not until 1976 that Fromm added two basic modes or orientations of existence that compete for the spirit of humanity. The **having mode,** which relies on the possessions that a person *has,* is the source of lust for power and leads to isolation and fear. The **being mode,** which depends solely on the fact of existence, is the source of productive love and activity and leads to solidarity and joy. People whose being depends solely on the fact that they *are* respond spontaneously and productively and have the courage to let go in order to give birth to new ideas. Fromm believed that everyone is capable of both the having and the being modes, but that society determines which of the modes will prevail (1976).

ASSESSMENT AND RESEARCH IN FROMM'S THEORY

An example of the way in which Fromm assessed and researched culture and society was published in 1970 (Fromm & Maccoby). Psychologists, anthropologists, historians, and other experts joined together in an interdisciplinary field study of a Mexican village. With the advent of technology and industrialization, these villagers had been lured away from their traditional values and life-style. Movies and television took the place of festivals and local bands. Mass-produced utensils, furniture, and clothing took the place of handcrafted items. Trained Mexican interviewers administered an in-depth questionnaire that was interpreted and scored for characterological and motivational factors. The Rorschach Inkblot Test, which purports to indicate repressed feelings, attitudes, and motives, was also given. These data showed that the three main classes in the village also represented three social character types: the landowners, productive-hoarding; the poor workers, unproductive-receptive; and the business group, productive-exploitative. The findings about the village's history, economic and social structure, belief systems, and fantasies illustrated and appeared to confirm

Fromm believed that the being mode is the source of productive love and activity and leads to joy.

Fromm's theory that character is affected by social structure and change. Fromm's work continues to have a signficient impact in Mexico (Millán & Gojman, 2000).

Michael Maccoby, who coauthored the Mexican village study, has done two more studies based on Fromm's character types. In the first, interviews of 250 managers in large corporations led to the identification of the "company man," a character type similar to the marketing orientation (Maccoby, 1976). Rather than emphasize actual job skills and knowledge, company men focus on superficial packaging of themselves, which they can adapt as one might change clothes to fit various situations. A potentially new character type, **self-orientation,** which is highly narcissistic and reflects social changes that have occurred in America since the 1960s, emerged in the second study of corporate leaders (Maccoby, 1981). This type tends to be cynical and rebellious, reflecting a breakdown in respect for authority and other traditional values. Self-indulgent and undisciplined, the self-oriented individual tends to lack loyalty and commitment to a work ethic. Maccoby's research supports Fromm's concept that historical and cultural forces shape the development of character types.

Fromm's work on the marketing character and his political and social ideas of health and pathology continue to be revisited and to generate interest (Saunders, 2001; Saunders & Munro, 2001). Scores on a consumer-oriented questionnaire developed to measure Fromm's marketing character correlate positively with anxiety and negatively with life satisfaction (Saunders & Munro, 2000). Still, Fromm's marketing character has become the dominant personality type of our age (Clark, 2005).

In the aftermath of September 11, 2001, Fromm's concepts of authoritarianism and escape from freedom have become increasingly relevant. Adorno and his colleagues (Adorno, Frenkel-Brunswick, Levinson, & Sanford, 1950) suggested that, as children, people with an authoritarian personality are overcontrolled, repressing their resentment and continuing to feel anger, and that as adults they are excessively obedient to authority and displace their hostility onto safe objects, such as minority groups. Rokeach (1960) suggested seven characteristics of the authoritarian personality: rigidity, compulsiveness, conformity, dogmatism, concreteness, literalness, and pedantry. Bob Altemeyer (1989) suggests that authoritarianism consists of three types of attitudes: submission to authorities, authority-sanctioned aggressiveness, and following social conventions. Authoritarian aggressiveness is related to the fear of a dangerous world and to self-righteousness, predictable post-9/11 attitudes and defenses (Crowson, Debacker, & Thoma, 2005). We can guard ourselves against authoritarianism by stressing the importance of freedom and emphasizing higher education, particularly in the liberal arts.

To help explore the emotions and behavior behind terrorist attacks and people's responses to them, Tom Pyszczynski, Sheldon Solomon, and Jeff Greenberg (2003) have developed a theory known as **terror management theory.** Combining insights from Fromm with existential psychology and evolutionary theory, they have built up a framework that is open to rigorous scientific testing. Terror management theory seeks to explain why people react the way they do to the threat of death and how this reaction influences their cognition and emotions. The theory suggests that an inborn annihilation anxiety, together with the unique human awareness of the inevitability of death, creates an ever-present possibility of terror. The fear induces us to construct a belief system to explain the nature of reality and reassure us of immortality through shared links to institutions, traditions, or symbols. When we live up to the standards of our faith, politics, and social norms, we manage the terror and feel safe. However, our worldviews are cultural constructs, requiring consensus for continuation and easily threatened by alternative belief systems. When we are reminded of the fallibility of our constructs, we feel frightened and seek to strengthen our beliefs. In addition, we may strike out at those who are different or those whom we blame for the threat or whom we believe deserve to be punished. Our innate annihilation anxiety is thus a major cause of racial and religious prejudice, as well as terrorism. Studies have substantiated a link between the fear of death and defense of one's cultural viewpoint, as well as negative thinking about people whose beliefs differ from ours. Studies also show that high self-esteem and worldviews that value tolerance mitigate against the likelihood of derogating others who are different.

> **Thinking Critically**
>
> What would Fromm say about terrorism? See the Thinking Critically box "Terrorism."

Terrorism is essentially a response from people who are in a position of weakness. Hostility and violence come to the fore when basic human needs (psychological, political, economic) are not met within the basic ideology and resources of the society. Random killing or acts of terrorism are unlikely to be effective, interfere with attempts at positive solutions, and invite a strong backlash. Nevertheless, where rapid cultural changes threaten traditional values, the stage is set for a fundamentalist retreat and efforts at an epic victory over evil.

The surge in American patriotism after 9/11 and the "war against terrorism" represent classic terror management strategies. So also are pleas for peace from those who urge a passive response to the attacks on the World Trade Center. Both reactions show that terror can lead to both positive and negative socializing responses. In one of several efforts to test terror management theory, two groups of people were polled on the merits of charity, an undisputed value in our society. Those who were polled in front of a funeral home (a subtle indicator of death) ranked charity as significantly more important than those who were polled on a street corner. If we remind ourselves that we value tolerance and believe that everyone has a right to his or her own values and opinions, reminders of death can increase tolerance. Terrorism can lead us to put more effort into creating a world that embodies our noblest values (Pyszczynski et al., 2003; Silberman, Higgens, & Dweck, 2005).

Evolutionary biologists and neuroscientists, discussed in the chapters on dispositional and biological bases of personality, are also being called upon to help us understand terrorism.

Thinking Critically

Terrorism

Is Fromm helpful in clarifying our response to terrorism? Fromm suggested that one way to escape from the problem of freedom is to submit to a new form of submission or domination. Is the relinquishment of personal freedoms—our willingness to give up our privacy, independence, and time in favor of greater security—an example of an effort to escape from freedom or a realistic response to the threat of terrorism? A second mechanism of escape is destruction and elimination of those perceived as responsible for the threat. Is the current "war on terrorism" an example of that mechanism? Are we seeing the emergence of a dystopia such as that described in George Orwell's *1984* in which constant surveillance invades personal privacy? Could such a dystopia develop in America?

The potential to develop scanners that could see the brain in action and screen for potential terrorists raises the question of the acceptable use of such scanners in security or law enforcement. Would brain scanning without a person's knowledge or consent be an appropriate noninvasive detection procedure or an invasion of privacy, an illegal search and seizure? What do you think? The ramifications of the explorations of cognitive neuroscientists are creating a new philosophical field of study: neuroethics, which will help clarify our constructive and destructive uses of these potentials. Fromm believed that the desire to destroy emerges when life forces are frustrated and that malignant forms of aggression can be substantially reduced when socioeconomic conditions favoring the fulfillment of human needs and potential are developed. How helpful is Fromm's analysis in clarifying the situation?

Cognitive researchers are using brain scanners to locate the neural sources of emotion, behavior, and belief. They have learned, for example, that the amygdala, a center of emotional learning in the limbic system, may play a role in the development of bias. They also have learned how easy it is to turn off the prefrontal cortex, the part of the brain that is involved in higher mental processes, considers social rules and empathy, and applies brakes to aggressive impulses. In time, with the ability to see aggression in action, a brain scanner might be developed that could screen for terrorists at border crossings or airports (Nutt, 2005).

Fromm's theory emerged during a particular time in the twentieth century when psychologists were ready to appreciate the contributions of sociology and anthropology and to focus on the importance of culture and society. Even with today's emphasis on neurophysiology and renewed interest in biology, Fromm's concepts continue to enhance our understanding of the impact of social forces and to underscore the importance of our being loving, productive, and in charge of our lives (Ortmeyer, 1998; Spiegel, 1994).

| PHILOSOPHY, |
| SCIENCE, |
| *and* ART |

Fromm's Theory

Fromm rejected **scientism,** or the exclusive reliance on a narrow conception of science, deeming it inadequate for the full comprehension of human nature. He was critical of a narrow scientific approach because it tends to be reductive and does not permit the final nuances of personality to emerge. He realized, perhaps more clearly than many, that the process of scientific activity begins with an epiphanic vision that is informed by the scientist's philosophy. Fromm's theory is a speculative and transcendental one, incorporating several vantage points that initially may appear contradictory.

We have seen how Freud's theory was a product of nineteenth-century thought, rooted and cast in the framework of a currently outdated biological determinism. Although Freud's concepts helped to shatter the nineteenth-century understanding of human nature, they require revision to meet the demands of the twenty-first century. Fromm took advantage of the emerging disciplines of psychology, sociology, and anthropology, as well as new findings in other areas, to revise Freud's theory and develop his own point of view.

Although Fromm's methods of research are empirical, based on observation, they could not be described as rigorous or precise scientific techniques. In the final analysis, Fromm, like many other followers of Freud, was philosophical in his emphasis. He considered that proof grows out of the internal coherence of a theory and the theory's ability to shed light on the human condition. This "coherence theory of truth" is characteristic of the philosopher (Rychlak, 1973).

Philosophical Assumptions

Which philosophical issues seem most important to Fromm? See the Philosophical Assumptions box "Examining Horney and Fromm."

Fromm wrote little about his technique of therapy. He indicated that he was a more active therapist than Freud, and he employed the term *activating* to describe the therapist's interventions to facilitate progress. Fromm emphasized that the therapist must *feel* what the patient is talking about and recognize the common humanity that both of them share. That element of empathy permits the patient to realize that inner feelings are shared by others.

There are clear ethical themes in the writings of Fromm. He tried to develop a norm or an ethic that presents the best answers to the problems we all face. He considered the behaviors that are most appropriate in unifying, harmonizing, and

Philosophical Assumptions

Examining Horney and Fromm

Many of the differences among personality theories can be attributed to fundamental differences in philosophical assumptions. Which of the basic philosophical issues, described in the introductory chapter and summarized on the inside back cover, seem to be clearly important to Horney and Fromm in the development of their theories? How, for example, does Horney's concept of basic anxiety influence her stand on heredity versus environment? How does Fromm's view of society influence his view of freedom versus determinism and optimism versus pessimism? Do their theories address any other philosophical assumptions? Rate Horney and Fromm on a scale from 1 to 5 on those philosophical assumptions that you feel their theories apply to most. Compare your ratings of Horney and Fromm with your own philosophical assumptions. Did your study of Horney and Fromm lead you to change any of your assumptions? Why or why not?

strengthening the individual to be ethical behaviors. Fromm's theory enlarges our concept of the application of personality theory to include efforts to inform and restructure society. His goals for the art of personality theory uniquely combine the scholarly and the ethical motives. In his discussions on guilt and ethics, Bacciagaluppi (1996) even suggests that Fromm anticipates some of the more recent theoretical and empirical contributions on the subject of guilt and provides an alternative framework for viewing data regarding aggression and guilt.

Although some of his writings may seem somewhat dated because they refer specifically to conditions surrounding the mid-twentieth century, his central ideas remain relevant to our contemporary situation. Many of Fromm's themes have been picked up by the humanist movement in psychology. His theory is coherent and sophisticated in its depth. His interdisciplinary approach and emphasis on humanistic ethics would be worth emulation by current students of politics and society (Wilde, 2004).

TO LEARN MORE about hypercompetitiveness and sports, and for a list of suggested readings, visit the *Personality Theories* textbook website at **college.cengage.com/pic/ engler8e.**

Summary

1. Horney described **basic anxiety** (p. 124) as anxiety that results from feelings of insecurity in interpersonal relations. Unlike Freud, she did not believe that anxiety is an inevitable part of the human condition. It results from cultural forces. Research on parenting styles and attachment emphasizes the importance of an affectionate and warm relationship between children and parents.

2. Basic anxiety is reflected in ten **neurotic needs or trends** (p. 124), which lead to **primary modes of relating** (p. 125) to others (**moving toward, moving against,** and **moving away**) and to three **basic orientations** (p. 125) toward life: the **self-effacing solution,** the **self-expansive solution,** and the **resignation solution.**

3. The **real self** (p. 126) represents that which a person actually is; the **idealized self** (p. 126) represents that which a person thinks he or she should be.

4. In a normal individual the real self and the idealized self closely coincide. In a neurotic individual they are more separate. In extreme cases of **alienation** (p. 127), a person may completely abandon the real self for the sake of the idealized self. Horney suggests that neurotics are governed by the **tyranny of the should** (p. 127).

5. Horney's view of women is almost a direct inversion of Freud's. Whereas Freud suggested the phenomenon of penis envy in women, Horney pointed out the phenomenon of **womb envy** (p. 128) in men. She emphasized the superiority of women as indicated by their capacity for motherhood, and she stressed that a woman's sense of inferiority is not constitutional but acquired. In her later writings Horney developed a theory that was not gender specific but applied to all humans.

6. Horney suggested systematic **self-analysis** (p. 129) as an important assessment tool. Her theory has stimulated research in areas such as feminine psychology, **hypercompetitiveness** (p. 130), **attachment theory** (p. 131), and **parenting styles** (p. 132).

7. Fromm identified the basic human condition as freedom; three common mechanisms of escape from it are **authoritarianism** (p. 136), **destructiveness** (p. 137), and **automaton conformity** (p. 137).

8. We create society to fulfill our basic needs. In turn, it structures how these needs may be met. Society also provokes the development of certain character orientations. In his discussion of the **marketing orientation** (p. 138), Fromm is thought to have developed a new type. The **productive orientation** (p. 138) depicts the mature individual, who is **biophilous** (p. 138)— that is, able to love and work in the broadest sense.

9. Assessment of and research on Fromm's theory have focused on culture and society and their influence on character. Since September 11, 2001, there has been a renewal of interest in **authoritarianism** (p. 140) and **terror management theory** (p. 141).

10. Fromm's concepts of authoritarianism and escape from freedom have shed light on the discussion of terrorism and have informed terror management theory.

11. Horney encouraged scientific investigation of and research on her theory. Fromm pointed out the dangers of **scientism** (p. 142). Both Horney and Fromm show deep philosophical commitments in their work. Horney's particular contribution to the art of personality theory has been in the area of psychotherapy; Fromm has illuminated our understanding of culture and society.

Personal Experiences

1. Horney defines *basic evil* as all of the negative factors in an environment that can provoke insecurity in a child. Examine these types of factors in your own life. List five specific conditions or episodes in your childhood that Horney might classify as a factor of basic evil. Which of the five do you think had the biggest impact on you? If you were a parent, which do you think you'd work hardest to protect your own child from? Explain your rationale.

2. According to Horney, a normal, well-adjusted person can resolve conflicts in life by balancing the self-effacing, self-expansive, and resignation solutions. Which orientation do you tend to gravitate toward? Or do you generally resolve conflicts by balancing all three? If you do incline toward one orientation, does this tendency help explain any patterns of conflict in your love relationships or patterns in how you tend to resolve such conflict?

3. Horney believed that we all have an idealized self, which represents who we think we should be. What do you conceive of as your idealized self? Is this self more forgiving, more thoughtful, braver, wealthier, and so forth, than your real self? Describe who your perfect self would be. Then consider what elements in your social environment contribute to your idealized version of yourself. What combination of social factors helped to create this concept of self—your parent's expectations, your schooling, your religion, your country?

4. Grade your parents' parenting. Which of the four styles described by Baumrind—indulgent, authoritarian, uninvolved, or authoritative—comes closest to describing the manner in which your parents raised you? How do you think that style of parenting impacted who you are as a person today, your values, your temperament? If you have siblings, respond to the following: Do you feel that the style of parenting used on you was different from

the style used on your siblings? What factors could help explain such a difference: birth order and age, gender? Was the difference fair? Finally, give your parents a grade for their overall efforts in parenting. If they don't receive an A, describe what they could have done to achieve that grade. What will you do differently when you are a parent?

5. Fromm identified five character orientations found in Western societies. Use Table 5.3 to figure out which orientation best describes your personality. Rank-order the five orientations, starting with the one that describes you best and ending with the one that describes you least. Next, rank the orientations of your friends and have them rank yours. Do your friends' rankings agree with yours? Try to account for any dissonance between these appraisals. What evidence do you and your friends provide to justify the rankings?

PART THREE

More Recent Trends in Psychoanalytic Theory

In many respects Freud's theory was a product of nineteenth-century thought, cast in the framework of a now-outdated biological determinism. Yet it was Freud who shattered the nineteenth-century image of human nature and opened the door to a new point of view. Many of his concepts moved us forward into the twentieth century, but they require revision if they are to continue to meet the demands of the twenty-first century and remain abreast of modern intellectual ideas. The thought of the analysts in Part III moves considerably beyond Freud yet remains consistent with basic psychoanalytic doctrine. In updating and revising Freud, they have been largely responsible for the continued relevance of his theory.

For the most part, these theorists believe that the changes they have made are consistent with basic psychoanalytic doctrine. The biological grounding of human existence remains, as does the power of sexuality. Repression and transference, keynotes of psychoanalysis, remain fast in their thought. More recent analysts, however, reformed and revised psychoanalysis so that it reflects the modern world and contemporary self-understanding.

CHAPTER 6

Ego Analytic Psychology

- **Anna Freud**
- **Erik Erikson**
- **Dan McAdams**

YOUR GOALS FOR THIS CHAPTER

1. Describe the contributions that Anna Freud made to psychoanalysis.
2. Identify four ways in which Erikson extended Sigmund Freud's psychoanalytic theory.
3. Explain how Erikson's theory enlarged our understanding of the ego.
4. Discuss the general characteristics of Erikson's **psychosocial stages** of development.
5. Discuss each one of Erikson's stages in terms of the Freudian psychosexual stage that it reflects, the emotional duality that it involves, and the particular ego strength that emerges from it.
6. Describe how Erikson explored the role of culture and history in shaping personality.
7. Discuss Erikson's findings in the area of sex differences.
8. Discuss Erikson's methods of research.
9. Describe empirical research based on Erikson's theory.
10. Evaluate Erikson's theory from the viewpoints of philosophy, science, and art.
11. Describe the contributions that McAdams makes to personality theory.

Sigmund Freud's theory sparked a great deal of controversy, and some of his original followers sought to develop separate theories. Jung, Adler, Horney, and Fromm discarded a number of concepts that Freud considered crucial to psychoanalysis. Others, however, have worked within the mainstream of psychoanalysis to refine and update Freud's ideas. The thought of Anna Freud and Erikson, discussed in this chapter, moves considerably beyond Freud but without abandoning his key concepts and principles. The focus changes from the study of the adult to the study of the child. The emphasis shifts from the id to the ego. There is an expansion of psychoanalysis as a therapeutic tool and greater appreciation of the role of society and culture in the development of personality.

This chapter briefly considers some inputs to psychoanalytic theory made by Anna Freud, focuses on the theory of her student Erik Erikson, and closes with the current contributions of Dan McAdams.

Anna Freud (1895–1982)

Anna, Freud's youngest daughter, was her father's intellectual heir, the only member of his family to follow in his profession. After her analysis by her own father, she worked closely with him as a highly skilled and respected colleague. After his death, she became an eminent lay psychoanalyst and international authority in her own right. Until her death in 1982, she was recognized as the guardian and elucidator of her father's revolutionary doctrine. She enlarged the application of psychoanalysis to new areas: the study of children and the exploration of the ego. She became an advocate for children and adolescents, insisting that their best interests need to be kept in the forefront. In doing so, she extended the influence of psychoanalysis into areas such as pediatrics, child care, education, and family law (see Goldstein, Freud, & Solnit, 1973, 1979).

In her efforts to clarify psychoanalytic theory, Anna Freud introduced some genuinely new and creative ideas. Her observations of children extended beyond normal or disturbed children growing up in average homes and included children who had met with extraordinary circumstances such as war, physical handicaps, and parentless homes. Her research opened the way to a new era of research in psychoanalytic child psychology under the auspices of the Hampstead clinic, with applications to a wide area of concerns associated with child rearing (c.f. Young-Bruehl, 2004).

Some of Anna Freud's observations concerning children overturned previous notions of their reactions. For example, it had been widely assumed that children have an instinctive horror of combat, blood, and destruction and that war has a devastating effect on young children. However, her case studies of the effects of World War II bombings on British children, written in collaboration with Dorothy Burlingham, a long-time friend and colleague (see Burlingham, 1990, and Jackson, 1991), revealed that although wartime may lead to negative reactions, the world of the child pivots primarily on the mother.

Anna Freud's therapy stressed protective, supportive, and educational attitudes. She suggested how the classic features of adult psychoanalysis could be utilized with children four years old and upward, but she recognized that child analysis could not be conducted like the analysis of an adult. Classical techniques such as free association, the interpretation of

Anna Freud (seen here with her father) was her father's intellectual heir and extended the interest of psychoanalysis to the study of the child and the exploration of the ego.

dreams, and analysis of the transference had to be changed to correspond with the child's level of maturity. She saw the need for a long preparatory period in which the analyst is established as a trusted and indispensable figure in the child's life. She also recognized that neurotic symptoms do not necessarily have the meaning in the life of a child that they have in the life of an adult. Her system of diagnosis, which conceives of personality as arising out of a developmental sequence, permitted her to distinguish between less serious manifestations of childhood distress, such as emotional problems of childhood that would be outgrown, and more serious disorders that threatened to fixate a child at a particular stage of development and thus jeopardize optimal personality growth. The latter, but not the former, in Anna Freud's opinion, mandated professional attention. She produced a classification system of childhood symptoms that reflects developmental issues, and she devised a formal assessment procedure known as a **diagnostic profile**. Such profiles have since been developed for infants, children, adolescents, and adults. The therapist uses the profile to organize and integrate the data that he or she acquires during a diagnostic assessment. The profile is intended to yield a complete picture of the various functionings of the patient's personality and an indication of their developmental appropriateness.

Anna Freud used the term **developmental line** to refer to a series of id-ego interactions in which children decrease their dependence on external controls and increase ego mastery of themselves and their world (1965). Her six developmental lines stress the ego's ability to cope with various internal, environmental, and interpersonal situations, and they complement her father's discussion of psychosexual development. As children grow, they progress from (1) dependency to emotional self-reliance, (2) sucking to rational eating, (3) wetting and soiling to bladder and bowel control, (4) irresponsibility to responsibility in body management, (5) play to work, and (6) egocentricity to companionship.

Anna Freud emphasized the importance of paying attention to a patient's maturation level and noted with regret that adolescence was a "stepchild in psychoanalytic theory"

(1958). She developed a concept of normality for the adolescent period, acknowledging that it is a period of disharmony but suggesting that the crisis it entails is "normative" and functional. She looked at the phenomena of impulsive acting out in child and adolescent analysis and clarified the types of acting out that are normal and that make a positive contribution during the prelatency and adolescence periods. It is not uncommon, for example, for an adolescent to temporarily escape the demands of society by skipping school or running away. This behavior, however, can be compounded by overreacting to it or by perjoratively labeling it.

In addition, Anna Freud learned from her work with children that there are realistic limits to analysis. Certain constitutional or environmental factors may not be open to real change through analysis, though their effects may be reduced. While recognizing the greater importance of environmental factors over internal ones in childhood disturbances, she was also impressed by the efforts of children to cope with and master extremely devastating situations.

Finally, Anna Freud systematized and elaborated on Freud's discussion of the *ego's defenses*. Whereas Freud concentrated on exploring the unconscious drives of the id, his daughter realized that in order for these to emerge in an analysis, the ego must become aware of the defenses that it is using to prevent the material from reemerging into consciousness. The ego's defenses may be inferred from observable behavior. Analysis of the defenses permits one to understand the child's life history and instinctual development. Anna Freud elaborated on the ego defenses outlined by her father and suggested some additional ones of her own (1946). She clarified the process of identification with the aggressor, in which a victim begins to react to his or her captor with gratitude and admiration. This phenomenon has since been recognized in prisoners of war and hostages. Anna Freud's graphic case descriptions illustrating these processes have become classic. Thus a schoolboy's involuntary grimace caricatures the angry face of his teacher and testifies to his identification with the aggressor.

Erik Erikson (1902–1994)

BIOGRAPHICAL BACKGROUND

Erik H. Erikson was born on June 15, 1902, near Frankfurt, Germany, the product of an extramarital relationship. He never knew his mother's first husband or his birth father. His mother subsequently married a pediatrician, Theodore Homburger, who adopted Erik and gave him a last name. In an act that Erikson later called "loving deceit," his parents concealed the fact of his adoption from him for several years. Thus the man who is famous for coining the term "identity crisis" did himself experience a significant identity crisis. Not only did he have to struggle with the usual quest for psychological identity, he was also unsure of his biological identity. The problem was compounded by the fact that he was raised in a Jewish home but his genetic background was Danish. Young Erik's Nordic features made him an outcast among his Jewish peers, ironically, at the same time his German classmates rejected him as a Jew. His resolution of the identity issue may have become apparent in 1939, when, in the process of becoming an American citizen, he added the surname by which we know him, assuming the identity of Erik Homburger Erikson. He also converted to Christianity.

In his discussion of psychosocial development, Erik Erikson makes explicit the social dimension implied in Sigmund Freud's work.

Erikson was able to find his professional identity in Vienna, where he and Peter Blos, a theorist and researcher on adolescence, established a progressive, nongraded school that gave children optimal freedom within an appropriate structure. After a short time, Anna Freud asked Erikson if he would be interested in beginning analysis with her and becoming a child analyst. Over the next few years, Erikson established himself as a key figure in psychoanalysis, publishing articles on the Montessori philosophy of education and psychoanalysis. The two complementary perspectives enabled Erikson to make a unique contribution to our understanding of child development.

Erikson left Vienna in 1933 and settled with his wife and family in Boston, where he became the city's first child psychoanalyst. In 1936 Erikson accepted a position in the Yale University Institute of Human Relations to teach at the medical school. In 1938, he learned of a unique opportunity to study child-rearing methods among the Sioux in South Dakota. Here he observed firsthand how childhood events are shaped by society and its customs, a theme he was to stress again and again in his later writings.

Between 1939 and 1960 Erikson held various positions in California and Massachusetts. In 1960 Harvard University offered him the position of professor in spite of the fact that he had never received a university or college degree. Erikson was a popular speaker at colleges and universities throughout the United States. He died on May 12, 1994, following a brief illness.

Erikson extended Sigmund Freud's psychoanalytic theory in four main ways. First, he increased our understanding of the ego, showing how it is a creative problem solver that emerges out of the genetic, cultural, and historical context of each individual. Second, he elaborated on Freud's stages of development, making explicit a social dimension that was implied in Freud's theory but never clearly stated. Third, he extended our concept of development to embrace the entire life span, from infancy to old age. Fourth, he explored the impact of culture, society, and history on the developing personality and illustrated this in psychohistorical studies of famous people.

AN ENHANCED UNDERSTANDING OF THE EGO

While Erikson was training in Vienna, a lively debate was going on between Anna Freud and Heinz Hartmann, another influential psychoanalyst. Whereas Anna Freud tended to restrict the ego's function to warding off drives, Hartmann was exploring the ego's adaptive responses to its environment. Even though Anna Freud had been his training analyst, Erikson found himself attracted to Hartmann's approach. As an educator, Erikson was interested in how one might strengthen and enrich the ego of young children. He found it difficult to conceive of the ego as adaptive if its role was limited to a set of defenses against inner drives.

In Erikson's theory, the ego is the part of the mind that gives coherence to experiences, conscious or unconscious. Erikson agreed with Sigmund Freud that many aspects of ego functioning are unconscious, but he believed the ego has an overall unifying purpose that leads to consistent behavior and conduct. The ego has the positive role of maintaining effective performance, rather than just a negative role of avoiding anxiety. Its defenses are adaptive as well as maladaptive (1974).

Erikson did *not* believe that we can best reconstruct the ego's functions from an understanding of its dysfunctions. He elaborated on its adaptive capacities, its ability to deal with stress, to resolve vital conflict, to recuperate, and to contribute to identity formation. In the final analysis, Erikson defined the ego as a strong, vital, and positive force: an organizing capacity of the individual that leads to "that strength which can reconcile discontinuities and ambiguities" (1975).

The development of the ego is clearly outlined in Erikson's psychosocial stages of the life cycle. Ideally, at each stage the ego develops certain strengths or basic virtues that enable it to move forward. These ego strengths lay the foundation for a set of ethical rules based on ideals that we can strive for, since Erikson also conceived of the superego and human consciousness in terms of an evolutionary process.

THE PSYCHOSOCIAL STAGES OF DEVELOPMENT

In his discussion of the psychosexual stages of development, Sigmund Freud concentrated on their biological character and tended to neglect the social dimension. Nevertheless, in Freud's stages children are doing more than coming to terms with their own sexuality. For Erikson, children are trying to understand and relate to the world and to others. In effect, Erikson made explicit the social dimension implied in Freud's work.

Each of Erikson's **psychosocial stages** centers on an emotional polarity or conflict that children encounter at certain critical periods. New environmental demands introject positive and negative emotional components into the development of personality. Both emotional components are to some extent incorporated into the emerging person, but if the conflict is resolved satisfactorily, the positive component is reflected to a higher degree. If the conflict persists or is not adequately resolved, the negative component predominates. Erikson's first four stages correspond to Freud's psychosexual stages (oral through latency). Erikson then subdivided the genital stage into four phases that represent growth and development throughout maturity.

Erikson's stages are *epigenetic* (from the Greek words *epi*, "upon," and *genesis*, "emergence"): One stage develops on top of another in a sequential and hierarchical pattern. At each successive level the human personality becomes more complex. Erikson stressed the prospective features of the life cycle, and he amended the logic of psychoanalysis so that early events are seen not only in terms of their contributions to later development but also as themselves directed by potentials that do not flower until later.

Erikson's psychosocial stages do not occur within a strict chronological framework. As in fetal development, however, each aspect of psychosocial development has a critical period of readiness during which, if it does not flourish, it is likely to flounder. In addition, the stages progress in a cumulative rather than a linear fashion. The behaviors of one stage do not disappear with the successive stage (1969).

Erikson made psychoanalytic concepts more consistent with contemporary scientific findings. His psychosocial stages are a gradual series of decisive encounters with the environment—interactions between biological development, psychological abilities, cognitive capacities, and social influences. Erikson saw the person as a way of being in the world. Thus the first stage, rather than a cathexis of libido onto an oral zone, is a complex of experiences centered in the mouth.

Each of the eight stages entails its own **life crisis,** a crucial period in which the individual cannot avoid a decisive turn one way or the other. Each stage also provides new opportunities for particular ego strengths, or basic **virtues,** to develop. These psychosocial gains result from the ego's successful adaptation to its environment and must be nurtured and reaffirmed continuously (see also Berk & Andersen, 2000; Green, Richardson, Lago, & Schatten-Jones, 2001; Pinquart & Sorensen, 2001; Roberts & Del Vecchio, 2000).

Trust Versus Mistrust: Hope

The emotional duality of **trust versus mistrust** is the key consideration of the first stage, which corresponds to Freud's oral, sensory, and kinesthetic one (Erikson, 1963). The basic psychosocial attitude to be learned at this stage is whether or not you can trust the world. For a protracted period of time children are highly dependent on others for their care. Certain frustrations are inevitable and socially meaningful, but too much of either frustration or indulgence may have negative effects. Basic trust implies a perceived correlation between one's needs and one's world. If infants receive unreliable, inadequate, or rejecting care, they will perceive their world as indifferent or hostile, and they will develop a high degree of mistrust. Granted, it is important that infants develop some sense of how much to trust and when to be ready for danger and discomfort. The danger lies in the extremes of trust and mistrust. This crisis is not permanently resolved during the first year or two of life, but a foundation is laid that influences the subsequent course of development.

An appropriate balance of trust and mistrust leads to the development of the ego strength *hope,* a basic human virtue without which we are unable to survive. Hope represents a persistent conviction that our wishes can be satisfied in spite of disappointment and failures (1964). Hope is the basis of faith, reflected in mature commitments.

Autonomy Versus Shame and Doubt: Will

Erikson's second psychosocial stage, **autonomy versus shame and doubt,** arises during the second and third years of life and corresponds to the anal-muscular stage in Freud's psychosexual scheme (1963). The primary emotional duality here is that of control over the body and bodily activities as opposed to a tendency for shame and doubt. "Just when a child has learned to trust his mother and to trust the world, he must become self-willed and must take chances with his trust in order to see what he, as a trustworthy individual, can will" (Erikson, as cited in Evans, 1967). The struggle for autonomy is not limited to sessions on the toilet but extends to many other areas of life as the ego begins to establish psychosocial independence. Toddlers, who are making rapid gains in neuromuscular maturation, verbalization, and social discrimination, begin to explore independently and interact with their environment. The negativism of the two-year-old whose favorite word is *no* is evidence of the child's struggling attempt at autonomy. A temper tantrum is simply a momentary loss of self-control. Cultures have different ways of cultivating or breaking the child's will, either reinforcing or rejecting the tentative explorations of the child. Doubts about their ability for self-control may give children feelings of inadequacy or shame.

Will, the virtue corresponding to this stage, is a natural outgrowth of autonomy. Clearly in the toddler years only rudiments emerge, but these will build into a mature sense of will power. Will is an unbroken determination to exercise freedom of choice and self-restraint (1964) and forms the basis for our subsequent acceptance of social laws.

Initiative Versus Guilt: Purpose

The emotional duality that Erikson envisioned for the phallic or genital-locomotor stage of psychosexuality (three to five years) is **initiative versus guilt** (1963). At this period, children are active in their environment, mastering new skills and tasks. Their dominant social modality is the *intrusive* mode: Their bodies vigorously intrude into space and onto other people. Preschoolers direct their activities toward specific goals and achievements. Their intrusion and curiosity extends not only to sexual matters but to many other concerns of life as well. The characteristic word of preschoolers is *why?* Parental responses to children's self-initiated activities determine the successful or unsuccessful outcome of this stage. If initiative is reinforced, a child's behavior will become increasingly goal oriented. Excessive punishment or discouragement may lead to feelings of guilt, resignation, and the belief that it is wrong to be curious about the world and ill-advised to be active in it.

Immense new faculties develop in children at this time as they begin to imagine goals for which their locomotive and cognitive skills have prepared them. Their use of language becomes more polished. Children begin to envision themselves as growing up and identify with people whose work and personalities they can understand and admire. Earlier fantasies are repressed or redirected, and the play of preschoolers becomes more realistic and purposeful. They begin to engage in projects. Children are at no time more open to learning than during these years. They are able to work cooperatively and to profit from teachers. Their learning is vigorous, leading away from their own limitations and into later possibilities.

Erikson believed that the Oedipus complex is both more and less than what Sigmund Freud made of it. Erikson preferred to call it an early generational complex. From the point of view of evolution, it is the child's first experience with the unrelenting sequence of generations, growth, and death. The same-sex parent becomes involved in the child's early genital fantasies at a time when the child's initiative is ready to turn away from the present situation to new goals. At the same time, the child's strong imagination and powerful locomotive skills produce gigantic, terrifying fantasies that awaken a sense of guilt and lead to the development of conscience (Evans, 1967). Thus the Oedipal stage results in a moral sense that establishes permissible limits and begins to attach childhood dreams realistically to the various possible goals of one's technology and culture.

The virtue that emerges out of the duality of initiative versus guilt is *purpose,* a view of the future giving direction and focus to our mutual efforts. Purposefulness slowly enables one to develop a sense of reality that is defined by what is attainable (1964).

Industry Versus Inferiority: Competence

The next stage in the child's life loosely parallels Sigmund Freud's latency period. Freud gave few clues as to what was happening to personality development during this period apart from suggesting that latency involves a move from premature sexual expression to a nonactive sexual phase. Erikson agreed that during latency certain passionate and imaginative qualities of earlier years calm down so that the child is free to concentrate on learning. However, he pointed out that learning involves more than just a basic form of striving that takes place throughout the life cycle and undergoes a special crisis during the school years. The focus moves sharply from the id to the ego as the child applies to specific and approved goals the drives that earlier motivated dreams and play. Yet the ego can remain strong only through interaction with cultural institutions. At this time society intervenes in a more formal manner to develop the child's capacities and potentials.

During the school years (six to eleven), the primary emotional duality is **industry versus inferiority** (1963). The term *industriousness* might be better than *industry* because it implies being busy with something, learning to make something and to make it well. Children in all cultures receive some form of systematic instruction at this time to teach them skills that will be needed in their society and to help them attain a sense of mastery.

New demands are placed upon children at this time. They are no longer loved simply for who they are; they are expected to master the technology of their culture in order to earn the respect of their teachers and peers. Their ability to conform and master the tasks of this level depends in large measure on how successfully they have traveled the preceding stages. If children emerge from the preceding stages with a basic sense of trust, autonomy, and initiative, they are ready for the industrious labor that "school" presupposes. But if their development has left heavy residues of mistrust, doubt, and guilt, they may have difficulty performing at an optimal level. From a psychoanalytic point of view, the child who has not adequately resolved his or her Oedipal complex may not be ready to fulfill the other demands of his or her society. If potentialities have been permitted to develop fully in the earlier stages, the child is in less danger.

The peril during this period is that feelings of inadequacy and inferiority will develop. Children begin to make comparisons between themselves and others and to perceive themselves in a more or less favorable light. Children know, or think they know, where they stand.

Children at this age are ready to learn to work and need to develop a sense of *competence*, the ego strength or virtue associated with this stage. Competence entails the ability to use one's intelligence and skill to complete tasks that are of value in one's society (1964).

Ego Identity Versus Role Confusion: Fidelity

For Sigmund Freud, the hallmarks of the genital stage were *lieben und arbeiten*, "to love and to work." Erikson agreed with the importance of these accomplishments, but he further divided Freud's final stage into four substages to underscore the point that "genitality is not a goal to be pursued in isolation" (Evans, 1967). In so doing, Erikson greatly enriched our understanding of adolescence and the adult years.

The primary duality during adolescence (twelve to eighteen) is **ego identity versus role confusion.** The process of forming an ego identity requires that one compare how one sees oneself with how significant others appear to expect one to be. "Ego identity, then, in its subjective aspect, is the awareness of the fact that there is a self-sameness and continuity to the ego's synthesizing methods and a continuity of one's meaning for others" (1963). Ego identity results in a sense of coherent individuality that enables one to resolve one's conflicts adaptively. If adolescents fail to answer the question "Who am I?" satisfactorily, they will suffer role confusion.

Erikson suggested that adolescence is a particularly crucial period. Along with rapid physical growth and changes, new psychological challenges occur. Previous continuities are

In contemporary society, scientific experimentation can be an important resource in encouraging children's sense of competence.

called into question as young people begin to reconnect the roles and skills that they have developed into a maturer sense of identity. This integration is more than the sum total of previous accomplishments. Erikson often spoke of adolescence as a moratorium between childhood and adulthood, and he considered such a waiting period particularly important in a complex society.

The greatest danger at this stage is role confusion, the inability to conceive of oneself as a productive member of one's society. Erikson pointed out that "a sound ego identity is the only safeguard against the anarchy of drives as well as the autocracy of conscience" (1958). Role confusion frequently arises out of the adolescent's difficulty in finding an occupational identity, but it may also express a general inability to find a meaningful place in one's culture. The development of a positive identity depends on support from significant groups. The adolescent who cannot find a meaningful adult role runs the risk of an **identity crisis,** a transitory failure to establish a stable identity. Some young people may drop out of mainstream society for a short period, as Erikson himself did. Others may adopt a **negative identity,** one that is opposed to the dominant values of their upbringing. Where support has not been forthcoming and the climate has not been favorable to the development of inner resources, a negative identity may provide the only way of demonstrating mastery and free choice in one's culture. Negative identifications may result in unfortunate consequences—social pathology, crime, or expressions of prejudice. However, Erikson wanted us to recognize that such developments are an important testimony to the adolescent's readiness for ideological involvement.

It is vitally important that a society present its young people with ideals they can share enthusiastically. The conspicuous absence of a sense of promise in any society, due to economic conditions, population trends, high unemployment, or other problems that thwart the occupational aspirations of young people, means that those adolescents will have a difficult time establishing a clear and positive ego identity. Capps (1996) suggests that Erikson's understanding of identity confusion and its ramifications has helped inform and nurture healing efforts for Vietnam veterans and other survivors of war by providing the therapeutic theory for readjustment and resocialization programs.

The virtue or ego strength developed at this time is *fidelity;* the adolescent is ready to learn to be faithful to an ideological point of view. Fidelity consists of "the ability to sustain loyalties freely pledged in spite of the inevitable contradictions of value systems" (1964). Without a constructive outlet for fidelity, the young person will either have a weak ego and suffer a "confusion of values" or search for a deviant group to be loyal to.

Intimacy Versus Isolation: Love

Young adulthood (eighteen to twenty-four) is marked by the emotional duality of **intimacy versus isolation** (1963). Intimacy refers to the ability to develop a close and meaningful relationship with another person. Erikson here applied Freud's dictum "to love and to work" as the model orientation. Isolation entails self-absorption and an inability to develop deep, committed relationships. Having grown beyond the beginnings of establishing an identity, the young adult is able to overcome the fear of ego loss and form a close affiliation with another individual. The task of young adulthood is to couple genitality with general work productiveness. Clearly, genitality is an inadequate definition of health. On the other hand, an individual's dedication to work should not be such that she or he loses the capacity to love.

Thus it is at this point that the virtue of *love* emerges as an ego strength (1964). This is not to deny the involvement of love in previous stages, but in young adulthood the individual is able to transform the love received as a child and begin to care for others. Love further represents a mutual devotion that is able to overcome the natural antagonism involved in any relationship between the sexes. Erikson acknowledged that there are different functions of the sexes, particularly with regard to procreation; however, the capacities of the mature ego can transcend these so that male and female cooperate.

Generativity Versus Stagnation: Care

The middle years (twenty-five to sixty-four) are characterized by the conflict of **generativity versus stagnation** (1963). Generativity entails more than parenthood; it is the ability to be productive and creative in many areas of life, particularly those showing a concern for the welfare of ensuing generations. The adult actively participates in those elements of culture that will ensure its maintenance and enhancement. Failure to do so leads to feelings of stagnation, boredom, and interpersonal impoverishment. An individual who does not have children can fulfill generativity by working with other people's children or helping to create a better world for them. A person is generative when making a contribution appropriate to her or his particular potential, be it children, products, ideas, or works of art.

Erikson suggested that because Sigmund Freud stressed early inhibition of the expression of the libido or sexual drive, he underestimated the importance of the procreative desires of human beings. Erikson considered a procreative drive to be instinctual and saw generativity as a further psychosexual stage whose frustration leads to symptoms of self-absorption and indulgence.

An elderly person who shares wisdom with younger generations helps to affirm the meaning of the life cycle.

The ego strength that emerges during the middle years is *care*. The adult needs to be needed. *Care* implies doing something for somebody. Care is also able to overcome the inevitable ambivalent feelings that are involved in the parent-child relationship. Once again, when the mature ego is able to transcend these emotions, the adult can fulfill obligations to youth.

Ego Integrity Versus Despair: Wisdom

Maturity, the final stage of life (sixty-five to death), is marked by **ego integrity versus despair** (1963). Ego integrity entails the ability to reflect on one's life with satisfaction even if all dreams are not fulfilled. Death is not feared but accepted as one among many facets of one's existence. Despair refers to regret over missed and unfulfilled opportunities at a time when it is too late to begin again. Ego integrity represents the fruit of the seven stages that have preceded. The virtue of this stage is *wisdom*. Wisdom enables an individual to bring life to an appropriate closure. It is the ability to stand back and reflect on one's life in the face of impending death (1964; see also Pinquart & Sorensen, 2001).

As he entered his own eighth stage, Erikson was able to further elaborate on that era, seeing it as a vigorous and active phase of continued generativity and integration rather than a passive one of reflection. Older adults can continue to contribute to the welfare of younger generations through financial assistance, mentoring, and in some cases, active parenting (Erikson, Erikson, & Kivnick, 1986). The wisdom of old age goes beyond self-integration and integrity to embrace other people of other times and places and to convey messages of human dignity and love (Erikson, 1982).

In an extended version of *The Life Cycle Completed,* Erikson's wife, Joan, who had been an active partner in his intellectual pursuits and was now in her nineties, enlarged on Erikson's vision of human development by introducing a ninth stage of very old age (Erikson, 1997). She describes the specific challenges presented to elders whose control over their bodies and lives is eroded by the inevitable wages of time. She discusses the important role of faith and hope in continuing to find joy and wisdom in life.

Table 6.1 on page 160 summarizes Erikson's psychosocial stages, indicates their relationship to Sigmund Freud's psychosexual stages, and lists their respective ego strengths.

ASSESSMENT AND RESEARCH IN ERIKSON'S THEORY

As a researcher, Erikson has been described as "the quintessential interdisciplinarian" (Smelser, 1996). He used cultural studies, psychohistories, and inquiries into sex differences in his development of unique methods of assessment. His research is based on direct

TABLE 6.1 THE LIFE CYCLE

PSYCHOSEXUAL STAGE	PSYCHOSOCIAL STAGE	EGO STRENGTH OR VIRTUE
Oral sensory and kinesthetic (infancy)	Trust versus mistrust	Hope
Anal-muscular (toddler years)	Autonomy versus shame and doubt	Will
Phallic or genital-locomotor (preschool years)	Initiative versus guilt	Purpose
Latency period (school years)	Industry versus inferiority	Competence
Genital (adolescence)	Ego identity versus role confusion	Fidelity
(Young adulthood)	Intimacy versus isolation	Love
(Adulthood)	Generativity versus stagnation	Care
(Maturity)	Ego integrity versus despair	Wisdom

SOURCE: Based on information in Erik H. Erikson, Childhood and Society (Norton, 1963), and Erik H. Erikson, Insight and Responsibility (Norton, 1964).

observation of a particular (configurational) kind followed by theoretical formulation (Coles, 1970).

The Study of Two American Indian Tribes

In 1938 Erikson went to the Pine Ridge Reservation in South Dakota to observe the children of the Sioux. He had become increasingly interested in the work of anthropologists and welcomed an opportunity to observe how the events of an individual's life are shaped by societal practices. Later, he traveled to northern California to observe a very different tribe, the Yurok.

The Sioux had originally been buffalo hunters. When the white settlers came, both the buffalo and the traditional Sioux way of life vanished amid bloody massacres. Defeated, the Sioux became withdrawn and apathetic. In part the present behavior of the Sioux was undoubtedly due to their painful history, but Erikson found additional reasons in Sioux child-rearing practices. Unlike most American middle-class parents, who impose firm structures on their children at an early age in the belief that this will help them to become productive adults, the Sioux actively encouraged their children to be free and delayed imposing restrictions on them. The Sioux mother was at ease with her tasks of mothering and liberally breastfed her infants. Sioux toddlers were allowed extensive liberties. Generosity was encouraged, property disregarded, and competition avoided. Boys were trained to be self-confident, boastful, spirited hunters of game and women. Girls were taught to be the wives and mothers of hunters. These child-rearing practices, probably well suited to the earlier life-style of the buffalo hunter, could not cultivate or sustain a more adaptive system of social roles. The adult Sioux, who had been given considerable freedom as a child but whose life was now severely restricted, could cope with the dilemma only by looking back to the glorious past. The future seemed "empty except for dreams of restoration."

The Yurok, on the other hand, showed "folkways of stinginess, suspicion, and anger" and an emphasis on acquiring and retaining possessions. Infants were weaned promptly at about six months and encouraged to be independent. Self-restraint was urged, and the child was swiftly taught to subordinate all instinctual drives to economic considerations. The Yurok, who fished along a salmon river, learned to live more easily with the white settlers because their values were similar in many ways and their present work (farming, lumbering, and fishing) was both useful and familiar to them.

In describing the behavior of these two American Indian tribes, Erikson deliberately avoided talking about basic character traits even though he was aware that traditional psychoanalysts would perceive "oral" and "anal" character structures in the Sioux and the Yurok, respectively. Erikson preferred to "concentrate on the configurations with which these two tribes try to synthesize their concepts and their ideals in a coherent design for living." He pointed out that each society uses childhood in a number of ways: to give meaning to the child's early experiences of its body and other people, to channel the child's energies in socially constructive ways, and to provide an overall framework of meaning for the anxieties that social living provokes (1963).

Psychohistories

Erikson also explored the contribution of culture and history to personality by examining the lives of significant historical figures. **Psychohistory** is "the study of individual and collective life with the combined methods of psychoanalysis and history" (1974). Sigmund Freud too had examined the lives of various famous people, but Erikson refined the method of psychohistory, and it is his name that is typically associated with the term.

In studying historical figures, Erikson explored how the ego strength of certain individuals is able to transform the conflicts that inhibit others so that they become leaders who make an impression on their era. Thus, in studying Martin Luther, an influential leader of the Protestant Reformation, Erikson did not focus on the pathological features of Luther's behavior as other psychiatric biographers had done. He concentrated on how Luther was able to overcome some of his limitations.

Erikson conceived of a seizure, which Luther is said to have experienced in the choir of his monastery, as a turning point in Luther's struggle for identity. Young Luther's exclamation "It isn't me!" expressed his need to repudiate certain roles in order to break through to what he intended to be.

The focus on a key episode is apparent in Erikson's effort to understand what led Gandhi to a position of militant nonviolence. Erikson saw Gandhi's decision to put his life on the line by fasting during a local labor dispute (which culminated in a strike in Ahmedabad in 1918) as a crisis through which Gandhi was able to transform a negative Indian identity of weakness into a positive and active political technique.

Erikson's use of psychohistory has been applied by other writers to the lives of significant figures, such as Robert Hogan's analysis of Malcolm X (1976). Malcolm X was a well-adjusted, superior student, yet an English teacher criticized his choice of a law career as unrealistic and suggested that he consider carpentry instead. Malcolm knew he was smarter than most of his white classmates, but society refused him the identity he wished to choose because he was an African American. Therefore, he turned to a negative identity, becoming a "hoodlum, thief, dope peddler, pimp," before assuming the role of the militant African

American leader of the 1950s and 1960s. The interdisciplinary approach of psychohistory provides a deeper exploration of the past than what is offered by separate disciplines (Lawton, 1990; Rousselle, 1990).

Sex Differences in Development

Erikson believed that the development of women is influenced by their awareness of their reproductive capacity, and he identified a woman's maternal potential as a key determinant of her personality. Unlike Freud, Erikson's clinical observations did not support the idea that a girl's awareness of her sex focused on a missing penis. Rather, in normative development, the focus is on a sense of vital inner potential. Investigations of children's play construction (1963) led him to conclude that girls and boys experience space differently. Girls emphasize **inner space** and qualities of openness versus closedness. Boys concentrate on **outer space** and qualities of highness and lowness. A woman's productive inner space is an inescapable factor in her development, whether social, historical, and other conditions lead her to build her life around it or not. Mayer (1996, 1998) suggests that Erikson's observations are a radical challenge to Freudian theory in that Erikson placed the experience of valuing femaleness at the center of how girls organize their sense of themselves as "gendered."

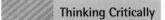

Thinking Critically

Do Erikson's stages work for women? See the Thinking Critically box "The Life Cycle."

However, Erikson, like Freud, employed a male paradigm in his theory. The "eight ages of man" are, in fact, for men. Although Erikson believed women could make significant contributions in the political and work world, he did not believe they find identity in work. Subsequent research has shown that Erikson's stages of development are more satisfactory in accounting for the development of males than of females (Forisha-Kovach, 1983). Wastell (1996) has described how Erikson's stages could be broadened by taking into account both male and female development.

Comments on Erikson's Research Methods

Erikson did not hesitate to develop techniques of study appropriate to his subject. Thus as a child psychoanalyst he used the media of children's play and their positioning of objects in space to explore their inner lives. In the clinical setting, it quickly became apparent to Erikson that "basic psychological insight cannot emerge without some involvement of the observer's impulses and defenses, and that such insights cannot be communicated without the ambivalent involvement of the participants" (1975). His anthropological fieldwork gave him further insight into how an observer necessarily participates in the lives of subjects and limits and structures the research. This finding, termed *participant observation* (Sullivan 1954), recognizes that we cannot speak of the observed without also speaking of the observer.

There are distinct parallels between the clinical evidence obtained and used by psychoanalysts in formulating their hypotheses and that used in the study of historical events. The discipline of psychohistory permits psychoanalysts to become aware of their own historical determinants and the historian to realize that in seeking to understand history we are also making history. The analyst asks the patient to free-associate and then reflect on those associations in order to perceive patterns and themes by which past experiences can be reconstructed. The study of a historical figure takes into account the coherence of statements, life, and time. Each event is considered in terms of its meaning for the individual at that particu-

The Life Cycle

Erikson articulated psychological stages to describe the life cycle. Some critics suggest that his life stages bear the hallmarks of a white, Western, patriarchal society and do not apply well to other cultures or even to our own today. Consider the emotional dualities of each of his stages and the virtues that emerge. Erikson's positive emotions (such as autonomy, initiative, industry) and virtues (such as will, purpose, and competence) are frequently seen as characteristics of healthy male development, and his negative ones (doubt, guilt, and inferiority) are seen as reflecting unhealthy feminine qualities. Gilligan's studies of girls' and women's development (1977, 1982, 1990) suggest that different positive values emerge in healthy female development. Connection, responsibility, and care replace autonomy, mastery, and power. What do you think? Do you think that Erikson's stages reflect a male bias? Do you think the stages of life occur differently for men and women?

lar stage of life and also in terms of its meaning for the life history as a whole. This means that early events need to be compatible with the developmental stage at which they occur and that there has to be a plausible continuity in the life history as a whole, just as the pieces of the developmental puzzle of an individual's life need to fall into place.

In psychoanalysis the significance of an episode, life period, or life trend is made clear by subsequent therapeutic crises that lead to decisive advances or setbacks. In biography, the validity of any relevant theme lies in its crucial recurrence in the person's development. In psychohistory we see how universal phenomena (such as the complex of emotions termed Oedipal) are reenacted in different ways by different people in different periods of history. Personal aims of an individual are framed in terms of the goals of the times and the relation of both of these to the psychohistorian's values (Erikson, 1974).

Some critics have suggested that the difficulty in distinguishing between historical fact and legend jeopardizes the conclusions of a psychohistorical study. Erikson was not distressed by such comments: "If some of it is legend, so be it; the making of a legend is as much of the scholarly re-writing of history as it is a part of the original facts used in the work of scholars" (1958). Such critics ask whether or not a theory corresponds to what we can observe: the empirical data. That criterion is characteristic of the scientist, but it is inappropriate for the historian or psychoanalyst engaged in a retrospective activity. The reconstruction of the past in these instances can be based only on present clues, which may or may not correspond with the actual past. After all, the historical data that survive, even the most well established, survive thanks to "a previous generation's sense of the momentous" (1969).

A given world image needs to be anchored "in facts and figures cognitively perceived and logically arranged, in experiences emotionally confirmed, and in a social life cooperatively affirmed," "to provide a reality that seems self evident" (1974). Thus Erikson considered proof to be a matter of the internal coherence or consistency of a theory and its ability to illumine the human condition.

Empirical Research in Erikson's Theory

Erikson's conception of developmental stages and tasks has profoundly influenced psychology and the way we describe our lives (Douvan, 1997). Adequate research on Erikson's stages of development would require extensive and costly longitudinal studies. Thus they have not been conducted. However, Marcia (1966, 1980) described four statuses implied in Erikson's concept of identity formation in adolescence by focusing on Erikson's belief that there are two components to identity formation: crisis (the struggle to reexamine old values) and commitment (making a decision and following its implications). Marcia developed an intricate interview formula to assess his statuses, which he termed *identity diffusion, foreclosure, moratorium,* and *identity achievement.* The identity status model provided by Marcia has generated a voluminous and productive amount of research literature on the processes of identity and the ways that environmental contexts affect it (Berzonsky & Adams, 1999).

Daniel Levinson has expanded on Erikson's concept of adult development and emphasized that the stages do not suddenly emerge and dissipate. Key developmental issues are always present and available for change. Thus in the transition phases of the adult life cycle, some or all of the developmental tasks can be readdressed and advanced again (Levinson, Darrow, Klein, Linson, & McKee, 1978). A parallel study of women was completed by his wife, Judy (Levinson & Levinson, 1996), and seeks to create a gender-specific conception of the adult development of women within a gender-free concept of human development that captures "what is most essentially human and common" to both genders. Archer (1989) concurs that the identity developmental pattern for both sexes is comparable. However, women's identity is more likely to be based on a number of factors (occupation, marriage, mothering), whereas men focus primarily on their profession (see also Patterson, Sochting, & Marcia, 1992).

Cross-cultural efforts have been made to explore Erikson's psychosocial stages. Research has included the importance of ethnicity in the development of identity of African Americans (Aries & Moorehead, 1989), Mexican Americans (Bernal et al., 1990), and other groups (Markstrom-Adams, 1992).

In an effort to clarify the ethnic identity of African Americans, Cross (1971) described stages of **Nigrescence** and suggested that as racial and ethnicity identity develops, there is a movement from a self-hating to a self-healing and cultural-affirming self-concept. Subsequent research indicated that the change is in the worldview, ideology, and value systems of African Americans rather than in their self-esteem. Cross (1991), therefore, revised his model and described the process of Nigrescence as the change from a preexisting (non-Afrocentric) identity to one that is Afrocentric. In the initial *preencounter* stage, the significance of the role of race and ethnicity in one's life is minimized. The *encounter* stage arises from experiences, which may be positive or negative, that force a reconsideration of one's attitudes about race. In the *immersion/emersion* stage, individuals immerse themselves in their African American identity and may denigrate whites. In the stage of *internalization,* racial identity is balanced with other demands of being a person (i.e., membership in other groups). The final stage, *internalization/commitment,* entails living according to one's new self-image, commitment to a plan of action, and transcendence beyond specific ethnic identity.

Parham and Helms (1985) developed a Racial Identity Attitudes Scale (RIAS) to measure the stages of Nigrescence outlined by Cross. The scale has been used extensively and has led to an expansion and restructuring of the concept of Nigrescence, in which each stage is seen as a distinct "worldview" by which people organize information that emerges while cognitive structures mature and are influenced by social forces (Helms, 1990). Although several other models of African American racial identity have been developed, based on observations in various cities (Thomas, 1971, in Watts; Milliones, 1980, in Pittsburgh), they are quite similar, indicating that the dynamics of black identity change are similar regardless of where it occurs.

Phinney's (1992) model of ethnic identity is explicitly based on Erikson's stages and Marcia's operationalization of those stages. She identifies three stages: *diffuse/foreclosed*, in which the issue of ethnic identity is unexplored or still to be addressed; *moratorium*, in which there is active searching for but not a clear acceptance of ethnic identity; and *achieved*, in which an ethnic identity has been embraced. Acceptance, clear understanding, and a deep sense of belonging to the group characterize the final stage. Cross-sectional findings indicate that individuals move toward the achieved stage as they grow older. Phinney's model aims to be universal, emphasizing factors thought to be present among ethnic identity of all ethnic groups.

Other models seek to depict the structure and nature of racial identity attitudes (Baldwin, 1985; Sanders-Thompson, 1991, 1995; and Sellers, Smith, Shelton, Rowley, & Chavous, 1998). These models suggest that the attitudes and beliefs of African Americans about the role of race in defining who they are has an important impact on how they experience life (Jones, 2001).

Measures of Erikson's concepts of generativity and stagnation have been valid predictors of parental behavior (Van Hiel, Mervielde, & Fruyt, 2006). Finally, Erikson's work has stimulated research on the final years of life. Hamacheck (1990) has suggested behavioral criteria to assess the level of development during Erikson's last three psychosocial stages.

| PHILOSOPHY, |
| SCIENCE, |
| *and* ART |

Erikson's Theory

The "coherence theory of truth" that Erikson employs is characteristic of the philosophical viewpoint in understanding personality (Rychlak, 1973). Unlike Sigmund Freud, Erikson does not insist on a simply scientific pretense for his work; he openly acknowledges the presence of philosophical statements in his theory, believing that a sound personality theory requires a sound philosophical base.

Moreover, Erikson, like Erich Fromm, believes that important moral commitments lie within the psychoanalytic framework. To facilitate the understanding of these moral commitments, Erikson explored the evolution of the superego and distinguished among infant morality, adolescent ideology, and adult ethics. In doing so, he showed how epigenetic principles apply to the development of conscience.

Philosophical Assumptions

Which philosophical issues seem most important to Erikson? See the Philosophical Assumptions box "Examining Erikson."

The ego strengths that Erikson outlines may be seen as ethical values toward which the human race can strive. Ultimately, he aims for a universally applied ethical standard, a contemporary version of the Golden Rule, which he translates as "What is hateful to yourself, do not do to your fellow man" (1964). Erikson's philosophical statements are explicit, unlike Freud's, which are implicit.

✳ Philosophical Assumptions

Examining Erikson

Many of the differences among personality theories can be attributed to fundamental differences in philosophical assumptions. Which of the basic philosophical issues, described in the introductory chapter and summarized on the inside back cover, seem to be clearly important to Erikson in the development of his theory? How, for example, does Erikson's discussion of psychosexual stages influence his view of heredity versus the environment and uniqueness versus universality? How does his emphasis on ego strengths influence his stance on freedom versus determinism? Does his theory address any other philosophical assumptions? Rate Erikson on a scale of 1 to 5 on those philosophical assumptions that you feel his theory applies to most. Compare your ratings of Erikson with your own philosophical assumptions. Did your study of Erikson lead you to change any of your assumptions? Why or why not?

Erikson's theory is highly comprehensive, accounting for many factors in personality development; he includes biological, cognitive, cultural, and historical variables in his discussion. It is also relevant, speaking to issues that concern us today. The fact that phrases such as "identity crisis," "life span," and "inner space" are part of our everyday vocabulary testifies to its pertinence. His theory has had a heuristic value, stimulating thinking among historians, theologians, and philosophers, as well as psychoanalysts. Many people, professionals and nonprofessionals alike, find that his theory compels.

This is not to say that Erikson ignores empirical data or shuns verification of his concepts. He recognizes that one's philosophy must reflect a sophisticated understanding of contemporary scientific methods. However, he points out that a narrow scientific methodology is not able to account for his findings and is not appropriate for the study of personality. He urges a broader approach for the social scientist, including the adoption of research methods similar to those described in his own writings. Initially his theory did not generate much laboratory research because of its lack of specificity and operational definitions; complex concepts such as *identity* do not readily lend themselves to precise measurement. Some research has been conducted on the identity crisis in adolescence, and for the most part the findings have been consistent with his theory. More recently, scholars such as McAdams have demonstrated considerable ingenuity in operationalizing such concepts as generativity in order to foster additional scholarship on them. Longitudinal studies could provide us with information on the validity of Erikson's concept of the developmental process, but such studies are expensive and lengthy. Researchers have largely focused on other personality theories that are easier to translate into operational terms.

In recent years, however, there has been a renewed interest in Erikson's work because of the way his theory links cognitive and personality development. Erikson explicitly states that changes in a person's thinking skills will lead to changes in that person's social interactions and personality. His work looks forward to current relational and interpersonal psychoanalytic thinking (Wallerstein, 1998).

Erikson's work has had an enormous impact in the clinical area. Not only have his formulations concerning ego development enriched formal psychoanalysis, but they have also found wide application in child psychology, education, psychotherapy, and vocational and marriage counseling. As the median age of our population rises, gerontologists turn to Erikson's work for insight into the needs of senior citizens.

Erikson has been called the "closest thing to an intellectual hero" in the United States (Hall, 1983). His work is imaginative, creative, and extremely compelling. More than any other theorist, he has helped to maintain the viability and relevance of Freudian psychoanalytic theory in the contemporary world.

Dan McAdams (1954–   )

Dan McAdams, who studied at Harvard during Erikson's tenure, sees a voice emerging in Erikson's *Childhood and Society* emphasizing "human cognition, imagery, consciousness, narrative, plans, and goals" and invoking "myths, legends, prototypes, scripts, narratives—the stories we live by" to outline the life-span development of personality and ego identity (McAdams, 1997). Building on Erikson, McAdams (1993, 2001a, 2001b) suggests that each of us develops identity and comes to know who we are by constructing a conscious or unconscious narrative of the self, which develops as we proceed through the stages of psychosocial development. McAdams (2001b) suggests that personality is a composite pattern of dispositional traits, characteristic adaptations (i.e., motives and developmental tasks), and integrative life stories. This individual life story is the focus of and vehicle for unity in the self in our postmodern period (2001).

The first years give us a legacy of either optimism or pessimism, setting the tone for our myths. In the elementary school years, motives and themes develop, usually organized around themes of *agency,* the striving for individual independence and power, and *communion,* the striving for intimacy and union (see Bakan, 1966). Throughout our stories, *nuclear episodes* signify highs, lows, and turning points and reflect our motivation at various stages of ego development. *Thematic lines,* repeated series of similar goals, are also key components of our life stories. The adolescent period of "emerging adulthood" (Arnett, 2000) requires us to face the problem of identity, and we become self-conscious in our myth-making. Vividly remembered personal events can be

Dan McAdams has expanded Erikson's theory through the study of life narratives and generativity and suggested a new framework for organizing research on personality into an integrative study of the whole person.

key self-defining memories with enormous power to change lives. We tend to remember a higher number of autobiographical events during the adolescent and young adult years, when we are preoccupied with forming identity (McAdams, 2001b). We also place our stories in the context of a specific ideological setting, incorporating ethical and religious principles that provide us with a perspective from which to judge our lives and those of others.

In middle age we develop a "generativity script" that links our individual personal myths to the collective myths of humanity. McAdams has focused on **generativity**, concern for and commitment to future generations, and developed a new model that draws on Erikson's theory, but he also makes some significant departures from it. Rather than supposing that there is a specific stage of generativity in adulthood, McAdams suggests that generativity becomes an important issue at that time because of increased cultural demand for it. Beginning with individual and shared *desires* that guide one to find occasions to care for others and cultural *demands* about assuming responsibility for the next generation as one gets older, generativity leads to conscious *concern* for the next generation. Generativity includes *beliefs* in the advisability of investing in the future of others and *commitments* to generative *actions*. It culminates in a *narration* of generative efforts that becomes part of one's life story (McAdams, 2001c). Generativity is expressed through creating a legacy, maintaining that which is worthy, and offering these gifts to the next generation.

Since the 1980s, considerable research has been conducted in the concept of generativity. McAdams and de St. Aubin (1992) have developed a self-report scale, the Loyola Generativity Scale (LGS), to measure differences in concern with generativity. It has been used in various research projects on generativity. Studies have examined age-related patterns and longitudinal changes in generativity motivation and accomplishment. They have looked at variations among different ethnic groups as well as the impact of generativity on parenting, political activity, and community involvements. Research suggests that a life-course perspective on generativity is more helpful then Erikson's original stage model, for it permits variations observed among different lives, cultures, and historical periods (McAdams, 2001c).

McAdams, Diamond, de St. Aubin, and Mansfield (1997) have found that the life stories of generative and less generative adults differ in fundamental ways (see Table 6.2). Interviews with participants were analyzed in terms of five themes previously identified as characteristic of commitment. Generative adults scored higher than nongenerative participants on all of the themes. The key difference between the two groups was that, in the stories of generative adults, negative events were frequently turned into positive ones. Such redemption sequences are also prominent in the stories of reformed ex-convicts (Maruna, 1997) and recovering alcoholics and addicts (McAdams, 2006; Singer, 1997). Generative adults were more likely to use themes found in biblical stories, ancient folklore, and myth in making sense of their lives than were their less generative peers.

> **Thinking Critically**
>
> How do you measure up on generativity? See the Thinking Critically box "Generativity: How Do You Measure Up?"

Most recently, McAdams (2006) has observed that the theme of redemption is the most powerful life story in America today, suggesting a key element in American identity and reflecting uniquely American ideas and values, such as being chosen and having a manifest destiny. The stories reveal both strengths and weaknesses in American's understanding of themselves and their behavior in the world.

McAdams uses both qualitative and quantitative measures in his personality and development research programs. In studying narratives, McAdams seeks a middle ground between the use of a strict system of content analysis in studying stories and the view that

Thinking Critically

Generativity: How Do You Measure Up?

Erikson believed that for both men and women the dominant task of the adult years is generativity. McAdams and de St. Aubin (1992) have developed a scale to measure differences in concern with generativity. How many of the following beliefs and activities do you engage in?

- Volunteering to work for a charity
- Trying to be creative in one's activities
- Assuming responsibility for others who are less fortunate
- Having children or adopting them
- Teaching important skills to others
- Having a positive impact on others
- Being committed to other people, groups, and activities
- Providing advice to other people
- Believing that one's contributions will survive after death
- Feeling needed by other people

Engaging in several leads to a high measure of generativity in the Generative Behavior Checklist. How would you measure up?

SOURCE: Based on information from McAdams, D. P., & de St. Aubin, E. (1992). A theory of generativity and its assessment through self-report, behavioral acts, and narrative themes in autobiography. Journal of Personality and Social Psychology, 62, 1003–1015.

stories are too fluid and culturally determined to be examined profitably. He calls this middle ground *psychosocial constructionism.* He performs a content analysis, identifying how frequently certain predetermined themes occur, but he also considers that the narratives warrant study on their own terms for the motifs that appear in them.

TABLE 6.2 THEMES INDICATIVE OF GENERATIVITY

Generative adults are more likely to use the following themes in making sense of their lives than are their less generative peers:

- A worldview characterized by the need to help others
- Values and beliefs that indicate moral steadfastness
- The belief that negative experiences can be transformed into positive outcomes
- Anticipation of the future with prosocial goals
- Early belief in having special advantages

SOURCE: Based on information from McAdams, D. P., Diamond, A., de St. Aubin, E., & Mansfield, E. (1997). Stories of commitment: The psychosocial construction of generative lives. Journal of Personality and Social Psychology, 72, 678–694.

McAdams and Pals (2006) have suggested five major principles for organizing current research and theory in personality psychology into an integrative study of the whole person. Their framework (summarized in Figure 6.1) recognizes that human lives are individual variations on a general evolutionary design. Psychological individuality may initially be seen as variations on a limited number of substantially inherited broad dispositional traits. Individuals also vary in their characteristic motivational, social-cognitive, and developmental adaptations, which are contextualized in time, place, and society. Human lives further vary in terms of the life narratives they construct to provide meaning and identity. At each of the three major levels of personality (dispositional traits, characteristic adaptions, and integrative life narratives), culture exerts different and increasing effects. Similar labels for traits are found across cultures, but culture shapes how traits are expressed. Cultural differences in goals and beliefs foster different patterns of characteristic adaptions. Finally, cultures provide options for life stories and shape how they should be told and lived. In addition to their own study of individual life narratives, McAdams and Pals's work encompasses other major trends in current personality theorizing discussed in this text, such as the Big Five model of personality traits (discussed in the chapter on factor analytic theories), and may provide a useful tool for future personality study and theorizing.

McAdams sees defining the self through a personal story as an act of psychological and social responsibility. A postmodern world can no longer dictate who we are and should be. Therefore, we must construct that meaning for ourselves. Conceiving of identity as a life story resounds with significant themes in cognitive, developmental, personality, and social psychology. Particular interest is being paid to the stories of women, persons of color, and members of other traditionally disenfranchised groups. Life stories are understandable within a specific cultural structure and also help us to differentiate ourselves as individuals. The multiplicity of narratives characteristic of our postmodern world is consistent with trends that stress particular expressions of human behavior but also provide unity and purpose. Stories and myths help to give us meaning and powerfully influence human behavior in social contexts. In some cases, however, if a particular myth is no longer functioning in a healthy way, it may be necessary to go back and construct a new self and

Thinking Critically

How would you write your life story? See the Thinking Critically box "Your Life Story."

Thinking Critically

Your Life Story

Erikson used psychohistories to examine the lives of significant people, and McAdams emphasizes defining the self through a personal story. You can deepen your self-understanding by understanding your own life narrative. Everyone has a favorite story they like to tell. What's yours? What's the one story that you tend to tell most often when meeting, or becoming acquainted with, new people? What's the predominant tone and theme of the story? Is it a somber story or funny? Action-oriented or self-reflective? What are you hoping to convey about yourself in the telling of it? Why is it such an important story to you?

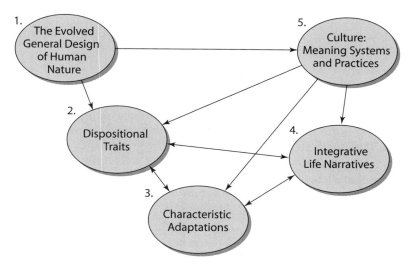

FIGURE 6.1 FIVE PRINCIPLES OF PERSONALITY PSYCHOLOGY

SOURCE: Adapted from McAdmas, D. P., and Pals, J. L. (2006). A new big five: Fundamental principles for an integrative science of personality. *American Psychologist, 61*(3), 204–217, p. 212.

new narrative materials from which we can make a new story. Intense therapy, such as psychoanalysis, can enable us to do that. The "narrative study of lives" has become a broad movement in the social sciences, transcending Erikson's original frame.

 TO LEARN MORE about the "sandwich generation" caring for family members at both ends of Erikson's psychosocial stages of development and about Erikson's psychosocial stages, and for a list of suggested readings, visit the *Personality Theories* textbook website at **college.cengage.com/pic/engler8e.**

Summary

1. Anna Freud emphasized the role of the ego, giving it a greater degree of autonomy. She also extended the interest of psychoanalysis to the study of the child.

2. Erikson extended Freudian psychoanalysis in four ways: He increased our understanding of the ego; he elaborated on Freud's stages of development; he extended the concept of development to include the entire life span; and he explored the impact of culture, society, and history on the developing personality.

3. Erikson emphasized the adaptive qualities of the ego, whereas Freud tended to emphasize defensiveness. He also described the social and historical forces that influence the ego's strengths and weaknesses, stressing its constructive rather than its repressive effects on development. He suggested that ego development reaches a climax during adolescence.

4. Erikson's **psychosocial stages** (p. 153) made explicit the social dimension that was implied in Freud's work. Each of Erikson's stages was established around an emotional conflict that people

encounter at certain critical periods. His stages were **epigenetic** (p. 153), progressing in a cumulative fashion. Each stage provided opportunities for a basic ego strength, or **virtue** (p. 153), to grow.

5. **Trust versus mistrust** (p. 154) is the emotional duality that corresponds to Freud's oral stage. It leads to the development of **hope. Autonomy versus shame and doubt** (p. 154) marks the anal-muscular stage and culminates in **will.** The phallic stage is characterized by **initiative versus guilt** (p. 155). The ego strength that emerges at this time is **purpose. Industry versus inferiority** (p. 156) is the hallmark of the latency period, whose ego strength is **competence.** Erikson subdivided the genital stage into four stages. The primary duality during adolescence is **ego identity versus role confusion.** The virtue developed at this time is **fidelity. Intimacy versus isolation** is characteristic of young adulthood and leads to the emergence of **love.** The middle years are characterized by a conflict of **generativity versus stagnation** (p. 158); the ego strength that emerges is **care.** The final stage is marked by **ego integrity versus despair** (p. 159), and the ego strength is **wisdom.**

6. Erikson engaged in several studies that show how culture and history shape personality. He compared the child-rearing practices of two Native American groups, the Sioux and the Yurok. He undertook a number of biographical studies on important historical figures such as Luther and Gandhi.

7. In his discussion of sex differences, Erikson explored boys' and girls' concepts of **inner** and **outer space** (p. 162).

8. Erikson developed techniques of study appropriate to his subject. There are parallels between the evidence used by a psychoanalyst and that used in a **psychohistorical** (p. 161) study. Each event is considered in terms of its coherence with the individual's life.

9. Empirical research on Erikson's theory includes Marcia's theory of adolescence, Levinson's expanding on the adult development of men and women, and research on ethnic identity such as that done by Cross, Parham and Helms, and Phinney.

10. The coherence method of truth that Erikson employs is characteristic of the philosopher. Erikson does not insist on a scientific pretense for his work. The philosophical statements entailed in his theory are explicit.

11. McAdams has expanded Erikson's theory in the study of life narratives and **generativity** (p. 168), and he suggested a new framework for organizing research in personality into an integrative study of the whole person.

Personal Experiences

1. Anna Freud developed a concept of normality for the adolescent period. She noted that many forms of adolescent acting out are normal and make a positive contribution to development. Did you act out during your adolescence? How did you do it? Did you skip school or run away? How did your parents react to your behavior? Was their reaction helpful or unhelpful to you? Erikson adds that some adolescents, such as Malcolm X, finding it difficult to establish a positive identity, establish a negative one. Did you go through a period of negative identity? Do you know others who did? What helped you to pass through that identity into a positive one?

2. Erikson feels that every stage of development entails its own life crisis, a critical time when a person must make a crucial decision about his or her life. Take some time to reflect on the stages of the life cycle that you have passed through. What do you consider to be your most *critical* life crisis thus far in your life? What about this period makes it so important? Why do you choose this period above all the others? Did it help you better understand yourself, your family, your friends, or perhaps life in general? Do you know other people who have had experiences similar to yours?

3. You probably are currently bridging the fifth and sixth stages of Erikson's psychosocial stages of development: ego identity versus role confusion and intimacy versus isolation. Given that you have relatively fresh, firsthand experience of these stages, how do you feel Erikson's theory relates to you? How do you feel you're coming along in understanding your identity, who you are as an individual? How do you feel about forming intimate relationships with others? Assess your love life. Do you feel ready to make a commitment to one other person, or are you happier dating multiple people? Try to explain your preference using your knowledge of these two stages. Do you agree with Erikson that your ability to form a secure identity directly impacts your ability to form healthy relationships and to make a strong, intimate commitment of love?

4. Look ahead at the stages Erikson characterized for the adult years: generativity versus stagnation and ego integrity versus despair. How do the adults you know seem to be negotiating the issues that Erikson describes? How do your grandparents fit into Erikson's conception of the later stages? How do you conceive of "adulthood"? Are you eagerly looking forward to it, or is it a prospect that induces anxiety or dread? Are you basing your feelings on examples of individuals who have been models of adulthood for you or on other sources, such as movies, television, or your peers?

5. Select one of Erikson's psychosocial stages of development, and analyze how this stage is portrayed in popular media. How is the age group you chose depicted in the movies and television shows you typically see? Compare the media portrayal of this stage with Erikson's discussion of it. Do the issues seem to be the same? If they do not, in what ways do they differ? Provide specific case examples to support your analysis. Are the people who would typically be in this stage portrayed in movies and on television in the manner that Erikson describes, or is there dissonance between Erikson's conception and the media portrayals? Do the media portrayals help to foster healthy or unhealthy development? Again, explain your analysis using specific examples from the media.

CHAPTER 7

Human Relations

- ## Object Relations Theory
  - *Melanie Klein*
  - *Margaret Mahler*
  - *Heinz Kohut*
  - *Otto Kernberg*
  - *Nancy Chodorow*
- ## The Stone Center Group

YOUR GOALS FOR THIS CHAPTER

1. Describe the major ideas of the **object relations** theorists.
2. Identify the essential components of Melanie Klein's theory.
3. What contributions did Margaret Mahler make to psychoanalytic theory?
4. Explain how Heinz Kohut clarifies **narcissism.**
5. Describe how Otto Kernberg accounts for **borderline personality disorders,** and discuss his method of treatment.
6. Describe what Nancy Chodorow means by the **reproduction of mothering,** and explain why social and historical forces are insufficient to account for gender development.
7. Identify the Stone Center group.
8. Describe the thesis of Jean Baker Miller's *Toward a New Psychology of Women.*
9. Describe the paradigm shift made by the Stone Center group.
10. Explain the significance of **connections,** and tell why **empathy** is central for growth within relationships.
11. Explain how **disconnections** are the major source of psychological problems.
12. Describe how psychotherapy can change and overcome the negative effects of disconnection.
13. Describe the neurobiological basis of relationships and relational-cultural theory.
14. Evaluate the human relations theories from the viewpoints of philosophy, science, and art.

S ome psychoanalytic psychologists emphasize the role of the ego in personality development; others consider how people develop patterns of living out of their early relationships with significant others. Human development occurs in the context of relationships with other people on whom we are dependent initially for our very survival and with whom we interact throughout our lives. Many, if not most, individual problems reveal themselves through difficulties in getting along with other people, and most significant problems that affect the entire human race are interpersonal in origin and require cooperative solutions. The global community cannot afford to neglect the challenge of understanding how human beings get along together, why human relations go awry, and how they can be rectified.

Object relations theorists—for example, Melanie Klein, Margaret Mahler, Heinz Kohut, Otto Kernberg, and Nancy Chodorow—seek to understand the interaction between intrapsychic dynamics and interpersonal relationships. Beyond object relations, a group of women scholars working out of the Stone Center at Wellesley College have suggested a new perspective for the understanding of human beings: relational-cultural theory, a perspective that has enormous potential to reshape our understanding. Whereas the object relations theorists emphasize the intrapsychic experience of relationships with others, the relational-cultural theorists emphasize the interpsychic experience of relationships, or the connections and disconnections that occur between people in relationships.

Object Relations Theory

In the 1950s and 1960s, American psychoanalysis was dominated by ego psychology. It emphasized conflict between internal structures and their defense in the individual psyche. Meanwhile, in Britain, Melanie Klein (1932) led child analysis in a direction different from that of Anna Freud (see also Caper, 2000) and initiated object relations theory. Freud had developed a drive-based structural model of the human psyche in which the objects of our drives, libidinal or aggressive, were a major element. Initially, he used the term *object* to refer to any target through which an infant seeks to satisfy the aim of a drive. Object relations theorists have shifted toward a relational structural model in which an inborn drive to form and maintain human relationships is the basic need from which other drives derive their meaning. In these theories, an **object** is the aim of relational needs in human development, and object relations are the intrapsychic experiences of those early relationships. The objects are primarily people, such as a primary caretaker and significant others. However, they may also be things, such as pacifiers, teddy bears, and blankets. From birth onward, object relations theorists suggest, individuals seek to develop human relationships and form attachments that may aid or hinder their development.

MELANIE KLEIN (1882–1960)

Melanie Klein initiated the shift in emphasis away from studying innate biological instincts and toward relations between people. She adhered to Sigmund Freud's drive theory but proposed that drives are psychological forces that seek people as their objects. Klein believed that, in dealing with their drives, children construct their own internal mental representations of

Melanie Klein

Margaret Mahler

Heinz Kohut

Otto Kernberg

Nancy Chodorow

Melanie Klein, Margaret Mahler, Heinz Kohut, Otto Kernberg, and Nancy Chodorow seek to understand the interaction between intrapsychic dynamics and interpersonal relationships.

other people and project them onto real people (externals). They then use subsequent experiences with those people to confirm or disconfirm their internal representations and to interpret their relationships with them. Klein also described how, primarily because of anxiety over aggressive impulses, children split objects and feelings into good and bad aspects in an effort to retain good ones as part of the self while getting rid of bad ones by projecting them onto others. This **splitting** of the object image into opposites in the internal world of fantasy permits children to treat the internalized object as clearly good or bad while continuing to trust and love the actual external person who is an intricate combination of both. To acknowledge both good and bad aspects in the actual person at this time is too threatening to the dependent and immature child. In time, this split between the nurturing and the frustrating mother becomes the starting point of a child's concept of "good-me" and "bad-me." The feeling of "good-me" stems from the nurturance that is seen as acceptance by the mother, and the feeling of "bad-me" stems from the frustration that is seen as rejection. In healthy development, the early frustration actually promotes the infant's separation and leads to individuation. Children learn to integrate "good" and "bad" aspects of the self and others and form consistent and adaptable concepts of the self and other people. Often, however, the activity of splitting clouds their subjective and objective perception and leads to distorted relations with other people.

According to object relations theory, personality is shaped by relationships with significant others. We begin life with certain genetic predispositions but with no sense of self or identity. Only through interactions with significant others do we take into ourselves parts of others and begin to build a self-structure. Our earliest object relations are the initial crucial building blocks of the self-system and the model upon which subsequent interpersonal relationships are developed. Thereafter, we tend to repeat in our other relationships those early self-object relations. Changes can be made, but making them is difficult. In emphasizing the interaction of unconscious fantasies and real experiences and the slow development of children's realistic relationships to the world, Klein made a major critical contribution to psychoanalytic theory.

Kernberg (1975) has suggested that it would also be appropriate to term object relations theory *human relations theory*. However, in a sense, the inclusive term *object* is more accurate because people develop relationships with nonhuman things, such as toys and pets, in addition to people. Some of our relationships are healthy and constructive, but others are not. We all know people who have strong but destructive relationships with other people, with food, with alcohol, or with other substances. Object relations theory suggests that the basic pattern of all these relationships is established early in life in our first relationships with significant others.

Klein was more interested in the reality of the "inner world" than in that of the "outer world." One result of her preference has been that object relations theory has been very helpful for understanding psychopathology, and the interest in object relations has become particularly important as a framework for understanding some of the syndromes that have become a part of our popular clinical literature, such as borderline and narcissistic personality disorders and various forms of abuse. More recently Klein's theory of psychodynamics has been used to inform the discussion of challenges and opportunities posed by racial reparative efforts for both whites and blacks (Balbos, 2004).

MARGARET MAHLER (1897–1985)

In object relations theory, human development is a lifelong process of emerging out of the dependent relationship of infant and mother and becoming an individual capable of entering into mature adult mutual relationships. Margaret Mahler (1975) explored the processes of separation and individuation by which the child emerges from a symbiotic, or intimate, fusion with the mother and assumes individual characteristics. Her findings confirm that the biological birth of an infant and the psychological birth of an individual are not the same. The former is a distinct event; the latter is a gradual unfolding process.

By studying and comparing severely disturbed and normal children, Mahler constructed a sequence of stages through which the ego passes in the process of becoming an individual. The process of **separation-individuation** optimally begins about the fourth month and leads to the formation of a stable self-concept near the end of the third year. *Separation* implies physical differentiation and separateness from one's primary caregiver. *Individuation* suggests psychological growth away from one's primary caregiver and toward one's unique identity. In Mahler's view the roots of identity, ego strength, and conflict resolution precede the Oedipus complex.

Prior to separation-individuation, there are two "forerunner phases," *normal autism* and *normal symbiosis,* in which the infant's ego develops from a state of absolutely primary narcissism to a recognition of an external world. At this time there is no real separation of self from mother, but developments may occur that promote or impede the subsequent individuation process. The separation-individuation process itself is composed of four stages: *differentiation,* the development of a body image separate from that of mother (five to nine months); *practicing,* perfecting motor abilities and developing physical independence (ten to fourteen months); *rapprochement,* increased awareness of separateness from mother, with an accompanying sensitivity to her absence that expresses a conflict between the urge to separate and the fear of loss and a recognition that mothers have both good and bad aspects (fourteen to twenty-four months); *consolidation,* unification of the good and bad in mother with the image of her as a separate entity in the external world and the beginnings of the child's own individuality and separate personhood as seen in the development of a self-concept based on a stable sense of "me" (two to three years). Mahler's concept expresses her belief that normal, healthy infants show a "drive for and towards individuation" that is demonstrated in the separation-individuation process. Mahler's theory is receiving attention currently because her concept of a separation-individuation process is so helpful.

Mahler's theory has had a significant impact in the therapeutic community in facilitating analytic work with patients who have disturbed object relations (cf. Pine, 2004). Historically, classical Freudian psychoanalysis has not been considered a treatment of choice for people with substance addictions or other addictive behaviors, such as obsessive gambling or shopping, overeating, or love addiction. Straussner and Spiegel (1996) have analyzed twelve-step programs, such as Alcoholics Anonymous, in terms of Mahler's separation-individuation process and found that such programs ameliorate the ego deficiencies and difficulties in relating to other people that their members tend to have. Followers of such programs, however, would suggest that their effectiveness cannot be fully explained at a theoretical level because the programs encompass psychophysiological and spiritual dimensions as well.

Heinz Kohut (1913–1981)

Object relations theorists emphasize the importance of effectively meeting early infantile needs. Heinz Kohut was very specific in his **self-theory** (1971, 1977a, 1977b). He maintained that children need to be **mirrored**—to have their talk and their accomplishments acknowledged, accepted, and praised. Little children believe that they are omnipotent and they also idealize their parents. Such **idealization** enables them to develop goals. In time, most children learn that their idealized notions are incorrect, and they substitute a more realistic assessment of both themselves and their parents. In part, this learning depends on parents responding positively to their children's unique, lovable, and commendable characteristics. If parents fail to respond in appropriate ways, children may be unable to develop a good sense of self-worth and may spend the rest of their lives looking without success for such acceptance. Narcissistic individuals are looking for an idealized parent substitute that can never be found.

With a well-developed self, one is aware of who one is, and that awareness gives significance and purpose to one's behavior. In ideal development, the **nuclear self,** a preliminary core self, emerges in the second year. Kohut believed that the nuclear self is bipolar. The two poles, archaic nuclear ambitions and subsequent goals, create a tension arc that fosters the development of early skills and talents. Supportive and empathetic family relations permit the nuclear self to grow and become more cohesive, leading to an autonomous self. The

Children need to be mirrored-to have their talk and their accomplishments acknowledged, accepted, and praised by their parents. Thus the author's granddaughter pauses in her study of her reflection in the mirror to reference her mother and solicit approval of the activity.

ideal **autonomous self** has qualities of *self-esteem* and *self-confidence,* establishes both general ambition and precise goals, and develops talents and skills in order to meet them. Furthermore, the autonomous self shows healthy independence and flexibility in interpersonal relations.

In object relations theory, trauma in the course of development can lead to pathological delay and the stunting of emotional growth and ego formation. Psychopathology is an expression of traumatic self-object internalizations from childhood that are acted out in our current relationships. Dysfunctional behavior is an immature effort to resolve early trauma. Kohut focused on narcissism and narcissistic character disorders that occur when an individual fails to develop an independent sense of self. He theorized that there is a narcissistic line of development that occurs distinct from and before ego and psychosexual development.

The term **narcissism** comes from the ancient Greek myth of Narcissus, who "unwittingly" fell in love with his own reflection in a pool of water. He talked to it and tried to embrace it, but all in vain as it fled at his touch. The passion with which he burned was self-consuming.

The narcissistic personality is characterized by an exaggerated sense of self-importance and self-involvement, behaviors that hide a fragile sense of self-worth. Sigmund Freud believed that narcissistic and borderline disorders could not be treated by psychoanalysis because they originated before the patient was able to talk and thus were not amenable to verbal analysis. Because the libido is withdrawn from external objects, resistance is insuperable and it is difficult to cultivate a transference. However, disruptions in family relationships and in society have led to an increase in these disorders and to more efforts to deal with them psychoanalytically. Kohut and others (such as Giovacchini, Kernberg, and Spotnitz) have expanded the psychoanalytic repertoire to include techniques designed to work through transferences and resistances that stem from pre-Oedipal phases of development.

Kohut (1971, 1977a) conceived of narcissistic feelings not as qualities specific to a certain stage of development but as an aspect of personality that gradually unfolds, permeates the entire life span, and leads to a distorted sense of self. He believed that disorders of the self arise from a failure in parental empathy and mirroring. The narcissistic disorders so prevalent today are characterized by recurrent self-absorption, low self-esteem, unimportant physical complaints, and a chronic sense of emptiness. Addiction, for example, is a "futile attempt to repair developmental deficits in the self" (1977b); Kohut's work offers a helpful perspective on the subject of addiction (Weegmann, 2003). Kohut pointed out that psychoanalysis cannot be useful unless the therapist deals first with the narcissistic disorder. Suggesting that therapists imagine themselves "into the client's skin," Kohut believed that therapists can cultivate feelings of being understood and appreciated in the patient so that the arrested growth of the patient's self can begin again. Thus Kohut stressed empathy and introspection over the conventional psychoanalytic blend of free association and evenly suspended attention. In the course of treatment, Kohut discovered that narcissistic patients develop idealizing or mirroring transferences to their analysts that reflect their early and troubled parent-child relationships. Therapy permits them to rework these relationships through to a better resolution.

Kohut (1977a) reminded us that the "presence of a firm self is a precondition for the experience of the Oedipus complex." He found that at the end of their analysis some of his patients who had primary self disorders acquired an Oedipal constellation. "This he considered to be the positive result of the consolidations of the self the patient had never achieved before" (Ornstein, 1993). Moreover, this development was associated with positive emotions, leading Kohut to believe that when children develop normally, the Oedipus complex may be a "joyful" experience. An Oedipus complex that is filled with conflict may be a sign that narcissistic parents have been unable to respond with empathy to their preschool-age child and may lead their child to turn to a fantasy life. Kohut (1977a, 1984) pointed out that the necessity for children to have nurturing and affectionate parents was just being given genuine notice by psychoanalysts, although it was well understood much earlier by neo-Freudians and humanists. Watson, Little, and Biderman (1992) found correlations between Baumrind's parenting styles (discussed in the chapter on psychoanalytic social psychology) and Kohut's theory, suggesting that an authoritative (rather than permissive or authoritarian) parenting style is less likely to foster narcissistic maladjustment.

Kohut (1984) pointed out that some parts of Freud's theory are "timebound," whereas other parts have a more "enduring validity." Eagle (1984) suggests that "if, as Kohut argues, forms of pathology are shifting more in the directions of narcissistic disorders; and if it is true and self psychology is uniquely appropriate to these phenomena; and if . . . the traditional theory of intrapsychic conflict is *inappropriate* to these phenomena, it follows that . . . the validity and applicability of traditional psychoanalytic theory [and I might add contemporary psychoanalytic theory] are culture—and era—bound . . . rather than . . . timeless and universal." Moreover, the increase in self disorders may be due to cultural forces such as an absence of stable beliefs and values and an attitude of cynicism that negatively affects teenagers and young adults.

Kohut transformed psychoanalysis from its preoccupation with sexuality into a more open inquiry of the self, its goals, ambitions, and relationships with others (Goldberg, 2003). Kohut's self-theory has resulted in some fruitful reinterpretations of Freud's classic case studies (see Magid, 1993), and his concept of the self object continues to generate discussion and research (e.g., Mollon, 2002). Haitch (1995) detects a common note with the work of theologian Paul Tillich in the concept of courage in faith, essential for fighting illnesses such as cancer and alcoholism. Such current interest in Kohut's work is testimony to its revitalization of psychoanalytic theory.

OTTO KERNBERG (1928–   )

The object relations perspective on psychopathology as immature and ineffective interpersonal relations is continued by Otto Kernberg, who agrees with Sigmund Freud and Kohut that many people who suffer from narcissistic disorders have parents who were indifferent, cold, and also subtly hostile and vengeful toward them (1975). Kernberg further underscores the atypical and high amount of self-reference in narcissistic individuals' interpersonal relationships and the dissimilarity between their seemingly exaggerated self-images and their insatiable need for approval from other people. Although their craving for admiration and approval may lead others to think that narcissists are dependent, Kernberg believes that they are actually unable to trust other people and are, therefore, powerless to depend on others.

Kernberg has also focused on **borderline personality disorder,** a serious mental illness more common than schizophrenia or bipolar disorder but less well known. Such patients are unable to engage in introspection, develop insight, and work through problems. They frequently have strong mood swings and are inclined to see significant others in their lives as all good or all bad. These patients display oral tendencies such as dependency needs or an incorporative style but also powerful aggressive tendencies, particularly with reference to their Oedipal struggles (Kernberg, Selzer, Koenigsberg, Carr, Appelbaum, 1989).

In the DSM-IV criteria, a person is considered to have a borderline personality disorder if he or she displays a pervasive five or more specific clinical features. Kernberg would prefer, however, a diagnosis and explanation of borderline based on a causal description of early, historical relationships that set up an abnormal self-structure and an abnormal representation of others. This development constitutes the syndrome of identity diffusion.

To account for the intense changes that are apparent in a borderline individual's interpersonal relationships, Kernberg further elaborates on the notion of splitting as failing to consolidate positive and negative experiences between oneself and other people. Borderline people swing back and forth between conflicting images, seeing one and the same person as both loving and hateful rather than being able to see one loving person who at times accepts and at other times rejects. Kernberg portrays this behavior:

> In one session, the patient may experience me as the most helpful, loving, understanding human being and feel totally relieved and happy, and all the problems solved. Three sessions later, she may berate me as the most ruthless, indifferent, and manipulative person she has ever met. Total unhappiness about the treatment, ready to drop it and never come back. (Sass, 1982)

Kernberg prefers to treat borderline patients face to face in intensive sessions two or three times a week. The therapist plays a more active role than is typical of classical psychoanalysis. Initially the stress is placed on current behavior rather than past events. Kernberg's method of treatment, which he calls **transference-focused psychotherapy,** differs from classical psychoanalysis in that a complete transference neurosis is not permitted to develop, nor is transference resolved through interpretation alone. Instead, the therapist clearly depicts and discusses the patient's seeming distortions of reality, such as a distorted view of the therapist (see also Clarkin, Levy, & Schiavi, 2005).

Kernberg (1992) has suggested some changes to Sigmund Freud's drive theory that help clarify some of the differences between his point of view and that of Kohut. He sees affects, psychophysiological structures that evolved to assist mammals in surviving (1996a), as the building blocks of drives; and he believes that the source of libido is the emotional state of sexual excitement that embraces all physiologically activated functions and body zones engaged in the erotic arousal of a parent-child relationship. For Kernberg, the basis of personality formation lies in uniting the neuropsychological causes of primitive emotions with the first interpersonal experiences of babies and children. He proposes that personality disturbances are caused by the psychic structures that are built under the influence of early emotional events with significant others. Genetic predispositions and early traumatic experiences affect brain circuitry (Kernberg, 2006). Whereas Kohut believed that narcissistic personality disorders are the result of empathic failures, Kernberg believes that personality disorders are the result of lack of integration of libidinal and aggressive object relations (see also Kernberg, 2004).

In Kernberg's theory, aggression is a major motivating force, and rage is the necessary emotion contributing to the feeling of aggression as a drive. In this respect, he believes that Kohut failed to recognize the importance of analyzing negative transferences. Patients with narcissistic or borderline disorders frequently express hate, rage, and envy. The analyst must be able to avoid reacting with counteraggression and to maintain a posture of technical neutrality in order to clarify and interpret the transference. The analyst must also be able to tolerate the ambiguity of his or her position (Kernberg, 1995a). Kernberg is careful not to let patients feel that their cure is essential to his own well-being, because such a belief tends to enhance feelings of omnipotence in a patient. The exercise of functional authority by the psychoanalyst is a necessary aspect of psychoanalytic work (1996b).

Kernberg believes that psychology needs to consider the cultural determinants of sexual excitement, as well as the intrapsychic and biological ones.

> If you live in an Arab country where women are all covered except for the eyes, the wind lifts the veil, and it is a primal scene! If you go to beaches in Western Europe where many go topless, then you have a different attitude toward erotic stimulation than if you were brought up in the Puritan atmosphere in the American mid-West 30 years ago. (Kernberg, 1992)

Kernberg (1994, 2003) recognizes that psychoanalysis in the United States has been hurt by declining interest, loss of prestige, health-industry intrusions on patients' privacy, and fewer prospective patients. Still, Kernberg (1996c) is optimistic about the future of psychoanalysis and encourages psychoanalytic institutes to foster more creativity in training candidates. Finally, Kernberg (2000) has explored the importance of *mature religiosity,* an integrated value system that entails the prevalence of love over hatred and of libido over the death drive.

NANCY CHODOROW (1944–   )

The significance of object relations theory for feminist and social theory has been explored by psychoanalyst and former professor of sociology Nancy J. Chodorow. In her initial work, *The Reproduction of Mothering,* Chodorow (1978) describes the cyclical process of the **reproduction of mothering** as a process by which the mother-daughter relationship instills in the daughter maternal capacities and a desire to take on the role of mother in future relationships.

Explanations of mothering rooted in biology or role socialization are insufficient. The capacity to mother does not come about as a result of a pregnant woman's physical or instinctual makeup or through deliberate role training. The early relationship between mothers and infants establishes a basis for parenting in children of both sexes and "expectations that women will mother." Mothering meets a woman's psychological need for reciprocal intimacy initiated during her own infancy when she and her mother saw one another as extensions of themselves. Mothers are also close to their baby sons, but they see their sons as dissimilar and do not experience the same feeling of "oneness" they have with their daughters. Boys' nurturing abilities are methodically limited and repressed as they are prepared to work outside the family.

The psyche develops differently in men and women. The process entails individual and emotional fantasy-related materials that arise in the course of psychoanalytic development, as well as social influences (1999a). The establishment of gender identity occurs in the pre-Oedipal period, and there are sex differences in the Oedipal experience because of this awareness. Women's personality develops in a way that emphasizes ongoing interpersonal relations, but men grow to see themselves as distinct and separate. This prepares the two sexes for different roles: nonrelationship activities for men and relational activities for women. The different development of women and men further re-creates women's mothering by preparing them to take "adult gender roles which situate women primarily within the sphere of reproduction in a sexually unequal society." Grown men, unused to a psychologically intimate relation, are satisfied with letting women mother (see Figure 7.1).

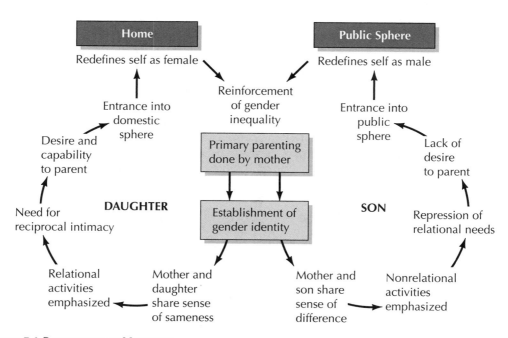

FIGURE 7.1 REPRODUCTION OF MOTHERING

Chodorow's reproduction of mothering is a cyclical process that produces daughters with mothering capacities and prepares men to repress relational needs.

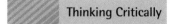

Thinking Critically

Should men and women share parenting? See the Thinking Critically box "Families Today."

Differential feminine and masculine development leads to discrepancies in the structure of parenting. Women's mothering ensures that parenting is done. However, the process creates stresses and pressures that subvert the sex-gender system. Chodorow (2000b) emphasizes the centrality and power of a woman's personal investment and sense of what it means to be a mother. Our current society fails to nurture that maternal subjectivity. An economy and philosophy that presumed the two-parent family and permitted and expected women to remain at home as full-time mothers has been replaced by an economy that often requires two adult incomes. The necessity to work, the requirements of the workplace, and our social beliefs as to what constitutes happiness jeopardize the mother-child relationship. Women need to be able to choose whether or not to become mothers and when and how to work.

Chodorow has shifted from a primarily social determinist stance toward a more psychological and internal point of view. She believes that it is "crucial" for us to recognize that "the ideologies of difference, which define us as women and as men, as well as inequality itself, are produced, socially, psychologically, and culturally, by people living in and creating their social, psychological, and cultural worlds" (1989; see also 2000a). Women and children's primary place in the home, combined with men's involvement in the public sphere, "defines society itself as masculine. It gives men power to create and enforce institutions of social and political control, important among these to control marriage as an institution that both expresses men's rights in women's sexual and reproductive capacities and reinforces these rights" (1978).

Chodorow (1989) points out that Freud's theory does not simply subjugate women. "Freud tells us how nature becomes culture and how this culture comes to appear as and be experienced as 'second nature.'" Although Freud's understanding of male attitudes toward women is clear and compelling, he himself acknowledged that his understanding of feminine psychology was "shadowy and incomplete." Nevertheless, he "condemned the conditions that lead to repression and hysteria in women" (Chodorow, 1991). Freud's writings testify to and account for clinical and sociohistorical sexual diversity in both men and women. Although he gave normative status to heterosexuality, it was within a culture characterized by male-dominant gender differentiation (Chodorow, 1994). Moreover, "Freud suggests that these processes do not happen so smoothly, that this reproduction of gender and sexuality is rife with contradiction and strains" (1989).

Chodorow (1996b) expresses concern about theories positing objectivized or universal stages, drives, or unconscious fantasies that transcend cultures to explain psychological experience. She points out that in the clinical experience, psychological meaning is created in the here-and-now, with singular evidence from each person's subjective childhood and individual transferences. A person's sense of gender is a fusion of personal and cultural meaning (1995) continually reconstructed. The emphasis on objective gender (general statements about how men and women construct the self) often obscures subjective gender (the personal sense of one's femininity or masculinity). For one individual, invulnerable anger may be a key dimension of masculinity; for another, femininity may be encompassed in feelings of shame and guilt. Such examples illustrate the immense variation and individuality of gender definition and construction. Emphasizing the linguistic, cultural, and political con-

Thinking Critically

Families Today

Psychoanalytic object relations theory emphasizes the importance of the mother-child relationship in human development. The mid-twentieth-century culture that called for full-time mothering and the economy that allowed it have been replaced by a variety of social and economic factors that no longer stress the mother-child relationship in the same way. Women entering the workplace has brought on the rise in dual-income households and the increase in child day-care services. Divorce and advances in reproductive technologies have led to an increase in single-parent households. Continually evolving views about gender roles and sexual orientation have paved the way for gay adoption rights and same-sex couples raising children of their own.

In her book *The Reproduction of Mothering,* Nancy Chodorow argues for the centrality of the mother-child role in the health and well-being of both women and their children, but the diversity of modern family structures and the ongoing fight for equal rights on the fronts of both gender and sexual orientation may threaten this focus. What do you think? Are women best suited to be the primary caregiver, or can men do just as good a job? Is a heterosexual man and woman the ideal parenting unit, or can same-sex couples and single parents raise children just as well? Jean Baker Miller believes that "if a society wants children, it should make proper provision for them" (2006). In negotiating this complicated issue, try to cite social policies and laws that would help promote your ideal vision of family and child rearing in the twenty-first century.

---

struction of gender risks omitting how individual psychological processes also construct gender for the individual. Autobiographical, fictional, and ethnographic literature, as well as feminist and gay-lesbian research, confirm Chodorow's clinical experience. They further suggest that although the specific *content* varies, the *process* of emotion, fantasy, and self-construction that contributes to gender subjectivity characterizes men as well as women, heterosexuals and nonheterosexuals, and people of varied racial and ethnic backgrounds (2002). Although Chodorow has been criticized for ignoring class, ethnic, racial, and sexual preference variations in family patterns, her work has led to further study of those areas (Monaghan, 1999).

Recently, Chodorow (1999b) has challenged the postmodern view that human beings are determined largely by cultural and historical forces by emphasizing the clinical individuality of personal gender and the mother-daughter relationship. She puts less stress on the social aspect of the reproduction of mothering (1999a). She underscores that culture and politics may affect, but do not determine, how women personally experience their bodies, their gender, and their relationships to their mothers and daughters (2004). Our human psychobiological makeup predisposes us to a psychological life that can be described in terms of certain processes and meanings that arise regardless of the different cultures and families from which we come.

Relational-Cultural Theory: The Stone Center Group

Since the late 1970s, a group of women, friends and colleagues, have come together in an effort to improve and cultivate a better understanding of the psychology of women and eventually of all human beings. Their work has effected a "virtual revolution" in psychoanalysis and gender (Sanville, 2003). The core group originally consisted of Jean Baker Miller, M.D., Irene P. Stiver, Ph.D., Judith V. Jordan, Ph.D., and Janet L. Surrey, Ph.D.; however, numerous other women are now central to the work, increasingly representing a more diverse community. Much of the work has been facilitated by the Stone Center for Developmental Services and Studies at Wellesley College in Massachusetts (now part of the Wellesley Centers for Women) under the leadership of Jean Baker Miller.

Most members of the Stone Center group are trained and practicing clinicians who started by looking at the experiences of the women they worked with and began to suspect that traditional theories of human nature and development misunderstood, disregarded, or devalued several aspects of women's experiences. Moreover, the conventional models were having an insidious effect on women. The theory that has emerged from the work of these women, relational-cultural theory (RCT), is unique in that it is primarily a collaborative effort. Although individuals may organize and express ideas a little differently, the generation and growth of their concepts have essentially come from the group. The original group of RCT theorists was largely white, middle class, heterosexual, and well educated. They ac-

Shown here are some contributors to the Stone Center group, which has been the catalyst of a new view of human development that focuses on connectedness. From left to right: back row—Yvonne Jenkins, Natalie Eldridge, Judy Jordan, Janet Surrey; front row—Maureen Walker, Jean Baker Miller, Irene Stiver.

knowledged that their perspective was limited by their own experience, and they did not try to suggest that their work was representative of all women. Increasingly, they have expanded their work by seeking the perspective of minority and lesbian women, who are also assuming leadership roles in the development of the theory. Although RCT was originally developed to understand women's experience, it is progressively being employed to better comprehend all human experience, including that of men. As a result RCT has become a broadly applicable theory with significant implications for psychotherapy as well.

A significant precursor to the theory that has emerged from the Stone Center was Miller's 1976 work *Toward a New Psychology of Women*. In that book, Miller argued that the psychological development of both sexes has been constrained and contorted by a "framework of inequity" in which one sex was thought to be of more worth than the other. The strict stereotypes portraying dominant males and subordinate females were hindering both men and women from reaching their full potential. Miller suggested a new foundation in which concepts traditionally associated with the two sexes (strength versus weakness, dependency versus autonomy) could take on new significance and purpose. Key to her message was the concept of affiliation and relationship. She asserted that women have critical strengths, as yet unrecognized by our society, that can bring a creative force to the human problems with which we are grappling. Her work undermined the male-focused paradigm of classical psychoanalysis and showed how concepts previously devalued because they have generally been associated with women (e.g., cooperation, giving, and nurturing) are in reality potential strengths. Miller pointed toward a new truth—that the initial development of all human beings begins in affiliation and relation (rather than self-enhancement)—and suggested the need to place our faith in building connections with others rather than in our own individual power, achievement, and self-sufficiency.

Research at the Stone Center is consonant with the work of Nancy Chodorow, who clarified the ways in which the early bond between mother and daughter creates boundaries between them that are different from those between mother and son—boundaries that are further entrenched by the child-rearing patterns of Western culture. The Stone Center's work is also similar to that of Carol Gilligan (1977, 1982, 1990), whose studies of girls' and women's psychological and moral development emphasize the importance of connection with, responsibility for, and care of others; however, the Stone Center places more emphasis on how growth emerges from mutual engagement.

Studies in gender differences suggest that the brains of men and women are wired differently. The female brain is "hardwired for empathy," the male for "understanding and building systems" (Baron-Cohen, 2003). Men and women therefore do not experience or express emotions in the same way. Traditional research on stress, conducted primarily on men, suggested a "fight or flight" response. However, newer studies at Harvard Medical School and the University of California at Los Angeles show that women, in response to stress, tend to bond with each other, a response conducive to health and longevity (Taylor et al., 2000). A meta-analytic review of sex differences in coping behavior (Tamres, 2002) also confirms that women are more likely than men to engage in coping strategies that entail social support. Throughout the industrialized world, girls have surged ahead of boys academically (Potrikus, 2003). These findings are consistent with the emphasis of RCT.

Research by the Stone Center group suggests that the basic organizing feature of women's growth is the feeling of *connectedness* to others (Miller & Stiver, 1997). The ability to make and build relationships is the source of a woman's sense of effectiveness and worth.

Women actively participate in the development of others, and they use their power to facilitate the growth and unfolding of both children and adults. Such participation in other people's psychological growth is an integral aspect of human life, providing a new psychological model of human development *"within relationships"* (Miller & Stiver, 1997).

The knowledge of how to develop relationships that facilitate growth is not confined to either gender, nor is it tied to an innate or biological source. As a general rule, however, society has assigned to women the role of participating in the psychological development of others, and thus it is primarily from the lives and experience of women that we can best learn about the possible impact of a relational approach to human development.

Shifting the Paradigm

In asserting that women's life experiences are an appropriate starting point from which to understand human nature, the women of the Stone Center are challenging long-standing assumptions of psychological development. Throughout Western history and culture, the paradigm of human nature has been a male one, emphasizing autonomy and independence. Becoming a self-sufficient individual is commonly seen as the goal of psychological development (see also Coy & Kovaks-Long, 2005). This aim is reflected in psychoanalysis, in which independence and separation are the model for health. Although Erikson's stages begin with relatedness, the model quickly moves into subsequent stages that stress autonomy and self-development. Women's strength in being able to relate to others has regularly been devalued and debased as a sign of weakness (Miller, 1991). According to the Stone Center group, basic beliefs about who we are develop within the mutual connection of interpersonal relationships, not in the process of separating from each other.

Initially, members of the group described their theory variously as "self-in-relation" or "the relational self." However, the virtue of setting up a new theory of "self" has itself been questioned, as they have shifted into an emphasis on relational development and the movement of relationships. "Connection" has replaced "self" as the key ingredient or focus of development (Surrey, 1990). It is **connections** that are the basic origins of growth and development and **disconnections** that derail us and block our growth. Reconceiving and recognizing the important role of relationships and connections changes the whole base of current psychological theory and thinking and requires major alterations in our concepts about what fosters growth and healing and what leads to problems and pain.

Thus the relational-cultural theorists (Miller & Stiver, 1997) are proposing a paradigm shift in our thinking about human nature that moves away from individualistic values to relational ones and that places connection at the center of our thought (see Table 7.1). Whereas earlier theorists described a process of separation-individuation, Surrey (1991) proposes the concept of **relationship-differentiation,** a process that entails increasing levels of complexity within the framework of human relationships. The two-directional dynamic of the mother-daughter relationship is an early model of relational development, providing us with a pattern for studying and learning about emotional connectedness and mutual empathy. The person unfolds in the matrix of significant relationships. Rather than entailing a task of separation, the path is one of developing capacity for entering into relationships and relational competence. Other aspects of growth, such as expressing one's own experience, develop within the prior situation of being in relation and do not negate the importance of relationship. In relationship, separate selves interact and coexist. Relationship does not always entail continuous physical connection, but there is continuous psy-

TABLE 7.1 P STONE CENTER GROUP PARADIGM

The Stone Center group paradigm for understanding human nature emphasizes human interconnectedness rather than separation and individuation.

	TRADITIONAL PARADIGM	STONE CENTER PARADIGM
Process of development	separation-individuation	relationship-differentiation
Goal of development	self	connections
Model	male	female
Health	self-sufficiency	relational competence
Ill health	dependency	disconnections
Values	individualistic	connecting

chological connection, and the awareness of the presence of the other is the basis of one's self-experiences. Within this new paradigm, the adolescent experience is not necessarily one of separation but rather of altering the relationship so as to facilitate and affirm the growth of both the adolescent and the parents (Surrey, 1991).

Connections

Human beings seek connections. Earlier drive theories of psychoanalysis suggested that human beings seek primarily pleasure or gratification. The very name *object relations* reflects a perception of other people as objects that fulfill or frustrate our drives. Traditionally, the

According to the Stone Center paradigm, basic beliefs about who we are develop within the mutual connection of interpersonal relationships.

view of our basic formative relationships has not been based on **mutuality,** a way of relating and sharing in which all are fully participating. Freud's model of human development stressed the competitive and aggressive qualities of the male relationship. Rather than focus on the Oedipus complex or a feminine version of it, Stiver (1991a) suggests that we look at the ongoing intense, often conflictual, relationships of mothers and daughters and fathers and daughters and study the different roles that mutual empathy and empowerment play in order to clarify the connections that we seek.

Central to the new emphasis is a reconception of **empathy,** which entails experiencing the feelings and thoughts of another while simultaneously knowing one's own different feelings and thoughts. Empathy has often been thought of as a setback to mature functioning, characterized by regression and symbiosis, in which there is a break of ego boundaries and a merging with another individual. Earlier, Kohut (1978) observed that "empathy is a fundamental model of human relatedness"; he even stressed the importance of empathy. However, he did not describe its origins or clearly envision it as a reciprocal interactional process. Jordan (1991) suggests that a more adequate definition of empathy envisions it as a process involving both cognitive and affective aspects that evolves to become increasingly complex, sophisticated, and mature. Developing the capacity to be empathetic requires modeling, practice, and mutual response.

Miller (1986) describes the type of empathic dialogue and interchange that fosters connection. Ann is telling Beth that a mutual friend, Emily, may have a serious disease:

> Tears are in Ann's eyes and her voice sounds sad and fearful. Beth says, "Oh, how sad." Beth's voice and expression are sad and there is also some fear in them.
>
> Ann then says, "Yes, but I have this other awful feeling—like fear. Like I'm scared—as if it could happen to me." Beth replies, "Me, too. It is frightening to hear this. Maybe we all feel as if it's happening to us."

An empathetic response adds to what was initially expressed and leads to a fuller acknowledgment and expression of thoughts and feelings. At first, Ann and Beth are hesitant about expressing the depth of their feelings; but as they each acknowledge and share their emotions, they are able to express them more profoundly, to imagine how Emily must be feeling, and to move from that to discussing how they would like to be with Emily during this difficult period. In the conversation that follows, Ann and Beth are able to explore their feelings and thoughts more fully. As the interaction proceeds, both become increasingly motivated and able to act. Because of the greater lucidity and accuracy that results from their conversation, they decide together to call Emily, visit her, and take other appropriate action.

In contrast, when Ann tries to share the news with her husband, Tom, a very different scenario occurs:

> Tom replies, "Well, it's a terrible thing. In the end, she'll have to do the best she can. She should get a second opinion. I hear the Sloan Clinic is very good on these kinds of cases. Have you called her back yet? Did you call my sister Helen about the birthday party she's trying to arrange for my mother next week? We should really do something about that if it's going to come off."

Tom does not respond to Ann's feelings. Instead he tells her what to do, what Emily should do, and then changes the subject, giving directions to Ann about an impending party. Whereas

Ann felt empowered after her conversation with Beth, she feels uncertain after the interchange with Tom. In addition to the feelings of fear and sadness that she was unable to express, she also feels that she has lost connection.

Mutual empathy fosters mutual empowerment (Miller & Stiver, 1997), which is characterized by *zest,* the feeling of authentic connection. In addition, mutual empathy leads to the ability to take *action* in the situation, to increased *knowledge* of ourselves and others, to a *sense of worth* and of the legitimacy of our feelings, and to the *desire to make more connections.* These *five good things* characterize a growth-fostering relationship (see also Frey, Beesley, & Newman, 2005).

Mutuality is thus a crucial element of growth that fosters relationships. It does not mean sameness or equality but rather a way of relating, a shared activity in which all are fully participating. In the creative process of mutuality, something new arises based on the contributions of each person. Individuality is not being sacrificed to the group; rather, we are being ourselves as much as possible while also responsibly responding to others. The self and other become "mutually forming processes" (Miller & Stiver, 1997).

Disconnections

The major source of psychological problems is *disconnection,* the break that is experienced when a person cannot engage in mutually empathetic and empowering relationships (Miller & Stiver, 1997). Disconnections can be either major or minor. Minor disconnections occur frequently and need not be problematic. They can even lead to growth and to improved connections, particularly if people feel safe enough to discuss the disconnection with someone who can hear and respond to the experience. The ability to reconnect after a disconnection is itself empowering. If disconnections continue over long periods of time, however, they are more difficult to resolve. They begin to appear to be natural, and a person may feel unjustified in being distressed over the disconnection. Disconnections pose the greatest problem in relationships of unequal power, because they hold the greatest potential for danger and harm to the less powerful individual. Attack or abuse in such relationships would be sources of major disconnections.

When other people do not share their feelings with us, we may feel alone in our emotions and angry because of their unresponsiveness. The situation will be compounded if we make an effort to reconnect and are further rebuffed. Because the feelings are ours, we may feel it is our problem, not the other person's. We move from feelings that are already difficult to handle, such as sadness or fear, to a much more complicated and confused combination of emotions.

Difficult feelings are best handled in connection with others. When children are not able to talk about their feelings—for example, their sadness at a death in the family—they feel frightened and confused. They also begin to believe that there is something wrong with them and their feelings. The ultimate outcome is psychological isolation, which is the most terrifying and damaging emotion that we can experience. More than just being alone, we are being actively prevented from connection and are powerless to change that situation. After experiencing repeated disconnections, individuals will still try to connect in whatever ways they possibly can. If they are powerless to change the relationship, they will try to change themselves. In order to be what others seem to want, they will deny their own feelings. On the surface, the person may seem to be compliant, but internally he or she experiences increasing disconnection and fear of trying to establish new connections. Anger is

In relationships of unequal power, disconnections can be quite threatening to the less powerful individual.

inevitable. It becomes difficult to form accurate relationship images of oneself or others. This leads to the *central relational paradox:* People who have experienced trouble in relationships continue to try to make new connections, but they are hindered from doing so because they cannot permit themselves to acknowledge the full range of their experience and feelings as they need to do in order to establish relationships.

Disconnections and violations happen to people at all ages; however, our most basic relational images are created early in life, when we are the most vulnerable to disconnection and least able to form new connections that might change the images. Thus abused or raped women who suffered from disconnections in childhood often believe they are unworthy and to blame for what happened to them. Much of the psychological suffering caused by depression, addictions, and eating disorders comes from trauma created by disconnected, distressed families. Dysfunctional relationships are at the core of many of our current social problems: incest, sexual abuse, and violence. In the past, clinicians commonly blamed the early mother-child relationship for problems primarily perpetuated by men and stemming from dysfunctional relationships between children and men rather than between children and their mothers. Too often, mothers were given full responsibility for child rearing without having necessary social support.

Disconnected families are characterized by three outstanding patterns (Miller & Stiver, 1997): *secrecy,* which denies "unacceptable" reality; *parental inaccessibility,* which precludes mutually empathetic relationships; and *"parentification,"* which requires the child to act prematurely as the grown-up. A conspiracy of silence often arises in a family in which incest occurs. In milder forms, children may be admonished not to discuss something "outside of the family." Adult children of alcoholics testify to inaccessibility in their childhood homes, as alcohol renders a parent either barely present or eruptive and angry. Depression may also leave a parent unable to connect with children. In such households, children may be required to assume parental responsibility while they themselves are still in need of active parenting. The three patterns both arise from and perpetuate chronic disconnections.

People learn to survive disconnections. They develop strategies for staying out of relationships, such as emotionally disengaging through inattention, preoccupation, withdrawal, or the use of alcohol or drugs (Hartling, 2003a). They may develop a strategy of role-playing in order to win approval and give the illusion of connection. Role-playing may appear to be adaptive, but it does not permit authentic engagement. People may replicate earlier traumatic family interactions, preventing the development of current authentic relationships. These survival tactics leave people suffering, disempowered, and out of touch.

> **Thinking Critically**
>
> How have you experienced disconnections? See the Thinking Critically box "Disconnections and Connections."

PSYCHOTHERAPY

Fortunately, people can establish new relationships that will enable them to overcome the negative effects of disconnection. Studies of resilience in children show that resilience is enhanced by having a close relationship with at least one person. Temperament may play a role if it is a temperament that facilitates relationships. Some people can make far-reaching changes. Women in battered-women's shelters, for example, may, through mutual empathy, join together to take appropriate legal and political action.

Psychotherapy can provide a path to increased authentic connections (Miller & Stiver, 1997). The Stone Center group believes that most psychological problems are a result of the basic relational paradox: They are consequences of the effort to avoid engaging in relationships. The Stone Center group emphasizes identifying the origins of disconnection; the goal of therapy is to help the patient make mutual empathetic connections. Essentially, relational-cultural therapy creates a new relationship between therapist and patient that is crucial to the process of healing.

Traditional clinicians are trained to distance themselves from their feelings in order to be objective and neutral. In contrast, Stone Center therapists remain open to their own experiences and permit themselves to be moved by their patients' feelings. When a clinician is able to feel along with a patient, the therapist herself changes. The patient is aware of this and knows that she has had an effect on the therapist by expressing her feelings and thoughts; she is now making a connection that contradicts her earlier experiences. It is a process of "moving in relationship"; the therapist and patient are moving toward mutual empathy.

The therapist's responsibility is to facilitate the process of moving in relationship. The clinician can let the patient know when and how the patient is affecting her. This helps people believe that they can experience and sort out feelings with another person. One can acknowledge how difficult it is to feel critical or angry feelings, particularly in a therapy situation. The ability to do so enhances the therapeutic relationship, which is not simply the means to the end but "both the means and the end" (Miller & Stiver, 1997).

The therapy technique used by the Stone Center group transforms traditional psychotherapy concepts such as transference. In classical analysis, the therapist maintains an attitude of neutrality and objectivity to facilitate the patient's process of projecting feelings toward people in his or her past onto the therapist. Conversely, the Stone Center group

Thinking Critically

Disconnections and Connections

Think back to the last argument or disagreement you had in which you experienced a sense of disconnection and the feeling that you were misunderstood. Retrace the dialogue, both verbal and nonverbal, as best as you can, citing specific phrases, gestures, or actions of the parties involved.

Now think back to the last time you experienced a strong sense of connection and the feeling that you were totally understood. Retrace that dialogue, both verbal and nonverbal, as best as you can, citing specific phrases, gestures, or actions of the parties involved.

Compare those two experiences. Can you identify the elements of the dialogues that led to your feelings of connection or disconnection, of being understood or misunderstood? What was your role in these situations? When you felt misunderstood, what if anything did you do to bridge the differences? Did you try to make the situation better or worse? Likewise, when you felt connectedness, what if anything did you do to foster that feeling? Can you detect patterns of behavior that might give rise to feelings of connection or disconnection?

---

believes that neutrality can hinder the process of therapy because it prevents the patient from seeing the differences between the current relationship and past ones. The safety that an empathetic relationship provides actually facilitates transference, letting the patient explore previous relational images and begin to change them. Rather than trying to interpret the transference, which could be perceived as criticism, the group believes that being empathetic to the power of the patient's earlier relational image and conveying respect for how she dealt with the earlier circumstances communicates the difference between the therapeutic relationship and earlier ones.

Freud viewed countertransference, the clinician's conscious and unconscious feelings about the patient, as an impediment. The Stone Center group believes that countertransference may either facilitate or impede the therapist's ability to connect with a patient. The clinician must pay attention to any feelings of disconnection she might be experiencing and must focus on moving back toward connection. It is important to take seriously the paradox that patients want to make connections but are afraid to establish them.

The Stone Center clinicians disclose more of their own feelings than do classical psychoanalysts. They recognize that silence and nondisclosure may have a negative effect on therapy and lead to disconnection. If a situation in the therapist's life makes it difficult for her to be fully attentive (e.g., a death in the family), it may help for her to admit this to the patient. Too much disclosure, however, can be burdensome and overwhelming to a patient (see also Miller, et al., 1999).

The process of therapy is difficult and demanding. Painful feelings emerge that would be impossible for a patient to explore except in an empathetic relationship with another person. The clinician's role, however, is not simply to be nice and caring. In order to move in relationship, the therapist must try to share the other person's experience in all its facets, including the cultural matrix in which it arises. The relationship of the therapist and patient is structured by the demands of therapy, and its goal is the growth of the patient (see also Stiver, Rosen, Surrey, & Miller, 2001). The limits of the therapeutic relationship must be recognized: It should not be seen as a friendship or a replacement for family.

Furthermore, although the relationship is mutual, a power differential obviously exists. The therapist needs to be aware of this and be willing to discuss it. The therapist and patient are partners in the therapeutic endeavor; the sole difference is that it is the therapist's responsibility to promote the movement toward more connection in the relationship.

Other Applications

Effective therapy leads to the ability to forge deeper connections with others and with the larger community. Following therapy, people are often motivated to begin to rectify deeper disconnections in the larger world. Therapy can be helpful when the culture has been hurtful (Walker, 2002). Because our surroundings affect us, both patients and therapists need to be among colleagues and peers with whom they can share their experiences. Twelve-step groups patterned after Alcoholics Anonymous are an effective example because of the mutual empathy and empowerment they foster.

The relational model reconceives many traditional concepts such as anger, dependence, courage, shame, and sexual desire and orientation. *Anger* is a necessary signal that something is wrong in a relationship and needs to be changed (Miller & Surrey, 1997). Women have a tendency to confuse anger with violence or oppression (Bernadez, 1988), and they have not been trained to assert themselves in appropriate and effective ways. *Dependence* is redefined as a process of letting other people help us to cope physically and emotionally with experiences and tasks when we do not have sufficient skill, confidence, or energy to do so by ourselves. This definition permits us to see ourselves as "enhanced and empowered through the very process of counting on others for help" (Stiver, 1991b). *Courage* can be redefined in a contextual relational manner so that it no longer refers to a solitary accomplishment but to an action taken in spite of fear and supported by the encouragement of others (Jordan, 1990, 2003a, 2003b, 2005). *Self-esteem* emerges from relational confidence rather than mastery or self-efficacy (Jordan, 1994). *Shame* is a deep yearning for connection while perceiving oneself as unworthy of it (Jordan, 1997b). The expression of *sexual desire* can be seen in a framework of empathic communication rather than one of achievement and performance (Jordan, 1997a). Rather than quickly dismissing the *fusion,* or intense intimacy, of lesbian relationships as pathological, one might view it as a pattern that allows women to express their relational strength (Mencher, 1997). *Power,* a capacity to produce change, has been reconceived, thanks to the modeling of people such as Mamie Bradley, the mother of Emmit Till. She refused to be shamed into silence following the racist murder of her son, who supposedly whistled at a white woman. Instead she delayed the funeral and allowed people to view his mutilated corpse and journalists to photograph the body and publish her son's story. She publicly shared her grief; her courageous action helped to fuel the civil rights movement and illustrated a power that is closer to love (Walker, 2003). Change, however, is not effected primarily through individual heroic acts, but rather through joining in community and changing from "power-over" actions to mutually empowering relationships (Miller, 2003; see also Aspy, 2004), which can strengthen resilience to trauma and help us to cope with the uncertainties of the current world (Hartling, 2003b).

Such reconception permits us to recognize how many behaviors of women that were previously seen as weakness or pathological are in fact "seeds of strength."

For example,

> a very poor immigrant woman of color had an alcoholic husband who beat her. She still managed to hold the family together and to foster her three children's growth in many ways. In clinical conferences and other settings she was labeled dependent or masochistic, or in more recent times her behavior might be called "enabling." The many abilities she demonstrated in surviving, and also making possible her children's development, were not investigated or even recognized. (Fletcher, Jordan, & Miller, 2000)

The Stone Center has been using the relational-cultural approach to study the workplace and large organizations in order to understand discrimination, appreciate gender differences, and revise social structures (Fletcher, 1996, Fletcher, Jordan, & Miller, 2000; Hartling & Sparks, 2003). Using structured observation of what people actually do in a natural work setting, one study sought to explore the specific ways women act in the workplace and their underlying beliefs about their actions. The study found that typically when women try to enact a model of relational growth, the rationale for their actions "gets disappeared" and is construed as private-sphere activity (see Figure 7.2). For example, in the context of an engineering firm, an effort to improve communication across departments may be seen as inap-

In relational-cultural theory, courage is no longer a solitary accomplishment but an action taken in spite of fear and supported by the encouragement of others. These women are training for a wilderness hike to benefit Elizabeth Stone House, a residence for women in emotional distress and a shelter for women who have been abused.

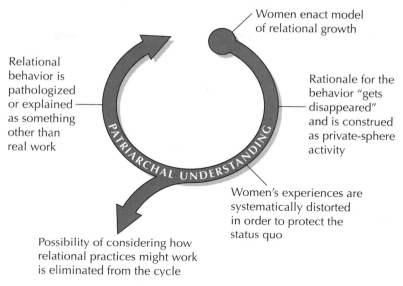

Women enact model
of relational growth

Relational
behavior is
pathologized
or explained
as something
other than
real work

Rationale for the
behavior "gets
disappeared"
and is construed
as private-sphere
activity

PATRIARCHAL UNDERSTANDING

Women's experiences are
systematically distorted
in order to protect the
status quo

Possibility of considering how
relational practices might work
is eliminated from the cycle

FIGURE 7.2 A "DISAPPEARING ACT"

When women try to enact a model of relational growth in the workplace, it "gets disappeared"
and is distorted.

propriate because such communication is not part of the job description. Patriarchal
understanding eliminates the possibility of considering how relational practices might
work in organizations, and women's experience is systematically distorted to socially enforce disconnection and protect the status quo. The behavior itself is either pathologized
or explained away as something other than real work (Fletcher, Jordan & Miller, 2000;
Robb, 2006).

In recent years, relational-cultural theory has also been used to explore parenting-in-
connection. Dooley and Fedele (1999) describe how a mother helped her young teenage son
move through the cycle of connection, disconnection, and reconnection when his best
friend's dog died. She encouraged him to contact the friend and give him a gift in memory
of the dog, suggestions that he initially rebuffed. However, she continued to encourage him
and permitted the mother-son relationship to be a safe context within which to move from
disconnection into stronger connection. Dooley and Fedele have developed the Mother-
Son Project to help mothers raise sons of all ages into adolescents who will tune in to, rather
than tune out of, relationships and into adult men who can stay connected.

Incorporating the specific experiences of women of color and lesbians has deepened
RCT (Jordan, 1997a). In particular, it has been possible to consider more fully the complicated issues of power and privilege that arise at the crossroads of racism, classism, hetero-
sexism, and sexism (Miller, 2003; Jordan & Hartling, 2002). Turner (1997) has shown how a
relational approach validates significant aspects of African American women's experience;
it is also enriched by including that experience (Jenkins, 2000). Study groups have also been
formed in which women with chronic illnesses or disabilities are the participants. Although
Stone Center group members believe that their general statements are meaningful, they

Thinking Critically

How can we foster dialogue in diversity? See the Thinking Critically box "Working with Diversity in Relationships."

realize that their relational approach must be integrated with the experience of marginalized groups such as Native and Asian American women (Portman & Garrett, 2005; Walker, 1999, 2001; Walker & Miller, 2001 West, 2005).

Tatum (1997) suggests that the practice of racism is like continually breathing in smog. It destroys both the oppressed and the oppressor. It is not an individual problem but a social one. A concerted effort must be made to develop understanding across different groups, emphasizing that empathy involves appreciating the differences of others as well as acknowledging similarities.

The Stone Center group continues to explore the ways that culture stratified by class, race, and gender affects the development of all groups (see Jordan, Walker, & Hartling, 2004; Walker & Rosen, 2004). In the last several years, work has focused on analyses of power imbalances of marginalization, and of the importance of sociopolitical context.

THE NEUROBIOLOGICAL BASIS OF RELATIONSHIPS

With the advent of functional brain imaging, research in neurobiology has provided substantial confirmation of the theoretical work of relational-cultural theory, supporting its central premise that relationships are at the core of human development. Alan Schore (1994) summarizes an abundance of studies showing how the relationship between mother and child actually influences the way the child's brain develops. When mother and baby are engaged in mutual responsiveness, both the mother's and the baby's brains change and grow. The mother's face stimulates chemicals in the brain, arousing and energizing regions of it. The prefrontal cortex matures through interaction with others. Our brains literally grow in connection and we are hardwired to connect. Daniel Siegel (1999) has further examined and explained how the prefrontal areas of the brain develop through social interpersonal experience. Parent-child interactions shape the social brain. Without the right kind of social developmental experiences, the mind cannot develop to its fullest potential.

The discovery of **mirror neurons,** initially seen in monkeys in the early 1990s and then linked to human evolution (di Pellegrino, Fadiga, Gallese, & Rizzolatti, 1992), gives us a glimpse of the workings of primal empathy. "Each time an individual sees an action done by another individual, neurons that represent that action are activated in the motor cortex" (Rizzolatti & Craighero, 2004 p. 172). Mirror neurons enable us to mimic other people's emotions and actions. They also help us sense what other people intend so that we can shape our responses to them, they contribute to a felt sense of connection. Mirror neurons lead to a host of human abilities, such as our being able to imitate and learn from each other, that permit the development and transmission of social culture (Ramachandran, 2000, see also Goleman, 2006). Research on autistics, who lack empathy and have trouble understanding others' feelings, indicates a dysfunctional mirror-neuron system.

Positive social interactions discharge brain chemicals that are pleasurable and energy mobilizing; negative interactions, such as shame and disconnection, release chemicals that decrease pleasure and inhibit energy. Ideally parents help children stay within optimal levels of arousal so that the brain develops resilience and can easily transition from positive to negative and back to positive emotion. Undue stress and early unresponsive relationships can lead to chemical alterations that cause neuronal cell death in emotional centers of the brain and permanent changes in receptors that enable us to feel pleasure (Banks, 2004).

Thinking Critically

Working with Diversity in Relationships

Stephen Bergman and Janet Surrey (1997) use the following questions to foster dialogue between men and women.

1. Name three strengths the other gender group brings to relationships.
2. What do you most want to understand about the other gender group?
3. What do you most want the other gender group to understand about you?

First answer the questions individually and then in groups of the same gender before attempting to share the answers with an entire group of members of both genders. In the discussion, pay particular attention to the impasses that arise and may lead to disconnection and to the ways in which the different groups seek to resolve them. The impasses in the groups are easier to recognize as different relational styles meet one another. Two common impasses that emerge in gender groups are the *dread/anger impasse,* in which men retreat and women begin to get angry, and the *product/process impasse,* in which women try to open up the process of communication and men try to fix a problem. It is important to experience the conflict without negatively expressing it and to work on staying in connection in order to foster understanding, curiosity, and empathy for the other group. This activity can also be adapted to working with members of diverse groups of different ethnicities, religions, and orientations.

SOURCE: Bergman, S. J., & Surrey, J. L. (1997). The woman-man relationship: Impasses and possibilities. In J. V. Jordan (Ed.), Women's Growth in Diversity, (pp. 260–287). New York: Guilford Press.

Others have also shown that disconnection resulting from social pain is detrimental to our brains and our mental health. Eisenberger and Lieberman (2005) have demonstrated that social pain (the pain from rejection) stimulates the same area of the brain (the anterior cingulated) as physical pain. The pain of social rejection is every bit as real as physical pain. Furthermore, the anticipation of social exclusion stimulates social pain. Research with persons who suffer from schizophrenia, posttraumatic stress disorder (PTSD), childhood violence, and/or sexual abuse also substantiates the damaging effects of negative social interactions. In a continuing or severely traumatic stressful environment, too many chemical neurotransmitters are released into the synapse between nerve endings in the brain, overwhelming and interfering with the brain's ability to regulate its receptors and eventually leading to alternating patterns of depletion and overstimulation that impair the brain's ability to communicate and respond adequately even in normal situations (Banks, 2001, 2004).

Social relationships are like air and water, essential for human well-being. We need growth-fostering connection with other people throughout our lives. Relationships characterized by mutual respect, mutual influence, and mutual caring support our physical, emotional, and neurological well-being. Healing involves building resilience in relationships and shifting our brain chemistry, shaping new neural pathways and connections. Fortunately, the plasticity of the brain, its ability to change in response to an appropriate environment, permits healing. Rather than reducing psychological problems to malfunctioning neu-rotransmitters and synapses simply treated by other chemicals such as drugs, neurochemi-cal discoveries support a relational posture and treatment in psychology (Robb, 2006).

Human Relations Theories

While grateful for the substantial support that has come from neurobiological re-search, human relations theorists do not insist on a scientific basis for their work. As clinicians, their work is based on empirical observation. They also emphasize the need for an interdisciplinary perspective, as is clearly seen in Chodorow's work.

Many variables—such as biological, cognitive, cultural, sociological, and his-torical factors—are addressed. The theories also speak to issues that concern us today, such as personality disorders that have become more pervasive and the need to rethink the issues of gender and parenting. The theories have a heuristic value, stimulating thinking among historians, sociologists, literary people, and philoso-phers, as well as psychoanalysts. Psychoanalysis is a good example of a science that has resisted the tenets of natural science and maintained aspects of the literary and descriptive language of everyday life (Jager, 1989).

This is not to say that these theorists ignore empirical data or shun verification of their concepts. However, they believe that a narrow scientific methodology is not appropriate for the study of personality, and they urge a broader approach for the social scientist, such as is illustrated in *organic inquiry,* a developing qualitative research method that draws on women's spirituality and transpersonal psychology (i.e., Clements, Ettling, Jenett, & Shields, 1998).

Their theories have not generated much laboratory research because of their lack of specificity and operational definitions. Complex concepts such as Klein's and Kernberg's *splitting* do not readily lend themselves to precise measurement. Longitudinal studies could provide us with information on the validity of some of their ideas, such as Chodorow's notion of the reproduction of mothering, but such studies would be expensive and lengthy. Researchers have largely focused on other personality constructs that are easier to translate into operational terms.

The *Mutual Psychological Development Questionnaire* (MPDQ), a standardized self-report inventory, has been developed by the Stone Center group to measure perceived mutuality in close relationships. The MPDQ permits empirical research that may help answer questions about how people perceive their intimate relation-ships and may also be useful in the clinical setting, although it was initially devel-oped using nonclinical populations. As the MPDQ is applied to relationships in other populations, it may help us understand gender, racial, and ethnic contextual factors that inform the relational aspects of psychological growth.

The development of the Relational Health Indices (RHI), which assess three dimensions of growth that foster connections within the relational model (engage-ment, authenticity, and empowerment), may help increase our understanding of the dynamics of human relationships, especially among women (Liang et al., 2002).

The work of the object relations and relational-cultural theorists has had an enormous impact in the clinical area. In 2001, the acknowledgment that the impacts of the terrorist attacks on September 11 were both psychological and physical, the awareness of and respect for effects of PTSD, and the recognition that immediately providing therapy and talking about a traumatic experience could begin to heal it were all innovative ideas that grew out of the relational movement (Robb, 2006). In a culture that has degraded the relational, this signified an incredible change. Much of the work of the human relations theories is being integrated into a variety of therapeutic approaches and has been particularly helpful in clarifying syndromes such as those presented by victims of trauma and abuse. Dysfunctional family systems—those having problems related to incest, addiction, or such traumatic experiences as Holocaust survival, for instance—can be more clearly understood in relational terms, as can the processes of recovery.

The current work in psychoanalysis is imaginative and creative. These theorists have helped to maintain the viability and relevance of Freudian psychoanalytic theory in the contemporary world. For all the criticism of psychoanalytically oriented theories that declares the lack of "'scientifically demonstrated' hypotheses—it is also a commonly overlooked fact that none of the modern competitive theories (cognitive, behavioral, or humanistic) have withstood similar rigid scientific tests to validate their claims to legitimacy as acceptable theories underlying the conceptualization and application of psychotherapy" (Kelly, 1991). Psychoanalysis is far from dead.

Philosophical Assumptions

Where do the human relations theories stand on basic philosophical issues? See the Philosophical Assumptions box "Examining Human Relations Theories."

The paradigm shift suggested by the Stone Center group is a major alteration in basic philosophical assumptions and underpinnings that has enormous potential to reshape the way in which human beings in Western cultures conceive of themselves. By putting the primary emphasis on the relationship as the origin and matrix of human development, the group challenges the "I"-centeredness

Philosophical Assumptions

Examining Human Relations Theories

Many of the differences among personality theories can be attributed to fundamental differences in philosophical assumptions. Which of the basic philosophical issues, described in the introductory chapter and summarized on the inside back cover, seem to be clearly important to object relations and relational-cultural theorists in the development of their theories? How, for example, does the object relations theorists' emphasis on intrapsychic dynamics and interpersonal relations influence their stance on heredity versus environment and optimism versus pessimism? How does the new paradigm proposed by the relational-cultural theorists at the Stone Center influence their view of freedom versus determinism and reactivity versus proactivity? Do their theories address any other philosophical assumptions or suggest any new polarities? Rate the object relations and relational-cultural theories on a scale of 1 to 5 on those philosophical assumptions that you feel their theories apply to most. Compare your ratings of object relations and relational-cultural theories with your own philosophical assumptions. Did your study of object relations and relational-cultural theories lead you to change any of your assumptions? Why or why not?

that has pervaded Western conceptualizations of and thoughts about the person and personality. This refocus not only has tremendous implications for understanding ourselves, but also has vast potential to be a very curative and healing force in human nature at a time when such a power is sorely needed.

 TO LEARN MORE about recent research at the Stone Center and about relationships in psychotherapy, and for a list of suggested readings, visit the *Personality Theories* textbook website at **college.cengage.com/pic/engler8e.**

Summary

1. **Object relations** (p. 175) theorists look at how people develop intrapsychic patterns of living out of their early relationships with significant others, particularly their mothers.

2. Melanie Klein introduced the concept of **splitting** (p. 176) and emphasized the interaction of unconscious fantasies and real experiences in the development of children's object relations.

3. Margaret Mahler explored the processes of **separation-individuation** (p. 177) by which the child emerges from a symbiotic fusion with the mother and develops individual characteristics. Mahler constructed a sequence of stages through which the ego passes in the process of becoming an individual.

4. Heinz Kohut accounted for **narcissism** (p. 179) and narcissistic character disorders that occur when an individual fails to develop an independent sense of self. Kohut has developed psychoanalytic techniques designed to work through transferences and resistances stemming from pre-Oedipal phases of development.

5. Otto Kernberg elaborated on the notion of splitting to describe the interpersonal relationships of patients with **borderline personality disorder** (p. 181), and he developed a method of treatment called **transference-focused psychotherapy** (p. 181). More recently, Kernberg has focused on aggression, and he has suggested changes to Freud's drive theory.

6. Nancy Chodorow believes that mothering by women reproduces cyclically, producing daughters with the desire and capacity to mother but sons whose nurturing abilities are limited and repressed. Social and historical forces are insufficient to account for gender development. A person's gender is a fusion of personal and cultural meaning.

7. The Stone Center group is a group of women who have developed a new collaborative theory of human development within relationships.

8. Jean Baker Miller's thesis is that both sexes have been constrained by a framework of inequity and that the concepts of affiliation and relationship are central to the development of human beings.

9. The Stone Center group makes a paradigm shift away from a concept of separation-individuation and individualistic values to a concept of **relationship-differentiation** (p. 188) and relational values.

10. According to the Stone Center group, **connections** (p. 188) are the basic origins of growth. **Empathy** (p. 190), experiencing the feelings and thoughts of another while being aware of

one's own different feelings and thoughts, fosters connections and leads to growth within relationships.

11. The Stone Center group sees the major source of psychological problems as **disconnection** (p. 188), which prevent people from engaging in mutually empathic relationships.

12. Psychotherapy can change and overcome the negative effects of disconnection by establishing new relationships that empower individuals. The emphasis is on creating a new relational experience that fosters healing.

13. Research in neurobiology provides confirmation of RCT. Our brains grow through interactions with others. **Mirror neurons** (p. 198) facilitate our felt sense of connection. Positive social interactions discharge pleasurable chemicals that build connection; negative social interactions lead to chemical changes destructive to emotional centers and neurotransmitter receptors.

14. The human relations theorists do not insist on a simply scientific basis for their work but make explicit philosophical assumptions. They include many variables in their discussion, believing that a narrow scientific methodology is not appropriate for the study of personality. Their work has had an enormous impact in clinical psychology.

Personal Experiences

1. In the context of object relations theory, an object is primarily a person, but it can also be something inanimate, such as a pacifier or blanket. What things did you form attachments to as a child? Try to list three of them. What purpose did those objects serve in your life? Why did you ascribe so much value to them? Do you still tend to form attachments to things today? If so, do you feel that your attachments to these objects are serving the same purposes and needs as your childhood attachments?

2. Much of object relations theory focuses on how we come to view ourselves through the eyes of other people. How we come to understand ourselves is in part determined by how people react to us. For example, if a little girl is consistently told she is pretty rather than smart, she will likely come to think of herself as the former rather than the latter—even though she could be both. Similarly, if a little boy is consistently called stupid, he will likely come to think of himself as such—even if in actuality he's of normal intelligence. Think of three words to describe yourself. Then think back to when you were a child. How did you first come to understand that these words were applicable to you?

3. Chodorow's reproduction of mothering theory suggests that daughters and sons are raised in different ways, such that a daughter's childhood prepares a girl for work in the private, domestic sphere and a son's childhood prepares a boy to work in the public sphere (see Figure 7.1). Ultimately, Chodorow believes, the way we raise our sons and daughters perpetuates gender inequality in society as a whole. Think about your own childhood in the context of Chodorow's theory. Were you raised in the manner that Chodorow discusses? If you have brothers or sisters, were there differences based on gender in how your parents treated them and you? Ask your parents about their childhood experiences. Compare your parents' childhood to Chodorow's theory. Are gender norms changing or staying the same?

4. The Stone Center group's relational-cultural theory challenges traditional Western conceptions of self. Previous theories suggested that human beings primarily seek self-gratification and self-sufficiency. The Stone Center group posits that human beings primarily seek relationships with others. Relational-cultural theory inverts traditional paradigms that claim "health" is predicated on self-sufficiency and "ill health" on dependency. According to RCT, "health" reflects relational competence, and "ill health" results from disconnection from others (see Figure 7.1). Test this theory for yourself. When do you feel most healthy and secure—when you and significant others are involved in mutually healthy relationships or when you are acting independently? Recall the time when you felt most depressed and the time you felt most happy. What was your relational context at each time?

5. How pervasive has the masculine model been in your upbringing and thinking? Relational-cultural theory suggests that many large organizations function from a masculine bias—that the patriarchal system disempowers women and distorts their values and experience. Think about the places where you've worked. Did women's ideas and preferences tend to be dismissed in favor of long-standing gendered models of private and public spheres? For example, have you seen a double standard in the assessment of male and female managers? Have you found yourself thinking in stereotypical terms? Try to explain the origin of your beliefs in the comparative abilities of men and women.

PART FOUR

Behavior and Learning Theories

One of the most puzzling questions in personality theorizing has been the dichotomy between internal and external determinants of behavior. How much of behavior is genetically hardwired and how much of it is environmentally shaped? A dominant trend in American psychology during the twentieth century was the behaviorist movement, with its emphasis on learning and experience as the primary forces that shape behavior. Rather than postulate complex personality structures and dynamics within the individual, behavior and learning theories focus on those factors in the environment that determine an individual's conduct. However, the either/or nature of this debate has been mitigated in light of more recent dispositional theories in which a combination of both biology and society, as well as other factors, is involved. There is now a greater recognition of the complex biological and social contexts that shape human behavior.

Most behavior and learning theories begin in the psychological laboratory, where infrahuman (lower-than-human) species, such as rats or pigeons, are studied. Theoretical speculation is avoided in favor of careful observation and experimentation. Behavior theorists have been committed to a rigorous methodology, trying to perfect the techniques of psychology and raise them to the sophistication of the natural sciences. This has permitted precision and economy in theory construction as well as clear empirical foundations for the major concepts of their theories. Part IV presents major contributions to the behavior and learning approach to personality theory and shows their outstanding influence.

CHAPTER 8

Experimental Analysis of Behavior

- **John Dollard and Neal Miller**
- **B. F. Skinner**

1. Describe how behavior and learning theorists study personality experimentally.
2. Identify the early contributions of Pavlov, Watson, Thorndike, and Hull.
3. Define and give examples of **habits, drives,** and **reinforcers.**
4. Describe the four main conceptual parts of the learning process.
5. Discuss findings from research into the learning process.
6. Explain how Dollard and Miller have integrated learning theory and psychoanalysis.
7. Describe Dollard and Miller's practice of psychotherapy.
8. Evaluate Dollard and Miller's theory from the viewpoints of philosophy, science, and art.
9. Explain why Skinner emphasizes **overt behavior** and avoids developing a theory of personality.
10. Describe the process of **operant conditioning,** and compare it with **classical conditioning.**
11. Distinguish among different schedules and types of **reinforcement,** and indicate their effectiveness.
12. Discuss Skinner's concept of **behavior modification,** and explain how it has been successfully employed.
13. Describe Skinner's concept of a utopian society.
14. Show how Skinner's position includes philosophical assumptions as well as scientific statements.
15. Evaluate Skinner's theory from the viewpoints of philosophy, science, and art.

John Dollard, Neal Miller, and B. F. Skinner are behavior and learning theorists who emphasize experience and learning as the primary forces that shape human behavior. Dollard and Miller's orientation has been called *psychoanalytic learning theory* because it is a creative attempt to bring together the basic concepts of Freudian psychoanalytic theory with the ideas, language, methods, and results of experimental laboratory research on learning and behavior. Skinner espoused a point of view now known as **radical behaviorism.** Believing that a stimulus-response theory of psychology can account for all of the overt behaviors that psychologists seek to explain, Skinner omitted the psychoanalytic underpinnings and simply relied on behaviorist principles. In doing so, he suggested that the term *personality* and personality theories are superfluous. However, his work includes points of interest to students of personality and has had an impact on subsequent developments in the field. Thus Skinner is typically included in books on personality theories.

Dollard and Miller's and Skinner's views on personality stem from experimental and laboratory procedures rather than clinical investigations. However, the principles that they developed have been widely applied in areas such as education, psychotherapy, industry, and corrections.

The Experimental Analysis of Behavior

Behavior and learning theories have their roots in a philosophical point of view known as **empiricism,** which suggests that all knowledge originates in experience. John Locke (1632–1704), one of the first empiricist philosophers, suggested that at birth the mind is a blank slate on which sensory experience writes in a number of different ways. Locke's phrase

John Dollard (left) and Neal Miller transformed Freud's concepts into the terms of learning theory and experimental psychology.

"blank slate" (or tabula rasa) expressed the philosophical view of empiricism in its classic form, just as Descartes's "I think, therefore I am" expressed the essence of rationalism.

Behavior and learning theories hold that valid knowledge arises out of experience and needs to be continually checked against it. Thus behavior and learning theories are largely based on the experimental analysis of behavior. The behavior of individual organisms is carefully studied in controlled laboratory settings, and the relationship between the behavior and factors in that environment is articulated.

Although behavioral theory is singularly American, the historical background of the approach begins in Russia, where Ivan Pavlov (1849–1936) demonstrated and articulated a form of learning known as **classical conditioning** (see Figure 8.1) (see also Dinsmoor, 2004). In a classic laboratory setting, Pavlov (1927) took a hungry dog and presented it with food, an **unconditioned stimulus** that normally elicits salivation, an **unconditioned,** or automatic, **response.** Then he simultaneously paired the food with the sound of a bell, a *neutral stimulus* that does not normally elicit salivation. The dog salivated to the paired food and sound of the bell. After several presentations of both food and bell, Pavlov was able simply to present the sound of the bell, and the dog salivated. The sound of the bell had become a **conditioned stimulus** that elicited a **conditioned response.** In other words, Pavlov showed that by pairing an unconditioned stimulus with a neutral stimulus, he could elicit a response that previously would have been elicited only by the original stimulus.

John Watson (1878–1958), the father of American **behaviorism,** expanded classical conditioning into a theory of behaviorism (Watson & Raynor, 1925) in which he recommended that psychology emphasize the study of overt rather than covert behavior. Watson's approach to classical conditioning was very important and laid the foundation for subsequent therapeutic techniques based on conditioning, such as those discussed later in this chapter. Behaviorism was quickly adopted by many American psychologists and became the dominant movement in psychology in America. Watson's thinking had a tremendous influence on advertising, and even today, the distinctive methodology of American psychology reflects Watson's emphasis on objectivity and extrospection.

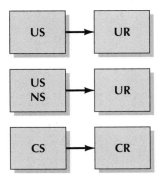

FIGURE **8.1** CLASSICAL CONDITIONING

In classical conditioning a neutral stimulus (NS) is paired with an unconditioned stimulus (US) that elicits an unconditioned response (UR) until it becomes a conditioned stimulus (CS) that elicits a conditioned response (CR).

Another figure in the history of learning theory is Edwin Thorndike (1874–1949), who conducted several experiments with animals in order to gain further understanding of the learning process. He formulated many important laws of learning (1913). The law that is particularly important for our purposes is the **law of effect,** which states that when a behavior or performance is accompanied by satisfaction, it tends to happen again. If the performance is accompanied by frustration, it tends to decrease. We now recognize that the law of effect is not necessarily universal. Sometimes frustration leads to increased efforts to perform. Still, most psychologists believe that the law of effect is generally true.

John Dollard (1900–1980) and Neal Miller (1909–2002)

BIOGRAPHICAL BACKGROUND

John Dollard and Neal Miller were both born in Wisconsin. They taught and worked together at the Institute of Human Relations at Yale University, which was founded in 1933 in an effort to explore interdisciplinary relationships among psychology, psychiatry, sociology, and anthropology. Both men underwent psychoanalytic training, each held a number of significant positions, and each authored several books or articles, in addition to their affiliation and collaboration at the Institute of Human Relations. Dollard and Miller's joint efforts resulted in a personality theory based on Clark Hull's reinforcement theory of learning and Freud's psychoanalytic theory. This integration resulted in a behaviorist theory that became representative of the mainstream of American psychology throughout most of the twentieth century.

John Dollard, born in 1900, was granted the A.B. from the University of Wisconsin and the M.A. and Ph.D. from the University of Chicago. His primary interests were in sociology and anthropology, and he was a strong advocate of interdisciplinary studies, which is evident in his 1937 field study, *Caste and Class in a Southern Town,* which depicted the position of black Americans in that period. The book, a courageous study (Miller, 1982) of black social immobility, was banned in Georgia and South Africa and later influenced civil rights activists and programs (Adams & Gorton, 2004). Dollard, an early pioneer in integrating the social sciences, died in 1980.

Neal Miller, born in 1909, was granted the B.S. from the University of Washington, the M.A. from Stanford, and the Ph.D. from Yale. His primary interests lay in experimental psychology. After thirty years on the faculty at Yale University, Miller taught for fifteen more years at Rockefeller University and then returned to Yale as a research affiliate in the psychology department. In 1964 he received the National Medal of Science, the highest scientific honor given in the United States, from President Lyndon Johnson. He died at age ninety-two in 2002 after an enormously productive and influential life as a psychologist, neuroscientist, statesman, and educator (Coons, 2002).

HABITS, DRIVES, AND THE LEARNING PROCESS

Dollard and Miller emphasize the role of learning in personality and place less stress on personality structure. They suggest (1950) that the structure of personality can be defined very simply as habits.

In the context of Dollard and Miller's theory, **habit** refers to some kind of learned association between a stimulus and a response that makes them occur together frequently. Habits are temporary structures because they can appear and disappear: Because they are learned, they can also be unlearned. This is a much simpler concept of the structure of personality than we have encountered before. The primary concern of Dollard and Miller's theory is to specify those conditions in the environment that encourage the acquisition of habits.

The primary dynamic underlying personality development and the acquisition of habits is **drive reduction** (1950). Dollard and Miller also drew heavily on Clark Hull (1884–1952), whose systematic theory of Pavlovian learning (1943), was based on the concept of drive reduction. A **drive** is a strong stimulation that produces discomfort, such as hunger. Hull believed that learning occurs only if a response of an organism is followed by the reduction of some need or drive. The infant learns to suck the breast or a bottle of milk in order to relieve hunger. If sucking the breast or bottle did not result in some drive or need reduction, the infant would not continue to perform that activity. Dollard and Miller point out that reducing a drive is reinforcing to an individual, and thus an individual will behave in ways that relieve the tension created by strong drives.

Primary drives are those associated with physiological processes that are necessary for an organism's survival, such as the drives of hunger, thirst, and the need for sleep. We rarely observe primary drives in a direct form because society has developed some means of reducing the drive before it becomes overwhelming. Thus primary drives, by and large, are satisfied through secondary drives. **Secondary drives** are learned on the basis of primary ones. Dollard and Miller consider them to be elaborations of the primary drives. An example of a secondary drive is being motivated to eat at one's usual dinner hour or wanting to earn money in order to buy food.

Dollard and Miller also distinguish between primary and secondary reinforcers. A **reinforcer** is any event that increases the likelihood of a particular response. **Primary reinforcers** are those that reduce primary drives, such as food, water, or need for sleep. **Secondary reinforcers** are originally neutral, but they acquire reward value when they are associated with primary reinforcers. Money is a secondary reinforcer because you can use it to buy food. A mother's smile or a word of praise is also a secondary reinforcer, associated with a state of physical well-being.

We acquire habits and develop specific behavioral responses through the process of learning. As infants each of us begins life with the basic equipment needed to reduce our primary drives: reflex responses and an innate hierarchy of response. **Reflex** responses are automatic responses to specific stimuli. All of us blink automatically to avoid an irritant to the eye or sneeze to eliminate an irritant to the nose. Such reflexes are important for our survival. **Hierarchy of response** refers to a tendency for certain responses to occur before others. For example, an animal runs to avoid a shock rather than cringe and bear it in pain. If a response is unsuccessful, however, an organism will try the next response in the hierarchy. Learning, in part, involves reinforcing and/or rearranging the response hierarchy.

Dollard and Miller (1950) suggest that the learning process can be broken down into four main conceptual parts (see Figure 8.2):

1. A **drive,** as we have already seen, is a stimulus impelling a person to act, but in no way does the drive direct or specify behavior. It simply impels.

2. A **cue** is a specific stimulus that tells the organism when, where, and how to re-

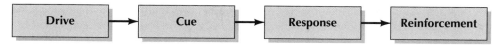

FIGURE 8.2 A SIMPLE DIAGRAM OF THE LEARNING PROCESS

In the process of learning, one *wants* something (DRIVE), *notices* something (CUE), *does* something (RESPONSE), and *gets* something (REINFORCEMENT).

spond. The ringing of a bell or the time on a clock is a cue to students to enter or leave the classroom.

3. A **response** is one's reaction to the cue. Because these responses occur in a hierarchy, we can rank a response according to its probability of occurring. But this innate hierarchy can be changed through learning.

4. **Reinforcement** refers to the effect of the response. Effective reinforcement consists of drive reduction. If a response is not reinforced by satisfying a drive, it will undergo **extinction.** Extinction does not eliminate a response but merely inhibits it, enabling another response to grow stronger and supersede it in the response hierarchy. If present responses are not reinforcing, the individual is placed in a **learning dilemma** and will try different responses until one is developed that satisfies the drive.

Dollard and Miller suggest that all human behavior can be comprehended in terms of the learning process. It is through the learning process that one acquires secondary drives. These drives may form a very complex system, but the underlying process by which they are developed is essentially the same: drive, cue, response, reinforcement. Even our higher mental processes can be understood in terms of the learning process. Thoughts are *cue-producing responses* in the brain. Reasoning consists of internal chains of drive, cue, response, and reinforcement, in which one thought serves as a cue for the next thought, and so forth. Even though cue-producing responses such as thoughts and images do not directly change the environment, they lead to other behaviors that do directly affect the environment. What is reinforced is determined by cultural patterns. Thus normal behaviors differ from society to society, as is apparent in the various behaviors of different social classes and immigrant groups in the United States, where different behavior patterns have been rewarded.

FRUSTRATION AND CONFLICT

Dollard and Miller have conducted extensive studies on different aspects of the learning process. A number of these studies have been in the area of responses to frustration and conflict (Miller, 1944, 1951, 1959). **Frustration** occurs when one is unable to reduce a drive because the response that would satisfy it has been blocked. For example, the child who is not permitted to take a cookie from the cookie jar is frustrated. If the frustration arises from a situation in which incompatible responses are occurring at the same time, the situation is described as one of **conflict.** Dollard and Miller used Kurt Lewin's (1890–1947) concept of approach and avoidance tendencies (Lewin, 1936) to distinguish among several different types of conflict in which an individual seeks to approach or avoid one or more goals. They developed ways of graphically presenting different types of conflict and of plotting the strengths of various forces involved in them. Thus the child who is required to choose between two attractive objects, a toy and a bar of candy, can be diagrammed as follows:

$$+ \qquad \longleftarrow \qquad \bigcirc \qquad \longrightarrow \qquad +$$
toy   child   candy

The circle represents the child, and plus signs represent each desired goal. (An undesired goal would be represented by a minus sign.) The arrows indicate that forces are moving the child in the direction of the goals (or away from them). The intensity of the force varies as the child moves closer to or farther from each goal.

The value of these graphic presentations lies in the fact that if we could measure the complex forces that impel human behavior and if we could develop formulas that encompass all of the variables involved, we could also predict a person's actions in reference to a particular goal. Human situations are so complex that such prediction is not possible at present. But Dollard and Miller's experiments with **infrahuman species** (Miller, 1944) have shown that we can be quite successful in predicting the behavior of simple laboratory animals under controlled conditions.

For example, in a classic experiment, rats were placed in a harness attached to a leash so that measurements could be made as to how hard they pulled on the leash to arrive at or avoid a particular goal (Brown, 1948). In one case, the goal was food. Here the experimenter noted that the pull on the leash became greater the nearer the animal came to the food. This enabled him to plot a gradient of approach. In another situation, rats were placed in a similar device in which they had learned to expect an electric shock at the goal. In this experiment, they were placed near the goal and permitted to run away. The experimenter noted that they pulled harder at the harness when they were near the goal than after they had gotten some distance away from it. This enabled him to plot a gradient of avoidance. It was discovered that both the tendency to avoid and the tendency to approach reach their highest point near the goal. However, the gradient of avoidance is steeper than the gradient of approach. The rats pulled harder at the harness to avoid the shock than they did to obtain the food.

Knowing these facts and having obtained these measurements, the experimenter was able to predict what a rat would do if it were placed in any particular position within a box from which it had learned that it would receive both food and a shock at the goal. If an animal were placed in the box at a position close to the goal, it would be likely to run away from the goal because the gradient of avoidance is stronger. But if it were placed in a position farther from the goal, it would be likely to begin to approach the goal until it reached the point where the gradient of avoidance became stronger.

Conflicts, in brief, result from some sort of opposition between our tendencies to approach or avoid certain objects and goals. Dollard and Miller distinguish among several different types of conflict. In an *approach-approach conflict,* the individual is simultaneously attracted to two goals that have positive value but are incompatible. (You are in love with two people at once and are forced to make a choice.) In an *avoidance-avoidance conflict,* a person faces two undesirable alternatives. (The hot plate is burning your hands but if you drop it you will spill the food.) In an *approach-avoidance conflict,* one goal both attracts and repels the individual. (Your date is both attractive and obnoxious.) These

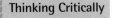

Thinking Critically

What types of conflict have you been facing? See the Thinking Critically box "Personal Conflicts."

conflicts may be diagrammed simply, as is shown in Figure 8.3. In everyday life, of course, the situation is seldom so simple. Therefore, it is often necessary to consider compounded situations of conflict, such as a *double approach-avoidance conflict,* in which an individual must deal simultaneously with multiple goals that both attract and repel.

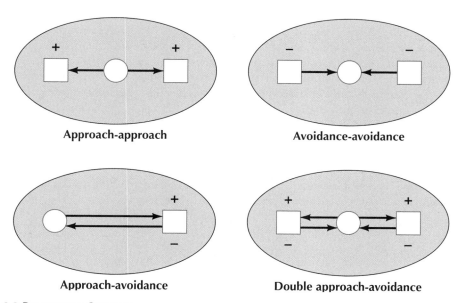

FIGURE **8.3** DIAGRAMMING CONFLICTS

The conflicts that Dollard and Miller describe may be diagrammed simply as shown here. The individual in conflict is represented by the circles. The various goals are represented by squares. The plus and minus signs and arrows indicate whether the person is attracted toward or away from the goal.

Thinking Critically

Personal Conflicts

Dollard and Miller's study of conflicts may be helpful to you in understanding your own personal conflicts and how you handle them. Make a list of the conflicts that you have had in the past year or that you are currently experiencing. Identify the types of conflicts that they represent: approach-approach, avoidance-avoidance, approach-avoidance, or compounded situations of more than one type. Make a diagram of them following the patterns shown in Figure 8.3. Consider the solutions of some of your past conflicts. As you got closer to the goal you were trying to approach or avoid, could you see how your tendency to move toward or away from it was increased? What were some other factors that influenced your resolution of the problem? In the case of current conflicts, try to identify some factors that may lead to an increase or decrease in your gradients of approach and avoidance.

THE INTEGRATION OF LEARNING THEORY AND PSYCHOANALYSIS

In their attempt to integrate learning theory and psychoanalysis, Dollard and Miller (1950) adapted many Freudian concepts and reconceived them in learning theory terms. They appreciated the importance of unconscious forces underlying human behavior, but they redefined the concept of **unconscious processes** in terms of their own theory.

There are two main determinants of unconscious processes. First, we are unaware of certain drives or cues because they are *unlabeled*. These drives and cues may have occurred before we learned to speak, and therefore we were unable to label them. Other cues may be unconscious because a society has not given them adequate labels. For example, we have essentially one word for snow, but certain Eskimo cultures have thirty or more different words for the various textures of snow. Such a society is certainly much more aware of the different variations in snow than we are. Distortions in labeling may also affect one's conscious perception. Through distorted labeling, an emotion such as fear may become confused with another emotion, such as guilt. Thus an individual may react in frightening situations as if guilty because of a distortion in labeling.

Second, unconscious processes refer to cues or responses that once were conscious but have been repressed because they were ineffective. Dollard and Miller point out that repression, like all other behaviors, is learned. When we repress, we do not think about certain thoughts or label them because they are unpleasant. Avoiding these thoughts reduces the drive by reducing the unpleasant experience.

Dollard and Miller also articulate many of the other defense mechanisms that Freud outlined: projection, identification, reaction formation, rationalization, and displacement. In each case, however, they are seen as learned responses or behaviors, and they are articulated in terms of learning. For example, identification entails imitating behavior that one has learned from another. Displacement is explained in terms of generalization and the inability to make proper discriminations.

Dollard and Miller posit four critical training stages in child development: the feeding situation in infancy, cleanliness training, early sex training, and training for control of anger and aggression. At each stage, social conditions of learning imposed by the parents may have enormous consequences for future development. The parallel to Freud's stages is obvious. The conflict situation of feeding in infancy is reminiscent of Freud's oral stage, cleanliness training is reminiscent of Freud's anal stage, and early sex training and the effort to control anger and aggression are elements of Freud's phallic stage.

Dollard and Miller agree with Freud that events in early childhood are vitally important in shaping later behavior. Further, they suggest that the logic of these events may be comprehended within the learning process as they have outlined it. Whereas Freud's stages unfold biologically, the outcomes of Dollard and Miller's stages are controlled by learning. Thus the infant whose cry when hungry brings immediate relief in the sense of being fed learns that self-generated activity is effective in reducing drives. The infant left to "cry it out" may learn that nothing self-generated can be done to reduce the drive and may begin to develop a passive attitude toward drive reduction. Thus, in their incorporation of Freud's theories, Dollard and Miller reconsidered and elaborated his ideas in light of learning theory principles.

It was easy to merge Freud's and Hull's theories because both of them are based on drive reduction and share the common feature of determinism. Dollard and Miller's work helps us appreciate the role of learning in the development of defenses and other psychoanalytic structures. However, there are significant differences between Freud's concepts and Dollard and Miller's articulation of them, so that the translation is not exact. For example, whereas for Freud anxiety, conflict, and repression are inevitable aspects of the human condition, for Dollard and Miller they are simply learned responses. Nevertheless, by transforming Freud's concept into the terms of learning theory and experimental psychology, Dollard and Miller rendered Freud more palatable to a large number of people. It is less threatening to believe that unconscious processes and defense mechanisms are learned and may therefore be unlearned than to conceive of them as largely universal and inescapable. In addition, Dollard and Miller's work stimulated a great deal of scientific research and experimental testing of Freud's concepts.

PSYCHOTHERAPY

We have seen that for Dollard and Miller behavior is learned in the process of seeking to reduce drives. Deviant behavior is also learned, but in the neurotic the behaviors that have been learned are frequently self-defeating and unproductive. The patient has strong, unconscious, and unlabeled emotional conflicts. The neurotic has not labeled the problem and therefore does not discriminate effectively, generalizing and applying old, ineffective solutions to current problems and situations. A young boy whose father was a tyrant may learn in early childhood to react meekly in order to avoid his father's wrath and may generalize his response to his father to later authority figures who in fact are not tyrants. In such situations, his meek response may not be the most appropriate one. Dollard and Miller (1950) suggest that "neurotic conflicts are taught by parents and learned by children."

Therapy involves unlearning old, ineffective, unproductive habits and substituting new, more adaptive, and productive responses. For example, fear, a learnable drive that reinforces responses that reduce it, can motivate either adaptive or maladaptive behavior. If thoughts on a certain topic provoke fear, and if the individual has learned to reduce the fear through responses that block the fear-eliciting thoughts, then this repression prevents the reasoning that could lead to adaptive behavior. Psychotherapy aims to reduce such fears so that reasoning and planning can occur. Training in *suppression* (the conscious, deliberate stopping of a thought or an action) can be helpful. The patient can be trained to suppress, rather than repress, thoughts or actions that reinforce old habits and at the same time be deliberately exposed to new cues that will evoke different responses.

Joseph Wolpe (1915–1997) was a psychiatrist whose method of treatment was also based largely on the application of learning principles established in the laboratory. He developed his methods of treatment after conducting a series of experiments with animals in which he created experimental neuroses in the animals and then attempted to cure them. Wolpe (1958, 1973) developed the principles of **reciprocal inhibition,** which entails the introduction of a competitive response that will interfere with the original maladaptive response, and **systematic desensitization,** in which a patient is conditioned to stop responding to a stimulus in an undesired manner and to substitute a new response. Relaxation is often a very successful competing response. Thus a patient may be taught to relax in the face of situations that were previously fear or anxiety producing. Other contemporary behavior therapists are discussed in the chapter on cognitive behavioral theories.

Dollard and Miller's theory of therapy represents a bridge to the more directive and active therapies of other learning theories such as Skinner's. It is pragmatic and action oriented. Whereas Freud thought it necessary to work through past problems for an analysis to be successful, Dollard and Miller believe that historical recollection is effective only if it is instrumental in creating change. If historical recollection is unnecessary for change to occur, it is only a short step to exclude that emphasis on the past and concentrate on the behaviors of the present, as Skinner and other subsequent learning and behavioral cognitive theorists do.

<table>
<tr><td>PHILOSOPHY,</td></tr>
<tr><td>SCIENCE,</td></tr>
<tr><td>and ART</td></tr>
</table>

Dollard and Miller's Theory

Dollard and Miller developed their theory of personality through laboratory studies and experimentation. They try to base their statements on empirical evidence and submit theoretical differences to observational tests. They recognize, perhaps more than many other theorists, that a theory is useful insofar as it leads to predictions that can be tested. As a scientific theory, therefore, Dollard and Miller's work has been very attractive to many psychologists because of its use in validating evidence.

Empirical evidence, however, has not always given as much support to Dollard and Miller's theory as the theorists imply. What an organism can learn is limited by **species-specific behavior**—complex, rather than reflex, behaviors that occur in all members of a species. Some stimuli are more relevant to a particular species than others; responses also differ. Pigeons peck, chickens scratch, and pigs root. It is difficult, if not impossible, to alter these behaviors. One cannot easily generalize from a rat to a human being.

As we have seen, Dollard and Miller have rendered many psychoanalytic concepts into the constructs of a scientific theory. Many consider this a substantial contribution to the viability of Freud's ideas. Whether psychoanalysis has gained or lost in the process, however, is a matter of considerable debate (Rapaport, 1953). Some would point out that in the process of translation Freudian concepts have lost considerable dynamism and have been emptied of their original intent. Others suggest that Freud's in-depth clinical study of humans illuminates the dynamics of human personality far more than Dollard and Miller's research with rats does.

Ideally, if we could measure forces that impel human behavior and develop sophisticated formulas that encompass all of the variables involved, we could predict complex human behavior; the applications of such a science would be mind-boggling indeed. Dollard and Miller's theory has been quite successful in predicting the behavior of simple laboratory animals under controlled conditions. However, the mazes that individual humans run, even within the same society, are very different (Dollard & Miller, 1941). Dollard and Miller's views have been important to the field of personality since they first published their major work, *Personality and Psychotherapy,* in 1950. They were among the first to seek to emulate a purely scientific model in understanding personality.

Philosophical Assumptions

Which philosophical issues are most important to Dollard and Miller? See the Philosophical Assumptions box "Examining Dollard and Miller and Skinner" on page 228.

Dollard and Miller combined the insights of Freud's psychoanalysis with the principles of learning theory, a combination that structured both the field of psychology and introductory psychology texts during much of the twentieth century. They collaborated on an exploration of the relationship between frustration and aggression (Dollard, Doob, Miller, Mowrer, & Sears, 1939) and introduced the concept of imitation (1941) that was later expanded upon by Albert Bandura. In recent years, the behaviorist position has been revamped to include an emphasis on cognition. These contributions, considered in the chapter on the social learning theories of Albert Bandura and Julian Rotter and the chapter on the cognitive-behavioral theories of Albert Ellis, Aaron Beck, and Arnold Lazarus, attest to the enduring significance of the learning approach that Dollard and Miller popularized.

B. F. Skinner

BIOGRAPHICAL BACKGROUND

Burrhus Frederick Skinner was born in 1904 in Susquehanna, Pennsylvania. His father was an ambitious lawyer; his mother was bright and of high moral standards. A younger brother, of whom he was fond, died suddenly at the age of sixteen. Skinner was reared in a warm, comfortable, and stable home, permeated with the virtues and ethics of small-town, middle-class America at the turn of the twentieth century. His parents did not employ physical punishments, but their admonitions succeeded in teaching their son "to fear God, the police, and what people would think." His parents and grandparents, to whom he was close, taught him to be faithful to the puritan work imperative, to try to please God, and to look

B. F. Skinner believed that the term personality was ultimately superfluous.

for evidence of God's favor through "success." Later, Skinner (1983b) suggested that childhood reinforcements shaped his own adult behavior.

As a child, Skinner was fascinated with machines and interested in knowing how things work. He developed a mechanical device to remind himself to hang up his pajamas, a gadget that enabled him to blow smoke rings without violating his parents' prohibition against smoking, and a flotation system to separate ripe from green elderberries. For many years he tried to design a perpetual motion machine, but it did not work. When his second daughter was born, he invented an aircrib to simplify her care and give her unrestrained movement in a temperature-controlled space (1985).

Skinner was also interested in animal behavior. He caught and brought home the small wildlife of the woodlands in northern Pennsylvania, such as snakes, lizards, and chipmunks. His interest in biology was later reflected in his training of animals. In the precomputer era of World War II, Skinner was given defense grants to study pigeons as prospective guidance systems for rockets.

Skinner was an excellent student. Majoring in English at Hamilton College, a small liberal arts school in upstate New York, he thought seriously of becoming a writer. He sent a few short stories to the poet Robert Frost, who encouraged him to write. He decided to take a year or two off to write, but he quickly became discouraged and decided he could not write because he "had nothing important to say."

During that interlude, he read books by Ivan Pavlov and John Watson, whose work impressed him, and he decided to begin graduate studies in psychology at Harvard. He received the Ph.D. in 1931. He taught at the University of Minnesota for nine years and was chairman of the department of psychology at Indiana University before he returned to Harvard in 1948, having established a reputation as a major experimental psychologist and having written an influential book, *Walden II* (1948), which describes a utopian society based on psychological principles.

Skinner died in 1990 after a battle with leukemia. He was eighty-six.

A Theory of Personality Without Personality

Skinner, the leading heir of the behaviorist position, took the beliefs and concepts of Watson's behaviorist theory to their logical extreme. He concurred with Watson that it is unproductive and foolish to refer to structures of the personality that cannot be directly observed. Thus Skinner developed a psychology that concentrates not on the person but solely on those variables and forces in the environment that influence a person and that may be directly observed. He presented behaviorism and learning theory in its purest and most extreme form.

For Skinner the term *personality* was ultimately superfluous because **overt behavior** can be completely comprehended in terms of responses to factors in the environment. The effort to understand or explain behavior in terms of internal structures such as a personality or an ego is to speak about "fictions" because such structures cannot be directly observed; it is very difficult to deduce operational definitions from them; and it is nearly impossible to develop systematic and empirical means of testing them (1953; see also Moore, 1992). Instead, Skinner suggested that we concentrate on the environmental consequences that determine and maintain an individual's behavior. One can consider the person as empty and observe how changes in the environment affect the individual's behavior.

Skinner did not deny genetic mechanisms or the role of evolution in behavior. He was well aware of them and acknowledged biological participation in behavior throughout his writings (see Morris, Lazo, & Smith, 2004). He further recognized that an adequate explanation of behavior would require interdisciplinary efforts studying both the organism and the effects of environment (1989). He avoided the study of underlying neurobiological mechanisms of behavior because at that time he could not study them scientifically (1974). In an era before the advent of sophisticated functional brain imagery, he focused on a behavioral analysis that was suited to the research tools he had at hand and from which he could begin to develop a science of behavior (Barash, 2005).

It was therefore unnecessary to posit internal forces or motivational states within a person as causal factors of behavior. Skinner did not deny that such states occur: They are important by-products of behavior. He simply saw no point in using them as causal variables because at that time they could not be operationally defined and their intensity could not be measured.

Rather than try to determine how hungry someone was, Skinner tried to determine what variables or forces in the environment affect an individual's eating behavior. What is the effect of the time period that has elapsed since the last meal was eaten? What are the consequences of the amount of food consumed? Such factors in the environment can be specifically defined, measured, and dealt with empirically.

Skinner also differed from other researchers in that he emphasized individual subjects. Typically, he studied each animal separately and reported his results in the form of individual records. Other experimenters draw their conclusions on the basis of the performance of comparison groups as a whole. Skinner, in contrast, believed that the laws of behavior must apply to each and every individual subject when it is observed under the appropriate conditions. He encouraged psychology to remain within the dimensional system of natural science, suggesting that to move away from that model makes it difficult to continue to call psychology a science (1983a).

THE DEVELOPMENT OF BEHAVIOR THROUGH LEARNING

At birth, the human infant is simply a bundle of innate capacities, but consequent behaviors can be comprehended in terms of learning. Thorndike's law of effect stated that when a behavior or performance is accompanied by satisfaction, it tends to be firmly established or increased. If the performance is accompanied by frustration, it tends to decrease. Omitting Thorndike's reference to internal states, Skinner derived a very simple preliminary definition of reinforcement. A **reinforcement** is anything that increases the likelihood of a response. It is the effect of one's behavior that determines the likelihood of its occurring again. If a young child cries or whines, perhaps parental attention will follow. If the behavior results in reinforcement, chances are the child will repeat that behavior pattern. If the behavior does not result in reinforcement—that is, if the child is ignored and does not receive attention—then it is likely that the behavioral response will cease and the child will behave in alternative ways to find patterns of behavior that are reinforced.

Operant Conditioning

Skinner (1938) distinguished between two types of behavior: respondent and operant. **Respondent behavior** refers to reflexes or automatic responses that are elicited by stimuli. Tapping the knee on the right spot makes the leg jerk forward. When our fingers touch hot metal, we reflexively pull our hand away. Such behaviors are unlearned: They occur involuntarily and automatically.

Respondent behaviors, however, may be conditioned or changed through learning. Respondent behaviors were involved in Pavlov's demonstration of classical conditioning. Pavlov's dog learned to salivate at the sound of a bell. An infant learns to suck at a nipple. These are reflexes or automatic responses that have come to be performed in the presence of the previously neutral stimulus through the process of association.

Operant behaviors are responses emitted without a stimulus necessarily being present. They occur spontaneously. Not all of a newborn's movements are reflex responses. Some of them are operant behaviors in which the infant acts on the environment. An infant swings an arm or moves a leg and certain consequences follow. These consequences determine whether or not the response will be repeated. Skinner believed that the process of **operant conditioning** is of far greater significance than simple classical conditioning. Many of our behaviors cannot be accounted for by classical conditioning. Rather, they are originally spontaneous behaviors whose consequences determine their subsequent frequency.

There is a clear distinction between respondent behavior and operant behavior. A respondent behavior is evoked or elicited by a stimulus. Operant behavior is emitted or freely made by the organism. The nature of reinforcement also differs. In classical conditioning, the stimulus is the reinforcement, and it precedes the behavior. In operant conditioning, the effect of the behavior is the reinforcement. Thus in operant conditioning the reinforcement follows the behavior.

Operant conditioning can be systematically described by depicting the behavior of a rat in an operant conditioning apparatus, a piece of laboratory equipment commonly known as a "Skinner box," which is designed to train animals and conduct controlled research. When a food-deprived rat is first placed within the box, it may behave in a variety of random ways. The rat may first walk around the box and explore it. Later, it may scratch itself or urinate. In the course of its activity the rat may at some point press a bar on the wall of the box. The bar pressing causes a food pellet to drop into a trough under the bar. The rat's behavior has had an effect on the environment. The food acts as a reinforcement, increasing the likelihood of that behavior occurring again. When it occurs again, it is reinforced. Eventually, the rat begins to press the bar in rapid succession, pausing only long enough to eat the food.

When a food-deprived rat is conditioned in a Skinner box to press a bar and is reinforced for that behavior with food, we can predict pretty accurately what the rat is going to do in subsequent sessions in the Skinner box. Furthermore, we can control the rat's behavior by changing the reinforcement. When the desired behavior occurs, it is reinforced. Appropriate reinforcement increases the likelihood of that behavior occurring again.

Shaping

Frequently the behavior that a researcher wishes to train an organism to perform is a complex, sophisticated one that the organism would not naturally be expected to do shortly after entering the box. Suppose you wished to train a pigeon to peck at a small black dot inside a white circle. If you were to wait until that behavior spontaneously occurred, you might wait a very long time. Therefore, Skinner employed a procedure termed **shaping,** in which he deliberately shaped or molded the organism's behavior in order to achieve the desired behavior.

Initially, the pigeon moves randomly about the box. When it moves in the direction of the circle, it is reinforced by a pellet of food in the trough below the circle. The next time it approaches the circle, it is again reinforced. Later, it is required to approach the circle more closely before it is reinforced. Later still, it is not reinforced until it pecks the white circle. Finally, the pigeon is reinforced only for pecking at the small black dot within the circle. Shaping facilitates **discrimination,** the ability to tell the difference between stimuli that are and are not reinforced, and **generalization,** the application of a response learned in one situation to a different but similar situation.

Through shaping, Skinner was able to induce animals to perform unique and remarkable feats. He taught pigeons how to play Ping-Pong and to guide missiles to their target. His pigeons never actually were put to work guiding missiles, but Skinner showed that it was possible for them to do so. Using behavior-shaping methods, other animal trainers have been able to produce unusual tricks and feats.

Thinking Critically

Can you identify examples of classical and operant conditioning in your life? See the Thinking Critically box "Classical and Operant Conditioning in Your Life."

Skinner believed that most animal and human behavior is learned through operant conditioning. The process of learning to speak one's native tongue involves reinforcing and shaping of operant behavior. The young infant emits certain spontaneous sounds. These are not limited to the sounds of its native tongue but represent all possible languages. Initially, the infant is reinforced for simply babbling. Later, the child is reinforced for making sounds that approximate meaningful words. Eventually the child is reinforced only for meaningful speech. Skinner (1986) suggested that verbal behavior evolved from signaling, imitating, and other nonverbal behaviors, following the rules of contingencies of

Animals have been taught to perform interesting and helpful feats through techniques that Skinner articulated. Prior to the advent of computers, dolphins were trained for service in World War II.

Thinking Critically

Classical and Operant Conditioning in Your Life

Through the process of association you have learned to pair a wide variety of objects with events that give meaning to your life and influence your behavior. Can you identify some examples of classical and operant conditioning in your life? Many of us have distinct preferences for or aversions to certain things. As a young child, I enjoyed sitting next to my father as he played the piano and we sang together. To this day, I find particular enjoyment in a songfest around a piano. Classical conditioning can also help us to understand the formation and durability of stereotypes, positive or negative prejudgments that we make about people on the basis of their membership in certain groups.

Operant conditioning is even more important in our lives than simple classical conditioning. Many of our behaviors involve complex shaped responses such as tying our shoes or playing a musical instrument. Think of the relationship between parents and children. What are some of the ways in which parents reward and encourage children?

Identify some behaviors that you perform because you find them reinforcing. Identify some that you have learned through operant conditioning. How big an impact do you think the examples you generated have on your personality? Which ones have been most and least influential? Can you also identify ways in which people from other cultures and societies shape their children? These deliberations should help you to recognize the pervasive importance of classical and operant conditioning.

---

reinforcement. Thus the process of shaping is involved in learning to speak, as well as in many other human behaviors.

SCHEDULES AND TYPES OF REINFORCEMENT

A practical necessity led Skinner to explore the effect of different schedules of reinforcement. In the 1930s, commercially made food pellets were not available. Skinner and his students found that it was a laborious, time-consuming process to make the eight hundred or more food pellets a day that were necessary to sustain his research. He wondered what the effect would be if the animal was not reinforced every time it performed the desired behavior. This question led to the investigation of various schedules of reinforcement.

Skinner (1969) described three **schedules of reinforcement** and their effectiveness. In **continuous reinforcement,** the desired behavior is reinforced each time that it occurs. A continuous schedule of reinforcement is extremely effective in initially developing and strengthening a behavior. However, if the reinforcement is stopped, the response quickly disappears or undergoes extinction.

In **interval reinforcement,** the organism is reinforced after a certain time period has elapsed, regardless of the response rate. Interval reinforcement may occur on a fixed or on a variable basis. If the schedule is **fixed,** the same time period elapses each time (such as five minutes). If it is **variable,** the time periods may differ in length. Interval reinforcement occurs frequently in the everyday world. Employees are paid at the end of each week. Students

Casinos use variable ratio schedules to keep many a gambler playing even though the money allotted for gambling has been lost.

are given grades at certain intervals within the year. Interval reinforcement produces a level of response that is more difficult to extinguish than responses that have been continuously reinforced. However, the level of response tends to be lower than the level produced by other kinds of schedules.

In **ratio reinforcement,** the rate of reinforcement is determined by the number of appropriate responses that the organism emits. A factory worker may be paid according to the number of pieces that he or she completes. Ratio schedules of reinforcement may be fixed or variable. If the schedule is **fixed,** the number of responses required prior to reinforcement is stable and unchanging. If the schedule is **variable,** the number of appropriate operant behaviors that must occur prior to reinforcement changes from time to time. A continuous schedule of reinforcement is most effective for initially developing and strengthening a behavior. A variable ratio schedule is most effective thereafter in maintaining the behavior. Responses maintained under the conditions of variable ratio reinforcement are highly resistant to extinction and less likely to disappear. Gambling casinos use variable ratio schedules to keep many a gambler at the table long after the money allotted for gambling has disappeared. Skinner suggested that a voluntary lottery could be systematically cultivated to replace state and national taxes.

When reinforcement is haphazard or accidental, the behavior that immediately precedes the reinforcement may be increased even if it is not the desired behavior. Athletes often engage in personal rituals before positioning themselves for play, because of an earlier fortuitous connection between a specific behavior and success. Such ritualized behaviors are *superstitious,* yet many ineffective habits and common superstitions have their origin in chance reinforcement. Some of these behaviors are culturally transmitted and reinforced.

Now that research has confirmed the effects of various types of reinforcement, we can systematically apply effective schedules of reinforcement to shape desired behavior.

Skinner (1953) described the effects of **generalized conditioned reinforcers** such as praise and affection, which are learned and have the power to reinforce a great number of different behaviors. Moreover, they can be self-given. As we grow older, we move from primary reinforcers to more generalized secondary types. Initially, young children will respond to food or to something else that meets their basic needs. Later, they respond to an allowance. At the same time, they associate these reinforcers with the praise and affection that accompany them. Eventually, children will work primarily for the reinforcement of praise, which can be self-given.

Skinner (1972) distinguished between positive reinforcement, punishment, and negative reinforcement. **Positive reinforcement** occurs when a behavior is followed by a situation that increases the likelihood of that behavior occurring in the future. **Negative reinforcement** comes about when a behavior is followed by the *termination of an unpleasant situation,* increasing the likelihood of that behavior in similar situations. To stop being labeled "acting white," some African American students underachieve in school (Fordham & Ogbu, 1986). Plastic surgery can help older people escape age discrimination. **Punishment** occurs when a behavior is followed by an unpleasant situation designed to *eliminate* it.

Skinner (1953) observed that punishment is the most common technique of behavioral control in our society. Children are spanked if they misbehave and lawbreakers are fined or imprisoned. Punishment may stop or block a behavior, but it does not necessarily eliminate it. The organism may seek other means of acquiring the same ends. Punishment creates fear, but if the fear is diminished, the behavior will recur. Punishment also can lead to undesired side effects: anger, hatred, or helplessness.

Skinner (1953, 1971) suggested using methods other than those based on aversive stimuli to eliminate undesirable behaviors. One may ignore the behavior until it undergoes extinction, or one may permit satiation to occur. **Satiation** entails permitting the behavior to occur until the individual tires of it. A child may be allowed to turn a light switch on and off until she becomes bored. One may also change the environment that provokes the behavior. Fragile objects may be placed out of a young child's reach. Finally, one can promote behaviors that counteract and inhibit the undesirable behaviors through positive reinforcement.

Skinner emphasized that positive reinforcement is most effective in initiating and maintaining desired behaviors. All too often we do not recognize how we inadvertently give positive reinforcement to a behavior that is not desirable. The child who is seeking attention may be *positively* reinforced by a parental scolding because the scolding affords the child attention. By identifying our reinforcement patterns, we can strengthen those that are most effective and develop more efficient means of controlling behavior.

PSYCHOTHERAPY AND BEHAVIORAL CHANGE

Skinner explained maladaptive or neurotic behavior in terms of environmental contingencies that sustain and maintain it. The neurotic or psychotic has been conditioned by the environment to behave in inappropriate ways. If we wish to change an individual's behavior, we can restructure the environment so that it will no longer sustain maladaptive behavior and instead will reinforce desirable behavior. Thus, in describing neurosis, Skinner did not find it necessary to refer to explanatory fictions such as repression or conflict, because maladaptive behavior can simply be reduced to the variables in the environment that reinforce and sustain it.

The role of therapy is to identify the behaviors that are maladaptive, remove them, and substitute more adaptive and appropriate behaviors through operant conditioning. Skinner concurred with Dollard and Miller that there is no need to review the individual's past or encourage reliving it. Therapy is not dependent on self-understanding or insight for behavioral change.

The contrast between Freud and Skinner emerges clearly in their attitudes toward therapy. As we have seen, Freud's intent was primarily scholarly. He sought to increase an individual's self-understanding, and psychoanalysis is relatively uninterested in specific behavioral change. Skinner's interest, on the other hand, was totally pragmatic and curative. **Behavior modification** seeks to eliminate undesired behaviors by changing the environment within which they occur.

Skinner's approach to behavior modification has been notably successful in areas in which traditional insight therapy has failed or is inappropriate. One of its more spectacular successes has been with mute individuals, who for obvious reasons are not amenable to traditional therapies, which are largely based on talking. Dr. O. I. Lovaas (1966) has used a systematic program of shaping to teach autistic and mute children to speak. First, he identifies something that is reinforcing to the child. Because food is generally reinforcing for children, it is commonly employed. Initially, Lovaas reinforces the child with a small piece of food every time he or she makes a sound. Gradually he shapes these sounds until they approximate words. Eventually, he reinforces the child only for communicating in full sentences, and so forth. The reinforcement of food is coupled with praise and affection so that the type of reinforcement grows from primary and secondary reinforcers to generalized conditioned reinforcers that can be self-applied. These methods are also generalized to include training in other desired behaviors. Because sustaining the newly learned behavior depends on maintaining a supportive environment, Lovaas includes parents and other significant figures in his program of behavior modification. Parents and other influential figures such as teachers are taught to systematically apply the same reinforcers to similar situations in the home or school. In this way the circle of the environment is widened to permit greater control.

Skinner's influence has extended into many areas of education. With Sidney Presley, Skinner developed the *teaching machine,* a device whereby students may be taught without the need for an ever-present human instructor. Skinnerian principles also underlie numerous systems of individualized and programmed instruction. In such programs, the work is broken down into small units, and the student must master each unit before being permitted to proceed to the next one. The student is, in effect, being shaped while mastering the material. There is immediate reinforcement in the sense of feedback to the student for correct and incorrect answers. Some computer-assisted instruction programs are based on Skinnerian principles, and many educational psychologists suggest the need for a more systematic application of his ideas in our schools.

Skinner's methods have been employed in schools for the mentally retarded, in mental institutions, in prisons and rehabilitation centers. In many of these, a **token economy** has been established. Tokens of some kind that may be exchanged for special privileges are used to reinforce appropriate behaviors. Making one's bed, getting dressed, talking to other patients, and other desirable behaviors are reinforced by tokens that individuals can exchange for candy, watching TV, and other amenities not routinely available.

Skinner's concepts and principles also have been applied systematically in industrial and business settings to boost productivity through a performance-improvement system based on accurate feedback and positive reinforcement.

SOCIAL UTOPIAS

Skinner's interest in the environment that shapes the individual and his bent toward a technological and reformist orientation led quite naturally to his interest in the design of an ideal environment or a utopian society. In 1948 Skinner wrote *Walden II,* a book that describes his concept of a utopia. **Walden II** was a behaviorally engineered society designed by a benevolent psychologist who employed a program of positive reinforcements. Because positive rather than aversive means were used to shape behavior, residents sought those reinforcers and willingly behaved in socially responsible and productive ways.

In 1971 Skinner wrote *Beyond Freedom and Dignity* and again argued for the creation of a behaviorally engineered society, pointing out that most major problems today—war, overpopulation, unemployment, inflation, and so forth—are caused by human behavior. What we need, he said, is a behavior technology that will enable us to cope with them. Such a technology cannot be established, however, unless we give up several cherished "fictions," such as the notions that people are responsible for their own behavior and that human beings are autonomous. For Skinner, human behavior is controlled by forces in the environment, and the concept of free will is a superstition. We feel free when we are abundantly reinforced and have learned effective behaviors. The clue to our behaviors and emotional states lies within the environment rather than the individual.

In Skinner's view (1984), operant conditioning is to the origin of behavior what natural selection is to the origin of species in Darwin's theory. Skinner's emphasis on the environment did not negate the impact of heredity, but it did stand in sharp contrast with the position taken by cognitive psychologists who suggest that certain learned behaviors are due to cognition rather than to environmental variables. Behaviorism may have lost its dominance in psychology because it could not assimilate the construct of *intentionality,* which is, according to many current psychologists, crucial to understanding human behavior and adaption (Hibbard, 1993).

In his utopian speculation, Skinner shifted from scientist to social philosopher. Presenting us with a form of social Darwinism, he suggested that "survival is the only value according to which a culture is eventually to be judged" (1971). During evolution, the environment shaped the behavior that survives in our genes. After birth, environmental conditioning shapes each one of us in this life. We need more, not less, control, Skinner argued. To his critics, he pointed out that human beings are already controlling and being controlled. The process of controlling should not be denied; instead, it should be studied and understood so that we can implement it effectively in developing the society that we want. We have the power to develop a behavioral technology. To ignore this is to run the risk not of no control but rather of continued ineffective or deleterious control.

Skinner mellowed with age and conceded that psychologists and other people do not possess the means or the motivation to implement his utopian schemes (1981). In the end, the very reasoning of behaviorism explains its lack of success. If, as behaviorism maintains, people do not initiate actions on their own but simply act in ways to which they have been conditioned, they cannot change in response to predictions. Problems such as pollution, energy depletion, nuclear contamination, and other environmental issues have not been dealt with effectively because they do not yet loom large enough to reinforce behavioral change. The survival of species may depend on our ability to use scientific forecasts to change cultural practices, but such understanding is precluded as a condition of behavioral change in Skinner's theory.

Skinner's Theory

PHILOSOPHY, SCIENCE, *and* ART

Skinner provided a great deal of experimental data and research to support his ideas. More than any other contemporary theorist, he stimulated research undertaken to validate the concepts of behaviorism (e.g., Staddon & Cerutti, 2003). Skinner's theory dominated American psychology, particularly in the 1970s. His work was characterized by the intensive study of individual subjects, primarily drawn from infrahuman species, the careful control of laboratory conditions through automated apparatus, and an emphasis on variables easily modified by manipulating the environment.

Skinner's concepts clearly evolved from experimental laboratory investigations, and he showed tremendous respect for well-controlled data. His constructs have been empirically tested and have held up well under the scrutiny of the scientific method. His theory is elegant in its simplicity. It is also admirable in its ability to predict and control behavior, particularly in infrahuman species. Although he set out to avoid theorizing, he presented a theory of human behavior, if not a theory of personality, and he even played the role of a social philosopher.

But Skinner did not always recognize the kinds of evidence on which his various statements are based. He frequently presented his social philosophy as if it were an empirical science with all the appropriate validating evidence. For example, Skinner observed that an individual may be controlled by the manipulation of the environment. This is an empirical statement that holds up under test. However, one cannot jump from that empirical observation to the conclusion that human beings are *nothing but* organisms controlled by their environment and claim that the conclusion is simply based on validating evidence. The conclusion entails a philosophical commitment that Skinner acknowledged (1972).

Skinner himself went beyond the development of a scientific theory. In designing his utopia he invoked ethical commitments. He suggested, for instance, that the value of a society lies in its ability to survive, that human beings should give up the conceits of freedom and dignity. These are ethical considerations, not empirical ones. As such, they need to be evaluated in terms of their adequacy as philosophy.

Skinner regretted that psychology persisted in its search for internal determinants of behaviors, suggesting that humanist psychology, the helping professions, and the recent emphasis on cognitive psychology represent three obstacles in the continued development of psychology as a science of behavior (1987). He continued to argue for psychology as an experimental science and an analysis of behavior in spite of

Philosophical Assumptions

Which philosophical issues were most important to Skinner? See the Philosophical Assumptions box "Examining Dollard and Miller and Skinner."

✺ Philosophical Assumptions

Examining Dollard and Miller and Skinner

Many of the differences among personality theories can be attributed to fundamental differences in philosophical assumptions. Which of the basic philosophical issues, described in the introductory chapter and summarized on the inside back cover, seem to be clearly important to Dollard and Miller and to Skinner in the development of their theories? How, for example, does Dollard and Miller's conception of the structure of personality in terms of habits influence their stand on freedom and determinism and proactivity versus reactivity? How does Skinner's view of human behavior as a product of operant conditioning influence his view of heredity versus environment and freedom versus determinism? Which issues are addressed in Skinner's utopian speculations? Do the theories of Dollard and Miller and of Skinner address any other philosophical assumptions? Rate Dollard and Miller and Skinner on a scale of 1 to 5 on those philosophical assumptions that you feel their theories apply to most. Compare your ratings with your own philosophical assumptions. Did your study of these thinkers lead you to change any of your assumptions? Why or why not?

controversy over the possible decline in the popularity of behaviorism (see Lambert, 1988; Place, 1988; Power, 1988).

Skinner's theory, as we have noted, works well in predicting and controlling behavior, particularly the behavior of infrahuman species. It also deals effectively with human behavior when that behavior occurs under situations of positive or negative reinforcement. In everyday terms we would say that it is effective in dealing with human situations that are surrounded by reward or punishment.

Skinner provided behaviorist explanations for complex human behaviors such as language acquisition, decision making, memory, and problem solving; however, his theory is less successful in these areas. For example, although there can be no question that operant conditioning, reinforcement, and shaping play large roles in the child's acquisition of language, these concepts alone do not fully explain how the child learns to speak (Chomsky, 1959; Hayes & Hayes, 1988). Skinner's theory does not account for the child's creative use of language. He did not tell us how it is possible for the child to come up with a new sentence never heard before. Nor do Skinner's concepts account for the meaningful errors that the child makes in learning to speak. The child who says, "I branged it home," may have never heard the verb *branged*. The error shows us that without the assistance of formal lessons in grammar, the child understands the use of the suffix *-ed* in expressing the past tense.

Concurring with Skinner that learning plays the central role in human behavior, Arthur Staats (1996) has developed **psychological behaviorism,** a detailed theory of personality that translates personality concepts into behavioral language (Cloninger, 2008). According to psychological behaviorism, personality characteristics, traits, temperaments, abilities, interests, and attitudes are due to a long-term, complex, continuous process of learning. In his practice of psychological interventions, Staats has also implemented token economies and developed the widely used procedure of **time-out** (1971), which avoids aversive punishment to eliminate undesired behavior by simply removing the individual from the situation in which the undesired behavior is occurring.

In efforts that may revitalize behaviorism, Murray Sidman (1994) and Steven Hayes (2001) have made some prudent additions to traditional Skinnerian radical behaviorism based on equivalence relations, which recognizes that human language requires deriving relations among events (e.g., if A = B and A = C then B = C). Human beings learn relations such as similarity, difference, comparison, and time and alter what they do in a particular situation based on its relation to other situations. Sidman, whose 1960 book, *Tactics of Scientific Research,* outlined the optimal methodology of behavior analysis, notes that people often react to words and symbols as if they are the things or events they refer to. Thus during the war in Iraq, impassioned people brought down the statue of Saddam Hussein, just as an earlier crowd had toppled a statue of Lenin. Hayes's relational frame theory brings a set of observable principles to bear on topics such as language, cognition, and emotion (although admittedly Skinner minimized the importance of cognition and emotion) and points toward new, effective forms of psychotherapeutic interventions. Steven Hayes's work is discussed in more detail in the chapter on cognitive behavioral theories.

Of all the theorists discussed in this book, Skinner and Freud have generated the most controversy and criticism. The theories of both offend us because they attack our illusion that we are in full control of our behaviors. Yet their responses to the concept of our lack of self-control differ widely because of the very different philosophical assumptions that undergird their work. Freud, a pessimist, offered us hope of gaining a small margin of control over the unconscious forces of which we have been unaware through the painful process of self-understanding. Skinner, an optimist, believed that the answer lies in recognizing our lack of control, renouncing our ambitions for inner control, and committing ourselves to being more effectively controlled by a behaviorally designed technology (cf. Altus & Morris, 2004; Barash, 2005).

Conclusions

Dollard and Miller developed a psychoanalytically oriented behavioral theory in which they combined the insights of Freud's psychoanalytic position with the principles of learning theory. Skinner took what he saw as the logical step that follows from Dollard and Miller's approach. If a stimulus-response theory of psychology can account for all of the overt behaviors that psychologists seek to explain, why not omit the psychoanalytic underpinnings and simply rely on behaviorist principles (Rychlak, 1973)?

The learning and behavior theories of Dollard and Miller and Skinner have strongly influenced American psychology. Throughout much of the twentieth century, the behaviorist movement was a dominant trend. The behaviorists' emphasis on a rigorous scientific approach set the model for subsequent psychological investigations. However, although their theories seem to be able to account for the learned behavior of animal species and for the learned habits and simple behaviors of human beings, behaviorists are less able to explain complex human behaviors. Blackman (1991) sees contacts between Skinner's emphasis on behavior as a biological phenomenon and Mead's social behaviorism and Vygotsky's general genetic law of cultural development. It is not surprising that the radical nature of Skinner's theory, which took the learning and behavior theory of Dollard and Miller to a logical extreme, led to the development of an alternative approach to learning and behavior (discussed in the chapter on social learning theories), that, while emphasizing situational factors, also reintroduces covert factors such as cognition.

 TO LEARN MORE about reinforcement schedules and advertising, and for a list of suggested readings, visit the *Personality Theories* textbook website at **college.cengage .com/pic/engler8e.**

Summary

1. Behavior and learning theories explore personality experimentally by studying behavior in laboratory settings. Their precise methods reflect an **empirical** (p. 207) point of view and the careful manipulation of variables under specified controlled conditions.

2. Early behaviorists include Pavlov, who explained the process of classical conditioning; Watson, whose theory recommended an emphasis on overt behavior; Thorndike, who formulated the **law of effect** (p. 209); and Hull, who clarified the concept of **drive reduction** (p. 210).

3. Dollard and Miller describe the structure of personality in terms of **habits** (p. 210) that may be learned and unlearned. They distinguish between **primary** (p. 210) and **secondary drives** (p. 210) and **reinforcers** (p. 210) as the primary motivating forces of personality.

4. The learning process can be broken down into four main conceptual parts: **drive** (p. 210), **cue** (p. 210), **response** (p. 211), and **reinforcement** (p. 211).

5. A number of experiments have been conducted on the learning process, especially in the areas of **frustration** (p. 211) and **conflict** (p. 211). Experiments with **infrahuman species** (p. 212) have been quite successful in predicting the behavior of simple laboratory animals under controlled conditions.

6. Dollard and Miller have adapted many Freudian concepts and integrated them into learning theory. Unconscious processes are reconceived as unlabeled drives and cues. The defense mechanisms and critical stages of development are also reconceived in terms of the learning process. The translation, though inexact, has helped to popularize Freud and stimulate experimental study of his ideas.

7. Dollard and Miller's therapy represents a bridge to the more directive and active therapies of other learning theories. Behavior therapy involves unlearning ineffective habits and substituting more adaptive responses.

8. Dollard and Miller's theory of personality seeks to emulate a scientific model and places a great deal of emphasis on empirical research.

9. Skinner chose to describe variables and forces in the environment that shape **overt behavior** (p. 218). He believed that the term *personality* and concepts of internal structure are ultimately superfluous and that behavior is best understood as responses to the environment.

10. **Operant conditioning** (p. 220) involves reinforcing and **shaping** (p. 220) spontaneous responses. It differs from **classical conditioning** (p. 208) in the nature of the behavior, which is freely made rather than elicited by a **stimulus** (p. 208), and in the nature of the **reinforcement** (p. 219), which follows rather than precedes the behavior.

11. Skinner described three **schedules of reinforcement** (p. 222): continuous, interval, and ratio. **Continuous reinforcement** (p. 222) is effective for initially developing a behavior. **Interval reinforcement** (p. 222) and **ratio reinforcement** (p. 223) are more effective for maintaining the behavior. Skinner described the effects of **generalized conditioned reinforcers** (p. 224), and he distinguished among **positive reinforcement** (p. 224), **negative reinforcement** (p. 224), and **punishment** (p. 224).

12. **Behavior modification** (p. 225) seeks to restructure the environment so that undesired behaviors are eliminated and more desired ones substituted. Skinner's approach has been successful in situations in which traditional insight methods are inapplicable. His methods have also been used in therapeutic communities, education, and industry.

13. Skinner advocated the development of a social utopia, a behaviorally engineered society in which a program of positive reinforcers would shape behavior.

14. Skinner's utopian speculations reflect philosophical assumptions as well as scientific generalizations by not allowing for any exceptions and by invoking values and ethical commitments.

15. Skinner's theory clearly evolved from experimental laboratory investigations and emulates a strict scientific approach. However, Skinner acknowledged the philosophical assumptions that underlie his theory.

Personal Experiences

1. Dollard and Miller emphasize the role of learning in personality and downplay personality structure. Try to identify an aspect of your experience that could serve as a good example of Dollard and Miller's concepts of habits and secondary drives.

2. Dollard and Miller broke down the learning process into four main conceptual parts: drive, cue, response, and reinforcement. Apply their model to describe how you learned something.

3. Skinner discussed three types of reinforcement: positive reinforcement, negative reinforcement, and punishment. These techniques are often evident in the context of child rearing. Which of them did your parents use most often in teaching you how to behave? What about your childhood friends? Did their parents and yours use similar or different strategies? Which technique do you think is the best strategy to employ in rearing a child? Does one stand out above all the rest, or do you feel that which strategy is best depends on the context?

4. Recall and describe three instances in which you experienced the dynamics of a "token economy"—for example, a small transaction between you and a sibling or a friend, a child-rearing strategy used by your parents, a behavioral strategy used by an elementary school teacher. Did the exchange have a productive and beneficial effect, or was the

dynamic more coercive and negative? Discuss the pluses and minuses of Skinnerian principles in the context of your life.

5. Skinner and Presley's teaching machine reduced the need for human instructors. With the continual development of technology and the ever-increasing efficiency of the Internet, their teaching-machine concept is manifesting itself in online courses and educational software programs. Describe your experience with "teaching machines." Have you found this technology effective, helpful? Or do you prefer the interpersonal dynamic arising from the presence of a human instructor? Take a moment to think about the future: How will you want your children to be taught?

CHAPTER 9

Social Learning Theories

- **Albert Bandura**
- **Julian Rotter**
- **Walter Mischel**

YOUR GOALS FOR THIS CHAPTER

1. Explain why an **agentic perspective** emerges in Bandura's theory, and describe what human agency entails.
2. Explain what Bandura means by **triadic reciprocal causation,** and identify the three factors that enter into it.
3. Describe **observational learning** by identifying three factors that influence modeling, four processes that enter into observational learning, and the role of reinforcement in observational learning.
4. Explain what is meant by **self-regulation.**
5. Discuss Bandura's contributions to the discussion of aggression, inhumane behavior, and moral disengagement.
6. Explain the concept of **self-efficacy.**
7. Describe Bandura's contributions to behavioral modification.
8. Evaluate Bandura's theory from the viewpoints of philosophy, science, and art.
9. Describe Rotter's **I-E Scale,** and discuss the construct it measures and the findings to which it has led.
10. Describe the four variables that Rotter includes in his formula for predicting behavior.
11. Discuss Mischel's initial work on **behavioral specificity.**
12. Describe the cognitive-affective system theory of personality known as **CAPS.**

Social learning theories, illustrated by Albert Bandura, Julian Rotter, and Walter Mischel, emerged out of the behavior and learning tradition. However, they have moved away from Skinner's reactive mechanical model of behavior to view the person as an agent or originator of experience. In doing so, they reintroduce internal cognitive variables, such as one's subjective interpretation of the environment, into the stimulus-response formula (S-R).

Initially exploring the impact of modeling, expanding to include self-regulatory and self-efficacy mechanisms, Bandura's social learning theory has developed into an agentic perspective that fosters personal and social changes and speaks to some of our most pressing global issues (Bandura, 2004a). The result is the correction of some of the flaws of behavior and learning theory and its transformation into a popular current approach in academic personality psychology (Pervin & John, 1997).

Social learning theories reflect the careful scientific procedures and methodology that characterize the behaviorist approach. However, they have moved from very simple laboratory situations to more complex ones and have increasingly used human rather than animal subjects. Laboratory conditions have been made more similar to the everyday life of people. Some of the contingencies under investigation are very complex, but laboratory procedures have become increasingly sophisticated in order to deal with them.

This chapter focuses on the theory of Albert Bandura and then briefly considers some contributions made to social learning theory by Julian Rotter and Walter Mischel.

Albert Bandura (1925–   )

BIOGRAPHICAL BACKGROUND

Mundare, a small town in Alberta, Canada, was the childhood home of Albert Bandura, an only son, born on December 4, 1925, to parents of Polish descent who already had five daughters. Bandura has written little of his early years. His family operated a drayage business, delivering supplies brought in by train to the different businesses in town. There was only one school in town. Because of a paucity of teachers and supplies, the students had largely to educate themselves, yet almost all of them went on to professional careers.

In college, Bandura initially enrolled in a psychology course because it met at a congenial time: His carpool companions, engineering and premed students, wished to arrive very early in the morning. He was captivated by the course and decided to major in the subject. He received his B.A. from the University of British Columbia in Vancouver in 1949 and his M.A. and Ph.D. from the University of Iowa in 1951 and 1952. There was a strong Hullian emphasis at Iowa, yet Bandura felt that the psychology department was very forward looking. He spent a year as a clinical intern at the Wichita (Kansas) Guidance Center and then accepted a position at Stanford University, where he rose through the ranks and has been ever since. He became a full professor in 1964 and in 1974 was awarded an endowed chair.

At Stanford, Bandura began field studies on social learning of aggression, particularly considering the role of modeling; this research led him to explore the components underlying observational learning. His research also investigates how people influence their own

Albert Bandura believes that human behavior is due to the interplay of behavioral, cognitive, and environmental factors.

motivation and behavior, especially through their perception of self-efficacy (see also Zimmerman & Schunk, 2003).

An active scholar and writer, Bandura has published several important books and a great many articles. He was elected president of the American Psychological Association in 1973. In 2006 the Gold Medal Award for Life Achievement in the Science of Psychology, presented by the American Psychological Foundation, was added to his many high honors. At the present time, he teaches undergraduate seminars at Stanford on the psychology of aggression and personal and social change and a graduate seminar on self-efficacy. He enjoys hiking in the Sierra, dining in Bay Area restaurants, and the San Francisco Opera.

AN AGENTIC PERSPECTIVE

An **agentic perspective** emerges in Bandura's sociocognitive view of personality. Whereas earlier learning theories primarily depended on principles of reinforcement to account for how human behavior is developed or changed, Bandura has increasingly viewed people as agents, or originators, of experience (2001). Causal influences on behavior do not simply go in one direction (1996), and people are more than reactive organisms shaped by their environment. Through evolution, human beings developed language and symbolization. This development permitted them to go beyond the dictates of their immediate surroundings and actively contribute toward their circumstances (2006a).

Bandura conceives of human agency as the ability to act and make things happen. Personal agency occurs within a larger network of sociostructural influences in which people construct and are constructed by social systems (2001). Both producers and products of their environment, people have cognitive, vicarious, self-regulative, and self-reflective capacities that influence behavior and provide some measure of control over it. Human agency (Bandura, 1999a, 2001, 2006a) entails *intentionality,* which enables us to behave purposefully; *forethought,* which permits us to anticipate outcomes; *self-reactiveness,* which allows us to motivate and regulate actions, behaving in ways that give us satisfaction and avoiding behaviors that bring self-censure; and *self-reflectiveness,* which gives us the ability to reflect on our thoughts and behavior and make changes as needed. We can exercise our agency individually, collectively, or by proxy when we authorize others to act on our behalf.

An agentic perspective encourages lines of research that can provide new insights into the social and behavioral shaping of the brain function and the agentic self. Brain imagery can show us how agentic causal beliefs and activities lead to the growth of a neurobiological substrate that fosters the development of psychomotor, social, and symbolic skills. Bandura does not deny the biological determinants of behavior. He recognizes that constitutional constraints influence an individual's social learning history; however, he focuses on the social and cognitive aspects of human development.

Thus the agentic self is socially constructed through experiences with the environment. The infant begins to perceive causal relations between events in the environment, gradually understands causation through action, and eventually recognizes the self as an agent of actions. Collectively this development leads to a conscious agentic species that can change evolutionary inheritances through genetic engineering and shape the future.

TRIADIC RECIPROCAL CAUSATION

Bandura's agentic perspective is reflected in his concept of **triadic reciprocal causation** (1978, 1986a), the regulation of human behavior by the interplay of behavioral, cognitive, and environmental factors. The three types of factors operate as "interlocking determinants" of one another. If we were to diagram the process, each factor would have arrows pointing toward it and toward the other two (see Figure 9.1).

Environmental stimuli influence our behavior, but individual personal factors such as beliefs and expectations also influence how we behave. The selection of a tuna fish sandwich for lunch is determined not simply by the menu and other environmental stimuli but also by one's attitude toward tuna fish and an expectation as to how it will taste. Further, the outcomes of our behavior change the environment. A rush on any particular item will cause a restaurant or household to run out of it and perhaps subsequently to order an extra supply.

Many psychologists have agreed with Bandura that behavior arises from the interactions of a person and the environment rather than from either factor alone. However, some earlier conceptualizations saw the person and situation as separate agents that combine to produce behavior, or they considered the behavior that the person and situation produce to be a by-product that does not enter into the causal process. Bandura believes that his concept is significant because it emphasizes the reciprocal nature of the interaction among all three factors (1989, 1991a).

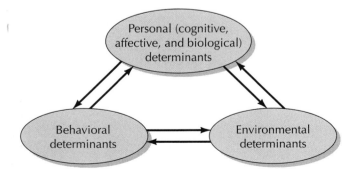

FIGURE 9.1 A DIAGRAM OF TRIADIC RECIPROCAL CAUSATION

Bandura suggests that the interplay of three factors—personal determinants, behavioral determinants, and environmental determinants—regulates human behavior.

While actions are regulated by their consequences, external stimuli affect behavior through intervening cognitive processes. While they are behaving, people are also thinking about what they are doing. Their thoughts influence how their behavior is affected by the environment. Cognitive processes determine which stimuli we will recognize, how we will perceive them, and how we will act upon them. Cognitive processes also permit us to use symbols and to engage in the type of thinking that enables us to anticipate different courses of action and their consequences. Because we act reflectively rather than automatically, we are able to change our immediate environment. In so doing, we arrange reinforcements for ourselves and influence our own behavior.

Processes relating to the self play a major role in Bandura's theory, but he does not conceive of the self as a psychic agent controlling behavior. Instead he uses the term **self-system** to refer to "cognitive structures that provide reference mechanisms," a "set of subfunctions for the perception, evaluation, and regulation of behavior" (1978). Thus the *self* in social learning theory is a group of cognitive processes and structures (personal determinants) by which people relate to their environment and that help to shape their behavior (see also Katzko, 2003).

Television viewing is a good example of the way in which behavioral, cognitive, and environmental factors may be interlocked. Bandura points out that "three factors—viewer preferences, viewing behavior, and televised offerings—reciprocally affect each other" (1978). The relative influence of the three interlocking factors varies in different individuals and in different situations. In a reciprocal interaction process, one and the same event can be a stimulus, a response, or an environmental reinforcer, depending on where in the sequence we begin our analysis. Thus it is useless to search for an ultimate environmental cause of behavior. Moreover, chance encounters frequently play a role in shaping the course of a human life. In a chance encounter, each separate chain of events has its own causal determinants, but their occurrence together arises fortuitously. The science of psychology cannot predict the likelihood of chance encounters, but it can clarify the factors that influence their impact (1986a).

LEARNING THROUGH OBSERVATION

In his early writing, Bandura (1977) emphasizes the power and pervasiveness of social modeling and the process of learning through observation or by example, without any direct reinforcement. He points out that most human behavior is learned by following a model rather than through the processes of drive reduction, classical or operant conditioning.

Bandura suggests that **observatonal learning** occurs either intentionally or accidentally. This is how children learn to play with their toys, to perform household chores, and to develop other skills such as riding a bicycle. Young children learn to speak by hearing the speech of others and extracting the embodied rules, which permits them to generate speech that goes beyond what they have heard. If learning a language were totally dependent on classical or operant conditioning, it could not be accomplished so readily, because a child would not be reinforced until after spontaneously uttering a sound that approximated a real word. In practice, parents repeat meaningful words over and over again to their children, who make use of those words as they learn to speak.

In many cases the behavior that is being learned is exactly the same as the modeled activity. Driving an automobile, for example, requires us to follow a prescribed method of action.

Observational learning is a key aspect of Bandura's theory. Here a young Native American watches the feet of an elder to learn how to dance during a traditional powwow.

However, new behaviors also can be learned through observation. Observers sometimes are able to solve problems correctly even after the model fails to solve the same problem. Thus observational learning exceeds mere imitation. Bandura suggests that learning through observation can produce innovative and creative behaviors when observers draw similar conclusions from different responses and create rules of behavior that permit them to go beyond what they have seen or heard. Through this type of synthesis, they are able to develop new patterns of conduct that may be quite different from those they have actually observed (1974).

Bandura's theory of observational learning is largely based on experimental analysis of the influence of modeling on behavior. In a typical modeling experiment, the participant observes another person performing a behavior or sequence of behaviors. Afterward the participant is observed to see whether or not the model's behavior is emulated. The participant's behavior is compared with that of a control group who did not observe the model to see if there are any significant differences. Bandura distinguishes between *imitation* (mimicking the model) and *modeling* (matching the structure or style of the behavior). His theory and research emphasize modeling rather than imitation.

Bandura's most famous study involved the use of a Bobo doll, a large inflated plastic figure about four feet tall (Bandura, Ross, & Ross, 1961). Young preschool-age children observed an adult playing with the doll in an aggressive fashion. The adult vigorously attacked the doll, hitting and kicking it while shouting things like "Sock him in the nose!" "Throw him in the air!" Other children did not see the adult playing with the doll aggressively. Later, when the children in the experimental group were given the opportunity to play with the Bobo doll themselves, their behavior was similar to that of the model in that it followed an aggressive style and was twice as aggressive as that of the children in the control group.

Through manipulating various independent variables in this kind of experiment, Bandura (1977) and his colleagues demonstrated three factors that influence modeling:

1. *Characteristics of the model.* We are more likely to be influenced by someone who we believe is similar to ourselves than by someone who is different. Simpler behaviors are more

readily emulated than complex ones, and certain kinds of behavior seem more prone to learning through observation than others. Hostile and aggressive behaviors are readily learned through modeling, especially by young children.

2. *Attributes of the observer.* People who are lacking in self-esteem or who are incompetent are especially prone to follow the structure and style of a model. So too are highly dependent individuals and those who have been rewarded previously for conforming behavior. A highly motivated individual will also emulate a model in order to master a desired behavior.

3. *Reward consequences associated with a behavior.* Participants are more likely to emulate a behavior if they believe that such actions will lead to positive short- or long-term results. Bandura believes that this variable is stronger than the other ones.

Learning through observation is not a simple matter of imitation. It is an active judgmental and constructive process. Four interrelated processes govern the development of observational learning: attentional processes, retention processes, motor production processes, and motivational processes (1977).

A number of variables influence *attentional processes*—the characteristics of the model, the nature of the activity, the nature of the subject. Some models are more noticeable than others and thus more readily copied. Charismatic models command considerable attention, whereas persons low in interpersonal attractiveness tend to be ignored. The people with whom one regularly associates limit and structure the kinds of activities and behaviors that one will observe. For example, those who live in an inner city where members of hostile gangs stalk the streets are more likely to learn aggressive modes of response than those who are reared in a pacifist commune. Television and the Internet have greatly enlarged the range of models available to people today. In contrast, our great-grandparents were pretty much limited to modeling sources within their own family and community. Personal qualities— our own interests, needs, wants, and wishes—also determine what we attend to.

Retention processes also influence observational learning. When you observe someone's behavior without immediately performing the response, you have to represent it in some way in order to be able to use it later as a guide for action.

Two types of symbols or representational systems facilitate retention: *verbal* and *imaginal.* You can remember "Big Mac" either by remembering the words themselves or by developing a visual image of two all-beef patties, special sauce, lettuce, cheese, pickles, onion, on a sesame-seed bun. These symbols may then be present to you when the actual stimulus is not.

Motor production processes are another prerequisite of observational learning. An individual has to convert the symbolic representation of the behavior into appropriate actions. The response has to be carried out in space and time in the same way that the original behavior was. Successful motor production requires cognitive organization of the response, initiation of the response, monitoring of the response, and refinement of the response. The skills that we learn through observational learning are perfected slowly through trial and error. We imitate the behavior of a model and then seek to improve our approximations through adjustment and feedback.

Motivational processes are also important. Social learning theory distinguishes between *acquisition,* what a person has learned and can do, and *performance,* what a person actually does. People do not enact everything that they learn. Most of us have the theoretical know-how to rob a store; we have seen robberies in real life or on television. However, most of us will not be applying our theoretical knowledge. We are more likely to engage in a modeled behavior if it will lead to consequences that we value and less likely to engage in it if the results are likely to be punitive. We also learn from observing the consequences of others' behavior. Finally, we can engage in self-reinforcement and self-regulation. We generate evaluative responses toward our own behavior, and they lead us to continue to engage in behaviors that we find self-satisfying and to reject those of which we disapprove or that make us feel uncomfortable.

No behavior occurs without sufficient incentive. Proper motivation not only brings about the actual performance of the behavior but also influences the attentional, retention, and motor production processes involved in observational learning. When we are not motivated to learn something, we do not pay attention, and so we choose to retain scant information. Moreover, we are not willing to practice hard or to engage in the kind of trial-and-error activities necessary for successful motor production. Thus motivation emerges as the primary component of learning through observation.

It is important to postulate the processes underlying observational learning in order to understand the phenomenon and to predict the circumstances under which learning will occur. In early development, children's modeling consists largely of instantaneous response. With age, children develop symbol and motor skills that enable them to follow more complex behaviors. Positing these processes helps us to specify the different variables that are involved in observational learning, develop hypotheses concerning them, and find ways of testing these hypotheses experimentally. In short, they enable us to make more accurate predictions. These constructs also help us to understand those instances in which an individual does not appear to learn from observation. Failure to reproduce a modeled behavior arises from insufficient attention, inadequate symbolization or retention, lack of physical capacities, skill, or practice, inadequate motivation, or any combination of these.

From Reinforcement to Self-Regulation

The importance of reinforcement, so necessary in the early behaviorist models of Dollard, Miller, and Skinner, gradually gives way to the emerging prominence of self-regulation in Bandura's theory. Bandura (1977) points out that almost any behavior can be learned without the direct experience of reinforcement. We do not have to be reinforced to pay attention to vivid images or loud sounds; the impact of the stimulus itself commands our attention. Nor do we have to be directly rewarded in order to learn something. Driving home from work each day, I pass a gas station along the route. One day, when I am nearly out of gas, I drive directly to the station, demonstrating that I had learned where it was even though I was not directly reinforced for doing so.

Observational learning occurs through symbolic processes *while* one is being exposed to the modeled activity and *before* any response has been made. Therefore, it does not depend on external reinforcement. When such reinforcement plays a role in observational learning, it acts as a facilitator rather than a necessary condition. The individual's anticipation of a reward or punishment influences how he or she behaves.

Extrinsic reinforcement is arbitrary or socially arranged rather than the natural outcome of the behavior. A medal for a good athletic performance and an A on a term paper are extrinsic reinforcements. Extrinsic reinforcement is clearly effective in creating behavioral change and has an important role to play in early development. Many activities that we need to learn do not become rewarding until we have become proficient in them. Without positive encouragements in the early stages, we would quickly become discouraged. Depending on the way in which rewards are used, extrinsic incentives can increase interest, reduce interest, or have no effect. What people make of incentives, rather than the incentives themselves, determines how extrinsic rewards affect motivation.

Intrinsic reinforcement is naturally related to the behavior. Some behaviors produce a natural physiological effect; for example, relaxation exercises relieve muscle fatigue. In other instances it is not the behavior itself or the feedback that is rewarding, but how we feel about it. Playing a difficult piece of music well leads to a feeling of accomplishment. The self-satisfaction sustains the practice of the behavior.

Vicarious reinforcement occurs when we learn appropriate behavior from the successes and mistakes of others. Vicarious learning can take the form of either a reward or a punishment. A child who sees a sibling being spanked for a misdemeanor quickly learns not to do the same thing.

Of the broad range of reinforcements that social learning theory considers, self-generated reinforcements become the most important. People have self-reactive capacities that permit them to control their own thoughts, feelings, and actions. People do not behave like weathervanes that shift in different directions according to the external pressures that are placed upon them. Instead, they regulate their own behavior by setting standards of conduct for themselves and responding to their own actions in self-rewarding or self-punishing ways.

Self-reinforcement increases performance primarily through its motivational function. One runner might be satisfied by completing a mile in five minutes; another would want to finish it in less time.

For a summary of Bandura's theory of observational learning see Table 9.1.

TABLE 9.1 OBSERVATIONAL LEARNING

Bandura's theory of observational learning rests on experimental analysis of the influence of modeling on behavior.

THREE FACTORS THAT INFLUENCE MODELING
- Characteristics of the model
- Attributes of the observer
- Reward consequences associated with a behavior

PROCESS OF OBSERVATIONAL LEARNING
- Attentional processes
- Retention processes
- Motor production processes
- Motivational processes

REINFORCEMENT IN OBSERVATIONAL LEARNING
- Extrinsic reinforcement
- Intrinsic reinforcement
- Vicarious reinforcement
- Self-reinforcement

Bandura (1991d) believes that human behavior, particularly in the adult, is motivated by the continual practice of **self-regulation,** or influencing one's own behavior. Self-regulation occurs through self-monitoring, self-judgment, and affective self-reaction. *Self-monitoring* entails paying attention to one's behavior. It permits one to diagnose and understand one's actions. It also helps one to be motivated and set goals for improvement. Attending to behavior gives feedback on performance. No simple process of mechanical tracking, self-monitoring entails self-referent processes that can influence what is observed and affect later courses of action. People vary in their self-monitoring capacities. *Self-judgment* entails evaluating one's behavior. Such evaluation is informed by personal standards that are developed through the reflective processing of the standards and behaviors of significant others as well as other social influences. People evaluate their activities in terms of their own achievement level and the performance level of other people. Perception of environmental circumstances also affects our judgment of behavior. *Affective self-reaction* governs subsequent courses of action. We have good and/or bad feelings about our behavior. Informed by these feelings and seeking to feel good about themselves, individuals create, for their own behavior, incentives and reinforcements, which in turn motivate them to behave in similar or different ways.

AGGRESSION, INHUMANE BEHAVIOR, AND MORAL DISENGAGEMENT

Bandura has made a major contribution to our understanding of aggression and inhumane behavior. Some of his experiments were specifically designed to investigate the influence of television viewing on the development of aggressive responses. In many different variations on his classic Bobo doll studies, Bandura studied the impact of a live model as opposed to a filmed model and a cartoon model. The aggressive film model was just as effective in teaching aggressive forms of behavior as the live model. The cartoon character was somewhat less influential but nevertheless successful. In each study, children who observed an aggressive model (live, film, or cartoon) performed more aggressive responses than did children who observed a nonaggressive model or no model at all (1973). Bandura (1973) has concluded that frequent exposure to aggression and violence on television encourages children to behave aggressively, and he has been very concerned about the aggressive models that our culture provides.

Bandura's demonstrations directed considerable attention to the possible relationship between violence in society and violence on television. It was suggested that several real-life instances of aggression and risk taking had actually been triggered by similar episodes on television or in the movies. For example, death was the result when teenagers copied a stunt from the movie *The Program* in which the "tough" hero lies down at night in the middle of a busy highway. Concern over such behaviors led to a number of studies throughout the 1960s and 1970s (Berkowitz, 1962; Liebert & Baron, 1973; Turner & Berkowitz, 1972). With the increased popularity of video and computer games, attention has turned to the effects of these media on aggression as well (Anderson & Bushman, 2002, 2003; Bartholow & Anderson, 2002; Sherry, 2001; Vesey & Lee, 2000).

No one disputes that learning influences children's aggressive behavior. However, Bandura has gone beyond a simplistic cause-and-effect relationship between viewing violence and violent behavior to a model of multicausality involving a complex interplay. Thus violence on television and in other media may be seen as having multiple effects, such as over-

Bandura believes that frequent exposure to aggression and violence in the media encourages children to behave aggressively, and he has been very concerned about the aggressive models that our culture provides.

whelming the nervous systems of young children (Winn, 2002), the teaching of aggressive styles of behavior, the reduction of restraints over aggression, the desensitization and habituation of viewers to violence, and the shaping of images of reality (Green, 1981; Thomas, Horton, Lippencott, & Drabman, 1977). Of the various options that might be taken to change current media practices, Bandura (1973) indicates that governmental control, public protest, and industry self-regulation have not been very effective. A privately funded public violence monitoring system and the encouragement and rewarding of desirable practices, such as the program *Sesame Street,* have more promise of dealing with the problem constructively. Informed by studies such as those initiated by Bandura, the American Academy of Pediatrics (2001) has recommended no television viewing by children under age two and the viewing of only one or two hours a day of nonviolent educational programs by older children.

Bandura (1986b) has also explored how **moral disengagement** permits individuals and institutions to perpetuate and encourage violence and other inhumane activities while justifying and exonerating their behavior. He has developed a conceptual model exploring the levels of internal control that permit people to disengage from moral behavior. Social cognitive theory bases moral agency in a self-regulatory system in which one controls one's behavior by monitoring and evaluating it in terms of internal standards and situational circumstances.

Initially, external sanctions from parents and others help to control our behavior as children. Eventually, through socialization, we develop moral standards and monitor our own actions. At various points in the self-regulatory process, however, moral self-sanctions can be selectively activated or disengaged (1986b). For example, destructive conduct may be made acceptable if it is linked to what a person considers a good purpose. Or one can justify reprehensible behavior by comparing it to other, more ruthless actions. Such mechanisms enable terrorists, for example, to engage in what otherwise would be unacceptable conduct. We can use euphemisms, or agreeable labels, to describe otherwise contemptible behavior. Genocide becomes "ethnic cleansing." Displacement or diffusion of responsibility also renders questionable conduct more acceptable. It is easy to justify cheating on taxes or using illicit drugs by viewing the laws as unfair or rationalizing that everyone else is doing it also. Ignoring, minimizing, or giving new meaning to our actions can further reduce the detrimental effects of behavior. Thus U.S. destruction in Vietnam in the 1960s and 1970s was conceived as saving the Vietnamese people from the enslavement of communism. Finally, it is easier to harm someone if we can dehumanize the individual or attribute blame to the victim. Victims of rape are often portrayed as provoking the act.

Moral disengagement supports destructive behavior by reducing prosocial feeling and prior self-censure and by encouraging cognitive and emotional reactions that favor aggression. Similar mechanisms are present in interpersonal aggression and delinquent conduct. Such disengagement permits individuals and a variety of industries, from the tobacco industry to gun manufacturers, to perpetuate socially destructive practices (1999b).

Bandura views deliberate purposeful acts of influential people who use their power for destructive and exploitative goals as more threatening to our welfare than impulsive acts of violence (1999b). The controversy that surrounded the release of Mel Gibson's powerful film, *The Passion of the Christ,* centered on its potential to increase ethnic violence. Bandura suggests that we need to develop effective social safeguards to counter such abuse. Pluralistic systems representing various points of view rather than monolithic systems may offer some protection. Corporations need be held accountable for the effects of their policies. Bandura suggests that today the Internet has the potential to increase participatory debate and mobilize collective influence in opposition to abusive practices. At the same time, it, too, is a tool that can be abused. Compassionate and humane behavior needs to be deliberately cultivated and fostered to make it more difficult for individuals and organizations to engage in inhumane practices.

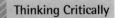

Thinking Critically

How does moral disengagement permit inhumane behavior? See the Thinking Critically box "Moral Disengagement and Reprehensible Conduct."

SELF–EFFICACY

A central mechanism of personal agency and self-regulation is **self-efficacy,** people's belief that they can successfully perform behaviors that will produce desired effects (Bandura (1977, 1997b). Efficacy beliefs work together with other social and cognitive determinants in enabling people to cope with everyday life. Self-efficacy is not to be confused with self-esteem. Self-esteem entails judgments of self-worth; self-efficacy entails judgments of personal capacity. Efficacy beliefs develop independently of performance and give us a basis for predicting whether one will engage in a behavior. Usually people do not try to do things they do not believe they can do.

Self-efficacy is a major component of social cognitive theory. It plays a central role in

Thinking Critically

Moral Disengagement and Reprehensible Conduct

World history provides numerous examples of reprehensible conduct facilitated by moral disengagement: Hutu and Tutsi genocide in Africa, "ethnic cleansing," by Saddam Hussein in Iraq, the "killing fields" of Cambodia, little girls being beheaded in Bangladesh for being Christian, guillotining of the aristocracy during the French Revolution, "ethnic cleansing" by Serbs in former Yugoslavia, treatment of Native American peoples by the U.S. government, treatment of prisoners at Abu Ghraib in Iraq. Choose three of these situations that you are familiar with, or others that come to mind, and identify mechanisms that facilitated moral disengagement.

Was the conduct given a moral justification, compared to more ruthless behavior, or labeled euphemistically? Was responsibility for the behavior displaced onto a higher authority or diffused onto a larger group? Were the consequences of the behavior ignored, minimized, or misconstrued? Were the victims dehumanized or held responsible?

---

governing our thoughts, motivations, and actions. It influences factors such as acquisition of knowledge, choice of activities, and levels of motivation. Perceived self-efficacy also has a generative capacity that activates and coordinates other cognitive, social, and emotional subskills.

In order to do something well, we need both skill and efficacy beliefs. Many people know how to drive; not all of them are able to successfully operate a car under extremely challenging or dangerous conditions. The belief in one's ability to drive does not necessarily coincide with one's actual proficiency.

Self-efficacy arises from past accomplishments that serve as indicators of ability, from vicarious experiences that alter our beliefs through comparison with others, and from social influences (e.g., verbal persuasion), as well as from physical and emotional states. These sources are selected, interpreted, and integrated into a total estimate of self-efficacy that in turn influences subsequent cognitive, motivational, emotional, and selective processes.

Over the course of our lives, our self-efficacy beliefs may change. Different periods of life create different challenges that can alter our development of agency and self-efficacy beliefs. Social conditions and life events, which may or may not be under our control, influence us. Nevertheless, we still have some choice over the environments we are exposed to and over our reactions to situations.

Efficacy beliefs are collective as well as individual. *Collective efficacy* refers to a group's shared belief in its ability to organize and carry out actions that will lead to fulfillment of certain group goals. The sources and functions of collective efficacy are similar to those of individual self-efficacy. Efficacy beliefs may vary cross-culturally. Some cultures may emphasize individuality and individual self-efficacy; others place the interest of the group above the individual and foster collective efficacy. A further distinction can be made between individual or group self-efficacy and communal mastery, the belief that one can succeed by being closely interconnected with others (Hobfoll, Schroder, Wells, & Malek, 2002). These beliefs also vary cross-culturally.

Efficacy beliefs influence our lives in several ways. They contribute to the development of academic confidence and success. Both students' beliefs in their ability to learn academic subjects and teachers' beliefs in their ability to motivate and encourage learning affect academic performance, as does the collective institutional conviction that the school is an important influence on students (see also D'Amico & Cardaci, 2003; Parker, Guarino, & Smith, 2002).

Anyone who is active in sports can readily acknowledge how efficacy beliefs affect almost all areas of athletic functioning. The ability to work hard at a sport, to persevere, concentrate, compete, avoid distractions, and cope with discouraging slumps is mediated by self-efficacy.

Self-efficacy structures vocational choices, educational preparation, and level of accomplishment. Research on self-efficacy in business decision making shows its powerful impact. Wood and Bandura (1989) had managers participate in a computer-simulated organization. The participants had to match employees' talents to particular subfunctions. They also had to learn and use new procedures to achieve challenging levels of organizational performance. The performance of managers who were led to believe that they could not be as effective as other managers and who received negative feedback deteriorated. The organizational functioning of those who were led to believe that they could acquire the skill and were given positive feedback improved. Lent and Lopez (2002) have explored the implications of efficacy beliefs in interpersonal contexts. Efficacy beliefs facilitate social support and adaptive coping strategies (Saltzman & Holahan, 2002).

Self-efficacy even modifies the biological systems of the body involved in health and disease. We can influence our health by controlling our behavior and environment. Although efficacy cannot entirely account for the course of an illness or disease, it can have a major impact. Nine large meta-analyses have been made on self-efficacy research findings studying varied realms of functioning and using varied methods and populations. The studies confirm the explanatory and predictive power of the concept (Bandura, 2004b).

It is important to foster the development of efficacy. In the future, women and ethnic minorities will increasingly make up more of the workforce. Many of these people avoid entering the fields of science, technology, and economics because they lack efficacy beliefs in their quantitative skills. The challenge is to improve their sense of efficacy, as society will be increasingly depending on them for accomplishments in these areas.

Growing global interdependence and rapid social and technological change require us to learn to exercise some control over our lives (Bandura, 1995). Efficacy beliefs structure the ways we select, construct, and manage our environment and adapt to changing social conditions. If we believe in "empowering" people, we must recognize that empowerment can arise only through a sense of efficacy that permits people to believe that they can effect changes personally and collectively.

PSYCHOTHERAPY AND BEHAVIOR MODIFICATION

The agentic perspective also informs Bandura's discussions concerning changing behavior. Bandura (1977) has added to the techniques of behavior modification the systematic use of *modeling* as an aid in changing behaviors. Modeling has been used to reduce fears in children and adults, to teach domineering and hyperaggressive children to be more cooperative, to teach language skills to autistic children, to increase communication facility in asocial psychiatric patients, to lessen anxiety and improve performance in college students, and to facilitate many other behavior changes. In each case, a model or models illustrate or explain an appropriate way of handling a situation, and the patient is encouraged to emulate the model. Thus, in order to eliminate a strong animal phobia, a subject might watch filmed and live models progressively interact with the animal in question and then be encouraged to engage in increasingly intimate interactions with the animal along with the model. Results have shown that modeling procedures are clearly instrumental in reducing and sustaining a reduction in fears and in making other behavioral changes. Modeling has been very effective in both group and individual psychotherapy and shown to benefit both the model and the observer (Yalom, 1995).

Bandura (1977) points out that people who behave in dysfunctional ways generally have a poor sense of self-efficacy. They do not believe that they can successfully perform the behaviors that will enable them to cope with everyday life. Their lowered expectations lead them to avoid situations that are threatening and in which they do not believe they could perform well. Where situations cannot be avoided, they try only a little and give up quickly. As a result, they do not engage in activities that might demonstrate their abilities and serve to change their sense of self-efficacy.

Bandura's therapeutic strategies are designed to help patients improve their perception of their own effectiveness through guided mastery experiences. Thus, in treating a group of *agoraphobics* (people who are afraid of public places), a variety of performance mastery aids were used. Initially, the therapists met with the agoraphobics in small groups and helped them to identify and rank those situations that aroused fear in them. Therapists also taught clients how to use relaxation techniques and how to substitute positive thoughts for self-debilitating ones. Then, through graduated field experiences, they encouraged clients to engage in successful interactions with their feared objects and settings. Appropriate responses and behaviors were modeled by therapists and former agoraphobics. Exposure to feared situations was taken gradually, one step at a time, in order not to overwhelm or discourage the client. Through successful experiences, the participants were able to improve their sense of self-efficacy and to increase the length of time they spent in intimidating situations. Gradually, the field therapists lessened their guided participation and support. Thus, through a variety of techniques, it was possible to increase self-efficacy and restore effective functioning (1986b).

In those cases in which behavior modification has focused only on change in the environment, Bandura points out that it usually has had only a short-term effect. As long as the person is under the control of the therapist or in a carefully monitored environment, the behavior is controlled. Once that external control and support is gone, the person may revert to his or her old style of behavior. Reciprocal causation assumes that behavior is controlled by both the person and the environment. It is possible, therefore, to indicate the conditions under which behavior will generalize and hold up over time and the conditions under which it will not. Change is maintained when (1) the new behavior has functional value for the individual, (2) there are strong social and environmental supports for the behavior, and (3) an individual's own self-evaluation becomes an important reinforcer. Thus cultivating effective practices of self-regulation is an important part of the therapeutic process.

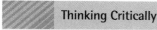

Thinking Critically

How can you use techniques of behavior modification to change your behavior? See the Thinking Critically box "Developing Self-Regulation."

Thinking Critically

Developing Self-Regulation

Techniques informed by social learning theory can be used to develop ways of changing your behavior. By carefully observing your behavior and the factors that lead to it, you can begin to see how to influence an undesired activity and change it. The environment can often be varied so that either the events that promote the activity or the consequences that follow it are changed. Through a strategy of behavioral programming, a person can gradually eliminate inappropriate behaviors and substitute more desirable ones.

In developing a program of self-regulation, the first step is to decide on a particular behavior pattern that you would like to modify, such as smoking. Carefully monitor and observe that behavior so that you can determine the conditions under which it is likely to occur. Your observation should be very specific. Are you likely to have a cigarette immediately upon awakening or after each meal with a cup of coffee? You need to count, chart, and evaluate each instance. It is helpful to keep a behavioral diary or chart. This is one way in which social learning theorists assess behavior. Next, make a list of graduated objectives that would shape you in developing a more appropriate behavior. Do not be overambitious. Select only one problem area and break it down into small, manageable steps. Consider the techniques that would help you achieve your objectives. If you tend to have a cigarette immediately upon awakening, substitute another activity, such as exercise. If you associate coffee with a cigarette, try tea instead. Are there any factors in the environment that you could change to facilitate the development of more appropriate behaviors? If you hang out with smokers in between classes, seek another spot to pass the time. Are there any models whose behavior you could emulate? Finally, you should develop a systematic schedule of reinforcements for appropriate behaviors that lead toward your objectives. How might you use the money you save from not buying cigarettes? Make sure that the reward is something that you value and are willing to work for. And then be sure that you employ it as a means of reinforcement.

Bandura (2004b) encourages the use of contemporary technologies to help modify behavior. Interactive computed-assisted feedback (see Figure 9.2) has been developed to promote good health and guide patients in their efforts to make life-style changes. This feedback can be enhanced by Internet connections that further inform and motivate. Interactive video games have helped young children cope with juvenile diabetes by helping them understand the condition and regulate the diet, insulin, and blood sugar of Packy and Marlon, two wacky diabetic elephants. Similar videos are being used to help children with asthma, cystic fibrosis, and other health issues. Self-management programs for geriatric populations are also being developed to help the elderly deal with arthritis and chronic diseases that accompany aging.

Serials dramatizing problems that people in various parts of the world deal with—such as family planning, AIDS prevention, spousal abuse, degrading dowry practices, literacy, and environmental degradation—have been useful tools, particularly in third-world areas

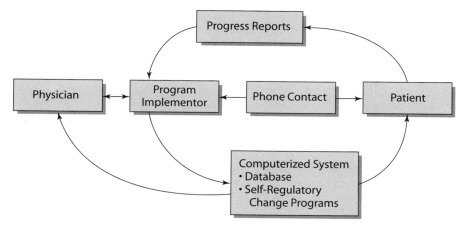

FIGURE 9.2 COMPUTER–ASSISTED SELF–REGULATORY DELIVERY SYSTEM FOR ALTERING HEALTH HABITS

SOURCE: *Bandura, A. (2004). Health promotion by social cognitive means.* Health Education and Behavior, *31(2), p. 153.*

(where radio versions can reach vast rural populations). Such serials inform, motivate, and link people to appropriate community resources. For example, a teenager in India who heard a radio serial drama in which a mother and daughter challenged restrictive cultural norms for women asked: "When Taru and her mother can fight harsh circumstances, why can't we?" (Bandura, 2006b).

Bandura has responded sharply to charges that behavior modification entails manipulation of human beings and denial of their freedom. He points out that procedures used to create a behavior pattern that is convenient to the influencer but of little value to the individual usually do not produce lasting results (Evans, 1976). Behavior modification increases rather than limits an individual's freedoms.

PHILOSOPHY,
SCIENCE,
and ART

Bandura's Theory

Heir to the behavior and learning tradition in American psychology, Bandura has developed one of the most popular approaches to the study of personality. It is particularly appealing to academic psychologists because it lies within the mainstream of American psychology. It strongly emphasizes experimental research and clearly emulates a scientific model. At the same time, it has increased clinical appeal.

Bandura's reintroduction of internal variables, his emphasis on triadic reciprocal causation, and his investigation of human participants allow his theory to deal with complex social responses more adequately than radical behavior and learning theories. B. F. Skinner's learning theory can account for the learned behavior of animals and very simple learned habits and behaviors of human beings; it does not explain complex human behaviors such as decision making and creativity well.

Philosophical
Assumptions

Which philosophical issues
were important to Bandura?
See the Philosophical
Assumptions box "Examining
Bandura, Rotter, and
Mischel" on page 257.

Bandura's account clearly includes those kinds of complex activities, permitting scientific analysis of a wide range of human behaviors. Bandura's work has helped to overcome the earlier behaviorist view of human nature as a machine whose output depends on the input provided. Indeed, Bandura's theory underscores the vast differences between a human being and a computer.

Bandura notes that psychology studies the complex interrelationships among biological, intrapersonal, interpersonal, and sociocultural factors of human behavior. Thus psychology is "the integrated discipline best suited to advance understanding of human adaptation and change" (2000).

Bandura's theory is clearly grounded in empirical research and is amenable to precise laboratory methods of investigation. It has stimulated research in other areas and has implications for personality assessment (Cervone, Shadel, & Jencius, 2001). It economically states major constructs in relatively simple terms. And it is compatible with our existing concept of the world.

We have also seen that learning and behavior theorists have sometimes failed to appreciate that scientific work is based on philosophical assumptions. Skinner, for example, for many years did not acknowledge the philosophical commitments that inform his work. Bandura recognizes that his scientific efforts rest on philosophical assumptions (1986a). At the same time, he avoids elevating his empirical conclusions into philosophical ones.

In spite of their desire to limit their activities to empirical science, learning and behavior theorists invariably raise philosophical issues and ethical questions (Rottschaefer, 1991). This is particularly evident in their efforts to apply their theories toward the improvement of human behavior and society. Bandura has developed significant new forms of psychotherapy, such as modeling. He has spoken candidly about the dangers of aggressive models. Other findings from observational learning theory have been taken from the laboratory and applied to problems in the everyday world, clearly demonstrating the practicality of Bandura's approach. His social cognitive theory has been applied to the most urgent global problems, such as burgeoning birthrates, and to the development of new models for health promotion (2000).

Individuals and collectives confident in their efficacy will be best equipped to take advantage of the expanding environment provided by electronic technology and global human connectedness to promote emotional well-being, education, health, work conditions, and productivity, and to change organizational and social conditions that affect the lives of people. The anonymity and pseudonymity of the cyber world, however, also facilitate moral disengagement (Bandura, 2004c). Social cognitive theory can help us develop guidelines for using new technologies and the Internet productively and creatively so that the impact of these forces is positive rather than divisive in our lives (Bandura, 2002).

Bandura has helped revitalize the learning and behavior approach by infusing it with an agentic perspective and by acknowledging some of its philosophical underpinnings. The scientific emphasis makes his approach an extremely popular one. His influence will undoubtedly continue to be substantial.

Like Bandura's, Julian Rotter's and Walter Mischel's work corrects some of the shortcomings of earlier behavior and learning theory and incorporates new findings in or from cognitive psychology.

Julian Rotter (1916–   )

INTERNAL VERSUS EXTERNAL CONTROL OF REINFORCEMENT

Rotter's most important concept is **locus of control,** the extent to which a person believes that reinforcements are controlled by his or her own behavior or by people or outside forces such as luck or fate. Rotter conducted a series of experiments designed to tell whether or not people learn tasks and perform differently when they see reinforcements as related or unrelated to their own behavior. The results of these experiments led him to develop the **I-E Scale,** an assessment tool that measures an individual's perception of control (1966). Internally controlled individuals (I) assume that their own behaviors and actions are responsible for the consequences that happen to them. Externally controlled people (E) believe that control is out of their hands.

Internal control and external control are the two extremes on the control-of-reinforcement continuum. Competence, mastery, helplessness, powerlessness, or alienation are but a few of the terms used to describe degrees of perceived control on the continuum.

Rotter's concept of locus of control is not the same as Bandura's concept of self-efficacy. *Self-efficacy* refers to the belief that one is able to perform certain actions. *Locus of control* anticipates whether one's actions will influence outcomes. Some have inquired whether self-efficacy and locus of control are indicators of a common core construct (Judge, Erez, Bono, & Thoresen, 2002). Rotter believes that his construct has an advantage over others because it is an integral part of a formal theory from which predictions can be made.

Although various measuring devices have been developed to assess locus of control as a stable personality characteristic, Rotter's scale remains one of the most widely used. The I-E Scale consists of twenty-three forced-choice items and six filler items. The participant indicates which of each pair of items applies best. The final score can range from 0 to 23; higher scores indicate greater externality. Although Rotter does not indicate any cutoff score that separates internals from externals, norms have been published for various groups to facilitate comparisons. On a national sample of high school students, the mean score was 8.50. The lowest mean score reported by Rotter was 5.94 among a group of Peace Corps trainees (1966).

The I-E Scale has been widely used in research and has led to a number of significant findings: Internality increases with age; as children grow older, their locus of control tends to become more internal; internality becomes stable in middle age and does not diminish in old age, contrary to popular views of the elderly as dependent. Certain parental practices help to foster a belief in internal control: warm, responsible, supportive conditions and the encouragement of independence (de Mann, Leduc, & Labrèche-Gauthier, 1992; Lefcourt, 1976).

Several studies have shown that internals are more perceptive and more ready to learn about their surroundings. They ask more questions and process information more efficiently than externals. They have greater mastery tendencies, better problem-solving abilities, and more likelihood of achievement (Agarwal & Misra, 1986). They learn faster how to co-operate (Boone et al., 2002). Thus internal prison inmates know more about the institution and conditions affecting their parole and are more likely to be paroled (Rotter, 1966). Internals are better versed about critical political events that may influence their lives (Ryckman & Malikiosi, 1975).

Internals are more likely to know about the conditions that lead to good physical and emotional health and to take positive steps to improve their health, such as quitting smoking, avoiding substance abuse, and engaging in regular exercise (Bezjak & Lee, 1990; Menec & Chipperfield, 1997; Powell, 1992; Rosolack & Hampson, 1991). They suffer less from hypertension and are less likely to have heart attacks. When they do become ill, they cope with the illness more adequately than externals (Strickland, 1978, 1979; see also Elkis-Abuhoff, 2003). Internals also derive more benefit from social support (Lefcourt, Martin, & Saleh, 1984) and are more likely to use contraception (Visher, 1986).

Internal locus of control appears to protect one against unquestioning submission to authority. Internals are more resistant to influences from other people. They make more independent judgments and try harder to control the behavior of others (Lefcourt, 1976). They tend to assume more responsibility for their own behavior and attribute responsibility to others.

Externals are more likely to conform (Singh, 1984) and prefer not to have to make a choice (Harrison, Lewis, & Straka, 1984). Externals tend to be more anxious and depressed, as well as more vulnerable to stress. They develop defensive strategies that invite failure in coping with a task and use defensive strategies afterward to explain their failures. They attribute their lack of success to bad luck or to the difficulties of the task (Drwal & Wiechnik, 1984; Lester, 1992). Pertinent to terror management theory, mortality salience decreases the perception of risk and increases risk taking in externals, while having the opposite effect in internals (Miller & Mulligan, 2002).

Some research has shown sex differences in locus of control, with females tending to be more external (de Brabander & Boone, 1990). The increase in external scores for women in the 1970s may reflect greater awareness of external constraints on their ability to meet their goals at work and in other settings (Doherty & Baldwin, 1985). However, family socioeconomic status is an even stronger correlate of locus of control (Young & Schorr, 1986), as well as not being a member of a vulnerable population, "such as children, medical patients, lower level employees, and the elderly" (Thompson & Spacapan, 1991).

Rotter believes that extreme belief in either internal or external locus of control is unrealistic and unhealthy. He has hypothesized a curvilinear relationship between locus of control measures and assessments of maladjustment (Rotter & Hochreich, 1975). However, it is clear that many favorable characteristics have been associated with internal locus of control, and it has been proposed that an internal orientation is more conducive to positive social adjustment and functioning.

The locus of control construct is durable and has had a major impact (Lefcourt, 1992). Some of the more recent research is cross-cultural (e.g., Banks, Ward, McQuater, & De Britto, 1991; Murk & Addleman, 1992; Saeeduzzafar & Sharma, 1991). Minority groups frequently test higher in external control. However, within the context of their culture, this does not necessarily indicate a poorer outcome. The association of positive outcomes with internal locus of control may not be universal (Hall & Barongan, 2002). One trend in more recent research on locus of control is to develop measures for specific domains such as health. This specificity may facilitate prediction, but it detracts from Rotter's initial concept of locus of control as a generalized expectation.

PREDICTING BEHAVIOR

Rotter's empirical observations about individual differences led to a more general motivational theory in which behavior potential, expectancy, reinforcement value, and the psychological situation are seen as four variables that can be measured and related in a specific formula that enables us to predict a person's behavior in any given situation (Rotter & Hochreich, 1975) through self-reports and behavioral observations.

Behavior potential refers to the likelihood that a particular response behavior will occur in a given situation. Rotter uses the term *behavior* broadly to refer to a wide class of responses that includes overt movements, verbal expressions, and cognitive and emotional reactions. In any given situation, an individual could react in a number of different ways. The behavior potential is specific both for the particular behavior and for the related reinforcement. Thus we must know what goal the behavior is related to before we can tell how likely it is to occur.

Expectancy refers to individuals' subjective expectations about the outcome of their behavior. It is an estimation of the probability that a particular reinforcement will occur if one behaves in a certain way in a given situation. What does Johnny expect will be the outcome of his temper tantrum? The answer to that question will influence the likelihood of a tantrum occurring.

Reinforcement value refers to the importance or preference of a particular reinforcement for an individual. Mary may be more willing to wash Dad's car if she thinks she'll receive ten dollars for the chore rather than just a verbal thank-you. Reinforcement value differs from individual to individual. Some children are more eager to please their parents than others. People also engage in activities for different reasons.

Julian Rotter (left) and Walter Mischel expanded social learning theories through research in topics such as locus of control and behavioral specificity.

Psychological situation refers to the psychological context in which the individual responds. It is the situation as defined from the perspective of the person. Any given situation has different meanings for different individuals, and these meanings affect the response. Rotter's concept of the psychological situation takes into account the importance of both dispositional and situational influences. An individual may have a strong need for aggression but may or may not behave aggressively in a particular situation, depending on reinforcement expectancies. Rotter believes that the complex cues of each situation arouse in individuals expectations for behavior reinforcement outcomes and for reinforcement sequences. The development of precise measuring techniques for these constructs, however, is only at a very early stage.

Walter Mischel (1930–   )

BEHAVIOR SPECIFICITY

Rotter's ideas about the significance of people's expectations in determining their behavior have influenced the thinking of Walter Mischel, whose work also reflects psychology's renewed interest in cognition. Mischel initially emphasized behavioral specificity in his discussion of human behavior. **Behavioral specificity** (Mischel, 1968) means that an individual's behavior is determined by the specific situation. Mischel initially thought that we behave consistently in the same manner in different situations only to the extent that these situations lead to similar consequences. When the consequences are different, we learn to discriminate among different situations and behave accordingly. Which reaction we show at any particular moment depends on discriminative stimuli: where we are, whom we are with, and so forth. Like other social learning theorists, Mischel emphasized behavioral specificity rather than trait consistency (trait theories are discussed in the part on dispositional theories).

Mischel's work stimulated a person-situation debate that commanded the attention of personality theorists for the next two decades. In the process, Mischel has tempered his position and conceded that it is overgeneralizing the concept of traits rather than the concept itself that is dangerous. Although it can be helpful to postulate a trait in explaining behavior, traits should not be seen as the sole determinants of behavior (1983). The debate underscored the need to study how personality and situations both contribute to behavior rather than simply attributing behavior to one or the other. Mischel (1973) attempted to reconstruct the idea of individual trait variations in light of concepts derived from the study of cognition and social learning. These have been further refined in his latest model (Mischel, 2004; Mischel & Shoda, 1995).

A COGNITIVE-AFFECTIVE PERSONALITY SYSTEM

In collaboration with Yuichi Shoda, Mischel has suggested a cognitive-affective system theory of personality, called **CAPS** for short (Mischel & Shoda, 1995). The theory considers both the stability of personality and the variability of behaviors across situations. In Mischel and Shoda's view, personality is a stable system that mediates the selection, construction, and processing of social information that generates social behavior. Individuals differ in their selection of situations to attend to, in their encoding of the situations, and in their emotional responses to them. These differences interact with other individual mediating processes, such as expectancies and behavioral scripts and plans, in determining behavior. Patterns of variability in behavior are not unwanted errors but reflections of the same stable underlying personality. This system makes it possible to account for both the unchanging qualities of the underlying personality and the expected variability of behavior across situations.

In order to accurately predict weather, meteorologists need to be aware of specific atmospheric processes that are responsible for changing weather patterns, not just overall climatic trends that tell us that Florida is usually warmer than New York. Similarly, personality theories must conceive of personality in terms of individual mediating processes, as well as predisposing behaviors. If we want to know why two people differ in the extent to which they display honesty across situations, it is not sufficient to simply look at differences in the levels of the trait of honesty that they possess. We need also to consider the unique pattern of where and when they differ in displaying the trait. The "self" that relates to Mother when visiting the family over the holidays is different from the "self" that relates to one's partner on the way home (Mischel, 2004).

In Mischel and Shoda's theory, individuals are described in terms of both the distinctive organization of their cognitions and feelings and the psychological features of situations. There is a stable pattern of variability within the individual that marks his or her distinctive behavior organization and profile. This conception of personality focuses on both the relationships between psychological features of situations and the individual's pattern of behavior variation across situations. One's **behavioral signature** is the personality consistencies found in distinctive and stable patterns of variability across situations. Focusing on the interaction between personal and situational variables allows researchers to make precise predictions concerning stability and change in behaviors. For example, Wright and Mischel (1988) were able to accurately predict that children with strong aggressive tendencies would act more aggressively in certain high-stress situations than children with low aggressive tendencies but that there would be little aggressive behavior from either group in specified low-stress situations. They focus on a conditional approach to dispositions, seeing them as clusters of behavior contingencies that link situations and behavior.

Mischel and Shoda believe that their approach accounts both for individual differences in behavior in general and for stable profiles of behavior variability across situations by seeing them as expressions of the same personality system. Their theory can also resolve the problem of consistency that has long been debated by personality theorists. People who are similar in their overall level of a trait such as honesty may show different, yet predictable, patterns in specific situations. The variation across situations is neither random nor representative of common differences in normative levels of behavior. Rather, it is a predictable indication of the organization of the personality system itself. Mischel and Shoda believe that this organization within a person remains fairly stable unless new development, learning, or biochemical changes occur.

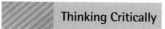

Thinking Critically

How does your behavior vary in different situations? See the Thinking Critically box "Behavioral Signatures."

The stable situation-behavior profiles generated by the personality system allow both the individual study of persons in their life contexts and also the general characterization of a group or type of individuals. They permit psychologists to describe individuals in terms of stable qualities that do not change across situations, as well as in terms of individual psychological processes that lead to different reactions in different situations. By assuming

Thinking Critically

Behavioral Signatures

Mischel, Shoda, and their colleagues asked students to imagine themselves in specific situations, such as receiving a bad grade on an important test, and then to complete items such as "I am _____ when _____." Their answers were less extreme than those of participants who imagined the same situations but responded simply to global items, such as "I am _____." Referring to a specific situational context helps to keep people from overgeneralizing about themselves or other people (Mendoza-Denton, Ayduk, Mischel, Shoda, & Testa, 2001) and to reveal people's distinctive, stable "behavioral signatures" (Mischel, 2004).

Vividly imagine yourself in a variety of situations; then describe yourself in those situations, using the format "I am _____ when _____." This activity should help you to curb extremities in your thinking and to avoid global conclusions, such as "I am a total failure."

Mischel and Shoda view personality traits as patterns of linkages between situations and actions. Given situation x, action y is likely. Describe yourself in a number of situations, following the pattern "Given situation x, I am likely to _____." This approach is similar to the way we usually describe other people's behavior. We specify the conditions in which the behavior will occur; for example, Marissa will attack when she is threatened. Identify occasions on which you may experience the same emotion but respond differently because of the situation.

that each partner's behavior provides the situational context for the other partner's cognitive-affective processing system, the CAPS approach has been used to organize research on attachment, rejection sensitivity, interdependence, and other interpersonal issues (Zavas, Shoda, & Ayduk, 2002).

Conclusions

Bandura's, Rotter's, and Mischel's theories are good examples of contemporary scientific approaches to personality. Cognitive and social learning theorists appreciate that we cannot understand an individual's behavior or personality without also asking what is going on in his or her mind. Moreover, they realize that the mind and its processes can be investigated scientifically. Bandura and Rotter have combined the insights of earlier behavior and learning theories with contemporary findings in the area of cognition and social psychology.

There are several interesting points of comparison among the social learning theorists. Bandura is more situational in his emphasis than Rotter or Mischel and Shoda. Rotter believes in a cross-situational locus of control but, like Bandura, does not place much emphasis on neurological and genetic factors. Mischel and Shoda

Philosophical Assumptions

Where do Bandura, Rotter, and Mischel stand on basic philosophical assumptions? See the Philosophical Assumptions box "Examining Bandura, Rotter, and Mischel."

☀ Philosophical Assumptions

Examining Bandura, Rotter, and Mischel

Many of the differences among personality theories can be attributed to fundamental differences in philosophical assumptions. Which of the basic philosophical issues, described in the introductory chapter and summarized on the inside back cover, seem to be clearly important to Bandura, Rotter, and Mischel in the development of their theories? How, for example, does Bandura's agentic perspective influence his stance on freedom and determinism? How does Rotter's view of locus of control influence his view of proactivity versus reactivity? Did Mischel's shift from an emphasis on behavior specificity to a cognitive-affective personality system indicate a shift of emphasis in heredity versus environment? Do their theories address any other philosophical assumptions? Rate Bandura, Rotter, and Mischel on a scale of 1 to 5 on those philosophical assumptions that you feel their theories apply to most. Compare your ratings of Bandura, Rotter, and Mischel with your own philosophical assumptions. Did your study of Bandura, Rotter, and Mischel lead you to change any of your assumptions? Why or why not?

make the compelling argument that personality must be understood from a biopsychological conceptualization of behavior in terms of variance rather than invariance.

Although these theories are based largely on research, most of the research has been conducted on European Americans. The focus on a linear cause-and-effect model is not characteristic of many minority groups, whose thinking is more likely to be circular and interpersonal (Krantrowitz & Ballou, 1992). As we have seen, learning and behavior theories tend to limit the kinds of phenomena psychologists can study and the ways in which they can investigate the phenomena. Their preoccupation with objective methodology and overt behaviors may constrain psychological investigation and prevent a more holistic understanding of human nature.

The validating evidence of the scientist is seldom as insightful or compelling as the epiphanic vision of the philosopher. This may be the price that social learning theories pay for the precision, power, and predictability of their work. Nevertheless, it has been their deliberate choice to restrict their assumptions and mechanisms to those that can be embraced by an exact scientific methodology. Thus, although they do not evoke deep insight or new philosophical understanding, they do provide precise, accurate, and measurable constructs. Moreover, the "dynamical" perspective afforded by Mischel and Shoda's CAPS theory (Shoda, Tiernan, & Mischel, 2002), in which elements change by virtue of their interaction, is emerging as a major integrative paradigm for personality (Vallacher, Read, & Nowak, 2002).

 TO LEARN MORE about research on the potential harm in playing violent video games, about a theory that expands Rotter's model of internal and external locus of control, and about observational learning, and for a list of suggested readings, visit the *Personality Theories* textbook website at **college.cengage.com/pic/engler8e.**

Summary

1. Albert Bandura introduces an **agentic perspective** (p. 235) to clarify that people actively contribute to their experience. Human agency entails intentionality, forethought, self-reactiveness, and self-reflectiveness.

2. Bandura suggests that the interplay of three factors—personal determinants, behavioral determinants, and environmental determinants—shapes human behavior. **Triadic reciprocal causation** (p. 236) is his name for this idea.

3. Bandura believes that most human behavior is learned through observation and modeling. Three factors that influence modeling are characteristics of the model, attributes of the observer, and reward consequences associated with the behavior. Four processes that enter into **observational learning** (p. 237) are attentional processes, retention processes, motor reproduction processes, and motivational processes. Extrinsic, intrinsic, vicarious, and self-reinforcement all play a role in observational learning.

4. **Self-regulation** (p. 242) is influencing one's own behavior. It entails self-monitoring, self-judgment, and affective self-reaction.

5. Bandura believes that frequent exposure to aggression and violence in the media encourages people to behave aggressively. He explores how moral disengagement permits individuals and institutions to continue inhumane behaviors.

6. **Self-efficacy** (p. 244) refers to people's beliefs that they can successfully perform behaviors that will produce desired effects.

7. Bandura added the systematic use of modeling as a therapeutic technique of behavior modification, and he developed strategies designed to help people improve their sense of self-efficacy. He also has conducted research in the area of self-control.

8. Bandura's theory clearly emulates a scientific model.

9. Rotter developed the **I-E Scale** (p. 251) to measure internal versus external control of reinforcement. The scale has been widely used in research and has led to a number of significant findings.

10. The four variables in Rotter's cognitive social learning approach are **behavior potential** (p. 253), **expectancy** (p. 253), **reinforcement value** (p. 253), and the **psychological situation** (p. 254). They can be measured and related in a specific formula that enables us to predict a person's behavior in any given situation.

11. Mischel's initial work on **behavioral specificity** (p. 254) indicated that an individual's behavior is determined by the situation.

12. According to **CAPS** (p. 254)—the cognitive-affective systems theory of personality—personality is a stable system that mediates the selection, construction, and processing of information that generates behavior. One's **behavioral signature** (p. 255) is the personality consistencies found in distinctive and stable patterns of variability across situations.

Personal Experiences

1. Bandura has explored the effects of the frequent exposure of children and adults to aggression and inhumane behavior in the media, and he has been concerned about the aggressive models that our culture provides. Have you ever seen a child emulate an aggressive model? Have you ever emulated an aggressive model? Has exposure to violence in the media affected your attitudes about or tolerance for violence? You can explore your own response by carefully monitoring your own television viewing and computer activity (i.e., playing computer games or surfing the Internet) and recording how many violent episodes you see in each show or activity. A "violent episode" is any behavior aimed at harming another living creature that wishes to avoid such treatment. Assaults on inanimate objects are considered violent if they indirectly cause harm, such as destruction of another's property. After each viewing period, record your mood and desire to express yourself aggressively on a scale of 1 (not at all) to 10 (a great deal). Do you see any correlation between your intensity of mood and the number of violent episodes you observe? Do your results confirm Bandura's position that exposure to aggression tends to increase aggression?

2. Explore Bandura's notion of moral disengagement in your own life. This chapter focuses on the larger implications of this idea, such as in cases of rape and genocide. In the context of what smaller events is moral disengagement evident in your everyday life? Do you tend to legitimize your own behavior while condemning the same behavior in others? More to the point, do you sometimes relabel acts to suit your own needs? For example, if you play a sport, have you ever characterized your teammates as "tough and competitive" and accused a competing team of playing dirty and breaking the rules? Have you ever labeled your views as "honest" while you label other people as being "judgmental" or "mean" for expressing theirs? List three instances in which moral disengagement may have influenced your behavior.

3. Self-efficacy, as explained by Bandura, relates to people's beliefs about how well they can successfully perform behaviors that will produce a desired effect. Beliefs about efficacy are both individual and collective and directly impact personal choices and values. To examine the influence that beliefs about personal efficacy can have on a person's life, ask five of your friends what they feel they do best. Does the skill they name relate to their field of study, to their favorite hobby, to their political beliefs? Do you agree with their self-efficacy assessments? Do they agree with your own self-efficacy assessments?

4. Rotter's most important concept is locus of control, the extent to which a person believes that reinforcements are driven by his or her own behavior (internal locus) or by other people or outside forces (external locus). Who among the significant persons in your life do you think has the strongest internal locus of control? Who has the strongest external locus of control? Describe the characteristics of these individuals. In what ways if any are their personalities distinctly different, or are they predominantly the same?

5. How well can you "read" your friends? In Rotter's theory, *behavior potential* refers to the likelihood that a particular response behavior will occur in a given situation. Behavior potential is one of four variables that can be used to predict a person's behavior. The

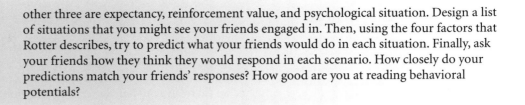

other three are expectancy, reinforcement value, and psychological situation. Design a list of situations that you might see your friends engaged in. Then, using the four factors that Rotter describes, try to predict what your friends would do in each situation. Finally, ask your friends how they think they would respond in each scenario. How closely do your predictions match your friends' responses? How good are you at reading behavioral potentials?

PART FIVE

Dispositional and Biological Theories

The oldest and most persistent approach to personality, one that is currently enjoying a renewed surgence, is the dispositional. People have always described one another by talking about their differences and putting them into general categories. People have been described as hot-tempered or placid, shy or aggressive, masculine or feminine, intelligent or dull, and so forth. Even though our specific actions may vary according to the situation we are in, we conceive of ourselves as the same person and recognize a certain regularity or pattern in our behavior. These qualities appear to be long-term dispositions or traits that can be used to characterize our personality. Part V concentrates on the contributions of dispositional theorists who emphasize the importance of long-term characteristics in personality, while recognizing today that traits interact with the environment to form behavior.

Contemporary research also substantiates that many identified personality characteristics have a biological basis. Psychology shied away from the biological basis of personality for much of the twentieth century after misguided political leaders, such as Hitler, used biological data to assert the alleged superiority of one group over another and attempted to eliminate supposedly inferior groups. However, recognition of biological differences does not necessarily lead to prejudicial behavior and may in fact lead to constructive behaviors and technologies that can enhance the quality of life for all groups. The resurgence of interest in the biological basis of behavior today holds promise of providing such life enhancements.

CHAPTER 10

Traits and Personology

- **Gordon Allport**
- **Henry Murray**

1. Discuss Allport's definition of personality.
2. Distinguish between **continuity** and **discontinuity** theories of personality.
3. Explain how **common traits** differ from **personal dispositions.**
4. Distinguish among three levels of personal dispositions.
5. Explain why Allport coined the term **proprium.**
6. Discuss the concept of **functional autonomy.**
7. Discuss Allport's concept of maturity.
8. Distinguish between **nomothetic** and **idiographic** approaches to the study of personality, and give examples of each.
9. Evaluate Allport's theory from the viewpoints of philosophy, science, and art.
10. Describe the study of **personology.**
11. Identify the units by which Murray suggests behavior can be studied.
12. Explain how Murray studied human **needs,** and identify Murray's twenty basic human needs.
13. Explain what Murray means by **press,** and give examples.
14. Discuss assessment and research in Murray's theory, and describe the **Thematic Apperception Test.**
15. Evaluate Murray's theory from the viewpoints of philosophy, science, and art.

G ordon Allport and Henry Murray were dispositional theorists who emphasized the complexity of personality and the need for an interdisciplinary approach to its study. Critical of narrow conceptions of personality and research, they believed that new methods of study were required to capture the richness and fullness of an individual's personality. Gordon Allport's theory emphasizes the uniqueness of the individual, the contemporaneity of motives, and a holistic view of the person. Allport paved the way for the humanistic approach, which we will consider in the next part of this book. Indeed, he was the first to coin the term *humanistic psychology* in 1930 (DeCarvalho, 1991). Henry Murray's theory is distinguished by its explicit discussion of motivation and the careful construction of a list of needs that characterize and direct human behavior.

Gordon Allport (1897–1967)

BIOGRAPHICAL BACKGROUND

Allport was born in 1897 in Indiana and grew up near Cleveland, Ohio. He described his practical but humanitarian home life as the son of a country doctor as one characterized by "plain Protestant piety and hard work." Allport wrote little about his childhood; he indicated that he spent much of it alone. He was adept at language but poor at sports and games.

After he graduated from high school, his brother Floyd, who also became a distinguished psychologist (see Nicholson, 2000), encouraged him to apply to Harvard, where Floyd had gone. As an undergraduate, Allport concentrated on both psychology and social ethics and in his spare time engaged in social service activities. He ran a boys' club in Boston's West End, served as a volunteer probation officer for the Family Society, and assisted other groups.

Upon graduation, he accepted an opportunity to teach English and sociology at Robert College in Istanbul, Turkey, in a venture that was an early forerunner of the Peace Corps. He enjoyed teaching and accepted a fellowship from Harvard for graduate study in psychology. He received his Ph.D. only two years later, in 1922. His dissertation, "An Experimental Study of the Traits of Personality," was also the first American study on personality traits.

Another fellowship for travel abroad gave an opportunity for Allport to meet Freud. Allport described their meeting as follows: When he arrived, Freud sat silent, apparently waiting for Allport to state the reason for his visit. Allport was simply curious. Then, an incident came to mind that he thought might interest Freud, because it concerned a small boy who had a phobia that appeared to be set very early in life. He told Freud about an event that had happened on the streetcar on the way to Freud's office. A small boy who was obviously afraid of dirt kept saying to his mother that he didn't want to sit on a dirty seat or next to a dirty man. When Allport finished, Freud looked at him and said, "And was that little boy you?" Allport was surprised, but he regained his composure and changed the subject. Still, he was shaken, and he never forgot the incident. He began to feel that Freud's ascription of most behaviors to unconscious motives was incorrect and that an alternative theory of motivation was necessary. In his own theory, Allport did not probe into the dark side of personality; he did not concur with Freud's emphasis on sexuality and unconscious motivations.

Gordon Allport emphasized that traits are bona fide structures within a person that influence behavior.

On his return from Europe, Allport became an instructor in social ethics at Harvard, where he developed and taught what was probably the first course offered in personality in this country. In 1926 he left to take up an assistant professorship in psychology at Dartmouth, but in 1930 he returned to Harvard, this time to stay. His contributions to Harvard were many. Most notably, he was an early advocate of interdisciplinary studies and a leader in the creation of the department of social relations, which combined degree programs in psychology, sociology, and anthropology. His professional honors were manifold, and he was a popular and respected teacher. He died in 1967, one month before his seventieth birthday.

THE NATURE OF PERSONALITY

Allport described and classified over fifty definitions of personality before he developed his own in 1937. After working with this definition for many years, he revised it in 1961. His final definition is: "Personality is the dynamic organization within the individual of those psychophysical systems that determine his characteristic behavior and thought." Each word in this definition is carefully chosen. Personality is *dynamic* (moving and changing), *organized* (structured), *psychophysical* (involving both the mind and the body), *determined* (structured by the past and predisposing of the future), and *characteristic* (unique for each individual).

For Allport, personality is not a fiction or an imaginary concept but a real entity. He wanted to suggest that one's personality is really *there.* He referred to the concept of personality as a hypothetical construct that is currently unobservable because it cannot be measured empirically. However, Allport suggested that personality is an inference that may someday be demonstrated directly as a real existence within the person, involving neural or physiological components. At one time the now dwarf planet Pluto was a hypothetical construct, postulated long before any telescope could observe it. In time, science was able to point directly to it. Allport also hoped that neurophysiological and psychological research eventually would show us the way to directly locate our present hypothetical construct of personality. In this connection, Allport was rather prophetic in recognizing that in the future much of psychology's research would focus on the brain.

Allport (1960) distinguished among continuity and discontinuity theories of personality and argued for a discontinuity theory. A **continuity theory** suggests that the development of personality is essentially the accumulation of skill, habits, and discriminations, without anything really new appearing in the person's makeup. Changes are merely quantitative relative to the amount of inputs. Such continuity theories are **closed systems.**

A **discontinuity theory** suggests that in the course of development an organism experiences genuine transformations or changes and consequently reaches successively higher levels of organization. Here growth is conceived as qualitatively different. Walking is considered very different from crawling, talking is viewed as discontinuous with babbling, and so forth, even though these behaviors emerge out of the earlier ones. If we picture personality as an organism into which inputs are introduced, a continuity theory merely sees the inputs accumulating. In contrast, a discontinuity theory suggests that at times during its development the organism reorganizes, regroups, and reshapes these inputs so that the structure of personality changes radically. Discontinuity theories view the person as open and active in consolidating and integrating experience. Change is qualitative rather than merely quantitative.

Theories that posit stages of personality development have the potential to imply discontinuity, because each stage entails a different organization of personality from the stage before it. Allport believed that Freud's psychoanalytic theory, though outlining stages of development, did not fully realize this potential because of Freud's primary emphasis on the individual and intrapsychic factors. Elements within Freud's theory pointed toward discontinuity, but the theory remained semiclosed.

TRAITS

With the possible exception of Raymond Cattell, Allport explored the concept of **trait** more fully than any other personality theorist. Allport proposed a biophysical conception of traits as neuropsychic structures (1937). He emphasized that traits are bona fide structures within a person that influence behavior; they are not simply labels we use to describe or classify behaviors.

Allport defined a trait as a determining tendency or predisposition to respond to the world in certain ways. Traits are consistent and enduring; they account for consistency in human behavior. Allport suggested that traits may be considered the ultimate reality of psychological organization. The trait, like personality, is not in principle unobservable. In time, trait theorists may be able to measure traits empirically.

Allport distinguished between individual traits and common traits (1937). In his later writings, to clarify his position, he used the terms *common traits* and *personal dispositions*.

Common Traits

A **common trait** is a hypothetical construct that permits us to compare individuals within a given culture. Although no two people can be said to possess identical traits, we can discover roughly comparable traits that allow us to compare the predispositions that are held in common with other persons. Normal people in any given culture tend to develop along similar modes or lines of adjustment. In a competitive society, most individuals develop a level of assertiveness or ascendance that can be compared with the level of assertiveness in others. There are several aspects of personality in respect to which all people in a given culture may be compared.

Personal Dispositions

Comparisons may be made among individuals, but in the last analysis no two individuals are exactly alike. A **personal disposition** is, like a trait, a general determining characteristic, but it is unique to the individual who has it. Although comparisons cannot be made among

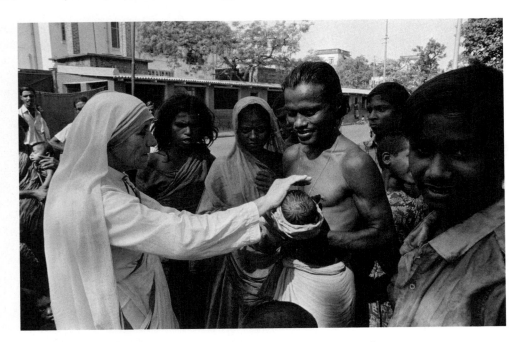

Blessed Mother Teresa of Calcutta's lifelong dedication to working with people in poverty may be seen as a manifestation of a cardinal trait.

personal dispositions, personal dispositions are necessary if one is to reflect accurately the personality structure of a particular individual. Whereas common traits place individuals into comparable categories, personal dispositions, if correctly diagnosed, more accurately describe an individual's uniqueness.

Each one of us has personal dispositions that are of greater or lesser importance. If a personal disposition is so pervasive that almost every behavior of the individual appears to be influenced by it, it is called a **cardinal disposition.** An example would be an extreme lust for power, so intense that almost every act of the individual can be seen to be governed by that desire. Allport believed that cardinal dispositions are quite rare. Nevertheless, some figures have been described as possessed of a cardinal disposition—for instance, Blessed Mother Teresa of Calcutta, whose life was marked by love and compassion for the poor.

Central dispositions are highly characteristic tendencies of an individual. They provide the adjectives or phrases a person might use in describing the essential characteristics of another individual in a letter of recommendation (e.g., intelligent, responsible, independent, sensitive, caring). Allport suggests that the number of central dispositions necessary to describe the essential characteristics of an individual normally varies between five and ten. **Secondary dispositions** are more specific, focused tendencies that are often situational in character and less crucial to the personality structure. A person may have a large number of these. A man might be domineering and aggressive at home in his role

Thinking Critically

What are your central dispositions? See the Thinking Critically box "Central Dispositions."

Thinking Critically

Central Dispositions

Think of a close friend or someone else whom you know well. On a blank sheet of paper, try to describe your friend's personality by jotting down those words or phrases that express his or her essential characteristics. Include those qualities that you consider of major importance in an accurate description. Then do the same thing for yourself. Count the number of words or phrases necessary to describe your friend or yourself. Chances are the number falls between five and ten. Allport suggests that the number of highly characteristic central dispositions along which a personality is organized generally falls within that range. In his own research the average was seven. Does your evidence support his hypothesis? Do you think this number reflects a certain level of complexity in human personality, or does it simply reflect the number of traits the observer is able to keep track of without getting overwhelmed or confused?

---

as father but behave submissively when confronted by a police officer who is giving him a ticket.

An important distinction between common traits and personal dispositions is the way in which each is established and assessed. The concept of common traits lends itself to traditional psychometric research (rating scales, testing instruments, and so on). The concept of personal dispositions requires new methodologies that permit the unique individuality of the person to emerge. We will explore this further in the section on assessment and research.

THE PROPRIUM

Allport's humanistic orientation can be seen most clearly in his concept of the *proprium.* Allport coined the term in order to avoid the terms *ego* or *self,* which he believed are often used as catchall phrases for those elements of personality that cannot be accounted for in any other way. Allport's **proprium** refers to the central experiences of self-awareness that people have as they grow and move forward. Allport purposely chose a term with the prefix *pro* to connote forward movement. *Proprium* is defined in terms of its functions or the things that it does. Allport described seven **propriate functions** (1961) that develop gradually as an individual grows from infancy to adulthood and constitute an evolving sense of self as known and felt (see Table 10.1).

Allport believed that there is a marked difference between the infant and the adult. The infant is a dependent, impatient, pleasure-seeking, "unsocialized horror," largely governed by unlearned biological drives, who can tolerate little delay in the fulfillment of those drives and reflexes. The infant has the potentialities for personality but "can scarcely be said to have personality" (1961). Given the appropriate security and affection, the child will grow in the direction of developing a proprium. The child will be transformed from a biologically dominated organism to a psychologically mature adult. The adult person is discontinuous from the child. The adult emerges from the child but is no longer governed by the child's needs.

TABLE 10.1 ALLPORT'S PROPRIATE FUNCTIONS

Allport's proprium is described in terms of its functions or the things that it does.

Bodily self	Knowing one's body and its limits
Self-identity	Awareness of inner sameness and continuity
Self-esteem	Pride in the ability to do things
Self-extension	Sense of possession and valuing of others
Self-image	Sense of measuring up to expectations of others
Self-as-rational-coper	Sense of self as active problem-solving agent
Propriate striving	Development of long-term purposes and goals

Not only is there a radical discontinuity between the child and the mature adult; Allport also suggests that there is a radical discontinuity between healthy adults and neurotics. The life of neurotics is marked by cognitive crippling. In their efforts to find security, neurotics react in rigid, inflexible ways. Such individuals continue to behave as children, dominated by infantile drives and conflicts. Their propriums are undeveloped and their motives remain tied to original needs.

FUNCTIONAL AUTONOMY

Closely related to Allport's concepts of the proprium and discontinuity is his concept of **functional autonomy,** the idea that adult motivation is not necessarily tied to the past. A given behavior may become a goal in itself regardless of its original intention. Thus adult motives are not necessarily related to earlier experiences in which the same motives appeared; they are contemporaneous with the behaviors themselves.

For example, let us imagine that young Johnny's father was a baseball fan. During his spare time and on Saturdays he played baseball with his son. Originally, Johnny played baseball with his Dad to gain his attention and to please him. During his school years, Johnny also played baseball with the other children in his neighborhood and was an active member of Little League. He discovered that he was competent in the game and, what is more, he enjoyed it. In high school and college, he played in the intramural sports program. Later, he was recruited to play with a major league. Today, as John is standing at bat for the Yankees or Dodgers, does it make sense to insist that his motive for playing baseball continues to be that of pleasing his father? Does it not seem more reasonable to suggest that he plays because he enjoys the game and the financial rewards that it brings? His present motives are entirely different and free from his original motives. There may be a historical tie, but there is no functional tie. John's motive is functionally autonomous.

Allport distinguishes between two types of functional autonomy: perseverative and propriate. **Perseverative functional autonomy** refers to acts or behaviors that are repeated even though they may have lost their original function; they are not controlled by the proprium and have no genuine connection with it. A teenage girl may, in a spirit of rebellion against her parents, begin to smoke cigarettes, which she knows will annoy them. As an adult, she may continue to smoke cigarettes, long after her period of teenage rebellion. Perseverative functional autonomy refers to repetitive activities such as compulsions, addictions to drugs or alcohol, and ritualistic or routine behaviors.

Propriate functional autonomy refers to those acquired interests, values, attitudes, intentions, and life-styles that are directed from the proprium. Abilities frequently convert into interests. The person selects those motives that are important and organizes them in a fashion that is consistent with his or her self-image and life-style.

Allport acknowledged that not all behaviors are functionally autonomous. Among the processes that are not are drives, reflexes, constitutionally determined capacities such as physique and intellect, habits, primary reinforcements, infantilisms and fixations, some neuroses, and sublimations. At times it is difficult to determine whether or not a motive is functionally autonomous. Further, certain motives may be autonomous only to a certain degree. Nevertheless, Allport believed that many of the motives of the healthy, mature adult may be considered to be governed by propriate functional autonomy. Allport's rationale for developing the concept of propriate functional autonomy is the desire to underscore the concept that we live in the present, not in the past.

A DEFINITION OF MATURITY

As we have seen, Allport believed that there is a radical discontinuity between the neurotic and healthy personality. Allport concurred with Carl Jung that too many personality theorists center their discussion of personality on the characteristics of the neurotic and view health simply as the absence of neurotic symptoms. In his discussion (1961), Allport posited six criteria of maturity.

1. EXTENSION OF THE SENSE OF SELF   Mature adults genuinely participate in important realms of human achievement. They are interested in others and consider the welfare of others as important as their own. Their sense of self is not limited to their own selves but embraces many interests.

2. WARM RELATING OF SELF TO OTHERS   Mature adults are able to relate intimately to other persons in appropriate situations. They are compassionate and able to tolerate many differences in human beings. In their relationships, they neither impose themselves on others nor hinder their own freedom of self-identity.

3. EMOTIONAL SECURITY (SELF-ACCEPTANCE)   Mature people are able to accept themselves and their emotional states. Their emotions, even though they are not always pleasant, do not lead them into impulsive acts or actions that hurt others. They are sufficiently secure in who they are to accept themselves and not wish to be somebody else.

4. REALISTIC PERCEPTION, SKILLS, AND ASSIGNMENTS   Mature adults do not need to create a fantasy world but live in the "real world." They are problem solvers and have developed the appropriate skills to complete their assigned tasks and work. Moreover, their work is not a burden to them; it is a responsibility whose challenge can be accepted without self-pity.

5. SELF-OBJECTIFICATION (INSIGHT AND HUMOR)   Self-insight is difficult to acquire. Mature people know what they can do, what they cannot do, and what they ought to do. They have no need to deceive either themselves or other people. An important corollary of insight is a sense of humor. Mature individuals are able to laugh at themselves rather than feel threatened by their human weaknesses. Such humor is to be distinguished from the ordinary

sense of the comic. The sense of humor to which Allport referred entails recognizing the ludicrous behaviors we share with others because of our common humanity.

6. UNIFYING PHILOSOPHY OF LIFE   Maturity entails a clear understanding of life's goals and purposes. In the mature person, this philosophy is clearly marked and outwardly focused. It is strongly informed by a set of values that may but does not necessarily include religious sentiments. In current parlance, Allport is describing **spirituality,** a search for meaning rather than an adherence to particular tenets as in a formal religion (Emmons, 1999). Further, a unifying philosophy of life is governed by a generic conscience. The *must* conscience of childhood is replaced by the *ought* conscience of the adult. Whereas the child's values are introjected from others, the adult's values arise from a chosen style of being and are based on propriate judgments.

Essentially, maturity for Allport is summed up by expression of the propriate functions to a high degree and freedom from one's past. Allport indicated that human beings are always in the process of *becoming* (1955). The urge to grow and fulfill oneself is present from birth. We have the ability to develop and follow a creative life-style. Further, with maturity we can consciously design and effect our plans without being hindered by unconscious forces of the past. His theory holds echoes of Jung's concept of self-realization and Adler's construct of the creative self and points toward the concepts of Rogers and Maslow. Maslow explicitly acknowledged Allport's influence on his interest in the study of self-actualized persons.

ASSESSMENT AND RESEARCH IN ALLPORT'S THEORY

Allport wrote extensively on methods of inquiry and investigation that are useful for the study of personality, and some of his own research in the area is considered classic. Allport pointed out that personality is so complex that every legitimate method of study should be included in its pursuit. He was critical of those who limit their research and do not encourage or permit the study of personality concepts that are not easily submitted to empirical test. At the same time, he was also critical of applying methods appropriate to the study of neurotic individuals to the normal individual.

Allport's view of personality as open and discontinuous does not lend itself very well to study by the traditional methods in academic psychology, which seek to discover general laws that apply to all individual cases. The emphasis, particularly in American psychology, has been on a **nomothetic** (from the Greek *nomos*, law, and *thetes*, one who establishes) approach, studying large groups of individuals to determine the frequency with which certain events occur and from this to infer common traits, general variables, or universal principles. Normality is often conceived as that behavior that occurs most regularly. Thus the behavior that is considered normal for a two-year-old is the behavior that is shared in common by most two-year-olds. Allport encouraged an **idiographic** (from the Greek *idios*, one's own, and *graphein*, to write) approach that centers on the individual, employing techniques and variables that are appropriate to understanding the uniqueness of each person and uncovering personal dispositions. Although such methods are difficult, time consuming, and often expensive to evolve, their aim is to account for the unique event that is theoretically just as open to lawful explanation as the frequent event.

In the 1940s, over three hundred letters written to a young married couple by a woman (Jenny Masterson) between her fifty-ninth and seventieth years came to Allport's attention.

He and his students analyzed these letters to determine Jenny's central dispositions. In studying these documents, Allport tried to note the frequency with which certain themes or ideas appeared. He asked other people to read the letters and assess Jenny in terms of her traits. He also discussed Jenny's personality in terms of different personality theories. Allport believed that the study of personal documents, such as diaries, autobiographies, and letters, could be a potentially valuable idiographic approach.

In his analysis of Jenny's correspondence (1965), Allport looked for recurring patterns and was able to identify eight unmistakable central dispositions that he believed were significant for understanding her personality: quarrelsome-suspicious, self-centered, independent, dramatic, aesthetic-artistic, aggressive, cynical-morbid, and sentimental. Allport then conducted a formal *content analysis* of the letters. The research technique of content analysis provides a systematic, objective, and quantitative way of describing written or spoken communications. Jenny's comments in the letters were classified into different categories (e.g., independence, hostility, affective, love of art, cynicism), and a frequency count was taken. The data were then subjected to a study by *factor analysis* (a complex statistical analysis). The findings of factor analysis were quite similar to Allport's own.

In his preface to *Letters from Jenny,* Allport wrote: "To me the principle fascination of the letters lies in their challenge to the reader (whether psychologist or layman) to 'explain' Jenny if he can. Why does an intelligent lady behave so persistently in a self-defeating manner?"

With Philip Vernon and Gardner Lindzey, Allport developed a Study of Values Scale, a dimensional measurement designed to examine individuality. The scale measures six common traits originally delineated by Spranger (1928): the theoretical, aesthetic, social, political, religious, and economic. Because the test reflects the relative strengths of these six values within one's own personality, one individual's score cannot be compared with anyone else's. The test has been widely used in counseling and vocational guidance and has proved to be a significant research tool in studies of selective perception.

Allport and Philip Vernon also initiated research into expressive behavior during the early 1930s. **Expressive behavior** refers to an individual's manner of performing. Every behavior has a coping and an expressive aspect. The *coping aspect* is what the act does to deal with or adapt to the task at hand. The *expressive aspect* is how the act is done.

Ordinarily we pay more attention to coping behavior than to expressive behavior. But expressive behavior, because it is more spontaneous, can be highly revelatory of basic personality aspects. Allport and others conducted considerable research on several expressive features of personality: the face, voice, posture, gesture, gait, and handwriting. They discovered that there is a marked consistency in a person's expressive behavior. In some instances, Allport was able to deduce certain traits and make accurate judgments about an individual's personality. Allport suggested that further research in this area would be highly desirable because a person's expressive manner and style may be the most important factor in understanding the personality.

Another outgrowth of Allport's personality theory has been his interest in religion as a healthy, productive aspect of human life. He initiated a major study of how religion was treated in college textbooks on psychology (Vande Kempe, 1995). In order to introduce religion into the comprehensive study of personality, Allport wrote *The Individual and His Religion* (1950), in which he presented religion as normal even though many other psychologists viewed it as a dysfunctional human phenomenon. Allport's distinction between intrinsic and extrinsic orientations in religion, a distinction between people who are motivated from within and those who are motivated by external forces, has contributed to research on understanding the relation between religion and prejudice. Churchgoers on the average are more prejudiced than nonchurchgoers, even though most advocates of treating all people equally are religiously motivated. Allport discovered a curvilinear relationship between religion and prejudice. The extrinsic attitude is correlated with prejudice, but the intrinsic is correlated with very low prejudice (1968). Allport fathered a line of theory and research on the social psychology of prejudice, focusing on the destructive effects of prejudice and discrimination against African Americans and other ethnic minorities.

In his authoritative study on prejudice (1954), Allport centered on racial and religious prejudice. However, identical forces occur with reference to women or any other minority. Allport suggests that first a group is compelled to respond in a specific way; then the group learn specific traits in order to adapt; and those same traits are employed as confirmation that the group is inferior. Thus, for example, women are often seen as weak when they communicate their need for relationships. The same need, however, could be seen as healthy and constructive for improving human relations among people of diverse cultures (Symonds, 1991). Allport's work on prejudice is "balanced, ahead of its time, and elegantly written" (Pettigrew, 1999). It shaped the study of prejudice in the twentieth century. Allport also demonstrated that social science can provide theoretical, empirical, and practical assistance to the comprehension and solution of social problems (Ruggiero & Kelman, 1999).

Allport's Theory

PHILOSOPHY, SCIENCE, *and* ART

Allport's personality theory is a highly creative one. Although many of his ideas are reminiscent of other theories, he combined others' insights with his own to develop a truly unique approach. His original concepts, such as personal dispositions, the proprium, and functional autonomy, are highly controversial and extremely stimulating. In his emphasis on the uniqueness of the individual and the contemporaneity of motives Allport foreshadowed the humanist theories of Rogers and Maslow. Indeed, the emphasis in his theory is not on the past but on forward movement.

Allport maintained that because personality is so complex, every legitimate method of study should be included in our efforts to comprehend it. He used rigorous scientific methods to establish common traits. At the same time, he pointed out that we need to develop alternative methods that help us understand the uniqueness of each individual. In his own research, Allport recognized the value of other methodologies and used information drawn from literature, philosophy, art, and religion, as well as from science. Allport believed that an open system of personality encourages the invention of new methods of research; these methods aim at rigor but do not forfeit the study of certain aspects of personality because present scientific methodologies cannot embrace such study.

Philosophical Assumptions

Which philosophical assumptions were most important to Allport? See the Philosophical Assumptions box "Examining Allport and Murray" on page 282.

Allport realized that to understand the whole human being, it is necessary to comprehend the individual philosophically as well as scientifically. "The philosophy of the person is inseparable from the psychology of the person" (1961). Indeed, any psychological stance, Allport pointed out, is implicitly linked to basic philosophical assumptions.

Allport's discussion of traits influenced a line of dispositional approaches to personality that culminated in the work of Raymond Cattell and the Big Five theorists discussed in the chapter on factor analytic theories, and of Hans Eysenck, whose work is covered in the chapter on biological traits. It also provoked debate concerning the importance of long-term dispositions as opposed to the influence of the particular situation, a debate that was initiated by Mischel and discussed in the chapter on social learning theories.

Allport's concept of functional autonomy has been the subject of a great deal of controversy and criticism. In presenting his theories to the public, Allport sought to teach and provoke interest rather than make statements that were above reproach. Thus it is often very difficult to differentiate between what he assumed and what he established through empirical procedures. The concept of functional autonomy is not a construct that lends itself to operational definition, predictions, or empirical tests. The phenomena that Allport explained as functionally autonomous can also be explained by rival constructs. Further, Allport did not clearly describe the developmental processes that underlie functional autonomy.

Still, Allport's concepts are highly congruent with recent developments in personality theory. His emphasis on discontinuity is picked up by humanist and cognitive theorists. His concepts of functional autonomy and propriate functions harmonize with recent expansions in psychoanalysis. The goal of psychoanalysis is to strengthen the functioning of the ego. The intent of the reconstruction of the past in psychoanalysis is to permit the patient to work through the past so that it loses its grip. By becoming aware of one's unconscious motivations, one is free to behave differently in the future if one so wishes. Thus the intent of psychoanalysis is congruent, if not synonymous, with the development of propriate functional autonomy.

Allport was not a practicing psychotherapist and did not develop a specific therapeutic technique. Nevertheless, many of his ideas, such as functional autonomy, propriate functions, and the radical discontinuity between normal and neurotic adults, have been useful to clinicians.

Allport did not develop a school of followers, but his theory has had considerable impact. His work offers a bridge between traditional academic psychology, which emphasizes psychometrics and nomothetic studies, and clinical psychology, which concentrates on a more idiographic approach to the understanding of personality. Allport's emphasis on personal documents has been a guiding light for their use in analyzing and understanding personality (Wrightsman, 1993). Furthermore, his early analysis of the language used to describe personality has been seen as laying the empirical and conceptual groundwork for the eventual development of the Five-Factor Model of personality (John & Robins, 1993).

There has been a resurgence of interest in idiographic approaches to the study of personality. Because of the emphasis on personal and unique determinants of behavior, an idiographic approach should provide greater accuracy in explanation and prediction. Lamielle (1981) argues "against continued adherence to the long dominant 'nomothetic' paradigm for personality research" because from it we cannot make any legitimate interpretations at the level of the individual. Lamielle suggests a strategy, which he terms *idiothetic*, that combines features of idiographic and nomothetic research in a way that does justice to individuals but that also invokes the use of norms. Pelham (1993) affirms that idiographic, or within-subjects, techniques grasp the truth of phenomenological reality where nomothetic, or between-subjects, techniques are unable to. Thus nomothetic research is not very helpful to a theory of personality that seeks to comprehend the uniqueness of individuals (Lamielle & Trierweiler, 1986). DeCarvalho (1990) has argued that Allport's complex and unifying suggestion in the late 1960s for a humanistic psychology was an exceptional happening in Western psychology that illuminates the conflict between an experimental as compared with an experiential approach to psychological exploration.

Henry Murray (1893–1988)

BIOGRAPHICAL BACKGROUND

Henry A. Murray was born in New York City on May 13, 1893. His parents were well-to-do, and Murray grew up as a privileged American boy in a time before automobiles, motorboats, or movies. Winters were spent in the city in a brownstone on what is now the site of Rockefeller Center. Summers were spent on Long Island, where he enjoyed outdoor physical activity, animals, and the woods in back of his home.

Murray did not believe that he qualified as a typical Freudian child. It was difficult for him to recognize the presence of an Oedipus complex in his life. His training analysis did not uncover any indications of hidden resentment toward his father. On the other hand, his childhood evokes several Adlerian themes. Murray recalled an incident at about four years of age when his mother suggested that the queen and her son pictured in a fairy-tale book were sad because of the prospect of death. Later he suggested that memory embodied feelings of having been abandoned (left to die) by his mother in favor of his siblings because he was difficult to care for. This led to an early development of self-reliance as well as tender feelings of pity toward his mother and others with emotional problems.

Unlike Allport, Murray received little formal training in psychology. After six years in two private schools in New York City, he went to Groton, a private preparatory school in Massachusetts. He obtained his B.A. from Harvard, where he majored in history but received only below-average grades. It appears he was more interested in going out for the

Henry Murray's term for the study of individuals was personology.

crew team. Yet he went on to medical school at Columbia University and graduated at the top of his class. Later he received an M.A. in biology from Columbia and a Ph.D. in biochemistry from Cambridge University.

In contrast to Allport, whose meeting with Freud left him somewhat skeptical about unconscious processes, Murray spent three weeks with Carl Jung in Zurich during an Easter vacation from Cambridge and emerged a "reborn man." He had "experienced the unconscious" and thereafter devoted himself exclusively to psychology and to probing the deepest recesses of personality.

Robinson (1992) suggests that Murray had a number of troubling intellectual and emotional shortcomings and, although he kept a traditional marriage, he was involved in a torrid affair with Christiana Morgan, a talented married woman who was also interested in the work of Carl Jung. Morgan made important contributions to the early development of psychoanalysis, especially in the area of feminism and also to Murray's theory of personality, for which she was never given proper recognition (Douglas, 1993); she also coauthored the Thematic Apperception Test (TAT), a significant projective technique widely used in personality assessment. Despite his affair with Morgan, Murray was a highly regarded professor of psychology at Harvard University from the 1920s to the 1960s, where he set up the Harvard Psychological Clinic expressly to study personality.

Murray gathered around him a group of capable young and mature scholars, many of whom are notable psychologists in their own right. He was awarded the Distinguished Scientific Contribution Award of the American Psychological Association and the Gold Medal Award of the American Psychological Foundation for his contributions to psychology. Murray died in 1988.

THE STUDY OF PERSONOLOGY

Murray, like Gordon Allport, emphasized the complexity of personality and the need for interdisciplinary research in personality. He suggested that the concept of personality is a hypothesis, a construct that helps us account for an individual's behavior. Unlike Allport, who saw personality as a real entity, Murray did not believe that the concept of personality refers to any real physical substance. An individual's personality is dependent upon brain processes, and hence the anatomical center of personality is the brain. There is an intimate relationship between cerebral physiology and personality. Neurophysiological processes are the source of human behavior.

In his study of **personology**—Murray's term for the study of individual "human lives and the factors that influence their course" (1938)—Murray emphasized the understanding of normal individuals in natural settings. He believed that psychologists should primarily concern themselves with the detailed and careful study of individual lives.

In studying the individual, Murray believed that it is useful to separate the total behavior of a person into identifiable and manageable units. His basic unit is a **proceeding**, a short, significant behavior pattern that has a clear beginning and ending. Proceedings are interactions between the subject and another person or object in the environment—for example, picking up a book, writing a letter, or holding a conversation. Proceedings may be internal (imagined) or external (real). A succession of proceedings constitutes a *serial*. Thus a friendship or a marriage consists of a serial of proceedings that needs to be studied as a whole. A planned series of proceedings is a *serial program*, which leads toward a goal such as becoming a lawyer. Serial programs may stretch into the future for months or even years. Each proceeding in the series may be seen as having a subgoal that brings the individual closer to the final goal. Serial programs are governed by a mental process known as *ordination*. Ordination enables us, once we understand our world, to develop a strategy for coping with it. Ordination also permits us to develop *schedules* or plans for resolving conflicting proceedings. A schedule, like a family budget, tries to accommodate all of the competing needs and goals by permitting them to be expressed at different times.

Some aspects of Murray's theory of personology were drawn from Freud's theory. However, Murray did not hesitate to redefine terms or to elaborate and enrich Freud's concepts. Thus he used the terms *id, ego,* and *superego* in describing the basic divisions of personality but added his own meaning.

Murray agreed with Freud that the id is the source of basic drives and needs, but he emphasized that the id contains positive impulses as well as negative ones. The superego is an internalized representation of the social environment, indicating when, where, how, and what needs can be expressed. The ego is the "organized, discriminating, time-binding, reasoning, resolving, and more self-conscious part of the personality" (1938). Its role is to facilitate the id in meeting its impulses; its effectiveness in doing so affects an individual's adjustment. Murray assumed a more active role for the ego, in line with the ego psychoanalysts discussed in the chapter on ego psychology.

HUMAN NEEDS

Murray's most significant contribution to the study of personality was probably his extensive research on human needs. He constructed what is undoubtedly the most careful and thorough list of human needs found in psychology.

Murray (1938) defined a **need** as a construct representing a force in the brain that organizes our perception, understanding, and behavior in such a way as to change an unsatisfying situation and increase our satisfaction. A need may be aroused by an internal state, such as hunger, or by an external stimulus, such as food.

An observer can infer a need from the following signs: a typical behavior effect or pattern, the search for and avoidance of certain kinds of press (to be discussed later in the chapter), the expression of a specific emotion, and signs of satisfaction or dissatisfaction with the effects of one's behavior. In addition, a person can usually confirm the presence of a need through subjective reports.

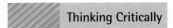
Thinking Critically

Which of Murray's needs are most important to you? See the Thinking Critically box "Evaluating Needs" on page 278.

From his intensive study of individuals at Harvard (1938), Murray constructed a list of twenty basic needs, which are listed and briefly defined in Table 10.2. Although this list has been revised and modified since that time, it remains highly representative of a comprehensive overview of human needs.

Not all of the needs are present in everyone, and needs vary in their strength and intensity. Murray believed that there is a hierarchy of needs, a concept later elaborated on by Maslow (discussed in the chapter on humanism). Where two or more needs conflict, the most important need will be met first. Some needs, such as the need for food or to eliminate waste, are *prepotent*, which means they become very urgent if they are not satisfied. Other needs may be met together. An actor may be able to meet achievement and exhibition needs in one and the same performance.

TABLE 10.2 MURRAY'S LIST OF NEEDS

Dominance	To govern and direct
Deference	To respect and conform
Autonomy	To behave independently
Aggression	To attack and fight
Abasement	To yield and surrender
Achievement	To succeed at a hard task
Sex	To be erotic
Sentience	To find joy in sensuousness
Exhibition	To show off and attract attention
Play	To have fun
Affiliation	To relate to others
Rejection	To exclude others
Succorance	To seek help
Nurturance	To give help
Infavoidance	To guard against embarrassment
Defendance	To protect one's self from abuse
Counteraction	To face failure with continued effort
Harm avoidance	To stay away from danger
Order	To organize things
Understanding	To seek comprehension

SOURCE: *Based on information in Murray, H. A. (Ed.),* Explorations in personality. *New York: Oxford University Press, 1938, pp. 142–242, 741–750.*

To characterize an individual's behavior simply on the basis of needs is to give a one-sided portrait. This is why Murray introduced the concept of **press,** forces from objects or persons within the environment that help or hinder an individual in reaching goals. Stimuli that arouse needs motivate us to look for or avoid certain kinds of press. Examples of press are cultural discord, family discord, poverty, accident, loss of possessions, presence of siblings, maltreatment by contemporaries, religious training, encouragement, friendship, sexual abuse, and illness. It is important to distinguish between *alpha press,* actual properties or attributes of the environment, and *beta press,* the individual's subjective perception of the environment. The beta presses are the determinants of behavior. Murray's concept of beta press can be seen as a precursor to the cognitive appraisal approach discussed in the

Thinking Critically

Evaluating Needs

Look over Murray's list of twenty needs and study their definitions. Think of instances in which the needs have arisen in your life, and make a list of the needs that seem to be important to you. In evaluating your own hierarchy of needs, it will be helpful if you consider specific events in your life when the needs were apparent.

Also consider the way in which diverse cultures and eras foster and encourage the development of different needs. Can you think of needs that you have today that may not be characteristic of people in other places and cultures? Imagine individuals living in the year 1000, the year 1900, and the year 2020. Do you think they would have the same needs or that their needs would differ depending on the context in which they lived? Do you think that Murray's list of needs is itself culture bound? Are you aware of any human needs that are not on Murray's list?

---

chapter on cognitive-behavior theories. It is our perceptions of stressful events that determine our stress responses.

ASSESSMENT AND RESEARCH IN MURRAY'S THEORY

Henry Murray was a pioneer in the area of assessment, an aspect of personality theory that is increasingly the focus of attention and concern. Like Allport, Murray emphasized an idiographic approach to personality, which focuses on the individual, rather than the usual

Murray is best known for his comprehensive list of human needs. Sometimes multiple needs—play, sentience, and nurturance, for example—can be satisfied by a single activity.

nomothetic approach, which deals with groups. The basic principle of Murray's concept of assessment was that multiple indicators are required to adequately assess an individual's performance. In other words, one single test could not adequately describe an individual. It is preferable to use multiple instruments administered by multiple assessors from different areas of specialization. Murray also believed that if feedback were provided to the individual, improved performance could be achieved.

In a unique interdisciplinary effort at Harvard, Murray led a staff of twenty-eight different specialists in studying fifty-two male undergraduates for a period of six months. Together they amassed a great deal of data through interviews, tests, questionnaires, and observations, using an array of clinical, psychoanalytic, experimental, physiological, and life history methods. By having several trained researchers observe the same individual, Murray believed he could cancel out personal errors in assessment. A diagnostic council permitted several observers to study the same subject and then integrate their findings into a final diagnosis. This type of interdisciplinary approach was unprecedented at the time.

Murray's concept of assessment has been generalized to programs and institutions; for example, multiple indicators of assessment have been used to accurately reflect their performance. Douglas Bray pioneered the use of assessment for personnel selection and the evaluation of performance at AT&T. The assessment center approach is widely used today for the selection of executives and leaders in industry and government.

Murray himself developed several techniques for assessing personality. The best known is the **Thematic Apperception Test (TAT),** developed by Murray and Christiana Morgan, which is widely used as a projective device. The TAT consists of a selection of ambiguous pictures (for example, see Figure 10.1). The subject is asked to make up stories for the pictures, telling what led up to the event, what is happening, what the characters in the picture are thinking and feeling, and how the event will turn out. The responses to the TAT suggest how the subject thinks in relation to the physical and social environment. Responses are noted in terms of predominant themes, and special attention is paid to those forces that emanate from the "hero" in the picture or from the environment. Through the data, the examiner can infer how the subject relates to other people and molds the environment to meet personal needs. There are special scoring guides, but many clinicians also develop their own systems of analysis.

Thinking Critically

What story would you tell? See the Thinking Critically box "The Thematic Apperception Test."

Because the stimuli are ambiguous and the participant is free to respond in any way, it is believed that any meaning the participant gives to the story must come from within. It is said that the participant projects meaning into the story, and thus the TAT is called a *projective test*. In the TAT we are dealing with imaginative projection rather than with a Freudian defense mechanism of projection. Participants unwittingly project their own attitudes and feelings onto the pictures and thereby reveal themselves.

TAT stories are interpreted in terms of *needs* and *press*. The interaction of need and press together with the outcome of a story make up a *simple thema*. Simple themas that run through several stories become *complex themas,* which help to characterize an individual's mode of functioning. Themas are merely symbolic; they are not considered literal translations of actual participant behavior. Their inference is a hypothetical construct that guides the clinician in evaluating an individual's personality dynamics.

The TAT has proven to be a valuable personality assessment device and is included

Thinking Critically

The Thematic Apperception Test

Look at the picture in Figure 10.1 and make up a narrative for it. What feeling does this picture evoke in you? What's the story of these two people? What just transpired in their lives to bring them to this moment? And what will happen to them in the future?

When you're finished, go to the section on Murray's theory and the TAT, and assess your response as objectively as possible. Which human needs are reflected in your story? What themes emerge? How are *needs* and *press* interacting in your narrative? And finally, what does the narrative say about you?

among the tests most often used across most settings (Watkins, Campbell, Nieberding, & Hallmark, 1995). A Children's Apperception Test (CAT) has also been developed by Percival Symonds. The TAT, along with Murray's system of needs, has influenced the development of varieties of the TAT and other assessment techniques, such as the Edwards Personal Preference Schedule and the Jackson Personality Research Form. TAT research has been extended into the study of borderline, narcissistic, and attention deficit disorders, as well as substance abuse (Abrams, 1999).

Murray's theory stimulated David McClelland to research extensively the need for achievement (NAch) (McClelland, Atkinson, Clark, & Lowell, 1953). Informed by Freud's concept of unconscious motivation, McClelland developed a modified version of the TAT to assess achievement motivation. High-need-achievement participants might respond to a picture of a young man with an open book sitting at a desk with stories of wanting to achieve and striving to do well. Low-need-achievement participants might talk about reading for pleasure or daydreaming. McClelland identified several behavioral differences between people with high and with low need achievement. He also found out that, just as individuals differ in their need to achieve, entire societies do so as well. His work eventually led to exploring conditions and developing techniques that cultivate the need for achievement in both children and adults (1961).

FIGURE 10.1

A Picture Exemplifying the Type of Pictures Included in the Thematic Apperception Test

Murray's Theory

Murray's pioneering studies helped to shape the growth of personality theory in this country. He was largely responsible for bringing Freud to the attention of academic psychologists and stimulating a great deal of scientific research on Freudian concepts. Although Murray tried to provide operational definitions and specific data, he recognized that he did not have sufficient data to justify calling his theory a scientific construct. The proceedings of his diagnostic council also fall short of today's typical standards in scientific research. Nevertheless, Murray was a forerunner in fostering scientific research in personality theorizing and a pioneer in the area of assessment.

Murray advocated an interdisciplinary approach to the study of personality, which was unprecedented. He was equally at home studying the literature of Herman Melville, the writings of Freud, and the latest empirical data as possible sources of knowledge about human nature. At the Harvard Psychological Clinic, he generated an atmosphere in which lively and creative minds could work together, exchanging ideas and developing syntheses. He spoke of the virtues of bringing different approaches and specialties together to shed light on human nature, and of the need to expand our scope beyond that of a narrow, limited model.

Other essays on personology, such as McAdams (1992a), stress that the "person can be said to be a history—a subjectively composed and construed life story that integrates one's past, present, and future."

Murray was uniquely successful in avoiding a one-sided picture of personality. He tried to strike a careful balance between constitutional elements and environmental factors. He recognized the importance of both past and future events. His theory embraces both behavioral and experiential aspects. Although he is not explicit about his philosophical position, his efforts are clearly rooted in a humanistic philosophy that encourages a comprehensive and holistic view of human nature. His concepts were "organismic when the rest of psychology was atomistic" (White, 1992). In his current efforts to provide a framework for an interactive synergistic model of psychotherapy, Theodore Millon specifically indicates that he is reviving Murray's personology (Millon, 2003).

Philosophical Assumptions

Which basic assumptions were most important to Murray? See the Philosophical Assumptions box "Examining Allport and Murray."

Murray's classification of needs is considered more useful than any other classification of its type. Most subsequent and current research on needs for power and achievement can be traced to his work. His emphasis on the brain's physiological processes foreshadows contemporary appreciation of the importance of biological and chemical forces in the human organism. Finally, Murray's Thematic Apperception Test, widely used as a diagnostic tool, represents a major contribution to the art of personality theory and continues to generate interest and research (Geiser & Stein, 1999). Several other personality tests are based on his work, such as Douglas Jackson's Personality Research Form (PRF).

☀ Philosophical Assumptions

Examining Allport and Murray

Many of the differences among personality theories can be attributed to fundamental differences in philosophical assumptions. Which of the basic philosophical issues, described in the introductory chapter and summarized on the inside back cover, seem to be clearly important to Allport and Murray in the development of their theories? How, for example, does Allport's distinction between common traits and personal dispositions influence his stance on universality versus uniqueness? How does his emphasis on the proprium influence his stance on proactivity versus reactivity? How does Murray's discussion of need and press influence his view of heredity versus environment? Do their theories address any other philosophical assumptions? Rate Allport and Murray on a scale of 1 to 5 on those philosophical assumptions that you feel their theories apply to most. Compare your ratings of Allport and Murray with your own philosophical assumptions. Did your study of Allport and Murray lead you to change any of your assumptions? Why or why not?

Conclusions

Together, Gordon Allport and Henry Murray stimulated a great deal of interest and research in personality in American psychology. Each emphasized the uniqueness of the individual. Allport's theory emphasized the contemporaneity of motives and a holistic view of the person. His concept of the proprium emphasized the difference between the child and the healthy adult. Murray explicitly discussed motivation; his careful construction of the list of twenty needs and his work in the area of assessment have contributed significantly to ongoing personality research. Both Allport and Murray emphasized that personality is very complex and urged that its study be both interdisciplinary and idiographic. Their work significantly informed humanistic psychology (Taylor, 2000). With the contemporary resurgence of interest in idiographic techniques, their pioneering efforts are even more appreciated.

 TO LEARN MORE about TAT and personality assessment, and for a list of suggested readings, visit the *Personality Theories* textbook website at **college.cengage.com/pic/engler8e.**

Summary

1. Allport described and classified over fifty definitions of personality before finalizing his own definition: "Personality is the dynamic organization within the individual of those psychophysical systems that determine his characteristic behavior and thought."

2. Allport distinguished between **continuity** (p. 264) theories of personality, which are closed and admit little change, and **discontinuity** (p. 265) theories, which are open and provide for extensive growth.

3. Allport distinguished between **common traits** (p. 265), hypothetical constructs that permit us to make comparisons between individuals, and **personal dispositions** (p. 265), which are unique to each person. Common traits and personal dispositions are studied by different research methods.

4. There are three levels of personal dispositions: **cardinal, central,** and **secondary** (p. 266).

5. Allport coined the term **proprium** (p. 267) to refer to the central experience of self-awareness that a person has in growing and moving forward.

6. The concept of **functional autonomy** (p. 268) implies that adult motivation is not necessarily tied to the past. There are two types of functional autonomy: **perseverative** (p. 268) and **propriate** (p. 269).

7. Allport was one of the first theorists to discuss the healthy personality. He posited six criteria of maturity.

8. The **nomothetic** (p. 270) approach to personality studies large groups of individuals in order to infer general variables or universal principles. The **idiographic** (p. 270) approach centers on the individual, using techniques that are appropriate to understanding the uniqueness of each person.

9. Allport respected and used the methods of rigorous science in establishing common traits, but he also recognized the value of other methods and the need to understand the individual philosophically as well as scientifically.

10. Murray's term **personology** (p. 275) refers to his unique interdisciplinary study of the individual, which employs a wide array of clinical, psychoanalytic, and experimental methods.

11. Murray separated a person's behavior into identifiable units. The basic unit is a **proceeding** (p. 275), a succession of proceedings is a **serial** (p. 275), a planned series is a **serial program** (p. 275), and a plan for resolving conflicting proceedings is a **schedule** (p. 276).

12. A **need** (p. 276) is a construct representing a force in the brain that organizes our perception, understanding, and behavior in such a way as to lead us to change an unsatisfying situation. Needs can be inferred from behavioral signs and confirmed through subjective reports. The twenty basic needs that Murray identified are: dominance, deference, autonomy, aggression, abasement, achievement, sex, sentience, exhibition, play, affiliation, rejection, succorance, nurturance, infavoidance, defendance, counteraction, harm avoidance, order, and understanding.

13. A **press** (p. 277) is a force from the environment that helps or hinders an individual in reaching goals. Murray distinguishes between *alpha press* and *beta press*. Examples of press are poverty, illness, and encouragement.

14. Murray urged an interdisciplinary and idiographic approach to the study of personology. He set up a diagnostic council in which several different specialists would study an individual and integrate their findings. The **Thematic Apperception Test** (p. 279) is a projective device in which a person makes up a story for ambiguous pictures. These stories may be interpreted in terms of needs, press, and thema.

15. Murray's interdisciplinary approach was unprecedented. It helps to underscore the values of an interdisciplinary approach to understanding personality and the limitations of a narrow model.

Personal Experiences

1. In the Thinking Critically box "Central Dispositions," you examined what you felt your central dispositions to be. Now let's build on that knowledge by trying to figure out your secondary dispositions. Describe how you would tend to react in each of the following situations: being wrongly accused of something; making a mistake at work that's discovered by your superior, discovering someone cheating on a test; finding out that your boyfriend or girlfriend is cheating on you; hearing someone talk badly about your friend; witnessing someone yell at your grandparent. Do you find your reactions in these situations to be in sync with or at odds with your central disposition? Explain your findings. What do they reveal about your values and beliefs?

2. Assess your own maturity. Allport put forth six criteria for maturity: (1) extension of the sense of self; (2) warm relating of self to others; (3) emotional security; (4) realistic perception, skills, and assignments; (5) self-objectification; and (6) unifying philosophy of life. Review the text discussion of these criteria; then assign each of the six a value ranging from 0 to 5. A value of 0 would indicate that you don't fulfill the criteria at all; a value of 5 would mean that you wholly fulfill the criteria. The highest possible score would be 30. Assess yourself and the people you know on this informal scale. What do your findings reveal? As a twist, after you evaluate your friends and family, have them assess themselves. Do your scores match theirs? Are you finding a trend based on personal bias? Explain your findings.

3. Examine how your friends' central dispositions relate to their expressive behaviors. Review your findings from the Thinking Critically box "Central Dispositions." Write down the main descriptors for each of your friends. Then start paying attention to their expressive behaviors over a few days to see if these behaviors inform their central personalities. Allport and Vernon examined several expressive features as they studied personality: the face, voice, posture, gesture, gait, and handwriting. You can do the same as you hang out with your friends. Does one expressive behavior inform the others? Are they connected or disconnected? Explain your findings.

4. What are your greatest needs? Refer to Table 10.2, which shows Murray's list of needs. Of the twenty needs listed, select the five that are most important to you. Then take some time to examine what in your life is creating these needs. For example, is your age a factor? where you are in relation to loved ones? geography? Does race, ethnicity, or gender play a part in this? Do you feel that those five will always be your greatest needs, or do you feel that your needs may change over time?

5. In the context of Murray's theory, the word *press* refers to a force from an object or person within the environment that could help or hinder an individual in reaching goals. Create a top-ten list of the presses in your life right now. First, establish what your three main goals currently are. Then write down the top ten presses that will impact, either negatively or positively, your achieving each goal. Have a couple of your friends do the same thing. Do you and your friends identify the same presses? Explain your findings.

CHAPTER 11

Factor Analytic, Genetic and Evolutionary Theories

- ▪ **Raymond Cattell**
- ▪ **The Big Five Personality Traits**
- ▪ **Genetic and Evolutionary Developments**

YOUR GOALS FOR THIS CHAPTER

1. Cite Cattell's definition of **personality,** and compare his personality theorizing with that of other theorists.
2. Distinguish between **source** and **surface** traits, give examples of each, and explain how Cattell identified traits through **factor analysis.**
3. Identify the terms most commonly used to describe the **Big Five.**
4. Discuss how the Big Five originated from the study of language and the study of personality questionnaires and ratings.
5. Describe the differences between the Big Five, the Five-Factor Model, and the Five-Factor Theory.
6. Discuss applications of the Big Five.
7. Define **behavioral genetics,** and distinguish between **genotypes** and **phenotypes.**
8. Explain how twin studies contribute to behavioral genetics.
9. Explain the concept of **heritability,** and discuss heritability estimates of the Big Five.
10. Discuss applications of genetic research.
11. Describe how **evolutionary psychology** influences personality theory.
12. Evaluate factor analytic trait theories from the viewpoints of philosophy, science, and art.

For many years, personality theorists debated whether personality is influenced by inner biological patterns or by the experiences an individual has had. This dispute, variously known as the issue of *heredity versus environment* or the controversy over *nurture versus nature,* was frequently conducted in a way that suggested that one or the other had to be the primary factor. Today, most theorists recognize that the answer is both and that each affects the other. Trait and temperament views recognize that the contributions of heredity and the environment are not merely additive but rather complex combinations.

Raymond Cattell used factor analysis, a sophisticated psychometric technique, to explore personality. Cattell's theory is complex and very difficult for the layperson to comprehend. This chapter provides an overview of important points that are helpful for understanding contemporary trends in trait and temperament theories. An important trend in personality theory is the emergence and development of what has come to be known as the Big Five personality traits. Cattell's theory and research on the Big Five wrestle with the issue of nature versus nurture, an interactionist view. Biological perspectives from the fields of behavioral genetics and evolutionary psychology have also enhanced our understanding of traits by helping to connect personality theory to natural science. The chapter concludes with a consideration of each of those areas.

Raymond Cattell (1905–1998)

BIOGRAPHICAL BACKGROUND

Raymond Cattell was born in Staffordshire, England, in 1905. His childhood was happy. England became involved in World War I when Cattell was nine. He later acknowledged that the war had a significant impact on him.

Cattell received his B.S.C. from the University of London in 1924 at the age of nineteen. He majored in chemistry and physics, but his interest in social concerns led him to pursue psychology, in which he earned a Ph.D. in 1929. His graduate work was also undertaken at the University of London, where he studied under Charles Spearman, a distinguished psychologist who developed the procedure of factor analysis that Cattell would later employ.

The following years were difficult. Employment was hard to come by for a psychologist, so Cattell worked at several part-time jobs. Meanwhile, he continued his own research. The depressed economy and his own poor health led to several lean years, during which he was haunted by poverty. His marriage broke up. Nevertheless, he remained steadfast in his dedication to his work.

In 1937, the University of London awarded Cattell an honorary doctorate of science for his contributions to research in personality. That same year he served as a research associate to E. L. Thorndike at Columbia University in New York. Subsequently, he became a professor of psychology at Clark University and later at Harvard, the University of Illinois, the University of Hawaii at Manoa, and Forrest Institute of Professional Psychology in Honolulu, Hawaii.

Cattell was especially proud of his work with mathematical techniques, through which he believed psychology could be studied as an objective, quantitative science. He made ex-

Raymond Cattell extensively used factor analysis to identify traits and study personality.

ceptional contributions in many areas, received several honors, and made significant advances to the study of personality. He died on February 2, 1998.

CATTELL'S DEFINITION OF PERSONALITY

Cattell began with a tentative definition of **personality:** "Personality is that which permits a prediction of what a person will do in a given situation" (1950). He believed that a full definition of personality must await further investigation into the types of concepts that are included in the study of behavior. His general statement may be expressed in the formula $R = f(P, S)$, which reads: A response (R) is a function (f) of the person (P) and the stimuli (S). Cattell observed that the response and the stimuli can be precisely determined in an experiment in which the experimenter carefully structures the situation. However, the person is a less well known factor that needs further exploration.

Cattell's definition of personality provides a striking and important contrast between his approach to personality research and that of other theorists, such as the Freudians. Freud developed psychoanalysis as a means of understanding one's self and developing a comprehensive theory of human nature. He was particularly concerned not with the efficacy of psychoanalysis as a predictive tool but with the compelling character of the vision of one's self or humanity that it provided. Cattell, in contrast, was concerned with the power of a construct to predict future events. His stance was that of the empirical scientist who derives from his or her theory propositions that are subject to empirical test. In a sense, prediction is more difficult than explanation, for it is easier to account for events that have happened than to predict them. On the other hand, a theory may have considerable predictive power and garner an impressive array of validating evidence, yet still fail to provide a comprehensive or compelling explanation. In his theorizing, Cattell provides an exemplary instance of a scientist who is concerned with validating evidence.

Cattell believed that the exploration of traits assists us in understanding the structure and function of personality. Knowledge of underlying traits allows us to make predictions about our own behavior and that of others. Although Cattell, unlike Allport, was interested in the physical and neurological components that influence behavior, he did not maintain that the traits he explored necessarily had any real physical or neural status.

SURFACE TRAITS VERSUS SOURCE TRAITS

Cattell reminded us that if a trait theory is to be useful, the traits postulated need to go beyond an individual's overt behaviors. Just as any successful hypothesis in science refers to future experiences that might occur if the hypothesis turns out to be useful, a successful trait construct goes beyond simply asserting that a particular behavior pattern exists. To argue that Dale is lazy because of a lazy disposition is to argue in a circle and not provide genuinely useful information. To argue that Pat is honest, thoughtful, and disciplined because of an underlying source variable or trait of ego strength is a much more useful way to proceed. The underlying trait of ego strength accounts for the surface manifestation and also permits us to speculate about other related characteristics, such as assertiveness or confidence, that Dale or Pat will display.

Thus, Cattell distinguished between surface traits and source traits (1950). **Surface traits** are clusters of overt behavior responses that appear to go together, such as integrity, honesty, self-discipline, and thoughtfulness. **Source traits** are the underlying variables that seem to determine the surface manifestation, in this case, ego strength.

The study of source traits is valuable for several reasons. Because they are probably few in number, source traits permit economy in describing an individual. Second, source traits presumably have a genuine structural influence on personality and thus determine the way we behave. Thus, knowledge of a particular source trait may permit us to go beyond mere description and make predictions about additional behaviors that we might further observe.

Source traits may have their origin in heredity or the environment. From extensive research using factor analysis techniques, Cattell identified sixteen basic source traits that he considered the "building blocks" of personality (1966). They are presented in Table 11.1 as bipolar dimensions. These source traits form the basis of Cattell's best-known and widely used assessment test, the Sixteen Personality Factor Questionnaire (16PF).

ASSESSMENT AND RESEARCH IN CATTELL'S THEORY

Cattell's personality theory made its major impact through his methods and techniques of researching and identifying traits. Cattell's primary tool was **factor analysis.**

Cattell began by gathering large masses of data from a great many individuals from a variety of sources, such as life records, self-report questionnaires, and projective tests. All of the data garnered from these sources were subjected to the complex, sophisticated statistical technique of factor analysis. Factor analysis is essentially a correlational procedure that describes large amounts of data in smaller, more manageable units by interrelating many correlations at one time. Hundreds, or even thousands, of variables can be considered in a

TABLE 11.1 CATTELL'S SIXTEEN BASIC SOURCE TRAITS

Cattell's sixteen source traits are the building blocks of personality. Some are indicative of an outgoing temperament; others indicate a more reserved disposition.

outgoing – reserved	trusting – suspicious
more intelligent – less intelligent	imaginative – practical
high ego strength – low ego strength	shrewd – forthright
assertive – humble	apprehensive – self-assured
happy-go-lucky – sober	experimental – conservative
strong conscience – lack of internal standards	group-dependent – self-sufficient
adventuresome – shy	casual – controlled
tough-minded – tender-minded	relaxed – tense

single study. Factor analysis is based on the assumption that if several variables correlate highly with one another, it is possible that a common dimension underlies them.

The first step in factor analysis is to make up a correlational matrix by computing a correlational coefficient for each variable to show how it relates to every other one. This tells us the degree to which each variable or measure covaries with the others. The second step is to scan the correlational matrix and look for any patterns that emerge. Computers are used in the process. The computer looks for a set of scores that seem to go together—that is, that are similarly high or low. When it finds such a cluster, it indicates that an underlying factor could account for the many relationships in the original matrix. A *factor* is a subset of highly intercorrelated measures.

The next step is to compute a correlation between each of the identified factors and each of the original variables. These correlations reflect what Cattell refers to as the "loading" of the variables on the factors and tell us to what degree each measure is related to each factor. A high positive correlation indicates that the measure is strongly related to the factor—that is, they covary together. A high negative correlation suggests that the measure is related but in an inverse way. The final step is to name the factors. Although the procedures for extracting factors are established mathematically, it is crucial to note that subjective judgment enters into the process of labeling and interpreting them.

Factor analysis enables researchers to draw conclusions such as that similar scores in reading, vocabulary, and spelling tests are due to a common underlying factor of verbal ability, whereas performance in addition, subtraction, and multiplication depends on mathematical ability. Many of the studies undertaken involve a great deal of mathematical computation. The advent of the computer made factor analysis a feasible technique for personality research.

Thus, beginning with hundreds of surface personality traits, Cattell discovered through factor analysis which of the traits cluster and occur together with the greatest frequency. These traits were then placed together under a common source trait, thereby reducing the number of traits to be dealt with and making them easier to handle.

Just as the study of individuals may be facilitated by the exploration of underlying traits, the study of groups and institutions that shape personality may be facilitated by the objective measurement of **syntality,** Cattell's term for the dimensions that permit us to describe and differentiate among groups and institutions (1948). Again, factor analysis is an important tool in identifying the syntality of social institutions, ranging from the family to larger cultural groups such as nations. Cattell's work in syntality has led to the development of sets of factors and matrixes that can enable us to begin to measure and examine the differences and relationships among people in various groups. Cattell believed that variations among cultural groups (for example, whether Americans are more extraverted than the British but less so than the Canadians) can be specified and quantified and thus help us anticipate behavior and develop appropriate responses, an important task in today's global world.

The Big Five Personality Traits

Cattell provided the theoretical groundwork for much of the current research in the measurement of personality. That work has culminated in the emergence of five factors that form a potential basic model for delineating the structure of personality. Some have even suggested that a consensus on the factors now exists, popularly known as the **Big Five** (Goldberg, 1990, 1993; John, 1990; McCrae & Costa, 1987).

Although somewhat different labels have been used for the Big Five factors, the most commonly used are *Neuroticism, Extraversion, Openness, Agreeableness,* and *Conscientiousness* (Loehlin, 1992). An acronym for remembering these factors can be formed by rearranging the first letters of each factor to form the word *OCEAN* (John, 1990, p. 96).

The Big Five is a contemporary theory that is inspiring a significant amount of research. Still, it is premature to say that there is a clear consensus. Although there is a high level of agreement that there are five dimensions, there is some disagreement (or dispute) concerning the exact nature of each of the five factors. Scholars do not even always use the same five terms.

Historically, the Big Five arose out of two different attempts to identify basic factors in personality. One was the study of language, which led to a descriptive model of personality traits that has been replicated across different languages. The other was the factor analysis of personality questionnaires, which led to an explanatory hypothesis, the **Five-Factor Model (FFM),** about dispositional biological traits that are substantially inherited. The two are similar in many ways, but they are not identical (John & Robins, 1993).

THE STUDY OF LANGUAGE

Initial support for the Big Five came from the analysis of language—specifically, vernacular terms used to describe personality. Sir Francis Galton (1822–1911), an English scientist, was one of the first to propose a "lexical hypothesis" suggesting that significant differences among people that affect how they interact with one another are encoded in words. Over time, people recognize and label those characteristics that are crucial for interpersonal relationships. These words are used frequently and reflect our understanding of the world and of other people (Goldberg, 1993).

Allport found 17,953 words in the English language that could be referred to as personality attributes (Hall & Lindzey, 1978). The words that people use to describe one another are observable attributes rather than underlying causal traits. However, within the vocabulary of synonymous terms, clusters develop that reflect the most important attributes. The fact that there are clusters leads one to ask how many terms we actually need to cover all of the characteristics. Lewis Thurstone, an early developer of factor analysis, was the first to suggest that as few as five might be sufficient to account for all of the adjectives that people use to describe one another (1934). He concluded that the "scientific description of personality" might be simpler than previously thought (1948).

Cattell (1943) used Allport's list as a basis for his factor analysis of the structure of personality and reduced the list to sixteen items (see Table 11.1). To hone the number to sixteen was an enormous task, considering the primitive calculators of the mid-1940s. Although Cattell launched the scientific research that led to the identification of the Big Five, he never adopted the model, believing that five was too small a number.

Whereas Cattell identified sixteen factors from his analysis, later researchers, using the same data, were able to consistently replicate only five. Tupes and Christal (1961) and Norman (1963) were among the first to identify factors similar to the current Big Five, and Goldberg (1981) reviewed research on them and argued for their power and consistency. Digman (1990) and John (1990) reviewed studies in diverse languages (such as Japanese, Chinese, and German) from different cultures and found cross-cultural support for the Big Five model.

THE STUDY OF PERSONALITY QUESTIONNAIRES AND RATINGS

The second source of support for five basic factors emerged from the factor analysis of personality questionnaires and ratings. This activity led to the Five-Factor Model (FFM). Questionnaires developed by Cattell and Eysenck were used, but most of the research in this area was done by Paul Costa and Robert McCrae, whose prodigious work and publications bolstered the acceptance of a five-factor model for understanding personality structure.

Costa and McCrae (1985, 1992a; McCrae & Costa, 1989, 1990) developed and refined an objective assessment device that expressly measures the personality dimensions of the FFM. The Revised NEO Personality Inventory, or NEO-PI-R, consists of thirty scales with eight items each. Participants are asked to indicate on a 5-point scale ranging from (*strongly agree* to *strongly disagree*) whether or not certain descriptions apply to them. In scoring and analyzing the inventory, six particular facets are considered within each of the five factors. These are summarized in Table 11.2. Each of these five factors captures the essential nature of a larger group of specific characteristics that are related to one another. Each of the five categories includes more specific traits, many of which may be further broken down. Thus a hierarchy of traits is created. For example, the factor of Extraversion encompasses the more specific trait of gregariousness, which could include the even more precise characteristic of friendliness. The more specific an attribute (and its measurement) is, the better we are able to predict specific behavior in a given situation. Thus a specific measure of friendliness lets us predict more accurately how much one will smile and talk in a social situation than does the more global measure of Extraversion. The NEO-PI-R inventory permits the assessment of personality at the level of the specific characteristics and also at the more general level. The NEO-FFI is a short but frequently used form of the test.

DIFFERENCES BETWEEN THE BIG FIVE AND THE FIVE-FACTOR MODEL

According to Saucier and Goldberg (1996), the Big Five, stemming from studies of language, simply provides a summary description of attributes. No assumption is made about whether

TABLE 11.2 FACETS ENCOMPASSED WITHIN THE FIVE-FACTOR MODEL

In scoring and analyzing the Revised NEO Personality Inventory (NEO-PI-R), six particular facets are measured within each of the five factors (Costa & McCrae, 1992a).

NEUROTICISM	EXTRAVERSION	OPENNESS	AGREEABLENESS	CONSCIENTIOUSNESS
anxiety	warmth	fantasy	trust	competence
angry hostility	gregariousness	aesthetics	straightforwardness	order
depression	assertiveness	feelings	altruism	dutifulness
self-consciousness	activity	actions	compliance	achievement striving
impulsiveness	excitement seeking	ideas	modesty	self-discipline
vulnerability	positive emotions	values	tender-mindedness	deliberation

or not the traits actually exist or about their possible causes. It is purely a description, not an explanation.

As seen by McCrae and Costa, the Five-Factor Model (FFM) is an interpretation of the Big Five factors (1989). It seeks to advance some additional claims that do not necessarily follow from the discovery of five basic dimensions in language. First, it asserts that we can describe personality structure in terms of five broad categories, each of which includes more specific attributes, and that individuals can be described by their scores on the measure of the broad concepts or the subsets. Second, it suggests that differences among people in these dimensions are stable over time, have a genetic basis, and are due at least in part to some still-to-be-specified internal mechanism. Thus the FFM sets forth additional, farther-reaching theoretical claims than does the Big Five.

Theorists differ on the extent to which the Big Five refers to real traits and the FFM refers to causal mechanisms that exist within the person. Although Cattell was interested in the physical and genetic components that influence behavior, he did not assert claims of such status for the traits he uncovered. Eysenck was very clear that his goal was ultimately to identify the causes of the components of personality (see the chapter on biological traits), but he clearly recognized the limits of factor analysis. Some researchers use the Five-Factor Model but do not subscribe to the theoretical claims. Most do not take a clearly causal stance and are very careful about specifying particular mechanisms.

FIVE-FACTOR THEORY

McCrae and Costa were cautious about moving from language-based descriptions of personality to conclusions about its basic structure. "No one would argue that an analysis of common English terms for parts of the body would provide an adequate basis for the science of anatomy, why should personality be different?" (McCrae & Costa, 1985). However, nowadays they make a distinction between the Five-Factor Model (FFM) and what they call Five-Factor Theory (FFT). The former is a hierarchical description of personality traits. The latter is an attempt to account for the body of research findings associated with the Five-Factor Model (McCrae & Costa, 1999, 2003).

The prodigious work and publication of Paul Costa (left) and Robert McCrae have bolstered the acceptance of a five factor model for understanding personality structure.

The mountain of research associated with the FFM includes case studies (Costa & McCrae, 1998, McCrae, 1993–1994), longitudinal studies (Costa & McCrae, 1992b), and cross-cultural studies (McCrae, Costa, del Pilar, Rolland, & Parker, 1998). It has inspired and reinvigorated trait psychology and led to significant findings concerning the origins, development, and functioning of personality traits (McCrae, 1992). McCrae and Costa's Five Factor Theory seeks to provide an overview of the functioning of the person throughout the life span based on that research. The core components of the personality system (indicated by rectangles in Figure 11.1) are *basic tendencies, characteristic adaptations,* and the *self-concept* (a characteristic adaptation of such importance that it has been elevated to a core component). Initially rooted in *biological bases* (genes, brain structure, and physical body), these interact with systems (indicated by ovals) that are outside personality per se, the *objective biography* and *external influences.* Arrows indicate the multiple paths of interaction among the various personality components. These paths may entail several dynamic processes (such as perception, coping, and planning), but FFT has little to say about them at this time while acknowledging that a complete theory of personality would need to elaborate on all of these topics. The figure can be seen as a diagram of personality at any given point of time, or it may be seen as an indication of how the person develops over time.

Key to McCrae and Costa's model is the distinction between basic tendencies and characteristic adaptations. Basic tendencies are biologically based, universal, and stable. Small consistent changes in some of the traits seen in longitudinal studies are seen as due to biological maturation. Characteristic adaptations leading to specific behaviors arise out of the interaction of basic tendencies and external influences. These can vary throughout the life

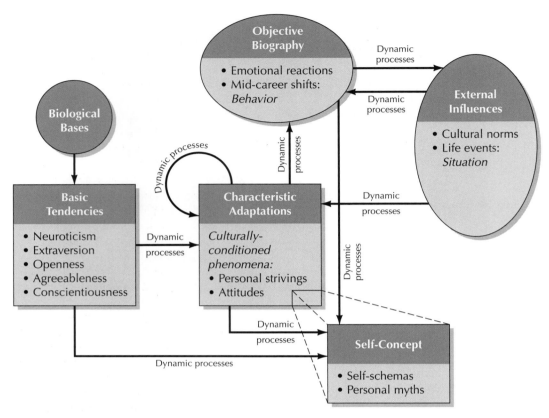

FIGURE 11.1 A REPRESENTATION OF THE FIVE FACTOR THEORY PERSONALITY SYSTEM
Core components are in rectangles; interfacing components are in ovals. Arrows indicate the multiple paths of interaction among the various personality components. The figure can be seen as a diagram of personality at any given point of time, or it may be seen as an indication of how the person develops over time.
SOURCE: McCrae, R., and Costa, P. in J. S. Wiggins, The Five-Factor Model of personality: Theoretical perspectives. Copyright (c) Guilford Publications, Inc. Reprinted by permission of Guilford Publications, Inc.

span and across cultures. Thus one's basic tendency for openness is biologically rooted and stable, but how one characteristically expresses it can change over time.

Comparing their work with that of other contemporary theorists, McCrae and Costa (2003) note that Mischel and Shoda's system (discussed in the chapter on social learning theories) is similar in its emphasis on the dynamic interaction of components. McAdams (discussed in the chapter on ego analytic psychology) also distinguishes among stable dispositional traits and changeable characteristic adaptations; however, McAdams sees them as separate levels, whereas in McCrae and Costa's model they are interconnecting components of a personality system.

APPLICATIONS OF THE BIG FIVE AND THE FIVE-FACTOR MODEL AND THEORY

Because the Five-Factor Model is based on the findings of the Big Five, hereafter we will generally refer to the Big Five with the understanding that, in some cases, research is specifically based on the Five-Factor Model and Theory. Research data support the construct validity of the Big Five measures and the role of the Big Five in determining certain behaviors (Paunonen, 2003).

Research on the Big Five has resulted in several applications. Most notably, research has been successfully used to predict job performance. Many of the traits reflected in the Big Five structure are related to those needed for positive achievement in work. For example, measures associated with the dimension of Conscientiousness are often helpful in predicting job success (Barrick & Mount, 1991), as are measures related to Agreeableness (Tett, Jackson, & Rothstein, 1991). Looking at some of the measures in terms of requirements for successful performance in specific occupations may permit employers to make intelligent decisions concerning job candidates. Successfully driving a truck, for example, requires an individual who is conscientious and emotionally stable; an impulsive, sociable individual is more likely to cause problems on the road (Hogan & Hogan, 1995).

Earlier use of personality measures by organizations led to considerable reservations about the practice because of problems of faking, low validity, and the potential for ethical abuse. However, newer data suggest that well-developed personality measures can successfully predict job performance and increase fairness in the employment process. Well-constructed personality questionnaires do not systematically discriminate against people with disabilities (Hayes, 1996), women, or the elderly, or people of minority-group status (Hogan & Hogan, 1995). Instead, they can be used as a force for "equal employment opportunity, social justice, and increased productivity" (Hogan, Hogan, & Roberts, 1996).

Personality measures can also contribute to the prediction of job satisfaction. Tokar and Subich (1997) used several different measures to survey the job satisfaction of adults employed in various occupations and concluded that personality dimensions contribute significantly to the prediction of job satisfaction. In particular, Extraversion and low Neuroticism were unique predictors. Holland (1996) has linked the five traits with his typology of persons and work environments to underscore that people work well when there is a good fit between their personality type and the characteristics of the work environment. Thus optimal use of human resources can certainly be facilitated by the framework of the Big Five (Goldberg, 1993).

The Five-Factor Model has become so compelling that a variety of instruments have been developed, and many existing instruments have been modified, to assess it (Widiger & Trull, 1997). Because it originated in the study of ordinary language, the structure is ideally suited for analyzing and understanding descriptions developed by individuals in working on their life histories, the constructs that emerge from Kelly's Role Construct Repertory Test (to be discussed in the chapter on personal constructs), and other idiographic or person-centered research (John & Robins, 1993). The five constructs can also be useful in showing us how concepts in personality theorizing are related. Thus Adler's *social interest,* Horney's *moving toward,* and Erikson's *basic trust* may all be seen as aspects of Agreeableness.

The five constructs have been replicated in both Western and non-Western languages. However, the factors that emerge across cultures do not completely coincide (Yang & Bond, 1990), suggesting that there are also important cultural differences in personality structure. When Shweder and Bourne (1984) permitted people in India and the United States to freely choose any terms to describe an acquaintance, trait terms were more frequently used by the Americans and situational action responses by the Indians. Thus people in the United States would be more likely to describe someone as helpful, whereas people from India would describe the actual instance of helping, such as, "My friend reaches out to help people when they fall down." These findings suggest that the Indian view of personality is less individualistic and more socially embedded than the American view.

McCrae and Costa (1997) compared data from studies that used six translations of the NEO-PI-R from different language families with the American factor structure. After the factors were rotated in an appropriate manner, the various samples (German, Portuguese, Hebrew, Chinese, Korean, and Japanese) revealed structures similar to the American factors. Because diverse cultures and languages were represented, McCrae and Costa believe that the result indicates that personality trait structure transcends cultural differences and may be universal. This is not to say that the five factors play the same role in every culture; indeed, they seem to emerge most easily in northern European languages (Saucier, Hampson, & Goldberg, 2000). But it is now possible to look at the specific cultural manifestations of common personality dimensions. Such cross-cultural replicability further points out the need for an evolutionary understanding of how differences among people have been encoded into everyday language. More recently, a cross-cultural study of maturational changes in personality across the life span has reaffirmed the stability of the model (McCrae et al., 1999), which has provided a basic foundation for considerable cross-cultural research in personality (McCrae & Allik, 2002).

The Personality Profiles of Cultures Project used a measure of the FFM to observe persons from over fifty cultures and test hypotheses about the universality of personality traits. The findings indicate that features of the FFM are common to all groups, suggesting a biological basis for personality traits as basic features of the human species (McCrae & Terracciano, 2005a). In addition, mean trait levels can be used to develop aggregate personality profiles of cultures and provide insight into cultural differences (McCrae & Terracciano, 2005b). These measurements do not converge with popular descriptions of national character. Such stereotypes are social constructions frequently used to foster negative discrimination; they do not accurately describe the people of a culture and measured against the assessed personality profiles may be seen to be groundless (Terracciano et al, 2005).

There are a number of conceptual and validity issues associated with cross-cultural studies: For example, might cultural bias interfere with a Western researcher's ability to actually understand human agency in non-Western cultures (Funder, 2004)? Most studies have not included culture-specific traits or studied samples that are very different in culture from the West. (Triandis & Suh, 2002). Therefore, critics continue to urge caution concerning the cross-cultural applicability of the FFM.

Research has also focused on the comprehensiveness of the Big Five and the Five-Factor Model, inquiring whether any significant personality characteristics are not encompassed in those structures (Becker, 1998; Paunonen & Jackson, 2000; Saucier & Goldberg, 1998). Concerns have been expressed that the models' dependence on language, self-report, and/or factor analysis limits their usefulness (Block, 1995; Eysenck, 1992; McAdams, 1992b). Nevertheless, consensus about the validity and cross-cultural generalization of the Big Five and the Five-Factor Model continues to grow (Mervielde & Asendorpf, 2000).

Development of the Five-Factor Model has had significant implications for the diagnosis and analysis of dysfunctional behavior (Livesley, Schroeder, Jackson & Jang, 1994). The

NEO-PI-R has been useful in diagnosing personality disorders. For example, Miller and Lyman (2003) studied measures in relation to psychopathy, or antisocial behavior. They correlated individuals' scores with an expert-generated FFM psychopathy prototype and self-reports of behavior, as well as with several laboratory tasks. Persons whose personality profiles consist of low Agreeableness and Conscientiousness and high Extraversion, along with mixed measures of the facets pertaining to Neuroticism (high in impulsiveness and angry hostility, low in anxiety, depression, self-consciousness, and vulnerability) were likely to behave in ways associated with psychopathy. They were more likely to abuse substances, engage in risky sex, and become involved in delinquent or criminal behavior. In addition, they were more aggressive in a laboratory task, were less willing to delay gratification, and showed a preference for aggressive responses. Such results join other studies in providing strong support for a dimensional approach to the assessment of personality disorders and show that the FFM is sufficiently broad to account for most of the variation in personality disorders (Clark, Vorhies, & McEwen, 2002; Schroeder, Wormworth, & Livesley, 2002).

The prevailing diagnostic system in America, the *Diagnostic and Statistical Manual of Mental Disorders—IV* (DSM-IV), classifies mental disorders as distinct categories, diagnosed on the basis of observable behaviors. The relationship between the five factors and DSM-IV personality disorders is a lively topic of current research (Costa & Widiger, 2002).

Thinking Critically

Do personality disorders and psychopathology represent a qualitative or a quantitative difference from normality? See the Thinking Critically box "How Abnormal Is Abnormal?"

The Five-Factor Model's emphasis on traits rather than types encourages us to look at normal and abnormal behavior as a continuum rather than as different types of behavior. The research revisits an important question: Do personality disorders and psychopathology represent a qualitative or a quantitative difference from normality? From the perspective of the Big Five model, one way to look at psychological disorders is to say that they represent extremes of normal characteristics. Thus people with disorders are quantitatively rather than qualitatively different from those without disorders. Although there are advantages and disadvantages to both the categorical and the dimension models of classification, empirical support is very compelling for the FFM (Widiger & Frances, 2002). Dimensional models are consistent with the evidence, and trait models can accommodate personality disorder categories.

Such a dimensional approach is consistent with the informal widespread clinical organization of mental illness as normal, neurotic, or psychotic, depending on the deterioration of an individual's reality testing and interpersonal relationships. Moreover, the informal clinical recognition that multiple causes and conditions find unique expression in an individual disorder is acknowledged in the Five-Factor Model because a high or low score on a Big Five trait is essentially a group of subfacet scores expressing unique combinations.

Still, it is not clear that the model is directly applicable to clinical use. Several obstacles must be overcome before clinicians can be expected to use the FFM in their practice (O'Connor & Dyce, 2002). People with the same overall score do not necessarily obtain the same score by responding in the same way to the items. One person's Neuroticism score could be elevated due to a stronger endorsement of somatic symptoms of anxiety (sweating palms, heart palpitations); another's score could be elevated by assenting to affective items (worry or anxiety). Is it appropriate to consider these two people the same? The facet structure within each of the five factors needs further development to capture clinical concepts. Trait

Thinking Critically

How Abnormal Is Abnormal?

Research on the relationship between the Five-Factor Model and DSM-IV personality disorders recalls an important question: Do personality disorders and psychopathology represent a qualitative or a quantitative difference from normality? The prevailing diagnostic system in America, the *Diagnostic and Statistical Manual of Mental Disorders—IV* (DSM-IV), classifies mental disorders as distinct categories, diagnosed on the basis of observable behaviors. Gordon Allport believed that there is a radical discontinuity between the neurotic and the healthy personality. Psychological disorders in the FFM, however, represent extremes of normal characteristics. Thus people with disorders are quantitatively rather than qualitatively different from those without disorders. In other words, because the five factors are the fundamental traits of personality, persons suffering from disorders simply have more or less of something we all have, rather than some unique or foreign ingredient in their personality.

What do you think? Are people who have personality disorders qualitatively or quantitatively different from normal people? What impact does your answer have on your beliefs and feelings concerning what separates you from individuals who warrant clinical diagnoses?

models do not account for all aspects of personality disorder, and attention needs to be given to the organizing and integrative functions of personality (Livesley, 2001). It is important to recognize that the focus of a diagnostic decision is the maladaptive expression of traits, not the basic traits themselves (Harkness & McNulty, 2002). No matter how extreme one's standing on a trait, it might not constitute a disorder unless it is associated with a characteristic problem in living or maladaptation.

Efforts have been made to translate the DSM-IV personality disorders into the hierarchical FFM as operationalized by the scales of the NEO-PI-R (Widiger, Trull, Clarkin, Sanderson, & Costa, 2002). Widiger, Costa, and McCrae (2002) have presented a four-step process of diagnosing personality disorders with the FFM that can assist in making the use of the FFM standard in research and clinical practice with personality disorders. They have also compiled a summation of characteristic problems in living associated with extremes of each of the five factors, as well as maladaptions for each of the subfacets. To date, most of the research has focused on personality disorders of Axis II of the DSM; however, it is rapidly being extended to other psychological and psychiatric disorders, and the scope has been enlarged to include treatment implications (Costa & Widiger, 2002). Thus the NEO-PI-R may be useful in determining types of treatment. For example, an extravert might do better in group therapy, but an introvert might be more comfortable in a one-on-one situation (Funder & Sneed, 1993). Thus the dimensional approach of the FFM may prove more reliable, valid, and useful than the categorical approach of the DSM (Monte, 1999; Widiger & Costa, 1994).

Genetics and Evolutionary Developments

THE GENETIC INFLUENCE ON TRAITS

Cattell was particularly interested in assessing the relative importance of heredity and environment to personality. The same interest has led other researchers to study genetic influences on traits. This research lends additional support to the Big Five theory. **Behavioral genetics** explores the cause of individual differences in human behavior in terms of heredity. The discipline makes an important distinction between the **genotype,** the genetic makeup of an individual, and the **phenotype,** the individual's observable appearance and behavior that arise out of the interaction of his or her genotype with the environment. Techniques of study have been developed to separate the phenotypic variation of a population into genetic and environmental aspects.

By focusing on a specific characteristic and comparing various individuals in different environments, behavioral geneticists can help us understand the relative contributions of heredity and environment. If children who are unrelated are adopted, raised in the same family, and grow up to be similar in regard to a trait such as extraversion, we may conclude that the shared family environment had a more important role in the development of that trait than did heredity. If the children tend to be dissimilar (as they in fact do), we might conclude that the genetic contribution was the more significant one.

Twin studies are the most popular design for behavioral genetic studies. Twins naturally arouse our curiosity and also provide a convenient population with which to explore the comparative contributions of nature and nurture. Twins are two separate individuals, yet they are very much alike. Myth and literature are replete with stories in which similar events happen to twins. There are documented instances in which twins raised separately after birth are reunited and discover that they have a great deal in common, such as using the same brand of toothpaste, owning the same make of car, or having similar jobs, hobbies, health problems, and so forth. How can we account for such occurrences?

The logic behind the method of studying twins can be easily understood. Identical, or *monozygotic* (MZ), twins develop from a single fertilized ovum or egg. They have the same genes and the same parents, and from a genetic point of view they are clones of each other. Any differences between MZ twins must be due to dissimilar experiences. Fraternal, or *dizygotic* (DZ), twins develop from two fertilized ova. They share the same parents but have different genes and are no more alike than regular siblings. Differences between DZ twins must be due to both genetic effects and separate experiences.

Cattell (1960) advocated the technique of *multiple abstract variance analysis* (MAVA), which studies twins and siblings who have been reared either together or apart. However, before the early 1980s, twin and adoption studies were done outside of the mainstream of psychology and had little impact on the field. The study of genetics emphasized animal studies. Selective breeding gave clear evidence for a genetic contribution to temperament. In the 1960s, two studies began to focus attention on human behavioral genetics and twin studies. Erlenmeyer-Kimling and Jarvik (1963) summarized the twin and adoption studies done up to that time and suggested that heredity is an important factor in IQ scores. Heston (1966) conducted an adoption study that revealed the importance of heredity in the development of schizophrenia. However, interest was quickly squelched when Jensen (1969) provoked tremendous controversy by suggesting that differences in IQ scores between blacks and whites may be due to genetics.

Although monozygotic (identical) twins are very similar, they are not exactly the same—as is illustrated by this picture of the text author (on the right) and her sister.

In the last several decades, the design of genetic studies has become highly sophisticated and varied, going far beyond the simple comparison of MZ and DZ twins. A wider range and greater number of studies have incorporated samples of adult twins and their offspring, as well as other combinations of siblings and families, both biologically related and adopted. New methods of testing hypotheses have increased the usefulness of available data. Earlier concerns regarding environmental effects and differences in the development of twins and singletons have been allayed. These are no longer seen as jeopardizing the effectiveness of the research for the purpose of genetic determination of traits. The analysis of blood tests for DNA markers has eliminated any questions about the zygosity of particular sets of twins because identical twins have the same markers.

Behavioral genetics uses the statistic of heritability to express the proportion of phenotypic variation that may be due to genetic variation. **Heritability** is an estimate of the degree to which a trait or characteristic is caused by the genotype rather than the environment. Geneticists look at a particular trait and compare the correlation between monozygotic (identical) twins on the trait with the correlation among singly born individuals. This comparison provides a ratio. For the characteristic of height, the ratio is .9; this means that 90 percent of the differences in height among people is genetic and the remainder is due to the environment. It is important to note that this does not mean that 90 percent of *your* height is due to your genes and the remaining 10 percent of your height is due to your environ-

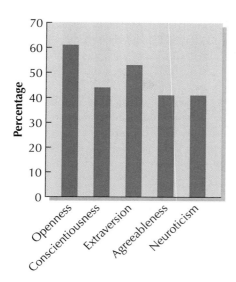

FIGURE 11.2 GENETIC INFLUENCE ON THE BIG FIVE

In a twin study assessing influences on the Big Five, Lang and Livesley (1996) found heredity estimates exceeding 40 percent for all of the factors. *SOURCE: Adapted from Lang, K. L., & Livesley, W. J. (1996). Heritability of the Big Five personality dimensions and their facets: A twin study.* Journal of Personality, 64, *577–597.*

ment. The ratio applies to an entire biological population growing up in a particular environment, not to individuals within the population. The fact that the heritability estimate of height is 90 percent means that almost all of the height differences are due to genetic factors.

Heritability estimates can be somewhat misleading by themselves because there are different ways to define and calculate heritability. These differences can produce varying numbers. Moreover, genes affect traits in a probabilistic rather than a predetermined manner. Nevertheless, heritability statistics help us know to what extent heredity can influence a trait. A significant degree of heritability does not mean that the environment has no role in the shaping of a trait, but it does place some boundaries on the extent of its potential contribution. Heritability studies can also clarify the degree to which a trait may be due to shared environmental experiences (i.e., a common family environment or the same diet) as opposed to experiences unique to the individual.

Summaries of the behavioral genetic twin study literature for the Five-Factor Model have been provided by Loehlin (1992) and Bouchard (1994). Earlier studies may have overestimated the genetic influence on personality, but heritability estimates exceed 40 percent for all of the factors. In Lang and Livesley's (1996) assessment of genetic influence on the Big Five, the specific estimates are Neuroticism, 41 percent; Extraversion, 53 percent; Openness, 61 percent; Agreeableness, 41 percent; and Conscientiousness, 44 percent (see Figure 11.2). Openness shows the greatest effect and Extraversion, the second greatest. The estimates of the influence of shared family environment are small. Most of the environmental variance was due to nonshared influences. These findings have also been replicated in cross-cultural studies.

APPLICATIONS OF GENETIC RESEARCH

Twin and adoption studies permit us to estimate genetic influences indirectly by noting how relatives resemble one another. However, new and sophisticated techniques are revolutionizing genetic research on personality by identifying specific DNA markers, segments of DNA whose locations are known on a particular chromosome, and genetic mechanisms that are believed to result in differences in behavior. The Human Genome Project, essentially completed in 2003, showed us that 99.9 percent of DNA sequences in the human genome is shared in all people. Only 0.1 percent varies, yet these differences affect psychological differences. There are an estimated 10 million variations, and over a third of them have been identified by finding random mutations in the DNA sequence that act as genetic milestones and make up the genetic or DNA markers. The variations are also called "snips," or SNPs (single nucleotide polymorphisms), and they tend to be inherited in small blocks of chromosomes known as hyplotypes. Scientists genetically analyzed DNA samples from persons from Africa, Asia, and the United States and developed the "HapMap," a catalog identifying variations and indicating where they occur in our genes and how they are distributed among people within and among populations in various parts of the world (Kotulak, 2005).

However, most behaviors are not the result of the action of a single gene. Rather, many genes having varying effects contribute to behavior variation and vulnerability to certain problems. The genes in these multiple-gene systems are labeled *quantitative trait loci* (QTL), and DNA markers are helping us identify and locate them. The challenge is to identify genes involved in complex behaviors that entail multiple-gene effects, as well as nongenetic contributors.

Research in the last decade of the twentieth century was able to make provisional associations between specific genes and traits of Extraversion and Neuroticism but was not able to conclusively demonstrate their connection. However, newer techniques, such as functional neuroimaging, have strengthened the relationship between certain genetic mechanisms and anxiety-related personality traits. Also, new computer models that improve on earlier self-report questionnaires may help us to better comprehend how common genetic

Just as physical similarities show up in intergenerational pictures of families, similar personality traits can be traced on genograms (see page 304).

polymorphisms change human behavior. In addition, the recognition that early environmental impacts can strengthen associations between genes and behavior may suggest that we are moving into an exciting new period of personality genetics (Epstein, 2006; cf. Canli, 2006). In the coming years, we will see new QTL mapping techniques that will permit us to use genetic markers as direct indicators of genotypes.

None of the data on the heritability of personality traits suggest that inheritance is either the primary factor or a more significant one than the environment. At best, research suggests that the heritability of many behaviors is in the range of 30 to 50 percent. This means that only about one-third to one-half of behavior variation is due to genetics; the majority of the variance is due to environment. Evidence of heritability varies from trait to trait, with traits associated with temperament having the highest degree of heritability and those relating to attitudes and beliefs having the least (Buss & Plomin, 1984; see also Jang, Livesley, Angleitner, Riemann, & Vernon, 2002). However, the more we know about a trait genetically as well as environmentally, the better equipped we will be to develop prevention and intervention strategies.

The fact that a behavior is genetically influenced does not mean that it cannot be changed. It just makes it harder to change. Nevertheless, genetic tendencies can be extensively altered by modifications in the environment, as each obese individual who diets and each recovering alcoholic who abstains demonstrate. Because many problems that may have genetic roots cannot be treated as effectively once they are fully formed (for example, psychopathology and alcoholism), early detection of people at risk provides our best means of prevention. Early identification of infants who inherit an inability to metabolize a certain protein (phenylketonuria [PKU]) has led to treatment through dietary restrictions that prevent the mental retardation that formerly resulted. However, the ability to detect potential problems early raises significant ethical questions about what should be done with that information.

Genes are not rigid blueprints that mandate our destiny. Their expression—how, where, and when they get turned on and off—is affected by changes in the womb, the environment, and other factors. Such extraneous factors have been implicated in mental disorders such as schizophrenia and bipolar disorder (Diamond, 2004). The more we explore about the genome, the more vulnerable to timing and experience genes seem to be. Rather than a linear cause-and-effect pattern, the relationship between genes, environment, and behavior may be one of circular interaction (Ridley, 2003). Indeed, a new paradigm may be needed to encompass the complexities of gene-environment interaction and covariances (Beckwith & Alper, 2002).

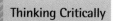

Thinking Critically

What does your family tree look like? See the Thinking Critically box "Using a Genogram to Chart Personality Traits in Your Family Tree."

Recent technological advances are leading to research strategies that will help us understand genetic influences on psychiatric disorders and behavior. Progress is being made in identifying genes and gene variations that play a crucial role in human behaviors and common severe behavioral diseases such as alcoholism, schizophrenia, and bipolar disorder. We now have the technology to scan a set of genes for genetic loci and variation across a large number of affected individuals and to identify uncommon variations that contribute to a phenotype. Such data are being collected for many major psychiatric disorders—for example, schizophrenia, bipolar disorder, alcoholism, and panic disorders (see Crabbe, 2002; Goldman & Mazzanti, 2002). However, locating a gene defect

Thinking Critically

Using a Genogram to Chart Personality Traits in Your Family Tree

Traits such as shyness, creativity, depressive disorder, alcoholism, and high intelligence frequently seem to run in families. Francis Galton, the founder of behavioral genetics, demonstrated a hereditary influence on intellectual abilities by tracing family trees of eminent individuals and noting that there were a proportionately higher number of accomplished persons in certain family trees.

You can chart personality traits in your family tree by drawing a genogram, a flow diagram that shows family relationships over generations using a standard format. You might wish to start by interviewing your relatives, asking what family traits have appeared in the family throughout the generations and how the traits may have varied in specific appearance. You may find some new things, pleasant and unpleasant. Try to roll with the punches, and be prepared for surprises.

Create the chart by drawing a symbol to represent yourself and other individuals (square for male, circle for female). A sample genogram is included in Figure 11.3. Put a slash or an X inside the shape if the person is deceased, and indicate the cause of death if it is relevant. Next to the symbol, indicate relevant data concerning the traits you are tracing and their expression. You can also indicate emotional relationships among members of families and their communities by using arrows to indicate positive feelings and (//) to signify disruptions. Do such activities help you to answer the question of whether genes have an impact on our personalities?

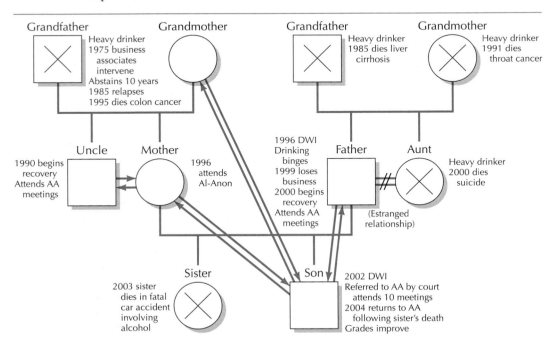

FIGURE 11.3 SAMPLE GENOGRAM TRACING THE TRAIT OF ALCOHOLISM IN A FAMILY TREE

does not necessarily indicate that a cure is close by or even possible. Nevertheless, identification of these gene variants is thought to have enormous potential for understanding and treating behavior.

However, even single-gene physical conditions, such as cystic fibrosis and Huntington's disease, have proven to be very complex. Unraveling the intricate genetics of personality is bound to be even more difficult. Still, "there is little doubt but that genes will eventually be associated with personality traits and mental illnesses." However, great care will need to be exercised in publicizing and applying this information so that it is not misused. Hasty and excited announcements of the finding of "homosexual," "depressive," "alcoholic," "aggression," or "criminal" genes do not contribute constructively to the understanding of these behaviors. Further, neither genetic nor environmental explanations of behavior excuse it or permit us to avoid responsibility for it. (Beckwith & Alper, 2002) (cf. DeCamp & Sugarman, 2004; Morse, 2006).

EVOLUTIONARY PSYCHOLOGY THEORY

Studies in heritability remind us of our close connections to the biological world and our evolutionary history. They lead us to ask how we have adapted to life and what role evolution plays in the development of personality. David Buss (1995) has suggested that **evolutionary psychology** may provide the conceptual tools for bringing together diverse threads in psychology and the study of personality.

Evolutionary psychology is a way of thinking about human behavior based on data drawn from biology, anthropology, sociology, cognitive psychology, and the neurosciences. Darwinian principles of evolution, outlined in *On the Origin of Species* (1859), are used to help explain human behavior. Darwin's theory of natural selection argues that any heritable characteristic that helps an individual survive and reproduce is more likely to be passed on than are other, less successful characteristics. Thus sexual selection favored characteristics that help people gain access to mates and led to competitive males. A preference for sweet-tasting foods, high in calories and providing necessary energy, was also adaptive behavior in an early hunting and gathering environment.

Since the 1960s, evolutionary psychologists have developed secondary theories to advance our understanding of human behavior. Altruistic behavior is explained by *inclusive fitness*—related individuals giving aid to others who share their genes. Such behavior helps related others to survive and pass the shared genes on (Hamiliton, 1964). *Reciprocal altruism* accounts for altruistic and cooperative strategies among nonrelatives when the benefits are greater than the costs (Trivers, 1971). *Parental investment theory* helps to explain why females tend to be more selective than males in choosing their mates. In their selection of a mate, females tend to value a male who is ambitious, industrious, and able to provide resources for the family, whereas men tend to choose a partner based on an appearance that indicates ample reproductive capacity. Also, women have a greater investment in making children because of the risks of giving birth as well as the long periods of gestation and lactation (Trivers, 1985).

Buss (2004) suggests that the current specific behavior patterns we see today (such as high male sexual drive and fear of snakes) are patterns that survived in our ancestors because they were more successful than other behaviors. Particular behavior patterns prevailed because they solved specific problems in the survival and mating processes. In the course of evolution, these behaviors became specialized psychological mechanisms programmed in the brain to give algorithmic (step-by-step) instructions for adapting to situations. The patterns exist in the form that they do because they solved a specific problem of survival or reproduction repeatedly throughout evolutionary history. Activated by situational clues, they have become the typical responses to particular happenings (Buss, 2004).

Cosimides and Tooby (1997) suggest that the mind is a set of information-processing machines developed by natural selection to solve adaptive problems faced by our hunter-gatherer ancestors. The brain is a physical system, acting as a computer whose circuits were designed by natural selection to solve problems that our ancestors faced during the evolutionary history of our species. Our conscious experience misleads us into thinking that our circuitry is simpler than it really is. Problems that we perceive as easy to solve are actually very difficult and require complicated, differentiated neural circuitry specialized for solving varied adaptive problems.

Evolutionary psychology seeks, through primate studies, hunter-gatherer research, and anthropological evidence, to reconstruct the problems of survival and reproduction that our ancestors faced in their early environments and the problem-solving mechanisms they created to meet those particular challenges. With this information, evolutionary psychologists hope to form a consensus on how the human brain and emotions have evolved. In our current culture, we face many of the same issues: sex, mating, making friends, making enemies, getting along, and getting ahead. Evolutionary psychologists further aim to develop behavior probabilities for our modern culture, showing us the biological basis behind our reacting the ways we do even though many of our behaviors are no longer adaptive for the problems that we face today.

We continue to engage in nonadaptive behaviors because cultural evolution has proceeded at a much faster pace than biological evolution. "Our modern skulls house a stone age mind" (Cosimides & Tooby, 1997). In an earlier era, using force in sexual behavior would have increased the likelihood of reproductive success, favoring aggressive male sexual behavior. Changes in attitude, which no longer make rape a viable option, have only recently occurred. Biological adaptation, however, is slow to follow cultural modifications. The impulse to kill, a survival strategy, becomes costly with the onset of civilization and tough criminal penalties and laws against it. When it becomes too costly, people are more likely to choose other alternatives (Buss, 2005). Understanding the biological and evolutionary basis of our motives lets us be more aware of them and better educated about the circumstances in which we are likely to act on them. Once we know how emotions and behaviors such as anger, hate, and prejudice have evolved, we can begin to change negative behavior patterns by being aware of and controlling them.

David Buss believes that evolutionary psychology may provide the conceptual tools for bringing together diverse threads in psychology and the study of personality.

From an evolutionary perspective, the Big Five traits represent strategic differences summarizing the "most important features of the social landscape that humans have had to adapt to" (Buss, 1995). Information from the social environment was incorporated into psychological mechanisms. Many of the significant features of our evolved psychological mechanisms are social in character because many of our significant problems are social. In the course of evolution, people who were able to correctly discern and act on individual differences had a selective advantage over those who were oblivious to them. Awareness of relative tendencies to be dominant or submissive assisted the development of individual strategies that, in the aggregate, produced a social hierarchy (Buss, 2004). Perception of the willingness of others to be cooperative or aggressive helped in forming alliances. Appreciation of another's expertise permitted one to solicit help. Recognition of the reliability of another enabled trust. Over time, people developed psychological mechanisms that were sensitive to these and other important differences. The Big Five persisted and became robust because of their usefulness in human adaption. Bringing an evolutionary perspective to them clarifies why they have been so pervasive.

Evolutionary psychology can help us overcome the false dichotomies that have often clouded discussions of the nature of psychological mechanisms by placing them in one or the other of two separate classes, such as genetic *or* environmental, cultural *or* biological, and so forth (Buss, 1995). Heritable individual differences may lead to different utilization of psychological mechanisms. Those who are muscular and strong learn different strategies for dealing with people than those who are lean and frail. They will probably have a greater success using an aggressive strategy than their frailer peers would. These differences can point individuals toward different ways of adapting; over time, these strategies become stabilized. What were previously considered to be separate dichotomies are more appropriately seen as aspects of one unified process of evolution.

David Buss (1995) distinguishes between evolutionary psychology and sociobiology. Adherents of sociobiology frequently advocate a view of human beings as "fitness maximizers," suggesting that psychological mechanisms aim to maximize inclusive fitness. Buss believes that this is a fallacy that confuses the origins of psychological mechanisms with their nature. Psychological mechanisms that evolved in the process of adapting to problems do not necessarily continue to ensure fitness. For example, the human preference for fatty foods at one time probably helped us adapt by increasing our caloric intake. Today, however, that preference is not necessarily in our best interest. Likewise, alcoholism may be an early beneficial nutritional strategy gone awry. In a scarce environment, the aroma of ethanol in naturally fermenting fruit helped to locate food that was good to eat (Dudley, 2000, 2002). According to Buss, it is more helpful to see human evolution in terms of adaptive problem solving than of fitness maximizing.

Evolutionary psychologists have been criticized for developing imaginary, unverifiable scenarios suggesting that nearly all that we do is a consequence of evolutionary adaptation and reducing behavior to genetic determination (Panksepp & Panksepp, 2000). There are also moral and political misgivings about the potential applications of evolutionary psychology (Rose & Rose, 2000). However, evolutionary psychologists are increasingly developing testable hypotheses and point out that if you change the environment and the culture you alter the effects of the genes. Describing how things came to be is not stating how they should be, nor is it dictating a social agenda (Workman, 2004). Employing an evolutionary approach to personality may help increase our understanding, assist us in making better choices, and bring some of the current diverse threads in psychology into a coherent whole (cf. Caporael, 2001; Schaller, 2002; Workman, 2004).

<table>
<tr><td>

PHILOSOPHY,
SCIENCE,
and ART
</td></tr>
</table>

Factor Analytic Trait Theories

Cattell's theory of personality is based on highly objective and precise scientific techniques. At its height it generated more empirical research than any other personality theory (Wiggins, 1984), although Cattell's findings were not always replicated. A perusal of the material on personality published in the *Annual Review of Psychology* in the 1970s and 1980s attests to the significant research that Cattell's theory generated.

Cattell's theory presaged the current emphasis on quantitative methods and empirical data. Few other theorists have been as precise or as operational in their definitions. Furthermore, few theorists have been as rigorous in subjecting their concepts of underlying personality variables to empirical test. In its adherence to a strict methodology and its generation of a vast quantity of research, Cattell's theory is a meritorious example of a scientific approach to personality.

To identify Cattell as a scientist is not to ignore the fact that his theory arises out of his philosophical commitment to an empirical approach. His theory suggests that he views the world as lawful, consistent, and controllable. Moreover, Cattell suggests that a system of ethical values, which he calls *beyondism,* may be developed on the foundation of science. Beyondism is based on the view that humanity is advancing biologically. Moral laws that will foster and ensure this evolutionary process need to be developed. Such ethics will enable us to adapt to a wider range of circumstances and will give us a better chance of survival. Strictly speaking, Cattell's new morality cannot be said to arise from science. Scientists may have discovered the process of evolution, but the judgment that such evolution is good and should be fostered is a value judgment that takes us outside the realm of validating evidence and into the realm of philosophy. The moral issues that Cattell raises, such as the advisability of selective breeding as a means of cultivating certain traits, deserve serious debate. Herein lies the value of science for Cattell and others who cherish the importance of validating evidence: Our intuition is subsequently checked by explicit logic and experimentation.

Cattell's theory is not as popular as other theories among psychologists, and it is almost totally unknown among the general public. In part this lack of popularity is due to its complexity, but it is also due to a feeling that factor analysis creates an artifact or a para-person that has no relationship to a real person. As we have seen, it is difficult for the conclusions of a scientific method to command the same degree of compellingness as a philosophical vision.

The Big Five, which is also based on factor analysis, has received a great deal of attention as a significant contribution to personality theory. In spite of its current popularity, however, there is no unanimous agreement concerning the Big Five. Cattell believes that five factors are too few, but Eysenck, who is discussed in the chapter on

Thinking Critically

Do you think we should engage in selective breeding? See the Thinking Critically box "Should We Selectively Breed Humans?"

Thinking Critically

Should We Selectively Breed Humans?

Cattell (1972) suggested that governments consider selective breeding as a means of cultivating desired traits in their populations. Incentives (such as tax breaks) could be used to encourage people who have demonstrated their ability to contribute constructively to society to have more children, and disincentives could be used to discourage others who have not demonstrated that ability.

Selective breeding has long been accepted as a way of developing superior animals, fruits, and vegetables. The labradoodle, a new breed of dog, combines the calm, even disposition of the Labrador retriever with the intelligence of the poodle. In many ways, people already selectively breed by choosing their mates on the basis of appearance, intellect, and so forth. Cattell argued that the goal is to create *not* an ideal person or master race but rather diversity that would maximize evolutionary progress and the survival of humanity.

Cattell has been roundly criticized for his ideas on government sponsoring of **eugenics,** improving the human race through genetic control. There is a great difference between informal considerations made by individuals and a formal scheme for deliberately breeding those mental and physical traits that are most desirable. Although hereditary considerations are important, critics argue that selective breeding is antithetical to American ideals of freedom and equality. In addition, some feel that it is presumptuous to assume that one has the authority to decide which genetic characteristics are most desirable. Answering such a question, in their opinion, cannot be done scientifically without presupposing personal values. What do you think?

---

biological traits, believes that three will suffice. Pervin (1994) expresses concern that there has been a premature consensus equating personality with the Five-Factor Model that does not do justice to the dynamic nature of personality. McAdams (1994) suggests that a personality psychology that is limited to traits provides us with only a psychology of the stranger, merely giving information about people that we need to know when we know nothing else about them. Nevertheless, the Five-Factor Model is an important one in personality theory, especially so because it has provoked a great deal of research, even though it may not be the final integrative model.

The present interest in behavioral genetics and evolutionary psychology is a helpful shift after the predominance that was placed on the environment by the behaviorist movement. However, we need to be careful not to move from a simplistic emphasis on the environment to an equally simplistic emphasis on biology (Plomin, Chipuer, & Loehlin, 1990). Moreover, an emphasis on genetics easily gives rise to controversial issues, such as that of selective breeding. In June 1997, Cattell was selected for the rare and prestigious American Psychological Foundation Gold Medal Award for Lifetime Achievement in Psychological Science. However, the award was

Philosophical Assumptions

Which basic philosophical assumptions seem to be most important to Cattell and the Big Five theorists? See the Philosophical Assumptions box "Examining Cattell and the Big Five Theorists."

⚜ Philosophical Assumptions

Examining Cattell and the Big Five Theorists

Many of the differences among personality theories can be attributed to fundamental differences in philosophical assumptions. Which of the basic philosophical issues, described in the introductory chapter and summarized on the inside back cover, seem to be clearly important to Cattell and the Big Five theorists in the development of their theories? How, for example, does Cattell's interest in prediction influence his stance on freedom versus determinism? How does his recommendation of selective breeding come out of his philosophical assumptions? How does research into the Big Five add to the discussion of heredity versus environment? Do these theories address any other philosophical assumptions? Rate Cattell and the Big Five theorists on a scale of 1 to 5 on those philosophical assumptions that you feel their theories apply to most. Compare your ratings of Cattell and the Big Five theorists with your own philosophical assumptions. Did your study lead you to change any of your assumptions? Why or why not?

delayed pending further investigation because of charges that some of his writings were racist. Cattell denied the accusation, arguing that his remarks had been taken out of context. Considerable controversy followed. In order to end the personal attacks, Cattell declined the award and asked that his name be removed from further consideration.

As research in behavioral genetics continues, some questions will be answered and others asked about the genetic components of traits and temperaments, their stability, and their cultural components (Woodall & Matthews, 1993). Evolutionary psychology will provide a helpful framework within which to examine the adaptive nature of temperament and traits and may help us reconceive of the duality of nature and nurture as two aspects of one evolving process (Buss, 1995). Advances in genetics, embryology, and developmental biology will contribute to this process (Lickliter & Honeycutt, 2003).

Cattell's theory and the Big Five that resulted from it are carefully constructed theories that are well rooted in empirical data. They have enormous potential for teaching us about human personality and for predicting behavior. Indeed, Cattell believed that, in time, by applying appropriate rules of reference, psychologists would be able to predict human behavior as accurately as astronomers predict the stars and planets. The rigorous methodology and approach of these theories, as well as of Eysenck's theory, are characteristic of the scientific enterprise at work.

 TO LEARN MORE about recent research on "mood genes" and about the Five-Factor Model, and for a list of suggested readings, visit the *Personality Theories* textbook website at **college.cengage.com/pic/engler8e.**

Summary

1. Cattell defined **personality** (p. 287) as "that which permits prediction of what a person will do in a given situation." His interest in personality theorizing was clearly oriented toward prediction.

2. **Surface traits** (p. 288) are clusters of overt behavior responses that appear to go together. **Source traits** (p. 288) are the underlying variables, which may have their origin in heredity or in influences of the environment. Cattell identified sixteen basic source traits that he considered the "building blocks" of personality. He used **factor analysis** (p. 288) to identify traits. Factor analysis is a correlational procedure that interrelates many correlations at one time and identifies common underlying dimensions.

3. The most commonly used terms to describe the **Big Five** (p. 290) are *Neuroticism, Extraversion, Openness, Agreeableness,* and *Conscientiousness.*

4. The study of language led to a descriptive model of personality traits that has been replicated across languages. The study of personality questionnaires led to an explanatory hypothesis of traits.

5. The Big Five is a summary description of attributes. The **Five-Factor Model** (p. 290) seeks to advance some further claims. There are differences concerning the exact nature of each of the five factors because of various ways of conducting a factor analysis. Researchers also differ on whether the five factors go beyond description to provide a causal analysis. The Five-Factor Theory seeks to account for the research associated with the FFM.

6. Research on the Big Five has been successfully used to predict job performance and job satisfaction, to diagnose personality disorders, and to determine therapy.

7. **Behavioral genetics** (p. 299) explores hereditary causes of individual differences. It distinguishes between the **genotype** (p. 299), genetic makeup, and **phenotype** (p. 299), observable appearance and behavior.

8. Twin studies are useful in behavioral genetics because they permit us to make comparisons that suggest the genetic determination of traits.

9. **Heritability** (p. 300) is an estimate of the degree to which variance in a trait is due to genetics. Heritability estimates exceed 40 percent for all of the Big Five.

10. Genetic research helps us learn about the genetic basis of traits so that we can develop prevention and intervention strategies for problematic conditions.

11. **Evolutionary psychology** (p. 305) helps us understand that psychological mechanisms such as the Big Five evolve because they solve specific adaptive problems in human ancestral environments.

12. Factor analytic trait theories are excellent samples of scientific theories of personality.

Personal Experiences

1. Cattell identified sixteen basic source traits indicative of an outgoing or a reserved temperament. Consider your own personality in light of Cattell's source traits (see Table 11.1). Do you have more of an outgoing or more of a reserved temperament? Gauge the temperaments of members of your family. How similar to you in temperament are they? What do your findings reveal about the factors of nature and nurture with regard to personality and temperament?

2. Table 11.2 lists facets encompassed within each factor of Costa and McRae's Five-Factor Model. Use Table 11.2 to informally gauge your five closest friends, noting which if any of the facets within a basic factor apply to them. Which factors best describe your buddies? Into what category do most of your friends best fit? Are you seeing a trend? If you are, what does it say about your tastes and values? If there is no discernible trend, what does that say about you?

3. You can get your own DNA analyzed. DNA markers may be assessed inexpensively from a drop of blood or saliva. Genetic tests available to the general public range from just under $100 to several hundred (Pollack, 2006). Typically customers swab the inside of the cheek to obtain a DNA sample and mail it to the company for analysis. Analysis of DNA permits identification of one's haplogroup. Defined by genetic markers, haplogroups link members back to a most common ancestor where the marker first appeared, indicating one's position on the tree of early human migrations and genetic evolution. Genetic markers also facilitate the identification of certain genetic inheritances that make one prone to particular disorders or illnesses. However, professional guidance is recommended to help one evaluate the accuracy of this information and how it might best be used.

4. Make up a list of characteristics that you would want to see in the person you choose to marry and raise a family with. Also consider the strategies that you have taken to make yourself attractive to a potential mate. Evolutionary psychologists suggest that reproduction and survival continue to be crucial factors in our attractiveness toward members of the opposite sex. If you are a man, do you find yourself attracted by women whose waist-to-hip ratios suggest a good ability to carry and give birth to children? If you are a woman do you find that a mate's ability to provide for a family is more important to you than physical attractiveness?

5. According to Buss and other evolutionary psychologists, behavior patterns we see today are patterns that survived in our ancestors because they were more successful than other behaviors. They prevailed out of evolutionary necessity and therefore became hardwired into our genetic makeup. How do you see this theory playing out in your life? Apply this theory to behavioral patterns you see between different ethnicities, races, classes, and genders. For example, does prejudice exist out of some natural imperative? How could this theory inform the way you approach people of a different economic class? How would this theory explain your self-destructive tendencies, behaviors that don't promote good health and survival, such as eating high-fat foods, drinking alcohol, smoking, and not getting enough sleep?

CHAPTER 12

Biological Traits

■ Hans Eysenck

1. Describe some of the historical predecessors to Eysenck's theory.

2. Explain how Eysenck constructed a model of personality.

3. Describe the superfactors that Eysenck identified through factor analysis, and compare them with those of Cattell and with the Big Five.

4. Describe how Eysenck measured traits.

5. Identify the hypothesized causal agents of **extraversion versus introversion, emotionality versus stability,** and **psychoticism** in Eysenck's theory, and indicate how his work relates to current research on the brain.

6. Describe the biological basis of behavior and neurosis in Eysenck's theory and current research.

7. Discuss Eysenck's contribution to understanding intelligence.

8. Describe some of the applications of Eysenck's theory.

9. Evaluate Eysenck's theory from the viewpoints of philosophy, science, and art.

I n his personality theory, Hans Eysenck sought to go beyond the descriptive factor analytic concepts of Cattell and the Big Five to provide a model of personality that can be
tested. He connected *superfactors,* which he identified through factor analysis, with psychophysical entities such as arousal and excitation. This model makes possible a great many
testable hypotheses that may be verified through experimental procedures. Adamant about
the need for psychology to follow the rigors of scientific procedure and to clearly specify
how its concepts may be disproved through falsification, Eysenck was highly critical of dynamic, humanistic, existential, and phenomenal approaches to personality that do not affirm the primacy of experiment and falsifiable theory.

Highly outspoken and unafraid of controversy, Eysenck advocated a **biosocial** approach
to personality, emphasizing biological and genetic factors as well as social and environmental ones. His superfactors are biological in nature and determined largely by genetic influences. They are the product of evolutionary forces. Thus Eysenck's work continues to focus
on many of the interests that were introduced in the factor analytic theories chapter.

Biographical Background

Berlin, Germany, was the birthplace of Hans Eysenck, who was born on March 4, 1916. Germany was losing World War I, and many suffered from the mass unemployment, high inflation, and political turmoil that followed that loss. Thus the war had a significant impact on
Eysenck, as it had on Cattell; fewer than half of his school classmates reached middle age.
His parents, well-known actors, divorced when he was two. He was raised by his maternal
grandmother. Eysenck's father encouraged him to become an actor, but his mother dis-
suaded him and he followed her "more sensible" advice.

In school, Eysenck, a Lutheran, had been taunted
with the label "white Jew" because he sympathized
with the plight of the Jews. Eysenck left Germany at
the age of eighteen. His hatred of the Nazi regime
led him to study politics and become a socialist.
Later he developed serious reservations about socialism and left the party, but he continued to be interested in political issues.

After traveling around Europe, Eysenck settled in
England and prepared to attend the University of
London. Someone suggested he study the newly
emerging science of psychology, to which Eysenck
replied, "What on earth is psychology?" (1982). When
assured, "You'll like it," he embarked on his distinguished career as a psychologist. Psychometrically

*Hans Eysenck sought to go beyond a descriptive analysis to
a causal analysis of personality.*

oriented, the University of London was an exciting place to study psychology, and in 1940 Eysenck received the Ph.D.

Eysenck was hired as a research psychologist at Mill Hill Emergency Hospital. There, he independently conducted a study on the reliability of psychiatric diagnoses and prescribed treatments at the hospital. Eysenck's undercover research demonstrated that there was very little agreement among psychiatrists concerning diagnoses and treatment. Later, using factor analysis, Eysenck concluded that disorders could be embraced under two major personality factors: neuroticism and extraversion-introversion. His findings led him to publish *Dimensions of Personality* (1947).

When World War II ended, Eysenck became director of the psychology department at Maudsley Hospital, the most prestigious teaching psychiatric hospital in England. There he established a program of behavior therapy as well as a program of study that was scientifically oriented and relied on the interdependence of clinical and experimental research. He also organized a behavior genetics division. In 1955, he was awarded a chair of psychology at the University of London. In 1988, he was awarded the Distinguished Scientist Award of the American Psychological Association. He also became a member of the Board of Scientific Affairs of the American Psychological Association.

A prolific writer whose output exceeded even that of Cattell, Eysenck wrote for both technical and lay audiences. Most of his work was in the area of individual differences. However, his diverse interests have led him to explore fields far different from simply the biological basis of traits and the experimental study of learning, memory, and conditioning. He wrote about psychopharmacology, sexual behavior, and the causes and effects of smoking and heart attacks and other related problems, as well as the psychological study of ideology, media influences, extrasensory perception, and astrology. He did not hesitate to criticize psychoanalysis, psychotherapy, and nonempirical theories of behavior. In turn, his theory has been both praised and denounced. Eysenck retired in 1985 but continued to lecture, conduct research, and write until he died at age eighty-one in 1997.

Historical Predecessors

In describing his theory of personality, Eysenck readily acknowledged that the model that culminated in his own work was a structure that had been built by several bricklayers who had contributed to the slow, steady process of research into temperament and personality (1981). One of the earliest efforts to describe personality in terms of dispositions was made by the Greek physician Hippocrates (460?–377? B.C.), who suggested that personalities could be classified according to a predominance of certain body fluids, or **humors,** which reflected the four elements of the cosmos. A predominance of blood led to a **sanguine** character, marked by sturdiness, high color, and cheerfulness. A predominance of mucus led to a slow, solid, and apathetic **phlegmatic** personality. A predominance of black bile led to a **melancholic** or depressed personality. Yellow bile infused the irascible and violent **choleric** personality. Twenty-one hundred years later, Immanuel Kant, a German philosopher (1724–1804), updated and popularized Hippocrates' doctrine of the four temperaments in his *Anthropologie.* He organized them according to two basic comparisons: feelings and activity. *Melancholic* represented weak feelings; *sanguine,* strong feelings. *Phlegmatic* represented weak activity; *choleric,* strong activity.

The primary difference between the views of Hippocrates and Kant and those of modern theorists is that the earlier ones depicted *types* rather than *traits*. Types or **typologies** imply distinct, discrete, and separate categories into which an individual can be placed. **Traits** refer to continuous dimensions that individuals possess to varying degrees. Modern trait theories recognize that individuals vary considerably with regard to the same characteristic. For instance, we can speak of two types of statures, tall or short. Within any given population, however, we find a continuous gradation of statures between tall and short. Most of the population tends to fall in the middle area between extremes of height.

Subsequently, Jung's depiction of two basic attitudes helped popularize the terms *extraversion* and *introversion* and link them with normal personality types. Jung also suggested a link between each of the attitudes and certain neurotic disorders. However, Eysenck believed that from the point of view of science, Jung's contribution to the study of personality types was primarily negative, because he permitted mystical notions to override empirical data.

Ernest Kretschmer, a German psychiatrist (1888–1964), was also interested in normal personality types and their abnormal complements. However, he is best known for his suggestion that people could be classified on the basis of their body measurements. Although Kretschmer's work was very influential, it was criticized because it was difficult to fit every individual into his framework.

William Sheldon (1899–1977), an American disciple of Kretschmer, described individuals in terms of traits based on physiques and temperaments (see Table 12.1). Sheldon's theory became very popular and continues to have some influence; it is also important because it marked the transition from earlier typologies and trait theories to a much more sophisticated approach to understanding personality. Sheldon laid the groundwork for and helped to create a significant movement in contemporary personality theory—*psychometric trait theory*—that found fruition in the work of Cattell and in the Five-Factor Theory of personality (discussed in the factor analytic theories chapter) and in Eysenck's approach, which is the focus of this chapter.

In surveying earlier efforts at characterizing temperaments that preceded his approach, Eysenck was impressed with a strong sense of historical continuity. Current work may be more comprehensive and developed with more sophisticated statistical methods under better controlled conditions, but it clearly continues an approach begun many centuries ear-

TABLE 12.1 SHELDON'S RELATIONSHIPS AMONG COMPONENTS OF PHYSIQUE AND TEMPERAMENT

PHYSIQUE		TEMPERAMENT	
COMPONENT	DESCRIPTION	COMPONENT	DESCRIPTION
Endomorphy	Predominance of soft roundness	**Visceratonia**	General love of comfort, relaxation, sociability, people, and food
Mesomorphy	Predominance of muscle, bone, and connective tissue	**Somatotonia**	Tendency to seek action and power through bodily assertiveness
Ectomorphy	Predominance of linearity and fragility	**Cerebrotonia**	Predominance of restraint, inhibition, and concealment

lier. Earlier theories may strike us as quaint and outdated, and in many respects they are; however, they presaged many concepts in modern psychology and continue to influence personality theorizing.

Constructing a Model of Personality

In Eysenck's view (1982), people are biosocial animals. Eysenck saw psychology as standing at the crossroads of the biological sciences (genetics, physiology, neurology, anatomy, biochemistry, pharmacology, etc.) and the social sciences (history, sociology, anthropology, economics, sociometry, etc.). At the same time, he believed that psychology must become more of a true science. The academic study of human behavior must follow scientific methods of research and investigation to arrive at valid conclusions. Eysenck was committed to the classical hypothetical-deductive method of physics in which one begins with a hypothesis or tentative explanation from which can be deduced predictions with which to test the hypothesis. He pointed out that science constantly searches for proof—confirmation or disconfirmation through the consistent use of the experimental method or another appropriate method of testing. Many psychologists, however, simply engage in literature, writing about human nature but not in a manner that permits us to arrive at agreed-upon truths. Psychology must disengage itself from dynamic, humanistic, existential, phenomenal, or other approaches that deny the primacy of experiment and falsifiable theory. Such methods are pseudoscientific and do not follow the rigors of scientific procedure, which Eysenck sought to apply to the study of personality.

Thus Eysenck insisted on a strict, carefully delineated, scientific model of personality that focused on two distinct aspects: (1) a description of personality derived from factor analytic studies and (2) a causal analysis based on experimental tests of deductions. This twofold approach reflected Eysenck's conviction that a model of personality must reflect the interaction of individual differences with the general normalities of human behavior (1981). Although it is possible to make general laws on the basis of observed regularities of human behavior, individuals behave differently in various situations. The laws of psychology need to reflect this interaction of individuality and generality.

In the past, experimental psychologists interested in establishing general laws and psychometricians interested in individual differences tended to go their own separate ways and to have little to do with each other. Eysenck believed that scientists in both areas need to work together cooperatively to develop a scientific psychology. Experimental psychology must understand individual differences in order to recognize and distinguish which responses in an experiment are due to the manipulation of an independent variable and which are due to individual differences in reaction to the same situation. Unless they can make this distinction, experimenters may mistakenly believe that varying responses invalidate the effects of the independent variable when they are actually due to individual differences. Psychologists who wish to explore individual differences need to use the concepts and methods of experimental psychology as tools to enable them to build a theoretical structure that links both approaches. By themselves, factor analytic studies cannot discover the cause of the factors they identify. They can simply give birth to further correlational studies. The only way out of this circle is to introduce outside criteria based on other theories that seek to identify the cause of the factors. Most such theories of causation will come from the area of experimental research. Using the tools of experimental psychology will permit personality theorists to make predictions that can be tested and thus make possible the development of a causal theory of personality. Thus psychometrics and experimental studies can complement and support each other; they can actively cooperate to develop a scientific model of personality.

Theories must consider the results of both correlational and experimental studies in making predictions and must carefully spell out the precise conditions under which a predicted event will occur. For example, what specific intensity and duration of stimuli are needed for the expected results to occur? Will the results vary with people of different personality temperaments? Under conditions of low stimulation, introverts may be more highly aroused than extraverts, but under high stimulation, the opposite may be true. Without specifying the exact measurements and conditions, we may not be able to interpret the results of an experiment. We may be misled into thinking that a theory has been falsified, when, in fact, the problem was with one of the conditions. The failure of a single prediction should lead not to a hasty abandonment of an entire theory but rather to a rethinking of the process and the conditions under which the predicted result was expected to occur. Scientific theories should not be abandoned simply because anomalies exist; they should be abandoned only when a better theory is available (1981).

Thus Eysenck was not troubled by the fact that his theory frequently encountered deviations from the expected predictions. The existence of such anomalies shows that the theory is scientific because it is subject to error and open to correction. "[W]hatever my model may be lacking, it certainly does not lack the quality of falsifiability" (1981). As part of the normal process of scientific development, a theory must take into account irregularities as they occur and account for them within the theory. When his model failed to hold up under experimental testing, Eysenck revised it. Thus when his preliminary attempt to develop a causal theory based primarily on a neural model of inhibition and excitation was experimentally disconfirmed, he changed it to a biological model of arousal. Table 12.2 shows the steps he took when constructing and revising his models.

TABLE 12.2 STEPS THAT EYSENCK TOOK IN CONSTRUCTING AND REVISING A MODEL OF PERSONALITY

See if you can identify these steps in the discussion of Eysenck's theory.

1. Hypothesize the relationship between various personality traits.

2. Conduct factor analytic studies to identify clusters of traits that indicate underlying superfactors.

3. Construct a biological theory to account for the behaviors associated with the underlying superfactors.

4. Generate hypotheses from the theory concerning specific testable psychophysical, neurological, or hormonal components.

5. Conduct experimental studies to validate the theoretical prediction.

6. Revise the theory where needed in light of the experimental studies.

SOURCE: These questions are reprinted from Personality and Individual Differences, 6, Eysenck, S. B. G., Eysenck, H. J., & Barrett, P. A *revised version of the psychoticism scale, 21–29. Copyright © 1985 with permission from Elsevier Science.*

The Identification of Superfactors

Eysenck drew from biology, historical typologies, learning theory, factor analysis, and experimental studies in order to understand personality. He used factor analysis in his work, but in a more deductive way than Cattell. In Cattell's research, conclusions were drawn from the clusters that appeared in the process of factoring. Eysenck began with a clear hypothesis about possible underlying variables and then used statistical analysis to test his hypothesis. Moreover, Eysenck considered factor analysis as at best a preliminary tool that paved the way for subsequent laboratory and experimental research to gain a causal understanding of the factors that had been posited.

THE HIERARCHICAL MODEL OF PERSONALITY

Eysenck defined personality as "a more or less stable and enduring organization of a person's character, temperament, intellect, and physique which determines his unique adjustment to the environment" (1970). He viewed personality as a hierarchy (see Figure 12.1). At the bottom of the hierarchy are *specific responses,* behaviors that we can actually observe, such as someone answering a phone. The next level is that of *habitual responses,* clusters of specific behaviors that characteristically recur in similar circumstances, such as buying groceries or giving parties. Above this are more generalized *traits,* clusters of related habitual responses such as the source traits that Cattell identified. At the top of the hierarchy, related clusters of traits make up broad general dimensions or basic types, such as extraversion or introversion. Eysenck's research focused on the identification of these superfactors. He sought not only to describe behavior in terms of basic typologies but also to understand the causal factors behind the behavior.

When Eysenck conducted a review of temperament theories, he observed that there were distinct patterns in the various typologies that had been used throughout history to describe personality. He sought to test the hypothesis that the behavior included in Hippocrates'

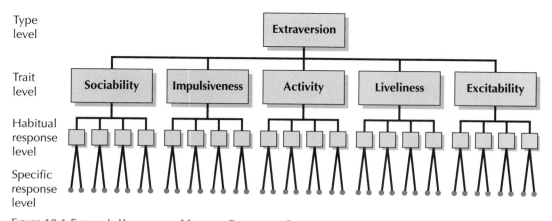

FIGURE 12.1 EYSENCK'S HIERARCHICAL MODEL OF PERSONALITY DEVELOPMENT

(SOURCE: From H. J. Eysenck, The Biological Basis of Personality, *1967, Courtesy of Charles C. Thomas, Publisher, Springfield, Illinois.)*

ancient typology could be accounted for by two fundamental personality dimensions, or superfactors: **extraversion versus introversion** and **emotionality versus stability.**

The extraversion versus introversion dimension reflects the degree to which a person is outgoing and participative in relating to other people. Extraversion-introversion is a continuous dimension that varies among individuals. Some people tend to be friendly, impulsive, and talkative whereas others tend to be reserved, quiet, and shy. These dimensions are similar to Jung's two basic attitudes.

The emotionality versus stability dimension refers to an individual's adjustment to the environment and the stability of his or her behavior over time. Some people tend to be well integrated and emotionally stable. Others tend to be poorly integrated, emotionally unpredictable, and neurotic. In Eysenck and Rachman's (1965) words: "At the one end we have people whose emotions are labile, strong and easily aroused; they are moody, touchy, anxious, restless, and so forth. At the other extreme we have the people whose emotions are stable, less easily aroused, people who are calm, even-tempered, carefree, and reliable." In both dimensions, most people fall somewhere in the middle of the two extremes. Eysenck suggested that these basic dimensions of personality may be summarized as shown in Figure 12.2. The inner circle shows Hippocrates' four temperaments. The outer ring shows the results of

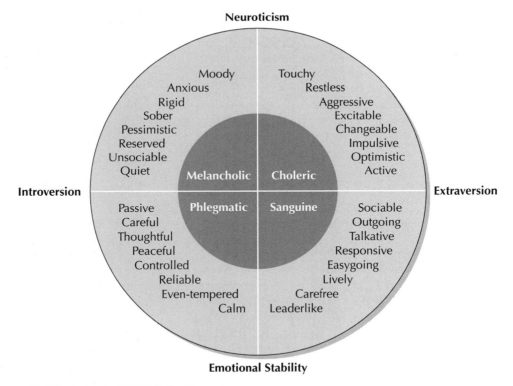

FIGURE 12.2 THE INTERCORRELATION OF TRAITS

The inner circle shows Hippocrates' four temperaments. The outer ring shows the results of factor analysis studies of the intercorrelations between traits done by Eysenck and others.

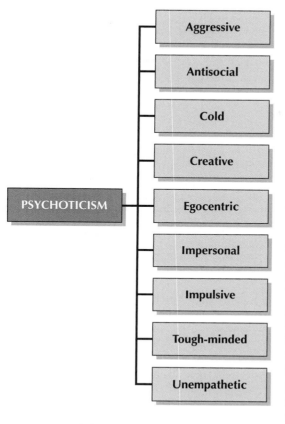

	Aggressive
	Antisocial
	Cold
	Creative
PSYCHOTICISM	**Egocentric**
	Impersonal
	Impulsive
	Tough-minded
	Unempathetic

FIGURE 12.3 PSYCHOTICISM

These traits together make up the superfactor of psychoticism (Eysenck & Eysenck, 1985).

factor analytic studies of the intercorrelations among traits. The traits, which are on a continuum, clearly reflect the two fundamental dimensions of emotional stability versus neuroticism and introversion versus extraversion.

Following his research in the first two superfactors, Eysenck investigated a third one: **psychoticism** (see Figure 12.3). Psychoticism is usually characterized by the loss or distortion of reality and the inability to distinguish between reality and fantasy. The person may have disturbances in thought, emotion, and motor behavior, as well as hallucinations or delusions. The psychoticism factor also includes some degree of psychopathy: disorders characterized by asocial and impulsive behavior, egocentricity, and an absence of guilt (Eysenck & Eysenck, 1976). Unlike the dimensions of extraversion-introversion and emotional stability-neuroticism, psychoticism is not a dimension with an opposite pole; rather, it is an ingredient present in varying degrees in individuals.

It is important to clarify that the personality dimensions of emotional stability–neuroticism and psychoticism merely indicate that one has a leaning in certain directions, a *constitutional predisposition;* they do not imply that the psychiatric illnesses will actually come about. Other prerequisite conditions, such as possible additional genetic factors (Eysenck, 1976) and sufficient environmental stressors (Eysenck, 1994c), would have to be present for a disorder to develop. Moreover, psychotic disorders are very different from neurotic disorders. Eysenck did not believe that neuroticism and psychoticism exist on a continuum. There are different routes to each of these conditions. A person may become more and more neurotic without becoming psychotic.

Eysenck originally conceived of extraversion as a blend of sociability and impulsivity. When he developed the idea of psychoticism, however, he transferred several impulsivity items from extraversion to psychoticism.

Although environmental factors have a significant role to play, Eysenck believed that individual differences in the three major superfactors are primarily due to genetic determinants. Recognizing a genetic basis for personality dimensions implies that they are universal. Thus we can expect that they may be found in the animal kingdom as well as in the human domain. We can also predict that the temperaments tend to be stable throughout an individual's life. We can further anticipate that they appear throughout history and in cross-cultural studies and that they surface in all types of various personality inventories and measures. Empirical studies give support to all of these hypotheses (Eysenck, 1985). "Identical factors have been found cross culturally in over 35 different countries covering most of the globe, from Uganda and Nigeria to Japan and mainland China, from the Capitalist countries of the West and the American continent to Eastern-bloc countries such as the Soviet Union, Hungary, Czechoslovakia, Bulgaria, and Yugoslavia" (Barrett & Eysenck, 1994). "Such cross cultural unanimity would be unlikely if biological factors did not play a predominant part" (Eysenck, 1990b).

COMPARISONS WITH CATTELL AND THE BIG FIVE

There are some significant differences between the theories of Eysenck and Cattell. Cattell's theory was primarily concerned with traits; Eysenck preferred to emphasize supertraits. Eysenck also believed that Cattell gave too much importance and value to factor analysis. Although factor analysis is a useful tool for suggesting clusters, there is a great deal of subjectivity involved in the use of the technique. Factor analysis basically tells us how many dimensions we need to accommodate items that are related to one another. However, just as the lines of longitude and latitude drawn on a map to help us identify specific cities and places are arbitrary, so the exact position of axes on which items are identified in factor analysis is also chosen rather than mandated.

In many respects, the factor theories of Eysenck and Cattell are quite similar. However, Cattell considered the scope of personality to be broader than did Eysenck. Further, Cattell's sixteen personality factors are *oblique,* which is to say that the various factors may also correlate with each other, whereas Eysenck's superfactors are *orthogonal,* or without further correlations. Indeed, Eysenck's supertraits, introversion-extraversion and emotional stability–neuroticism, are essentially the same as further intercorrelations among Cattell's sixteen personality traits, which produce a lesser number of orthogonal or second-order factors. Cattell criticized Eysenck for limiting the scope of personality in his questionnaire items, but Eysenck noted that those questions are specific to the dimensions they seek to assess and do not represent the whole of personality. He believed the traits that Cattell stressed are more limited than his own superfactors (1972).

Eysenck agreed with the champions of the Big Five that the most important traits are supertraits that can be further subdivided into more specific ones. However, he described the Big Five as a "hodge-podge" of factors and superfactors (1990a). The Big Five factors of Extraversion and Neuroticism are similar to Eysenck's dimensions of introversion-extraversion and emotional stability–neuroticism. Low measures on Agreeableness and Conscientiousness (which Eysenck sees as primary traits rather than superfactors) are aspects of Eysenck's factor of psychoticism (1990a). Openness is a cognitive ability trait and, like intelligence, ought not to be seen as a temperament and should be measured by an appropriate IQ test rather than by self-reports or adjective questionnaires (Eysenck, 1991).

Critics continue to debate the merits of the "big three" versus the Big Five (Saggino, 2000). Eysenck would have us believe that the relative merit of these positions has to come from a realm other than that of factor analysis. When experimental research shows that a relationship can be found between a trait and a psychophysical measure, "then we can begin to think that this factor has a claim to reality and is more than just a statistical artifact" (1982). Thus Eysenck sought to go beyond Cattell's descriptive theory by developing a testable theory of individual differences (1997). In this sense, he would applaud those who seek to establish links between the Five-Factor Model and causal mechanisms that exist within the person.

THE MEASUREMENT OF TRAITS

Accurate measurement is an important component of both the descriptive and the causal aspects of Eysenck's work. Without reliable and accurate ways of quantifying concepts, we are not able to translate them into adequate operational procedures. Eysenck was very active in developing appropriate measures for quantifying his concepts.

Traits can be measured in several ways. People can be asked to rate themselves, providing answers to a paper-and-pencil questionnaire or in a structured interview. Psychologists can rate others through the use of controlled observation in a naturalistic setting or in an arranged specific one. A researcher can set up an experiment in real life or in the laboratory. The specific technique chosen must fit the requirements of the theory, the situation, and the participant. Thus one would not give a questionnaire to a two-year-old but would rely on parental ratings or controlled observation. In general, a combination of methods is used to ensure greater reliability and validity.

Personality inventory questionnaires became very popular during the first part of the twentieth century. A number of them were developed to measure characteristics such as intelligence, emotional instability, and extraversion-introversion. Eysenck (1957) was critical of early ratings and inventories used in personality assessment. He observed that inventory constructors mistakenly assumed that individuals answer questions truthfully. In some cases, people deliberately answer a question falsely to avoid being judged in a negative way. Moreover, people do not always know the truth about themselves. In one experiment, 98 percent of the subjects "claimed to have a better than average sense of humor" (1957). The fact is that in a normal bell-shaped curve, about 50 percent of the population score in the average range.

The problem with personality inventories stems from the fact that there is no objective outside criterion against which to make measurements. Eysenck (1957) noted that psychologists were able to overcome some of the difficulties involved in questionnaires when they gave up the notion of *interpreting* the answers and simply dealt "with the objective fact that a person puts a mark on one part of the paper rather than in another."

Eysenck constructed improved personality inventory questionnaires using a method that he called **criterion analysis.** He began with a hypothesis concerning a possible underlying variable—for instance, emotional stability versus neuroticism. He then identified two criterion groups: a group of people who have been clearly identified as emotionally stable and another group who have been identified as neurotic. He gave each group a questionnaire and observed how many yes and no answers there were in each group to each question. If it was clear that there was a greater tendency for one group to answer a particular question in the affirmative or negative, then that question may be a good item for distinguishing between the two groups. Table 12.3 shows some sample questionnaire items.

Eysenck made it clear that he was concerned not with the *reasons* for the answers, but simply with the fact that there are significant differences in the two groups' answers. By studying the differences in answers to multiple questions, it is possible to determine probabilities and develop a questionnaire that will distinguish between the two groups and rank each individual along a continuum. The use of criterion groups helps to show how sensitive a question is to a particular variable, such as emotional stability versus neuroticism. The approach is strictly empirical and makes use of complex statistical analysis.

Contemporary questionnaires and rating procedures are much more sophisticated and more carefully constructed than earlier ones. Tested by complex statistical studies and

TABLE 12.3 SAMPLE QUESTIONNAIRE ITEMS FOR PERSONALITY RESEARCH

Here are some sample questions for Extraversion, Neuroticism, and Psychoticism from the Eysenck Personality Questionnaire-Revised.

1. Do you usually take the initiative in making new friends?

2. Does your mood often go up and down?

3. Do you prefer to go your own way rather than act by the rules?

4. Are you mostly quiet when you are with other people?

5. Are your feelings easily hurt?

6. Do you take much notice of what people think?

7. Can you easily get some life into a rather dull party?

8. Are you a worrier?

9. Would you like other people to be afraid of you?

The following personality dimensions are indicated if specific questions are answered in the ways shown: Extraversion: 1-Yes, 4-No, 7-Yes; Neuroticism: 2-Yes, 5-Yes, 8-Yes; Psychoticism: 3-Yes, 6-No, 9-Yes.

SOURCE: *The questions are reprinted from* Personality and Individual Differences, *6, Eysenck, S. B. G., Eysenck, H. J., & Barrett, P. A revised version of the psychoticism scale, 21–29. Copyright © 1985, with permission from Elsevier Science.*

experimentation, and with careful procedures for establishing reliability and validity, the resulting instruments can be useful tools for the psychologist who wishes to measure personality. Eysenck constructed a number of paper-and-pencil self-report inventories to measure the dimension of introversion-extraversion. Among them are the Maudsley Personality Inventory, the Eysenck Personality Inventory, and the Eysenck Personality Questionnaire. The Eysenck Personality Profiler measures traits at both the primary factor and the superfactor levels (Eysenck & Wilson, 1991). These inventories, as well as revived and abbreviated versions, have been used in an extraordinarily large number of research projects in Britain, the United States, and abroad.

Looking for Causal Agents of Behavior

In his discussion of personality, Eysenck went beyond a descriptive analysis to a *causal* analysis that hypothesized the agents that may cause certain behavior patterns.

EYSENCK'S HYPOTHETICAL CAUSAL EXPLANATIONS

In his early descriptive research, Eysenck pointed out that individuals differ in the reactivity of their brains and central nervous systems and in the speed with which they develop conditioned responses. His first causal explanation (1957) traced the difference between extraversion and introversion to variations in central nervous system levels of inhibition and excitation. He suggested that individuals with weak excitatory and strong inhibitory potentials are likely to become extraverted, whereas individuals with strong excitatory and weak inhibitory potentials are likely to become introverted. The less sensitive, less aroused, and more inhibitory brain processes of extraverts require them to continually look for outside stimuli in order to overcome their own passivity. These individuals are insensitive to low-intensity stimulation because their strong inhibitory processes suppress it. They need to seek more stimulation and can tolerate much higher levels of it before their cortical processes act protectively to inhibit further increases. The more sensitive, more aroused, and less inhibitory introvert needs to withdraw from the outside world in order to avoid being overwhelmed. These individuals are quickly satiated at rather low levels of stimulation.

Clark Hull's drive theory (briefly described in the chapter on experimental analysis of behavior) helped to clarify the relationship between excitation and inhibition. As drives intensify, reinforced learned habits are strengthened. However, responses that are continuously repeated lead to a type of neural fatigue and to inhibition that lowers the effect of the original drive. Eysenck (1964) described how you can experience this inhibition by tapping your index fingers as rapidly as possible. In a little while, one of your fingers will take an "involuntary rest pause," interrupting the rhythm for just a brief fraction of a second.

Relating the relationship between excitation and inhibition to extraversion and introversion, Eysenck predicted that introverts can be more readily conditioned than extraverts because they have a higher drive (excitatory processes) and weaker inhibitory processes. This prediction was tested by Frank (1956), who found that introverts could be more easily conditioned to blink an eye in response to a tone. However, subsequent efforts to replicate Frank's findings were unsuccessful, leading Eysenck (1967) to specify additional parameters that must be met for the predicted result to occur. This is just one example of anomalies that have arisen in the course of trying to test his theory. Such anomalies led Eysenck to develop further conditional explanations that complicate his original position. However, they also led to his second causal model.

In 1967, Eysenck revised his theory and hypothesized that specific biological functions were responsible for excitation and inhibition. This second explanation traced the difference between extraversion and introversion to levels of cortical arousal and the difference between emotional stability and neuroticism to levels of visceral brain activity.

Eysenck (1967) suggested that introversion-extraversion is related to arousal thresholds in the ascending **reticular activating system** (RAS) of the brain and that emotional stability–neuroticism is related to differences in **visceral brain** (VB) activation (see Figure 12.4). The primary function of the RAS is to regulate levels of arousal ranging from sleep to states of high alertness. Destruction of these tissues causes an animal to sleep almost continuously, whereas stimulation will cause it to become more aroused. Thus the RAS controls the brain's level of excitability and its responsiveness to stimuli.

Eysenck believed that introverts may have higher levels of RAS reactivity than extraverts. Thus, given identical stimulating conditions, the state of arousal would be higher in introverts than in extraverts. The high level of arousal may create a constraint on their behavior and contribute to the specific traits, such as reserved and careful, that generally characterize introverts. In the same way, the low levels of arousal experienced by extraverts may lead to an absence of constraints and a predominance of impulsive and outgoing behavior normally associated with extraversion.

Eysenck hypothesized that emotional stability versus neuroticism is due to differences in visceral brain activity. The visceral brain includes the limbic system and the hypothalamus,

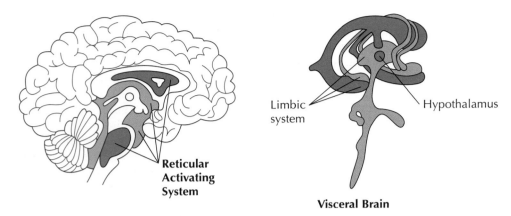

Limbic system

Hypothalamus

Reticular Activating System

Visceral Brain

FIGURE 12.4 THE RETICULAR ACTIVATING SYSTEM AND THE VISCERAL BRAIN

The anatomical structures that Eysenck hypothesizes may be responsible for inherited differences in introversion-extraversion and emotional stability–neuroticism.

which are both involved in motivation and emotional behavior. They exert their influence through the autonomic or involuntary nervous system. Eysenck theorized that individuals who have a low threshold of visceral brain activation—and thus are readily viscerally aroused—may be very emotional in their behavior and more susceptible to neurotic disorders. In short, Eysenck suggested that there is a causal connection between biological functions of the brain and the basic personality dimensions of emotional stability–neuroticism and introversion-extraversion.

The 1967 theory of the biological basis for introversion-extraversion placed the emphasis on excitation rather than inhibition. This emphasis led to a shift in efforts to test the model away from the hypothesized effects of inhibition and toward the effects of RAS arousal. McLaughlin and Eysenck (1967) offered a test of the new model by combining it with the Yerkes-Dodson law of motivation and performance. The Yerkes-Dodson law maintains that the relationship between motivation and performance is curvilinear. As motivation increases, performance increases until an optimal point is reached, after which increasing motivation decreases performance. Optimal performance generally occurs at moderate levels of arousal. You can confirm this from your own experience. Without sufficient motivation, we simply do not put forth the effort to accomplish a task; however, too much pressure may lead to such a high level of motivation that it actually interferes with performance. The relationship between motivation and performance also varies with the difficulty of the task. A higher level of motivation may be required to complete a very simple task in order to sustain concentration and avoid boredom. A lower level of motivation leads to better performance on a very difficult, complicated task.

McLaughlin and Eysenck (1967) predicted that, given a very difficult task, stable extraverts would have the strongest performance and neurotic introverts would have the weakest. The high level of arousal and motivation of the introvert would interfere with successful task performance; the low arousal and motivation of the extravert would facilitate it. The researchers made predictions for the other types as well and for varying levels of task difficulty. They sorted participants by the four types and gave them either an easy or a difficult learning task that involved paired nonsense syllables. On the whole, the results were as predicted, sustaining Eysenck's theory of arousal, especially in reference to the stable extraverts. However, another irregularity arose. Normal introverts did not do as well as neurotic ones. Even though the difference was not statistically significant, it raised further questions provoking additional clarification of the theory.

As noted early in this chapter, one of the strengths of Eysenck's model of personality is his willingness to adjust his theory so that it specifies the exact conditions under which certain generalizations are true. Eysenck's theory allows for specific prediction and testing. For example, if introverts have strong excitatory brain processes and relatively weak inhibitory effects, they should and do react more quickly in certain structured laboratory situations such as eye-blink conditioning (Eysenck & Rachman, 1965). Electrocardiogram studies and other electrophysiological studies also lend some support to Eysenck's theory (1970). Neuroimaging is a potent supplement to the available techniques of personality research because it can link simultaneous behavior and processing to particular regions of the brain. It has even been possible to indicate introversion or extraversion by comparing the amount of salivation produced when lemon juice is applied to someone's tongue with the amount created without lemon juice. Introverts produce considerably more salivation than extraverts (Corcoran, 1964). This suggests that the same physiological functions control

Thinking Critically

Are you an introvert or an extravert? See the Thinking Critically box "The Lemon Test."

Thinking Critically

The Lemon Test

You can get some rough measures of introversion-extraversion and develop a greater appreciation for the underlying physiological functions of Eysenck's superfactors by trying this simplified version of the lemon test developed by Corcoran (1964). Tie a length of thread to the center of a double-tipped cotton swab so that when you hold it by the string the swab hangs perfectly horizontally.

Swallow three times and immediately put one end of the cotton swab onto your tongue. Hold it in your mouth for thirty seconds. Remove the swab and put four drops of lemon juice on your tongue. Swallow and immediately place the other end of the swab on the same spot in your mouth. Hold it there for thirty seconds and then let the swab hang.

If you are an extravert, the swab will remain close to horizontal. If you are an introvert, one end will hang down noticeably, indicating that you produced a large amount of saliva in response to the lemon juice.

Try this with several participants whom you have previously identified as introverts or extraverts and compare your results. The lemon test is predicated on the assumption that the same physiological functions control both salivation characteristics and introversion-extraversion characteristics. What other physiological characteristics can you come up with that may also be controlled by the same functions that control introversion-extraversion, and what kind of predictions can you make that could be tested?

both salivation characteristics and introversion-extraversion characteristics. Research has also shown that introverts are more sensitive to stimulant drugs, whereas extraverts are more sensitive to depressant drugs (Eysenck, 1970).

It was more difficult to develop a causal theory for psychoticism than for introversion-extraversion and emotional stability–neuroticism. Efforts to identify the biological factors that underlie the superfactor of psychoticism are still very preliminary. However, Eysenck (1982) believed that psychoticism may be related to a person's sex-**hormone** balance. Androgens are present to a considerably lesser degree in women than in men. Men in general receive higher scores on measures for psychoticism. As a group, criminals and psychopaths also score high on measures for psychoticism, and this group for the most part is male. Prior to menopause (at which point their androgen levels increase), women are less likely to become schizophrenic than are men. Schizophrenics and people who score high on psychoticism have lower levels of serotonin, a chemical neurotransmitter in the brain. These factors led Eysenck to suspect that psychoticism may be traced to hormonal differences and variations in neurotransmitter levels.

New Research on Brain Functioning

There has been enormous growth in research on the biochemistry of the brain and its functions since Eysenck's speculative theory. New technology in brain imaging, such as PET (positron emission tomography), MRI (magnetic resonance imaging), and fMRI (functional magnetic resonance imaging), allow us to actually peek into the working brain, monitoring activity as it is happening. Such images reveal distinctly different patterns of activity in the brains of normal, manic depressed, and schizophrenic individuals (see Figure 12.5). Richard Davidson and his colleagues at the University of Wisconsin in Madison are using such images to study emotion (Mattmiller, 1998). They have identified "processing centers" in the brain for negative and positive emotions. Other studies focus on the amygdala, a portion of the inner brain that regulates fear. The changes that occur in the brain of an alcoholic or an addict when potent cravings are triggered have been pinpointed, as have areas activated at the sight of food in the brains of thin and obese people (Young, 2005). Areas of the brain involved in impulsive violence (Mattmiller, 2000) and in depression have been examined, as have those affected by antidepressants and other medications (Land, 2003).

Building upon Eysenck's model, Jeffrey Gray (1985) suggested that the septum, hippocampus, amygdala (LeDoux, 1996), and parts of the right frontal cortex make up a *behavioral inhibition system* (BIS) that regulates avoidance behavior and negative emotions. It arouses fear and causes withdrawal in the face of new, unexpected, threatening, or punishing stimuli. Individuals differ in the sensitivity of the BIS, which may be associated with levels of neuroticism and anxiety (cf. Shiyong, Danling, Zhen, Hongyan, & Jie, 2005). A second system, the *behavioral approach system* (BAS), has been associated with extraversion. Including areas of the forebrain and higher cognitive centers, the BAS regulates approach behavior and positive emotions (Gray, 1987). Seeking rewards and incentives, its functioning involves activity in the left frontal cortex (Davidson, 1992, Sutton & Davidson, 1997) and neural pathways transmitting dopamine (Depue, Luciana, Arbisi, Collins, & Leon, 1994).

In time, advanced techniques in imaging may help us to identify parts of the brain that regulate temperamental factors such as shyness, boldness, or fearfulness. It is increasingly

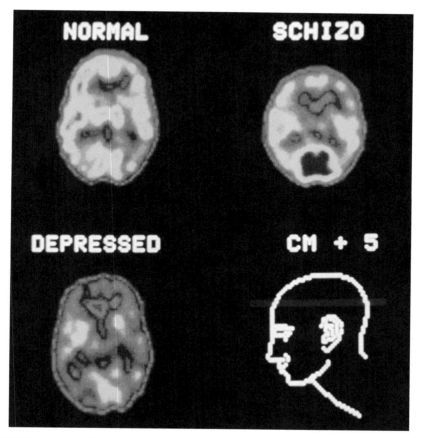

FIGURE 12.5 PET SCANS OF THE HUMAN BRAIN

New technologies in brain imaging allow us to actually peek into the working brain. These PET scan images reveal distinctly different patterns of activity in the brains of normal, depressed and schizophrenic individuals. The diagram at the lower right indicates the cross-section of the brain being imaged.

likely that major personality dimensions have biochemical roots and will someday be explained in those terms. Joseph LeDoux, whose investigation of the origins of human emotions (1996) suggested their evolution as a complex neural system that facilitated survival, further suggests that synapses, the spaces between neurons, are the channels by which we think and remember. They are also the means by which our most fundamental traits, beliefs, attitudes, and ultimately our sense of self are encoded (LeDoux, 2002). Todd Feinberg and Julian Keenan are conducting experiments to map the place in the brain where the sense of self is formed (Feinberg, 2002; Keenan & Gallup, 2004). Self-transcendence, an adaptive characteristic in aging, is also being mapped (Kaasinen, Maguire, Kurki, Bruck, & Kinner, 2005). John Cacioppo urges a collaborative effort among social science, cognitive science, and neuroscience in mapping the brain and understanding personality(Cacioppo & Berntson, 2005). Eysenck's theory anticipated these developments.

There is also ample evidence that our human brains and personalities are undergoing a major transformation due to the widespread use of technologies that we have developed. Media images, television, computers, the Internet, and cell phones are changing the functioning of our brain. Images have replaced language as the basic means of communication. Our abilities to concentrate, focus, inhibit impulsive behaviors, delay gratification, and think in the abstract have been affected as our brains have been "rewired," so to speak (Resta, 2003). However, research also demonstrates the plasticity of our brains. Practice and discipline can forge new circuits. Our brains continue to be capable of change throughout our lives, fostering the development of appropriate therapies and brain fitness programs (cf. Edmondson, 2006).

THE BIOLOGICAL BASIS OF BEHAVIOR AND NEUROSIS

Tying both introversion-extraversion and emotional stability–neuroticism to biological bases permitted Eysenck to distinguish among four extreme types of personality based on the particular combination of the processes of reticular activating system arousal and visceral brain activation. These four types are summarized in Figure 12.6. Eysenck's typology indicates extremes rather than discrete types. His work, also being dimensional, lends support to a dimensionally based factor model of personality disorders (Larstone, Jang, Livesley, Vernon, & Wolf, 2002), such as encouraged by advocates of the Big Five, albeit the number of categories is disputed.

Because introverts have sensitive nervous systems, Eysenck believed that they are more easily civilized. The ease with which they become conditioned also makes them more vulnerable to anxiety-based neuroses, which are conditioned emotional responses. Extraverts, on the other hand, have less sensitive and more inhibitive cortical processes; they seek additional stimulation and are slow to develop conditioned responses. Because socialized behavior depends largely on a well-conditioned conscience developed in childhood, extraverts are more likely to develop psychopathic disorders. Thus Eysenck suggested that neurotics become so because their cortical and emotional states interfere with the learning of appropriate responses or facilitate the learning of maladaptive ones. Neuroticism could be viewed as excessive stimulation discharged by the visceral brain, leading to a

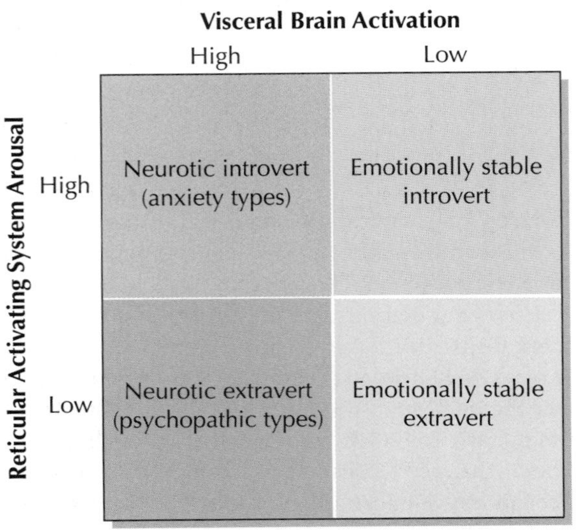

Visceral Brain Activation

	High	Low
High	Neurotic introvert (anxiety types)	Emotionally stable introvert
Low	Neurotic extravert (psychopathic types)	Emotionally stable extravert

(vertical axis label: Reticular Activating System Arousal)

FIGURE **12.6** THE BIOLOGICAL BASIS OF PERSONALITY

Tying his dimensions to biological bases permitted Eysenck to distinguish among four types of personality. *SOURCE: Based on information in H. J. Eysenck,* The Biological Basis of Personality. *Springfield, Ill.: Charles C. Thomas, 1967.*

high degree of emotionality that may combine with an extremely high or low cortical arousal of the reticular activating system to form a particular neurosis.

Behavior itself is not inherited; certain structures of the nervous system are. The phenotype, the individual's observable appearance and behavior, arises out of the genotype's interaction with the environment. The genotype evolves into inherited anatomical structures, which include the cortex, the autonomic nervous system, the ascending reticular activating system, and the visceral brain. Individuals differ widely in the particulars of these structures. These differences lead to the development of different habitual levels of arousal and thresholds for emotional response, which can be seen in laboratory experiments. Through interactions with a particular environment, these tendencies lead to the various emotionally stable or unstable, introverted or extraverted phenotypic patterns of behavior and primary traits that have been identified through factor analysis (Eysenck, 1970). Expressed in a formula, $P_B = P_C \times E$, "Behavioral personality equals the constitutional personality times environment."

The distinction between the genotype and the phenotype is an important one. Eysenck did not suggest that genes determine the outcome for any given individual. Genes are not certain predictors for specific patterns of behavior or development. Many genes express themselves only under certain conditions. Our genetic predispositions are affected by the specific experiences we have from conception onward.

Thus, even though people differ in the extent to which they are genetically predisposed to neurosis, Eysenck believed that neurotic behaviors themselves are learned. In this respect he shared similar views with the behavior and learning theorists on the origin and treatment of neurotic disorders and was a staunch advocate of behavior therapy. However, his recognition of the biological basis of personality is also consistent with biological therapies: Physical or chemical interventions, such as drugs, may affect the brain or other body functions and thus provoke or inhibit certain behaviors.

INTELLIGENCE

A final superfactor that Eysenck believed plays a major role in personality is *intelligence*. Intelligence is not always considered a personality trait or discussed in the context of temperament. However, it is a dimension of personality that is generally considered to be very significant. Indeed, Eysenck wrote, "If we were reduced to describing a person in just three figures, then I have no doubt that we would get the closest approximation to his real nature by using these figures for an assessment of his intelligence, his extroversion, and his neuroticism" (1965).

From Francis Galton's early unsuccessful efforts to develop tests of intelligence based on head size, muscular strength, and visual acuity, the efforts to define and measure intelligence accurately and fairly have been fraught with difficulties (Gould, 1996). Eysenck (1994b) distinguished between *biological intelligence*, the physiological, neurological, and anatomical bases of intelligence, and *psychometric intelligence*, the numerical measure designed to reflect intelligence. Psychometric intelligence is generally defined in terms of IQ. It is made up of Spearman's *g* factor, the general factor with which other measures of intelligence tend to correlate highly, and various primary factors that have been identified subsequently by Thurstone (1948), Guilford (1967), and others. Psychometric intelligence is largely due to biological intelligence, but it is also influenced by environmental and social factors. It is clear that there are biological bases to intelligence because of the clear genetic

origins of individual differences in this area. Eysenck mentioned that we sometimes also refer to *practical* or *social intelligence,* the successful application of one's intelligence to life experiences. Practical intelligence depends on many other factors beyond IQ. In general,
practical intelligence is too broad a concept to be scientifically helpful. Thus Eysenck primarily emphasized the biological and psychometric definitions of intelligence and tried to
relate them to personality using a theoretical-experimental model. He believed that his efforts to connect these concepts of intelligence experimentally would be more fruitful than
limiting the discussion to a theoretical psychometric approach, as was done previously.

Earlier studies that tried to develop a correlation between the psychometric measure of
intelligence and personality were unsuccessful. Eysenck (1994b) believed they were doomed
to failure because they were based on a "simple blunderbuss approach" in which correlations were made at random without any preliminary a priori hypothesis.

There are a number of different variables that, if carefully sorted and specified in advance, begin to indicate a relationship between intelligence and personality. One such variable is work speed. When tests are timed, extraverts have an advantage, whereas in extended
tasks, introverts, characterized with higher cortical arousal, feel less constrained and can be
more careful. When a test is administered over a long period of time, the performance of
extraverts declines toward the end of the testing period. This is not to say that introverts and
extraverts differ in their total IQ scores but that different test administration conditions affect them differently, especially those relating to time pressures.

A second variable is cognitive style. The cognitive style of extraverts tends to be faster,
less accurate, and less reflective than that of introverts. This difference in cognitive style becomes more apparent as the task to be performed becomes more ambiguous. Howard and
McKillen (1990) successfully tested this hypothesis by administering a perceptual maze test
under ambiguous and unambiguous conditions. Their study was characterized by the careful construction of a specific hypothesis, the development of appropriate measures relating
to well-delineated aspects of both personality and intelligence, and a focus on how the
problem was solved rather than simply on the solution itself (see also Zhang, 2001).

We can conclude from such studies that intelligence is not related to personality per se
but that performance on IQ tests may be related to personality variables. However, simple
attempts to correlate a personality test with an IQ measure will not be successful. It is necessary to deduce hypotheses from well-established theories of performance and develop experimental conditions to test them. Global IQ scores must be separated into distinct factors
such as mental speed, persistence, and error checking. Each of these can be correlated with
separate aspects of personality, such as extraversion-introversion and emotional stability–
neuroticism. Conditions must be arranged to test for the differentiated parameters. Eysenck
believed that this approach—combining psychometrics with experimental psychology—
will prove more promising for the study of intelligence (1994b).

Because intelligence has a clear genetic basis, it must also have a biological basis, which
would account for differences between individuals. Eysenck believed that the physiological
mechanism for intelligence is related to **evoked potential.** Sensory (such as auditory or visual) stimulation activates neurons that send messages to the nervous system, causing electrical activity in the brain. This electrical activity, or evoked potential, can be measured by
an electroencephalogram, a simple noninvasive procedure in which electrodes are placed
on the skull, a stimulus is presented, and the evoked potential is recorded as waves or cycles
per second (see Figure 12.7). These waves vary in complexity. More complex evoked potential patterns are present in people of high intelligence; those with lower intelligence show

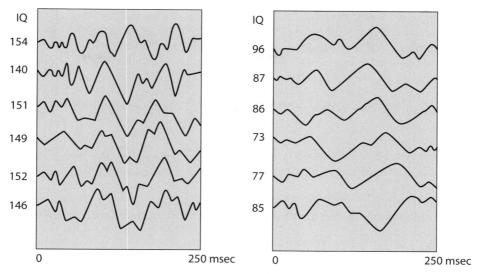

FIGURE 12.7 EVOKED POTENTIAL WAVEFORMS FOR HIGH IQ AND LOW IQ SUBJECTS

Evoked potential waveforms under auditory stimulation of six high-IQ and six low-IQ subjects.
SOURCE: Adapted from Eysenck & Eysenck, 1985.

simpler evoked potential patterns. These variations are evidently due to the frequency of errors made within the brain in transmitting the incoming messages provoked by the stimulus. Low rates of error are associated with more complex evoked potential patterns. Simpler evoked potential patterns are associated with higher error rates. Eysenck believed that as information is relayed through the cortex, errors may occur at the synapses. The tendency to make errors contributes to a low IQ; a low tendency to make errors contributes to a high IQ. Eysenck also anticipated that high-IQ individuals have shorter reaction and inspection times (Eysenck & Eysenck, 1985). It is important to note that all of these expectations can be formulated into hypotheses, which can then be subjected to experimental test.

Eysenck believed that his work with evoked potential could revolutionize the field of intelligence research (1982). In time, Eysenck hoped that we could develop a simple physiological reaction test that could measure intelligence with the same accuracy and validity as more complex IQ tests. Such a direct physiological measure of intelligence would help us to avoid the cultural bias that has haunted the history of test development and to ensure fairness in selection processes that currently employ measures of intelligence. However, although the measures correlate well with ability test scores, they have revealed little about the cognitive processes behind them.

Applications of Eysenck's Theory

Eysenck's research has the potential for considerable social applications. Eysenck believed that a scientific model of personality can help us to accurately predict social behaviors in light of various personality constructs. Figure 12.8 outlines the causal steps involved in making such predictions.

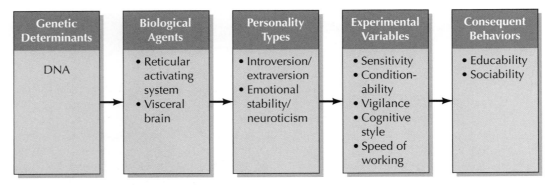

Genetic Determinants	Biological Agents	Personality Types	Experimental Variables	Consequent Behaviors
DNA	• Reticular activating system • Visceral brain	• Introversion/ extraversion • Emotional stability/ neuroticism	• Sensitivity • Condition-ability • Vigilance • Cognitive style • Speed of working	• Educability • Sociability

FIGURE 12.8 FROM GENETIC DETERMINANTS TO BEHAVIOR

Causal factors and relationships that contribute to personality types and consequent behaviors.

EDUCATION

One area in which Eysenck's research, especially that on intelligence and performance, has significant implications is education. Teachers have long recognized that children's personalities influence their responses to the classroom situation and to the particular method of teaching that is used.

Most innovations in education and other areas, such as criminal justice, are initially welcomed with enthusiasm but quickly discarded once it appears that they are no more successful than those that preceded them. The problem, Eysenck (1996) pointed out, is that they are not tested in a manner that clearly establishes the conditions under which they will succeed. All individuals are exposed to the new method under the assumption that it will have the same effect on everyone. This assumption, however, is unfounded. The laws of psychology must pertain to individuals, not simply to a general model of a person, as though people were clones of one another.

For example, in education there has been considerable debate over the merits of *discovery* learning, in which students are encouraged to explore for themselves and to construct facts and theories rather than having concepts formally presented to them as in *reception* learning. Empirical studies did not show a significant difference in the results of the two methods because the research did not clearly articulate the conditions under which the difference would become apparent. When assessment of the approaches took into account the personalities of the students (Leith, 1974), it became apparent that children who are extraverted learn best in a situation that emphasizes discovery, whereas children who are introverted profit more from the traditional approach.

These findings have tremendous significance for education. In the lower grades, there tends to be a more relaxed atmosphere and an emphasis on discovery methods. In the higher grades, the classroom is more formal, and reception modes of presentation are more prevalent. By the time a student enters college, the lecture method has become pervasive. Is it any wonder that the "good students" at that level are generally introverts (Leith, 1974)?

Honey and Mumford (1992) have developed a Learning Style Questionnaire (LSQ) based on a model developed by David Kolb (1984). Correlations of the LSQ and personality factors have been

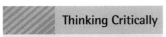

Thinking Critically

How do you learn best? See the Thinking Critically box "Study Places."

Thinking Critically

Study Places

Eysenck's model of personality has implications for learning preferences and academic performance. Consider the atmosphere in which you prefer to study. When you go into a library or another place with the intent to study, what do you look for? If you are an introvert, you will probably look for a solitary, quiet place where there are few distractions. If you are an extravert, you may prefer an open area where others are present and there is some noise. Those were the predictions and findings of Campbell and Hawley's (1982) research based on Eysenck's theory. Earlier recommendations for study areas usually favored the preferences of the introvert without recognizing that individual differences matter. What other implications do you imagine the dimensions of introversion and extraversion might have for study preferences, such as number of study breaks, deadline pressures, and so forth?

investigated by Jackson and Lawty-Jones (1996). The results support a hypothesis that personality is causally related to learning styles, but further refinement is needed to make the LSQ a more precise tool.

The potential for education is highly significant. People learn best at medium rather than high or low levels of arousal, but individuals vary in how much stimulation they need to reach that ideal medium level on the "U-shaped curve." Introverts need very little; extraverts need a lot. Individuals who are highly reactive or have naturally high levels of arousal are at risk of learning neurotic behavior more quickly and thoroughly. In addition to the implications of introversion and extraversion, research must be done on the impact of other factors, such as emotional stability, psychoticism, age, and stages of development. As Eysenck (1996) pointed out, in both the United States and the United Kingdom, there is concern that the educational process is not serving our children very well. Teachers at every level could be helped to become aware of the differing impact that individual personality variables have on learning style and performance; appropriate measures could be generated to assess those variables; and educational methods could be developed and utilized to take advantage of the findings.

CREATIVITY

Eysenck (1993) developed a theory designed to relate creativity to personality in a more explicit manner than had been done before. He used his dimensions of personality to explain many of the behaviors identified with creative achievement. He suggested that there is a causal chain connecting individual DNA configurations to creative behaviors. His theory was very speculative, but like the rest of his work, it was formulated in such a manner as to be testable.

Eysenck distinguished between creativity as a dispositional personality trait, *originality*, and creativity as it refers to exceptional *creative achievement*. The trait of originality is normally distributed within the population. Creative achievement such as Einstein's theory of relativity, on the other hand, is very rare, occurring in a J-shaped distribution. Many people are creative, but only a small number of people are responsible for most major creative works in science and the arts. Originality is a necessary but not a sufficient condition for creative achievement. Other factors include cognitive abilities (pertinent forms of intelligence), environmental variables (such as a socio-cultural-economic climate favorable to the particular creative act), and personality factors (such as motivation and persistence). These work together synergistically to generate creative achievement.

High scores on the dimension of psychoticism are positively correlated with creativity as a trait and as an achievement. Eysenck's hypothesis that psychoticism is causally related to creativity is further confirmed, he believed, by evidence that psychotics, high P (psychoticism) scorers, and creative achievers employ an identical cognitive style (1993). The cognitive style shared by psychotics, high P scorers, and creative achievers is to be *overinclusive* in their thinking. The process of finding answers to problems is directed by notions of what is and what is not relevant. Some people demonstrate a wide concept of relevance, or overinclusive thinking; other people have a narrower concept. These differences can be assessed by the use of a word-association test that takes note of unusual and unexpected responses. The overinclusive cognitive style generates a greater number of ideas, increasing the likelihood of new, divergent, and creative responses. Hypotheses linking overinclusive cognitive style and psychoticism have been confirmed in subsequent studies (Abraham, Windmann, Daum, & Gunturkin, 2005).

The difference between an overinclusive cognitive style and the style most people use has to do with selectivity in human information processing in which past memories influence present perceptions. Reliance on past experience is helpful in that it creates patterns and structures how we perceive new information. However, it also limits novel ideas. It leads us to automatically associate "cup" with "saucer." The normal inhibitory processes that limit associative connections appear to be weakened in creative persons, as well as in psychotics and high P scorers. This may be due to a relative lack of cortical inhibition that can be further traced to varying levels of dopamine and serotonin in synaptic transmission. The final link in the chain from creativity to genetic inheritance would appear to be the hippocampus, a structure in the brain related to learning, recognizing novelty, and remembering.

Eysenck acknowledged that although there is some factual support for his theory, it was extremely speculative. The details may be in error, and some of it may have to change. However, the theory has the advantage of suggesting paths of research and generating testable hypotheses that are subject to experimental test and falsification. It is a theoretical model that can be adjusted in light of subsequent experimental research.

PERSONALITY, BIOLOGY, AND GENETICS

Eysenck was long convinced that personality has a strong genetic component. Earlier in the twentieth century, many people advocated crude eugenics programs and crusaded for and succeeded in passing laws based on genetic notions—for instance, laws that restricted the entry of "inferior" immigrants into the United States and permitted the sterilization of persons considered to be feebleminded. In Nazi Germany, the same pattern of thinking culminated in the mass extermination of "inferior groups." The horror and shock that accompanied news of the events of the Holocaust was partly responsible for the subsequent strong emphasis that psychology placed on behaviorism, which emphasized the environment and minimized heredity.

In describing the biosocial nature of human behavior, Eysenck wrote:

Human behavior [has] both biological and social causes; it's time the pendulum started swinging back from an exclusive preoccupation with social causes to an appropriate appreciation and understanding of biological causes. . . . Biological causes act in such a way as to predispose an individual in certain ways to stimulation; this stimulation may or may not occur, depending on circumstances which are entirely under environmental control. (1967)

Modern methods of analyzing the various factors that determine phenotypic behavior have a wide variety and scope. Some of these methods are discussed in the chapter on factor analytic theories. Today, analysis goes beyond the simple determination of heritability to look at interaction with the environment.

Eysenck contributed a recommendation on measurement to the study of heritability. He suggested that, rather than using one score from one measure of a general factor, a full battery of tests measuring the same factor be given. A factor analysis of the intercorrelations of all the scores from those tests could then be computed and the resulting score used. Eysenck believed that this procedure would prevent results from being confounded by scores that actually measure other intervening factors. Using just one measure increases the chance that other, irrelevant variables will affect the results. By using such measures, Eysenck suggested, for example, that the broad heritability of intelligence is 80 percent (1982).

Drawing on his own research and that of others, Eysenck maintained that there is evidence for strong genetic determinants of differences in intelligence, personality, social and sexual behavior, criminality, mental disorder, and many other aspects of human social interaction. "Clearly we cannot inherit behavior, whether it is the kind of behavior that gives rise to the trait theories of personality or the problem solving type of behavior that gives rise to the concept of intelligence and primary aptitudes" (1982). All that we can inherit is "genes coding for structural proteins and enzymes that influence metabolic, hormonal and other physiological processes which may inadvertently modify the risk of 'criminal' [or other] behavior in a particular environment" (Bohman, Cloninger, Sigarodson, & von Korring, 1982). Therefore, we need to look for anatomical, physiological, and neurological structures and functions that underlie the diversity that we observe. Further research should lead us to the underlying biological structures that are the product of genetic influences and evolutionary forces.

Even though Eysenck believed that the differences in personality are essentially due to genetic factors and that environmental factors are not as important as popularly believed, he also found that the relationship between heredity and behavior is not a simple one. Eysenck's superfactors are polygenetic—that is to say, several genes interact together to make up the trait. The individual effect of each separate gene may be small, but together they create the greater impact. This is why it is unrealistic to think that we are going to be able to easily identify single genes that underlie specific behaviors, behavioral problems, or disorders. It also helps us to understand the importance of making clear distinctions, such as recognizing that although the personality dimension of psychoticism and the psychiatric disorder of psychosis may share some common genetic elements, other genes may also contribute to the fully developed illness (1976).

Eysenck (1982) suggested three main lines of evidence that support a genetic factor in criminal behavior. First, cross-cultural studies show that criminal, antisocial, and psychopathic behavior is related to psychoticism, a dimension of personality that has already been shown to have a large genetic component. Second, studies of twins indicate that monozygotic twins are likely to have a higher concordance of criminal behavior than are dizygotic twins. (As a twin, I must remind you that this does not mean that twins are more likely than other people to be criminals, simply that if one monozygotic twin displays antisocial tendencies, the other is likely to as well; see also Rhee & Waldman, 2002.) Third, studies show that adopted children tend to resemble their biological parents more than they do their adoptive ones.

Heritability studies only provide information about differences within groups and have little predictive value for the individual. Nor does the identification of a specific gene by itself permit prediction about behavior. A variation in the dopamine D2 receptor gene has been linked to attention deficit hyperactivity disorder (ADHD) as well as to a wide range of impulsive, compulsive, and addictive behavior. Such an individual may be more at risk, but there is no certainty. Individuals with high levels of dopamine (a neurotransmitter associated with pleasure) receptors seem to be more responsive to natural reinforcers, making it easier for them to balance the desire for pleasure with the desire to achieve other positive life goals (Volkow, 2007). Although our genes are clearly implicated in many antisocial behaviors, genetic research also makes a clear case for the importance of the environment since the effects of genes are influenced by and can be changed through environmental intervention (Baker, Bezdjians & Raines, 2006; Parens, Chapman, & Press, 2006).

Psychotherapy

It would be a mistake to conclude that because genetic factors play a large part in the initiation and maintenance of negative behaviors, such as neurotic disorders and criminal activities, we can do little about them. Even though people differ in the extent to which they are genetically predisposed to certain types of behavioral tendencies, the behaviors themselves are learned. In this respect, Eysenck shared with the behavior and learning theorists similar views on the origin and treatment of neurotic disorders and was a staunch advocate of behavioral therapy and modification.

Eysenck's interest in psychotherapy began with his survey entitled "The Effects of Psychotherapy" (1952), described in the introductory chapter, which created an enormous impact that continues to haunt some quarters. Although Eysenck was not saying that psychotherapy was useless, he was saying that there was no acceptable evidence for its efficacy. In many cases, simply waiting for spontaneous remission to occur was just as effective. Eysenck suggested that psychologists rely on experimental studies of learning and emotion and develop methods of treatment from them rather than emulate classical Freudian psychoanalysis. His paper gave a tremendous impetus to behavior therapy. There are many problems with studies of psychotherapy (methodological questions, adequacy of control, criteria of improvement, etc.); therefore, Eysenck believed that subsequent refutations of his position need not be taken seriously because of their suspect data and flawed methodology (1982).

Behavior therapy began as a way of taking academic knowledge stemming from experimental laboratory studies and the theories behind them and applying that knowledge to psychiatric problems. Eysenck (1982) held that treatment methods should be based on experimental laboratory data. Although most of that work originated with animals, theories of learning and conditioning can be applied to human clinical problems.

Learned-helplessness experiments with animals provide a good example. In learned-helplessness experiments, dogs who have been conditioned to jump across a small hurdle to avoid an electric shock when a light blinks continue to jump long after the potential of shock has been taken away. They continue to associate the blinking light with the shock. The animals can be taught to stop jumping by preventing the response and by *flooding*. The hurdle is raised so high that the dog cannot jump over it; the light blinks; and the dog experiences fear, panic, and anxiety in the shock-free environment. Eventually, the dog calms down. After the treatment is repeated a few times, the dog no longer jumps even when the conditioned stimulus (the light) is presented.

Similarly, individuals with obsessive-compulsive disorder continue their behavior long after it has become self-defeating and purposeless. An effective treatment has been used with patients who needed to wash their hands immediately after any suspicion that they have been soiled. After describing the procedure and getting permission, the therapist directed the patients to dirty their hands. The patients were not permitted to satisfy their strong need and desire to wash their hands. After realizing that they could tolerate the resultant fear, panic, and anxiety, the patients' obsessive-compulsive responses subsided (1982).

In a similar fashion, Eysenck was able to help depressed patients. Animal studies have linked depression with insufficient positive reinforcement. To counteract their depression, patients are trained to increase the rate of positive reinforcement they receive by interacting with the environment in a positive way (constructive communication, problem solving, self-assertion, etc.) in spite of their depressed mood.

Eysenck viewed his theory and approach to behavior therapy as less rigid and more inclusive than that of Skinner. Skinner avoided the use of terms such as *anxiety* in his strategy, describing them as mentalistic. Eysenck did not see any problem with introducing anxiety as an intervening variable. He believed that such mediational concepts are helpful and even desirable in understanding and analyzing human behavior (1982).

Eysenck (1982) distinguished between the terms *behavior therapy* and *behavior modification*. Behavior therapy is basically informed by classical conditioning and primarily used to treat neurotic disorders on an individual basis. Behavior modification is based on operant conditioning, deals with undesired behaviors, and is generally applied to groups in a closed environment, such as schools, prisons, and hospitals. Eysenck's efforts were directed toward behavior therapy, but he believed that behavior modification can be a useful tool.

Thinking Critically

How effective is psychotherapy? See the Thinking Critically box "Measuring the Efficacy of Psychotherapy."

Referring to concerns that have been raised about the ethics of using behavior therapy and modification, Eysenck pointed out that, in a misguided effort to apply findings and change behavior, some "treatments" (that should more accurately be termed "torture") have been developed and used in prisons and other settings. Appropriate training is needed to prevent uninformed practitioners from putting together collections of methods and labeling them as behavior therapy. On the other hand, Eysenck questioned the ethics of psychodynamic therapists who treat patients with time-consuming and costly methods that create stress and other potential negative effects and that have never been proven to be effective.

Eysenck's emphasis on the biological basis of personality was also consistent with biological therapies: Physical or chemical interventions, such as drugs or hormones, affect the brain or other body functions and thus provoke or inhibit certain behaviors. Medication

Thinking Critically

Measuring the Efficacy of Psychotherapy

Ever since Eysenck stunned the therapeutic communities with his initial report on treatment outcomes, the question "How effective is psychotherapy" continues to concern us. Although each method of psychotherapy must be evaluated in terms of its own goals and purposes (review the discussion in the introductory chapter), in a era of third-party providers and concern with assessment and getting one's money's worth, the topic of measuring the efficacy of psychotherapy continues to daunt us. Consider some of the following questions regarding this issue. Who should determine the effectiveness of therapy? (Client? therapist? insurance company? other?) When should the measure of therapy be made? (During therapy? immediately after? six-month follow-up? years later?) How should therapy efficacy be measured? (Objective questionnaire? subjective client appraisal? interview? measurable behavior changes?) What are your thoughts on this issue, and how would you defend your position?

can influence the underlying biological system and thus change an individual's subjective experience and behavior. Again we see Eysenck's concern with individual differences. Recovering alcoholics have to be extremely careful with drugs or medications that are mood altering or impact the central nervous system as they can activate areas of the brain implicated in addiction and trigger a relapse (Davis, 1991). Effects of drugs are patient-specific; so are different types of therapies. Certain types of therapies may work better with certain types of patients. Extraverts, for example, may do well in a group situation, whereas introverts may be more comfortable in a one-on-one setting.

Eysenck's interests extended to other health areas as well (1995). He associated the probability of developing certain health problems such as heart disease or cancer with various personality traits (1989, 2000). A relationship has been established between stress and cancer and coronary heart disease. Changing life patterns may make it less likely that people will die of those diseases. Thus Eysenck described appropriate behavioral therapy to increase one's chances for longevity (1995). These writings are not as clearly tied to his theory as are some of his other writings. However, they anticipate the current interest on the healthful versus damaging effects of personality on health. Once again, the importance of genetic factors does not mean that individuals have no control. Biological and emotional factors may predispose us to, for example, cardiovascular disease, obesity, and/or addition; however, in the light of this information, we can avoid potentially dangerous situations, eat a healthy diet and learn appropriate new responses.

Advances in neuroscience suggest that psychotherapy be viewed as a process of modifying the brain's functioning. Genetic influences are but one factor that influences human behavior. Environmental experiences change the brain and rewire it through learning. Therapy, which deals with memory and emotion, targets areas of the brain that are highly plastic and amenable to neurogenesis and change (Davidson, Jackson, & Kalin, 2000). The therapeutic relationship creates a bond that facilitates movement toward health (McCabe & Priebe,

2004). Neuroscience can be used to inform effective strategies and techniques for implementing change (Cappas, Andres-Hyman, & Davidson, 2005). Such strategies are highly consistent with Eysenck's therapeutic position.

Eysenck reminded us that most human problems are psychological and due to human actions. Problems such as war, famine, and pollution are caused in large measure by human behaviors and can be controlled only by a better understanding of human nature. Part of that understanding entails acknowledging that individuals differ in their traits and intellectual abilities. A commitment to equal rights need not entail the naive belief that biologically we all are similarly endowed. The fact is that we are not genetically equal; our social and political commitments to equality must rest on other grounds. However, while recognizing the tragic consequences of earlier eugenic efforts, Eysenck unabashedly supported a meritocracy in which the most competent people are chosen for important social positions and occupations. To do otherwise, he said, is to run the risk of a "mediocracy" and to fail to protect ourselves (1975).

| PHILOSOPHY, |
| SCIENCE, |
| *and* ART |

Eysenck's Theory

In his initial tirade against the Freudians, Eysenck wrote, "I have usually been against the establishment and in favor of the rebels. I prefer to think that on these issues the majority were wrong and I was right." Today most trait researchers concur that evidence from behavior genetics and psychophysiological models lends support to Eysenck's major contention that traits have underlying biological components, eradicating the likelihood that traits are mere social constructions (Matthews & Gilliland, 2001).

Eysenck believed that his greatest contribution to personality theory was to connect ideas that had been vaguely anticipated by earlier philosophers with causal theories of behavior. In his theory, concepts such as extraversion-introversion and emotionality-neuroticism are clearly tied to a biosocial model. Eysenck's theory of personality sought to avoid the circular arguments often involved in studies of personality that are limited to factor analysis and to root itself as well in experimental research. "Ultimately," Eysenck wrote, "all theories will suffer disproof and replacement by a better theory. Until that day comes, and I don't expect it to be all that far distant, my theory may serve as an example of what personality theories ought to be like" (1982).

Essentially, Eysenck's approach, like that of Cattell and the Big Five theorists, is a nomothetic rather than an idiographic one. However, as Eysenck reminded us, this does not jeopardize the concept that each individual is unique. The uniqueness is found in the particular combination of traits within an individual, even though the traits themselves are common to everyone. Eysenck reminded us, "To the scientist, the unique individual is simply the point of intersection of a number of quantitative variables" (1952). Thus his typology may well be complemented by studies of the unique individual, but Eysenck would want such studies to be governed by a strict rubric of scientific methodology.

Because research in biology and on the nervous system is growing at such a rapid pace, it is understandable that Eysenck's theory was based on a view of the nervous system and the brain that has become outdated. Nevertheless, it set the stage for connecting the genotype with behavior and the environment through physiological, hormonal, and neurological mediators (Nybourg, 1997). Eysenck's theory also undoubtedly oversimplifies a very complicated system. The efforts to test his theory were frequently plagued by anomalies. Eysenck was extremely willing to adjust his theory and model of personality to accommodate irregularities and to specify the exact conditions under which certain generalizations are true. The problem is that as more adjustments are made, the basic model becomes less powerful as a theory and risks becoming just a collection of explanatory concepts. Nevertheless, Eysenck ambitiously tried to encompass fields as divergent as psychometrics, experimental psychology, neurophysiology, and genetics into his theory, and it would be naive and unrealistic to imagine that a simple theory composed of only a few dimensions and laws could encompass such a wide range.

Eysenck's theory is a superb model of a scientific approach to personality. There is considerable support for his "type" approach. Sophisticated techniques of brain imagining were not available to Eysenck when he speculated how the brain works, and he acknowledged that his hypothesis "must stand and fall by empirical confirmation" (1965). Although contemporary research has not provided evidence to support Eysenck's specific description, it clearly confirms Eysenck's conviction that the brain and its processes are central to understanding behavior and personality.

Eysenck's concept of scientific activity was, however, somewhat narrow. There are alternative ways of gathering empirical data and operationally defining terms, which Eysenck disallowed even though other scientists would permit them. Moreover, Eysenck's own procedures were not as objective or purely scientific as he contended. For example, the data of factor analysis may be interpreted in various ways. Also, the conclusions of factor analysis studies are only as good as the original data. The average individual has undoubtedly been more directly influenced by the trait approach to personality than by any other approach. Most people have been assessed by some device based on the trait approach—for instance, an intelligence test, an achievement test, or an aptitude test. Such psychometric measuring devices and techniques have not been used without criticism. Most of the constructs supposedly indicated by these tests cannot be measured directly. Often the validity of the tests is assumed rather than demonstrated.

Philosophical Assumptions

Which philosophical issues were most important to Eysenck? See the Philosophical Assumptions box "Examining Eysenck's Theory."

On the other hand, the judicious use of appropriate assessment techniques can be invaluable in developing individual and group potential. Accurate understanding of one's limitations and abilities is important for developing one's potential.

Trait and temperament theories are controversial because, among other things, they imply that some personality differences are genetically based. Eysenck said that people "are created equal in the sight of God and as regards the judicial system, but they are not created equal as far as beauty is concerned, or strength, or intelligence or a great many other things" (as quoted in Evans, 1976). This is not to say, however, that heredity is the sole determinant of personality. All of the theorists discussed in this chapter emphasize the interaction of biology and society.

☼ Philosophical Assumptions

Examining Eysenck's Theory

Many of the differences among personality theories can be attributed to fundamental differences in philosophical assumptions. Which of the basic philosophical issues, described in the introductory chapter and summarized on the inside back cover, seem to be clearly important to Eysenck in the development of his theory? How, for example, does Eysenck's discussion of the biological bases of behavior and of behavior therapy and modification influence his view of heredity versus the environment? How does his insistence on a scientific approach to personality influence his stance on freedom versus determinism? Does his theory address any other philosophical assumptions? Rate Eysenck on a scale of 1 to 5 on those philosophical assumptions that you feel his theory applies to most. Compare your ratings of Eysenck with your own philosophical assumptions. Did your study of Eysenck lead you to change any of your assumptions? Why or why not?

Heredity may place limits on an individual's potential, but environment probably determines where within that range his or her actual behavior will fall.

Problems arise when people use biological differences to draw unwarranted claims about certain groups, such as implying that one group is superior and should have power over another group. The answer lies not in eradicating differences but rather in avoiding using them as excuses for prejudice and discrimination (Hall & Barongan, 2002). The recognition of similarities and differences among all people enables the effective development and application of a social philosophy that intends to provide equal opportunity for all people in our global community to achieve their potential. Such a recognition underscores the desirability of a reciprocal relationship between the philosophy, science, and art of a personality theory. Scientists should be aware of the ways in which philosophical assumptions inform their work and, in turn, of the ways in which their findings influence ethical and social decisions.

Modern neuroscience and contemporary technologies raise ethical issues, but they are not actually new issues nor will they be resolved by science. "Responsibility," Michael Gazzaniga reminds us, "is a socially constructed rule . . . a moral value that we demand of our fellow . . . human beings" (2005). Neuroscientific knowledge may enrich our ethical understanding, but we must be held responsible for the social, legal, and ethical consequences of our developing technologies (Rose, 2005).

TO LEARN MORE about the link between creativity and mental illness and about hierarchical models of personality, and for a list of suggested readings, visit the *Personality Theories* textbook website at **college.cengage.com/pic/engler8e.**

Summary

1. Some of the historical predecessors to Eysenck's theory are Hippocrates, Kant, Wundt, Jung, Kretschmer, and Sheldon.

2. Eysenck sought to construct a model of personality by giving a description of personality based on factor analysis and then identifying the biological causes of personality through experimental studies.

3. Eysenck identified the superfactors of **extraversion-introversion** (p. 320), **emotional stability–neuroticism** (p. 320), and **psychoticism** (p. 321). There are similarities but significant differences between Eysenck, Cattell, and the Big Five theorists.

4. Eysenck rigorously employed scientific methods in assessment. He criticized the shortcomings of early versions of ratings and inventories, constructed more accurate questionnaires, and developed a number of self-report inventories to measure the dimensions he has identified.

5. Eysenck suggested that extraversion-introversion is related to arousal thresholds in the ascending **reticular activating system** (p. 325) of the brain and emotional stability–neuroticism to differences in **visceral brain** (p. 325) activity and that psychoticism may be due to **hormone** (p. 328) levels. Although his model of how the brain works has become outdated, his work anticipated current developments in brain research.

6. Eysenck connected personality and neurosis to biological bases and to the interplay between the genotype and the environment. Research continues identifying genetic markers and brain mechanisms.

7. Eysenck believed that intelligence is related to **evoked potential** (p. 332).

8. Eysenck's theory found applications in many fields, such as education, the study of creativity, criminal justice, and psychotherapy.

9. Eysenck's theory is an excellent model of a scientific approach.

Personal Experiences

1. Sheldon suggested that there is a correlation between physique and temperament. He identified three body types and equated them to three personality types. Using Table 12.1, test Sheldon's theory in your own life. Think of ten friends and family members. Place each one into the physique type that best fits; then check to see if Sheldon's temperament correlation for that body type sufficiently matches your friend or family member. Do Sheldon's typologies seem to fit? If they do, consider the degree to which other people's perceptions of body type play into our own personalities. Sheldon suggested that parents and teachers assist children in developing aspirations and expectations that are consistent with their physique and temperament. Do you agree with his recommendations?

2. Eysenck drew from Hippocrates' four humors, the ideas of the philosopher Kant, and the theories of modern personality psychologists to illustrate his own theory about the relationship of emotionality versus stability. Eysenck's work shows how the factors in this relationship lie on a continuum—that is, they are not fixed and rigid. Thus a person's

position on the continuum shows particular tendencies in constitutional predisposition, not psychological certainties. Use Figure 12.2 to help you assess where you fall on the emotional stability–neuroticism scale. Where do your closest friends and family members fall?

3. Eysenck defined psychoticism as the loss or distortion of reality and the inability to distinguish fantasy from reality. According to Eysenck, pyschoticism does not have a polar opposite; rather, psychoticism is present in all individuals to one degree or another. Using Figure 12.3, identify the three traits of psychoticism that are most applicable to you. In effect, try to identify, in Eysenck's terms, the traits most likely to predispose you to a psychotic episode. Then look back to the Thinking Critically box "How Normal Is Abnormal?" in the chapter on factor analytic theories. How does your response to Eysenck's psychoticism scale inform the qualitative versus quantitative debate about normality versus abnormality?

4. Do you see evidence that human brains and personalities are undergoing a major transformation due to the development of new technologies? Compare your parent's and grandparents' ability to use, and comfort with, computers and other new technologies with your own. Do you find new gadgets easier to master than your parents or grandparents do? How do you account for the difference? Do you see any difference in your and their abilities to concentrate, think in the abstract, or inhibit impulsive behavior? Might new technologies have anything to do with whatever difference you see?

5. What type of learner are you? There has been much debate over the merits of *discovery learning,* in which students are encouraged to explore their environment and construct facts and theories for themselves, versus the merits of *reception learning,* in which concepts are formally presented to them. Research indicates that children who are extraverts learn best in a situation that emphasizes discovery and children who are introverts profit more from the traditional receptive approach. Categorize yourself according to Eysenck's four dimensions in Figure 12.2. Does your self-appraisal seem to support the research on discovery versus reception learning: If you are an extravert, do you learn better with the discovery method? If you are an introvert, do you learn better with the reception method? How would you want your own kids to be taught?

PART SIX

Humanistic and Existential Theories

The humanistic theories of Abraham Maslow and Carl Rogers emerged in the 1950s in an effort to correct the limited concepts of human nature of both classical psychoanalysis and radical behaviorism. Maslow and Rogers disagreed with the dark, pessimistic, and largely negative picture of personality presented by Freudian psychoanalysis. They also disagreed with the picture of the person as a machine or robot that characterized the early behavior and learning approach.

Maslow and Rogers emphasized a view of the person as an active, creative, experiencing human being who lives in the present and subjectively responds to current perceptions, relationships, and encounters. The humanistic view of personality is a positive, optimistic one that stresses the tendency of the human personality toward growth and self-actualization. It finds current expression in the movements of positive psychology and transpersonal psychology.

Rollo May's existential theory also began to appear in the 1950s. It represented a singular effort to bring together the psychoanalytic tradition in psychology and the existential movement in philosophy. May was deeply aware that technology does not provide satisfactory answers to fundamental questions of human existence. In today's postmodern society our Social Security numbers have become more important than our names. In the midst of rapid technological change, the person appears to have been lost. In combining the insights of psychoanalysis and existentialism, May developed a theory that is clearly expressive of our concerns in the initial decades of the twenty-first century.

CHAPTER 13

Humanism

▪ Abraham Maslow ▪ Carl Rogers
▪ *Positive Psychology*
▪ *Transpersonal Psychology*

braham Maslow has been described as the spiritual father of humanistic psychology. An articulate, persuasive writer, he described humanistic psychology as a
"third force" in American psychology. He criticized both psychoanalysis and radical behaviorism for their limited conceptions of human nature. "The study of crippled, stunted, immature, and unhealthy specimens," he wrote, "can only lead to a crippled psychology"
(1970). The study of human nature as a machine, typical of radical behaviorism, cannot
comprehend the whole person. Maslow offered his view as a complement rather than an alternative to these two other forces. He did not reject the contributions that psychoanalysis
and behaviorism have made, but he believed that the picture of human nature needs to be
rounded out. In particular, Maslow sought to emphasize the positive rather than the negative side of human nature. The brighter side of humanity is emphasized in his concept of
the self-actualized person.

According to Carl Rogers, a person's behavior is completely dependent on how he or she
perceives the world and its events. Rogers's theory of personality describes the **self** as an important element of experience. It is largely due to Rogers's efforts that the self has reemerged
as a useful construct for understanding personality. In much of behaviorist thought the
concept of the self had been ignored as a remnant of earlier religious or philosophical views.
Rogers presented the self as a scientific construct that helps to account for what we observe.
Self is Rogers's term for those psychological processes that govern our behavior. At the same
time, his theory emphasizes the organism or the total person.

Abraham Maslow (1908–1970)

BIOGRAPHICAL BACKGROUND

Abraham Maslow was born in 1908 in Brooklyn, New York, the first of seven children. His
parents were Russian immigrants. As his father's business improved, Maslow's family moved
out of the slums and into lower-middle-class neighborhoods. The young Maslow found
himself the only Jewish boy in the neighborhood and a target of anti-Semitism. Embarrassed by his physical appearance and taunted, isolated, friendless, and lonely, he spent a
great deal of his early years cloistered in the library in the companionship of books.

Maslow was not close to either of his parents. He was fond of his father but afraid of him.
He described his mother as schizophrenic and later wondered how he had turned out so
well in spite of his unhappy childhood. His mother clearly favored his younger brothers and
sister and mercilessly punished her eldest son at the least provocation. Recalling a painful
memory, Maslow told how his mother once killed two stray cats he had brought home by
smashing their heads against the wall. Later, Maslow admitted that he hated his mother and
all that she stood for (Hoffman, 1988). They were never reconciled and he did not attend her
funeral. His mother's brother, however, was a kind and devoted uncle who spent a great deal
of time with him and may have been responsible for Maslow's mental stability.

Later, Maslow suggested that life didn't begin for him until he married and began studying at the University of Wisconsin. He discovered John Watson and was totally absorbed in
behaviorism, which he saw as a very practical way of improving society. Maslow received
a solid grounding in empirical laboratory research. His doctoral research concerned the

Abraham Maslow has been called the spiritual father of humanistic psychology.

sexual and dominance characteristics of monkeys.

After receiving the Ph.D. from Wisconsin in 1934, Maslow returned to New York and began to teach at Brooklyn College. New York was a vibrant place for a young psychologist during the 1930s. Many European psychologists, psychiatrists, and others of the intelligentsia who had come to America to escape the Nazis were in New York. Maslow eagerly met and learned from them. He was influenced by Erich Fromm, Karen Horney, and Alfred Adler. He was also impressed by the anthropologist Ruth Benedict, who inspired him with her optimism about the potentialities of society.

Within such an eclectic climate, it was probably inevitable that Maslow's interest in behaviorism would diminish. The birth of his first daughter was the "thunderclap that settled things" once and for all. All of his experimentation with rats and primates did not prepare him for the mystery of the child. Behaviorist theory might explain what was observed in the laboratory, but it could not account for human experiences. The advent of World War II also profoundly affected Maslow. His attention turned more fully to research on the human personality in an effort to improve it, "to show that human beings are capable of something grander than war and prejudice and hatred" (Hall, 1968).

Maslow remained at Brooklyn for fourteen years. In 1951, he moved to Brandeis University, where he stayed until one year before his premature death in 1970. Maslow had become a very popular figure in the field of psychology. Shortly before his death he had embarked on a fellowship that would have enabled him to undertake a large-scale study developing a philosophy of economics, politics, and ethics informed by humanistic psychology.

HUMAN MOTIVATION: A HIERARCHICAL THEORY

Maslow believed that human beings are interested in growing rather than simply restoring balance or avoiding frustration. He described the human being as a "wanting animal" who is almost always desiring something. Indeed, as one human desire is satisfied, another arises to take its place. In the drive to self-actualize, or fulfill one's potential, the individual moves forward toward growth, happiness, and satisfaction.

Maslow (1970) distinguished between motivation and metamotivation. **Motivation** refers to the reduction of tension by satisfying deficit states or lacks. It entails **D-needs** or deficiency needs, which arise out of the organism's requirements for physiological survival or safety, such as the need for food or rest, and motivate the individual to engage in activities that will reduce these drives. Motivation and the D-needs are powerful determinants of behavior. **Metamotivation** refers to growth tendencies. It entails **B-needs** or being needs, which arise out of the organism's drive to self-actualize and fulfill its inherent potential.

B-needs do not stem from a lack or deficiency; rather, they push forward to self-fulfillment. Their goal is to enhance life by enriching it. Rather than reduce tension, they frequently heighten it in their quest for ever-increasing stimuli that will bring a life lived to the fullest.

Motivation and the D-needs take precedence over metamotivation and the B-needs, because they dominate the organism when both types of needs are thwarted. Unsatisfied deficiency needs hinder movement toward the B-needs (see Sumerlin & Bundrick, 1996). An individual who is desperate for food is unlikely to be concerned with spiritual goals like truth or beauty. Within the D-needs, physiological needs are stronger than safety needs. Thus, in *Les Misérables,* Jean Valjean risks his safety and future by stealing a loaf of bread.

Maslow (1970) proposed a **hierarchy of needs** based on the principle of relative potency. The five basic needs are: physiological needs, safety needs, belonging and love needs, self-esteem needs, and self-actualization needs (see Figure 13.1):

1. *Physiological needs.* The strongest needs of all are the physiological ones that pertain to the physical survival and biological maintenance of the organism. They include the need for food, drink, sleep, oxygen, shelter, and sex. If these biological needs are not met for a protracted period of time, an individual will not be motivated to fulfill other needs.

2. *Safety needs.* Safety needs are the organism's requirements for an orderly, stable, and predictable world. The young child, who is helpless and dependent, prefers a certain amount of structured routine and discipline. The absence of these elements makes the child anxious and insecure. Individuals who live in unsafe environments or suffer from job insecurity may need to spend a great deal of time and energy trying to protect themselves and their possessions.

3. *Belonging and love needs.* Once the physiological and safety needs are met, needs for love and belonging arise. The individual seeks affectionate and intimate relationships with other people, needing to feel part of various reference groups, such as the family, neighborhood, gang, or a professional association. Maslow noted that such needs are increasingly more difficult to meet in our technological, fluid, and mobile society.

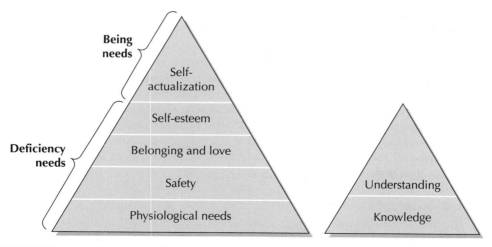

FIGURE 13.1 MASLOW'S HIERARCHY OF NEEDS

4. *Self-esteem needs.* Maslow described two kinds of esteem needs—the need for respect from others and the need for self-respect. Self-esteem entails competence, confidence, mastery, achievement, independence, and freedom. Respect from others entails recognition, acceptance, status, and appreciation. When these needs are not met, an individual feels discouraged, weak, and inferior. For most people, the need for regard from others diminishes with age because it has been fulfilled and the need for self-regard becomes more important.

5. *Self-actualization needs.* If the foregoing needs have been met, the needs for **self-actualization** may emerge *if* the individual has the courage to choose them. These needs are difficult to describe because they are unique and vary from person to person. In general, *self-actualization* refers to the desire to fulfill one's highest potential.

As each need is satisfied, the next higher-order need attains importance. Some individuals, because of their circumstances, find it very difficult to satisfy even the needs at the bottom of Marlow's hierarchy. The higher one is able to go, however, the greater is the physiological health and self-actualization one will demonstrate.

Self-actualization is possible only if the lower needs have been sufficiently met so that they do not detract from or engross a person's basic energies. Rather than organize their behavior toward tension reduction, individuals whose deficiency needs are satisfied may, in fact, seek states of increased optimal tension in order to enhance their opportunities for self-actualization. Higher needs may become as compelling as food to the hungry. In short, those who are living on a B-level have a radically different motivation from those who are still striving to satisfy deficit states.

In addition to the hierarchy just outlined, Maslow posited the important human needs to *know* and *understand* (1970). These form a small but powerful hierarchy of their own, in which the need to know is more potent than and prior to the need to understand. Children, by nature, are curious; when their cognitive impulses are satisfied, they seek further comprehension and understanding. Clinical studies also convinced Maslow that in some individuals aesthetic needs are very important: "They get sick [in special ways] from ugliness, and are cured by beautiful surroundings; they *crave* actively, and their cravings can be satisfied *only* by beauty" (1970). These needs are not sharply delineated from the needs of the earlier hierarchy; they overlap with them and are interrelated.

Maslow (1970) encouraged a more careful study of all situations that foster and fulfill the satisfaction of our basic needs: among them, constructive marriages, close friendships, healthy parent-child relationships, positive educational settings, and satisfying employment. Following physiological and safety needs, affiliation is the primary psychological need (cf. Coy & Kovacs-Long, 2005). For Maslow, every human relationship is potentially a therapeutic one. Indeed, studies show that good relations may protect us from stress by making our immune systems more resilient (Goleman, 1992). One task of psychology is to try to identify those qualities that promote good human situations rather than poor ones. We can then better foster relationships that enable us to grow.

THE STUDY OF SELF-ACTUALIZED PERSONS

Maslow has been described as preoccupied with healthy persons rather than with neurotics. This focus on healthy personality makes Maslow stand out from other theorists. He conducted an extensive, although informal, study of a group of persons whom he considered to be self-actualized. The study generated such interest among other psychologists that Maslow published his findings as an initial, tentative attempt to study optimum health and as a focal point for further empirical research (1970).

Thinking Critically

Whom did Maslow include? See the Thinking Critically box "Who's Among the Self-Actualized?"

Maslow defined *self-actualizing persons* as those who are "fulfilling themselves and doing the best that they are capable of doing" (1970). His subjects consisted of friends and personal acquaintances, public figures living and dead, and selected college students. Studying these individuals, their personalities, characteristics, habits, and abilities enabled Maslow to develop his definition of optimal mental health.

By ordinary standards of laboratory research, what Maslow did in his study was not true research. He was quick to acknowledge that his investigation was not conducted along strict scientific lines. His descriptions were not based on standardized tests, nor were his conclusions obtained from controlled experimental situations. Moreover, his definition of a self-actualized person tended to be a subjective one: The self-actualized person was one whom Maslow deemed to be self-actualized. Nevertheless, Maslow pointed out that the canons of rigorous scientific procedures would

Thinking Critically

Who's Among the Self-Actualized?

Look at the following list of persons whom Maslow identified as self-actualized: Jane Addams, Sholom Aleichem, Robert Benchley, Martin Buber, George Washington Carver, Pablo Casals, Eugene V. Debs, Albert Einstein, Ralph Waldo Emerson, Benjamin Franklin, William James, Thomas Jefferson, Abraham Lincoln, Camille Pissarro, Eleanor Roosevelt, Albert Schweitzer, Baruch Spinoza, Adlai Stevenson, Harriet Tubman. If you do not recognize some of these names, look them up in the Biographical Names section of a collegiate dictionary. Although Maslow indicated that self-actualization is a potential for everyone, would a review of his list indicate that it is most likely to include American presidents or politicians or great creative figures or scientists in the West? How many women do you find? How many people from non-Western cultures are included?

Not everyone agrees with Maslow's choice of examples of self-actualized persons. Eleanor Roosevelt, a very controversial figure, had to overcome crippling roots of being born into a privileged family destroyed by alcoholism. Abraham Lincoln suffered from serious bouts of depression. Others point out that as currently delineated, Maslow's concept would not include many genuinely creative persons such as Wolfgang Mozart, Karen Horney (whose lower needs were by no means fully satisfied), or Martin Luther King Jr. Perhaps his choice reflects his subjective preference and bias. Would you consider Mohandas Gandhi, the Dalai Lama, Nelson Mandela, Mother Teresa, Christopher Reeve, or Oprah Winfrey self-actualized? Can you think of any modifications of Maslow's criteria for self-actualization that would need to be made before his goal of self-actualization truly could be said to be a potential for everyone? Can you think of other individuals whom you would consider self-actualized?

not have encompassed or permitted research into the areas that he was studying. Further, he presented his data as only an initial observation and effort to study health as opposed to neurosis. Maslow hoped that future studies would yield more information as to the nature of self-actualization and confirm or disprove his own expectations.

Following his investigation, Maslow described several characteristics of self-actualized persons (1970). These are listed in Table 13.1. The self-actualized person frequently experiences what Maslow called a **peak experience**—an intensification of any experience to the degree that there is a loss or transcendence of self. Peak experiences are often termed mystical or religious, but Maslow emphasized that they do not necessarily entail traditional religious labels or interpretations. A peak experience may be provoked by a secular event as well. Events that may be mundane and ordinary to others, such as viewing a work of art or reaching a sexual climax, may be the sparks that trigger a peak experience for you.

During a peak experience, the individual experiences not only an expansion of self but also a sense of unity and meaningfulness in life. For that moment, the world appears to be complete and the person is at one with it. The experience lingers on and transforms one's understanding so that things do not seem to be quite the same afterward. Research using a questionnaire about peak experiences has confirmed the characteristics Maslow described

TABLE 13.1 CHARACTERISTICS OF SELF-ACTUALIZERS

Maslow identified fifteen characteristics of self-actualized persons that emerged from his study (1970). These have been grouped under four key dimensions.

AWARENESS

Efficient and accurate perception of reality
Continued freshness of appreciation without preconceptions
Tendency to have peak experiences
Clear ethical awareness and standards but not necessarily conventional ones

HONESTY

Philosophical sense of humor that pokes fun at our shared human pretensions
Deep feeling of kinship with all humanity
Selective and deep interpersonal relations with small circle of intimates
Democratic character structure accepting of all people

FREEDOM

Detachment and a need for privacy
Autonomous and independent of culture and environment
Creativeness characterizing whatever they do
Spontaneity, simplicity, and naturalness

TRUST

Problem- rather than self-centered
Acceptance of self, others, and nature for what they are
Resistance to cultural conformity

Intense concentration on an activity may provoke a peak experience, in which there is a loss or transcendence of self.

(Privette, 1986). Maslow believed that *all* human beings, not only self-actualizers, are potential peakers. People at any stage can have peak experiences, even though Maslow considered such experiences moments of self-actualization. Maslow distinguished between "transcenders" and the "merely healthy": Transcenders are inclined to have peaks; the merely healthy tend not to. Some people have peak experiences, but they suppress them and therefore do not recognize them when they occur. In other cases, one may inhibit a peak experience, thereby preventing its occurrence.

Self-actualizers are able to distinguish between the goal that they are striving for and the means by which they are accomplishing it. For the most part, they are focused on ends rather than means. At the same time, they often consider as ends activities that are simply means for other people. They can enjoy and appreciate the journey as well as the destination.

The picture Maslow drew of the self-actualized person is a composite. No one person that he studied possessed all the qualities of the self-actualized. Each person demonstrated the characteristics to varying degrees. Maslow's definition of self-actualization implied not perfection but a higher level of functioning. As such, self-actualizers may show many human failings. They frequently have silly, wasteful, or thoughtless habits. At times they are vain and take too much pride in their achievements. They may sometimes lose their tempers. Because of their concentration on their work, they may appear absentminded, humorless, or impolite. At times their kindness toward others leads them to permit others to take undue advantage of them. At other times they may appear to be ruthless and inconsiderate in their relations with other people. Sometimes they are boring, even irritating. In short, they are not perfect.

The number of people who achieve self-actualization is relatively small, less than 1 percent of the entire population. Concepts such as "the self-actualized person" may apply to only a select few. Obviously, the possibility of self-actualization is limited or even closed to large numbers of the human population, whose environment and life-style have yet to meet the lesser needs depicted in Maslow's hierarchy, let alone the higher needs. This is not to say, however, that some groups of people are by nature unable to self-actualize. Maslow did point out that some people can be healthier than their environment. He concluded that they have some kind of inner freedom but did not specify how or why.

Maslow's Theory

PHILOSOPHY,
SCIENCE,
and ART

Maslow's theory clearly points away from pure science and toward the broader outlines of philosophy. He reminded us that human beings create science, establish its goals, and use its technology for their own purposes. Maslow believed that it is misleading to think science is value-free, since its procedures are employed for human purposes. We may use science to create mechanistic robots out of human nature, or we may use it to increase human freedom and potential. Maslow suggested that we conceive of science as a problem-solving activity rather than a specific technology. Only the goals of science can dignify or validate its methods.

Philosophical
Assumptions

Which philosophical assumptions were most significant for Maslow? See the Philosophical Assumptions box "Examining Maslow and Rogers" on page 372.

Maslow's study of self-actualized persons lacks the rigor and distinct methodology characteristic of strict empirical science. His work underscores the fact that the canons of rigorous scientific procedures do not necessarily encompass or permit research into important human questions. The tension between the demands of the subject matter of psychology and the requirements of good science continues to concern psychologists.

Maslow suggested the need for a broader definition of science and the development of methodologies appropriate for the human participant. His "third force" became a very powerful force in psychology, and its impact was reflected in the creation of a new division of the American Psychological Association: Humanistic Psychology. Maslow's hierarchy of human needs continues the interest in human needs explored historically by Henry Murray (whose theory is discussed in the chapter on traits and personology).

Interest in human needs and self-actualization continues today in the *self-determination theory* (SDT) of Edward Deci and Richard Ryan (1991, 2002; Ryan & Deci, 2001, 2006), which suggests that people are active organisms with innate tendencies to fulfill their potential and rise above challenges. The social environment can support or hinder these natural tendencies, and negative human behaviors are seen in terms of thwarted needs. Over the past two decades, Deci and Ryan's SDT macro theory has generated considerable research. Laboratory experiments and field studies have been performed in diverse real-world settings to explore motivational issues that underlie the self-regulation of behavior. Additional mini theories have been developed to further explain the phenomena that have emerged from research and to enlarge SDT (Deci & Ryan, 2004). This work expands Maslow's concepts of self esteem and self-actualization and testifies to its ongoing relevance. Current research also explores variations within and between cultures in the perception and expression of human needs (Diener, Oishi, & Lucas, 2003). In an effort to address feminist, existential, and environmental critiques that Maslow's hierarchy is too individualistic and male, Steven Hanley and Steven Abell have suggested a modification that emphasizes the importance of relatedness (2002).

Maslow's portrayal of the self-actualized person is optimistic, generating much confidence in human potential. Yet some critics suggest that his picture may be simplistic, neglecting the hard work and pain that are involved in growth and development and ignoring the phenomenon of tragedy. Maslow's research originated in an era of growth and prosperity accompanied by a seemingly limitless view of human potential. But is this picture realistic? In fact, the likelihood of self-actualization may be more remote than Maslow indicated. Perhaps it is naive to hope to reduce all conflict and more realistic to assume that we can merely strengthen the ego, enabling it to be more effective in its executive functions. Freud, we recall, was pessimistic about reducing human conflict.

Some critics further suggest that Maslow's view of the self-actualized individual is based on American values of individual achievement. Because of cultural training, many people in Western societies tend to believe that personality is best rooted on a high sense of positive self-esteem. Thus parents in middle-class America are encouraged to take steps to develop positive self-esteem in their children, especially their sons (Josephs, Markus, & Tafarodi, 1992; Markus & Kitayama, 1991), and psychological disorders such as anxiety and depression are often seen as a failure to develop such autonomy, achievement, and feelings of self-worth. However, people in many non-Western cultures cultivate very dissimilar personalities. In Japan and China, an autonomous self is not stressed, and children are taught to cooperate and not to demonstrate their superiority so as to avoid diminishing other people (see Kitayama & Markus, 1992). As a result, people perceive themselves to be part of a whole and define themselves in terms of the group. When Kitayama and his coworkers compared the responses of Japanese and American university students who were asked to indicate the frequency and origin of certain emotions, Japanese students associated positive feelings with good interpersonal relations rather than personal achievements, whereas the opposite was true of the Americans (Kitayama & Markus, 1992).

Likewise, even within the same culture gender differences may apply. Thus in North America a woman's self-esteem tends to be based on interpersonal relations, whereas a man's tends to be based on personal accomplishments (Josephs et al., 1992). Lerman (1992) reminds us that Maslow did not demonstrate how the environment frequently fails to permit the gratification of basic needs of women and other subjugated groups. She believes, however, that there is a place in his and other humanist theories for contributions from a feminist examination of the environment and its potential impact on the well-being of humanity. Nicholson (2001) observes that Maslow recognized that psychology had become too masculine and struggled to "soften" it without undermining its rigorous groundwork. In Maslow's hierarchy, self-esteem and self-actualization needs emerge only after relational needs are met (Coy & Kovaks-Long, 2005).

However, others (such as Chang & Page, 1991) believe that cross-cultural comparisons among Maslow, Rogers, Lao Tzu, and Zen Buddhism point more toward a universality of human experience in that they all share the assumption that people have an actualizing tendency that fosters positive growth. Hamer's research posits a link between genes and spirituality (2005). Miller (1991) suggests that placing self-actualization in the context of transpersonal psychology removes its elitism and fosters cross-cultural comparisons with Eastern concepts. Rather than emphasize one concept of an ideal, Coan (1991) suggests we look at the diverse ways in which people can realize their potential.

Clearly, more attention needs to be given to the processes within the individual and various cultures and societies that permit self-actualization and creativity to flower. In Maslow's words, "How good a human being does society permit?" (1970). In what instances can an individual overcome and compensate for needs that have not been met in life? As it stands, Maslow's discussion of self-actualization is descriptive rather than functional. He describes the characteristics of the self-actualizer but does not tell how these characteristics may be concretely acquired.

By articulating the concept of peak experiences, Maslow believed that he had brought all major religions under the rubric of the natural science of psychology. He felt that a study of positive forces that foster self-actualization and an improved culture should be a primary focus of psychology. Like Maslow, Carl Rogers picks up on the concept of self-actualization and its development in his humanistic theory.

Carl Rogers (1902–1987)

BIOGRAPHICAL BACKGROUND

Carl Rogers was born in 1902 in Oak Park, Illinois, a suburb of Chicago. He was the fourth of six children. Rogers's parents, educated and conservative middle-class Protestants, instilled in their children high ethical standards of behavior and emphasized the importance of hard work.

Rogers had little social life outside of his large family, but this did not bother him. He was an avid reader and developed a certain level of independence early in life. When he was twelve, the family moved to a farm. Farm life spurred his interest in science and increased his ability to work independently. He was fascinated with the literature on scientific agriculture that his father brought home. Rogers worked hard at his chores on the farm. He raised lambs, pigs, and calves. He also collected, studied, and bred moths. A superior student, Rogers entered the University of Wisconsin, a family alma mater, with the full intent of studying agriculture. However, in his second year, he decided to prepare for the ministry. After his graduation in 1924, he married Helen Elliot and moved to New York City to begin preparation for the ministry at Union Theological Seminary.

Rogers's fate, however, was not to become a minister. During his final years at college, Rogers found himself departing from his parents' fundamentalist ways of thinking (see Thorne, 1990). The liberal philosophical approach toward religion fostered at Union Theological Seminary and the insights Rogers gained from participation in several YMCA conferences led him to feel that he could not work in a field that would require him to profess a specific set of beliefs. This was a difficult period for both Rogers and his parents, but it nurtured Rogers's growing conviction that one must ultimately rely on personal experi-

Carl Rogers is perhaps best known for the method of psychotherapy he developed.

ences for developing a philosophy of life (see also Dolliver, 1995). His interests were turning toward psychology; therefore, he transferred to Teachers College at Columbia University, where he was introduced to the philosophy of John Dewey and began his training in clinical psychology.

In 1931, Rogers received the Ph.D. and joined the staff of the Rochester Guidance Center, where he helped develop a highly successful child study department. Here, Rogers first met what was to be many years of opposition from members of the psychiatric profession who felt that psychologists and counselors should not be permitted to practice or have any administrative responsibility over psychotherapy. In 1939, when Rogers was made the director of the center, a vigorous campaign was waged to unseat him. No one criticized his work, but the general opinion was that a psychologist simply could not do this kind of work. Fortunately, the board of trustees backed Rogers.

In 1940, Rogers accepted an appointment as professor of psychology at Ohio State University. He worked with intellectually adept graduate students and began to clearly articulate his views on psychotherapy using college students as his primary database. In 1945, he moved to the University of Chicago, where, as professor of psychology and executive secretary of the counseling center, he again championed his view that psychologists and counselors could effectively conduct therapy. Rogers's efforts, along with others', led to the reconciliation of psychiatry and psychology as two professions in search of a common goal. This reconciliation and challenge were reflected in Rogers's appointment as professor of psychology and psychiatry at the University of Wisconsin in 1957. In 1963, Rogers became a fellow at the Center for Studies of the Person in La Jolla, California. Throughout his life, Rogers referred to himself as a counselor.

In his final years, Rogers sought to bring together in encounter groups people from conflicting political factions, such as Protestants and Roman Catholics in Belfast, Ireland. As his son David observed, "Over his career, he moved from one-on-one psychotherapy, to small groups, to nations" (Goleman, 1987). He was planning to return to South Africa to lead a second encounter session with blacks and whites when he died in 1987 of a heart attack following surgery for a broken hip.

ROGERS'S THEORY OF PERSONALITY

Influenced by a philosophical movement called **phenomenology,** Rogers (1959) maintained that each individual exists in the center of a phenomenal field. The word *phenomenon* comes from the Greek *phainomenon,* which means "that which appears or shows itself." In philosophy, phenomenology seeks to describe the data, or the "given," of immediate experience. In psychology, phenomenology has come to mean the study of human awareness and perception. Phenomenologists stress that what is important is not the object or the event in itself but how it is perceived and understood by the individual. The **phenomenal field** is the total sum of experiences. It consists of everything that is potentially available to consciousness at any given moment. As you read you may not be aware of the pressure of the chair on your buttocks, but when attention is drawn to this fact you become conscious of it.

The organism, or person as a whole, responds to the phenomenal field. Rogers's emphasis here is on the individual's perception of reality. In this respect he was consistent with the recent emphasis on cognition in psychology. For social purposes, we agree that the perceptions commonly shared by others in our culture are the correct perceptions. However, reality is essentially a very personal matter. Two individuals walking along at night may see an object by the road and respond very differently. "One . . . sees a large boulder and reacts with fright. The other, a native of the country sees a tumbleweed and reacts with nonchalance" (1951, p. 484). The individual's perception rather than the reality itself is most important. Suppose a young boy complains that his father is dogmatic, authoritarian, and dictatorial but an impartial observer concludes that the father is open and democratic. Rogers would point out that what the father is really like is meaningless; what is important is how the boy perceives his father. It follows that the best vantage point for understanding an individual is that of the individual.

Rogers pointed out that the individual is the only one who can fully know her or his field of experience. He acknowledged that it is not always easy to understand behavior from the internal frame of reference of another person. We are limited to the individual's conscious perception and communication of experiences. Nevertheless, such an empathic understanding of the experiences of another is useful in understanding a person and therefore useful in understanding personality processes.

Actualization

The primary tendency of the organism is to maintain, actualize, and enhance itself. This actualizing tendency is part of a universal life force (Van Kalmthout, 1995); it follows lines laid down by genetics and may also be influenced by temperament (Ford, 1991). The particular type of seed that is planted determines whether or not the flower will be a chrysanthemum or a snapdragon, but the environment can greatly influence the resulting bloom. The process of actualization is neither automatic nor effortless; it involves struggle and even pain. The young child may struggle with the first step, but it is a natural struggle. Thus each organism, or living being, moves in the direction of maturation as it is defined for each species.

Behavior is the "goal-directed attempt" of the organism to meet its needs as it perceives them (Rogers, 1951). This goal-directed behavior is accompanied by emotions that, unless they are excessive or inappropriate, facilitate the behavior. Rogers's view of emotions is a very positive one. Fully experiencing one's emotions facilitates growth, whereas the denial or distortion of emotions may permit them to raise havoc in our lives. Rogers suggested that actualization occurs most freely when the person is open and aware of all experiences, be they sensory, visceral, or emotional. Our inner experiences are intrinsically growth-producing. An **organismic valuing process** subconsciously guides us toward productive growth experiences provided that it has not been overlaid with external rules and societal values that preclude healthy self-actualization (1964).

In Rogers's theory, the actualizing tendency follows lines laid down by genetics; however, the environment can influence adult behaviors. Thus even genetically identical twins can grow up to become very different people.

The Self

Out of the interaction of the organism and the environment, and in particular the interaction with significant others, there gradually emerges a structure of self, or a concept of "who I am" (1951). As young children interact with their environment in the process of actualization, they acquire ideas about themselves, their world, and their relationship to that world. They experience things that they like or dislike and things that they can or cannot control. Those experiences that appear to enhance one's self are valued and incorporated into one's self-image; those experiences that appear to threaten the self are denied and rendered foreign to the self.

The **self-concept** is a portion of the phenomenal field that has gradually become differentiated. It is composed of those conscious perceptions and values of "me" or "I," some of which are a result of the organism's own valuing of its experiences and some of which have been introjected or taken over from important others. Because the self-concept comes in part through others, the potential for dissociation or estrangement exists (and usually occurs to some degree). As a result, the actualizing tendency may be perverted into behaviors that do not lead to actualization. The self-concept, then, is an object of perception. It is the person as she or he perceives herself or himself. Thus we have a distinction between the organism or real self in the process of actualization, and the self as perceived, or object. The "self" that one forms may be at variance with the real experience of one's organism because it includes values that are taken over from other people rather than the actual experiences of the organism.

For example, a young boy quickly learns that his parents withdraw their affection when he hits his baby brother. Even though hitting his brother is a satisfying act, the boy forfeits his satisfaction in order to conceive of himself as lovable to his parents. He denies that he wants to hit his brother. When children deny or distort their experiences, they are no longer aware of them. They begin to experience the attitudes of others, such as their parents, as if these were the direct experiences of their own. Through such distortion, an individual may come to experience any expression of anger as bad and therefore may no longer accurately perceive that at times its expression is satisfying. In such cases the experiences of the self and that of the organism do not coincide.

Rogers did not believe that the self-structure must be formed on the basis of denial and distortion. The child values experiences as positive or negative. If a parent is able to accept the child's feeling of satisfaction and also accept her or his *own* feelings that certain actions are inappropriate, the parent can help the child curb actions without threatening the integrity of the child's self-concept. The parent can make it clear that the action of hitting the baby is wrong. Nevertheless, the feelings of satisfaction from the aggression and the child's desire are recognized and accepted.

The experiences that occur in our lives are symbolized, ignored, denied, or distorted. If an experience is *symbolized*, it is accepted into consciousness, perceived, and organized into a relationship with the self. Experiences are denied or distorted if they appear to be inconsistent with the self-structure. Young women who are brought up to believe that aggression is unfeminine may deny or distort their natural feelings of anger and find it difficult to be assertive because they seek to behave in ways that are feminine. Likewise, men frequently deny or distort natural feelings of being nurturing because they find them inconsistent with being masculine. In short, the individual's awareness is highly dependent on the self-concept.

Congruence and Incongruence

There is a need for the self as perceived and the real self, the organism, to be congruent. A state of **congruence** exists when a person's symbolized experiences reflect all of the actual experiences of the organism. When one's symbolized experiences do not represent all of the actual experiences, or if they are denied or distorted, there is a lack of correspondence between the self as perceived and the real self. In such a situation, there is **incongruence** and possible maladjustment. Diagrammatically, we can show this with overlapping circles, much as we depicted Horney's distinction between the real self and the ideal self (see Figure 13.2).

When an individual denies or distorts significant sensory and visceral experiences, certain basic tensions arise. The self as perceived, which primarily governs behavior, is not an adequate representative of the true experiences of the organism. It becomes increasingly

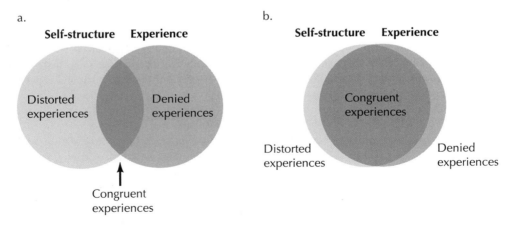

FIGURE 13.2 THE TOTAL PERSONALITY

Rogers believed that a person is free from inner tension and is psychologically adjusted when the self-concept is congruent with experience. Diagram *a* depicts a state of psychic tension. Diagram *b* depicts a state of relative congruence, wherein most elements of experience are integrated into the self.

difficult for the self to satisfy the organism's needs. Tension develops and is felt as anxiety or uncertainty.

Rogers (1951) offered the following example. A young mother conceives of herself as a "good and loving mother." She cannot recognize her negative, rejecting attitudes toward her child because they do not coincide with her self-image. Nevertheless, these negative attitudes exist, and her organism seeks aggressive acts that would express these attitudes. She is limited in expressing herself only through channels that are consistent with her self-image of being a good mother. Because it is appropriate for a good mother to behave aggressively toward her child when the child's behavior is bad, she perceives a great deal of the child's behavior as bad and punishes the child accordingly. In this manner, she can express her negative attitudes but retain her self-image of being a good mother.

When the self-concept is congruent with the experiences of the organism, the person is free from inner tension and psychologically adjusted. Rogers made it clear that he did not advocate the free and unrestrained expression of all our impulses and emotions. Part of the reality of the organism's experience is that certain social and cultural values require suppression of certain activities. Nevertheless, one's self-concept can include both the desire to behave one way and the desire to behave in other, more socially accepted ways. If parents can accept their feelings of rejection for their children as well as their feelings of affection, they can relate to their children more honestly.

When people become aware of and accept their impulses and perceptions, they increase the possibility of conscious control over their expression. The driver who is adept on icy roads knows the importance of steering "with the skid" in order to gain control over the car. In the same manner, by accepting all experiences, a person acquires better self-control.

Development of Personality

Rogers did not posit any specific stages of personality development from infancy to adulthood. He concentrated on the way in which the evaluations of others impede or facilitate self-actualization. Although the tendency to actualize follows genetic determinants, Rogers noted that it is subject to strong environmental influences.

The young child has two basic needs: the need for positive regard by others and the need for positive self-regard. **Positive regard** refers to being loved and accepted for who one is. Young children behave in such a way as to show their strong need for the acceptance and love of those who care for them. They will undergo significant changes in their behavior in order to attain positive regard.

In an ideal situation, positive regard is unconditional. It is given freely to children for who they are regardless of what they do. **Unconditional positive regard** is not contingent on any specific behaviors. A parent can limit or curb certain undesirable behaviors by objecting only to the behaviors and not disapproving of the child or the child's feelings. A parent who sees a child scribble on the wall may say, "Writing on the wall destroys it. Use this blackboard instead." Here, the parent limits remarks to the behavior itself. But the parent who says, "You are a bad boy (girl) for writing on the wall," has shifted from disapproval of the behavior to disapproval of the child. Such regard is no longer unconditional.

Conditional positive regard is given only under certain circumstances. Children are led to understand that their parents will not love them unless they think, feel, and act as their parents want them to. In such cases, the child perceives the parent as imposing **conditions of worth,** specifying the provisions under which the child will be accepted, such as being pretty or earning top grades. Such conditions of worth may lead the child to introject values of others rather than of the self and lead to a discrepancy between the self-concept and the experiences of the organism.

Positive self-regard follows automatically if one has received unconditional positive regard. Children who are accepted for who they are come to view themselves favorably and with acceptance. It is very difficult, however, to view oneself positively if one is continually the target of criticism and belittlement. Inadequate self-concepts such as feelings of inferiority or stupidity frequently arise because a person has not received adequate positive regard from others.

In the course of development, any experience that is at variance with the emerging self-concept is denied entrance into the self because it is threatening and evokes anxiety. If children are taught that it is wrong to feel angry, they may begin to perceive the emotion of anger itself rather than certain *expressions* of anger as dangerous or incorrect.

Research on social cognition concurs with Rogers's belief that self-perception is important in personality development and that congruence is needed for psychological health. Moreover, research has shown that people try to verify their self-concept even if the self-concept is negative. Thus people who have a negative self-concept often choose partners who think unfavorably about them. Perhaps disapproving judgments increase their perception that their world is predictable. In this view, people "may go to great lengths to maintain the perception that they are in touch with social reality, however harsh that reality may be" (Swann, Stein-Seroussi, & Giesler, 1992).

Rogers believed that supportive parents and a creative environment can facilitate psychological adjustment (1951). Longitudinal studies have suggested a positive correlation between Rogers's prescribed child-rearing practices and a composite index of creative potential in early adolescence (Harrington, Block, & Block, 1987). Individuals who have experienced a positive development are more likely to become fully functioning people. Rogers did not provide as extensive a description of the self-actualized individual as Maslow did. However, he suggested five criteria with which to judge whether someone is a **fully functioning person.** These criteria are summarized in Table 13.2.

PSYCHOTHERAPY

Carl Rogers is best known for the method of psychotherapy that he developed, known originally as **client-centered** or **nondirective therapy** and more recently as **person-centered psychotherapy.** Rogers not only originated this type of therapy but also carefully studied it

---

TABLE **13.2** CRITERIA FOR BEING A FULLY FUNCTIONING PERSON

1. *Openness to experience:* Aware of all experiences without a need to deny or distort them.

2. *Existential living:* Able to live in the moment without preconceived structures.

3. *Organismic trust:* Trust in one's own experience; not bound by other people's opinions.

4. *Experiential freedom:* Free-choice agent; assumes responsibility for decisions and behaviors.

5. *Creativity:* Able to adjust creatively to changes and seeks new experiences and challenges.

According to Carl Rogers, the young child has two basic needs: the need for positive regard by others and the need for positive self-regard.

to determine what makes it work. As a scientist, he tried to define operationally the conditions that underlie successful therapy to generate hypotheses that can be empirically tested. He led a large-scale research program at the Counseling Center of the University of Chicago on the outcomes of psychotherapy (Rogers & Dymond, 1954), specifying the conditions that lead to change and describing cases in which change did and did not occur. Rogers's leadership in demanding empirical validation of psychotherapy was a significant contribution, particularly considering his phenomenological and idiographic orientation.

Attitudes Necessary for Therapeutic Change

Rogers's studies suggested that three attitudes on the part of therapists are necessary and sufficient for change. By *necessary,* Rogers meant that these attitudes are essential and must be evident to the client. By *sufficient,* he meant that no other conditions are required for change to occur. Not only did Rogers maintain that these three attitudes underlie his method of therapy, but he also suggested that they underlie any good relationship and any successful therapeutic technique and that they lead to the development of the same attitudes in the client (1961).

What are these attitudes? The first is **empathy,** the ability to experience another person's feelings as if they were one's own but to never lose sight of the "as if." Through empathy, the therapist is able to put him- or herself in the client's shoes without trying to wear those shoes. The therapist understands the client's internal frame of reference and communicates this understanding, largely through statements that reflect the client's feelings.

The second attitude is **acceptance.** The therapist does not posit any conditions of worth. Acceptance is nonjudgmental recognition of oneself and the other person. Through acceptance the therapist lets the other person be. In a climate of acceptance or unconditional positive regard, the client will be able to explore feelings and experiences that were previously denied or distorted, and the client can set aside conditions of worth, relax his or her defenses, and become open to organismic experiencing. As a result, the client's self-concept gradually becomes more congruent with the actual experiences of the organism.

The third attitude is **genuineness.** An effective therapist is genuine, integrated, free, and deeply aware of the dynamics of the therapeutic relationship. The therapist need not be a model of perfect mental health and may have shortcomings and difficulties in other situations. But within the relationship of therapy, the therapist needs to be congruent.

Given these attitudes on the part of the therapist, Rogers believed that positive, constructive personality changes would occur. He is assuming, of course, that the individual's environment permits change and that the individual is accessible to counseling (i.e., is not suffering from a psychosis that would prevent the expression of feelings and problems).

Responses to Emotional Communications

Rogers did not use any special techniques, such as free association or dream analysis, in his therapy. The direction of the therapy is determined by the client. In Rogerian therapy, if there were any instructions, they would be, "Talk about whatever you would like to talk about." The client determines what will be discussed, when, and to what extent. This is why Rogers's form of therapy has been labeled "client-centered." The client who does not want to talk about a particular subject is not pressed to do so. The client does not even have to talk at all. Rogers felt strongly that his clients had the ability to understand and to explore their problems and that given the appropriate therapeutic relationship—that is, an attitude of acceptance—they would move toward further self-actualization.

In Rogerian therapy, the therapist communicates the attitude of acceptance through statements that reflect the client's feelings. We can understand this technique better by distinguishing among different kinds of responses to emotional communications. Rogers developed a number of studies in which he explored how people communicate in face-to-face situations in everyday life as well as in therapy (Rogers & Roethlisberger, 1952). Consider the following hypothetical communication: "The doctor keeps telling me not to worry, but I'm frightened of this operation." There are many different ways to respond to such a statement. Rogers discovered that most responses fall into one of five categories used in the following order of frequency in everyday life: (1) **evaluative,** (2) **interpretative,** (3) **reassuring,** (4) **probing,** and (5) **reflective.** Each type of response tends to lead toward a different consequence (see Table 13.3).

TABLE 13.3 RESPONSES TO EMOTIONAL COMMUNICATIONS

Rogers's research showed that most responses to emotional communications fall into one of the five categories in the left column. In the middle column is an example of each type of response to the following emotional communication: "I'm really worried about Stephen. His grades have fallen, and I think he may be into drugs." The third column indicates the likely consequence of each type of response.

TYPE OF RESPONSE	EXAMPLE	CONSEQUENCES
Evaluative: Places a value judgment on the person's thoughts, feelings, wishes, or behavior	"You mustn't feel that way. Worrying never helped any situation."	Detracts from a basic attitude of acceptance
Interpretative: Identifies the real problem or underlying feelings	"That's because you feel guilty because you smoked some pot when you were young."	If wrong or ill-timed, may lead to feeling misunderstood
Reassuring: Attempts to soothe the person's feelings	"Most kids go through periods like that; it's probably nothing to worry about."	May be seen as an attempt to minimize the situation
Probing: Seeks further information	"What is he doing that makes you think he's into drugs?"	May be taken as an infringement of privacy
Reflective: Captures the underlying feelings	"You're very concerned about him."	Encourages elaboration and exploration

Thinking Critically

How can you develop a more reflective response? See the Thinking Critically box "Friendlier Arguments: Using Reflection to Resolve Conflicts."

While evaluative responses are the most common, they are judgmental and tend to detract from an attitude of basic acceptance of the other individual. Reflective comments which capture the underlying feelings are most likely to encourage further elaboration and exploration. However they are the least commonly used response.

Rogers believed that meaningful therapy is not confined to the professional therapist's or counselor's office. Any interpersonal relationship can become therapeutic when the three necessary and sufficient attitudes are present. Most people could use practice in cultivating reflective responses inasmuch as they are the most fruitful but least used responses.

Supportive Versus Reconstructive Psychotherapy

Different methods of psychotherapy vary in their ambitions. Some therapies aim at strengthening adaptive behaviors, and others seek to reorganize the basic personality structure. At one end of the spectrum, psychoanalysis stands as an example of **reconstructive psychotherapy.** Through analysis of the resistances and transference the analyst seeks to remove defenses so that the analysand can communicate true feelings and integrate his or her personality. On the other hand, many psychotherapeutic techniques are best characterized as **supportive psychotherapy,** because they seek to strengthen adaptive instincts and defenses without necessarily tampering with the underlying personality structure. Clearly, reconstructive psychotherapy is a much more intensive undertaking, which accounts for the long duration of psychoanalysis. Although he was not averse to providing insight when the occasion merits it, Rogers's approach tends to be supportive rather than reconstructive.

One technique is not better than the other; rather, we need to recognize that for different people, in different circumstances, and perhaps even at different times in their lives, one approach may be more suitable than another. Rogers pointed out that we all can benefit

Thinking Critically

Friendlier Arguments: Using Reflection to Resolve Conflicts

Rogers suggested the following exercise as a way of cultivating a more constructive way of approaching and dealing with personal differences and disagreements. The next time you become deeply engrossed in a conversation or an argument, agree to obey the following rule: Each person may speak only after reflecting the thoughts and feelings of the previous speaker accurately and to that person's satisfaction. What initially sounds simple proves difficult but leads to a much more constructive discussion, for it focuses on mutual understanding rather than on simply presenting different points of view.

Understanding is particularly difficult when one is dealing with a group of people of different genders, backgrounds, races, native languages, and/or cultures. Try this activity with many diverse people, and see how it helps to improve your communication.

Why do you think empathy has been found to be a key element of effective therapy?

from counseling. Although we may not be suffering from overt problems that seriously affect our lives, we may not be functioning as well as we would like.

CHANGES IN ROGERS'S VIEW OF THERAPY

Rogers's earlier writings on therapeutic techniques stressed the idea that the potential for better health lies in the client. The counselor's role was essentially that of making the kinds of reflective responses that would enable the client's potential to flower. Later, Rogers shifted from his emphasis on technique to therapist genuineness and use of self in therapy (Bozarth, 1990).

In later years, Rogers was less interested in individual counseling and more interested in group counseling, as well as broader social concerns. He was a leader in the field of encounter groups and sponsored some interracial and intercultural groups. Under the guidance of a facilitator, rather than a traditional leader, *encounter groups* seek to create an atmosphere in which members can express their feelings, focus on their experience, and acknowledge how they are perceived by others in the group. Encounter groups were a forerunner of the support and help groups that many people today find very useful.

Rogers challenged some of the concepts on which our society is based, such as that power is power over other people or that strength is the strength to control. Instead he suggested that influence is gained only when power is shared and that control is constructive when it is self-control. He wrote about education, particularly higher education, describing a plan for radical change in teacher education and researching the effects of teachers' attitudes on students' learning. He emphasized the importance of combining experiential with cognitive learning. He also explored various forms of partnership unions or alternatives to marriage, as well as other interpersonal relationships in contemporary society. His later workshops have been depicted as entailing a spiritual dimension, perhaps reflecting Rogers's (1980) openness to mysticism and his belief that subjective experiences were compatible with science.

ASSESSMENT AND RESEARCH IN ROGERS'S THEORY

Rogers was exceptionally open to the empirical test of his theories. The private, confidential character of clinical treatment has made it very difficult to study in its natural setting. With the permission of his clients, however, Rogers introduced the tape recorder and film camera into the treatment room. He did not believe that they detract from the therapy. Within a short time, both client and counselor forget about the recording equipment and act naturally and spontaneously. Today computers aid in the monitoring process (Scherl & Haley, 2000).

The recordings Rogers made have provided a group of actual transcriptions of therapeutic sessions that can be observed and studied. The sessions have been analyzed in various ways. A classification system permits us to note the kinds of statements made by both the client and the counselor. Rating scales monitor the progress and change that occur during therapy from the viewpoints of both the client and the counselor.

Thus in describing the case of Mrs. Oak, Rogers was able to illustrate in her therapeutic experience and in her performance on a variety of test and research instruments, such as pre- and post-therapy Thematic Apperception Tests, the process of her psychotherapy and its results (Rogers & Dymond, 1954). In his analysis, changes in the perceived self and the self-ideal, as well as changes in their relationship, were readily apparent. In the beginning of therapy, the self-ideal bears little resemblance to the perceived self. However, during the process, congruence increases, so that at the conclusion and in the follow-up study, there is marked congruence.

One method that Rogers used for studying changes in a person's self-concept is the **Q-sort technique,** developed by William Stephenson. The Q-sort test uses a packet of one hundred cards containing descriptive statements or words that can be used to describe the self. The person is given the cards and asked to sort them according to his or her self-perception into a prearranged order, which resembles a normal curve of distribution. The Q-sort technique has been used to measure changes that occur throughout therapy. In short, Rogers provided an impetus to developing means for ongoing empirical research on the processes of therapy and the self.

From his studies, Rogers concluded that there is a clear predictability to the therapeutic process. Given certain conditions, such as the three therapist attitudes mentioned earlier, certain predictable outcomes may be expected. The client will express deep motivational attitudes and begin to explore and become more aware of attitudes and reactions. The client will begin to accept him- or herself more fully and will discover and choose more satisfying goals. Finally, the client will begin to behave in a manner that indicates greater psychological growth and maturity.

Rogers's Theory

PHILOSOPHY,
SCIENCE,
and ART

Rogers did a great deal to bring the human being back as the primary focus of psychological study. In doing so, he clearly reasserted the philosophical character of personality theorizing. At the same time, he was very careful to distinguish between his philosophical assumptions and his scientific hypotheses. For instance, in Rogers's theory the self is not a philosophical concept but a name for a group of processes, which can be studied scientifically. The usefulness of the concepts of self and self-actualization continues to attract discussion and debate (see Geller, 1984; Ginsberg, 1984; Heine, 2001).

Still, Rogers's emphasis on subjectivity and the individual's internal frame of reference made scientific research difficult. Researchers have traditionally stressed the role of the external observer because, as we have seen, introspective reports are much more difficult to validate than extrospective reports. Rogers was criticized for using self-reports in his research, and many scientific psychologists have rejected Rogers's notion of the self because of his methods.

However, Rogers encourages us to invite the person as a co-investigator in personality research (Bohart & Byock, 2005). The concept of self, which he revitalized, is increasingly described as a complex psychological construct stemming from interpretations of cognitive, affective-motive, and attitudinal facets. Within individuals, there is one self with varied interrelated aspects as compared with a multiplicity of selves.

Tendencies to suppress data or to supply socially acceptable data instead of the truth do exist in subjective reporting. However, if we are aware of these tendencies toward error, we can take steps to avoid them. In this sense, introspection is no

From his work with clients, Rogers concluded that there is a clear predictability to the thera-peutic process as the perceived self and the self ideal become more congruent.

different from any other scientific method. Extrospection is also open to a great deal of error: Sense organs may be defective or deluded. Psychologists have known for a long time that there is hardly a perfect correspondence between the stimulus, or the evidence of the world that reaches our senses, and our perception of the world. Introspection does not involve the sense organs to the same extent as extrospection and so in some respects may be more trustworthy. Thus Rogers's emphasis on introspection was a useful correction of the emphasis on extrospection that characterized American psychology. Introspective self-reports have gained wider acceptance with social and cognitive behavior theorists with the present emphasis on cognition.

Nevertheless, a major criticism of Rogers's position is that it is based on a simplistic concept of phenomenology and does not reflect a sophisticated understanding of the complexity of the processes underlying human awareness. It also does not take into account a child's immature cognitive structures and inability to make clear distinctions between feelings and actions. To say that the best vantage point for understanding an individual is that of the individual minimizes how frequently human beings deny or distort the truth about themselves to themselves. Many of us seem bent on self-deception rather than on self-understanding. Although Rogers acknowledged that there are experiences of which a person may be unaware through the processes of denial and distortion, he did not believe that repression is inevitable and held that an atmosphere of acceptance is sufficient to lift repression. Critics suggest that this belief is naive and that Rogers failed to recognize the power and intensity of unconscious forces.

Rogers's own example of the two men, one of whom saw a boulder and the other a tumbleweed, depicts the limitations of his approach. In spite of how an object is perceived, or even if it is not perceived, its reality has an impact. After all, "contact with a boulder will hurt no matter how it is perceived." "Reality is not wholly determined internally" (Lerman, 1992). Research in feminist psychology shows that individuals' personalities are intimately related to the world they live in and the conditions of worth that are imposed upon them. The reality of women's subjugation (and of other oppressed groups) influences what they can be, how they conceive of themselves, and their personality development (Miller, 1976). Thus Lerman (1992) points out that Rogers does not seem to fully appreciate the impact of external influences. Patriarchy has, in fact, limited options for women. A woman's belief that she is entitled to leave an abusive situation does not necessarily imply that she will be able to leave safely. Changing women's self-perceptions will not, in itself, eliminate external barriers.

Moreover, Rogers's view of the development and actualization of self may be highly culture-bound. He has been accused of encouraging selfishness (Marin, 1975; Wallach & Wallach, 1983) and making interpersonal relations "instrumental" and "competitive" (Geller, 1982). His portrait of the healthy self as an actualizing being, differentiated from others and dependent on achievement, may not be relevant to non-Western cultures in which the self is delineated in terms of relation to others, particularly within the family (Heine, 2001; Markus & Kitayama, 1991). This may be strange, because Rogers (1963) indicated that one of the outcomes of self-actualization is harmonious and deep social relations. Das (1989) argues that Rogers's view can be seen as complementary to the concept of self-realization in Vedandic Hinduism and the two major schools of Buddhism—Thervada and Mahayana. Hermsen (1996) has suggested that the concept of self, central to Rogers's psychotherapy, may be helpful in developing a synthesis of the psychology of religion, psychotherapy, and Taoism, while recognizing the cultural differences.

At the same time, a phenomenological view gives balance to psychology by providing a human voice in an expanding electronic world of computerization and reminds us that psychology is principally a human science (Mruk, 1989). Even though Rogers worked prior to the diagnosis of posttraumatic stress disorder, his account of threat-related psychological processes is consistent with contemporary trauma theory, and his therapy provides ways of helping traumatized persons. (Joseph, 2004).

Rogers's careful empirical study of the therapeutic process has shed considerable light on the phenomenon and practice of therapy. Scientific research has helped to clarify the types of situations and relationships that are conducive to change and validates his basic conditions for change (Elliot, Greenberg, & Lietaer, 2003, Norcross, 2002). Rogers's discussion of the therapist's attitude of acceptance is a helpful correction of Freud's overemphasis on transference. It is the real, personal relationship between therapist and client that fosters personality change. Rogers's most lasting contribution may be the therapeutic impact of the art of listening (Cain, 1990): an attitude of openness and readiness to hear, which is generally taken for granted and sounds so easy but in fact is exceedingly difficult to do. Rogers, in encouraging empirical validation of his theories, facilitated the development of person-centered therapeutic techniques. He was a pioneer in working with interracial and intercultural groups, and his approach can be modified for applicability in multicultural counseling (MacDougall, 2002) by modifying responses to cultural considerations (see also Kirschenbaum, 2004).

Rogers (1961) criticized the social and philosophical implications of a rigid behavioral science, such as that proposed by B. F. Skinner, who advocated the development of a technology to control human behavior (see the chapter on experimental analysis of behavior). Rogers believed that kind of society would destroy our personhood. He acknowledged that science brought us the power to manipulate; if we value the ability to control other people, our scientific technology can tell how to achieve this goal. On the other hand, if we value individual freedom and creativity, our scientific technology can facilitate these ends as well. In either case, the goal that directs the scientific enterprise lies outside of the scientific enterprise. The basic difference between a behavioristic approach and a humanistic approach is a philosophical choice (1980).

> **Philosophical Assumptions**
>
> Which philosophical assumptions were most important to Rogers? See the Philosophical Assumptions box "Examining Maslow and Rogers."

Rogers suggested that we need to be explicit about the goals we want our scientific endeavor to serve. In his role as scientist, he studied the predictability of the therapeutic process, not to control his client's behavior but to help his client be less predictable and more free, responsible, and spontaneous.

Psychologists have welcomed Rogers's reintroduction of the importance of subjectivity and perception in determining behavior, a theme consistent with the current cognitive emphasis. His therapeutic techniques have been widely applauded and adopted in education, industry, and social programs (Kirschenbaum

☀ Philosophical Assumptions

Examining Maslow and Rogers

Many of the differences among personality theories can be attributed to fundamental differences in philosophical assumptions. Which of the basic philosophical issues, described in the introductory chapter and summarized on the inside back cover, seem to be clearly important to Maslow and Rogers in the development of their theories? How, for example, does Maslow's hierarchy of human needs influence his stance on universality versus uniqueness? How does his portrait of the self-actualized person reflect his stance on proactivity versus reactivity? How does Rogers's incorporation of a phenomenological view influence his position on freedom versus determinism? Does his client-centered psychotherapy reflect an optimistic or pessimistic point of view? Do the theories of Maslow and Rogers address any other philosophical assumptions? Rate Maslow and Rogers on a scale of 1 to 5 on those philosophical assumptions that you feel their theories apply to most. Compare your ratings with your own philosophical assumptions. Did your study of Maslow and Rogers lead you to change any of your assumptions? Why or why not?

& Jourdan, 2005). Moreover, Rogers's theory prompted a great deal of further study and research, particularly concerning his concept of the self and the process of psychotherapy. Kohut incorporated many of Rogers's ideas into psychoanalytic self-theory and clinical method (Kahn & Rachman, 2000). Rogers's emphasis on human potentiality and freedom provides an attractive alternative to theories that emphasize the idea that we are largely controlled by external or unconscious forces. His theory has tremendous appeal for those who share his humanistic and optimistic philosophy of the human being.

Positive Psychology

The humanistic view of psychology that Maslow and Rogers advocated is a positive one. Martin Seligman and Mihaly Csikszentmihalyi have taken up the challenge of developing a framework for a twenty-first-century science of **positive psychology.** Noting that a focus on pathology has prevented psychology from focusing on the positive features of human beings that make life worth living, they have called upon leading psychologists to articulate an attractive vision of the good life based on empirical studies (Seligman & Csikszentmihalyi, 2000). The mission of positive psychology is to adapt the best of the scientific method to understanding the complex behavior of people in a way that emphasizes the systematic building and amplifying of human strength and virtues.

Positive psychology focuses on experience, traits, and institutions. The study of positive subjective *experience* involves research on contentment and satisfaction with the past, happiness and flow in the present, and optimism and hope for the future. Understanding *traits* entails the identification and study of positive virtues for individual growth, such as wisdom and knowledge, courage, humanity and love, justice, temperance, and transcendence. The study of *institutions* looks into positive strengths that promote better communities, such as responsibility, leadership, teamwork, work ethic, parenting, justice, and tolerance (Seligman, 2002). In short, positive psychology is the scientific inquiry into virtues and strengths that make it possible for individuals and communities to thrive.

Positive psychologists hope to develop a classification of human strengths—to be called *Values in Action (VIA) Classification of Strengths Manual*—that can serve as a counterpart to the *Diagnostic and Statistical Manual of Mental Disorders* developed by the American Psychiatric Association (Peterson & Seligman, 2003). The VIA classification seeks to operationally define, measure, and suggest interventions for the positive virtues that make up a good character. Twenty-four facets that contribute to six primary virtues have been identified (see Table 13.4). Some of these have already been studied and described using a wide range of instruments for assessment (Lopez & Snyder, 2003).

Research in positive psychology includes topics such as the positive experience (Why is one moment better than another?), the positive personality (What distinguishes happy positive people from unhappy negative ones?), and the positive social context (How do positive communities and institutions evolve and develop?). Previous studies on positive personal traits such as subjective well-being, optimism, happiness, and self-determination are incorporated into the new framework. Fostering excellence and encouraging positive mental and physical health are key elements of the framework for cultivating positive lives. At the same time, cultural expectations influence one's sense of satisfaction. In the United

TABLE 13.4 CLASSIFICATION OF STRENGTHS AND VIRTUES

Positive psychologists have identified twenty-four strengths under six basic virtues to be defined, measured and cultivated.

WISDOM AND KNOWLEDGE	JUSTICE
Curiosity/interest in the World	Citizenship/duty/teamwork/loyalty
Love of learning	Fairness and equity
Judgment/critical thinking/open-mindedness	Leadership
Ingenuity/originality/practical intelligence/street smarts	TEMPERANCE
Social intelligence/personal intelligence/emotional intelligence	Self-control
	Prudence/discretion/caution
Perspective	Humility and modesty
COURAGE	TRANSCENDENCE
Valor and bravery	Appreciation of beauty and excellence
Perseverance/industry/diligence	Gratitude
Integrity/genuineness/honesty	Hope/optimism/future-mindedness
HUMANITY AND LOVE	Spirituality/sense of purpose/faith/religiousness
	Forgiveness and mercy
Kindness and generosity	Playfulness and humor
Loving and allowing oneself to be loved	Zest/passion/enthusiasm

SOURCE: Seligman, M. E. (2002). Authentic happiness. New York: Free Press, pp. 140–158.

States, self-respect, self-knowledge, and self-expression lead to satisfaction, whereas in Japan, meeting social and family standards, having discipline, friendliness, and cooperation are key elements (Baird, 2004).

According to behavioral geneticist David Lykken (1999), humans have a basic "set point" or level of happiness that is largely genetic. However, research suggests that there are ways of living that increase feelings of happiness. Positive, optimistic, grateful, and loving thoughts, as well as exercise, meditation, and lovemaking, increase the level of neurotransmitters that help us to feel good. Positive life events, like negative ones, do not just happen to people; they are actively generated (Davidson, Shahar, Lawless, Sells, & Tondora, 2006). Contrary to what might be expected, as people become well-off financially they do not necessarily become happier (Layard, 2005). Joy comes primarily from relationships with other people. The more connected we are to others, the less likely we are to become despondent (Durkheim, 1897). Rather than imagining how we would feel, we can predict our happiness in a future situation more accurately by asking people of similar backgrounds who have had the same experience how happy their decisions made them (Gilbert, 2006). Training oneself to turn negative thoughts around, keeping a gratitude journal, and other positive behaviors help us to have a positive attitude and give us more energy.

Csikszentmihalyi (1990) suggests that people are most happy when they are in a state of flow and entirely involved in what they are doing. An optimal state of intrinsic motivation,

flow is a state of oneness with the activity and situation at hand. Flow entails heightened focus, productivity, and happiness. People in a state of flow are so engaged in what they are doing that they may even lose track of time. To achieve a state of flow, there has to be a balance between the challenge of the task and the skill of the performer: If the task is too easy or difficult, flow does not happen. Companies in the corporate world, such as Microsoft and Toyota, are drawing on Csikszentmihalyi's concept to figure how they can get the best out of their workers and connect with customers (Csikszentmihalyi, 2003). The movement of positive psychology has international appeal as well. The small Himalayan kingdom of Bhutan has declared its GNH (gross national happiness) quotient a higher priority than its GDP (gross domestic product) (Revlan, 2007). Other countries, such as Britain and Canada, are also developing indices of well-being.

Positive psychology is empirically oriented though open to philosophical viewpoints. It fosters the growth of interventions to facilitate individual growth and the development of empirical instruments to measure results. But do its formula (Seligman, 2002) $H = S + C + V$ (happiness equals your set point, conditions of life, and volunteer activities) and all of its research findings provide any information that is really new (Lanchester, 2006)? Concerns also have been expressed regarding positive psychology's emphasis or character strength at the possible expense of goodness and its dependence on quantitative self-reports, which may be misleading (Pawelski, 2004). Efforts are under way to use qualitative assessment to provide greater depth and help grasp complexities. In spite of the criticism, positive psychology has received an enthusiastic reception and is perceived as having enormous and promising practical implications (Seligman, Stein, Park & Peterson, 2005).

Transpersonal Psychology

Near the end of his life, Maslow urged the promotion of a "fourth force" (the three other forces being psychoanalysis, behaviorism, and humanistic psychology) to deal with spiritual and religious issues that had been previously neglected or given insufficient weight. Such a fourth force has emerged in the perspective of **transpersonal psychology,** a branch of psychology that studies the transcendent or spiritual dimensions of persons. The term *transpersonal* means "beyond the personal." Transpersonal psychology is concerned with those states and processes in which people experience a deeper or wider sense of who they are and a sense of greater connectedness with others, nature, and the "spiritual" dimension. Transpersonal psychology assumes that such experiences involve a higher mode of consciousness that transcends the ordinary self and ego. Western psychology has traditionally centered on prepersonal and personal aspects of personality rather than on transpersonal and spiritual dimensions. Transpersonal psychology combines findings from modern psychology with insights from the world's Eastern and Western contemplative traditions.

Jung used the term *transpersonal* in reference to the collective unconscious (see the chapter on analytical psychology). Maslow's research on self-actualized persons and peak experiences gave transpersonal psychology a major impetus. Transpersonal psychology recognizes its roots in psychoanalytic, behaviorist, and humanistic psychologies. It seeks to extend and place them in a new context without denying their validity. It also maintains that mystical and religious experiences—basic concerns of humanity for thousands of years—are valid approaches that can be studied scientifically. Transpersonal psychology moves from the personal to the transpersonal. Growth and maturation entails working through one's personal humanity in an inclusive manner to express the divinity within.

Transpersonal psychology emphasizes health and human potential, seeking a balance of the whole person: intellectual, emotional, spiritual, physical, social, and creative. It acknowledges that human beings have sexual and aggressive impulses but suggests that they also have drives toward wholeness and connecting with the divine. Looking to the sayings and deeds of great people (heroes and heroines, saints and prophets, artists in all creative media), transpersonal psychology conceives of the individual as moving forward toward the development of full humanity. One's personal history and individual personality (including one's traits, tendencies, and attributes) are merely the external shell of a transpersonal existence through which the soul and spirit can reveal itself.

The understanding of spirituality in transpersonal psychology differs from the popular conception of spirituality as belief or participation in an organized religion. Maslow included spirituality in his drive toward self-actualization. Transpersonal psychology maintains that people are born with needs for spiritual and transcendent experiences. **Spirituality** involves a person's relationship to existential issues that go beyond everyday reality. When our desire for spirituality is not met, we may turn to false "spiritualities" such as alcohol and drugs, codependent relationships, and fanatical causes. Other spiritual problems may include loss of faith, near-death experience, and spiritual crises due to sudden and intense spiritual disruption into one's life. Many of these concerns are not usually considered by mainstream psychology; however, with the encouragement of transpersonal psychologists, a new category, "religious or spiritual problem," was incorporated into the DSM-IV.

> **Thinking Critically**
>
> Is spirituality an appropriate topic for psychological study? See the Thinking Critically Box "Should Psychologists Study Spirituality?"

Many of the phenomena that interest transpersonal psychologists have previously been dismissed by traditional psychologists as signs of various forms of mental illness or as regressions to infantile states of psychological development. Religious and spiritual experiences have been perceived and treated as regressive or pathological, a confusion that Ken Wilber has termed the pre/trans fallacy (1977). Transpersonal psychologists suggest that there is a difference between prerational psychiatric problems and authentic transpersonal problems.

Charles Tart (1975) pioneered empirical research into altered states of consciousness, and Ken Wilber has been a major contributor to transpersonal psychology (although he has since separated himself from the movement in favor of developing an "integral theory of consciousness"). In a project that "opened up the horizon far beyond anything conceived in Western scientific psychology" (Puhakka, 1999), Wilber (1977) developed a model of consciousness that integrates the philosophies and psychologies of the ancient and modern West and East. In his theory, "Spirit" replaces the personal self at the center of development and evolves (through us) through prepersonal, personal, and transpersonal manifestations as it journeys toward self knowledge. At the highest transpersonal level, the *superior viewpoint,* dualities disappear and the Spirit pervades everything, including and extending beyond the human self.

Transpersonal psychology seeks to establish itself as an academic discipline and has been integrated into some psychology departments in the United States and Europe. This inclusion has helped to counter the description of it as a type of New Age exploration or a reli-

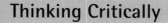

Thinking Critically

Should Psychologists Study Spirituality?

Psychology emerged as a science in the late nineteenth century and sought to establish itself as a credible science by focusing on objective empirical data and emulating established sciences such as physics in its methodology. Transpersonal psychology draws upon the spiritual, a topic that many psychologists have shunned because it is not seen as based on empirical data. Do you think psychologists should study the spiritual and spirituality? Does the nature of spiritual phenomena render them out of bounds for scientific study? Should psychology alter its methods of study in order to adequately encompass the spiritual? How might that best be done?

gious or spiritual movement. Although it has not been granted formal status by the American Psychological Association, a Transpersonal Psychology Section has been established in the British Psychology Society. Jennings (1999) suggests that transpersonal psychology, using Jung's typology, expresses the neglected interior function in American psychology, needs to be incorporated into it, and offers great potential and promise for the development of psychology in the third millennium.

TO LEARN MORE about unconditional positive regard and transpersonal psychology, and for a list of suggested readings, visit the *Personality Theories* textbook website at **college.cengage.com/pic/engler8e.**

Summary

1. Abraham Maslow has been called the spiritual father of humanistic psychology. He criticized psychoanalysis for being pessimistic and negative, and behavior and learning theories for being mechanistic.

2. Maslow distinguished between **motivation** (p. 350) and **metamotivation** (p. 350), which entail **D-needs** (p. 350) and **B-needs** (p. 350), respectively. Motivation and the D-needs take precedence over metamotivation and the B-needs.

3. Maslow's **hierarchy of needs** (p. 351) includes physiological, safety, belonging and love, self-esteem, and **self-actualization** (p. 352) needs.

4. Self-actualized persons fulfill themselves and do the best that they are capable of doing. Maslow described key characteristics of self-actualizers as awareness, honesty, freedom, and trust. A **peak experience** (p. 354), entails a transcendence of self.

5. Deci and Ryan have developed self-determination theory (SDT).

6. Some critics suggest that Maslow's picture of self-actualized persons is simplistic and neglects the hard work that is involved in growth and development. Others suggest it is based on American values and a Western male paradigm of individual achievement.

7. Maslow's theory points in a direction away from pure science. His work underscores the fact that rigorous scientific procedures may not encompass or permit research into important human questions.

8. Rogers's humanist theory is influenced by **phenomenology** (p. 359), which emphasizes that what is important is not an object or event in itself but how it is perceived. In psychology this means an emphasis on human awareness and the conviction that the best vantage point for understanding an individual is that of the individual him- or herself. The **phenomenal field** (p. 350) is the total sum of experiences an organism has; the organism is the individual as a process; the **self** (p. 361) is a concept of who one is. Self-actualization is the dynamic within the organism leading it to actualize, fulfill, and enhance its potentials. Emotions accompany and facilitate the process of actualization. Fully experiencing emotions facilitates growth, and repression is unnecessary.

9. **Congruence** (p. 362) exists when a person's symbolized experiences reflect actual experiences. The pressure of denial or distortion in the symbolization leads to **incongruence** (p. 362).

10. The young child has a strong need for **positive regard** (p. 363). Ideally, positive regard is **unconditional** (p. 363). If it is contingent upon specific behaviors, it is **conditional positive regard** (p. 363) and posits **conditions of worth** that may lead a child to introject the values of others and experience incongruence.

11. Rogers is best known for his method of person-centered therapy. The three attitudes on the part of the therapist that he thought were necessary and sufficient for change are: **empathy, acceptance,** and **genuineness** (p. 365).

12. Rogers distinguished among five responses to emotional communications: **evaluative, interpretative, reassuring, probing,** and **reflective responses** (p. 366). Each of them has different effects. Rogers encouraged the cultivation of reflective responses.

13. **Person-centered psychotherapy** (p. 364) tends to be **supportive** (p. 367) rather than **reconstructive** (p. 367). In his later writings, Rogers stressed the need for the therapist to be present as a person in the relationship and showed more interest in group counseling and social change. He encouraged the empirical test of his theories and developed methods of assessing and predicting therapeutic change.

14. Rogers was very careful to distinguish between his philosophical assumptions and his scientific hypotheses. He criticized Skinner's view of science and his goal of controlling human nature rather than increasing human freedom, responsibility, and spontaneity. He pointed out that technology may be used to foster many different goals. His own position has been criticized for its reliance on a simplistic phenomenology and for being highly culture-bound. It has been praised for increasing understanding of interpersonal relationships. Rogers's careful empirical study of the therapeutic process has shed considerable light on the phenomenon of therapy and counseling.

15. **Positive psychology** (p. 373) seeks to study and understand the complex positive behavior of people in order to emphasize the systematic building and amplifying of human strengths and virtues.

16. **Transpersonal psychology** (p. 375) is concerned with those states and processes in which people experience a deeper or wider sense of who they are and a sense of greater connectedness with others, nature, and a "spiritual" dimension.

Personal Experiences

1. Maslow proposed that there is a hierarchy of needs that we need to meet in order to reach our full potential. The needs he outlined, starting with the strongest and most basic, are as follows: physiological, safety, belonging and love, self-esteem, and self-actualization. At what level on Maslow's hierarchy would you position yourself? Assess which of your needs have been met thus far in your life. Review Figure 13.1 and the discussion of each need. If there's a need that has not been adequately met, how is it impacting your life? Consider your friends and what they have told you. Can you detect needs in their lives that have not been adequately met?

2. Maslow identified fifteen characteristics of self-actualized persons (see Table 13.1). How many people do you know who seem to have achieved self-actualization? Does anyone you know meet Maslow's criteria? If so, who? If there are a few people, are you noticing any generalizable trends? Are these self-actualized individuals old, young, male, female? Explain your findings.

3. Rogers focused on the way in which the opinions of others impede or facilitate self-actualization. He stressed the importance of positive regard—being loved and accepted for who one is. Rogers distinguished between unconditional and conditional positive regard. Regard is unconditional when parents communicate to a child that the child's behavior is bad, not the child. Regard is conditional when parents tend to communicate that the child is a bad person. Think back to your childhood. How did your parents scold you when you did something wrong? Did they tell you that you were bad or that your behavior was bad? Informally poll your friends and family about their parents' scolding styles. Are there any discernible trends in child rearing that you can detect, such as by generation, gender, or class? Explain your feelings.

4. Would Carl Rogers recognize you as a fully functioning person? The five criteria to be met are (1) openness to experience, (2) existential living, (3) organismic trust, (4) experiential freedom, and (5) creativity, (see Table 13.2). After assessing yourself, assess your friends. Do you believe that any of them meet all five criteria? Note which categories each person fulfills and falls short of. Then ask your friends to assess themselves and you. Compare assessments. Are they relatively similar? Explain your findings.

5. What type of communicator are you? Rogers described five types of responses to emotional communication: (1) evaluative, (2) interpretative, (3) reassuring, (4) probing, and (5) reflective (see Table 13.3). Think about a conversation you've had in the recent past that dealt with an emotional issue. How did you handle the situation? Into which of Rogers's five types does your response fit? How do you tend to respond in emotional situations? If you're not sure, ask your closest friends and family—the persons most likely to receive your responses. Now that you're becoming aware of different emotional responses, think about how you would prefer to be responded to. In a crisis, which type of response do you think you'd prefer to receive?

CHAPTER 14

Existential Psychoanalysis

▪ Rollo May

YOUR GOALS FOR THIS CHAPTER

1. Identify two major traditions that May combines.
2. Describe the philosophy of **existentialism.**
3. Explain the existentialist approach to scientific methodology.
4. Describe the central problem May believed we face.
5. Explain how May conceived of **anxiety,** and tell how it is intensified in contemporary culture.
6. Discuss the source of the human dilemma according to May.
7. Identify four ontological assumptions May made concerning human beings, and explain how they can give us a structural basis for a science of personality.
8. Discuss what is involved in rediscovering selfhood.
9. Show how May confronted the **paradoxes** involved in each of the following goals of integration: love, **intentionality,** the **daimonic,** courage and creativity, power, freedom and destiny.
10. Explain how May defined **myth** and why he believed we need new myths.
11. Describe the existentialist approach to psychotherapy.
12. Describe May's methods of assessment and research.
13. Evaluate May's theory from the viewpoints of philosophy, science, and art.

Existentialism and psychoanalysis grew out of the same cultural situation. Both seek to understand anxiety, despair, and the alienation that people feel from themselves and society. During the last half of the nineteenth century, there was a strong tendency to thinking of people as cogs in the industrial system in which they worked. This mechanistic view had a psychological counterpart in extreme repression within the individual. It was Freud's genius to speak to, and help cure, the problem of repression (May, Angel, & Ellenberger, 1958). However, the problem went deeper than neurotic repression in the individual. Kierkegaard, Nietzsche, and other forerunners of the existentialist position believed that forces of disintegration were gradually destroying individuals' inner emotional and spiritual life, producing despair and alienation from self and society.

Rollo May's work brings together the psychoanalytic tradition in psychology and the existentialist movement in philosophy. As we have seen, Freud's writings, though transcending his own era, nevertheless clearly reflect tendencies of nineteenth-century philosophy that are considered inappropriate today. In combining the insights of psychoanalysis and existentialism, May not only clarified the continued relevance of many of Freud's contributions but also developed his own original stance. In doing so, he helped underscore the importance of philosophy and the understanding of values for the psychologist and the theory of personality. His work has earned him the title of father of American existential psychology (Bugental, 1996a).

Biographical Background

Rollo May was born on April 21, 1909, in Ada, Ohio, and grew up in Marine City, Michigan, where a middle-American anti-intellectual attitude prevailed. His father commented several times that a psychotic breakdown experienced by Rollo's older sister was due to "too much education." May felt that the comment was "inhumane and destructive" and came to hate the disease of anti-intellectualism. However, he indicates that in other respects his father was a very sympathetic man (1983).

May graduated from Oberlin College in Ohio, where he received the A.B. in 1930. In college he marveled at the simple yet beautiful lines of an antique Greek vase displayed on a table in one of the classrooms and resolved to go to Greece, which he did immediately after his graduation. He worked in Greece for three years, teaching at Anatolia College in Salonika and traveling during the summer. He spent two summers with a group of modern artists, painting and studying peasant art. The impact of Greek philosophy and mythology is clear in his writings. He also went to Vienna and studied briefly with Alfred Adler, whose approach influenced him considerably.

Europe's tragic view of human nature prevented May from ever accepting a mechanistic concept of the person (see also Bugental, 1996b). Upon his return to the United States, American psychology seemed "naive and simplistic." So he enrolled at Union Theological Seminary in New York—not with the intent of becoming a preacher, but with the intent of asking questions. There he could raise penetrating inquiries into the meaning of despair, suicide, and anxiety, issues largely ignored by psychologists. He also hoped that in doing so he might learn about their counterparts: courage, joy, and the intensity of living (1983; see

Rollo May's work brings together the psychoanalytic tradition in psychology and the existentialist movement in philosophy.

also Abzug, 1996). At Union, he began a lifetime friendship with the eminent Protestant theologian Paul Tillich (1886–1965), an association that enriched the lives, work, and writings of both men.

May's parents were divorced while he was at Union, so he interrupted his studies and returned to East Lansing, Michigan, to take care of what remained of his family—his mother, a younger sister, and a brother. During that time, he served as an adviser to students at Michigan State College. He was able to return to New York and receive the B.D. in 1938. During his senior year at Union, his first book, *The Art of Counseling,* was written. Thereafter, May served briefly as a parish minister in Montclair, New Jersey, before going back to New York to study psychoanalysis at the William Alanson White Institute for Psychiatry, Psychoanalysis, and Psychology. He enrolled at Columbia University and received its first Ph.D. in clinical psychology.

May's life was sharply interrupted when he came down with tuberculosis in his early thirties. At that time there was no medication for the disease. May spent three years at the Saranac TB Sanatorium in upstate New York, not knowing whether he would live or die. During his illness, he read, among other works, *The Problem of Anxiety* by Freud and *The Concept of Dread* by Sören Kierkegaard, the founder of the existential movement in philosophy. He appreciated Freud's careful formulations but felt that Kierkegaard "portrayed what is immediately experienced by human beings in crisis" (1969). May's illness helped him to appreciate an existential point of view. His own book *The Meaning of Anxiety* (1977) is widely recognized as the first in America to encourage a genuine union between psychology and philosophy and to demonstrate the importance of values for psychology.

May's professional life was busy and productive. He served as a counselor to college students at City College of New York, developed a private practice in psychoanalysis, and became a member of the White Institute. He taught at The New School for Social Research, New York University, Harvard, Yale, and Princeton. He has numerous publications and was honored with several awards. May died in 1994.

The Existential Attitude

Existentialism is a movement in contemporary philosophy and psychology that sprang up spontaneously in different parts of Europe and among different schools of thought. It has its roots in the resistance movements during World War II and in the philosophies of Sören

Kierkegaard (1813–1855), Martin Heidegger (1889–1976), and Jean-Paul Sartre (1905–1980). The word *existentialism* comes from the Latin *exsistere*, which means "to stand out" or "to emerge." The existential approach focuses on the human being as he or she is emerging and becoming.

Western philosophy has traditionally looked for the **essence** of being, the unchangeable principles and laws that are believed to govern existence. Mathematics is the purest form of this approach. In psychology, the essentialist attitude expresses itself in the effort to understand human beings in terms of forces, drives, and conditioned reflexes. Existentialists point out that a law can be true yet not be real. "Two unicorns plus two unicorns equals four unicorns" is a logically true statement, but it does not talk about anything that is real. Existentialism seeks to bridge the gap between what is abstractly true and what is existentially real (May et al., 1958).

The existential attitude can be a bewildering one that defies simple definition. We can illustrate it, however, by comparing two possible postures that a person might have at a football game. The first is that of a spectator up in the stands; the second is that of a player on the field.

Both spectator and player are involved in the football game, but there is considerable difference in their involvement. The spectator may become very agitated and excited as the game proceeds, urging and cheering on a favorite team. But the outcome of the game does not depend on the activity of the spectator, who remains outside the game as an observer. The outcome does depend very much on how the player behaves and performs on the field. The player cannot stand back and observe the game while being involved in it.

The posture of existentialism is that of the player, and the game of existentialism is the game of life. In life, existentialists point out, we cannot play the role of detached or uninvolved spectators because we are already participants in the game.

Existentialists suggest that there is no truth or reality for us as human beings except as we participate in it, are conscious of it, and have some relation to it. Knowledge is not an act

of thinking but an act of doing. Existentialists do not necessarily rule out essences but insist that "existence precedes essence." May, for example, did not deny the validity of concepts such as conditioning or drives. He simply pointed out that we cannot adequately explain a person on that basis because when we try to, we end up talking about abstractions rather than the living person. It is all right to have concepts, but we must recognize that they are only tools and not substitutes for the living person. Thus, when we use concepts, we must make it clear that we are abstracting them from the living person and we are not talking about the real person.

The existential attitude can be illustrated by comparing the postures of a football player and of a spectator at a football game.

Psychologists have generally tended to study those phenomena that lend themselves to control and analysis and permit one to formulate abstract laws. They are not particularly concerned with whether or not the phenomena are real or even close to everyday life. Indeed, in some laboratory experiments, the phenomenon under consideration is far removed from real life. Existentialists believe that psychologists' preoccupation with lawfulness and predictability stands in the way of understanding the real person. May pointed out that the behavior of a neurotic is quite predictable because it is compulsive, whereas the healthy person is "predictable" in that behavior is dependable and consistent, but at the same time a healthy person can be flexible and spontaneous. The existentialist approach has been criticized for rendering the individual unlawful and unpredictable. It is true that existentialists do not see the human being in terms of our traditional conceptual theories, looking instead at the structure of a particular person's existence and its own lawfulness.

The existentialist approach is not antiscientific. It arose out of a desire to be not *less* but *more* empirical, but it does urge a greater breadth to our scientific methodology. Contrary to the conventional approach of the scientist in which the more complex is explained by the simpler, existentialists believe that a reductionistic approach misleads and that the "simpler can be understood and explained only in terms of the more complex" (May, 1969). When a new level of complexity emerges, it becomes crucial for understanding the forms that have preceded it. What makes a horse a horse is not what it shares with the organisms it evolved from but what constitutes its distinctive "horseness" (1983). Science, therefore, must look for the distinguishing characteristic of what it is trying to understand—namely, the human being.

The existentialist view takes the inquiry to a deeper level to look at the structure in which those concepts are rooted. It seeks to develop an empirical science that deals with the whole of our knowledge of what it means to be human. As such, it looks at the unity of the person prior to any split into subject versus object, body versus mind, nature versus nurture, or any other conceptual "either-or" dimensions. It asks what it means to be and to exist under these particular psychological, cultural, and historical conditions.

In studying the structure of human existence, the very nature of the subject shapes the science that investigates it. Existentialists have made clear the limits of objectivity in our understanding and the need to broaden the scope of our methodology. Objectivity is a goal that many psychologists have prized and sought to achieve. They believe that unless we are objective, our emotions and prejudices will come between us and the facts, clouding our reasoning processes. Students of psychology are encouraged to take a detached, objective stance. At times, however, objectivity prevents understanding. Some truths, such as understanding what it means to be, are discovered not by objectivity but by intense personal involvement. The existentialist attitude strongly resists the tendency to treat a person as an object.

In their insistence that human knowledge is ultimately interpersonal, May and other existentialists are indebted to the thought of Martin Buber (1878–1965), whose book *I and Thou* made a classic distinction between knowing that is transpersonal (I-Thou) and knowing that is objective or subjective (I-it). In his book, Buber describes an entirely different way in which the world, particularly the world of persons, reveals itself to us. Knowledge is not simply objective (of an external object) or subjective (of the self) but also interpersonal, arising out of the encounter of human beings with one another. Understanding through encounter is just as real as understanding through objectification.

Existentialism begins with personal existence. It asks, "What does it mean to be a self?" It questions the purpose and nature of existence. It views individuals as agents with free choices who are responsible for their actions. Each one of us carves out his or her own destiny. We are literally what we do. The existentialist posture leads to an emphasis on choice and responsibility and to the view that a worthwhile life is one that is authentic, honest, and genuine.

Our Predicament

May pointed out (1967) that the central problem that we face is a feeling of *powerlessness,* a "pervasive conviction that the individual cannot do anything effective in the face of enormous cultural, social, and economic problems." Our feelings of powerlessness are compounded by anxiety and the loss of traditional values.

POWERLESSNESS

The problem of powerlessness goes much deeper than the fact that this is an age of uncertainty and social upheavals. May believed that the unwanted war in Vietnam and the continued unrest in the Middle East illustrate how we can become caught in a historical situation in which no one person or group of persons feels capable of exercising significant power. With our increased technology, power has become impersonal, an autonomous force acting on its own behalf (1967).

In the early 1950s, May observed that many of the patients who came to see him were suffering from inner feelings of emptiness (1953). He noted that the neurotic frequently acts out what others are temporarily unaware of. May anticipated that the experience of emptiness and powerlessness he was seeing in his patients would in time become epidemic. The 1970s saw considerable talk about human potentialities, yet very little confidence on the part of individuals about their power to make a significant difference (1975). This feeling of paralysis accompanied us throughout the remainder of the twentieth century and into the twenty-first.

May believed that the most striking example of the individual's sense of insignificance and powerlessness is the impotence many of us feel concerning the threat of nuclear war or accident. The potentiality for such disaster rapidly increases along with a recognition that it could begin through a simple incident such as a computer malfunction. The threat of nuclear war and other unsettling social conditions are but symptoms of the deeper problem. Contemporary men and women feel helpless and insignificant. Our impotence leads to anxiety and repression, leading in turn to apathy, which is a form of protection. Impotence and apathy, however, also breed violence and hostility that further alienate us from one another and only serve to increase our isolation (1972). Since September 11, 2001, the threat of terrorism has further heightened our feelings of powerlessness.

ANXIETY

It has become commonplace to describe our age as an age of anxiety. However, prior to 1950, only two books had been written that concerned themselves specifically with presenting an objective picture of anxiety and suggesting constructive ways of dealing with it: Freud's *The Problem of Anxiety* and Kierkegaard's *The Concept of Dread.* After May wrote

The Meaning of Anxiety, which was first published in 1950, hundreds of works followed on the same topic. May's efforts helped to spur research into this area. *The Meaning of Anxiety* was revised in 1977, and at that time May pointed out that the tremendous interest in anxiety that attended its initial publication had indicated the need for an integrated theory of anxiety. May's work is distinguished by its efforts to synthesize the insights of both psychology and philosophy. After that time, he applied his analytic synthesis to the dilemmas of love and will, power and innocence, creativity, and freedom and destiny.

Some psychologists prefer to use the term *stress* in place of anxiety. May believed that this tendency is unfortunate and inaccurate. The word *stress* has become popular because it comes from engineering and physics; it can be defined easily and measured accurately. The problem with the concept of stress is that it does not adequately describe the apprehension we ordinarily refer to as anxiety. Moreover, it puts the emphasis on what happens to a person, whereas anxiety is distinctly bound up with consciousness and subjectivity (1977).

May proposed the following definition of **anxiety:** "Anxiety is the apprehension cued off by a threat to some value that the individual holds essential to his or her existence as a person" (1977). Anxiety is an inevitable characteristic of being human (1983), a given. Anxiety is objectless "because it strikes at that basis of the psychological structure on which the perception of one's self as distinct from the world of objects occurs" (1977). Thus in anxiety, the distinction between self and object breaks down.

The potential for anxiety is innate, although the particular events that may become threatening are learned. Fear is the expression of anxiety in a specific objectified form. May suggested that anxiety is intensified in our contemporary competitive culture by the interpersonal isolation and alienation that have emerged out of a particular pattern in which one's self is viewed as an object and self-validation depends on winning over others (1977). Anxiety, therefore, is another symptom of the deeper problem. Kagan (1994) reminds us that the primary source of anxiety in our time is not the major source of anxiety in all of time, reflecting a universal truth about human nature. A particular culture may elevate one facet of anxiety to a dominant position, but only temporarily. The situations that provoke anxiety in our time would be incomprehensible to a Tibetan villager.

Our current stepped-up efforts to dispel anxiety actually end up increasing it. May reminded us that we cannot live in an empty condition for a sustained period of time (1953). We need something to fill the gap, be it a destructive authority, drugs, or alcohol. In the twentieth century, the emotional vacuum in Europe permitted fascist dictators to seize power. Today, many young people "waste" themselves on alcohol and drugs. The problem is that human consciousness, responsibility, and intentions have not been able to keep up with all of the rapid changes in contemporary society. If we were able to recognize our historical situation and its psychological implications, we might be able to move from self-defeating activities to constructive ones.

THE LOSS OF VALUES

The source of our problem lies in the loss of the center of values in our society (May, 1967). Ever since the Renaissance, the dominant value in Western society has been competitive prestige measured in terms of work and financial success. Such values are no longer effective in the postmodern world, in which we have to learn to work with other people in order to survive. Individual competition no longer brings the greatest good to one's self or to the community. Instead, it creates problems where previously it did not.

Our ability to stand outside of ourselves and relate to ourselves permits us to create values that help to shape our lives (1967). For several centuries, we were able to validate ourselves by our power over nature. Then we began to supply the methods that had been so successful in understanding and controlling nature to ourselves. In so doing, we rendered ourselves impersonal objects that could be exploited. Along with the loss of the dominant value of individualism, we lost a sense of the worth and dignity of the human being. We became estranged from nature and from one another. Today, many people are more comfortable conversing with a computer than with another human being. The loneliness and isolation that were potential in Western society have become widely apparent in our time.

The answer to our dilemma is to discover and affirm a new set of values. There are those who would suggest that we need to reaffirm the traditional values, embodied in earlier philosophies and religion, that we have permitted to go by the wayside.

Thinking Critically

How do times of change and crisis lead us to rethink our values? See the Thinking Critically box "After 9/11."

Here, May's existential stance becomes apparent. Because we have no "essence," there are no given or preestablished values to which we can turn. Our values are established in the course of our existence, and our destiny now includes the historical situation in which we have placed ourselves (1981). There can be no simple reaffirmation of our human "essence," because there is none; the human being is forever in the process of becoming. We have to choose our values in the process of living. Significant times of change and crisis, such as the aftermath of the terrorist attacks of September 11, lead us to rethink, reaffirm, and/or choose new values.

The choice is ours, and so is the responsibility. We can withdraw in anxiety, giving up our distinctive human capacity to influence our own development through our awareness; we can surrender to the power of the technology that we created; or we can muster the courage that we need to preserve our sensitivity and responsibility and consciously work together in developing a new society (1975).

Rediscovering Selfhood

May (1953) believed that *consciousness of self* is the unique mark of the human person. Self-consciousness enables us to distinguish between ourselves and the world, to learn from the past and to plan for the future, to see ourselves as others do, and to have empathy with

Thinking Critically

After 9/11

Significant times of change and crisis, such as the aftermath of the terrorist attacks of September 11, 2001, lead us to rethink, reaffirm, or choose new values. How have the terrorist attacks led you to rethink your willingness to give up your privacy, independence, and time in favor of greater security? your attitude toward profiling? your desire to continue or change current immigration policies? Are there other values and issues that you have been rethinking in light of those events?

others. However, such self-consciousness comes at the risk of anxiety and inward crisis. It means that we must stand on our own and develop an identity apart from that of our parents and forebears. We can even stand against them, if necessary.

Unlike the acorn that grows automatically into an oak tree, the human being, in self-actualizing, must do so consciously through choice and affirmation. Selfhood is not automatic but arises in a social context and grows in interpersonal relations. However, May's emphasis is not on the extent to which we are created by others, but rather is on our capacity to create and experience our own selves.

Some psychologists avoid the concept of self because it separates humans from animals and complicates scientific experimentation. May, along with Rogers and Maslow, believed that in doing so psychologists miss an important feature of the human experience. Our capacity for self-relatedness is prior to, not established by, our science. It is presupposed in the fact that one can be a scientist. May wanted to see us develop a science to illuminate the concept of self.

ONTOLOGICAL ASSUMPTIONS CONCERNING THE PERSON

Many psychologists emphasize the study of behavior, but May believed that they need to ask questions on a deeper *ontological* level—the level of being. They need to ask what is the nature of the person as a person and how can we best describe human existence.

As a clinician, May frankly admitted that he made certain ontological and philosophical assumptions about what it means to be a human being (1967). First, he assumed that all living organisms are potentially centered in themselves and seek to preserve that center. In psychotherapy, a patient is engaged in the process of such preservation. Second, human be-

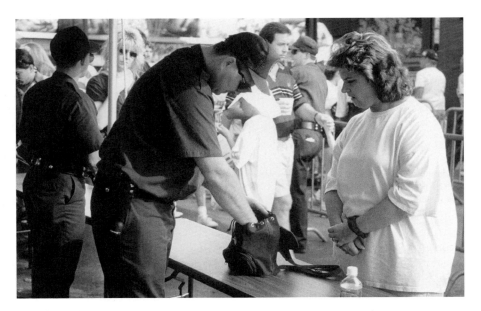

Since the terrorist attacks of September 11, 2001, people have been willing to submit to inconvenience, surveillance, and loss of privacy in hopes of greater security.

ings have the need and the possibility of going out from their centeredness to participate with other people. This entails risk and is illustrated in psychotherapy in the encounter with the therapist. Third, May suggested that sickness is a method whereby an individual seeks to preserve his or her being, a strategy for survival, even though that method may be limiting and may block off potentials for knowledge and action. Finally, May asserted that human beings can participate in a level of self-consciousness that permits them to transcend the immediate situation and to consider and actualize a wider range of possibilities. These ontological assumptions can give us a structural basis for a science of personality. They precede analytic activity and make it possible. In turn, our analytic activity can help to illumine them.

Psychological concepts need to be oriented within an ontological framework. Thus May suggested that the concept of *unconscious experience* can be understood in terms of self-deception and experiences that an individual cannot actualize. May interpreted the Oedipal myth and conflict as indicative of the problems involved in a person's relation to the world through the emergence and development of consciousness (1967). The main question in the drama does not concern murder and incest but is "Shall Oedipus recognize what he has done?" It is significant that Oedipus plucks out his eyes and thereby blinds himself, rather than, for example, attacking his genitals. What is at issue is seeing reality and the truth about oneself.

May believed that the theme of exile in the story is very important. Oedipus was exiled as a baby, and at the end of the drama he exiles himself. Being aware that one is responsible for one's life, a person can confront life and death. This is why the symbol of suicide is centrally placed in the existentialist approach.

REDISCOVERING FEELINGS

In rediscovering selfhood, most people have to start back at the beginning and rediscover their feelings (1953). Many of us have only a vague idea of what we are feeling at any given time. We react to our bodies as if they were separate and distinct. While denying our own emotions, we ascribe feelings to machines, describing them as "friendly," "affectionate," and so forth. We need to recognize that we play an active role in creating our bodies and feelings. Awareness of one's body and feelings lays the groundwork for knowing what one wants. Surprisingly few people are actually clear about what they want. Being aware of one's desires does not imply that one must act on them. But we cannot have any basis for judging what we will and will not do unless we first know what we want to do.

Becoming a person requires not only getting in touch with one's feelings and desires but also fighting against those things that prevent us from feeling and wanting (1953). The development of a human being is a process of differentiation from an original unity with the mother toward freedom as an individual. The physical umbilical cord is cut at birth, but the infant is still dependent on its mother. Unless the psychological cord is severed in due time, the individual's growth is stunted. In order to advance and be oneself, a person has to become free of domineering and authoritarian powers even if that requires taking a stand against one's parents or other authorities. It is our infantile ties of dependency that keep us from being clear as to our feelings and wants. The early struggle against authority is external; as we grow, the problem becomes internal. Thus as adults many of us continue to act as if we still have to fight the original forces that enslaved us when in fact we are now enslaving ourselves.

FOUR STAGES OF CONSCIOUSNESS OF SELF

May (1953) suggested that there are four stages of consciousness of self. The first is the *stage of innocence* before consciousness of self is born. This stage is characteristic of the infant. The second is the *stage of rebellion* in which the individual seeks to establish some inner strength. The "no" of the toddler and the "no way" of the adolescent illustrate this stage, which may involve defiance and hostility. The rebellious individual seeks freedom but does not comprehend the responsibility that accompanies it. The third stage is *ordinary consciousness of self.* This is the stage most people refer to when they speak of a healthy personality. It involves being able to learn from one's mistakes and live responsibly. May referred to the fourth stage as *creative consciousness of self.* It involves the ability to see something outside one's usual limited viewpoint and gain a glimpse of ultimate truth as it exists in reality. This level cuts through the dichotomy between subjectivity and objectivity. Not everyone achieves each stage of consciousness. The fourth stage, achieved only rarely, is somewhat analogous to Maslow's peak experience. Nevertheless, it is the level that gives meaning to our actions and experiences on the lesser levels.

The Goals of Integration

May conceived of the human being as conscious of self, capable of intentionality, and needing to make choices. In his existential analysis of personality, May sought to undercut the traditional dualism of subject and object that has haunted Western self-understanding ever since Descartes, who said that we are conscious of ourselves either as a subject or as an object. May considered the self as a unity. In his discussion of the goals of integration, May further revealed an intent to discuss key issues in personality in such a way as to avoid the tendency to abstract the real person and life itself into artificial dualisms and constructs. Instead of abstract conceptualizations, we need to recognize and confront the paradoxes of our own lives (1981). In **paradox** two opposing things are posited against and seem to negate each other, yet they cannot exist without each other. Thus, good and evil, life and death, beauty and ugliness appear to be at odds with each other, but the very confrontation with the one breathes life and meaning into the other. "Harmony," as Heraclitus reminded us, "consists of opposing tension, like that of the bow and the lyre" (May, 1981). The goals of integration include confronting one's potentialities for the daimonic, power, love, intentionality, freedom and destiny, and courage and creativity.

THE DAIMONIC

In a world that vaunts rationality, May (1969) reintroduced the concept of the daimonic and insists that we come to terms with it. The **daimonic** is "any natural function which has the power to take over the whole person." Sex, anger, a craving for power, all of these may become evil when they take over the self without regard for the integration of the self. We can repress the daimonic but we cannot avoid its consequences. In repressing it, we become its pawns.

The daimonic is potentially creative and destructive at the same time. By becoming aware of it, we can integrate it into ourselves. We can learn to cherish our internal demons and permit them to give us the salt of life. The daimonic begins as impersonal; by bringing it into consciousness, one makes the daimonic urges personal. With a more sensitive understanding of these forces in one's body and life, the daimonic pushes one toward the universal structure of reality. The movement is from impersonal to personal to a transpersonal dimension of consciousness (1969).

POWER

A basic factor in our contemporary crisis is the feeling of insignificance and powerlessness. Human life can be seen as a conflict between achieving a sense of the significance of one's self on the one hand and the feeling of powerlessness on the other. We tend to avoid both sides, the former because of evil connotations associated with being too powerful and the latter because our powerlessness is too painful to bear.

Violence has its breeding ground in impotence and apathy. As we make people powerless, we encourage their violence rather than control it. Violent deeds such as the taking of hostages are done by those who seek to enhance their self-esteem. Powerless people sometimes invite exploitation in order to feel significant or seek revenge in passive-aggressive ways, such as the ways of drugs and alcohol.

May pointed out that the argument against violence on television would be stronger if it were made against the passive character of television viewing rather than against the emulation of aggressive models. Televised entertainment cultivates the spectator role rather than active participation; as such, its greatest danger may lie in the cultivation of feelings of impotence that contribute to violent behavior.

"The culture admittedly has powerful effects upon us. But it could not have these effects were these tendencies not already present in us, for, . . . we constitute the culture" (1983).

Power is an ontological state of being. The potentiality to experience and to express power is present in all of us. No one can escape experiencing power in desire or in action. Our goal is to learn how to use our power in ways that are appropriate for the situation, to be assertive rather than aggressive. We must find social ways of sharing and distributing power so that every person can feel significant.

LOVE AND SEX

Love used to be seen as the answer to human problems. Now love itself has become the problem (1969). The real problem is being able to love. Our world is schizoid, out of touch, unable to feel or to enter into a close relationship. Affectlessness and apathy are predominant attitudes toward life, forms of protection against the tremendous overstimulation of modern society.

According to May, televised entertainment cultivates the spectator role, which leads to feelings of impotence and contributes to violent behavior.

May believed that our highly vaunted sexual freedom has turned out to be a new form of puritanism in which emotion is separated from reason and the body is used as a machine. Pornography and commercialization have also turned sex into a vehicle for power. We have set sex against *eros,* the drive to relate to another person and create new forms of life. It is now socially sanctioned to repress eros, and we rush to the sensation of sex in order to avoid the passion and responsibility that eros commands. The sexual freedom established during the 1960s and 1970s has not led to the increase in happiness that many thought would follow a freeing of sexual mores. The premature awakening of sex so prevalent in our time can lead us to dodge awakening at other levels (1991). In the midst of wide availability of information and birth control, unwanted pregnancies and sexually transmitted diseases continue. Why? The real issue is not on the level of conscious rational intentions but in the deeper realm of intentionality, where a deep defiance mocks our withdrawal of feeling.

May (1969) suggested that only the experience and rediscovery of *care,* the opposite of apathy, will enable us to stand against the cynicism that characterizes our day. The mythos of care points to the need to develop a new morality of authenticity in human relations.

INTENTIONALITY

May believed that we must put decision and will back into the center of our picture of personality. His intent is not to rule out deterministic influences but to place the problem of determinism and freedom on a deeper level. May does this by introducing the concept of **intentionality** (1969), which underlies will and decision.

By intentionality, May meant "the structure which gives meaning to experience." A distinctly human capacity, intentionality is an imaginative attention that underlies our intentions and informs our actions. It is the capacity to participate in knowing. How a piece of paper is perceived will differ depending on whether one intends to write on it or to make a paper airplane. It is the same piece of paper that provides the stimulus and the same person responding to it, but the paper and experience will have a different meaning.

Intentionality bridges the gap between subject and object because it is the structure of meaning that permits a subject to understand the world as object. Perception is directed by intentionality. Contrary to the popular belief that truth is perceived through a detached objective stance, May held that we cannot know the truth until we have taken a stand on it. Both the detached type and the asocial personality avoid confronting their intentionality. When you face your intentionality, then you can decide whether or not to act it out in your behavior.

FREEDOM AND DESTINY

The existentialist attitude is sometimes mistakenly criticized for portraying the individual as absolutely free with no restraints whatsoever. May, however, reminded us that freedom can be considered only together with destiny (1981). Freedom means "openness, readiness to grow, flexibility, and changing in pursuit of greater human values" (1953). It entails our capacity to take a hand in our own development. Freedom is basic to the existentialist understanding of human nature because it underlies our ability to choose and to value. However, freedom can be experienced only in juxtaposition with human destiny.

May (1981) defined destiny as the vital design of the universe expressed in each one of us. In its extreme form, our destiny is death, but it also expresses itself in our individual talents, our personal and collective histories, and the culture and society into which we were born. Destiny sets limits for us, but it also equips us to perform certain tasks. Confronting these limits yields constructive values. Freedom is not to be confused with rebellion, although rebellion is a necessary step in the evolution of consciousness and freedom. People earn their right to be free by an inner act of rebellion structured by the culture in which they live. In the Western world, freedom is experienced as individual self-expression. In the East, it is experienced as participation in a group. These are two very different situations, but both permit the experience of freedom.

Freedom is in crisis today because we have viewed it without its necessary opposite. We have become irresponsible with our laissez-faire free-enterprise system and culture of narcissism. We have lost sight of the fact that we can exist only as a community. The tendency to believe that nothing is fixed and that we can change everything we wish is not only a misperception of life but also a desecration of it. When people cannot or will not accept their destiny, it is repressed and often projected onto others, such as the perception of one's enemy as totally bad (1981).

May pointed out that "freedom and determinism give birth to each other. Every advance in freedom gives birth to a new determinism, and every advance in determinism gives birth to a new freedom" (1981). Freud's and Darwin's theories, deterministic as they were, opened the door to new possibilities. However, the word **determinism,** borrowed from physics, is not very adequate for the rich nuances of human experience. To the extent to which one is unaware of one's responses, the term *determinism* may be appropriate, yet May suggested that we reserve it for inanimate objects, such as billiard balls, and use the term *destiny* for human beings. Determinism is merely one aspect of destiny. The shift from determinism to destiny occurs when a person is self-conscious about what is happening to him or her (1981).

Are we responsible for our destiny? May reminded us that responsibility is inseparable from freedom. To acknowledge one's destiny is to accept personal responsibility. In the terms of our psychology, freedom is the capacity to pause between a stimulus and a response. The key word here is *pause.* The significance of the pause is that it breaks the rigid chain of cause and effect. In the debate between situational and dispositional factors, May reminded us that there is a third alternative. Human beings can choose when and whether they are to be acted upon or do the acting. In moving between being controlled and controlling, one moves on a deeper level of freedom, the freedom of being (1981).

The past and future live in the psychological present. On the deepest level, the question of which age we live in is irrelevant. Instead the question is how, in our awareness of self and the period we live in, we are able through our choices to attain inner freedom and live according to our own inner integrity (1953). One reason we are reluctant to confront our destiny is that we are afraid it will lead us to despair. But despair may be a prelude to better things. Indeed, authentic despair is the emotion that forces us to come to terms with our destiny and permits us to let go of false hopes (1981).

COURAGE AND CREATIVITY

Courage is the capacity to move ahead in spite of despair. In human beings, courage is necessary in order to make being and becoming possible. Courage is not a virtue but a foundation that underlies and gives reality to all other values. The paradox of courage is that we must be fully committed but we must also be aware at the same time that we might be wrong. Creative courage is the discovery of new forms, symbols, and patterns on which a new society can be built. The creative person must fight the actual order so as to bring about what is new. Thus creativity brings upon us the wrath of the gods, the anger of the authority of the past. Psychologists frequently ignore creativity because, as an act of encounter between two poles, it is very difficult to study. Yet our contemporary crisis requires creativity if we are to deal with it effectively (1975).

A CRY FOR MYTH

In his book *The Cry for Myth* (1991), May argued passionately that many of the problems we confront, such as increases in suicide, anxiety, depression, substance abuse, and the growth of cults, stem from the absence of myths that would help us make meaning in what has become a "senseless world." May defined **myths** as "narrative patterns that give significance to our existence" and deemed them essential for psychological health. Our current myths no longer play that role; rather, they increase our frustrations.

We do not generate the necessity for myths. That necessity comes from our destiny as humans, our language, and a mode of knowing one another. May described the pseudomyths that are filling the vacuum created by the lack of genuine myths for people living today in the West. Our denial of myth in the West reflects our overemphasis on left-brain activities, rationalistic speech, and "our refusal to confront our own reality and that of our society."

The myths that we create are both conscious and unconscious, personal and collective. Thus each of us develops our own unique narrative in which we play the primary role, and by which we model our lives. That myth may follow infinite patterns but generally also reflects a primary motif of classical myths, such as that of Satan, who appears over and over again under many different names in our literature. This is because "myths are archetypal patterns in human consciousness": being born, dying, making choices, and so forth.

The need for myth is also the need to belong to a community and to have heroes who act as role models as compared to celebrities who are simply well known. Martin Luther King Jr. and Mother Teresa are heroes whom we can identify with, as compared to celebrities such as Donald Trump and Paris Hilton.

"Myth leads to fact rather than the reverse" (May, 1991). The American myth of the frontier permitted many people to make a new, more constructive, beginning of their lives. But there was also the myth of the Lone Ranger, which eventually became the myth of lonely individualism that characterizes the narcissistic personality and expresses itself in our loneliness and violence.

The most influential myth in America has been that of Horatio Alger, which couples individualism with success and leads people to be driven, competitive, tense, and predisposed to stress and depression. Meanwhile anxiety disorders and depression have soared, and we must rediscover myths that can help us combat them. If not, our gambling (which defrauds primarily the poor) and use of drugs will continue to skyrocket.

Dante's *Divine Comedy* tells us we must go through hell before we can love and live "life as community." May reminded us that "a person's hell may consist of confronting the fact that his mother never loved him; or it may consist of fantasies of destroying those a person loves most, like Medea destroying her children; or undergoing the hideous cruelty released in wartime when it becomes patriotic to hate and to kill" (1991). What is important is not the particulars of one's own hell but the journey itself.

In the nineteenth century, Ibsen anticipated the twentieth and tolled the death of hyper-individualism. Counterposing humans and subhuman trolls, his *Peer Gynt* describes the conflicting life of a man who wishes to be honored and taken care of by one woman. The struggle renders him passive, dependent, and powerless.

Goethe's *Faust* is the myth of patriarchal society and power that has dominated the West. Much as we would like to believe that our tremendous technology is leading to progress, the tale of Faust reveals that, in a patriarchal society, men have a serious problem with the feminine dimension of life. Washington politics, some say, demands a Faustian pact from even its finest people. Vince Foster Jr., President Bill Clinton's boyhood chum and later his aide, is said to have commented before he committed suicide, "Before we came here, we thought of ourselves as good people" (Farmer, 1993). Faust steered Gretchen into condemnation. In the twentieth century, May suggested, Germany itself became Faust and tumbled to its death in Nazism, a guilt that is shared by all in the West. One does not have to commit the specific evil to be guilty. We are guilty because we are human, and the only way we can save ourselves is to assume responsibility.

Myths motivate us because they imply new potentialities and interpretations. Our current distress with parental sexual abuse of children is a new form of the Oedipal myth. May was amazed that Sophocles' sequel to *Oedipus Rex, Oedipus in Colonus,* is neglected in American psychoanalytic circles because in that drama the blind Oedipus comes to terms with what he has done. Oedipus knows that he is not guilty because he was unaware that the man he murdered was his father, but he must assume responsibility for his action.

Finally, May asked if we can construct a new myth for our survival. The Peer Gynt and Faust myths teach us that we must develop a myth of equality between men and women to undermine the primarily male, left-brain concepts of reason and hyperindividualism that have misled us. We need myths that give meaning to a woman's

> ### Thinking Critically
>
> What is your personal guiding myth? See the Thinking Critically box "Cultural Myths and the Media."

Thinking Critically

Cultural Myths and the Media

May says that human beings need myths—guiding narratives that help us to make sense out of our lives—in order to find meaning. In developing our myths, we draw upon cultural forces, such as the media. Pick out someone from literature, film, or TV who has been an influential hero or role model in our culture. How has that particular figure helped to shape our thinking of who we should be in our culture? Are there figures in our contemporary culture and media that undercut our efforts to develop a personal narrative that brings out the best in ourselves? Is it hard to find in the media today positive images worthy of emulation?

May suggests that we should be working to create myths that support efforts to make the best of life rather than undermining them. What can we do to contribute to a culture that fosters the development of positive myths?

life other than just in the context of her relationship to men. The Navajo have a myth in which women, by their power of creativity, save the world from chaos, much as Ma Joad in Steinbeck's *The Grapes of Wrath* holds a migrant family together.

May believed we can develop a new myth out of our explorations of the heavens. On Christmas Eve 1968, three astronauts circled the Moon and read from the Bible, making that experience sacred. Those astronauts could become heroes in a myth in which they look back from space upon Earth and recognize that the borders over which people kill each other do not really exist. Pictures of Earth from space tell us that we must develop a new myth that fosters world community and learn to live in one global family (see also Kaplan, 1994). May's theory is summarized in Table 14.1.

Psychotherapy

The existential approach to psychotherapy maintains that the central goal of therapy is to help promote understanding of the self and one's mode of being in the world. Psychological constructs for understanding human beings are, therefore, placed on an ontological basis and take their meaning from the present situation. Drives, dynamisms, or behavior patterns are understood only in the context of the structure of the existence of the particular person.

TABLE 14.1 MAY'S EXISTENTIAL PSYCHOANALYTIC THEORY

The existential attitude: There is no truth or reality except as we participate in it.

Our current predicament:

Powerlessness
Anxiety
Loss of values

Rediscovering selfhood entails:

Becoming aware of feelings and desires
Moving through four stages of consciousness:
  Innocence
  Rebellion
  Ordinary consciousness
  Creative consciousness

The goals of integration

Integrating the daimonic
Experiencing our power
Rediscovering care
Facing intentionality
Freedom in juxtaposition with destiny
Courage and creativity
Developing a new myth

May pointed out that *being* in the human sense is not given once and for all. As humans we have to be aware of ourselves, be responsible for ourselves, become ourselves. "To be *and* not to be" (May's rephrasing of Hamlet) is a choice we make at every moment. An "I am" experience is a precondition for solving specific problems (1983). Otherwise, we merely trade one set of defenses for another.

Becoming aware of one's own being is not to be explained in social terms. The acceptance of the therapist may facilitate the "I am" experience, but it does not automatically lead to it. "The crucial question is what the individual himself, in his own awareness of and responsibility for his existence, does with the fact that he can be accepted" (1983). Nor is the emergence of an "I am" experience identical to the development of the ego. It occurs on a more basic level, an ontological one, and is a precondition for subsequent ego development.

In order to grasp what it means to exist, one also needs to grasp the option of nonbeing. Death is an obvious form of the threat of nonbeing, but conformity is an alternative mode that May found very prevalent in our day. People give up their own identity in order to be accepted by others and avoid being ostracized or lonely, but in doing so they lose their power and uniqueness. Whereas repression and inhibition were common neurotic patterns in Freud's day, today *conformism* is a more prevalent pattern. Such denial of one's potentialities leads to the experience of guilt. Ontological guilt does not come from cultural prohibition but arises from the fact of self-awareness and the recognition that one has not fulfilled one's potentialities. Facing such guilt in the process of therapy leads to constructive effects.

Thus the central task of the therapist is to seek to understand the patient's mode of being and nonbeing in the world. It is the context that distinguishes the existential approach rather than any specific techniques. The human being is not an object to be managed or analyzed. Technique follows understanding. Various psychotherapeutic devices may be used, depending on which method will best reveal the existence of a particular patient at any given time.

May believed that free association is particularly useful in revealing intentionality. The relationship between the therapist and patient is seen as a real one. When transference occurs, May pointed out that it distorts the therapeutic encounter. The therapist seeks to help the patient experience existence as real. This does not imply simply adjusting to one's culture or relieving anxiety but rather experiencing one's existence or mode of being in the world.

May warned against the use of drugs in psychotherapy. For the most part, he believed they have a negative effect because, in removing the patient's anxiety, they may remove the motivation for change and thereby deny an opportunity for learning and destroy vital resources. Anxiety is an inevitable characteristic of being human. An absence of anxiety may be pathological in that it denies reality. Occasionally, May employed techniques developed by *gestalt* therapists such as Fritz Perls. An emphasis might be placed on nonverbal behaviors to show the inconsistency between verbal and nonverbal statements. If a patient states that she is frightened but has a smile on her face, the therapist might point out that a frightened person does not smile and seek to explore the meaning of the smile. A patient might be asked to fantasize that a significant other was sitting in an opposite chair, to have a conversation with that person, and then to reverse roles. Such techniques are designed to help the patient confront and experience actual present feelings. Finally, May's approach emphasized commitment, believing that patients cannot receive any insight until they are ready to decide and take a decisive orientation to life (see also Bugenthal, 2000).

Assessment and Research in May's Theory

May believed that in their efforts to be "scientific" many psychologists have lost sight of the real person that they seek to understand. However, although May was critical of some of the so-called scientific forms of psychology, he was by no means antiscientific. His aim was to speak out against concepts of personality that dogmatically foreclose avenues of research.

In the 1950s, May criticized psychologists for having singled out for study those aspects of human behavior that overlap with animal behavior and can ultimately be described in physiological or stimulus-response terms. In doing so, May pointed out that psychologists neglected the problem of symbols, even though the use of symbols is part of the distinct human condition (May et al., 1958). Although cognitive psychology studies symbols and other events that occur in the mind, May did not look to cognitive psychology for answers because its conceptions are also too limited for the psychological problems of our time (1981).

May criticized contemporary psychological research for being impressed with data and numbers at the expense of theory. Psychologists tend to be contemptuous of imagination and speculation, yet the most important scientific discoveries (Copernicus's concept of the universe, Darwin's theory of evolution, Freud's construct of unconscious forces, Einstein's theory of relativity) were made not by accumulating facts but by perceiving the relationship among them (1983). Human nature can be understood only within a theoretical framework.

The existential approach suggests three basic changes in psychological methods of research on personality. First, "we must cut through the tendency in the West to believe we understand things only if we know their causes, and to find out and describe instead what the thing is as a phenomenon—the experience, as it is given to us, in its 'givenness.' First, that is, we must know what we are talking about. This is not to rule out causation and genetic development, but rather to say that the question of *why* one is what one is does not have meaning until we know *what* one is" (1967). This phenomenological approach is very similar to the view maintained by Rogers.

Second, psychologists must recognize that all ways of understanding what it means to be a human being are based on philosophical assumptions and myths. We need to examine these presuppositions continually, for it is one's philosophical concept of human beings that guides one's empirical research. Here May also reminded us of Rogers's and Maslow's emphasis on science serving previously chosen goals.

Finally, we must ask the question of the nature of person as person, the ontological question of what it means to be. Understanding the being of another person occurs on a very different level from knowing specific things about the person. This is the classical distinction between *knowing* and *knowing about*. Our culture tends to believe that something is not real unless we can reduce it to a mathematical abstraction. But according to May, this denies the reality of our own experience. May suggested that it would be more scientific to first try to see clearly what we are talking about and then try to find symbols to describe what we see with a minimum of distortion (1983).

At this time, much of our research is governed by the myth of the technological man, which May described as "a set of assumptions of postulating that the human being is governed by what he can rationally understand, that his emotions will follow this understanding, and that his anxiety and dread will thus be cured" (1969). May tried to help us develop a new form, a new myth that will be more adequate for our day. After all, he reminded us, "Anyone can do the research . . . .The original contribution lies in seeing a new *form* for the problem" (1967). May believed that new forms of symbols and myths for understanding human nature are more likely to come from our art, literature, humanities, and religion than from our present psychology (1983; also see DeCarvalho, 1992).

Two particular areas that May researched are anxiety and dreams. He undertook a study of unmarried mothers in order to illuminate the meaning of anxiety (1969). Because he believed that there might be damaging effects in inducing anxiety experimentally, he took what was an anxiety-creating situation at that time in our society and studied it to reveal a pattern that would be characteristic of other anxiety-creating situations as well. May believed that the more intensely we study the individual, the more we arrive at data that lie below individual differences and are applicable to human beings in general. His study led to some rich observations concerning the meaning of anxiety itself, the origin of neurotic anxiety in a particular parent-child relationship in which rejection is covered over with pretenses of love so that it cannot be appraised realistically, and the greater prevalence of neurotic anxiety among women of the middle class (cf. Kirby, 2004).

May believed that dreams reflect how we perceive, cope, and give meaning to our world. Our dream life reflects our intentionality and deepest concerns. It permits the person to experience rather than merely explain important symbols and myths. In analyzing dreams, May took them phenomenologically as self-revealing givens, patterns of data within themselves. He looked for consistency over a period of time and noticed that latent meanings in earlier dreams often become manifest in the later dreams. The latent meaning of dreams was thus reconceived by May as a dimension of communication that the patient is unwilling or unable as yet to actualize.

Each dream has a theme and a motif. The *theme* is the unity and inner consistency that is a part of the dreamer. It is characteristic of all dreams and reflects the unity of a person's character. The *motif* is the central thread running through the various dreams and the goal one is moving toward. The purpose of interpreting a dream is not to tell the individual what it means but to expand the individual's consciousness so that what is going on can be more fully and deeply experienced. In dreams we successfully resist the temptation to intellectualize and, instead, wrestle with our real problems.

After May had painted a portrait of one patient from her dreams, he compared his picture with that which had emerged in the course of her three-year analysis with Dr. Leopold Caligor by comparing his findings with the doctor's case notes. He found a remarkable consistency between the two accounts, confirming his hypothesis that one can get an accurate and meaningful picture of a person from the symbols and myths created in dreams.

Victor Frankl (1905–1997), a contemporary of Rollo May, also emphasized the search for meaning. A survivor of Auschwitz, a concentration and extermination camp during World War II, Frankl was most impressed with the meaningfulness that could be found in suffering itself, and he recognized that the survivors (of those given a chance to survive) were most likely those who held on to a vision of the future. The form of therapy, *logotherapy,* that he developed sets forth the need of *a will to meaning* balancing the then predominant physiological view with a spiritual perspective. Like May, Frankl (1997) emphasized the need to discover and choose meaning and value and describe the *existential vacuum* or emptiness created by meaninglessness that leads us to fill our lives with stuff that does not provide lasting satisfaction. The current movement of positive psychology (discussed in the chapter on humanism) draws inspiration from the work of Frankl and May as well as Maslow and Rogers.

PHILOSOPHY,
SCIENCE,
and ART

May's Theory

May clearly recognized that science derives from prior philosophical forms and is fundamentally dependent on them. He believed that the reason we don't understand the truth about ourselves is not that we haven't amassed enough data, conducted the right experiments, or read enough books, but that we "do not have enough courage." Scientific facts and technical proofs rarely help us answer the questions that really matter. We have to "venture" (1953).

In psychotherapy May was "the implacable friend," insisting that his patients "grapple with the disabling forces inside of them and fight their way back into life" (Harris, 1969). He was not afraid to risk reintroducing concepts vehemently rejected by mainstream psychologists—intentionality, the will, the daimonic. He reintroduced these concepts because he believed that they are vital to an understanding of what it means to be human today. There is a prophetic note to his writing, reminiscent of Erich Fromm, and his thinking frequently has a theological quality. Indeed, there are those who suggest that May took up where Paul Tillich, the theological giant of the twentieth century, left off (Harris, 1969). May acknowledged that for him the great periods in history were not those when psychological concerns were dominant but those when philosophical and religious concerns were uppermost (1983).

May did not give us a series of hypotheses that may be tested by empirical procedures. Instead, he gave us a philosophical picture of what it means to be a person in today's world. Reasons are offered in support of his affirmations, but they do not serve as proof; they cooperate as pieces of evidence in favor of a certain picture of reality. To reduce our understanding of personality to scientific, causative, and abstract terms means that we will lose some significant content and fail to understand the full reality of a human being. May, Maslow, and Rogers were contemporaries, and their work influenced one another's theories. May encouraged us to examine the philosophical assumptions of our scientific endeavor so that we can maintain a creative dialogue between our science and our philosophy. In a climate that encourages scientific reductionism, psychospiritual absolutism, and postmodern relativism (Schneider & May, 1995), May's prime legacies are the "embracing of life's paradoxes and the maximizing of freedom" (Schneider, 1999; see also Schneider, 2005).

May's philosophical picture of human nature is coherent, relevant, comprehensive, and compelling. He successfully avoided dualisms that have troubled us since the philosophy of Descartes. The existential framework that informs his theory is more compatible with our world than are the philosophical assumptions of nineteenth-century science that informed Freud's work. An existential philosophy provides a helpful background for discussing what Freud meant to say about the nature of psychic functioning. Although Freud was not an existentialist, existentialism provides categories that clarify Freudian thought and intent. Thus May fruitfully reconceived many Freudian concepts.

Philosophical Assumptions

Which philosophical issues were most important to May? See the Philosophical Assumptions box "Examining May."

Whereas Freud's philosophy was an extension of the assumptions inherent in the scientific community of his time, May began

✳ Philosophical Assumptions

Examining May

Many of the differences among personality theories can be attributed to fundamental differences in philosophical assumptions. Which of the basic philosophical issues, described in the introductory chapter and summarized on the inside back cover, seem to be clearly important to May in the development of his theory? How, for example, does May's existential philosophy influence his view of freedom versus determinism and uniqueness versus universality? Where does he stand on optimism versus pessimism? Does his theory address any other philosophical assumptions? How does his concept of paradox influence his philosophical assumptions? Rate May on a scale of 1 to 5 on those philosophical assumptions that you feel his theory applies to most. Compare your ratings with your own philosophical assumptions. Did your study of May lead you to change any of your assumptions? Why or why not?

as a philosopher. His image of human nature provides a welcome antidote to the technological view of the person that permeates radical behavior and learning theories as well as the naive optimism of the humanists. May differed from traditional learning and behavior theories in his open examination of his philosophical assumptions. He differed from the humanists in his insistence that we directly confront our own evil.

For the most part, academic psychologists have tended to ignore May's theory because they cannot treat it as a scientific hypothesis. Concepts such as intentionality and the daimonic are nearly impossible to define operationally and test empirically, but the findings of an empirical test do not establish a philosophical assumption; they may not even significantly relate to it. Nevertheless, the very strength of May's theory, the fact that it has its roots in a new philosophical conception of human life, may also be its greatest liability. May runs a strong risk of being given short shrift by the psychological establishment and having little impact on personality theorizing. This is ironic because in many ways the humility and openness to change that are characteristic of May's theory are more in keeping with the nature of the scientific enterprise than is the attitude of those who seek to limit and confine research. By ignoring May, psychologists deprive themselves of the challenge of reexamining their own philosophical assumptions and, perhaps, reconceiving the goals and methods of their science.

TO LEARN MORE about a new existential theory that focuses on fear of death and how a life-threatening illness can actually make life more meaningful, and about powerlessness and anxiety, and for a list of suggested readings, visit the *Personality Theories* textbook website at **college.cengage.com/pic/engler8e.**

Summary

1. May's work brings together the psychoanalytic tradition in psychology and the existentialist movement in philosophy.

2. **Existentialism** (p. 382) emphasizes existence rather than **essence** (p. 383). It suggests that there is no truth or reality except as we participate in it. Knowledge is an act of doing.

3. Existentialists believe that the psychologist's preoccupation with lawfulness and predictability stands in the way of understanding the real person, and they urge greater breadth to our scientific methodology. They seek to study the structure of human existence and to look at the unity of the person prior to any split into subject and object.

4. The central problem we face, according to May, is a feeling of powerlessness in the face of enormous problems.

5. May defined **anxiety** (p. 386) as the apprehension cued off by a threat to an essential value. It is intensified in contemporary culture by the interpersonal isolation and alienation that have come out of the way in which we view ourselves. Many of our present efforts to dispel anxiety actually end up increasing it.

6. The source of the human dilemma lies in the loss of the center of values in our society. A distinguishing mark of the human animal is that of creating values. The need today is to discover and affirm a new set of values.

7. May assumed that (a) all living organisms are centered on themselves and seek to preserve that center; (b) they can go out from their centeredness to participate with other people; (c) sickness is a means of preserving one's being; (d) human beings can engage in a level of self-consciousness that permits them to transcend the present and consider alternatives. These ontological assumptions precede our scientific activity and make it possible, but our analytic activity may in turn illumine them.

8. Rediscovering selfhood involves rediscovering our own feelings and desires and fighting against those things that prevent us from feeling and wanting. There are four stages of consciousness of self: innocence, rebellion, ordinary consciousness of self, and creative consciousness of self.

9. May discussed key issues in personality in ways that avoided abstraction and facilitated the confronting of **paradoxes** (p. 390). Love, which used to be seen as the answer to human problems, has now become the problem. We are unable to love. We need to experience and rediscover care. May introduced the concept of **intentionality** (p. 392) to bridge the gap between subject and object and to place the problem of determinism and freedom on a deeper level. He reintroduced the concept of the **daimonic** (p. 390) and insisted that we must come to terms with it. He emphasized our need to be courageous and creative. We also need to rediscover our power and express it in constructive ways. May pointed out how our freedom needs to be considered in light of our destiny.

10. May defined **myth** (p. 394) as "narrative patterns that give significance to our existence." He believed pseudomyths, such as that of Horatio Alger, are filling the vacuum created by the lack of genuine myths of people living today in the West. We need new myths to give our lives meaning, provide heroes, and suggest new possibilities. Two possible new myths that we need are equality between women and men and a global community with no boundaries.

11. In psychotherapy the existentialist seeks to understand the patient's mode of being in the world. It is the context that distinguishes the existential approach rather than any specific tech-

nique. The psychotherapeutic devices of both Freud and gestalt psychotherapists have been used.

12. May criticized contemporary psychological research for being impressed with data and uninterested in theory. We need continually to reexamine our presuppositions and raise ontological questions. Two specific research activities that May engaged in were a study of unmarried mothers and the study of a dream sequence.

13. May's theory is not a scientific theory of personality giving us a series of hypotheses that may be tested by an empirical procedure. Instead May suggested a philosophical picture of human nature that is coherent, relevant, comprehensive, and compelling.

Personal Experiences

1. In order to better understand the existential view of knowing other people, describe in three different ways someone with whom you have a close relationship. First, give an objective description of the other person, indicating as accurately as possible his or her age, appearance, background, and occupation, and providing other important information. Second, give a subjective description of how you feel about the individual. Express what your thoughts and emotions are when you are in the other's presence and how you feel when you are apart. Third, write the story of your relationship with the other person. Tell how you met, what you have said to each other at various times, and some of the things you have done together. When you are finished, compare the different descriptions. Which one best conveys a real sense of that individual and your relationship? Which do you think is most consistent with the existential posture?

2. To understand May's concept of powerlessness on a societal level, it's helpful to think about how powerlessness impacts your own life. Recall a time when you felt powerless. Perhaps such a feeling was prompted by a divorce or a death in the family, or by something of less obvious significance, such as getting into a fight with a bigger sibling or being picked on at school. How did being powerless make you feel: angry, hostile, humiliated, defensive, anxious, depressed, withdrawn? Write down any emotion that seemed tied to the condition of your powerlessness. Then with this personal instance fresh in mind, try to think about the implications of powerlessness in society as a whole. Do you agree with May's thesis? If so, how? If not, why?

3. Although May's concept of powerlessness was formed during the Cold War, when fear about nuclear war was widespread, similar feelings of powerlessness may be just as pervasive today because of the threat of terrorism. Try to compare people's sense of powerlessness now with their sense of powerlessness in the days of the Cold War. Ask ten adults over the age of thirty to answer these two questions: (1) Were you more anxious and fearful living during the Cold War with the threat of nuclear destruction than you are living today with the constant threat of terrorism? (2) Can you identify what has increased or decreased your feelings (for example, government policies, globalism, the Internet)? The answers you receive will give a sense of whether May's theories are becoming more or less a fact of modern life.

4. According to May, we find it increasingly difficult to truly love and form close, intimate relationships. Do you agree with this observation: "Love used to be seen as the answer to human problems. Now love itself has become the problem." Mine your personal experiences for evidence to support or rebut this claim. Do you yourself have trouble allowing others to be close to you? Are you wary of revealing your true self, of being honest and therefore vulnerable? How about your friends? Your family? Are you surrounded by loving, happy relationships, or are the people you know struggling to find intimate connections? How would you relate all that you observe to May's ideas?

5. What is the predominant myth of your life—the story that you tell yourself that motivates you to continue striving to be a better person? For example, perhaps you tell yourself that you are a rebel. Even though you conform to social and institutional norms, such as by wearing clothes, going to school every day, abiding by traffic rules—even though you conform more often than not—you might choose to stress to yourself the idea of nonconformity, of rebelliousness, for the purposes of moving more productively and assertively throughout your life. As May stresses, we all need personal and collective myths in order to be productive, both as individuals and as a collective. What myth motivates you?

PART SEVEN

Cognitive Theories

Cognitive theories of personality, exemplified here by the personal constructs of George Kelly and the cognitive-behavioral theories of Albert Ellis, Aaron Beck, and Arnold Lazarus, explore the processes by which an individual becomes aware of the world and makes judgments about it. Cognitive theories stress that behavior is determined not simply by the environment but primarily by an individual's attitudes, expectations, and beliefs.

Other theorists recognize the importance of cognition but do not make it the mainstay of their theory. Freud emphasized emotional processes of the heart rather than intellectual processes of the mind. The behavior and learning tradition initially was concerned with the analysis of environmental stimuli and the individual's final overt response to the environment rather than with the intermediate subjective processes that led to the behavior. Increasingly, however, contemporary theories of personality emphasize the ways in which we construct ourselves and give meaning to our world.

CHAPTER 15

Personal Constructs

■ George Kelly

1. Explain why Kelly suggested that we view ourselves as scientists.
2. Describe the philosophical position of **constructive alternativism.**
3. Discuss Kelly's fundamental postulate, and identify eleven **corollaries** that support it.
4. Explain how Kelly reconceived traditional concepts in personality theorizing.
5. Describe the **Rep Test.**
6. Discuss Kelly's view of and contributions to psychotherapy.
7. Identify some of the criticisms of Kelly's theory.
8. Evaluate Kelly's theory from the viewpoints of philosophy, science, and art.

Reading Kelly is like entering a new terrain because he avoided many of the concepts traditionally present in personality theorizing. Kelly was forthright in describing the differences between his approach and that of others. "It is only fair," he wrote, "to warn the reader about what may be in store for him. In the first place, he is likely to find missing most of the familiar landmarks . . . .For example, the term *learning,* so honorably embedded in most psychological texts, scarcely appears at all. That is wholly intentional; we are for throwing it overboard all together. There is no *ego,* no *emotion,* no *reinforcement,* no *drive,* no *unconscious,* no *need*" (1955). It is not that these concepts are entirely omitted from Kelly's work; rather, they are given new meanings and incorporated into his philosophy of constructive alternativism.

Biographical Background

George Kelly was born on a farm in Perth, Kansas, in 1905. His father was a Presbyterian minister, but ill health prevented him from actively leading a church congregation. Kelly's parents were devout fundamentalists who practiced their faith, prescribed hard work, and rigorously shunned the evils of dancing, drinking, and card playing. As an only child, Kelly received extensive attention and love. His mother, in particular, was devoted to him.

Kelly's early education was somewhat sporadic. He attended a one-room country school and was taught by his parents at home. He was sent to Wichita, Kansas, for high school, where he attended four different schools. He studied for three years at Friends University and received the B.A. degree one year later (1926) from Park College. Kelly had majored in physics and mathematics and planned a career in mechanical engineering. However, his interests were turning to social problems. While holding a number of different jobs related to engineering and education, he pursued the M.A. degree in educational sociology at the University of Kansas.

In 1929, Kelly was awarded a fellowship for study at the University of Edinburgh in Scotland. He earned the B.Ed. degree there based on his previous academic experience and his year of residency in Scotland. Kelly wrote his dissertation on the problem of predicting teaching success and discovered that his interests were turning to psychology. On his return to the United States, he enrolled as a doctoral student in psychology at the State University of Iowa. He received the Ph.D. in 1931 with a dissertation on speech and reading disabilities.

Kelly began his career as an academic psychologist in the middle of the Depression of the 1930s. Opportunities for work in physiological psychology, his specialty, were scarce, so he turned his attention to clinical psychology, a growing field. During the next twelve years, Kelly taught at Kansas State College at Fort Hays and developed a program of traveling psychological clinics that sought to identify and treat emotional and behavioral problems in students in the state's public school system. His experience with the clinics was crucial to his later development and theorizing. Not committed to any one theoretical approach, Kelly experimented with several different methods in his work with students referred for counseling. His position gave him a unique opportunity to try out innovative as well as traditional clinical approaches. His work with the clinics sparked several ideas that later found application in his own theory of personality and therapy.

George Kelly's theory of personality is based on his philosophical position of constructive alternativism.

World War II briefly interrupted Kelly's academic career. He enrolled in the navy as an aviation psychologist, headed a training program of local civilian pilots, and worked for the bureau of medicine and surgery, gaining recognition for his clinical services. After the war, a significant demand for clinical psychologists appeared as returning servicemen required help with personal problems. Clinical psychology came to be seen as an essential part of health services. Kelly played a leading role in fostering the development and integration of clinical psychology into the mainstream of American psychology. After teaching one year at the University of Maryland, he joined the faculty of Ohio State University as professor and director of clinical psychology. During the next twenty years at Ohio State, Kelly built a distinguished program of clinical psychology and refined and published his theory of personality.

In 1965, Kelly received a prestigious appointment to the Riklis Chair of Behavioral Science at Brandeis University. This appointment would have given him great freedom to pursue his research, but he died in 1967.

Kelly did not publish a great deal, but he lectured extensively in the United States and abroad, and he exerted a significant influence on psychology through his personal impact on his students and friends. In his later years, he spent considerable time suggesting how personal construct theory could be applied to help resolve social and international problems. He held several important positions, such as president of both the Clinical and the Counseling Divisions of the American Psychological Association. He assisted in developing and also served as president of the American Board of Examiners in Professional Psychology.

The Person as Scientist

George Kelly invited us to look at ourselves and other people as scientists, an image that he noted psychologists are quick to ascribe to themselves but perhaps not as readily to other people. Kelly suggested that the posture we take as we attempt to predict and control the events in our world is similar to that of the scientist who develops and tests hypotheses. In our efforts to understand the world, we develop **personal constructs** that serve as hypotheses that make the world meaningful to us. This is the core of Kelly's **personal construct theory.** If these constructs appear to fit our subsequent experience, we find them useful and hold on to them. Thus, if we construe the world or certain events as hostile, we will act in certain ways to protect ourselves. If our protective behaviors appear to be useful ways to cope with the events, we will continue to hold on to the hostile interpretation. If the pattern or construct does not lead to behaviors that help us adjust to events in our world, we will seek to alter or change the construct in order to develop a better one. Just as the scientist employs hypotheses to make predictions about certain consequences, people employ their constructs to predict what is going to happen to them in the future. Subsequent events are then used to indicate whether the predictions and underlying constructs were correct or were misleading.

Because of the emphasis he placed on the ways in which people construe the world, Kelly is often perceived as a cognitive theorist who stressed the process of knowing as the primary factor in personality development (see also Warren, 1990). One could also easily defend labeling Kelly a humanist (Epting & Leitner, 1992; Epting & Paris, 2006) or a phenomenologist. Kelly repeatedly protested that his was not a cognitive theory: "I have been so puzzled over the early labeling of personal construct theory as 'cognitive' that several years ago I set out to write another short book to make it clear that I wanted no part of cognitive theory" (Mahler, 1969, p. 216). He felt that his theory belied any such classification and should be considered independently. However, interest in Kelly's approach has grown in recent years because it has been seen as compatible with the growing interest in cognition that characterizes contemporary psychology.

The cognitive movement in contemporary psychology rejects the behaviorist view that people react passively to stimuli. It explores the various ways in which we respond to the environment by actively processing the information we receive into new forms, categories, and "mental representations of the world" (Klatzky, 1980) and thereby actively construe reality (Soffer, 1993). Kelly's theory is cognitive because he stressed that an individual's behavior is determined not simply by the environment or heredity but also, and primarily, by attitudes, expectations, and beliefs.

Constructive Alternativism

Kelly's theory of personality is based on his philosophical position of **constructive alternativism**: the assumption that any one event is open to a variety of interpretations. The world, in and of itself, does not automatically make sense to us. We have to create our own ways of understanding the events that happen. In effect, there is no reality outside our interpretations of it. Take, for example, the situation of a boy who is late for school. His father may think that the boy is late because he is lazy. His mother may suggest that her son is forgetful and daydreams on the way to school. His teacher may view the pupil's tardiness as an expression of his distaste for and hostility toward academic work. His best friend might see it as an accident. The boy himself could construe his lateness as an indication of his inferiority. The event itself is merely a datum, but it gives rise to many different alternative constructions that may lead to different actions. For Kelly, the individual's complex constructions are the appropriate object of study. The objective truth of a person's interpretations are unimportant because they are unknowable. What is important is their implications for behavior and life.

In our efforts to understand the world, we develop constructs or patterns that make the world meaningful to us. We look at the world "through transparent patterns or templates" of our own creation (Kelly, 1955). It is as if each person can view the world only through sunglasses of his or her own choosing. No one construct or pattern is final and a perfect reflection of the world. There is always an alternative construct that might do a better job of accounting for the facts that we perceive. Thus our position in the world is one of constructive alternativism, as we change or revise our constructs in order to understand it more accurately.

For example, at the beginning of a semester, students develop certain constructs or ideas about the subjects that they are studying. Usually, these constructs are based on a very limited sample of the actual course or the instructor's behavior. One student may conclude that a particular course will be a snap, requiring a minimum of time and preparation. Another student may conclude that the same course will be a challenge, requiring considerable effort. As the semester progresses, each student acts on and gradually tests the preliminary hypothesis for its accuracy. The lectures, reading assignments, written papers, and tests are all subsequent events that confirm or disprove the initial assumptions. By the middle of the semester, the students have a much clearer idea of the accuracy of their original constructs concerning the course.

> **Thinking Critically**
>
> How do you use the scientific method in your everyday life? See the Thinking Critically box "How We Behave as Scientists."

A student's behavior in a college course is simply an example in miniature of what happens to us all throughout our lives. As was pointed out earlier, the world is not a fixed given that can be immediately comprehended and understood. In order to understand the world, we have to develop constructs or ways of perceiving it. During the course of our lives, we develop many different constructs. Further, we continually test, revise, and modify them. Because none of our constructs is ultimate, alternative constructs that we could choose from are always available. Thus a person is free to change constructs in an effort to make

Thinking Critically

How We Behave as Scientists

Kelly (1955) suggested that each one of us behaves as a scientist in our efforts to understand the world. You can gain a deeper appreciation of your own attempts to understand other people by analyzing a recent situation and your effort to understand it in terms of the scientific method. Suppose one night, when you arrive home, you observe that there are tears in your roommate's eyes. You might conclude that your roommate is upset about something. However, when you inquire what the problem is your roommate says "Nothing is the matter" and points to a pile of onions recently chopped for tonight's stew.

Analyze this situation, or another one, in terms of the scientific method. What was the problem? What hypothesis did you develop? What prediction did you make about possible experiences you could have if the hypothesis were useful? How did you test your hypothesis, and what conclusions did you draw?

Anderson and Kirkland (1990) suggest that in his metaphor of the personal scientist, Kelly provides a constructive alternative to the mechanistic metaphor of the machine. What do you think?

sense out of, predict, and control the world. This validation process is central to the psychology of personal constructs (Landfield, 1988).

Fundamental Postulate and Corollaries

In order to present and explain his theory, Kelly (1955) set forth one basic assumption, or fundamental postulate, and then elaborated on it with eleven **corollaries** (see Table 15.1). The *fundamental postulate* reads:

> A person's processes are psychologically channelized by the ways in which he anticipates events.

Probably the most important word in Kelly's primary assumption is *anticipates*. Essentially, Kelly suggested that the way in which an individual predicts future happenings is crucial to behavior. As scientists, people seek to forecast what is going to happen. They orient their behaviors and ideas about the world toward the goal of accurate, useful predictions. According to Kelly, the future, rather than the past, is the primary impetus for behavior.

Each of the eleven corollaries that Kelly presented to elaborate his fundamental postulate focuses on a primary word that sums up the essence of these supportive statements and his theory:

1. *Construction:* "A person anticipates events by construing their replications" (Kelly, 1955). The term *construe* means to place an interpretation on an event. As we have

TABLE 15.1 KELLY'S FUNDAMENTAL POSTULATE AND COROLLARIES

FUNDAMENTAL POSTULATE: "A person's processes are psychologically channelized by the ways in which he anticipates events."

COROLLARIES

1. *Construction:* People anticipate events by interpreting them.

2. *Individuality:* Each person construes events differently.

3. *Organization:* People develop an organized system of constructs.

4. *Dichotomy:* Constructs are of a bipolar nature.

5. *Choice:* People choose from among alternatives the most useful construct.

6. *Range:* Each construct has a limited range or focus.

7. *Experience:* Constructs are changed in the light of experience.

8. *Modulation:* Constructs are open to change and alteration.

9. *Fragmentation:* People may use constructs that seem to be incompatible.

10. *Communality:* Communication is based on similar personal constructs.

11. *Sociability:* Social interaction entails understanding constructs.

seen, the universe is not an automatically knowable given. We must create constructs, or ways in which to understand it.

2. *Individuality:* "Persons differ from each other in their construction of events" (Kelly, 1955). No two people interpret events in the same way. Each of us experiences an event from our own subjective point of view. This corollary underscores Kelly's belief that it is the subjective interpretation of an event, rather than the event itself, that is most important.

3. *Organization:* "Each person characteristically evolves, for his convenience in anticipating events, a construction system embracing ordinal relationships between constructs" (Kelly, 1955). Our interpretation of events in the world is neither haphazard nor arbitrary. Each one of us organizes constructs in a series of ordinal relationships reflecting our belief that some constructs are more important than others. The fact that our constructs fall into an organized pattern means that we develop a system of constructs rather than simply a number of isolated ones.

4. *Dichotomy:* "A person's construction system is composed of a finite number of dichotomous constructs" (Kelly, 1955). In making an interpretation about an event, we not only make an assertion about it, but we also indicate that the opposite quality is not characteristic of it. A dichotomy is an opposition; Kelly suggested that all of our constructs are of a bipolar form. When we construe that a person is strong, we also imply that the person is not weak. The dichotomous form of our constructs provides the basis for constructive alternativism. Riemann (1990), however, suggests that bipolarity is an important but not necessary aspect of personal constructs.

5. *Choice:* "A person chooses for himself that alternative in a dichotomized construct through which he anticipates the greater possibility for extension and definition of his system" (Kelly, 1955). The choice corollary is a very important one. It underlines Kelly's belief that a person is free and able to choose from among the various alternatives the construct that will be most useful.

6. *Range:* "A construct is convenient for the anticipation of a finite range of events only" (Kelly, 1955). Each construct has a certain range or focus. The construct of *tall versus short* is useful for describing people, trees, or horses, but practically useless for understanding the weather. Some people apply their constructs broadly, and others limit their constructs to a narrow focus.

7. *Experience:* "A person's construction system varies as he successively construes the replication of events" (Kelly, 1955). People change their interpretation of events in the light of later experience. Such reconstruction forms the basis for learning.

8. *Modulation:* "The variation in a person's construction system is limited by the permeability of the constructs within whose range of convenience the variants lie" (Kelly, 1955). The extent to which a person's constructs may be adjusted or modulated depends on the existing framework and organization of the constructural system. Constructs are *permeable*—that is, they are open to change and alteration. But, some constructs are more permeable than others. Concrete constructs are rather difficult to change because of their specificity in definition and range. The construct *good versus evil* might be narrowly conceived by one individual so as to contain relatively few experiences. In that case it would be very difficult for the individual to

change the construct. For another individual, the same construct might be much more permeable and easily penetrated by new experiences.

9. *Fragmentation:* "A person may successfully employ a variety of construction subsystems which are inferentially incompatible with each other" (Kelly, 1955). There are times when people employ constructs that appear to be incompatible with each other. Because of this, we are often surprised by other people's behavior, and we cannot always infer what people are going to do tomorrow from the way they behave today. Such fragmentation is particularly likely to occur either when a person's constructs are impermeable and concrete or when they are undergoing change.

10. *Communality:* "To the extent that one person employs a construction of experience which is similar to that employed by another, his psychological processes are similar to the other person's" (Kelly, 1955). This does not mean that their experiences are identical, but our ability to share and communicate with other people is based on the fact that we share similar personal constructs with them.

11. *Sociability:* "To the extent that one person construes the construction processes of another, he may play a role in a social process involving the other person" (Kelly, 1955). Our ability to interact socially with other people entails understanding a broad range of their constructs and behaviors. Thus other people are also important for testing one's construing system (Walker, 1990).

The Reconstruction of Old Concepts

Kelly avoided many of the concepts traditionally associated with personality theorizing. He gave familiar landmarks and terms new meanings and subordinated them to his theory of personal constructs.

Some of Kelly's constructs refer to self-identity or the identity of others. The **self-construct** is based primarily on what we perceive as consistencies in our own behavior. For example, we believe that we are honest, sincere, friendly, and so forth. The self-construct is developed out of our relationships with other people. When we construe other people, we also construe ourselves. When we think of another person as "hostile" or "aggressive," we are making those qualities and their opposites a dimension of our own experience. Our self-interpretation is linked to our role relationships with other people.

A **role** is a process or behavior that people engage in based on their understanding of the behavior and constructs of others. We do not have to be accurate in our constructions to enter into a role. A student may play a certain role with a professor believed to be unduly demanding and unfair when in fact the professor is not. Nor does a role have to be reciprocated by the other person. The professor may remain fair in spite of the student's misconstruction. What is needed in order to play a role is simply some construct of the other person's behavior.

Kelly's use of the term *role* should not be confused with its use in social psychology. In social psychology, *role* usually refers to a set of behavioral expectations—mother, teacher, physician, ruler, and so on—set forth by a particular society and fulfilled by its members. In Kelly's theory, the role is defined by the individual in an effort to understand the behavior of other people and relate to them. One's self-construct may be seen as a core or basic role structure by which one conceives of oneself as an integral individual in relation to other people.

For Kelly, the person is a process, an organism in continual activity, whose behavior is governed by a system of personal constructs. *Development* is based on one's choice of constructs and viewed in psychological rather than biological terms (Vaughn & Pfenninger, 1994). *Learning* and *motivation* are built into the very structure of the system. Kelly believed that no special inner forces—such as drives, needs, instincts, or motives—are needed to account for human motivation. Human nature in and of itself implies motivation because it is alive and in process. Nor need behavior be accounted for in terms of external forces, such as stimuli and reinforcements. Learning is synonymous with all of the psychological processes themselves. It is simply inappropriate to conceive of an individual as motivated by other internal or external forces. Kelly (1958) declared that "there are pitchfork theories on the one hand and carrot theories on the other. But our theory is neither of these. Since we prefer to look at the nature of the animal itself, ours is probably best called a jackass theory."

Not all constructs are verbalized; therefore, conscious and unconscious processes may be accounted for by our capacity to form constructs that are not put into words. *Emotions* are also subsumed under the general framework of personal constructs. Although some critics (e.g., Bruner, 1965; Rogers, 1965) suggest that Kelly's theory is too intellectual and mentalistic, Kelly refused to divide the person into cognitive and emotional states. Feelings and emotions refer to inner states that need to be construed. They arise when constructs are in a state of change.

Traditional psychological concepts such as anxiety, guilt, and aggression were also reconceived by Kelly in accordance with his personal construct theory. *Anxiety* is "the recognition that the events with which one is confronted lie outside the range of one's construct system" (1955). In other words, we feel anxious when we can no longer understand ourselves and the events of our lives in terms of our past experiences. Such discrepancy can lead to construct change. If a change is merely incidental, the individual may experience some fear, but if the change is comprehensive, the individual will feel deeply threatened.

Guilt is a "perception of one's apparent dislodgement from his core role structure" (1955). In our relationships with significant others, we develop a *core role* in which we construe ourselves in certain ways, such as loving or responsible. If we behave, either intentionally or unintentionally, in a way that violates the core role structure, we will experience guilt.

Aggression entails "the active elaboration of one's perceptual field" (1955). Aggression involves action: the deliberate placement of oneself into situations that call for decisions. Such aggression is distinguished from hostility, in which an individual forces other people or events to fit into the current personal construct system. In Kelly's theory, *hostility,* the "conflicted effort to extort validational evidence in favor of a type of social prediction which has already proven itself a failure" (1955), is the opposite of aggression. Kelly uses the term *aggression* in the way most of us would use *assertiveness.*

Assessment and Research in Kelly's Theory

Clinical experience with public school and college students provided the basis for Kelly's theory of personal constructs. Although these students may have had problems, they were essentially functioning normally in the academic setting. In assessing the students who came to him, therefore, Kelly primarily used the interview. "If you don't know what is going on in a person's mind," Kelly wrote, "ask him; he may tell you!" (1958). Kelly might have asked his clients to respond to questions such as, "What kind of child were you?" "What kind of a person do you expect to become?" and "What do you expect from therapy?" Such questions, and their answers, were useful in elaborating the construct system.

At other times, Kelly would ask his clients to write a character sketch of themselves as if they were the primary character in a play. Written in the third person and beginning "The client's name is," the character sketch was to be written as if by an intimate and sympathetic friend who knew the individual better than anyone else. Such character sketches were also helpful in determining the individual's constructs and relations with others.

In order to understand further how a person interprets the world, Kelly developed the Role Construct Repertory Test, known more simply as the **Rep Test** (see Figure 15.1). Essentially, the Rep Test permits a person to reveal constructs by comparing and contrasting a number of significant persons in her or his life. The Rep Test has also been used to explore the complexity of an individual's construct system and changes in the construct system throughout the life span (Crockett, 1982). Such research has focused on **cognitive complexity,** the

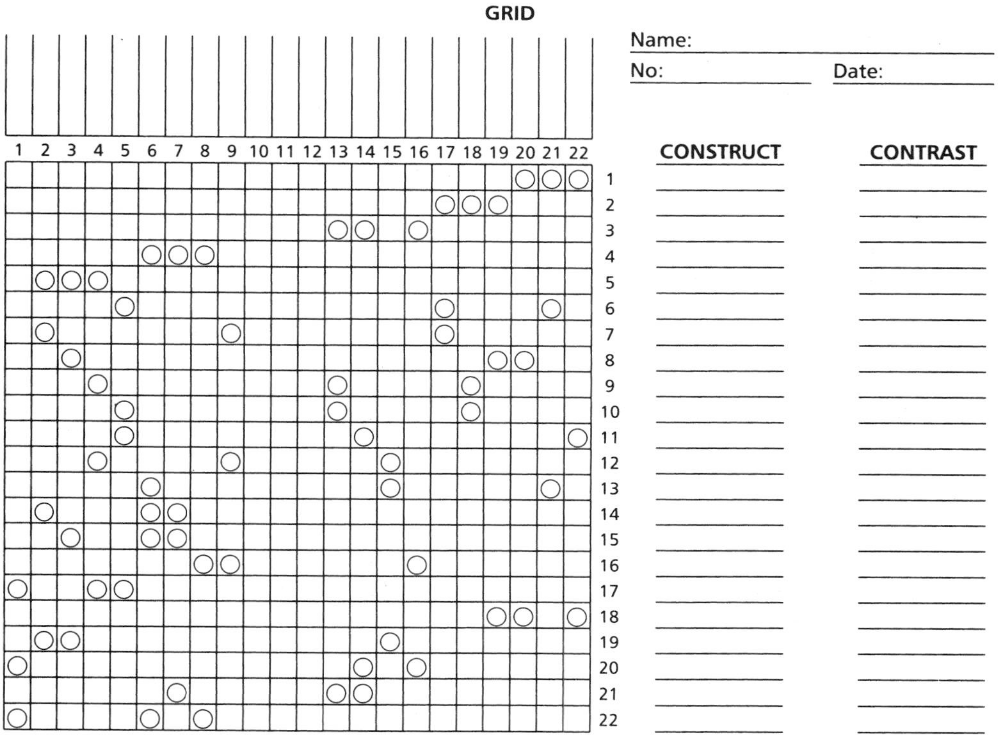

FIGURE 15.1 REP TEST GRID

SOURCE: *Reprinted from* The Psychology of Personal Constructs, *Volume One, by George A. Kelly, Ph.D., by permission of Mrs. Gladys Kelly. Copyright 1955 by George A. Kelly.*

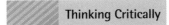

Thinking Critically

How can you explore your constructs? See the Thinking Critically box "Assessing Personal Constructs: The Rep Test."

ability to perceive differences in the way in which one construes other people. Individuals who are high in cognitive complexity are better able to predict what others will do and to relate with them.

The philosophical aspect of Kelly's theory may help account for the fact that his work initially generated little research. Most of the empirical studies based on his work concern the Rep Test (Bannister & Mair, 1968). Other studies, such as Bannister and Fransella (1966) and Bannister and Salmon (1966), suggest that the Rep Test and Kelly's constructs can help us understand the disturbance of thought in schizophrenia. They conclude that the thought constructs of a schizophrenic are less interrelated and more inconsistent than other people's, particularly regarding interpersonal constructs.

As psychologists pay increased attention to the role of cognitive factors in personality, personal construct theory has generated more and more research (Chambers & Epting, 1985; Chambers & Graves, 1985; Chambers & Stonerock, 1985; Tobacyk & Downs, 1986). Recent research has used the Rep Grid to assess values and beliefs (Horley, 1991) and to analyze content and structural form in personality description (Donahue, 1994). In addition, computer-based methods of analysis have been developed (Bringmann, 1992; see also Ford & Adams-Webber, 1991).

Website and software programs have been developed to facilitate working with the Rep Test. The Rep Test has the potential to be a fruitful source of cross-cultural research. The fact that it evokes personal constructs can help us to explore the universal and cultural aspects of organization and categorization that affect the development of personal constructs in diverse peoples.

Psychotherapy

According to Kelly (1955), psychological disorders arise when a person clings to and continues to use personal constructs in spite of the fact that subsequent experience fails to validate them. Such a person has difficulty anticipating and predicting events and is unable to learn from experiences. The neurotic flounders in an effort to develop new ways to interpret the world or rigidly holds on to constructs that are useless. Instead of developing more successful constructs and solving problems, the neurotic develops symptoms.

Kelly conceived of his therapeutic methods as "reconstruction" rather than psychotherapy. He sought to help his patient reconstrue the world in a manner that would foster better predictions and control. The first step in his therapy is usually that of "elaborating the complaint." In this step, the therapist seeks to identify the problem, discover when and under what conditions it first arose, indicate what changes have occurred in the problem, discover any corrective measures that the client may have already taken, and find out under what conditions the problem is most and least noticeable. Elaboration of the complaint usually reveals many aspects of the person's construct system, but Kelly conceived of a second step as that of elaborating the construct system itself. Such elaboration gives a fuller picture of the elements encompassed in the complaint, allows more alternatives to arise, broadens the base of the relationship between therapist and client, and reveals the conceptual framework that created and sustained the symptoms.

Thinking Critically

Assessing Personal Constructs: The Rep Test

The following activity will acquaint you with the Rep Test and also tell you about some of your own personal constructs.

Make up a list of representative persons in your life by choosing the individuals who most suit each description below. Using the form provided (Figure 15.1), write the name of the person in the grid space above the column with the number corresponding to the description.

List of Representative Persons

1. Write your own name in the first blank.

2. Write your mother's first name. If you grew up with a stepmother, write her name instead.

3. Write your father's first name. If you grew up with a stepfather, write his name instead.

4. Write the name of your brother who is nearest your own age. If you had no brother, write the name of a boy near your age who was most like a brother to you during your early teens.

5. Write the name of your sister who is nearest your own age. If you had no sister, write the name of a girl near your own age who was most like a sister to you during your early teens.

   From this point on do not repeat any names. If a person has already been listed, simply make a second choice.

6. Your wife (or husband) or, if you are not married, your closest present girl (boy) friend.

7. Your closest girl (boy) friend immediately preceding the person mentioned above.

8. Your closest present friend of the same sex as yourself.

9. A person of the same sex as yourself who you once thought was a close friend but in whom you were badly disappointed later.

10. The minister, priest, or rabbi with whom you would be most willing to talk over your personal feelings about religion.

11. Your physician.

12. The present neighbor whom you know best.

13. A person with whom you have been associated who, for some unexplained reason, appeared to dislike you.

14. A person whom you would most like to help or for whom you feel sorry.

15. A person with whom you usually feel most uncomfortable.

16. A person whom you have recently met and would like to know better.

17. The teacher who influenced you most when you were in your teens.

18. The teacher whose point of view you found most objectionable.

(Continued next page)

19. An employer, supervisor, or officer under whom you served during a period of great stress.
20. The most successful person whom you know personally.
21. The happiest person whom you know personally.
22. The person known to you personally who appears to meet the highest ethical standards.

After you have written the names in the space above the columns, look at the first row. There are circles under three persons' names (20, 21, 22). Decide how two of them are alike in an important way and how they differ from the third person. Put an X in each of the two circles under the names of the persons who are alike. Then write on the line under the column headed "Construct" a word or phrase that identifies the likeness. Write the opposite of this characteristic under the heading "Contrast." Now go back and consider all the other people you listed on your grid. If any of them also share the same characteristic, put a check mark under his or her name. Repeat this procedure until you have completed every row on the form.

When you have completed the form, take a close look at your results. First consider the nature of the constructs you listed. How many different constructs did you list? What kind of constructs were they? Did you tend to make comparisons on the basis of appearance (skinny versus fat) or personality characteristics (thoughtful versus unthoughtful; honest versus dishonest)? Do any of the constructs overlap? You can discover this by examining the pattern of checks and X's in the various rows. If the pattern for one construct (such as honest versus dishonest) is identical to that of another construct (such as sincere versus insincere), you can suspect that these two constructs may really be one and the same for you. To how many different people did you apply each of the constructs? A construct that is applied to a large number of people may be more permeable than one that is restricted to only one person. Are the constructs divided in terms of their application to persons of the same age or sex? This may give you some idea of the limits on the range of your constructs. Now take a look at your list of contrasting constructs. Are there any constructs that you list only as a difference and never as a similarity? If so, you may be reluctant to use that construct. If you list a contrasting pole for one person only, perhaps that construct is impermeable and limited to that person. Are any names associated only with contrasting poles? If so, your relationship to those persons may be rigid and unchanging even though you get along with them. Finally, compare your own column with those of the other people on the list. Which of the three people are you most like?

This analysis will not give you definitive answers; it will simply provide a starting point for further questions. Rather than consider the results on the grid as final, use your findings as the basis for additional study of yourself. For example, if you discover identical patterns for two constructs, such as honest versus dishonest and sincere versus insincere, you might ask yourself, "Do I believe that all honest people are sincere?" In other words, use your findings for further questions. Numerous possibilities for self-exploration are initiated by the Rep Test.

SOURCE: Reprinted from The Psychology of Personal Constructs, Volume One, by George A. Kelly, Ph.D., by permission of Mrs. Gladys Kelly. Copyright 1955 by George A. Kelly. Additional quotes reprinted by permission of W. W. Norton and Company, Inc.

Many of the techniques that Kelly employed to effect psychotherapeutic change are similar to those used by other therapists. However, in part through exposure to the psychodrama of J. Moreno (Stewart & Barry, 1991), Kelly made a unique contribution to therapeutic methodology by developing and fostering the use of **role-playing.** In the course of therapy, if a client mentioned difficulty with a particular interpersonal relationship, such as an overly demanding boss or unsympathetic professor, Kelly would suggest that they pretend they were in the boss's or the professor's office and reenact the troublesome scene. Afterward, alternative methods of handling the scene would be explored and the scene itself reenacted and changed in the light of alternative ways in which the client might deal with it in the future. Kelly encouraged the use of role reversal, having the client play the role of the significant figures while he played the client. Role reversal allows the client to understand his or her own participation more fully and also to understand the framework of the other person.

Thinking Critically

How can you use role play to understand your interpersonal relationships? See the Thinking Critically box "Role-Playing."

Kelly also used fixed-role therapy, in which he had the client enact the role of someone else for a more protracted period of time. Beginning with the client's own character sketch, developed during the phase of elaborating the construct system, the therapist creates a fictitious role for the client to play that is different from the normal role and is designed to help the client explore possible ways of reconstruing experiences. The client is introduced to the fictitious role and asked to try to think, talk, and behave like that other person for a period of a few days or weeks. Obviously, the role must be carefully contrived ahead of time. It must be realistic and not too threatening for the client. Eventually the client may discover that the construct system of the character played is more effective and may adopt some of those constructs. More importantly, the client learns that change is a real possibility. Fixed-role therapy has proved to be a very creative way to reconstrue the self under professional guidance. Mair (1988) believes that Kelly was reaching toward a new conception of inquiry in which the narrative form becomes very important and psychology is seen as a storytelling discipline.

Kelly believed that his theory had wide implications for social and interpersonal relationships. By actively considering alternative constructions, Kelly suggested, it is possible for us individually and collectively to envision new, more creative ways of dealing with a problematic situation. Take the problem that arises when a teacher observes an inattentive student who does not listen, turns in work late, and appears to put forth very little effort. The teacher might conclude that the pupil is lazy. Kelly would ask us to pose the question: Is this the most fruitful interpretation that the teacher can make, or is it simply a cop-out? Perhaps a different construction would give the teacher more latitude in creatively dealing with the problem. At the same time, the student may have a construction of the classroom situation that is hindering rather than facilitating learning. The student may, for instance, perceive that teachers are out to prove the stupidity of their pupils and play an obliging role.

Kelly acknowledged the integral relation of values and theory. Indeed, his metaphor of the scientist may be seen as a proscription instead of a description of human nature (Walker, 1992). Kalekin-Fishman (1993) believes that Kelly's theory escapes the limitation of radical individualism and enriches our understanding of sociocultural processes by emphasizing shared social construction of reality. As such, it may help us build a bridge to the social constructionists and deal with the problem of alienation.

Thinking Critically

Role-Playing

Kelly's method of role-playing can be fruitfully employed as a way of understanding one's own interpersonal relationships. Ask a close friend to help as you play the role of an important figure in your life. You might wish to play the role of your mother, father, instructor, boss, or boy or girl friend. Identify a problem situation or a potential problem. First consider how your parent, or whoever, would handle the situation. Then act it out, with your friend playing yourself. It is important that you try to look at the situation and behave as you believe your mother, or the other figure, would. Afterward, discuss with your friend what happened, and consider alternative ways of handling the scene. What are the benefits and drawbacks of role-playing as a therapeutic technique?

Kelly also encouraged the use of group therapy to help solve individual and common problems. The technique of role-playing is particularly well adapted to groups, in which several people may assist an individual in acting out a scene. By the end of his life, Kelly was suggesting ways in which his theory could be applied to help solve social and international problems. Much of our difficulty as Americans in international relations has been our problem as a nation in understanding how different events are construed or interpreted

Kelly made a unique contribution to therapeutic methodology by developing and fostering the use of role-playing.

variously by people in other countries. An enrichment of Kelly's theory, termed *perspectivism,* conceives of other people as equal partners and promotes tolerance of multiple perspectives (Warren, 1992). In this way, personal construct theory can underlie a theory of social action because its central task is to help people reconstrue their lives (Butt, 1995; see also Cormack, 2005).

| PHILOSOPHY, |
| SCIENCE, |
| *and* ART |

Kelly's Theory

Although Kelly encouraged us to think of the person as a scientist, his discussion of the way we validate personal constructs involved the compelling character of philosophical insights as well. Kelly's theory suggests that a construct is validated if the anticipations it gives rise to occur. *Validation* refers to the compatibility between one's predictions and one's observation of the outcome, both of which are subjectively construed. This form of everyday validation does not precisely parallel the controlled procedures of science. A scientist testing hypotheses does not look for events that will verify the hypotheses but rather sets up conditions that might falsify them. In a well-designed experiment one's anticipations are of little consequence to the outcome of the hypothesis (Rychlak, 1973, 1990). In Kelly's theory people are philosophers as well as scientists, or, at least, the scientific activities in which they engage are predicated on a philosophical stance. Kelly candidly acknowledged that his view of the person as a scientist was based on the philosophical position of constructive alternativism.

Philosophical Assumptions

Which philosophical issues were most important to Kelly? See the Philosophical Assumptions box "Examining Kelly."

Kelly's theory is better known in England and Europe than in the United States. Industrial/organizational psychologists, management development specialists, and occupational counselors have computerized the Rep Test and grid and have seen enormous potential for the instrument as an assessment device in industry. In spite of the fact that Kelly's own writings were scholarly and academic in tone, replete with their own technical vocabulary, his personal construct theory lends itself well to industrial/organizational psychology, in which there is a need for the psychologist to speak the language of the employee rather than that of the psychologist (Jankowicz, 1987). Translated into lay terms and concretely applied to the everyday lives of individuals, Kelly's theory is particularly relevant in the workplace.

Kelly emphasized the rationality of the human being. He believed that as the scientific world becomes increasingly sophisticated, the constructs we form are increasingly more successful approximations of reality. Nevertheless, he did not believe that the world or the person is ultimately knowable through a scientific methodology. Science is simply a construct system that helps us explain events. It is one system of constructs among many alternatives. Because we cannot posit any objective reality apart from our understanding of it, we cannot assert that science can ever comprehend the real person. It can, however, provide useful constructions that assist us in making predictions. This point of view characterized Kelly's attitude toward his own philosophizing and theorizing as well, as he readily acknowledged and expected that his own theory would ultimately be succeeded

Philosophical Assumptions

Examining Kelly

Many of the differences among personality theories can be attributed to fundamental differences in philosophical assumptions. Which of the basic philosophical issues, described in the introductory chapter and summarized on the inside back cover, seem to be clearly important to Kelly in the development of his theory? How, for example, does Kelly's view of the person as scientist influence his view of proactivity versus reactivity? How does his fundamental postulate shape his view of uniqueness versus universality? Where does he stand on freedom versus determinism? Does his theory address any other philosophical assumptions? Rate Kelly on a scale of 1 to 5 on those philosophical assumptions that you feel his theory applies to most. Compare your ratings with your own philosophical assumptions. Did your study of Kelly lead you to change any of your assumptions? Why or why not?

by an alternative construction (1970). "At best," he wrote, "it is an ad interim theory" (1955).

In spite of the "ad interim" character of Kelly's theory, it has attracted considerable attention and controversy. Kelly has been brought to task for his overly intellectual view of the individual and therapy, his neglect of developmental antecedents, his failure to deal adequately with human emotions, and his insistence on dichotomous concepts. The biggest criticism of Kelly's work has been that he ignored the full range of the human personality in his effort to do justice to the human intellect (Bruner, 1965; Rogers, 1965). He has been praised, however, for providing a model of uniqueness versus universality; "construct systems can have unique content elements but follow common principles of functioning" (Pervin, 1996).

Kelly's personal construct theory was a forerunner of modern social cognitive models (Rafaeli-Mor & Steinberg, 2002). Although Kelly insisted that his theory was not a cognitive one, his work foreshadowed the contemporary interest in cognitive factors in personality. As such, some critics suggest that Kelly's theory is a "classic that was ahead of its time" (Rorer & Widiger, 1983, p. 426). At the same time, psychologists who are influenced by information processing models often conceive of Kelly's constructs as schemas, scripts, or neural networks when in fact Kelly's personal constructs are structures of the phenomenal field. Mancuso (1996) suggests that Kelly's personal construct theory shares assumptions with social constructionism and narrative psychology and can help to illumine the emerging discussions on narrative as a highly suitable mode for personality expression. The theory has made distinct contributions to education, human learning, artificial intelligence, and human-computer interaction. Most theoretical clinical models now include a constructivist branch (Patrick, 2005). Kelly's theory is also making inroads in sociological areas due to its emphasis on the need to consider together both the social (communality) and the personal (individuality) reality (Fransella, 2003).

According to Kelly, the identification of universal truths is an impossible task. All ethical behavior has been humanly constructed (Raskin, 1995). Kelly's work was seminal to the current modern-postmodern debate on the construction of meaning (Raskin, 2001).

By viewing personal constructions as the primary factor governing personality, Kelly developed a theory that encompasses cognitive, emotional, behavioral, perceptual, and motivational aspects of personality. Perhaps this is why Kelly was entertained by various efforts to classify his theory. After he gave a lecture at Harvard, Kelly noted that "Professor Gordon Allport explained to the students that my theory was not a 'cognitive' theory but an 'emotional' theory. Later the same afternoon, Dr. Henry Murray called me aside and said, 'You know, don't you, that you are really an existentialist'" (in Mahler, 1969, p. 216; see also Soffer, 1993).

However one wishes to classify Kelly's theory, his emphasis on construction is compatible with recent trends in cognitive psychology, and, thus, his theory is likely to continue to attract attention. Moreover, his techniques of assessment and role-playing have proved to be very useful tools in psychotherapy, education, and industry.

 TO LEARN MORE about constructive alternativism, and for a list of suggested readings, visit the *Personality Theories* textbook website at **college.cengage.com/ pic/engler8e.**

Summary

1. Kelly suggested that we view ourselves as scientists because, in our efforts to understand the world, we develop **personal constructs** (p. 408) that act as hypotheses that make the world meaningful to us.

2. Kelly's theory is based on the philosophical position of **constructive alternativism** (p. 409), the assumption that any one event is open to a number of interpretations.

3. Kelly's fundamental postulate is "A person's processes are psychologically channelized by the ways in which he anticipates events." Kelly elaborates on his fundamental postulate with eleven **corollaries** (p. 411): construction, individuality, organization, dichotomy, choice, range, experience, modulation, fragmentation, communality, and sociality.

4. Kelly gave new meanings to many traditional concepts in personality theorizing, such as **self-construct** (p. 413), role, learning, motivation, and emotion.

5. Kelly developed the **Rep Test** (p. 415), which permits a person to reveal his or her constructs by comparing and contrasting a number of different persons in his or her life.

6. In his psychotherapy Kelly sought to help his patients reconstrue the world by first elaborating the complaint and then elaborating the construct system. His unique contribution was the technique of **role-playing** (p. 419).

7. Kelly has been criticized for being too intellectual and for failing to deal with the whole of personality or the emotions.

8. The way in which we validate personal constructs involves philosophical insights as well as scientific methods.

Personal Experiences

1. Kelly believed that all people are scientists to a certain extent. All people try to predict and control events in their world much as scientists do in developing and testing hypotheses. In attempting to understand and control our worlds, according to Kelly, we develop personal constructs, which we use to help ourselves predict events as they unfold in our lives. For example, if we construe the world as hostile, we act in certain ways to adapt and protect ourselves; likewise, we adapt accordingly if we view the world as inherently good, or dangerous, or romantic, and so forth. If a personal construct helps us to handle a situation effectively, we continue to use that construct. If a personal construct proves faulty, we begin changing the construct to better suit our needs. So how do you construe the world? What are two of your personal constructs? What evidence do you have to support your use of them?

2. Illustrate Kelly's concept of constructive alternativism in your own life. Oftentimes, we perceive the world and events from only our own perspective, using our own personal constructs. Doing so deprives us of other people's perspectives and other potentially valid opinions. It is always useful and constructive to take into account views that may differ or conflict with our own. According to Kelly, any event is open to a variety of interpretations. That is why watching movies and reading stories is so engaging: Moviegoers and readers often have differing views and interpretations of characters' beliefs and actions. Examine a recent event in your life from multiple perspectives. It could be a fight you had with your significant other, a debate with friends, something you witnessed on campus or at a party. Whatever instance you choose, list all the different people who were involved in the scene, and then write a brief paragraph in each person's voice expressing each person's perspective.

3. Your self-construct, according to Kelly, is based primarily on what you perceive as consistencies in your behavior. For example, you may believe that you are funny, honest, generous, and outgoing. Your self-construct emerges from your relationships with other people. So put your self-construct to the test. Write down the three characteristics that you feel capture the essence of your self-construct. Then ask at least five people who know you to list on a piece of paper the three characteristics that they feel best define who you are. Ask them to respond in writing and anonymously, to increase the likelihood that you will get honest answers. See how closely your view of yourself matches the views of those around you. Assess why the responses are similar or different.

4. A role, in Kelly's usage, is a process or behavior that people engage in based on their understanding of the behavior and constructs of others. So in order to understand the various roles that you play, you must be aware of your perceptions of the people who illicit those roles from you. Think about your perceptions of your closest friends. Does your behavior change depending on who you're with? For example, are you more outgoing with one friend and more quiet and laid-back with another? And how does your perception of each friend influence your behavior? Do you try to match what you perceive a friend's demeanor to be, or do you try to counterbalance it? Assess this dynamic with those closest to you. Kelly points out that one's perception of someone else does not

need to be accurate; in fact, it can be completely wrong. Keep that in mind as you assess each relationship.

5. In the Thinking Critically box entitled "Role-Playing," you were asked to engage in a role-playing session with a close friend, but you may also practice role-playing on your own. Choose one aspect of your personality that you would like to work on. For example, if you believe you are quick-tempered, you may want to try to become more patient and calm. To do this, you would, in essence, play the role of a calm person. For part of a day, constantly consider the way you think a calm person would act and behave, and then actively try to think and behave in exactly that way. Don't tell anyone you're doing this; you don't want your friends to behave differently around you. Instead, just go about your day, continually behaving in a calm and patient manner regardless of circumstances. After the allotted time period is over, assess how well the role-playing worked. Do you feel it had short-term benefits? If so, do you think such benefits could be sustained in the long term?

CHAPTER 16

Cognitive-Behavioral Theories

▪ Albert Ellis ▪ Aaron Beck ▪ Arnold Lazarus

Substantial information for this chapter, some of which was used verbatim, comes from Nancymarie Bride, RN, LPC, a certified clinical mental health counselor in private practice in Westfield, NJ.

I n recent years, behavioral cognitive therapies have revolutionized the fields of psycho-therapy and counseling. Albert Ellis, Aaron Beck, and Arnold Lazarus are primarily clinicians who have developed techniques and strategies for helping people cope better with their problems. These theorists were frustrated with the relatively long (and to them ineffi-cient) process of psychoanalysis; they devised counseling methods that are often very brief, client-centered, and to the point. Rather than take a long time to bring out issues that are related to events in the distant past, they deal directly with elements of the client's immedi-ate present and attempt to change existing thoughts or client values. In their writing, they primarily talk about the type of therapy that they do. Nevertheless, their counseling and therapy strategies are based on underlying theories (although they are not necessarily clearly articulated or a primary concern of these thinkers, who emphasize practical advantages over theoretical orientations). Although these theories are a little difficult to extract from their writings, we can try to examine them as theories of personality (cf. Ziegler, 2000). They emphasize and cultivate conscious forces, recognizing that a primary goal in life and analysis is to become more aware and conscious. The significance of these clinicians is ap-parent when we note that a survey of clinical and counseling psychologists on the "Ten Most Influential Psychotherapists" (D. Smith, 1982) placed Ellis second, Beck seventh, and Lazarus fifth.

Albert Ellis (1913–2007)

BIOGRAPHICAL BACKGROUND

Albert Ellis (1991a) did not believe that his childhood experiences shaped his becoming a psychotherapist. Born September 27, 1913, in Pittsburgh and raised "on the streets of the Bronx," Ellis said that he was a "semiorphan" because his father (before his parents were di-vorced) did a great deal of traveling and spent little time with him and his younger brother and sister. He believed that his mother was totally unprepared to raise children. As a result, Ellis suggested, "I was almost as instrumental in raising my mother (and, to an even greater degree my younger brother and sister) as she was in raising me."

Neglected by his parents, he was also ill (with nephritis, chronic inflammation of the kidney, which led to severe headaches), frequently hospitalized, and not permitted to en-gage in active childhood play. Shy and introverted, he was readily exceeded by his brave ex-traverted brother. To top things off, during the Great Depression, the family just barely managed without having to go on welfare.

With an incompetent mother, a brother who "acted out," and a sister who "whined," you might think that the stage was set for a pretty miserable childhood. Nevertheless, Ellis "re-fused to be miserable." In his immediate family, only his sister suffered from depression and anxiety, leading him to speculate that emotional disorders are due to genetics as well as en-vironmental factors. Fortunately, when they became adults, Ellis's rational emotive behav-ior therapy (REBT) was able to help her.

He went to the High School of Commerce in New York with the intent to quickly become a millionaire, but upon graduation the Great Depression shattered that dream. He enrolled in City College, where he ended up majoring in English. He did a great deal

Albert Ellis developed an A-B-C theory of personality that influences his rational emotive behavior therapy.

of writing, supporting himself with odd jobs. When he could not get any of his six novels published, he decided to focus on nonfiction.

It was sex that launched him into clinical psychology. Wanting to write about promiscuity, he did a great deal of reading in erotic fiction and nonfiction. Friends began to ask him to assist them in solving some of their problems. He found that he was good at helping and enjoyed doing it, and he decided to begin graduate training. At Teachers College of Columbia University he received his M.A. degree and matriculated for the Ph.D. Ellis wanted to write his dissertation on love, but two members of the department censored the topic, leading him to deliberately choose and successfully defend a dull and harmless topic, *A Comparison of the Use of Direct and Indirect Phrasing with Personality Questionnaires.* He thereby became very knowledgeable about personality inventories.

Returning to his love of research on sex, Ellis wrote a great many articles and books that became very popular. Together with the work of Alfred Kinsey, Bertrand Russell, and others, he instigated the social-sex revolution of the 1960s. Ellis spent two years in analysis and was subsequently "unofficially" trained by his analyst, who was associated with the Horney Institute for Psychoanalysis, which at that time did not permit the training of psychologists. Ellis found he was an effective analyst but gave it up in 1953 because he was looking for a more "efficient" method. Ellis had rapidly risen to a position of high authority in the state of New Jersey, but "prudes" in the state system objected to his research on sex, so he left New Jersey in 1952, became a well-known practicing psychologist in New York, and continued to write. In 1955, Ellis introduced a new approach—*rational psychotherapy*—so called to emphasize its focus on rational rather than irrational thinking. When wrongly criticized for neglecting emotions, Ellis changed the name to rational-emotive therapy (RET). In the late 1960s and early 1970s, Ellis began to remake RET, "making it both simpler and more complex" (1991b). In 1991, he amended the name once again to **rational emotive behavior therapy** to acknowledge the behavioral aspect that was always emphasized. Because the term is rather cumbersome, we will primarily refer to it by its acronym, **REBT.**

REBT is the first primarily cognitive-behavioral therapy, and Ellis was proud to have been its founder (2006). His career soared in the 1960s because of the popularity of his books and therapy method, and he founded the Albert Ellis Institute in New York. The institute has grown enormously, and the therapy it proposes has been widely adopted throughout the world.

Partially disabled with diabetes, poor hearing, weak vision, and other physical handicaps during most of his life (1997), this incredible busy, productive, and controversial man, even in his tenth decade, used his own basic principles to help himself continue to actively practice, train, write, and conduct workshops. He died on July 24, 2007.

PHILOSOPHICAL ORIGINS

The philosophic origins of REBT go back to the Stoic philosophers, particularly Marcus Aurelius (121–180) and Epictetus (60–120), who wrote in the *Encheiridion* (or Handbook), "People are not disturbed by things, but by the view which they take of them," a position that is the cornerstone of REBT. Ellis was also influenced by Immanuel Kant's writings on cognition and ideation, as well as by the philosophers of science, such as Bertrand Russell, who emphasized the importance of testing hypotheses.

In psychology, the modern precursor of REBT was Alfred Adler, whose emphasis on inferiority feelings, goals, education, and social interest is also apparent in Ellis's work. Adler's (1927) motto "Everything depends on opinion" is an essential tenet of REBT.

Ellis considered himself largely a postmodern constructivist (1998a). REBT emphasizes that conscious and unconscious absolutistic philosophical tenets tend to lead to dysfunctional behaviors and emotions. Ellis concurred with Kelly (1955) that people have strong inborn tendencies both to self-actualize and also to defeat themselves. However, they can use their constructive inclinations to defeat their defeatism and further their potential. Ellis believed that spiritual goals and values can be potentially harmful as well as helpful, especially when they are absolutist or go beyond normal human aims and entail supernatural ideas, such as surrender to a higher power. He preferred "profoundly meaningful, purposive and spirited goals" chosen with caution and care in reference to the particular situation (2000).

THE THEORY OF RATIONAL EMOTIVE BEHAVIOR THERAPY

Ellis (1978) pointed out that from the beginning REBT denoted a theory of personality that arises from its theory of personality change (see also Ellis, 1994c; Ziegler, 2000).

Ellis (1958) suggested that human beings are "sign-, symbol-, and language-creating" animals who use four fundamental processes: *perception, movement, thinking,* and *emotion.* These are all necessarily interrelated. Thinking entails not only brain activity (such as remembering, learning, and problem solving) but also perception, emotion, and movement. Therefore it would be more accurate to say that a person "perceives-moves-feels-THINKS about" a problem than to simply say that he or she "thinks" about it. Likewise, emotion is not one thing but a combination of related phenomena. Thus cognitions, emotions, and behavior are consistently interactional and transactional.

The theory behind REBT is a comprehensive cognitive-affective-behavioral one (Ellis, 1962). Because thoughts and emotions frequently overlap, much of what we consider emotion is a type of evaluative thinking. Perhaps evaluative thinking is somewhat less dispassionate than that which we usually label "thinking," but nevertheless it may be seen as a type of thought. Because humans are raised in a social culture in which thinking and emoting are closely interrelated, thinking and emotion tend to develop into a cause-and-effect relationship, "so that one's thinking *becomes* one's emotion and emoting *becomes* one's thought." These processes tend to merge into a type of "self-talk"—"internalized sentences" that shape our thoughts and emotions. Although it is possible to have a momentary outburst of emotion without thought, in order to sustain the emotion one has to back it up with some form of thought (1958). Thus the basic personality theory of rational emotive behavior theory suggests that human beings create their own emotional consequences.

Ellis believed that people have strong innate inclinations to live and be happy, to seek pleasure and to avoid pain. They are goal-oriented, active, and changing creatures with a strong compulsion to fulfill their potential. Nevertheless, people of all ages have irrational thoughts, unsuitable feelings, and dysfunctional behaviors that tend to sabotage the effort to achieve their potential. People are born with a distinct propensity to engage in self-destructive behavior, and they learn, through social conditioning, to exacerbate rather than to lessen that propensity. Most of these self-sabotaging tendencies may be summed up by stating that humans are born with a strong tendency to want, to "need," and to condemn first themselves, then others, and then the world when they do not immediately get what they supposedly "need." They consequently think "childishly" or "humanly" all their lives, and they are able only with enormous difficulty to achieve and maintain "mature" or realistic behavior (1976).

People grow up in social groups and spend much of their energy trying to impress, live up to the expectations of, and outdo the performances of other people. On the surface they are "ego-oriented," "identity seeking," or "self-centered." Even more importantly, however, they usually define themselves as "good" or "worthwhile" when they believe that others accept and approve of them. Ellis says that it is realistic and sane for people to find or fulfill "themselves" in their interpersonal relations and to have a considerable amount of what Adler called social interest.

However, what we call emotional disturbance is frequently associated with people's caring too much about what others think and stems from their believing they can accept themselves only if others think well of them. When disturbed, people escalate their desire for others' approval and the practical advantages that normally go with such approval into an absolute *dire need* to be liked, and they can hardly avoid becoming anxious and prone to depression (Bernard, 1986; Ellis, 1962, 1987b, 1988; Ellis & Dryden, 1997; Ellis & Harper, 1975). It is our tendency to exaggerate the importance of others' acceptance that often causes our inappropriate emotions (Ellis, 1985a, 1985b; Ellis & Becker, 1982; Ellis & Dryden, 1997).

According to the **A-B-C theory of personality** underlying rational emotive behavior therapy, when a highly charged *emotional consequence* (C) (such as being very frightened) follows a significant *activating event* (A) (such as being chased by a large dog as a child), A may seem to but actually does not cause C. Instead, in subsequent situations, emotional consequences are largely created by B, the individual's *belief system* (Oh dear, all dogs are dangerous and that is horrible). "If two people get labeled 'stupid,' and one laughs at the statement and the other feels depressed, we cannot explain these radically different Consequences by A (the Activating Event) but rather by B (the Belief System) *about A*" (1978). Although the sequence may appear to be linear, the theory is actually interactive and bidirectional (1996).

When an undesirable emotional consequence occurs, such as severe anxiety, it can usually be traced to the person's irrational beliefs. When these beliefs are effectively challenged (at point D) by *disputing* them rationally and behaviorally (Some, but not all, dogs are dangerous; thus while it pays to be prudent, you don't have to be afraid of and avoid all dogs), the disturbed consequences are minimized and greatly decreased (see Figure 16.1).

Emotional disturbance results from the interdependence of cognition, emotion, and action. Thus it is too simplistic to say that irrational beliefs cause or determine unhealthy

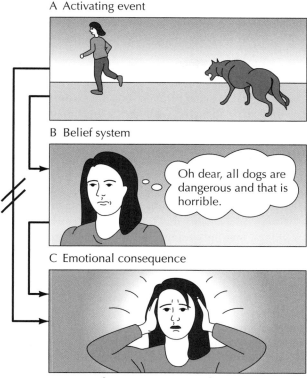

A Activating event

B Belief system

Oh dear, all dogs are dangerous and that is horrible.

C Emotional consequence

A does *not* cause C; rather, B does.

<figure>FIGURE 16.1 ELLIS'S A–B–C THEORY</figure>

According to the A-B-C theory of personality, when a highly charged emotional consequence (C) follows a significant activating event (A), in subsequent similar situations A may seem to, but actually does not, cause C. Instead, subsequent emotional consequences are largely created by B—the individual's belief system.

negative emotions. Rather, we are dealing with a complex of thoughts, feelings, and action tendencies that are more likely to become disturbed when they are grounded in dogmatic **musturbatory belief systems** consisting of **absolute musts,** such as "I *absolutely must* perform well and be lovable!" "Other people *absolutely must* treat me considerately and fairly!" and "My life conditions *absolutely must* be comfortable and not too frustrating" (1978, 1996).

Ellis acknowledged that his choice of the word *irrational* to describe beliefs that are not only unrealistic and illogical but also, and primarily, self-defeating was not the wisest choice and suggested that instead these beliefs be called *dysfunctional beliefs* (1996).

If people think and work hard at understanding and contradicting the "absolute musts" of their musturbatory belief systems, they can make amazing curative and preventive changes in their disturbance-creating tendencies. Instead of thinking "I must always have the approval of other people," they can think "I like to have the approval of other people, but I know I am not always going to get it." Thus the personality theory behind REBT "may at first sound grim and pessimistic" (1987a; Ellis & Dryden, 1997), but it is actually very realistic. It is also highly optimistic and pragmatic. Ellis debunks as myths the notions that personality disorders mainly stem from parental rejection, that feelings of worthlessness usually arise from constant criticism, or that sexual-abuse victims invariably continue to suffer as adults (1995). Posttraumatic stress disorder victims may compound their severe distress by having dysfunctional beliefs (1994b).

How do people get their belief systems? Ellis increasingly believed that heredity has a large influence, for as human beings we inherit a great many biological hedonistic predispositions and a high degree of "teachability." Ellis believed that "probably 80 percent of the variance of human behavior rests on biological bases and about 20 percent on environmental training" (1978). We inherit a tendency to raise cultural *preferences* into *musts* and social *norms* into absolute *shoulds*.

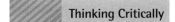

Thinking Critically

How can you identify your irrational beliefs? See the Thinking Critically box "A Self-Help Form."

There are so many variables (both internal and external, conscious and unconscious) that lead to the origin and maintenance of personality that Ellis believed there are no simple answers concerning the existence of traits or explanations of certain behavior. Although behavior is somewhat determined by internal and external forces, Ellis believed people do have *some,* albeit limited, free will and capability of changing their behavior patterns. Although he recognized that we can make some general statements about what people have in common, he also believed that each individual is unique and must assume responsibility for his or her behavior. In spite of his strong emphasis on heredity, Ellis would place himself firmly in the proactive camp.

RATIONAL EMOTIVE BEHAVIOR PSYCHOTHERAPY

Albert Ellis took a very directive approach and argued strongly for the view that people must judge their behavior not in terms of what others may believe but in terms of what they sense is right for them. The goal of therapy for Ellis was to enable clients to commit themselves to actions that are congruent with their true value systems. The goal of therapy should not be to understand the causes or to remove the symptoms of pathological behavior, but rather it should be to free individuals to develop constructive and confident images of their self-worth. Clients should be led to appreciate their "true identity" and encouraged to venture forth to test their personal tastes and values.

If clients are helped to focus on their irrational thinking and inappropriate emoting and behaving by a highly active, directive, didactic, philosophic, homework-assigning therapist, they are more likely to change their symptom-creating beliefs than if they mainly work with a dynamically oriented, client-centered, existentialist, or classical behavior-modification therapist (Ellis, 1978, 1985a, 1987a; Ellis & Dryden, 1997).

The principle therapeutic techniques that are used in rational emotive behavior therapy are cognitive, emotive-evocative, and behavioral therapy. **Cognitive therapy** attempts to show clients how to recognize their *should* and *must* thoughts, how to separate rational from irrational beliefs, and how to accept reality. It assumes that clients can think, can think about their thinking, and can even think about thinking about their thinking. In one-to-one sessions, the therapist not only listens but also gives information and seeks to stimulate the client to explore his or her own philosophy of life. In group therapy or workshops, members are encouraged to discuss, explain, and reason with one another.

A Self-Help Form

The Institute for Rational-Emotive Therapy has developed a Self-Help Form that can be useful for individuals trying to identify irrational beliefs that lead to emotional disturbance or self-defeating behavior.

First you are asked to identify an activating event that precipitates a negative consequence or condition that you would like to change. For example, the prospect of having to drive on a high-speed highway makes me very anxious and leads me to avoid such trips.

Then you identify those irrational beliefs that lead to your self-defeating feelings and behavior. For example:

1. I *must* do things perfectly.
2. I am a *worthless person* if I become anxious.
3. I *must* be approved and accepted by other people.
4. People *must* live up to my expectations, and if they don't it is terrible.
5. It is *awful* or *horrible* when major things don't go my way.

Next you develop a dispute for each of your irrational beliefs. For example:

1. Why *must* I do things perfectly?
2. Where is it written that I am a worthless person if I become anxious?
3. Why do people *have to* approve or accept everything I do?
4. Many people do not live up to my expectations. It's disappointing, but not terrible.
5. Is it really *awful* or *horrible* when major things don't go my way? Or only a hassle or inconvenience?

Finally, work on coming up with an effective rational belief to replace your irrational beliefs. For example:

1. I'd *prefer* to do very well, but I don't always *have* to.
2. I can be a worthwhile person and still feel a little anxious.
3. Although it is nice to be approved and accepted by everybody, it isn't absolutely necessary. I won't die of rejection.
4. It's disappointing when people don't live up to my expectations, but it is not the end of the world.
5. It's pretty inconvenient when major things don't go my way, and I don't *like* it, but I can stand it.

After you have come up with some effective rational beliefs for some of the activating events that used to create problems for you, notice the different types of feelings and behaviors that you experience. By thinking rationally when negative events occur, you will be more likely to feel healthy feelings, such as disappointment or frustration—rather than *disturbed* feelings such as rage, anxiety, or depression. Regularly practice and repeat these rational beliefs to yourself—out loud—in order to help yourself feel better and behave more rationally.

SOURCE: *This exercise is based on the REBT Self-Help Form published by the Institute for Rational Emotive Therapy, 45 E. 65th Street, New York, NY 10021.*

Emotive-evocative therapy employs role-playing, psychodrama, humor, and other ideas such as unconditional acceptance to reduce disturbance-creating ideas to absurdity; to convince clients that others can accept them with their failings; and to get in touch with their "shameful" feelings so they can zero in on the exact things they are telling themselves to create these feelings.

Behavior therapy is employed in REBT not only to help clients change maladaptive patterns of behavior but also to help change their cognition. Thus clients can be told to deliberately fail at a small task in order to survive a failure and thus learn that it is not dangerous. Clients may be persuaded to momentarily stay in a difficult situation, such as an uncomfortable job or marriage, in order to work on the problem. REBT therapists give specific active homework assignments and may suggest that clients develop penalties for failure to do their assignments.

Cognitions, emotions, and behaviors are consistently interactional and transactional (1958). Through the use of **desensitization**—a process whereby anxieties and fears are reduced by gradual, repeated, imagined, or real exposure to the noxious stimuli paired with relaxation, skill training, and other behavioral techniques—individuals who are anxious about driving on major high-speed highways might first be taught how to deeply relax (a skill that can be learned, but takes practice) and then to imagine themselves driving on a highway as safe, competent drivers. If there is any question about their driving ability, they might be encouraged to take a driving class. Other goal-oriented steps might be encouraged as well to help them maintain a reasonable speed, and so forth. Some REBT therapists prefer **implosive** (or sudden, instead of gradual) confrontation of phobic situations, depending on the circumstances. REBT embraces experiential-encounter techniques, and Ellis invented some of his own.

The rational-emotive theory of psychotherapy asserts that there are many kinds of psychological treatment and that most of them work to some degree. An efficient system of therapy includes (1) economy of time and effort, (2) rapid symptom reduction, (3) effectiveness with a large cross-section of clients, (4) solution-oriented discussions, and (5) long-term results that last. Ellis (1997) says that rational emotive theory is realistic and unindulgent. It gets to the core of and ruthlessly persists at undermining childish demandingness, the main element of serious emotional disturbance.

Unlike many other systems of psychotherapy, Ellis's system emphasizes the biological aspects of human personality. Although Ellis held that people have vast untapped resources for growth and in many important ways are able to change their social and personal destinies, he also held that they have exceptionally powerful innate tendencies to think irrationally and to harm themselves (Ellis, 1976).

The rational therapist assumes that people imbibe goals, standards, and values from their parents and culture and then add their own musts and demands to these ideals. Along the way, they also construct illogical ideas or irrational modes of thinking; without doing so, they could hardly be as disturbed as they are. It is the therapist's function not merely to show clients their irrational ideas or thinking processes but to persuade them to change and substitute for them more rational ideas and thought processes. Rational emotive behavior therapy employs many techniques, such as role-playing and free association and other expressive emotive techniques, but the therapist does not isolate her- or himself but rather acts "as his or her own person" (1997) so that these relationship-building techniques really get to the core of illogical thinking and induce clients to think in a more rational manner.

Ellis (Ellis & Dryden, 1997) points out that eclecticism is "hardly new to REBT." His willingness to draw creatively from many areas of effective psychotherapy is impressive.

The rational emotive behavior therapist keeps pounding away, time and again, at the illogical ideas that underlie the client's fears. This means showing the client, for example, that it is not fear of failure but fear of being blamed, of being disapproved of, of being unloved, of being imperfect, of being a failure.

Like most Western therapies. REBT tends to adopt a more universalist (and also more individualistic) position than would be appropriate to the cultures that many of the world's people are reared in. However, dysfunctional beliefs occur in all cultures, albeit in various forms. Ellis (1991b) worked with clients of Asian background and encouraged trying to understand cultural issues in therapy. Early Buddhist and Zen Buddhist concepts have been incorporated into the practice of REBT (Christopher, 2003). Because REBT specializes in uncovering dysfunctional beliefs, it can make a significant contribution to the study of cultural diversity.

In recent years, REBT has been adapted for use with children and adolescents as well as intergrated into family systems therapy (DiGiuseppe, 1998). Its psychoeducational format permits its use as a preventative tool with groups, in workshops, and in classrooms. Ellis hoped it would be incorporated in schools and become more educational rather than primarily therapeutic (Overholser, 2003). As he became disabled and older, Ellis also turned his attention to using his techniques to cope with the challenges of disability (1997), aging (1998b, 2002), and the threat of terrorism (2002, 2004). With substance abuse and dependence being the most prevalent mental health disorder in the United States, REBT is also being used to help manage addictions (Bishop, 2000).

Ellis recognized the importance of empirical research for supporting and maintaining the effectiveness of REBT (1996). The vivid informality of his descriptions could easily mislead us into thinking that his ideas are not scientific. Because they are interdependent, his concepts are more difficult to measure and study than single isolated concepts, but that is not to say that they are untestable. We can observe the different complexes entailed in absolute musts as compared to preferences and also the consequent thoughts, feelings, and actions and convert these into variables for empirical study, an activity that Ellis would strongly encourage.

Aaron Beck (1921–   )

BIOGRAPHICAL BACKGROUND

Aaron T. Beck was born in Providence, Rhode Island, on July 18, 1921. He is the third surviving son and youngest child of Russian Jewish immigrants to the United States. His mother's depression following the death of her only daughter in an influenza epidemic lifted when her youngest child was born, and Beck would joke that his ability to cure his mother at an early age illustrated his need to control. Young Aaron developed a near fatal illness following an infection of a broken arm, which led him to be anxious and to believe that he was inept and stupid. At an early age, he began to work cognitively through some of his problems and fears. Later, his theory and therapy would help others overcome the types of negative beliefs that he himself experienced. His father encouraged his interest in science and nature, but his career interests did not coalesce until he had almost finished college. Beck graduated

Aaron Beck views personality as shaped by schemas, cognitive structures consisting of core beliefs and assumptions about how the world operates.

from Brown University magna cum laude in 1943 and was elected to Phi Beta Kappa. The Yale School of Medicine granted him the M.D. in 1946, and the American Board of Psychiatry and Neurology certified him in psychiatry in 1953. The following year, he joined the faculty of the Department of Psychiatry of the University of Pennsylvania Medical School, where he has been ever since. In his early years at the university, he received training in psychoanalysis from the Philadelphia Psychoanalytic Institute.

Following his education, Beck, concerned with the lack of scientific basis for psychoanalysis, embarked on research intended to substantiate psychoanalytic concepts. In a study of depressed people's dreams, Beck hypothesized that their dreams "would contain more hostility than those of nondepressed people . . . .Instead their dreams reflected three common themes: defeat, deprivation, and loss" (1991). While psychoanalytically treating a patient, Beck also discovered that, in spite of the instruction to free-associate, the patient was not sharing with him certain thoughts that preceded and were responsible for her feelings. Prior to feeling anxious, she had had the thought, "I must be boring him." Soliciting and focusing on these fleeting, unreported, involuntary thoughts led him to identify in his patients specific cognitive patterns—preconscious internal communication systems that frequently distorted reality yet affected emotions and behavior. He began to believe that "depressed people did not seek failure; rather they distorted reality to the point where they could not recognize success when it happened" (Greenberg, 1981). These failures of traditional psychoanalysis led him eventually to develop cognitive therapy as a way of understanding and treating depression.

In addition to his teaching duties at the University of Pennsylvania, Beck has researched issues such as depression, suicide, anxiety and panic disorders, substance abuse, marital problems, and personality disorders. He has received a number of honors for his contributions to the comprehension and therapy of depression, anxiety, and suicidal behaviors. His alma mater, Brown, gave him an honorary Doctor of Medical Science in 1982 and the Distinguished Alumnus Award in 1990. In 1987, he was elected a fellow of the Royal College of Psychiatrists. He received the prestigious Lasker Award for Clinical Medical Research in 2006. Beck has written or coauthored over five hundred articles and sixteen books. He has also developed a number of assessment instruments.

PHILOSOPHICAL ORIGINS

Cognitive therapy's theoretical foundation is derived from three main sources: the phenomenological approach to psychology, structural theory and depth psychology, and cognitive psychology. The phenomenological approach, demonstrated in the writings of Adler (1936), Horney (1950), Sullivan (1953), and Rogers (1959), holds that an individual's view of self and the personal world is central to behavior. The structural theory and depth psychology of Kant (1798) and Freud, particularly Freud's concept of the hierarchical structuring of cognition into primary and secondary processes, influenced cognitive theory. More recent developments in cognitive psychology also have had an impact, such as George Kelly's (1955) use of "personal constructs" and his emphasis on the role of beliefs in behavior change, even though Kelly himself did not like being called a cognitivist.

Cognitive theory was originally developed to facilitate treatment for depression, and it is still one of the best effective treatments for that disorder. Aaron Beck, however, moved cognitive therapy from a set of cognitive-behavioral techniques to an empirically based school of psychology (Clark & Beck, 1999).

THE THEORY BEHIND COGNITIVE THERAPY

Cognitive therapy is based on a theory of personality that maintains that how one thinks largely determines how one feels and behaves. It is similar in many ways to rational emotive behavior theory and therapy. Both Ellis and Beck believe that people can consciously change how they reason, and both view the client's underlying assumptions as targets of intervention. However, REBT bases its concepts of personality dysfunction primarily on philosophical, existential, and humanistic bases, and cognitive therapy tends to support its concepts with empirical outcome studies (Ellis, 2003; Padesky & Beck, 2003). Cognitive processes are able to be observed by clients and studied by researchers. Thus the validity of cognitive therapy can be studied (Fox, 2006). Whereas Ellis confounded and persuaded clients that the philosophies they lived by were irrational, Beck "turned the client into a colleague who researches verifiable reality" (Wessler, 1986, p. 5).

Cognitive Schemas

Beck's approach recognizes the importance of schemas. **Schemas** are cognitive structures that consist of an individual's fundamental core beliefs and assumptions about how the world operates. Before birth our biology and chemistry preprogram us with certain types of proto-schemas (referring to survival, bonding, autonomy, etc.), which vary in strength from person to person (Beck & Hollon, 1993). The environment facilitates or inhibits the emergence of the schema in a way that may or may not assist in adaptation. Schemas, therefore, develop early in life from personal experiences and identification with significant others. People form concepts about themselves, others, and the world that shape personality. Schemas may be adaptive or maladaptive. They may be general or specific. The behavioral and emotional patterns that make up personality, therefore, are derived from individual rules about life and beliefs about the self. Examples of schemas are "Unless other people approve of me, I am worthless" or "Unless I can do something perfectly, I should not do it at all." Schemas are much more stable than cognitions, but they are somewhat dependent on a person's moods.

The schemas of depressed individuals are characterized by negative and pessimistic beliefs that reflect primal concerns of loss and deprivation and focus on one's being helpless and unlovable. Individuals who are predisposed to anxiety or depression have latent primal threat or loss modes that remain in a chronic state of readiness so that a relatively minor stressful event can activate them. The dominance of the primal loss mode of thinking interferes with the person's ability to develop more adaptive, constructive modes of thinking and also leads to biased information processing and other cognitive errors. In Beck's cognitive theory, the root of many psychological problems does not lie deep in the unconscious; it lies in problems of thinking patterns nearer to conscious awareness.

Automatic Thoughts

Beck distinguishes between automatic and controlled thoughts or levels of cognitive processing. **Automatic thoughts** are involuntary and unintentional. They often occur at a preconscious level and are difficult to stop or regulate. In contrast, controlled thoughts are voluntary, intentional, fully conscious, and more amenable to regulation. Automatic thoughts function as self-monologues, inner voices that may support or berate us. A woman engaged in an endless depreciating self-monologue telling herself that she is unattractive and worthless may be led to behave in self-defeating ways, such as promiscuity, because she does not believe she has anything better to offer. Beck discovered that specific themes and contents in the automatic thoughts of individuals suffering from different personality disorders leading them to interpret events in various but typical ways. A depressed person's self-monologue following someone's departure might reflect helplessness or being unloved, and a paranoid individual's automatic thoughts would construe the same situation as a form of persecution or abuse.

> **Thinking Critically**
>
> How can you recognize automatic thoughts? See the Thinking Critically box "Automatic Thoughts Diary."

Thinking Critically

Automatic Thoughts Diary

Beck attributes many psychological problems to unexamined automatic thoughts and systematic distortions. He suggested that clients keep a "Daily Record of Dysfunctional Thoughts" to help them identify distressing thought patterns and substitute more constructive ones. You can keep such a diary by answering in a journal the following questions whenever you experience a negative feeling such as depression or anger.

1. In what situation did the feeling occur?
2. What (automatic) thought passed through your mind?
3. What type of cognitive distortion can you identify in your thinking? (See Table 16.1.)
4. How could you rationally and constructively respond to the thought?
5. How might your new response change your emotion?

Being aware of our tendencies to make certain cognitive distortions can be helpful, because if we are aware of our tendencies, we can take steps to control them. Did you discover any cognitive distortions other than those included in Table 16.1?

SOURCE: Beck, Aaron T. (1991), Biographical Sketch, unpublished manuscript. Used with permission.

Cognitive Distortions

Systematic errors in reasoning called **cognitive distortions** appear during psychological distress (Beck, 1967). Examples are given in Table 16.1. Distortions in cognitions arise when stressful events trigger an unrealistic schema. Each individual has a set of idiosyncratic vulnerabilities that predispose the person to psychological distress in a unique way and that are related to the individual's personality structure and cognitive schemas. Such *errors in logic* frequently entail a primitive yet systematic negative style of thinking, in which the cognitive distortions are linked together in a sequential chain of negative processing that becomes automatic (see Table 16.2).

Sociotropic and Autonomous Dimensions of Personality

Beck further describes personality in terms of two dimensions that have particular relevance to the tendency toward depression. The **sociotropic dimension** is characterized by dependence on interpersonal relationships and a need for closeness and nurturance. This

TABLE 16.1 COGNITIVE DISTORTIONS

Beck provides several definitions and examples of cognitive distortions.

COGNITIVE DISTORTION	DEFINITION	EXAMPLE
Arbitrary inference	Drawing a specific conclusion without supporting evidence or even in the face of contradictory evidence	After getting a C rather than an A on the first test, a student erroneously concludes that she would not be able to pass the course.
Selective abstraction	Conceptualizing a situation on the basis of a detail taken out of context and ignoring all other possible explanations	An individual who is nervous about getting into an accident while driving will zero in on all the reports about traffic accidents while listening to the morning news, reconfirming the belief that driving is a dangerous activity.
Overgeneralization	Abstracting a general rule from one or two isolated incidents and applying it too broadly	Hearing about a robbery in the city leads one to conclude that everyone is being robbed.
Magnification and minimization	Seeing an event as more significant or less significant than it actually is	A high school girl thinks that if she is not asked to go to the senior prom, her life is over.
Personalization	Attributing external events to oneself without evidence of connection	Parents assume that they are to blame every time their children misbehave.
Dichotomous thinking	Categorizing situations in extremes	A person sees his or her performance on a task as either a complete success or a total failure.

TABLE 16.2 A SEQUENCE OF AUTOMATIC THOUGHTS

A patient, engaged in an argument with his brother, later accessed the following sequence of automatic thoughts. What cognitive distortions can you identify?

I'm talking too loudly.

He's not listening to me.

I'm making a fool of myself.

He's got a lot of nerve ignoring what I am saying.

Should I tell him off?

He would probably make me look totally foolish.

He never listens to me.

He does not respect me.

SOURCE: A. T. Beck (1999), Prisoners of Hate, New York: Perennial.

dimension is organized around closeness, nurturance, and dependency. The **autonomous dimension** is characterized by independence and organized around goal setting, self-determination, and self-imposed obligations (Beck, Epstein, & Harrison, 1983). Although "pure" cases of sociotropy and autonomy exist, most people display features of both, depending on the situation. Thus sociotropy and autonomy are modes of behavior, not fixed personality structures. Beck's research shows that dependent individuals become depressed when their relationships are disrupted. Autonomous people become depressed when they fail to achieve a certain goal.

The Cognitive Triad

According to Beck (1967), the depressed individual has a negative view of him- or herself, the world, and the future. These three perceptions form the **cognitive triad.** The world seems devoid of pleasure or gratification. The depressed person's view of the future is pessimistic or nonexistent. The increased dependency often observed in depressed patients reflects the view of self as incompetent, an overestimation of the difficulty of normal life tasks, the expectation of failure, and the desire for someone more capable to take over. Indecisiveness similarly reflects the belief that one is incapable of making correct decisions. The physical symptoms of depression—low energy, fatigue, and inertia—are also related to negative expectations.

COGNITIVE PSYCHOTHERAPY

Borrowing some of its concepts from psychodynamic therapy and a number of techniques from behavior therapy and client-oriented psychotherapy, **cognitive therapy** consists of a set of well-defined therapeutic techniques that serve as an integrative model for effective psychotherapy (Alford & Beck, 1997). Cognitive therapy seeks to remove systematic biases in thinking by correcting faulty information processing, thus helping clients to modify assumptions that maintain maladaptive behaviors and emotions. Cognitive and behavioral methods are used to challenge dysfunctional beliefs and to promote more realistic thinking. The ultimate goal is to deactivate the more automatic primal modes and to strengthen more constructive reflective modes of thinking (Beck & Clark, 1997).

Cognitive therapy fosters change in clients' beliefs by conceiving of beliefs as testable hypotheses to be examined through behavioral experiments jointly agreed upon by client and counselor. The cognitive therapist does not tell the client that the beliefs are irrational or wrong. Instead, the therapist asks questions that elicit the meaning, function, usefulness, and consequences of the client's beliefs. It is up to the individual client to decide which beliefs to keep and which ones to eliminate.

Cognitive therapy is not as simple as replacing negative thoughts with positive self-statements. Change can occur only if the client experiences **affective arousal.** In the language of cognitive therapy, hot cognitions happen when a person experiences arousing emotions and reality testing at the same time. A **hot cognition** is the actual phrase, fear, or critical self-blaming thought, such as "Oh, what a klutz I am." An examination of personal experience and logic at the same time allows the client to change the inner attitude or belief.

Cognitive therapy is present-centered, directive, active, problem-oriented, and best suited for cases in which problems can be delineated and cognitive distortions are apparent. It is not designed for personal growth or developmental work. It consists of highly specific learning experiences designed to teach clients to monitor their negative, automatic thoughts or cognitions; recognize the connections between cognition, affect, and behavior; examine the evidence for and against distorted automatic thoughts; substitute more reality-oriented interpretations for these biased cognitions; and learn to identify and alter the beliefs that predispose them to distort their experiences (Beck, Rush, Shaw, & Emory, 1979).

Various cognitive and behavioral techniques are used to enable the client and the therapist to work together to effect genuine change. Anxious clients commonly "catastrophize" and anticipate the worst possible outcome of a situation. Using the cognitive technique of *decatastrophizing* and asking the client to anticipate the worst possible outcome of a situation can help to place it in a more realistic perspective. *Role-play,* or the rehearsal of a situation that will later happen in real life, is also a helpful behavioral technique. These are just a few of many techiques included in the repertoire of the cognitive-behavioral therapist.

Beck's cognitive therapy uses many techniques in common with Ellis's rational emotive behavior therapy, such as desensitization. However, Beck does not dispute the client's cognitive distortion as actively and directly as Ellis does. His is a gentler form of therapy (Beck would never interrupt a patient in midsentence), but also very effective.

Beck has used his cognitive and therapeutic principles to analyze destructive behavior and to explore the dynamics of thoughts, emotions, and behavior in the causes and prevention of hatred (1999). He shows that the basic elements of destructive behavior, be it domestic abuse, prejudice, terrorism, war, genocide, or some other form, share familiar patterns with reactions to the frustrations of everyday life. Hate and violence stem from diminishing and dehumanizing other people, common patterns in dysfunctional interpersonal relations. Under frustration, our minds can be taken over by a type of primitive thinking that leads us to behave in irrational ways. We can develop a negative "frame" toward another, leading us to feel mistreated and to behave in an aggressive manner toward the assumed foe. In war people are encouraged to forsake a healthy pattern of judging others along a broad continuum of various shades of good and bad and to engage in dichotomous thinking based on notions of "we are totally good" and "they are totally evil." Terrorists, for example, view themselves as righteous and committed to a noble cause. Beck also offers solutions and suggestions showing how human rationality can help us change our thinking in order to live better, more loving lives.

ASSESSMENT AND RESEARCH IN BECK'S THEORY

Aaron Beck developed an instrument to measure depression called the **Beck Depression Inventory,** which is widely seen as the finest psychometric instrument for this objective. Equally important have been his longitudinal studies on suicide and its deterrence. Other assessment devices that Beck has published include the Beck Anxiety Scale, Beck Hopelessness Scale, Beck Scale for Suicide Ideation, and Beck Self-Concept Test.

Ninety percent of the studies testing the cognitive model have supported it. Outcome studies have corroborated the power of the cognitive theory of depression (Stricklin-Parker & Schneider, 2005). Other studies show that cognitive therapy is helpful in panic disorders, obsessive-compulsive disorder, substance abuse, personality disorders, marital problems, sex offenses, schizophrenia, and suicide prevention (Beck, 1991, 2005a; Beck & Rector, 2000; Block, 2004). Effectiveness is usually determined on the basis of percentage of improvement and maintenance of gains at follow-up and in terms of comparison with other types of therapy (including pharmacotherapy) or other controls (Beck & Hollon, 1993).

Beck encourages his critics to test his theory and his results. He acknowledges that more decisive tests of the kinds of cognitive change or causal structures entailed in his theory would have to consider that some cognitive schema may be latent and therefore difficult to assess unless primed or activated; that the model is a *diathesis-stress* one, which sees disorders as joint functions of a diathesis, or predisposition, and environmental stress, so that simply assessing cognitions in the absence of live events would not be sufficient; and that attention must be given to idiographic methodologies that would be sensitive to individual vulnerabilities (Beck & Hollon, 1993).

Many books have been published on cognitive therapy, and two scholarly journals focus on the topic. Most big cities in North America and numerous cities in other nations have centers for instruction in cognitive therapy. In an age of Prozac and other antidepressants, the population of people seeking cognitive therapies has changed to people with more complicated problems than simple anxiety or depression (Goode, 2000). Cognitive therapy is showing significant promise with patients for whom medication is insufficient and is also being tested with patients with severe psychiatric disorders. Beck believes that his approach is useful with more serious psychotic disorders, even schizophrenia (Beck & Rector, 2000). He believes that cognitive therapy may work with schizophrenics because it helps them to organize their mental processes and gain access to their logical thinking abilities (Goode, 2000). In spite of the effectiveness of many medications, Beck reminds us, "People are missing the boat if they say that because it can be treated by drugs, depression [and other psychological disorders] are primarily biological in nature. . . . People who receive psychotherapy learn something; people on drugs don't" (Greenberg, 1981). In a public dialogue with the Dalai Lama, Beck enumerated several points of similarity between Buddhism and cognitive therapy (2005b).

Donald Meichenbaum has taken Beck's cognitive restructuring and behavioral methods and developed techniques such as Stress Inoculation Training (Meichenbaum & Deffenbacher, 1988). He is a leader in the application of operant conditioning principles in settings ranging from classrooms to institutions for exceptional individuals. Meichenbaum's work on "self talk" and cognitive behavior modification is gaining increased recognition.

Because of his work in controversial domains, Aaron Beck is often seen as a "maverick." His "approach is so straightforward in shunning traditional complexities that Dr. Beck says it befuddles many psychiatrists. 'Analysts view me as a behaviorist and behaviorists view me as an analyst.' . . . He says simply, 'I am a researcher'" (Greenberg, 1981). In any event, his work on depression, schizophrenia, and borderline personality disorder has had a significant impact.

Arnold Lazarus (1932–   )

BIOGRAPHICAL BACKGROUND

Johannesburg, South Africa, was the birthplace of Arnold A. Lazarus on January 27, 1932. When he was born, his older sisters were seventeen and fourteen and his brother was almost nine. "'A skinny kid, who was bullied a lot,'" Lazarus took to lifting weights, and at seventeen he left school thinking he would open a health and training center. Two years later, he was convinced it would be smarter to return and finish his education (Dryden, 1991).

All of his degrees are from the University of Witwatersrand in Johannesburg: a B.A. in psychology and sociology in 1955, a B.A. with honors in psychology in 1956, an M.A. in experimental psychology in 1957, and a Ph.D. in clinical psychology in 1960. At first he thought he would major in English, but he was fascinated by psychology.

In the 1950s, while Lazarus was a student at the University of Witwatersrand, the psychotherapeutic climate was predominantly Freudian and Rogerian. Visiting lectures by Joseph Wolpe, a general medical practitioner who was applying "conditioning methods" with his patients, led to the formation of a small group of "neobehaviorists." The members of this group knew that performance-based methods were usually better in clinical practice than purely verbal and cognitive approaches. Whereas the psychotherapeutic establishment viewed behavior as the outward manifestation of more fundamental psychic processes, the neobehaviorists stressed that behavior per se is often clinically significant. People can acquire insight and change significant beliefs and still use maladaptive coping behavior and self-destructive behavior.

To legitimize behavioral intervention as an essential part of clinical practice, Lazarus in 1958 introduced

Arnold Lazarus's multimodal therapy is informed by his theory of the BASIC-ID.

the terms *behavior therapy* and *behavior therapist* (Lazarus, 1958). His doctoral dissertation, "New Group Techniques in the Treatment of Phobic Conditions," was the first study to explore the use of systematic desensitization in groups and included the development of objective scales for assessing phobic avoidance (Dryden, 1991).

In 1959, Lazarus began private practice. In 1963 he was elected to the presidency of the South African Society for Clinical and Experimental Hypnosis.

Growing distress with apartheid led the Lazaruses to the United States, and in 1967 Lazarus began working with Joseph Wolpe as a professor in the Department of Behavioral Science at Temple University Medical School in Philadelphia. However, it quickly became apparent that Wolpe's and Lazarus's interests and thinking were headed in different directions. After teaching briefly at Yale University in 1970 and publishing *Behavior Therapy and Beyond* (1971), Lazarus assumed the rank of Distinguished Professor of Psychology at Rutgers University in 1972.

Lazarus has received several honors and been president of many professional organizations. He has written eighteen books and over 250 journal articles. He has lectured widely and is often cited as "one of the most influential psychotherapists of the twentieth century" (Dryden, 1991). In 1992 he received the Distinguished Psychologist Award, Division of Psychotherapy, from the American Psychological Association. In 1996 he was awarded the highly prestigious Cummings PSYCHE Award, and in 1997 he received an award from the Division of Clinical Psychology for Distinguished Professional Contributions. In 1999 he received two Lifetime Achievement Awards. He retired from Rutgers in 1998 and is now president of the Center for Multimodal Psychological Services in Princeton, New Jersey, and executive director of the Lazarus Institute in Skillman, New Jersey.

The Development of a Theory and the BASIC-ID

In 1966 Lazarus published an article that challenged narrow stimulus-response formulations of the early 1960s and focused on dyadic transactions, or significant interpersonal relationships, as a significant part of the maintenance of maladaptive behavior. This was the first step in a significant movement away from the radical behaviorism of an earlier period. Contemporary behavior theory and therapy has moved from the individual to the group and to society at large.

No one exemplifies these developments more than Lazarus (Franks, 1997), whose multimodal therapy is one of the "most methodologically sophisticated expressions" of behavior therapy to date. Spurning psychoanalytic methods in favor of the apparently more favorable pattern of early stimulus-response conditioning therapy, Lazarus soon became disillusioned with the then current behavioral strategies. Slowly and carefully, he developed a new set of clinical strategies that has come to be known as **multimodal therapy.**

The importance of feeling, behavior, and thought (Affect-Behavior-Cognition) is well documented in the writings and practices of behavior theorists and therapists, but Lazarus felt that they gloss over other significant modalities, such as our senses, our tendency to form pictures of events, and crucial interpersonal factors. A comprehensive appraisal based on the observation that clients are usually troubled by a multitude of specific problems called for an examination of behavior, affect, sensation, imagery, cognition, and interpersonal relationships. The first letter of each word forms the acronym BASIC-I.

Behavior entails overt behaviors. *Affect* refers to the emotions. *Sensation* entails the wide realm of sensory stimuli. *Imagery* may entail a memory or the deliberate imaging of a relaxing image or scene. *Cognition* includes the intuition, ideology, concepts, and judgments that make up our basic attitudes, values, and beliefs. *Interpersonal relations* entails one's social life and issues of intimacy with others (1976). *D* was added to the acronym to stand for *drugs* (neurological and biochemical factors that influence behavior). Lazarus is aware that some clients may require medication, but *D* has also come to stand for all aspects of physical well-being. With the addition of drugs, the acronym became **BASIC-ID** (see Figure 16.2).

THEORY OF PERSONALITY

Lazarus believes that the seven modalities—behavior, affect, sensation, imagery, cognition, interpersonal processes, and drugs/biology—may be said to make up human personality. The BASIC-ID is presumed to comprise human temperament and personality, and it is assumed that everything from anger, disappointment, greed, fear, grief, awe, contempt, and boredom to love, hope, faith, and joy can be accounted for by examining components and interactions within a person's BASIC-ID.

Lazarus holds that each person is a product of genetic history, environment, and learning. He gives great importance to the concept of individual physical **thresholds.** People have different thresholds, or tolerance levels, for pain, frustration, or stress. These thresholds are unique and individual. Psychological interventions can bolster physical thresholds, but genetics, which also influences thresholds, cannot be significantly changed.

Thinking Critically

Which modalities do you favor? See the Thinking Critically box "Using the Basic-ID."

People tend to favor some BASIC-ID modality; thus, we may speak of a "sensory reactor" or an "imagery reactor" or a "cognitive reactor." This does not imply that a person will always react in a certain way, but over time, a tendency to value certain response patterns can be noted. As Bandler and Grinder (1976) say, visualizers tend to "make pictures" out of what they hear. In terms of split-brain research (Galin, 1974; Kimura, 1979), imagery reactors are probably right-hemisphere dominant, whereas cognitive reactors are frequently left-hemisphere dominant (see Ornstein, 1997).

The habits that make up a personality are acquired through genetics, but also through association and conditioning. A good bit of human thoughts, feelings, and behaviors is due

1	**B** ehavior	What the individual does
2	**A** ffect	The predominant emotions
3	**S** ensation	Specific sensory stimuli
4	**I** magery	Predominant fantasies and images
5	**C** ognition	Primary attitudes, values, beliefs, and opinions
6	**I** nterpersonal	Relationships with other people
7	**D** rugs/**Biology**	Physical well-being

FIGURE 16.2 THE BASIC-ID

In Lazarus's theory, seven modalities, known as the BASIC-ID, make up personality. The first letters of each modality forms the acronym BASIC-ID.

Thinking Critically

Using the BASIC-ID

In Lazarus's theory, one's personality is reflected in the basic BASIC-ID. You can identify your preferences and compare the relative strength of the seven modalities that make up your BASIC-ID by rating yourself on the sample questions below using a scale from 6 (*highly characteristic of me*) to 0 (*highly uncharacteristic of me*).

1. **Behavior:** Are you active, a doer, very busy?
2. **Affect:** How emotional are you?
3. **Sensation:** How intently do you monitor your bodily sensations?
4. **Imagery:** Do you think in pictures, fantasy?
5. **Cognition:** Do you like to make plans, anticipate?
6. **Interpersonal:** Are you gregarious, intimate?
7. **Drugs/Biology:** Are you healthy? Do you abuse drugs or alcohol?

In reference to a specific problem, asking the following can also help to access the BASIC-ID:

1. **Behavior:** When you have the problem, what are you usually doing at the time?
2. **Affect:** How are you feeling? Fearful, depressed, discouraged . . . ?
3. **Sensation:** Do any parts of your body feel tense or uncomfortable?
4. **Imagery:** What pictures come to mind when you dwell on your problem?
5. **Cognition:** What thoughts, irrational and rational, do you have about the problem?
6. **Interpersonal:** Who are the other people involved in your problem?
7. **Drugs/Biology:** Do you ever resort to alcohol or sleeping pills while experiencing the problem?

---

to the simple conditioning of family life. Many aversions appear to result from an association of one stimulus with another. Bandura (1969, 1977) speaks of imitation, observational learning, modeling, and vicarious processes as means of acquiring life-styles and habits that make up our personalities. As Bandura's (1978) principle of reciprocal determination underscores, people do not react automatically to external stimuli. Their thoughts about those stimuli will determine which stimuli are noticed, how much they are valued, and how long they are remembered. Lazarus's view of the role for the unconscious is related to the recognition that different people have different levels of self-awareness. He states that nonawareness (subliminal) or nonrecognition of thoughts and feelings does not prevent these nonconscious processes from influencing a person's attitudes and behaviors. Lazarus simply does not deal with traditional psychoanalytic notions and concepts in his writing.

MULTIMODAL THERAPY

Multimodal therapy rests primarily on the theoretical base of social learning theory (Bandura, 1969, 1977, 1986a) while also drawing from general systems theory (Bertalanffy, 1974; Buckley, 1967) and group communications theory (Watzlawick, Weakland, & Fisch, 1974).

Lazarus's search for systematic therapies led him to the awareness that changing a client's cognitive modality often called for more than the correction of misconceptions. Lazarus needed to help clients change the messages conjured up by their imaginations. He added *goal rehearsal,* imagining yourself fulfilling your goal, *time projection,* imagining yourself projected into the future, and other coping imageries to his repertoire (see Lazarus, 1978, 1982).

Lazarus takes a holistic approach to his clients. Initially (Lazarus, 1973, 1976) the term *multimodal behavior therapy* was used to describe BASIC-ID assessment and treatment, but because emphasis is on comprehensive coverage of all the modalities, it is misleading to single out any one dimension over another. In a critical review of multimodal therapy, Kwee (1981) underscores its historical development from a narrow band of stimulus-response conditioning therapy by way of broad-spectrum behavior therapy to its present multimodal therapy and concludes that "whether or not multimodal therapy can be classified as behavior therapy is less important than the method itself" (p. 65).

Detailed accounts of multimodal assessment and therapy have been presented in several textbooks (for example, Carlson & Sperry, 2000; Corsini & Wedding, 2005; Nelson-Jones, 2001; Norcross & Goldfried, 2005; and O'Donohue, Fisher, & Hayes, 2003), and encyclopedias (Lazarus, 2001, 2004). Books, articles, and chapters on multimodal therapy have been written or translated into German, Italian, Portuguese, Spanish, and Dutch. Multimodal therapy has also been proven effective beyond the traditional therapeutic settings and can be found in day hospitals, nursing homes, and self-help support programs (Brunell & Young, 1982; O'Keefe & Castaldo, 1981; Roberts, Jackson, & Phelps, 1980).

Another fundamental multimodal therapy assumption is that without new experiences there can be no change. The multimodal therapy methods, therefore, are *performance based.* Woody puts it very clearly when he says that an effective therapist "must be more than a 'nice guy' who can exude prescribed interpersonal conditions—he must have an armamentarium of scientifically derived skills and techniques to supplement this effective interpersonal relations" (Lazarus, 1971).

Multimodal therapy is predicated on the assumption that the more disturbed the client is, the greater the specific excesses and deficits there will be throughout the BASIC-ID. Lazarus bases his model on actualization and self-determination rather than on pathology. His theory places primary emphasis on the uniqueness of each person. Maximum flexibility rather than fixed rules is demanded of the therapist in selecting and matching therapeutic interventions to each client (1994, 1996a, 1996b, 1997). The fundamental question is always "what is best for this particular client?"

Although multimodal therapy draws heavily from several systems (both rational emotive and cognitive), there are distinctive features that set multimodal therapy apart: (1) its holistic approach of giving attention to the full BASIC-ID; (2) the use of **modality profiles,** or a specific list of problems and proposed treatments spanning the client's BASIC-ID; (3) the use of a **structural profile,** or a quantitative assessment of the relative involvement of each of the elements of the BASIC-ID; (4) the use of **bridging,** a multimodal technique used by counselors to deliberately begin work in terms of their client's preferred modality (with a feeling-sensory client it can be detrimental to insist on cognitive restructuring right at the onset of treatment; multimodal therapy starts where the client is and bridges into more challenging areas as the therapeutic relationship develops); and (5) the use of **tracking,** or paying careful attention to the "firing order" of the different modalities. The "firing order" refers to "how the modalities interact to cause the client's problems" (Lazarus, 1985) or the order in which the modalities appear. Most people report a reasonably stable range of firing order much of the time. Recognition of these patterns permits intervention at any point in the firing sequence. Tracking also enables one to select the most appropriate intervention techniques.

Multimodal therapy offers a precise and disciplined behavioral retraining process. Behaviorists are sometimes insensitive to the individual's interpersonal needs and affective reactions. Multimodal therapy helps them to meet this challenge (Lazarus, 1989, 1997).

TECHNICAL ECLECTICISM

Lazarus is also very well known for advocating **technical eclecticism** (1995, 1996c, 2008). He maintains that good treatment methods may be derived from many sources without necessarily agreeing with the theories that generated them. He further believes that if therapists or counselors use only the methods included in their favored theoretical view, they will invariably neglect effective techniques that are used by therapists or counselors of other persuasions. Thus Lazarus may borrow techniques that were generated by Gestalt therapy, Transactional Analysis, or existential therapy without embracing the theory held by their founders and disciples. Lazarus says he prefers to operate out of social and cognitive learning theory because "its tenets are grounded in research and are open to verification and disproof.... [moreover] I have yet to find any effective procedure that cannot be readily explained in terms of social and cognitive learning theory" (Dryden, 1991). He sees the main difference between other colleagues and himself as his "willingness to go the extra mile for the client" (Lazarus, 2002; see also Lazarus & Zur, 2002).

Lazarus further maintains that the greater number of coping skills clients develop, the less likely they will backslide. Thus Lazarus's method is performance based. He starts by observing behavior and develops a reeducation plan custom-made for each client.

Lazarus's eclectic multimodal theory and therapy, performance-based and tailor-made for each client, is demonstrably effective; however, the inherent limitations of controlled evaluations make it difficult to attend to the particularities of individual cases (Davison & Lazarus, 1994).

| PHILOSOPHY, |
| SCIENCE, |
| *and* ART |

Cognitive Behavioral Therapies and Theories

Although cognitive behavioral therapies and theories clearly emphasize the art of psychotherapy and counseling, one can find some key underlying philosophical assumptions. Ellis's roots in Stoic philosophy and his realistic attitude of both pessimism and optimism concerning human nature (that human beings have a strong tendency to sabotage themselves but at the same time have enormous potential for change and self-actualization) are important philosophical assumptions. Beck's strong roots in phenomenology, the structural theory and depth psychology of Kant

Philosophical Assumptions

Which philosophical issues are most important to Ellis, Beck, and Lazarus? See the Philosophical Assumptions box "Examining Ellis, Beck, and Lazarus."

and Freud, and more modern developments in cognitive psychology lead him also to concur that people have great potential to change. Lazarus further agrees with the crucial significance of emotional freedom and rational thinking. These theorists recognize that behavior is both determined and free, that both hereditary and environmental factors influence behavior, and that although there are similarities among people, each one of us develops a unique way of coping with life's problems. Although learning is important in shaping our behaviors, people can also act primarily on their own initiative.

In neurotic clients, dysfunctional beliefs (Ellis) and cognitive schemas (Beck) function as philosophical assumptions. The client is compelled by them and tenaciously clings to them out of that compulsion. The therapist helps the patient to treat the dysfunctional beliefs and cognitive schemas as working hypotheses and to test them. In the process, they may be successfully falsified and changed, leading the client to new epiphanies and alternative beliefs and schemas.

The emphasis on behavior, "rational" thinking, and science in behavioral and cognitive theories of personality clearly fits and perpetuates the preferred philosophical models and functions of white male Euro-Americans. It may not be suitable for the diverse ways of knowing and being of other populations. For example, the emphasis on thinking as primary and the need to challenge beliefs may be inappropriate for Asians, who emphasize emotional harmony with cultural norms (Kantrowitz & Ballou, 1992). Work is being done to re-vision therapy through diverse lenses, recognizing that as individuals, families, and groups we are all embedded in and bound by class, culture, gender, and race. Examples of psychological illness and effective healing can be found from minority as well as majority cultures from all over the world (Goldrick, 1996, 1998).

Cognitive-behavioral methods of therapy and counseling have received considerable empirical and scientific support (cf. Westen, Novotny, & Thompson-Brenner,

Philosophical Assumptions

Examining Ellis, Beck, and Lazarus

Many of the differences among personality theories can be attributed to fundamental differences in philosophical assumptions. Which of the basic philosophical issues, described in the introductory chapter and summarized on the inside back cover, seem to be clearly important to Ellis, Beck, and Lazarus in the development of their theories? How, for example, does Ellis's A-B-C theory of personality influence his stance on freedom versus determinism? How does Beck's view of the origin of cognitive schemas influence his position on heredity versus environment? How does Lazarus's identification of the BASIC-ID shape his view of uniqueness versus universality? Do their cognitive-behavior therapies reflect an optimistic or pessimistic point of view? Do their theories address any other philosophical assumptions? Rate Ellis, Beck, and Lazarus on a scale of 1 to 5 on those philosophical assumptions that you feel their theories apply to most. Compare your ratings with your own philosophical assumptions. Did your study of Ellis, Beck, and Lazarus lead you to change any of your assumptions? Why or why not?

Much of the therapeutic work of Ellis, Beck, and Lazarus can be done in groups, a cost-saving factor that is very attractive in a climate of managed care.

2004). In particular, Ellis's research at the Albert Ellis Institute confirmed his approach to counseling; Beck's research studies into many areas of maladaptive behaviors and his development of assessment inventories demonstrate the effectiveness of his cognitive therapy; and Lazarus's development of objective scales for assessing phobic avoidance, pre- and posttreatment assessments, and research on the BASIC-ID demonstrate the effectiveness of multimodal therapy. At the same time, cognitive theories are more alike in practice than individual author positions might suggest. The movement is toward integration, incorporating concepts and techniques from various theoretical perspectives and appreciating the significance of diverse cultural lenses.

The current emphasis on managed care has led to an increase in short-term psychotherapy that is directed toward the active resolution of specific problems and is frequently limited to a specific number of sessions (see also Sanchez & Turner, 2003). "Not unreasonably managed care demands demonstrably effective interventions that are valid, short-term, of minimal cost, and consumer-friendly" (Franks, 1997; see also Lazarus, 2000). Some critics are concerned that managed-care companies are making decisions on the basis of cost effectiveness rather than medical desirability and that these decisions may be jeopardizing the quality of mental health care (Goleman, 1996; Yalom, 2002). At the same time, the demands of managed care have led to the development of innovative models for meeting the challenges of providing adequate psychotherapy and keeping costs reasonable (MacKenzie, 1996). Lazarus reminds us that short-term therapy can be practiced without shortchanging the patient (1997).

It is in the application and art of psychotherapy and counseling that these behavioral cognitive therapies and theories really shine. Extremely practical, down to earth, directive, and eclectic, these theorists are determined to help people change and to improve their life-styles. And they are effective! Moreover, much of the work that they do can be done in groups—a cost-saving factor that is important in this climate of economic concerns. Twelve-step programs frequently employ cognitive tools to foster behavioral change, as does the currently very popular *choice theory,* the new reality theory developed by William Glasser (see Glasser, 1998, 2000). Although Ellis, Beck, and Lazarus are criticized for being simple, incomplete, and one-sided as philosophers of human nature, Ellis and Beck were praised as "legends" at the 2000 APA convention, and there is little reason to doubt that all three will continue to have an enormous impact in the areas of therapy and counseling.

Mindfulness

In a new development that is coming to be known as the "Third Wave" of behaviorism, researchers such as Steven Hayes, Marsha Linehan, Robert Kohlenberg, and Zindel Segal are paying less attention to changing the *content* of thoughts and focusing more on changing their *context,* a process that Segal calls disidentifying with thoughts (Segal, Williams, Teasdale, 2002). Typically we identify with our thoughts and feelings, rather than seeing them as simply reactions. For example, if we think a stupid thought, we conclude "I am stupid." Without trying to prove or disprove such conclusions (as cognitive-behavioral therapists have tended to do), these theorists teach **mindfulness,** a discipline of noting thoughts and feelings without becoming enmeshed in them. Hayes uses the illustration of treating thoughts and feelings as if they were leaves being observed as they float along a stream. Mindfulness involves accepting thoughts and emotions and defusing from judgments. It is not a distraction or avoidance technique. It requires practice, and specific techniques can be used to cultivate it.

Acceptance and commitment therapy (ACT), developed by Hayes, helps individuals identify a set of personal core values, or chosen life directions, based on what matters most to them, and then commit to behaviors that will advance those values in spite of potentially painful emotional obstacles (Hayes, Strosahl, & Wilson, 1999). Acceptance and mindfulness practices, together with commitment and strategies to change behavior, help increase psychological flexibility, which permits us to be fully in touch with the present and to continue or change our behaviors, depending on the situation, in the service of chosen values. ACT assumes that most psychological suffering is caused by experiential avoidance. The choice is not between pain and problems or no pain and no problems. It's between old, familiar, deadening pain and problems or new, challenging, enlivening pain and problems that help us move forward.

Hayes also developed an explanation of how the mind works. Relational frame theory (Hayes, Barnes-Holmes, & Roche, 2001) explains that in our attempts to solve problems through verbal refutation we draw on the same language skills and cognitive processes that lure us into persistent but futile attempts to combat our inner demons, instead of making healthy contact with the thoughts and feelings we seek to avoid. Acceptance is not resignation or tolerance but an "active vital embrace of the moment" (Hayes & Smith, 2005). When we gently push our fingers into a Chinese finger trap (rather than persisting in trying to pull them out), we make room for them. In their practices, Hayes and his colleagues encourage clients to engage in specific experiential techniques and activities in order to learn to accept their thoughts and feelings and to identify their core values and behave in ways that will reflect them. Clinical research studies have yielded evidence of the positive impact of ACT and provided support for its underlying theory (Hayes, Masuda, Bissett, Luoma, & Guerrero, 2004).

Mindfulness introduces to the West a technique of detachment reminiscent of Eastern practices (to be discussed in the chapter on Zen Buddhism) and points toward a potentially fruitful convergence of East and West.

TO LEARN MORE about cognitive distortions and mindfulness, and for a list of suggested readings, visit the *Personality Theories* textbook website at **college.cengage.com/pic/engler8e**.

Summary

1. The philosophical origins of Ellis's **rational emotive behavior therapy** (p. 428) go back to the Stoics. The most important modern precursor is Alfred Adler.

2. Ellis suggested that human beings are "sign-, symbol-, and language-creating" animals who use four interrelated processes: perception, movement, thinking, and emotion. Evaluative thinking gives rise to "self-talk"—"internalized sentences" that shape our thoughts and emotions. According to Ellis, people have a strong innate tendency to engage in dysfunctional behaviors, but they also have the potential to change and self-actualize. Emotional disturbance usually arises when people care too much about what others think of them.

3. The **A-B-C theory of personality** (p. 430) suggests that people develop irrational and **musterbatory belief systems** (p. 431) when a highly charged emotional consequence (C) follows a significant activating event (A). A may seem to but does not actually cause C. Instead, emotional consequences are largely created by inappropriate irrational beliefs (B's).

4. Humans have an innate tendency to raise cultural preferences into *musts* and social norms into absolute *shoulds*.

5. The goal of rational emotive behavior therapy is to free individuals to commit themselves to actions that are congruent with their true value systems. The principal therapeutic techniques are **cognitive, emotive-evocative,** and **behavior therapy** (pp. 432–434).

6. The philosophical origins of Beck's cognitive theory are the phenomenological approach to psychology, structural theory and depth psychology, and cognitive psychology.

7. Cognitive therapy is based on a theory of personality that maintains that how one thinks largely determines how one feels and behaves. Personality reflects the individual's cognitive organization and structure, which are both biologically and socially influenced.

8. **Schemas** (p. 437) are cognitive structures that consist of an individual's core beliefs and assumptions about how the world operates. **Automatic thoughts** (p. 438) are involuntary, unintentional, preconscious thoughts that are hard to regulate. **Cognitive distortions** (p. 439) are systematic errors in reasoning.

9. The **sociotropic dimension** (p. 439) of personality is characterized by dependence on interpersonal relationships and a need for closeness and nurturance. The **autonomous dimension** (p. 440) is characterized by independence.

10. The **cognitive triad** (p. 440) is a depressed individual's negative view of him- or herself, the world, and the future.

11. Beck's **cognitive therapy** (p. 440) consists of therapeutic techniques designed to help the client experience **affective arousal** (p. 441).

12. Beck developed assessment instruments to measure depression, anxiety, hopelessness, and other emotional disorders. Unlike other behaviorists, Beck believes it is essential that people understand that their unrealistic views of the world and of their lives are responsible for their depression.

13. Lazarus's theory developed out of an emphasis on interpersonal relationships. He developed the personality-appraisal tool known as the **BASIC-ID** (p. 445). These letters stand for seven modalities: *behavior, affect, sensation, imagery, cognition, interpersonal relations,* and *drugs.*

14. Lazarus says people have different physical **thresholds** or tolerance levels, and tend to favor some BASIC-ID modality.

15. **Multimodal therapy** (p. 444) is performance based. Features that set it apart from other therapies are the use of **modality profiles** (p. 447), **structural profiles** (p. 447), **bridging** (p. 447), **tracking** (p. 448), and Lazarus's emphasis on **technical eclecticism** (p. 448).

16. Although behavioral cognitive therapies and theories are informed by philosophy and science, it is in the application and art of psychotherapy and counseling that they really shine.

17. The "Third Wave" of behaviorism is an emphasis on **mindfulness** (p. 451), noting thoughts and feelings without becoming enmeshed in them.

Personal Experiences

1. According to Ellis, we inherit a tendency to raise cultural preferences into *musts* and cultural norms into *shoulds.* Individually, we then create our own musturbatory belief systems consisting of absolute musts—things that we consider non-negotiable, that "absolutely must" happen. For example, a man feels that he *must* not be made fun of or embarrassed, instead of thinking that he would *prefer* not to be. In instances in which he is embarrassed, his emotional disturbance is elevated, not necessarily because of the instance itself but because of his absolute belief about embarrassment. Do you have personal absolute *musts?* Do you have *musts* about fairness, about going particular places, about being treated in a certain way, or about doing certain things? Sometimes it's difficult to think of *musts* on your own, so it may be helpful to enlist the insight of close friends and family. Ultimately, being aware of, and being able to contradict, your absolute *musts* will help you to quell the disturbance-related tendencies of those *musts.*

2. According to Beck, schemas are cognitive structures that consist of an individual's core beliefs and assumptions about how the world operates. Like Kelly's personal constructs, schemas shape the way we perceive and react to the world around us. Beck believes that

schemas develop early in life from personal experiences and identification with significant others. Try to better understand your personal schemas. First, what's your general perception of the world? Do you see life as hopeful, fun, exciting, sad, hostile? Once you identify your general life schema, recall one event, one condition, and one person from your childhood that contributed to the formation of this schema. Which do you feel was most influential? Do you feel this schema might have been different without that one influence?

3. Cognitive distortions are systematic errors in reasoning that appear when stressful life events trigger unrealistic perceptions. Table 16.1 provides descriptions and examples of six types of cognitive distortion. Referring to this table, supply a personal example of each type. In doing so, you'll be better able to assess your thought processes when confronting stressful situations.

4. You can facilitate and help to replenish the modalities that make up your BASIC-ID, according to Lazarus, by asking yourself on a regular basis the following questions and using your answers help strengthen your modalities:

   Behavior: "What fun things can I do?"

   Affect: "What positive emotions can I generate?"

   Sensation: "What sensory experiences can I enjoy?"

   Imagery: "What empowering and pleasant mental images can I conjure?"

   Cognition: "What positive self-talk can I employ?"

   Interpersonal: "Which amiable people can I associate with?"

   Drugs/Biology: "What specific health-related activities can I engage in?"

5. Here is a strategy to try in order to cultivate a state of mindfulness. The next time you are troubled by bothersome thoughts, imagine that you are standing on a bridge and that your negative thoughts and feelings are leaves floating down the stream below. Suspend judgment and become a detached observer. It might help to say to yourself, "I observe that I am feeling . . ." If you find yourself having negative thoughts about yourself, you might summarize them in one word, such as "stupid." Repeat the word over and over as quickly as you can for about a minute. After about twenty seconds, the word will have been defused, losing its emotional force and credibility.

PART EIGHT

A Non-Western Approach

Persons of all cultures have engaged in the effort to understand themselves and have developed scholarly concepts to account for the similarities and differences among them. As Westerners, we are frequently unaware of or tend to depreciate other psychologies, such as those that come from Eastern traditions. Although we have made great progress in the collection of information and have learned a great deal about ourselves, we are still far from an adequate understanding of what it means to be human beings. Our modern technology and culture have given rise to practices that may relieve many forms of human illness and suffering, but they have yet to provide satisfactory answers to the most fundamental questions of human existence.

Many movements of Eastern thought raise questions about the ultimate meaning and purpose of human life and have developed theories of personality insofar as they have investigated what it means to be a human being. In many respects these thought systems do not resemble philosophy or religion as much as they resemble the art of psychology and psychotherapy (Watts, 1961). Their basic concern is with the human situation: the suffering and frustrations of people. They emphasize the importance of techniques to accomplish change. Eastern thought aims at transformations in consciousness, feelings, emotions, and one's relation to other people and to the world. Neither original Buddhism nor Zen, the focus of this section, is "religious." These philosophies are not concerned with God, prayer, the soul, the hereafter, or any of the other trappings of religion. Instead they constitute a practical psychology of daily living to minimize stress and anxiety.

There are many varieties of Eastern thought: Hinduism, Buddhism, Confucianism, Taoism, and Sufism, among others. This text introduces one of them, Zen Buddhism, in order to help us recognize that the assumptions that constitute the consensus about reality in the modern-day Western world are not necessarily universal and shared by other cultures. From the viewpoint of many of these movements, several of our contemporary Western ideas about personality are very alien. No wonder we often have difficulty communicating, as long as we tacitly assume that our comprehension of human behavior is universally shared.

CHAPTER 17

Zen Buddhism

YOUR GOALS FOR THIS CHAPTER

1. Discuss the origins of **Zen** by describing the story of the **Buddha,** the teachings of Buddhism, and the main branches of thought that stemmed from early Buddhism.

2. Discuss the principle of **dependent origination.**

3. Discuss the three characteristics of existence: **anicca, dukkha,** and **anatta.**

4. Explain what is meant by **satori.**

5. Discuss the five **skandhas,** and explain what is meant by the statement that they are empty.

6. Describe the Eight Consciousnesses, and explain what is meant by the "seeding" of the **alayavijnana.**

7. Describe **zazen,** and contrast **shikantaza** with the **koan** method.

8. Learn to actually practice Zen meditation.

9. Compare the modes of liberation or psychotherapeutic change developed by the East and the West.

10. Evaluate Eastern theories of personality from the viewpoints of philosophy, science, and art.

This chapter was authored by Prof. Yōzan Mosig of the University of Nebraska–Kearney.

A professor once asked a Zen master to teach him about Zen. The master agreed and offered him a cup of tea. He accepted. The master prepared the tea and filled his guest's cup, continuing to pour tea until it was overflowing. The professor exclaimed, "What are you doing? Can't you see that the cup is already full?" "Ah," replied the master, "it is just like your mind, which is full with your ideas and misconceptions. How can I teach you something about Zen? Before you can receive more fresh tea, you must first empty your cup."

Only if you empty your cup and approach the material in this chapter with an open mind will you be able to appreciate and understand it.

The Introduction of Zen to the West

Daisetz Teitaro Suzuki (1870–1966) is often credited with singlehandedly introducing Zen Buddhism to the West. A follower of the Rinzai school of Zen (described below), Suzuki seldom mentioned the Soto school, although it was and is the main form of Zen in Japan. Alan Watts (1915–1973) later popularized the ideas of Suzuki in America. As a result, Rinzai Zen became well known in the West and Soto Zen remained almost unknown. Paradoxically, the Zen of D. T. Suzuki, though stressing enlightenment (satori) as the goal of Zen, never provided a practice method or any practical guidance to experience it.

In the 1960s and 1970s, due to the efforts of several Soto Zen masters, such as Shunryu Suzuki and Dainin Katagiri in America and Taisen Deshimaru in Europe, Zen spread. These masters, among others, deserve credit for being the true introducers of Zen in the West.

The Origins of Zen

Zen is a school of Buddhism that claims to represent the purest essence of Buddhist teachings. The origins of Zen trace back to the story of Siddhartha Gautama, born about 563 B.C.E. in northern India, the son of a king. Upon his birth, the story goes, a local sage prophesied that the child would become either a great sage or a conquering monarch. His father, preferring the latter, decided to accustom the child to a life of luxury and comfort, as befitted a future king. Siddhartha grew up a virtual prisoner in the palaces his father built for him, married a princess from a neighboring kingdom, and had a son.

Wanting to know the kingdom he was to rule one day, he finally got his father's permission to leave the palaces and see the country, but he was greatly disturbed by seeing on successive occasions a very old man, a severely ill person, and a funeral procession. These were his first encounters with old age, sickness, and death, since information about such aspects of the human condition had been withheld from him. Recognizing impermanence and suffering, he was so moved that he vowed to forsake his kingdom and to dedicate his life to finding a solution to the problem of suffering. He left in the middle of the night, leaving behind his wealth as well as his family, knowing that they would be cared for. He was twenty-nine years old.

For six years, Siddhartha sought out and trained under the greatest Yoga teachers of northern India. He learned and practiced their meditation techniques and achieved the

The joy and radiance of an enlightened master are evident in this photograph of Dainin Katagiri-roshi (1928–1990), who brought Zen to the American Midwest.

most advanced states of altered consciousness his teachers had accomplished. But he was dissatisfied, for he realized that regardless of the nature of the mental trance he experienced, it provided only a temporary escape—not a permanent cure for human suffering. He tried all the methods and studied under all available teachers, even engaging in intense ascetic practices and self-mortification designed to liberate the mind from the demands of the body, but to no avail.

In desperation, leaving the ascetic practices that brought him near to death from starvation, he accepted food, regaining his strength, and sat down under a great peepul tree (an Indian fig tree, which would become known as the *bodhi tree* or tree of enlightenment). He determined not to rise again until he found the answer to the problem of suffering. After seven days of intense concentration, he reached a profound flash of awakening, and the nature of reality as well as the solution to the problem that had tormented him were clear. From that moment on, he became known as **Buddha,** the Awakened One. He was then thirty-five years old. He spent the following forty-five years of his life traveling, teaching others, and sharing his great discovery. He made no claims of divine origin or of having received a divine revelation. When asked whether he was a god, or a supernatural being, he always replied no. When asked what he was, he said, "I am Awake" ("I am Buddha"). Radiant, peaceful, compassionate, and charismatic, he continued his work until he died at the age of eighty, in about 483 B.C.E.

The Buddha's teachings, preserved initially through an oral tradition, were eventually written down in the form of three collections or "baskets," known as the **Tripitaka.** The oldest version of these is believed to have been written in Pali, an ancient Indic language. It constitutes the scriptures of one of the two main branches of Buddhism, sometimes called the **Hinayana,** or "small vehicle," and represented today by the **Theravada** school. The Theravada canon is dominant today in parts of Southeast Asia. The second major canon, the **Mahayana,** uses primarily the Sanskrit version of the Tripitaka, in addition to which it recognizes a large number of additional scriptures not in the Pali canon, some attributed to the historical Buddha and others to diverse authors. The total number of scriptures in Buddhism surpasses 85,000, a massive body of literature. Mahayana (or "great vehicle") Buddhism is dominant in East Asia. Zen belongs to the Mahayana tradition, developing from roots in India through the filter of Taoism in China, passing from there to Korea and to Japan, and to the rest of the world.

A primary difference between Theravada and Mahayana Buddhism lies in their ideals of personal development. The former stresses renunciation of worldly life and a monastic life-style, seeking to develop the practitioner into an *arhat,* a sage who through practice and discipline is liberated from suffering. The latter accepts that enlightenment is possible also for lay practitioners. Its ideal is the **bodhisattva,** a person who vows to dedicate life to the salvation of all sentient beings, not accepting full liberation until all others are free from suffering. Of the two key virtues in Buddhism, wisdom and compassion, Theravada stresses the former, while Mahayana emphasizes the latter. This does not necessarily represent a contradiction.

The Teachings of the Buddha

What the Buddha discovered at the time of his awakening is very profound, complicated, and difficult to understand, yet amazingly simple, direct, and self-evident. To appreciate his great insight, it is helpful first to reflect on the philosophical background in India two and a half millennia ago.

There were then more philosophical schools and positions in India than ever developed in ancient Greece. These ranged from a form of Vedic mysticism that postulated a universal creator, or Brahma, and individual souls (**atman**) who transmigrated through many lives in order to become purified and rejoin the universal Brahma, to those who believed that all that existed was the material substance evident to the senses, and that at death the individual was totally extinguished. One extreme was the eternalist position, where a person's soul or atman continues eternally, and the other the annihilationist position, postulating that a human being is completely destroyed at death. The Buddha discovered a position between these extremes. He called this position **dependent origination.** He also advocated a life-style that avoided the extremes of self-indulgence and self-mortification. His position became known as the "Middle Way."

DEPENDENT ORIGINATION

The teaching of dependent origination is at the core of the Buddha's **Dharma** (meaning "Doctrine," "Truth," or "Law"). Simply stated, dependent origination is a law of causality that says: "This is, because that is; this is not, because that is not; when this arises, that arises; when this ceases, that ceases." Despite the apparent simplicity of this law, it is a far-reaching truth that leaves nothing untouched and causally connects everything in the universe, for it implies that all phenomena, whether they be external or internal events, come into existence depending on causes and conditions without which they could not be (Szehidewicz, 2000). These causes and conditions can themselves be either internal or external.

As Hanh (1988) suggests, consider the page of the book you are reading. This piece of paper can be, because a tree was, since the tree had to be in order to be cut down to make the paper. This same piece of paper is also because there was rain and sunshine; without them the tree could not have grown. The same is true for the seed and the fertile soil, and the logger who cut the tree down. Without them, the tree would not have been there for the paper to be. But for the logger to be, his parents had to be, and the food they consumed, and all the conditions that made their lives possible, and those lives upon which theirs depended, and on, and on. There is no end to this causal interconnectedness. Everything in the universe is connected to this piece of paper. If the component conditions are seen as elements, we can say that this piece of paper is composed of nonpaper elements: Conditions other than the paper itself are necessary for the paper to exist. The paper cannot exist by itself. Neither can you or anything else in the universe.

The same is true of cognitive or mental states. For every emotion, every perception, every thought, there are necessary causal conditions without which they would not have come into being. Everything is dependently arisen; everything exists only if the necessary conditions are there. This means nothing is ever truly independent or separate from everything else. Dependent origination is not simply A causing B, but simultaneously A being a necessary condition for B to occur, and B being necessary for A to arise. Thus the best label is that used by Katagiri (1988, 1998), "interdependent co-origination," or Hanh's (1988, 2007) "interbeing," where things and mental states "inter-are." Modern general systems theory, derived from our relatively recent awareness of the interconnectedness of ecological factors, approximates this, although the theory lacks the generality and universality of the Buddha's position (Macy, 1991).

The concept of dependent origination results in an understanding of existence as a process of change, the result of an infinite web of causal conditions, with birth and death marking neither the start nor the end. The conditions that result in our present existence represent a beginningless chain; the consequences of our actions become causal conditions whose effects will continue after we die. Although there is no separate, immutable self or soul that can continue forever, the process of which we are a part continues forever (Katagiri, 1988). The Buddha talked about "rebirth." By this expression he did not mean reincarnation in the Vedic sense, where a soul (atman) inhabits a succession of bodies. He meant continuation in the sense in which a wave is "reborn" in the ocean after apparently "dying" on the seashore. All the water is still there, and the process continues endlessly, but no "soul" travels from one wave to the other. There are no transmigrating souls, only a continuing karmic process. Who we are lives on in the effects we have on others and on our world (Varela, 1997).

THE THREE CHARACTERISTICS OF EXISTENCE

The Buddha realized that there are three characteristics of existence: *anicca, dukkha,* and *anatta.* **Anicca,** or "impermanence," means that everything is always changing. Nothing is immutable or permanent. Children grow, people age, things break down, spring follows winter, rivers flow, subatomic particles fluctuate, galaxies spin: Everything is in a state of flux. Impermanence is not good or bad, it's just the way things are. Understanding and accepting impermanence leads to the avoidance of unrealistic expectations. Ultimately there is nothing we can hold on to or keep forever. Attachment and aversion will not change this.

Dukkha, usually translated as "suffering," refers to the dissatisfaction and distress that results from both attachment and aversion. The Buddha's solution to the problem of suffering, which has been called "the most important psychological discovery of all time" (Mosig, 1989), represents an application of the far-reaching principle of dependent origination. If suffering is, it must have come into being as the result of causal conditions, and if suffering is to cease, those conditions must cease. The Buddha's solution was expressed in the form of **Four Noble Truths** (Sheng-yen, 2000).

The first Noble Truth describes the problem of suffering, the universal dissatisfaction that characterizes human existence: our perception of pain, illness, old age, and death; not getting what we want and being exposed to what we don't want; not being able to keep forever what we love and not being able to eliminate what we hate.

The second Noble Truth begins the application of dependent origination to the problem, identifying the causal conditions on which suffering depends. Suffering and dissatisfaction, the "dis-ease" of human existence, cannot be by themselves; they arise from our craving, our "thirsting" and desiring for things to be other than what they are. Old age is not suffering; it is just old age. Suffering arises because we do not want to be old. This thirsting for things not to be as they are comes in two "flavors": attachment (which includes greed and possessive love) and aversion (including anger, resentment, and hate).

The third Noble Truth derives a solution through the application of the same principle. Because human suffering arises out of craving, to bring our "dis-ease" to an end we must cease the self-defeating liking and disliking that causes it; we must stop the "picking and choosing" that is "the sickness of the mind" (Seng T'san in Sheng-yen, 1987). Although we cannot get rid of illness, physical pain, aging, and death, we can eliminate the anxiety we cause ourselves with our cognitive processing. In doing so, we can achieve freedom from unnecessary psychological pain (Hanh, 1999; Kalupahana & Kalupahana, 1982). To eliminate suffering, we must get rid of craving.

The answer to how we can do this is contained in the Buddha's fourth Noble Truth, which is known as the **Eightfold Path.** It consists of *Right Understanding* (understanding the interconnectedness and impermanence of everything, and specifically the Four Noble Truths); *Right Thinking* (cultivating thoughts of selfless detachment, compassion, and non-harming, and extending these to all sentient beings); *Right Speech* (abstaining from lying, slander, gossip, and injurious speech, speaking only that which is positive and constructive, otherwise maintaining a "noble silence"); *Right Action* (acting in ways that will benefit and not cause suffering to others or oneself); *Right Livelihood* (avoiding ways of making a living that are based on the exploitation of the suffering of animals or people); *Right Effort* (cutting off unwholesome thoughts before they can be transformed into actions and nurturing wholesome ones); *Right Mindfulness* (maintaining full awareness of our actions and experiences in the present moment, and their likely consequences); and *Right Concentration* (the disciplining, concentration, and one-pointedness of mind resulting from the practice of meditation) (Piyadassi, 1974; Rahula, 1974; Sheng-yen, 2000).

The first two components of the Eightfold Path are related to wisdom; the following three, to moral conduct; and the last three, to mental discipline. The different aspects of the Path are themselves interdependent. Without wisdom one would not see the necessity of undertaking the Path, without moral development one would not be ready to undertake it, and without mental discipline one would not be able to do it! The moral conduct aspects of the Path relate also to the concept of karma. **Karma** means volitional action, whether of word, deed, or thought. Every action has effects or consequences that "rebound." One could hardly expect to free oneself from suffering while inflicting it on others.

The third characteristic of existence, **anatta,** or "nonself," sets Buddhism apart from practically all other religious, philosophical, and psychological theories and positions.

> Buddhism stands unique . . . in denying the existence of a soul, self, or *atman.*
> According to the teaching of the Buddha, the idea of a [personal] self is an

imaginary, false belief which has no corresponding reality, and it produces harmful thoughts of "me" and "mine," selfish desire, craving, attachment, hatred, ill-will, conceit, pride, egoism, and other defilements, impurities and problems. It is the source of all the troubles in the world, from personal conflicts to wars between nations . . . [T]o this false view can be traced all the evil in the world. (Rahula, 1974, 51)

Craving is one of the links in the chain of dependent origination, and suffering is the end product. The doctrine of anatta links craving to the false idea of a separate ego or self. It is important to realize what is meant by the "self" that the Buddha rejected as illusory. Not only are human beings said to lack a soul or self, so is everything else: rivers, mountains, this book, and your pencil. This means they cannot have any reality apart from the interconnected net of causal conditions that make their existence possible. All things (including human beings) are composites; they are composed of parts and have no real existence other than as temporary collections of parts. There is no separate essence, self, or soul, that could exist by itself, apart from the component parts and conditions (Katagiri, 1999).

What we call a "person" is the composite of five groups of elements, or **skandhas.** The skandhas are *form, feelings, perceptions, impulses,* and *consciousness.* Just as an automobile is a temporary collection of car parts, a person is a temporary arrangement of the five skandhas. There is no separate, independent self or soul that would be left if we removed form (which includes the body), feelings, perceptions, impulses, and consciousness. While these elements are together, the functioning gestalt we call a person exists; if they are removed, the gestalt ceases to be. For this reason, the self can be said to be "empty": a view of the self radically different from Western perspectives (Page & Berkow, 1991; Szehidewicz, 1999, 2000; Mosig, 2006).

Close your hand into a fist and look at it. What do you see? A fist. Is it real? It certainly seems to be. Now open your fingers. What happened to the "real" thing called "fist" that was there a moment ago? Where did it go? Consider your self, your ego. Is it real? Certainly. Or is it? What would remain of it if you removed form, feelings, perceptions, impulses, and consciousness? Just as the term *fist* is a convenient label to designate a transient arrangement of the fingers, the term *self* or *I* is nothing but a label for an impermanent arrangement of the skandhas. There is no little person inside the head, no inner ego or self, other than the temporary gestalt formed by the skandhas. This is the Buddha's concept of anatta, and why the self is an illusion.

The concept of anatta does not negate the person, nor does it diminish it. Rather, it empowers the individual by erasing the boundaries of separateness that limit the personal ego or self. The person becomes transformed from an isolated and powerless individual struggling against the rest of the world, into an interconnected integral part of the universe. The person's boundaries dissolve, and the person *becomes* the universe. This is the realization known as enlightenment, the emergence of the big self, the Self with capital S, which is boundless.

Consider a wave in the ocean. It has no reality apart from the water. Although its form seems to last as it continues to move on the surface of the ocean, it is composed each moment of different water particles. It seems so real, yet we can see that there is no thing called "wave" there at all; there is only the movement of the water. The wave has no separate "self," no reality apart from the water. The separation is just an illusion created by our perceptions and by the words we use to describe them. Now assume that the collection of elements forming the wave resulted in the phenomenon of consciousness. As long as the wave was unaware of the nature of the ocean, believing itself to be separate and independent of it, it might develop attachments and aversions, fears, jealousies, and worries about its size, its purpose, its importance, or its destination. Any such concerns would vanish instantly upon realizing the water-nature of the ocean, and its oneness with it. In the same way, all human problems disappear when the illusion of a separate self is eliminated.

The transcendental wisdom of realizing the universal oneness generates compassion and caring for everyone as oneself. To hurt or help another is to hurt or help oneself. True wisdom is automatically manifested as universal compassion, and true compassion manifests itself as wisdom. Wisdom and compassion "inter-are." In the final analysis, wisdom is compassion, and compassion is wisdom (Mosig, 1989).

The ultimate state of mind in Buddhism is **nirvana,** not a place like heaven, but a mental state, in which all cravings, desires, and dualistic ideas have been completely extinguished, through the complete realization of anicca and anatta. The Buddha taught that liberation is within the grasp of everyone. Just as he said that there had been many fully enlightened beings or buddhas before him, he indicated that there would be countless buddhas after him.

Vasubandhu and the Eight Consciousnesses

The psychological insights of the Buddha have been explicated by a number of commentators. One of the most important ones was Vasubandhu, an outstanding Buddhist scholar living in the fourth century. He was a founder of the school known as the Vijnanavada ("path of knowledge") or Yogacara ("application of yoga"), and the author of one of the most important books of Buddhist psychology, the Abhidharmakosa (de La Vallee Poussin, 1989–1990).

According to Vasubandhu, all that can be experienced to exist is "mind only," or the mental processes of knowing. There is experience, but there is no subject (no atman) having the experience. **Vijnana,** or "consciousness," the last of the five skandhas, is a multilayered concept, including both conscious and unconscious aspects.

There are Eight Consciousnesses, not just one (see Figure 17.1). The first five correspond to the five basic sense fields and share the same level of depth. They are the consciousnesses of seeing, hearing, smelling, tasting, and touching. Below is the **manovijnana,** or "thought consciousness," the integrating basis of the five sense consciousnesses. In a way, manovijnana functions as a sixth sense that allows for the awareness of thoughts, as well as for memory, evaluation, conception, and imagination. Next comes **manas,** or "mind," where the information is given further cognitive processing. It is at the level of manas that we become aware of being aware, which results in the delusion that we must be a self having the awareness. The illusion of a subjective "I" or "ego" is the source of all our psychological problems. Finally comes the vast **alayavijnana,** or "storehouse consciousness," which is the passive or potential ground out of which emerge the other seven consciousnesses. It is the repository of all potential activities of the other consciousnesses. These potentials exist in the form of "seeds" (*bija*) (Hanh, 1974; Epstein, 1985; Mosig, 2006). These "seeds," upon development, produce all sorts of mental phenomena. Furthermore, in the alayavijnana, the "seeds" affect each other in various ways. They are "watered" by conscious activities, so that,

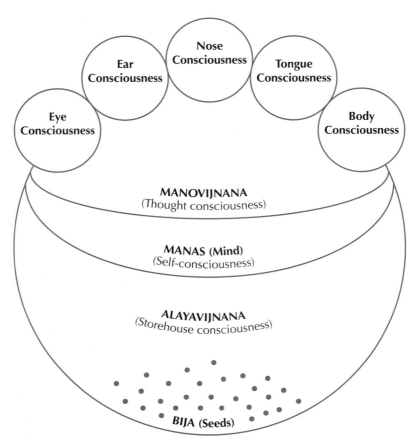

FIGURE 17.1 THE EIGHT CONSCIOUSNESSES OF THE VIJNANAVADA SCHOOL (YOGACARA) FOUNDED BY VASUBANDHU AND ASANGA IN THE FOURTH CENTURY C.E.

The Eight Consciousnesses are conceived not as separate but rather as eight manifestations of an ongoing process, such as the illumination of a room to which individual bulbs contribute.

for example, engaging in kind or compassionate thoughts makes the seeds of compassion ripen and grow (i.e., become more powerful), so that it will be easier to think compassionately next time. Allowing oneself to indulge in anger or hatred waters the corresponding seeds, so that it becomes easier to grow angry and to experience hate. This is why mindfulness of thoughts is so important, and why the "right effort" aspect of the Eightfold Path deals with cutting off negative or destructive thoughts as soon as they appear, while nurturing positive ones. This develops positive mental habits rooted in the seeds of the alayavijnana and has far-reaching effects on the life and well-being of the individual.

The alayavijnana is a vast unconscious realm, which is often compared to a stream, constantly flowing and renewing itself. If the individual is likened to a wave in the ocean, then the alayavijnana is the unconsciousness (or subconsciousness) of the ocean, providing the continuity of the karmic process. Jung's collective unconscious is the closest concept in

Western psychology, with the archetypes being somewhat analogous to the "seeds"; but the Buddhist concept is more vast and more dynamic, allowing as it does for the interactive "seeding" of the unconscious (Hanh, 1991; Mosig, 2006).

The Eight Consciousnesses should not be conceived as separate but rather as eight manifestations or functions of an ongoing process. Think of a room illuminated by several lightbulbs. The illumination is one ongoing phenomenon, integrating the contributions of the individual bulbs. In this example, the electricity that activates them is the equivalent of the alayavijnana. There are Eight Consciousnesses, yet they are ultimately one (Epstein, 1985).

Bodhidharma and the Transmission of Zen to China

Zen Buddhism was introduced to China around 520 C.E. by the Buddhist monk Bodhidharma. Upon his arrival in China, Bodhidharma met with the emperor, a devout but superficial Buddhist who asked, "I have built temples, support the monks, and have had the scriptures translated, tell me, what will all of this bring me?" "It will bring you nothing," replied Bodhidharma. "Then tell me, what are the sacred things in Buddhism?" "There are no sacred things—only vast emptiness." Irritated, the emperor asked, "And who are you to stand in front of me and talk to me like this?" "I do not know," said Bodhidharma, and he left. The emperor was functioning at the relative plane, whereas Bodhidharma made repeated references to the absolute one, where there are no "things," nothing can be sacred or profane, and there is no "I" or "self" to know.

Bodhidharma is said to have practiced sitting meditation for nine years in a cave by the Shaolin Temple, teaching the monks with his example. He is also said to have summarized his teaching as "a special transmission outside of the scriptures; no reliance upon words and letters; direct pointing to the heart of man, and the realization of enlightenment" (Hoover, 1980). This statement emphasizes that the scriptures must be practiced and not just read, for words by themselves are as useless as a picture of a cake is to satisfy hunger. Only an enlightened teacher can verify the awakening of a disciple, which is thus transmitted "from mind to mind" (or "from heart to heart").

As Zen Buddhism passed into China, it adopted expressions from **Taoism,** which helped to convey Buddhist ideas. The philosophy of Taoism, attributed to the Chinese philosopher Lao-tse (approximately fourth century B.C.E.), the author of the *Tao Te Ching* ("The Way and Its Power"), is essentially compatible with that of Buddhism. Lao-tse referred to the absolute as the **Tao,** or the "Way" of Nature, which is inexpressible in words, and stressed the desirability of harmonizing with nature. Many references to the "Way" (Tao) appear in Chinese Zen literature, usually to express the Buddha-nature (Cleary, 1998).

In China, the Tao was thought to manifest itself in the form of two forces: **yin** and **yang.** Yin stands for the feminine, receptive, internal, negative aspect of nature. Yang represents the masculine, active, external, positive aspect. Yin and yang are not merely opposites but exist in a state of dynamic complementation, expressing the unity of the Tao. In Buddhist terms, we can say that yin and yang are dependently arisen, so that yin is yin because of yang, and yang is yang because of yin. The yin and yang symbol thus becomes a convenient expression of the principle of dependent origination, its dynamic quality corresponding to the impermanence and constant change that the Buddha saw in the universe. The white dot in the black yin signifies that there is yang in the yin, and the black dot on the white field reflects the yin in the yang.

The Practice of Zen

We need to distinguish between Zen as a school of the Mahayana division of Buddhism and Zen as an experience. To speak of the latter is immediately to distort and misrepresent it. Zen masters have often said that those who say what Zen is do not know what it is, whereas those who know what it is do not talk about it but teach the practice of Zen so that others will be able to experience it.

The practice of Zen entails a systematic training of the mind designed to create in the disciple a state of mind that will permit the realization of enlightenment. The indispensable form of Zen practice is **zazen,** which is traditionally practiced sitting cross-legged on a firm, round cushion or *zafu,* maintaining a precise physical posture for a period of time. Eastern psychologies, and especially Zen, do not regard the mind and the body as separate but as intimately interconnected, to the point that one could more properly refer to a "body-mind" than to a body *and* a mind. The posture of the body in zazen is extremely important and is expressed in the mental state that accompanies it.

The main position recommended for zazen is the full lotus, with the right foot placed on the left thigh and the left foot on the right thigh. This position expresses the oneness of duality. Even though we have two legs, in this posture they become one. The head, neck, and spine are kept in a straight vertical line, which is the hallmark of all proper zazen postures. When one sits correctly, the body is held in perfect balance. Everything exists in the right place and in the right way. In such a position, a person can maintain physical and mental balance and can breathe naturally and deeply. The state of consciousness that exists when one sits in the correct posture is, itself, enlightenment.

The harmonization of the mind with the posture of zazen is usually accomplished through awareness of one's breathing. The mind tends to act like a monkey or a misbehaving child, constantly engaging in discursive thought. As the practitioner notices that the mind is climbing the treetops, he or she returns awareness to the breath and continues to repeat this process.

Zazen can be practiced by young and old. The preferred body posture is the full lotus, which requires a measure of flexibility. The lotus posture and the hand position (cosmic mudra) represent non-duality and oneness with the universe.

Any thoughts, ideas, visions, or unusual experiences that may occur while one is practicing zazen are to be dismissed as *makyo,* delusions or hallucinations. The student is to attach no significance to them. Zazen is not the pursuit of mystical experiences. Zazen done properly is just sitting, body and mind together, right here and now—*just sitting.* Although some recommend that beginners count their breaths, follow a mental sound or mantra, use some sort of visualizations, or ponder a paradoxical riddle during zazen, these are "unnecessary training wheels" (Kosko, 1993).

Zazen is not a means to reach enlightenment, so it is not a tool to be discarded once the mind has become awakened. At that point, zazen becomes a manifestation of this realization. "The reason why you have to practice zazen is that if you do not practice zazen, things stick to you, and you cannot let go of them" (Katagiri, 1988). In the same way that showering allows us to wash away dust and dirt, practicing zazen allows us to let go of past regrets and future worries. Just as it would not occur to us to discontinue showering because the body is now clean, we should not regard any mental state as an indication that zazen is no longer necessary.

In the **Rinzai** school of Zen, **koans** are often used as themes for Zen meditation. The term *koan* literally means a "public document." It consists of an apparently paradoxical anecdote, statement, or question that has no logical, rational, or intellectual solution, as long as the student continues functioning at the level of the *relative,* the realm of duality. The koan statement is perfectly clear to an enlightened individual able to experience the *absolute* realm of nonduality. Because language is a tool developed to express dualistic concepts, it is totally inadequate to convey a nondualistic experience or understanding. For this reason, any attempt to provide an answer based on language or discursive Aristotelian-style logic is futile.

The koan usually describes actions or words by an enlightened teacher attempting to jolt a student out of discursive thinking into an intuitive realization. The use of such incidents as meditation aids is relatively recent in the long history of Zen Buddhism. Examples of koans are "What was your face before your parents were born?" and "What is the sound of one hand clapping?"

Students using a koan typically have individual daily interviews (called *sanzen*) with the master, to express their current understanding of the koan. Students' answers are almost invariably rejected, and they are sent back to meditate on the koan until they become one with it and arrive at a breakthrough, transcending dualistic thinking. Once they have broken through the koan, they are assigned another one, and the process is repeated. It may take weeks, months, or years for a student to work through a particular koan (Puhakka, 1998).

Teachers of the **Soto** school of Zen also use koans, but not as meditation themes. Zazen in Soto Zen is essentially **shikantaza,** themeless, just sitting. Shikantaza is not based on trying to realize anything (Loori, 2004; Coupey, 2006). It is a pure practice that allows any effects to take place without being sought after. A Soto Zen teacher may use a koan as a focal point for a *teisho,* a "dharma talk" offered by a master to his students to enhance their understanding. A koan can be seen as a miniature exaggeration of the problem of life. Just as the koan seems to defy logical comprehension and resolution, so life itself cannot be held or contained within the categories constructed by dualistic thinking.

A number of studies have examined the physiological responses that occur during the practice of Zen meditation (Murphy & Donovan, 1988; Austin, 1998, 2006). In experienced meditators, the respiratory rate has been found to typically slow down during zazen, from the normal of 18 to 20 breaths per minute to 4 to 6 per minute or less, with a marked

Thinking Critically

Do you realize that your mind is constantly chattering like a restless monkey? To find out what you can do about it, see the Thinking Critically box "Meditation."

increase in the tidal volume of air displaced. The electroencephalographic record shows a predominance of alpha along with theta waves, although zazen is normally practiced with the eyes partially open. Oxygen consumption shows a marked decrease, and metabolic rates slow down (Hirai, 1989). Although some of these changes can be brought about through simple relaxation, they are not critical to the experience of zazen. Simple relaxation cannot produce the transpersonal awareness and present-centering that result from a proper meditative practice. There is a considerable body of literature supporting the notion that zazen, as well as other Eastern meditative disciplines, can lead to better health and an increased ability to deal with stress and tension (Kabat-Zinn, 1990; Brazier, 1995; Miller, Fletcher, & Kabat-Zinn, 1995; Epstein, 1995, 1999; Urbanowski & Miller, 1996; Finn, 2000; Austin, 2006; Rizzetto, 2006). Such practices emphasize internal rather than external control, as well as the unity of mind and body, and they are gaining recognition from contemporary Western medicine for their efficacy.

Zen practice has many other forms, which serve to extend the mindfulness of zazen to daily life. **Kinhin** is a slow walk performed between consecutive periods of zazen, while maintaining concentration and mindfulness. The kinhin walk allows for rest and normalization of circulation in the legs when one is doing several sittings. Just as during zazen one just sits, so when walking in kinhin one just walks. In a more informal form of walking meditation, a person, alone or in a group, just walks (in the park, around the block, or wherever), maintaining awareness of the breath and of everything experienced during the walk, but without labeling or discussing what is being experienced. In order to maintain **mindfulness** when walking in this manner, it is recommended that the person notice the number of steps taken while inhaling, and also the number while exhaling (Hanh, 1985). Counting the steps and maintaining awareness of the breathing keeps the individual focused on the present, and this mindfulness is extended to everything encountered. If you try this exercise, you may be amazed at how many things you notice during your walk that you had never noticed before.

Gathas, short verses to help focus attention on the task at hand by mentally dedicating the activity to the benefit of all sentient beings, may also be used. This practice makes every activity into something sacred and clarifies that no activity is more or less valuable than any other activity. As we engage in it, it is our life at that moment.

Another form of Zen practice is the **gassho,** the putting together of the hands, palm to palm. The gassho position is a symbol of nonduality. It reminds us that mind and body are one. One hand stands for you, the other for the person you are greeting, or for the entire universe, and you become aware that you and the other are one. When you put the hands together in gassho, just do gassho. Zen teaches to do each action completely and for its own sake.

Chanting sutras is Zen, too; here the important thing is to just chant, expecting nothing out of it. These are **autotelic** activities—activities that contain their own goal. Chanting is not a form of prayer. It is not aimed at a superior power, nor does it petition anything. When chanting, just experience the sound.

A practice that many Westerners find difficult at first because of their cultural upbringing is bowing. In Zen, bowing is not an act of worship but an action expressing respect and gratitude. You may put your hands in gassho and bow to give thanks or to show appreciation for another, or merely as a greeting. Bowing in front of an altar, whether it be a standing bow or a full prostration, is an exercise that helps to subdue the ego and expresses

Thinking Critically

Meditation

Unlike Western personality theories, Zen cannot be grasped by thinking, critically or otherwise. It must be experienced. Here are instructions on how to practice zazen.

Wear loose-fitting clothes. Find a quiet, temperate, and neat place where you are not likely to be disturbed. Put a mat or folded blanket on the floor close to a wall, and place a cushion six or eight inches thick on top of it. Facing the wall, you should sit on the edge of the cushion, which should support the base of your spine. The cushion should allow you to sit straight and be stable, with your spine and your two knees forming three points of a tripod. The knees must be on the mat, not elevated from it.

Place your legs in one of the following positions (in descending order of stability and desirability): *full lotus* (right foot on left thigh and left foot on right thigh), *half lotus* (one foot on the opposite thigh, the other tucked underneath), *quarter lotus* (one foot on the opposite calf, the other tucked underneath), *burmese* (both legs flat on the mat), or *seiza* (kneeling, with the cushion on edge between your legs). If none of these are possible for you, sit on a cushion at the edge of a chair (keep your back straight, do not lean on the backrest). Put your hands on your knees, palms up. Breathing deeply, slowly arch your body back and then forward, and then sway from side to side in *decreasing* arcs, until you are perfectly centered. Then put your right hand on your lap (resting on your left foot, if you are in a lotus position), palm up, and the left hand on top of it, with the thumbs slightly touching over your middle fingers. Your hands should now be forming an oval, with the blades (edges of the palms) touching the stomach a few inches below the navel. The arms are relaxed and extend slightly forward, without touching the sides of your body.

Push your lower back slightly forward; then straighten your back, pushing upward with the top of your head. Keep your neck straight and tuck your chin slightly in. There should be a straight line now from the bottom of your spine to the top of your head. Your nose and navel should be in a vertical line, and your ears and shoulders on a horizontal line. Your eyes should remain slightly open, with your gaze cast downward at a 45-degree angle. Don't look at a specific spot—just let your eyes rest; don't try to see or visualize anything. Your mouth should be closed, with lips and teeth touching. Rest the tongue against the roof of the palate. Swallow any saliva, creating a vacuum inside your mouth. Breathe in and out through your nose, and let the air go down to your lower abdomen so that you are breathing with the diaphragm. Breathe naturally; don't force the breath.

Keep your mind with your breath. When you inhale, be aware of your lower abdomen going out. When you exhale, notice your lower abdomen going in. Maintain this awareness. If you become distracted, don't get upset. If thoughts arise, notice them and let them go, gently returning to your breath. Keep repeating this. Just sit there, doing nothing, just being present in the reality of your life, beyond likes and dislikes. Sit firmly and immovable, like a mountain. At the end of your sitting period, release the posture of your hands, and put them on your knees, palms up. Gently sway from side to side in *increasing* arcs, exhaling each time as you sway to one side and then the other; then undo the position of your legs and stretch them out. Stand up slowly and carefully.

Sit every day, expecting nothing, for at least five minutes, working up to forty as time allows. Early morning and end of day are the best times to practice.

gratitude. All the statues found in a Zen temple are symbolic of mental states and abilities; they do not represent external deities. In Zen you can bow to anything—people, statues, animals, your meditation cushion, a cup of tea. The important thing when bowing is to just bow, expecting nothing out of it (Maguire, 2003).

Eating also can be a form of Zen practice, whether it be with the traditional *oryoki* bowls often used in Zen centers and monasteries, or in the everyday setting of the Western dining room. The key element in this is the maintenance of mindfulness. When you eat, just eat. Give your food your undivided attention. You can take care of other matters when their turn arrives.

Many aspects of Japanese culture show the imprint of Zen. This is true of the tea ceremony, the Noh theater, the art of calligraphy, ink-brush painting, haiku poetry, flower arranging, the *shakuhachi* flute, as well as the martial arts such as karate, aikido, swordsmanship, and archery. These are meditative arts based on the discipline of zazen. These and other forms of Zen practice are not substitutes for zazen but serve to extend the mindfulness of zazen to everyday life (Mosig, 1988, 1990, 1991). The martial arts in particular necessitate the development of two mental states associated with Zen: "no-mindedness" (*mushin*), the ability to react without conscious thought, and the "immovable mind" (*fudoshin*), the ability to remain calm and undisturbed regardless of the circumstances (Mosig, 1988).

But you do not need to bow, chant, play the shakuhachi, write haikus, recite gathas, learn calligraphy, or engage in a martial art in order to practice Zen. All those manners of Zen expression, however helpful they may be, are ultimately superfluous and can be dispensed with. The only Zen practice that is completely indispensable is zazen, which needs to be practiced over and over and over (Maezumi, 2001).

"Nothing happens next. This is it."

It is important to find a master or a teacher to learn the correct way to practice Zen. The most important thing to look for in a teacher is not the depth of his or her enlightenment—that is secondary. The most important point is how much of the truth the teacher has experienced has been "digested" and manifests itself in the teacher's life (Katagiri, 1988). Only a teacher who has received "Dharma transmission"—in other words, whose experience has been verified and authenticated by an enlightened master—is in a position to verify and authenticate the awakening of others.

Five Approaches to Zen Practice

There are five basic approaches to Zen practice. **Bompu Zen** is Zen practiced for a profit, such as mental health, stress management, improved sports performance, inner peace, or effective salesmanship. Today most Westerners who take up the practice of zazen do so with some benefit in mind. They are also likely to quit if the expected results are not experienced in a short time. **Gedo Zen** is practice unconnected with the Buddha's teachings. It is exemplified by New Age practitioners who engage in zazen in order to reach higher levels of consciousness, visions, or mystical experiences. People of diverse religious backgrounds may also attempt to use Zen to deepen their religious experiences. **Shojo Zen,** or "small vehicle" Zen, is zazen practiced for the sake of one's own liberation from suffering or for one's personal enlightenment. It is similar to the approach to meditation in the Theravada tradition. **Daijo Zen** is Zen practiced for the sake of liberating all sentient beings, seeking enlightenment to help others. This approach is the one found in most Mahayana schools, including Rinzai Zen. **Saijojo Zen,** meaning "great and perfect practice," is zazen practiced for the sake of practicing zazen, with no idea of gain and no expectations. This is the *shikantaza,* or "just sitting," emphasized in Soto Zen. It is called great and perfect because it is not based on trying to realize anything. It is a pure practice that allows any effects to take place without being sought after.

An analogy to learning to swim may make these distinctions clearer. You could learn swimming in order to improve your health (*bompu*), in order to have a mystical experience of oneness with the ocean (*gedo*), in order to save yourself from drowning (*shojo*), in order to save others from drowning (*daijo*), or just in order to swim (*saijojo*). Notice that the last approach does not preclude improved health, oceanic experiences, or salvation from drowning for oneself or others. Instead, it pursues swimming for its own sake and allows any benefits to come of themselves. Thus it is the pure and perfect practice of just swimming.

Enlightenment

The reflective illumination or awakening of Zen is known as **satori.** Satori, or enlightenment, cannot be communicated with words, any more than words could communicate the experience of color to someone who is blind. In the Rinzai school, satori is regarded as the goal of Zen practice, and zazen as a method to achieve it. Practitioners sit in meditation, attempting to circumvent linear, rational thought through the use of a koan.

The Soto school, in comparison, stresses that satori is not a goal to be attained but is identical with the practice of zazen, which must be engaged in with no gaining idea in mind. Dogen Zenji (1200–1253), founder of the Soto school in Japan, interpreted the Buddha's statement that everyone has the Buddha-nature as *everyone is the Buddha-nature*. This is because the Buddha-nature is not something outside or inside of the individual but is the absolute universal reality. Each and every one of us is the universe, whether we realize it or not. Satori means to wake up to this fact, to the way things are and have always been, a transformative experience that entails the realization of the universal Self (Deshimaru, 1999; Okumura, 2000).

To clarify satori, Loori (1988) tells the story of the ugly duckling who felt terrible because he was so different from the other ducks, who made fun of him. One day, as he was looking at his reflection in the water, he noticed the reflection of another ugly duckling just like him. As he looked up, he discovered a group of swans, and *in that moment* he realized that he himself was a swan. He instantly became a perfect and complete swan. Suddenly everything was right and he was free from all his psychological suffering. He was enlightened, yet nothing had changed for he had always been a perfect swan. The difference, though, was transformative, for he was liberated from the delusion of his imperfection.

Okumura (1985) wrote, "Satori is nothing but being aware of, or being alert in, whatever activity you are doing right now, right here. Any activity is not a step, means, or preparation for other things, but rather should be done for its own sake, being accomplished in each moment." This description is a far cry from the mystical misconceptions often connected with the subject of enlightenment.

It is just as important to let go of the good as of the bad features of the past. As Okumura (1997, p. 1) points out:

> If we did something good yesterday, we should forget it and face what is in front of our eyes today. What we did yesterday is not reality anymore. We cannot be proud of what we did in the past and think we are great people because we did such and such. Even if we make mistakes, we shouldn't be caught up in them. Let go of them and start again. Start right from this posture in silence, right from the ever fresh life force that is free from any defilement. Moment by moment, we start again and again.

This is the enlightened state, in which human evaluations are no longer important.

The activities of an enlightened individual are autotelic. Such enlightened functioning is similar to Csikszentmihalyi's "flow" (1985, 1990). When we become totally immersed in an activity, we can "flow" with it to the point that we lose awareness of ourselves as separate from the activity.

When an enlightened person eats, that person just eats, when resting, just rests, in the same manner that one just sits when practicing zazen. The awakened one does not discriminate between activities, knowing that no task is intrinsically better or worse than any other. Whatever is being done, painting a landscape or cleaning the toilet bowl, is one's life at that moment. Giving the activity full attention is to be able to flow with it, without attempting to get it out of the way to do something else that may be more enjoyable. One is thus fully living one's life. Zen is the art of losing the self (the ego) in the everyday flow of autotelic activities (Okumura, 2000; Triet, 2000).

The awakening of Zen can be precipitated by any stimulus or event occurring at the right time in the life of a person who is ready to experience it. Recorded instances provide the subject matter for numerous Zen stories (Cleary, 1998). The manner in which a given inci-

The performance of work, when done with mindfulness, is a meditative experience in the Zen tradition.

dent manages to trigger the awakening of a specific individual cannot be understood intellectually, and any attempt to imitate another's realization experience is futile.

Satori must be personally experienced. A master can point the way but cannot experience it for the student. If we are hungry or thirsty, another person's eating or drinking will not fill our stomachs or moisten our throats. This is why Zen masters insist that they have nothing to teach or impart. All they can do is show how Zen is practiced and exemplify it in their lives.

Enlightenment is not the end of Zen practice. If it were, it would represent the outcome of a selfish interest in one's own happiness and fulfillment. Practitioners seek enlightenment not for themselves but for the benefit of all sentient beings. Zen teaches that in the enlightenment of one person, all sentient beings are enlightened, for all boundaries are illusions. It has been said that Zen training is like climbing a mountain. Satori is being on top of the mountain. But after reaching the top, coming down the other side of the mountain and returning to the "marketplace" to help everyone else is the bodhisattva spirit, exemplified in the enlightened master.

Eastern Thought and Psychotherapy

Psychotherapeutic applications of Eastern and Western psychology have been examined by a number of authors (e.g., Watts, 1961; Goleman, 1981; Loy, 1992; Young-Eisendrath & Muramoto, 2003; Magid, 2005; Mosig, 2006; Mruk & Hartzell, 2006; Zhang, 2006). Both aim at effecting a positive change in the mode of functioning and the life-style of the individual. However, Western psychotherapy is designed to effect such change in persons experiencing psychological or behavioral disorders, whereas Eastern disciplines affect also above all the practical everyday life of normal or healthy individuals. Buddhist psychology is concerned with the alleviation of the unnecessary suffering caused by the delusion of the separate self in human beings in general. The delusion of separateness results in cravings, grasping, clinging, greed, selfishness, hatred, fear, feelings of alienation, loneliness, helplessness, and anxiety, which afflict those who are "healthy" as well as "unhealthy" (Mosig, 2006).

Western psychotherapy, in its efforts to heal the neurotic individual, attempts to strengthen the ego, or to foster the development of a stronger "self," yet it is this very notion of self that Buddhist psychology sees as the root cause of human suffering. Eastern psychotherapy attempts to dissolve the experience of the self-as-separate-entity and replace it with a feeling of interconnectedness, the nonself or selfless Self implied in the Buddhist concept of anatta. This radical change is seen as the key to liberation from dukkha, the dissatisfaction and suffering of human existence (Mosig, 2006). Nevertheless, it is not enough for the healthy, liberated individual to eliminate the delusion of the separate self. While understanding universal interconnectedness and absolute reality, the emptiness or nothingness of Buddhism, the person needs at the same time to experience reality in the relative sense, in which individual identities exist. The integration of the two levels of awareness, the absolute and the relative, is essential for the normal functioning of the healthy human being in society. When crossing the street, it is not enough to contemplate an approaching car and to realize that we are one with it. Although it is true that the car, the road, our bodies, and everything else are nothing more than temporary collections of countless particles (or fluctuations of energy, at the quantum level of analysis) and that all there is is an ocean of energy in which car, road, and person have no more reality than the transient shape of a wave on the surface of the ocean, unless we act in the relative plane and get out of the way of the car, the collection of skandhas that allows this awareness to occur will be promptly dissolved. What is needed is appropriate action in the relative world while maintaining awareness of the big picture. The larger awareness guides the individual in compassionate action and eliminates unnecessary worries and suffering about impermanent events, which can now be accepted as the momentary contents of reality (Mosig, 2006).

The different conceptions of the self in Western and Eastern psychology have clear implications for psychotherapy and everyday life. Despite their differences, an integration of Western and Eastern approaches may be possible or even necessary (Mruk & Hartzell, 2006; Young-Eisendrath & Muramoto, 2003). It could be argued that the self needs to be strengthened before it can be abandoned. Culture may play a critical role in this process. The delusion of the separate self is likely to be stronger in persons raised in individualistic societies, such as those of Europe and America, and may be weaker in collectivistic societies, such as those of China or Japan, where the harmony (*wah*) of the group takes precedence over the needs of the individual. Western approaches may be extremely valuable in giving the person (primarily in individualistic societies, but to some extent also in collectivistic ones) sufficient self-confidence and maturity to discard ego-centeredness. This in turn prepares the individual to transcend the isolation of the separate self through the realization of the universal

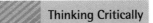

Thinking Critically

Would you like to be able to enjoy everything you have to do? To find out how, see the Thinking Critically box "Mindfulness and the Search for a Higher Synthesis."

Thinking Critically

Mindfulness and the Search for a Higher Synthesis

At this point you would be asked to relate Zen Buddhism on each of the philosophical assumptions described in the first chapter. However, such an activity would be contrary to the spirit of Zen, which aims at a higher synthesis and asks that we experience rather than analyze. Can you see how the experience of Zen undercuts traditional dualisms such as freedom versus determination, uniqueness versus universality, proactivity versus reactivity? Can you suggest ways in which thinking in terms of these dualisms may stand in the way of our experiencing ourselves? Can you further suggest ways in which people in the West can benefit from the teachings of the East?

As an additional experiential exercise to appreciate the power of mindfulness in Zen, try the following. Select a task you normally dislike or avoid. For example, let's say that you hate to wash dishes. The next time the opportunity presents itself, approach this task as something to be done as a meditative experience. Do the job with full concentration, without rushing through it to get it out of the way in order to do something else that you regard as more interesting or enjoyable. While you are washing dishes, this is your life at the moment. No activity is intrinsically better or worse than any other activity; it is merely the content of your life at the moment. Pick up each dish, each cup, each glass, each utensil, and carefully wash it, one after the other, as if you were polishing precious jewels. Look at each item in your hands and actually see it. Don't allow your attention to wander. Don't think of anything else. Be there, in the present moment. Maintain awareness of your breath, of your inhalations and exhalations, while you do the washing—it will help you to stay in the present moment. Don't look at the clock. Don't talk with someone else while doing this. Just wash the dishes, one at a time, carefully, mindfully, with your whole being. Afterward you may wish to reflect on this experience. Was the task distasteful? Was it enjoyable? What would your life be like if you did everything with mindfulness? What is keeping you from it? You will find other mindfulness exercises in Buswell (2007), Hanh (1975, 1993, 2005a) and Kabat-Zinn (1990).

---

interconnectedness stressed by Buddhist psychology as the gateway to wisdom and compassion (Mosig, 2006).

There may be another way in which Western psychotherapy has failed, and that is in terms of the development of a method to enhance and protect the mental health of the practicing clinician. Western psychotherapists have rightly stated that it is not possible to bring someone to a higher level of mental health than one has accomplished oneself, but Western psychotherapy has failed to develop the equivalent of zazen as a method to dissolve the delusion of the ego in therapists and patients alike. Therapists need to heal themselves before they are in a position to help others. They need to develop inner peace and the capacity for compassionate action in order to be able to be islands of refuge for those immersed in psychological pain. This is the mental characteristic known as the "immovable mind" of Zen, the natural outcome of the practice of zazen. Echoing Zen master Katagiri's words: If we don't practice zazen, painful events stick to our consciousness and we cannot let go of them.

With the current meeting of East and West, more Western psychotherapists are discovering the value of adopting a meditative discipline as part of their training and, in general, of regarding meditation as a powerful therapeutic tool (e.g., Hirai, 1989; Kabat-Zinn, 1990; Fickling, 1991; Fuld, 1991; N. J. Miller, 1991; Brazier, 1995; Epstein, 1995; Urbanowski & Miller, 1996; Young-Eisendrath & Muramoto, 2003; Mruk & Hartzell, 2006).

Perhaps one of the most significant developments in the field of psychotherapy over the past couple of decades has been the introduction in the West of several Eastern systems of treatment. Reynolds (1980) identified several Japanese forms of psychotherapy, which he called the "quiet therapies" because their main therapeutic tool is some form of silent meditation, in contrast with the "talking cures" so prevalent in the West. **Morita therapy** was developed by Japanese psychiatrist Shoma Morita in the early 1900s and is founded on the theoretical concepts and practice of Zen, as shown by Rhymer (1988). The method consists of isolated bedrest (to force patients to come in touch with themselves), followed by periods of light and then heavier manual work, and a period of retraining to help patients rejoin normal life. During part of the treatment patients keep a diary that is annotated by the therapist. Standard hospitalization lasts usually from forty to sixty days (Reynolds, 1976).

The Moritist method requires that patients acknowledge their feelings and take full responsibility for their actions, being trained to behave appropriately despite any feelings that might arise. In other words, they learn to gradually develop a degree of "immovable mind," realizing that if they do not react to their feelings, these feelings have no power over them. This is similar to a person sitting in zazen and learning that whatever thoughts, stimuli, or feelings pop up in consciousness and are noticed but not reacted to will pass away, demonstrating their impermanent character. Instead of attempting to remove symptoms, Morita therapy regards patients as students and teaches them to live constructively despite any symptoms or feelings that may be present (Dearborn, 2001).

Morita therapy seems to be most effective with neuroses grouped under the name **shinkeishitsu,** which overlap primarily with anxiety disorders in the standard DSM-IV classification (Morita, 1998). The rates of success of Morita therapy, as reported by Rhymer (1988), are very high: over 90 percent when significant improvement and cures are combined.

Naikan introspective therapy emphasizes the development of a sense of responsibility and obligation in the patient, consonant with the principle of interconnectedness or dependent origination stressed in all Buddhist schools, as well as with the sense of societal and familial responsibility associated with Confucian ethics. For instance, the patient may be instructed to sit in introspective meditation, recording all the things her mother has done for her, and on a following day, all the things she has done for her mother, and similarly with respect to her father, her siblings, her teachers, and others in her life. What emerges is a deep insight into the imbalance of the relationships and a desire to repay others for their care and support (Reynolds, 1980; Krech, 2000; Silva, 2006).

Morita and Naikan therapies have demonstrated their effectiveness in the West and are regarded with growing respect in psychotherapeutic literature (Bankart, 1997; Walsh, 1995). The two approaches have been successfully combined into the "Constructive Living" system championed by Reynolds in the United States, a system rapidly growing in popularity here and abroad (Reynolds, 1995).

The value of Zen meditation as therapy and as an adjunct to other forms of psychotherapy has been documented by Hirai (1989) and others. A more general application of mindfulness therapy is advocated by Hanh (1991, 1992), in which awareness of emotions (such as anger) is used to transform the energy of the emotion into constructive channels. Kabat-Zinn (1990) has also developed a program based on mindfulness meditation for stress reduction and is currently helping develop similar programs across the country. We are likely to continue to see the increasing impact of Zen and other Eastern disciplines on Western psychotherapy in the future (Magid, 2005; Mosig, 2006; Mruk & Hartzell, 2006; Zhang, 2006).

PHILOSOPHY,
SCIENCE,
and ART

Eastern Theories

An extensive literature on Buddhist psychology exists, including diagnosis and psychotherapy. In the East, the emphasis is relational rather than individual; the person is considered not in isolation but in relation to others, to society, and to the larger cosmos.

Most certainly, Eastern concepts of personality do not qualify, nor do they aspire to qualify, as science. The very needs to evaluate and to demonstrate a personality theory's usefulness constitute a bias that is foreign to Eastern thought. Although Eastern theories are sometimes considered a philosophy or a religion, they do not entail the same logic or speculation that characterizes Western religion and philosophy. Zen and Eastern personality theories in general are in many ways closer to science than to philosophy or religion, but because they do not utilize the scientific method of investigation, it is perhaps most accurate to describe them as art.

Eastern theories are highly practical. They offer a variety of techniques for cultivating a deeper understanding of the self. These practices move the individual away from intellectual, rational consciousness and cultivate a deeper awareness that transcends everyday consciousness. Systematically training the body and the mind, Eastern disciplines aim at enabling the individual to perceive the truth that lies in the interconnected reality in which he or she lives.

There has been a steady growth of interest in the ideas and practices of the East. The influence of Eastern concepts is apparent in the work of several personality theorists included in this book: Jung explicitly incorporated Eastern concepts into his theory; Fromm and Horney turned to the East to enrich their theories and practices; and the same is true to some extent of Allport, Rogers, Maslow, and many others, particularly in the emerging field of transpersonal psychology. By looking for the commonalities between Buddhism and Western thought, especially existentialism, we may be taken to even greater insights. Exciting new holistic meta-theories of personality integrate Western psychology's obsession with early development and self-esteem with Eastern traditions concerned with self-transcendence and enlightenment. Today, with increasing opportunities for cooperation, it is vitally important that East and West appreciate each other's attempts to understand the self. To do so can only enrich both.

TO LEARN MORE about Eastern and Western psychotherapies, and for a list of suggested readings, visit the *Personality Theories* textbook website at **college.cengage .com/pic/engler8e.**

Summary

1. Siddhartha Gautama, the **Buddha** (p. 458), renounced everything he had and left home in search of a solution to the problem of human suffering. After six years he attained enlightenment. **Theravada** (p. 458) and **Mahayana** (p. 458) Buddhism grew out of his teachings. **Zen** (p. 457) Buddhism, a branch of the Mahayana, adopted expressions from **Taoism** (p. 465) in China and spread from there to Japan and the rest of the world.

2. The principle of **dependent origination** (p. 459) says, "This is, because that is; this is not, because that is not; when this arises, that arises; when this ceases, that ceases." It causally connects everything in the universe.

3. The three characteristics of existence are **anicca** (p. 460), "impermanence"; **dukkha** (p. 460), "suffering"; and **anatta** (p. 461), "nonself." The Buddha's solution to the problem of suffering was expressed in the form of **Four Noble Truths** (p. 460).

4. **Satori** (p. 471) is an awakening to the reality of the universe that cannot be grasped through intellectual analysis but must be experienced personally.

5. The five **skandhas** (p. 462) are form, feelings, perceptions, impulses, and consciousness. A person is a temporary arrangement of these elements and has no reality separated from them.

6. There are Eight Consciousnesses. The first five correspond to the basic sense fields: seeing, hearing, smelling, tasting, and touching. Below them is **manovijnana** (p. 463), the integrating basis of the five sensory consciousnesses. Next comes **manas** (p. 463), where the illusion of a separate "I" or "ego" arises. Finally comes **alayavijnana** (p. 463), the "storehouse" from which all potential activities ("seeds") of the other seven consciousnesses emerge. The seeding of the alayavijnana is accomplished by "watering" the positive seeds (by attending to them and acting on them) while not "watering" the negative seeds (refusing to act on them while maintaining awareness of their presence).

7. The practice of Zen entails systematic training of the mind through **zazen** (p. 466), sitting meditation, and the extension of the mindfulness and concentration of zazen to daily life. The **Soto** (p. 467) school of Zen views the practice of zazen as "just sitting," or **shikantaza** (p. 467). The **Rinzai** (p. 467) school uses **koans** (p. 467)—apparently paradoxical statements, questions, or anecdotes—as a focus of concentration during zazen. The Rinzai school sees zazen as a method to reach enlightenment. The Soto school stresses that practice and enlightenment are one and the same.

8. It is necessary to actually practice zazen in order to understand it. Detailed instructions are given in the Thinking Critically box on meditation.

9. Western psychotherapy emphasizes change for neurotic or disturbed individuals. Eastern disciplines are primarily concerned with change in the consciousness of normal or healthy people, pointing out that the distress of both is caused by **maya** (p. 474), or illusion.

10. Eastern theories do not entail the speculation or the kind of logic characteristic of Western theories. For our purposes, it is most accurate to characterize them as art.

Personal Experiences

1. The Buddha said that *anicca* is one of the three characteristics of existence. *Anicca,* or "impermanence," means that everything in life is always changing, that nothing lasts forever. This notion may at first sound to you like common sense. But how often do you actually acknowledge anicca in your own life? Recall the last three times when you experienced a lot of stress or anxiety. Think about the causes of those feelings. How much of your stress was due to changes in your life? To a breakup with a girlfriend or boyfriend, graduation, moving to college, switching roommates or living quarters? Consider whether consciously acknowledging change as an inevitable aspect of life would have helped you cope with each circumstance.

2. *Dukkha,* "suffering," refers to the dissatisfaction and distress that results from both attachment and aversion. In the Buddhist context, attachment relates to greed and possessive love; aversion, to anger, resentment, and hate. Both of these afflictions arise from our desire, our craving, for things to be other than what they are. Which of these two causes of distress and dissatisfaction do you feel most applies to you? Do you tend to be possessive in love relationships or over things such as clothes, money, or food? Do you tend to get angry or resentful when things don't go your way? Do you at times feel that events have turned out unfairly and you're not getting the acknowledgment, status, or some other compensation that you deserve? Take some time to closely examine the sources of your discontent. According to Zen principles, taking time to examine one's own life is a necessary means of freeing oneself from such distress.

3. Examine the Buddha's fourth Noble Truth, the Eightfold Path. Review the description of each of the eight principles. How well are you currently following this path? For each principle, rate yourself on a scale of 1 to 5, 1 being *least applicable* to your life and 5 being *most applicable.* The total scale would then rate out of a maximum of 40. See how closely you're following the path. To get a better sense of how you compare with others in how closely you seem to follow the Buddha's path, have your friends or family members read the text and rate themselves as well. You may uncover trends in age, gender, race, and so forth. This can be a fun way to begin exploring Buddhism if this is the first time you've been exposed to it.

4. In Buddhism, *karma* means volitional action, or an action that someone consciously chooses to do whether by word, deed, or thought. Every action has effects or consequences that "rebound," or ultimately come back to the person who initiated the act. Do you believe in karma? If you see someone cheating, do you believe that such a negative act will ultimately come back to haunt the cheater? Think back to a time when you decided against doing something bad for fear it would come back to haunt you in some way. Do you tend to think this way often? If you do, why do you think that is? What does that say about your approach to life and to the universe? If you believe that "whatever comes around goes around," is there any need to take punitive action ourselves? Would the world be a better, more peaceful place if we let "life" literally take care of itself?

5. The third characteristic of existence described by the Buddha is *anatta,* or "nonself." The doctrine of anatta links craving to the false idea of a *separate* ego or a self apart from the

body. The Buddha rejects the idea of a "self" that can have independent reality, and instead sees the self as a pattern of interactions between impermanent elements (the skandhas). The self exists only as a configuration that cannot be by itself, independently of the skandhas. Freud regards the ego, in a way, as a homunculus, a little man inside the head, while the Buddha sees it as an impermanent, flowing process. The two theories, one a primary element of Western philosophy and the other a primary component of Eastern thought seem to oppose each other. Try to objectively assess where you stand between these two poles. Write down all of the things that are important to you as a person: your ethics and values, your sources of joy, and your sources of distress. After creating a comprehensive list, make two columns—one for ego and the other for anatta. Then start placing each item on your list in one of the two columns. If you feel that a source of joy is better served by the belief in a separate ego, put it in the "ego" column. If it's better served by the belief in anatta, put it in that column. After assigning the items in your list to one column or the other, examine both columns. Do your personal philosophical beliefs position you closer to the Eastern or to the Western philosophical pole?

Personality Theory in Perspective

1. Compare different personality theories' emphasis on philosophy, science, and art.
2. Compare different personality theories' stand on basic philosophical issues.
3. Discuss the history of the terms **psyche** and **psychology** from their origins in Greek thought to their present-day use.
4. Indicate how Western psychology has narrowed the definition of **empirical.** Explain how the scientific method may separate us from experience rather than illuminate it.
5. Describe some signs of change on the horizon.
6. Explain why it is important to conceive of personality theories as philosophy and art, as well as science.

T his final chapter seeks to place the personality theories we have studied into perspective by making some comparisons and contrasts among them and by pointing to a problem in contemporary personality theorizing, suggesting a view toward the future.

Personality Theories

Although personality theories are a branch of academic scientific psychology, they also entail philosophy and art. As scientists, personality theorists seek to develop workable hypotheses that enable us to understand human behavior. As philosophers, personality theorists seek to give us insight into what it means to be a person. As artists, personality theorists seek to apply what is known about people and behavior to foster a better life. Some critics evaluate theories simply in terms of their efficacy as science. Yet, as we have seen, few of the theories described in this text demonstrate purely scientific concerns. This text has described a variety of theories ranging from Freud's emphasis on the ego to Eastern psychology's denial of it. Most theories reflect a great variety of concerns and need to be evaluated in terms of the criteria that suit their goals.

Some of the theories we have considered clearly reflect philosophical concerns. The psychoanalytic tradition, for instance, tends to be philosophical, rather than scientific, in its approach. Psychoanalytic theorists, by and large, are clinicians who develop their theoretical structures within the context of therapy. Although their methods and results are frequently empirical—that is, based on observation—they could not be described as rigorous or precise scientific techniques. Psychoanalytic theorists tend to consider proof as arising from the internal consistency of a theory and the ability of the theory to illumine the human condition. Their work is ultimately evaluated in terms of its coherence, relevance, comprehensiveness, and compellingness. The theories of Sigmund Freud, Carl Jung, Alfred Adler, Erich Fromm, and Rollo May represent a deep commitment to an underlying philosophy of life. More recent psychoanalytic theorists appreciate the need to validate their constructs and are thus open to scientific test. But psychoanalytic theory remains largely philosophical. This is best seen in the work of Erik Erikson, who did not insist on a scientific rationale for his work but tried to make his philosophical assumptions explicit.

Other theories make a greater effort to be successful scientific theories. Behavior and learning theories are expressly scientific in their approach. Committed to a rigorous methodology, behavior and learning theories shun theoretical speculation in favor of careful observation and experimentation. Thus, John Dollard and Neal Miller emphasized empirical research in their efforts to combine psychoanalytic theory with the behaviorist tradition. B. F. Skinner's view also evolved from experimental laboratory investigations. This emphasis has continued in the work of cognitive and social learning theorists, like Albert Bandura and Julian Rotter, whose theories are superb examples of a rigorous scientific approach to personality. Their methodologies have produced precise and economical theories and have given strong empirical support to their constructs. Psychometric trait theories also demonstrate a deep commitment to scientific methodologies and validating evidence; Raymond Cattell, Hans Eysenck, and the Big Five theorists are excellent examples of theorists who try to comprehend personality through a scientific model.

Some theorists deliberately seek an interdisciplinary approach. Henry A. Murray was one of the first to recognize the value of an interdisciplinary methodology; the diagnostic council that he established at Harvard was unprecedented in its vision and scope. Jung, Fromm, Gordon Allport, and Abraham Maslow all drew upon several areas of research—art, literature, history, philosophy, and science—in their efforts to understand human nature. Carl Rogers very carefully distinguished between his philosophical assumptions and his scientific hypotheses, emphasizing the need for a balanced view.

Other theories are primarily concerned with the art of personality theory, or the practical applications. We saw how Eastern thinkers do not seek to demonstrate the validity of their constructs or engage in philosophical speculation; rather, they are concerned with offering a variety of practices for cultivating a deeper understanding of the human situation. Likewise, Ellis, Beck, and Lazarus are best known for their contributions in the area of counseling. Freud, Horney, Adler, Rogers, and Kelly also made substantial contributions to the understanding and practice of psychotherapy.

None of the personality theories that we have studied can be appropriately labeled as simply philosophy, science, or art. For instance, although behavior and learning theories largely seek to present a scientific conception of personality, they also reflect basic philosophical assumptions that influence their scientific hypotheses and their practical applications.

Initially, behavior and learning theorists were unable to recognize the philosophical roots of their approach. In recent years, however, they have acknowledged the philosophical assumptions that undergird their work. It is now widely recognized that even the most scientific approach to understanding personality addresses philosophical questions and suggests philosophical answers. Indeed, the basic difference among personality theories appears to be one of philosophical stance.

Philosophical Issues

Personality theories, then, can be compared in terms of where they stand on each of the basic philosophical issues outlined in the introductory chapter. For example, theorists differ as to whether they believe people are basically free to control their own behavior or whether they believe that behavior is essentially determined by forces over which people have little, if any, control. Both Freud and Skinner saw the individual as determined but for very different reasons. For Freud, the individual is motivated by internal unconscious forces. For Skinner, the individual is shaped by forces within the environment. Theorists also differ in the extent to which they would like their theories to be used to cultivate freedom in human nature or to exercise greater control over it. Skinner sought to develop a technology to control human behavior, whereas Rogers tried to increase a client's sense of freedom and responsibility.

As we have seen, another of the most puzzling questions in personality theorizing has been the dichotomy between hereditary and environmental determinants of behavior. Theorists differ over whether they believe that inborn characteristics or factors in the environment have the more important influence on a person's behavior. Dispositional theorists stress the importance of long-term personality traits in understanding behavior; behaviorists emphasize situational factors. These philosophical differences also lead to different recommendations for action. An emphasis on inborn factors sometimes leads to the support of selective breeding; an emphasis on situational factors may lead to efforts to change the environment. Thus Cattell urged consideration of *eugenics,* the study of improving hereditary qualities by genetic control, and Bandura encouraged *euthenics,* the study of advancing human life by improving living conditions. The most recent theories stress an interactionist and biosocial view.

A third major issue is that of uniqueness versus universality. Allport clearly grappled with this issue. He recognized that common traits permit us to make generalizations and comparisons among individuals, but in the final analysis he held that each individual is particular and unique. Eastern theories point out that we need to see through the illusion of individual existence, called maya. Jung described a twofold process of individuation and transcendence.

Proactivity versus reactivity is a fourth dimension that influences personality theories. Allport discovered in a study of psychological terms with the prefixes *re-* and *pro-* that most theories tend to be reactive. Concepts such as "repression" and "regression" in psychoanalysis and "reflex" and "reinforcement" in stimulus-response theory suggest an emphasis on the past and a preoccupation with homeostasis. Humanist theories, in contrast, suggest that the human being is motivated toward heterostasis—that is, growth and self-actualization. Cognitive theories also emphasize the present and the future rather than the past, viewing the individual as purposeful and active rather than passive.

Finally, personality theories can be compared according to whether they are optimistic or pessimistic about the possibility of change. Freud is generally seen as a pessimist because he believed that adult behavior is deeply structured by early childhood. Dispositional theorists believe that some constitutional factors place firm limits on personality change. Behavior and learning, cognitive, and humanist theorists, however, are usually very optimistic concerning the possibility of change.

These basic issues are typically presented as bipolar dimensions. However, Rollo May reminded us that they are actually paradoxes of human existence that seek resolution in a creative synthesis. An either/or position is generally misleading. Personality theorists must avoid being impaled on either horn of the dilemma as they try to reflect the truth of human existence.

In any event, a response to a theorist can take one of three forms. We can agree with the theorist and adopt his or her philosophical categories as part of our scientific activity. We can object to a theorist's own philosophical grounds and maintain that another view is more compelling. Or we can maintain that none of these views is adequate. If we adopt the third position, we are then faced with the responsibility of suggesting an alternative philosophical framework that provides a more convincing model for understanding personality.

The Challenge of Contemporary Personality Theorizing

Although psychology is a young science, it represents the oldest of human concerns. Our Western tradition initially fostered a mystical view of the self, emphasizing the spiritual side of the person. The effort to comprehend the human personality within the framework of a scientific methodology is largely a product of the twentieth century.

The term **psychology** comes from the ancient Greek word **psyche,** first introduced by the poet Homer to express the essence of a human being, or "the self." During the early Christian era, as philosophy and rhetoric replaced poetry and mythology, the term *psyche* came to be identified with *pneuma,* or "spirit." It later became identified with the more rationalistic and intellectual concept of *nous,* or "mind." By the time of the Enlightenment, *psyche* had become synonymous with *consciousness* or *mental processes.* As we have seen, John Watson, the founder of behaviorism, subsequently pointed out that states of consciousness are not objectively verifiable. He deemed them unfit as data for science and encouraged psychologists simply to study behavior. Under Watson's leadership, psychology was transformed from the largely introspective study of consciousness into the study of overt or observable behaviors. Thus, in the typical American university a strange situation prevailed throughout most of the twentieth century. Students of psychology discovered that, for the most part, they were not engaged in the study of the psyche; they were engaged in the study of behavior.

Behaviorism came to be the dominant position of psychology in American universities. Psychologists sought to pursue psychology as an experimental science that emulated the natural science of physics. The mainstream of American psychology still tends to emphasize extrospective observation and a rigorous scientific methodology. This emphasis is found in the cognitive approach, which has superseded behaviorism as the dominant trend.

Not all of the personality theorists that we have considered agree that a rigorous scientific method is the best way to understand personality. Indeed, some (Allport, Maslow, Rogers, and May, for example) have been very critical of the narrow view of psychology as an experimental science. Their critiques have fostered trends toward a more humanistic approach and an interest in alternative means of studying the person.

Unfortunately, however, humanistic psychology became a "divisive force." Psychologists tend to be divided as to whether they belong to a "humanistic" or a "scientific" camp. Thus, "the early promise of this approach, as emphasized by Abraham Maslow and Carl Rogers, was never realized in the mainstream of psychology" (Ornstein, 1977; see also Boneau, 1992). Humanistic psychology and mainstream psychology share the same problem: How do we overcome the tension between the demands of good science and the demands of the subject matter (Giorgi, 1987)?

The behaviorist and cognitive positions, with their emphasis on extrospective observation and experimental research, continue to represent the strongest and most predominant modes of psychological study in the American academy today. Those theorists who choose not to imitate the mainstream run the risk of being considered less respectable because of their lack of allegiance to a purely scientific approach and methodology. They are tolerated, particularly when they are willing to subject their findings to scientific scrutiny, but their theories are not fully recognized as sound.

We have seen that the keynote of science is observation. Scientific theories rest on empirical data—that which is based on experience. In Western psychology, however, the term

empirical has been rendered practically synonymous with "relying on or derived from extrospective observation." Empirical data have been largely limited to objective findings. Other data of experience or observation, such as subjective introspection, have been discouraged or depreciated, largely because it is so difficult to test these findings experimentally.

Historical, philosophical, and mythological data, because they invariably entail subjective as well as objective elements, are often viewed as incompatible with science. According to this conception, a competent scientist generally does not permit subjective assumptions to interfere with his or her work. The scientist remains detached, objective, and value free, which Maslow and Fromm said is an error. As a result, Western psychology has tended to isolate itself. It has divorced itself from other possible modes of investigation on the grounds that their findings, because they are difficult to test experimentally, are not objective and are therefore incompatible with science.

David Bakan has pointed out that the rigorous scientific methodology of the Western experimental psychologist may, at times, actually stand in the way of the empirical and divorce us from experience rather than illuminate it (1969). In a well-developed experiment the experimenter does not deal with the everyday world; instead, she or he creates a **paraworld** of quantified, logico-mathematical imaginary constructs. In this paraworld, events are carefully chosen and precisely controlled in order to avoid the haphazard occurrences of the everyday world that might jeopardize the results. Further, in a well-designed experiment all the possible alternatives and outcomes are anticipated in advance. The experimenter can predict within limits what is going to happen as a result of the manipulation of the variables in the experiment. So the more carefully designed an experiment is, the more separate it becomes from the world of experience that it seeks to clarify. The Western psychologist's reliance on a rigid experimental method may, therefore, interfere with the possibility of learning from experience.

The emphasis on extrospection and rigorous scientific methodology also limits the findings of psychology to those that can be demonstrated within the experimental laboratory. It circumscribes the study of personality to merely those aspects about the person that can be comprehended in specifically scientific terms. Because of this, many questions about the ultimate meaning, purpose, and goal of human living, questions that traditionally have been and could be included in the study of personality and that are addressed by some theorists, are ruled out of inquiry.

Few theories of personality resemble an ideal scientific theory. Their assumptions lack explicitness, making it difficult for us to derive empirical statements that would permit us to move from abstract theory to empirical observation. Many personality theories, although provocative, have failed to generate a significant amount of research, thus depriving us of some of the "most important evaluative comparison" that can be made among theories (Hall & Lindzey, 1978; see also Hall, Lindzey, & Campbell, 1998). Yet those personality theories that successfully emulate a scientific model can be criticized as gaining their precision, accuracy, and predictive power at the price of evoking little depth of insight or new understanding.

In part, the problem results from the fact that theories of personality explore phenomena that by their very nature elude a narrow definition of science. At the heart of the experimental method is the search for cause and effect. Theories that emphasize motivation or free will make it difficult to look for underlying causes and limit the possibility of prediction and control. Moreover, they call into question the value of experimentation as a primary means of gaining insight into the human condition.

We need to recall that American psychology struggled valiantly to become a respectable science. This struggle entailed severing early ties with philosophy and modeling itself along the lines of the natural sciences. Sound training in experimental design and statistical methods characterizes the curriculum of academic psychology. Because of the earlier struggle to gain recognition as a science, many psychologists, particularly those with a behaviorist orientation, are suspicious of recent efforts by personality theorists to defy strict scientific methodology and reassert the philosophical character of psychology.

As a result, at the end of the twentieth century, much of the current research in personality was fragmented (cf. Berthenthal, 2002; Magnusson & Törestad, 1993; Sarason, 1989) and isolated (Ehrenreich, 1997), limited to a special domain that can be precisely defined, articulated, measured, and tested. Feshbach (1984) suggested that "the study of personality has not moved in the direction of actualization; rather it appears to have become constricted, dissociated, and overly defensive." A particular variable, such as locus of control, subjective well-being, birth order, or cognitive style, is isolated for study, leading to a multiplicity of interesting and reliable empirical findings.

Many current texts in personality, after providing a brief introduction to theories, concentrate on major research issues such as intelligence, anxiety and stress, perceived control, aggression, altruism, sex roles, and gender differences. But as May reminded us, contemporary psychological research is preoccupied with data and numbers at the expense of theory. The most important scientific discoveries were made not by accumulating facts but by perceiving relationships among the facts (May, 1983). Retief (1986) points out that "data and methods, no matter how profuse and sophisticated they may be, can lead nowhere on their own: it is obvious that good theories are needed to guide them. . . . Psychology has made a firm commitment to method: the time for an equal commitment to theory is overdue." Human nature can be understood only within a theoretical framework. The real contribution lies in seeing a new *form* that avoids the misconceptions of an existing mythology (see also Millon, 2000b, 2003; Noble, 1993).

A new framework is needed within which the study of personality can develop into a more cumulative science (Shoda & Mischel, 1996). Recently, McAdams (1996a, see also McAdams & Pals, 2006), whose work is described in the chapter on ego psychology, has suggested an integrative framework of three levels for studying personality: personality traits, goals and motives, and personal life stories. He believes that his framework will enable us to place recent advances in the study of personality within the cultural context of modernity. McCrae and Costa (1999) presented a personality system of integrating components similar to that of Mischel and Shoda (1995; Mischel, 2004). As time goes on, it will be interesting to see the response to these efforts to provide a comprehensive new theory. There is a lot to integrate, for the range of concepts included in personality theories is very wide. Indeed, the two biggest emerging trends, the neurobiological underpinnings of personality and the spiritual dimensions of personality, are coming from polar realms and tend to draw upon very different methodologies that often seem to be clashing with each other.

The reluctance to reassert the philosophical character of psychology to some extent reflects a realistic fear that our present disillusionment with science may foster a tendency to disregard the substantial contributions that it has made to our understanding. We developed the experimental method as a tool because we discovered that we could increase our understanding and act more efficiently if our activities were guided by information about the determined aspects of our everyday world. Although it may be true that the experimental method cannot establish truth, it has provided a very pragmatic means of testing some of our assumptions and yielded incredibly useful information.

Still, we should recognize that a purely experimental approach is not the only option available to the personality theorist, and we should be aware of the effects of a narrow scientific conception of psychology. Moreover, we must not allow the popularity of the experimental approach in the American academy to close our eyes to the importance of other methods or to the reality of the phenomena that other methods draw to our attention. We should seek a higher perspective in which science and philosophy are no longer in opposition to one another but complement each other.

Many contemporary personality theorists urge us to be *more,* not less, empirical—that is, *more* empirical in the original sense of the term, "based on experience." They point out that our traditional scientific methods may not only fail to do justice to the experiential data but may also camouflage it. They suggest that when we limit our analysis to those phenomena that can be comprehended in terms of current experimental methodology, we prejudice our results. By becoming "less scientistic," psychology could become "more scientific" (Bakan, 1969).

Although psychology represents the oldest of human concerns, the science of psychology and the effort to comprehend the human personality within the framework of a scientific methodology are largely a product of the twentieth century. We have seen (in the introductory chapter) that Wilhelm Wundt conceived of psychology as an experimental science that ought to emulate the natural science of physics. Psychology may have failed as a scientific enterprise because it did not develop its own methodology but borrowed it from the physical sciences (Kruger, 1986). Many psychologists have been moving away from the social sciences toward the biological sciences and clinical practice. This has led to an increased isolation of scientific psychology from the insights and problems of other social sciences (Harzem, 1987). In contemporary sciences from biology to physics, the concept of *pattern* has replaced earlier concepts, such as cause and effect, as the key principle of explanation. Psychology has yet to incorporate that view (Rychlak, 1986).

There are signs of change on the horizon. Rychlak (1981) and Valentine (1988) argue for a teleological (goal-oriented) perspective. Motivation has reemerged as a central player in personality theory (Pervin, 1996). The renewed interest in idiographic methods of research is heartening. In 1988, the *Journal of Personality* devoted an entire issue to psychobiography and life narratives. These are contemporary forms of case histories and studies of the unique life stories of individuals such as those explored by Freud, Erikson, Murray, and Allport. MacIntyre (1984) has suggested that narrative history may be "the basic and essential genre for the characterization of human actions." Davidson (1987) suggests that if psychology reconceives itself as based on an analysis of motivational/intentional relations, it will place itself in a closer and more appropriate relationship to the sociocultural sciences than to the physical sciences. McClelland (1996) points out that when the study of personality is expanded to include topics such as values, motives, and life stories, it becomes a much more exciting area to explore.

The narrative form is increasingly being seen as the most appropriate form for understanding the construction of self in a postmodern era (Atkinson, 1990; Freeman, 1992; McAdams, 1995, 1996a, 1996b; Miller, Potts, Fung, & Hoogstra, 1990). "Instances of cultural diversity take on a different hue when viewed from a narrative perspective" (Howard, 1991). A study of Japanese children's personal narratives may help us to understand how those children are trained in empathy (Minami & McCabe, 1991). Gardner (1992) suggests that psychology turn toward literature and other artistic studies in an effort to help understand issues such as self, will, consciousness, and personality. His suggestion stirred considerable discussion (see Markova, 1992; Oatley, 1992; Potter & Wetherell, 1992; Sternberg, 1992; and Woodward, 1992). Students of personality would do well to emulate van Krogten's interpretive-theoretical research method modeled in his *Proustian Love* (1992), in which he presents a complex theory on the psychology of love built on principles originating from a study of Proust's *Remembrance of Things Past*. "The stories we live by" (McAdams, 1993, 2001a) and the scientific method itself (Suchecki, 1989) are being seen as mythical texts. There is a long-standing connection between stories and spirituality; stories help us to attend, to remember, and to be aware of ourselves as members of a community (Kurtz & Ketchum, 1992). This resurgence of new interest is seen in the development of a new peer-review e-journal, *Pragmatic Case Studies in Psychotherapy,* in 2005.

Mahers (1991) argued that the meager real increase in our understanding of the psychology of personality in recent years may be due to methodological procedures and our underlying notion of human behavior. These notions and procedures induced us to "invent artificial problems to solve" instead of focusing on real ones, "namely the identification of the processes that govern" human behavior "in the natural habitat." As psychologists increasingly argue that psychology needs to be relevant, to "adequately explain the immediate causes influencing people's lives" (Retief, 1989), and to take a proactive role in helping us to understand our values and moral development in a postmodern society (Krimerman, 2001; Neufeldt, 1989; Packer, 1992), narrative thought is being seen as a major form of cognition and an important part of moral education (Vitz, 1990).

No more can we assume that science considers facts and ethics consider values. Ethics are the result of social life and need to be studied "in their own right." "When we do this, the outline of a different kind of ethical justification becomes apparent, one that legitimatizes multiple objective moralities rather than a universal moral system" (Packer, 1992).

As we focus on cultural diversity, we also must recognize that ideas such as actualization, individuation, and autonomy and the psychotherapies rooted in them are not likely to be immediately germane to other portions of U.S. society or to people who relate to diverse other societies that do not cultivate or prize these notions. Many theories of personality "imply that their stance is apolitical, while in actuality, they serve a highly political function—in service of the continued acceptance of the specifically patriarchal status quo of present society in the United States" (Lerman, 1992). Sexism and racism as ideologies that try to justify white male supremacy need to be challenged (Anderson, 1991). We need to specifically ask of personality theories whether they embrace the diversity and complexity of women and other minorities and insist that they begin to address those issues (Espin & Gawelek, 1992; Heine, 2001). As technologies are increasing our communication with people of diverse cultures and values, we need to recognize that "there is no distinct American identity. America exists as it does because of the relationships of which it is a part" (Gergen, 1992).

Burkitt (1991) suggests that we try to understand people as social selves rather than self-contained individuals. It may be desirable to develop indigenous psychologies more appropriate to various cultures (Naidu, 1991; Puhan & Sahoo, 1991) or at least a pluralistic psychology aiming to transform dehumanizing social contexts (O'Hara, 1992).

Concentration on the biological basis of personality will also increase. As we turn to genetics and neurobiology, we will be looking at temperaments or traits that are innate and explore how these are changed by social and developmental events (Woodall & Matthews, 1993). An evolutionary perspective will also be apparent, looking at how personality traits adapt and have helped to ensure the survival of the human race (Buss, 1991). Personality theory cannot afford to ignore principles derived from genetics, biology, and evolution (Epstein, 1996). Indeed, contemporary personality theories are more "threatened" by developments in neuropsychology, biochemistry, and computer technology than by rival personality theories (Loevinger, 1996). The psychology of personality can continue to play an integrative role (Barone, Herson, & Van Hasselt, 1998) as it is influenced by new models such as chaos theory and self-organizing systems (Barton, 1994; Pervin & John, 1999; Robertson & Combs, 1995).

The spirit of the new physics combats the estrangement and segmentation of life in the twenty-first century and supplants it with a view of reality in which the human consciousness is just one form of consciousness within a wider cosmic consciousness. Such a quantum worldview goes beyond the two poles of the individual and the relationship by demonstrating that human beings can be the persons they are only within a framework. "The quantum self thus mediates between the extreme isolation of Western individualism and the extreme collectivism of Marxism or Western mysticism" (Zohar & Marshall, 1990). Both the artist and the physicist invite us to change our perception of the world and illuminate revisions of reality (Shlain, 1991). Arnold Mindell (2000) has developed a theory of process-oriented psychology that connects psychology and dream work with math and quantum physics to create the basis for a new integrated science. Combining elements from Jungian psychology, cognitive and behavioral models, and non-Western psychology, his theory may mark the beginning, in psychology, of a unified theory such as the unified field theory in physics. A therapeutic universal narrative is now coming into consciousness from many diverse fields of science and telling us that it is futile to be disconnected. The cosmos is "one system of which we're one part integrated into the totality. . . . The fate of the earth is our fate as we're part of the same totality" (Coelho, 1993; see also Coelho, 2002). See Figure C.1.

Boneau (1992) predicts that students and faculty will be leaving psychology "to become interdisciplinary cognitive scientists and neuroscientists." However, he adds, these subjects are only concerned with parts of a larger picture. We "need to have a science of humanity, a discipline concerned with understanding and explaining the human individual coping in a social-cultural-environmental context. . . . That is not what psychology is now, but perhaps it should be."

It is not wise for a field of investigation that claims to explore the human condition to refuse to deal with a wide variety of concepts and data simply because they are difficult to state in narrow, preconceived scientific terms. The crises in living that we face today mandate that we marshal whatever means are available to assist us in self-understanding. A true portrait of personality must come to terms with all the experiences that are central to being a person, even though they may be difficult to conceptualize, test, or express. Lopsided theories err not simply because they present us incomplete portraits that are often biased or stereotyped but because they fail to develop concepts that adequately represent human potential. Lopsided portraits deprive us of important aspects of our own consciousness. Moreover, they permit us to dehumanize and demonize the "other" while failing to recognize the dark side of ourselves. Thus they can be used to justify terrorist acts, prisoner abuse, and other horrific acts that we commit in the name of a moral imperative (Zajonc, 2003).

This book has suggested that personality theorizing invariably entails more than science;

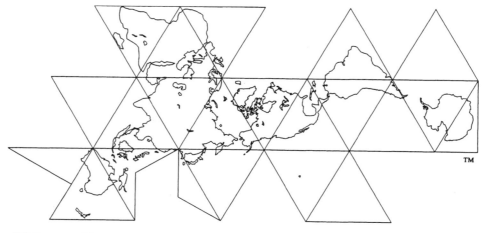

FIGURE C.1 DYMAXION MAP

Here is a map that seeks to portray the world that we all share. *SOURCE: The Fuller Projection Map design is a trademark of The Buckminster Fuller Institute, © 1938, 1967, 1992. All rights reserved.*

it also involves philosophy and art. Every activity that we engage in rests on certain philosophical assumptions. Contemporary personality theorizing is tied to and limited by certain assumptions that characterize our view of the world. Frequently, these assumptions are implicit rather than explicit—that is, they are not clearly recognized. Nevertheless, they profoundly influence our concept of the world and its inhabitants. Only by making our assumptions explicit and continually reexamining them can we place ourselves in a better position to understand ourselves. Herein lies the value of the scientific method: It has provided us with a means of testing and consensually validating our theoretical speculations. What we need to do is twofold. We need to evaluate our philosophical assumptions in the light of contemporary scientific information, and we need to judge our scientific findings in the light of their adequacy as philosophy. In the final analysis, however, neither the speculations of science nor the speculations of philosophy can express the ultimate meaning of

Pictures of the earth from space show us that the borders over which people kill each other are not really there. We must develop new ways of understanding and living that foster world community.

personality. The ultimate expression of personality does not lie in the constructs of science or psychology. It lies in the art of living.

 TO LEARN MORE about philosophical issues in personality theory, and for a list of suggested readings, visit the *Personality Theories* textbook website at **college.cengage .com/pic/engler8e.**

Summary

1. Psychoanalytic theories tend to emphasize philosophy. Behavior and learning theories emphasize science. Numerous other comparisons are possible.

2. Basic philosophical issues on which personality theories can be compared are freedom versus determinism, heredity versus environment, uniqueness versus universality, proactivity versus reactivity emphases, and optimism versus pessimism. For instance, humanist theories stress an individual's responsibility and free will, but psychoanalytic and behaviorist theories see the individual as determined.

3. Although psychology is a young science, it represents one of the oldest human concerns. **Psyche** (p. 485) is an ancient Greek term that originally referred to "the self." Later it came to mean "spirit" and, finally, "mind." Through the influence of the behaviorist movement, **psychology** (p. 485) came to be the study of behavior, emphasizing a rigorous scientific method based on extrospective observation.

4. In Western psychology the term **empirical** (p. 486) has been rendered synonymous with "relying on or derived from extrospective observation." The rigorous scientific methodology of the Western experimental psychologist may at times tend to divorce us from experience, rather than illumine it, by separating us from the everyday world.

5. Some signs of change are the emphasis on the narrative form, the introduction of values, an emphasis on cultural diversity, and a possible reconceptualization of psychology.

6. Personality theories need to be seen as philosophy, science, and art in order to do justice to the full range of human existence and potentiality.

Glossary

A-B-C theory of personality In Ellis's rational emotive behavior therapy, the theory that a highly charged *emotional consequence* (C) is caused not by a significant *activation event* (A), but by the individual's *belief system* (B).

absolute must In Ellis's theory, a dogmatic, unrealistic demand placed on oneself.

acceptance A nonjudgmental recognition of oneself, others, and the world.

active imagination In Jung's psychotherapy, a method for getting in touch with the archetypes.

affective arousal The arousal of emotions in conjunction with cognitions.

agentic perspective Bandura's view of persons as agents of experience.

alayavijnana Sanskrit for "storehouse consciousness," the last of the Eight Consciousnesses.

alienation In Horney's theory, a state in which the real self and the idealized self are disjunct.

amplification In Jungian therapy, an analytical method whereby one focuses repeatedly on an element and gives multiple associations to it.

anal stage Freud's psychosexual stage in which the major source of pleasure and conflict is the anus.

analytical psychology The school of psychology founded by Carl Jung.

anatta Pali for "nonselfness," the lack of a permanent separate self, one of the three characteristics of existence according to the Buddha.

androgyny The presence of both masculine and feminine qualities in an individual and the ability to realize both potentials.

anicca Pali for impermanence and transiency, one of the three characteristics of existence according to the Buddha.

anima In Jung's theory, an archetype representing the feminine side of the male personality.

animus In Jung's theory, an archetype representing the masculine side of the female personality.

anxiety An emotional state characterized by a vague fear or premonition that something undesirable may happen. In May's theory, the apprehension cued off by a threat to some value that the individual holds as essential to his or her existence as a person. In Sullivan's theory, any painful feeling or emotion that may arise from organic needs or social insecurity.

archetype In Jung's theory, a universal thought form or predisposition to perceive the world in certain ways.

assessment Evaluation or measurement.

atman Sanskrit for soul, self, or ego.

attachment theory A theory developed by Bowlby concerning the tendency to bond with other people and experience distress following separation and loss.

attitude A positive or negative feeling toward an object. In Jung's theory, a basic psychotype. In Cattell's theory, a surface dynamic trait.

authoritarian ethics In Fromm's theory, a value system whose source lies outside the individual.

authoritarianism In Fromm's theory, a way of escaping from freedom by adhering to a new form of submission or domination.

autoeroticism Self-love. In Freud's theory, the child's sexual activity.

automatic thoughts In Beck's theory, involuntary, unintentional, preconscious thoughts that are difficult to regulate.

automaton conformity In Fromm's theory, a way of escaping from freedom by adopting the personality proffered by one's culture.

autonomous dimension In Beck's theory, a personality dimension characterized by independence.

autonomous self In Kohut's theory, an ideal self with qualities of self-esteem and self-confidence.

autonomy versus shame and doubt Erikson's psychosocial stage, corresponding to Freud's anal stage, in which the child faces the task of developing control over his or her body and bodily activities.

autotelic Containing its own goal, an activity done for its own sake.

avoiding type In Adler's theory, people who try to escape life's problems and who engage in little socially constructive activity.

basic anxiety In Horney's theory, feelings of insecurity in which the environment as a whole is dreaded because it is seen as unrealistic, dangerous, unappreciative, and unfair.

basic evil In Horney's theory, all of the negative factors in the environment that can provoke insecurity in a child.

basic human condition In Fromm's theory, the basic human condition of freedom.

BASIC-ID In Lazarus's theory, an examination of the seven modalities—behavior, affect, sensation, imagery, cognition, interpersonal relationships and drugs—that make up human personality.

basic needs In Fromm's theory, primary needs that must be met in order for an individual to develop fully.

basic needs therapy Therapeutic procedures that seek to meet the primary needs of people.

basic orientations In Horney's theory, fundamental modes of interaction with the world.

Beck Depression Inventory An instrument developed by Beck to measure depression.

behavior The activity of an organism. In learning theory, a response to stimuli. In Rogers's theory, the goal-directed attempt of the organism to meet its needs as it perceives them.

behavior modification A form of therapy that applies the principles of learning to achieve changes in behavior.

behavior potential In Rotter's theory, a variable that refers to the likelihood that a particular behavior will occur.

behavior therapy A form of therapy that aims to eliminate symptoms of illness through the learning of new responses. In Ellis's theory, helping clients change maladaptive patterns of behavior and ways of thinking.

behavioral genetics Study of heritable causes of individual differences.

behavioral signature In Mischel's theory, personality consistencies found in distinctive and stable patterns of variability across situations.

behavioral specificity Michel's view that behavior is determined by specific situations.

behaviorism A movement in psychology founded by John Watson, who suggested that psychologists should focus their attention on the study of overt behavior.

being mode In Fromm's theory, a way of life that depends solely on the fact of existence.

Big Five The five factors that typically surface from personality questionnaires and inventories: Openness, Conscientiousness, Extraversion, Agreeableness, and Neuroticism.

biophilia hypothesis In Wilson's theory, an intense need to belong to the rest of the living world.

biophilous character In Fromm's theory, a character orientation that is synonymous with the productive orientation.

biosocial Eysenck's approach to personality, which emphasizes biological and genetic factors as well as social and environmental ones.

B-needs Maslow's term for being needs that arise from the organism's drive to self-actualize and fulfill its potential.

bodhisattva Sanskrit for "enlightenment being," a person who has vowed not to accept final liberation from suffering until all sentient beings are liberated; the ideal of the Mahayana tradition.

bodily self In Allport's theory, a propriate function that entails coming to know one's body limits.

Bompu Zen Zen practiced for a profit, such as stress management or increased mental health.

borderline personality disorder A serious mental illness characterized by instability and displaying five or more specific clinical features.

bridging A multimodal technique used by counselors to deliberately begin work in terms of their client's preferred modality.

Buddha "Awake" or "Enlightened One." One who has fully awakened to the Truth.

CAPS Acronym for Mischel and Shoda's cognitive-affective system theory of personality.

cardinal disposition In Allport's theory, a personal disposition so pervasive that almost every behavior of an individual appears to be influenced by it.

castration anxiety In Freud's theory, the child's fear of losing the penis.

catharsis An emotional release that occurs when an idea is brought to consciousness and allowed expression.

central disposition In Allport's theory, a highly characteristic tendency of an individual.

central relational paradox The phenomenon by which people who have experienced trouble in relationships continue to try to make new connections but are hindered in doing so.

cerebrotonia In Sheldon's theory, a component of temperament characterized by a predominance of restraint, inhibition, and the desire for concealment.

character orientations In Fromm's theory, social character types shared by people in Western societies.

choleric One of Hippocrates' temperaments, referring to an individual who tends to be irascible and violent.

classical conditioning A form of learning in which a response becomes associated with a previously neutral stimulus.

client-centered therapy A therapeutic technique developed by Rogers that focuses attention on the person seeking help.

cloning Creating a genetic twin of an individual.

closed system A concept of personality that admits little or nothing new from outside the organism to influence or change it in any significant way.

cognition The process of knowing.

cognitions In Beck's theory, a person's awareness.

cognitive complexity The ability to perceive differences in the way in which one construes other people.

cognitive distortions In Beck's theory, systematic errors in reasoning.

cognitive neuroscience A field that concentrates on how mental activities occur in the brain.

cognitive processes Ways in which we experience the world and relate to others in the course of personality development.

cognitive theories Theories of personality that emphasize cognitive processes such as thinking and judging.

cognitive therapy In Ellis's theory, showing clients how to recognize their "should" and "must" thoughts, how to separate rational from irrational beliefs, and how to accept reality. In Beck's theory, a set of well-defined therapeutic techniques that seeks to remove systematic biases in thinking.

cognitive triad In Beck's theory, a negative view of the self, the world, and the future.

coherence One of the criteria for judging philosophical statements: the quality or state of logical consistency.

collective unconscious In Jung's theory, a shared, transpersonal unconscious consisting of potential ways of being human.

common traits In Allport's theory, hypothetical traits that permit the comparison of individuals according to certain shared dimensions.

compatibility A criterion for evaluating rival hypotheses: the agreement of the hypothesis with other previously well-established information.

compellingness One of the criteria for evaluating philosophical statements: the quality of appealing to someone with a driving force.

compensation Making up for or overcoming a weakness.

compensatory function In Jung's theory, an effort to complement one's conscious side and speak for the unconscious.

compensatory mechanisms In Adler's theory, safeguarding tendencies that ward off feelings of inferiority.

complex In Jung's theory, an organized group of thoughts, feelings, and memories about a particular concept.

comprehensiveness One of the criteria for evaluating philosophical statements: the quality of having a broad scope or range and depth of coverage.

conditional positive regard In Rogers's theory, positive regard that is given only under certain circumstances.

conditioned response A response that becomes associated with a stimulus through learning.

conditioned stimulus A previously neutral stimulus that becomes associated with a response.

conditions of worth In Rogers's theory, stipulations imposed by other people indicating when an individual will be given positive regard.

conflict In Freud's theory, the basic incompatibility that exists among the id, ego, superego, and the external world. In Dollard and Miller's theory, frustration that arises from a situation in which incompatible responses occur at the same time.

congruence In Rogers's theory, the state of harmony that exists when a person's symbolized experiences reflect the actual experiences of his or her organism.

connections In relational-cultural theory, the basic origins of growth and development.

conscience In Freud's theory, a subsystem of the superego that refers to the capacity for self-evaluation, criticism, and reproach.

conscious In Freud's theory, the thoughts, feelings, and wishes that a person is aware of at any given moment.

consensual validation Agreement among observers about phenomena.

constellating power In Jung's theory, the power of a complex to admit new ideas into itself.

constitutional traits In Cattell's theory, traits that have their origin in heredity or the physiological condition of the organism.

constructive alternativism In Kelly's theory, the assumption that any one event is open to a variety of interpretations.

continuity theory A theory that suggests that the development of personality is essentially an accumulation of skills, habits, and discriminations without anything really new appearing in the makeup of the person.

continuous reinforcement A schedule of reinforcement in which the desired behavior is reinforced every time it occurs.

control group In an experiment, a group equally matched to the experimental group and used for comparison.

conversion disorder A reaction to anxiety or stress expressed through physical symptoms; the modern term for hysteria.

corollaries In Kelly's theory, eleven statements that elaborate on the fundamental postulate.

correlation A statistical tool for making comparisons by expressing the extent to which two events covary.

covert behavior A behavior that can be observed directly only by the individual actually experiencing it.

creative self In Adler's theory, that aspect of the person that interprets and makes meaningful the experiences of the organism and establishes the life-style.

criterion analysis A method of analysis employed by Eysenck that begins with a hypothesis about possible variables and conducts statistical analyses in order to test the hypothesis.

critical periods Periods during which an organism is highly responsive to certain influences that may enhance or disrupt its development.

cue In Dollard and Miller's theory, a specific stimulus that tells the organism when, where, and how to respond.

Daijo Zen Zen practiced for the sake of liberating others.

daimonic In May's theory, any natural function that has the power to take over a person.

defense mechanism In Freud's theory, a procedure that wards off anxiety and prevents its conscious perception.

definition A statement that is true because of the way in which we have agreed to use words.

delayed reinforcement Reinforcement that is delayed after a response.

denial In Freud's theory, a defense mechanism that entails refusing to believe a reality or a fact of life.

dependent origination The Buddhist concept of interconnected causality.

dependent variable In an experiment, the behavior under study.

desensitization A process whereby anxieties and fears are reduced by repeated, gradual, imagined, or real exposures to the noxious stimuli paired with relaxation, skill training, and other behavioral techniques.

destructiveness In Fromm's theory, a way of escaping from freedom by eliminating others and/or the outside world.

determinism The philosophical view that behavior is controlled by external or internal forces and pressures.

developmental line In Anna Freud's theory, a series of id-ego interactions in which children increase ego mastery of themselves and their world.

Dharma Sanskrit for the truth or law of the universe discovered by the Buddha; the Buddha's teaching.

diagnostic profile A formal assessment procedure developed by Anna Freud that reflects developmental issues.

directive A term used to describe therapies whose course is primarily structured by the therapist.

disconnection The break that is experienced when a person cannot engage in mutually empathetic and empowering relationships.

discontinuity theory A theory of personality that suggests that in the course of development an organism experiences genuine transformations or changes so that it reaches successively higher levels of organization.

discrimination In behavior theory, the ability to tell the difference between stimuli that are and are not reinforced.

displacement In Freud's theory, a defense mechanism in which one object of an impulse is substituted for another.

D-needs Maslow's term for deficiency needs that arise out of a lack.

dream See **latent dream; manifest dream.**

dream analysis A technique used by Freud and other analysts to uncover unconscious processes.

dream work In Freud's theory, the process that disguises unconscious wishes and converts them into a manifest dream.

drive The psychological correlate of a need or stimulus that impels an organism into action. In Freud's theory, a psychological representation of an inner bodily source of excitement characterized by its source, impetus, aim, and object. In Dollard and Miller's theory, the primary motivation for behavior.

drive reduction A concept formulated by Hull that suggests that learning occurs only if an organism's response is followed by the reduction of some need or drive.

dukkha Pali for suffering, dissatisfaction, imperfection, incompleteness; one of the three characteristics of existence according to the Buddha.

dynamic traits In Cattell's theory, traits that motivate an individual toward some goal.

dynamism In Sullivan's theory, a pattern of energy transformation that characterizes an individual's interpersonal relations.

eclectic Selecting the best from a variety of different theories or concepts.

ego The self. In Freud's theory, a function of the personality that follows the reality principle and operates according to secondary processes and reality testing. In Jung's theory, one's conscious perception of self.

ego-ideal In Freud's theory, a subsystem of the superego consisting of an ideal self-image.

ego identity versus role confusion Erikson's psychosocial stage of adolescence in which one faces the task of developing a self-image.

ego integrity versus despair Erikson's psychosocial stage of maturity that entails the task of being able to reflect on one's life with satisfaction.

ego-psychoanalytic theory Psychoanalytic theory that emphasizes the role of the ego in personality development.

Eightfold Path The Buddha's prescription for living constituting the fourth Noble Truth; the "Middle Way" leading to nirvana.

Electra complex A term that some critics have used to express the feminine counterpart to the male Oedipus complex.

emotionality versus stability One of Eysenck's personality dimensions, involving an individual's adjustment to the environment and the stability of his or her behavior over time.

emotive-evocative therapy In Ellis's theory, helping clients to get in touch with their feelings.

empathy The ability to recognize and understand another's feelings.

empirical Based on experience and observation.

empiricism The philosophical view that human knowledge arises slowly in the course of experience through observation and experiment.

environmental-mold traits In Cattell's theory, traits that originate from the influences of physical and social surroundings.

epiphany A manifestation of the essential nature of something.

equilibrium Balance or harmony.

erg In Cattell's theory, a constitutional dynamic trait.

erogenous zones Areas of the body that provide pleasure.

Eros In Freud's theory, life impulses or drives forces that maintain life processes and ensure reproduction of the species.

essence In philosophy, the unchangeable principles and laws that govern being.

eugenics Improving the human race through genetic control.

evaluative response In Rogers's theory, a response that places a value judgment on thoughts, feelings, wishes, or behavior.

evoked potential Electrical activity in the brain.

evolutionary psychology The branch of psychology that considers the impact of evolution on psychological mechanisms.

excitation and stimulation In Fromm's theory, the need to actively strive for a goal rather than simply respond.

existential dichotomy In Fromm's theory, a dilemma or problem that arises simply from the fact of existence.

existentialism A philosophical movement that studies the meaning of existence.

expectancy In Rotter's theory, the individual's subjective expectation about the outcome of his or her behavior.

experimental method A scientific method involving a careful study of cause and effect by manipulating variables and observing their effects.

exploitative orientation In Fromm's theory, a character type in which a person exploits others and the world.

expressive behavior In Allport's theory, an individual's manner of performing.

extinction The tendency of a response to disappear when it is not reinforced.

extraversion An attitude of expansion in which the psyche is oriented toward the external world.

extraversion versus introversion One of Eysenck's personality dimensions, involving the degree to which a person is outgoing and participative in relating to other people.

extrinsic A quest that serves other purposes outside the original goal.

factor analysis Employed by Cattell, a procedure that interrelates many correlations at one time.

falsification The act of disproving.

family atmosphere In Adler's theory, the quality of emotional relationships among members of a family.

family constellation In Adler's theory, one's position within the family in terms of birth order among siblings and the presence or absence of parents and other caregivers.

family therapy Treating psychological problems in the context of the family.

feeling One of Jung's functions, involving valuing and judging the world.

fictional finalism In Adler's theory, a basic concept or philosophical assumption that cannot be tested against reality.

finalism In Adler's theory, a principle that reflects the concept of goal orientation.

Five-Factor Model (FFM) A hypothesis for understanding personality structure based on five factors.

fixation In Freud's theory, a concept in which there is an arrest of growth, and excessive needs characteristic of an earlier stage are created by overindulgence or undue frustration.

fixed reinforcement A schedule of reinforcement in which the time period or number of responses before reinforcement is identical.

flow A state of oneness with the activity and situation at hand, entailing heightened focus, productivity, and happiness.

Four Noble Truths The essence of the practical teaching of the Buddha, specifying the nature of suffering, its cause, its cessation, and the path to accomplish liberation from suffering.

frame of orientation and object of devotion In Fromm's thought, the need for a stable thought system by which to organize perceptions and make sense of the environment.

free association In Freud's psychoanalysis, a technique in which a person verbalizes whatever comes to mind.

freedom of movement In Rotter's theory, the degree of expectation a person has that a particular set of responses will lead to a desired reinforcement.

frustration In Dollard and Miller's theory, an emotion that occurs when one is unable to satisfy a drive because the response that would satisfy it has been blocked.

fully functioning person A term used by Rogers to indicate an individual who is functioning at an optimum level.

functional autonomy In Allport's theory, a concept that present motives are not necessarily tied to the past but may be free of earlier motivations.

functions In Jung's theory, ways of perceiving the environment and orienting experiences.

fundamental postulate In Kelly's theory, the basic assumption that a person's processes are psychologically channelized by the ways in which he or she anticipates events.

gassho Japanese for "palms of the hands pressed together," expressing the unity of the person and the universe, a gesture commonly used for greeting in many cultures in the East.

Gedo Zen Zen practiced without connection to the Buddha's teachings, generally in order to attain mystical experiences.

generalization A statement that may be made, when a number of different instances coincide, that something is true about many or all of the members of a certain class. In behavior theory, the application of a response learned in one situation to a different but similar situation.

generalized conditioned reinforcers In Skinner's theory, learned reinforcers that have the power to reinforce a great number of different behaviors.

generativity In McAdams's theory, concern for and commitment to future generations.

generativity versus stagnation Erikson's psychosocial stage of the middle years, in which one faces the dilemma of being productive and creative in life.

genital stage Freud's psychosexual stage in which an individual reaches sexual maturity.

genotype The genetic makeup of an individual.

genuineness A therapist's attitude characterized by congruence and awareness in the therapeutic relationship.

gestalt Configuration or pattern that forms a whole.

gestalt principle The notion that the whole is more than the sum of its parts.

gestalt psychology A branch of psychology that studies how organisms perceive objects and events.

getting type In Adler's theory, dependent people who take rather than give.

goal of superiority In Adler's theory, the ultimate fictional finalism, entailing the desire to be competent and effective in whatever one strives to do and to actualize one's potential.

gradient The changing strength of a force, which may be plotted on a graph.

habit In Dollard and Miller's theory, the basic structure of personality: a learned association between a stimulus and response.

habitual responses In Eysenck's theory, clusters of specific behaviors that characteristically recur in similar circumstances, such as buying groceries or giving parties.

having mode In Fromm's theory, a way of existence that relies on possessions.

heritability An estimate of the degree to which a trait or characteristic is caused by the genotype rather than the environment.

heterostasis The desire not to reduce tension but to seek new stimuli and challenges that will further growth.

heuristic value The ability of a construct to predict future events.

hierarchy of needs Maslow's theory of five basic needs ranked in order of strength: physiological, safety, belonging and love, self-esteem, and self-actualization.

hierarchy of response In Dollard and Miller's theory, a tendency for certain responses to occur before other responses.

Hinayana Sanskrit for "small vehicle," a designation for the southern schools of Buddhism concerned with personal liberation. One of the two major divisions of Buddhism.

historical dichotomy In Fromm's theory, a dilemma or problem that arises out of human history because of various societies and cultures.

hoarding orientation In Fromm's theory, a character type in which the person seeks to save or hoard and protects him- or herself from the world by a wall.

homeostasis Balance or harmony.

homosexuality Primary attraction to the same sex.

hormones Chemicals released into the blood stream by the endocrine glands.

hot cognitions In Beck's therapy, experiencing arousing emotions and reality testing at the same time.

humanist theories Theories of personality that emphasize human potential.

Humanistic Communitarian Socialism The name of Fromm's ideal society.

humanistic ethics In Fromm's theory, a value system that has its source in the individual acting in accord with the law of his or her human nature and assuming full responsibility for his or her existence.

humors In earlier psychology, bodily fluids thought to enter into the constitution of a body and determine, by their proportion, a person's constitution and temperament.

hypercompetitiveness In Horney's theory, American society's sweeping desire to compete and win.

hypothesis A preliminary assumption that guides further inquiry.

hysteria An earlier term for an illness in which there are physical symptoms, such as paralysis, but no organic or physiological basis for the problem.

id In Freud's theory, the oldest and original function of the personality, which includes genetic inheritance, reflex capacities, instincts, and drives.

idealization In Kohut's theory, the tendency children have to idealize their parents.

idealized self In Horney's theory, that which a person thinks he or she should be.

identification In Freud's theory, (a defense mechanism in which a person reduces anxiety by modeling his or her behavior after that of someone else, and (the process whereby the child resolves the Oedipus complex by incorporating the parents into the self.

identity crisis In Erikson's theory, transitory failure to develop a self-image or identity.

idiographic In Allport's theory, an approach to studying personality that centers on understanding the uniqueness of the individual.

I-E Scale A questionnaire developed by Rotter to measure internal versus external locus of control.

imagoes In McAdams's theory, main characters that represent our primary social roles and cravings for power and love.

immediate reinforcement Reinforcement that immediately follows a response.

implosive A sudden, instead of gradual, confrontation of a phobic situation.

imprinting A bond of attraction that develops among members of a species shortly after birth.

incongruence In Rogers's theory, the lack of harmony that results when a person's symbolized experiences do not represent the actual experiences.

independent variable In an experiment, the factor that is manipulated by the experimenter.

individual psychology The school of psychology developed by Adler.

individuation In Jung's theory of self-realization, a process whereby the systems of the individual psyche achieve their fullest degree of differentiation, expression, and development.

industry versus inferiority Erikson's psychosocial stage, corresponding to Freud's latency period, in which children face the task of learning and mastering the technology of their culture.

inferiority complex In Adler's theory, a neurotic pattern in which an individual feels highly inadequate.

inferiority feelings In Adler's theory, feelings of being inadequate that arise out of childhood experiences.

infrahuman species Species lower than human organisms.

inhibition The prevention of a response from occurring because it is in conflict with other strong unconscious responses.

initiative versus guilt Erikson's psychosexual stage, corresponding to Freud's phallic stage, in which children face the task of directing their curiosity and activity toward specific goals and achievements.

inner space In Erikson's theory, tendency on the part of girls to emphasize qualities of openness versus closedness in space.

insight A form of therapeutic knowing that combines intellectual and emotional elements and culminates in profound personality change.

insight therapy Therapeutic procedures that seek to increase self-understanding and lead to deep motivational changes.

intentionality In May's theory, a dimension that undercuts conscious and unconscious, and underlies will and decision.

interpersonal psychiatry The school and theory of psychiatry founded by Harry Stack Sullivan.

interpretative response In Rogers's theory, a response that seeks to interpret a speaker's problem or tell how the speaker feels about it.

interpsychic Between psyches or persons.

interval reinforcement A schedule of reinforcement in which the organism is reinforced after a certain time period has elapsed.

interview Sullivan's term for the interpersonal process that occurs between the patient and therapist.

intimacy versus isolation Erikson's psychosocial stage of young adulthood in which one faces the task of establishing a close, deep, and meaningful genital relationship with another person.

intrapsychic Within the psyche or individual self.

introversion An attitude of withdrawal in which personality is oriented inward toward the subjective world.

intuition One of Jung's functions, entailing perception via the unconscious.

IQ Intelligence quotient: a number used to express the relative intelligence of a person.

karma Sanskrit for volitional action.

kinhin Japanese for the meditational walking performed between periods of zazen.

koan Japanese for "public document," an apparently paradoxical story, anecdote, or statement expressing the realization of a Zen master.

latency period Freud's psychosexual stage of development in which the sexual drive is thought to go underground.

latent dream In Freud's theory, the real meaning or motive that underlies the dream that we remember.

law of effect A law formulated by Thorndike that states that a behavior or a performance accompanied by satisfaction tends to increase and a behavior or performance accompanied by frustration tends to decrease.

L-data In Cattell's theory, observations made of a person's behavior in society or everyday life.

learning dilemma In Dollard and Miller's theory, the situation an individual is placed in if present responses are not reinforced.

libido In Freud's theory, an emotional and psychic energy derived from the biological drive of sexuality. In Jung's theory, an undifferentiated life and psychic energy.

life crisis In Erikson's theory, a crucial period in which the individual cannot avoid a decisive turn one way or the other.

locus of control In Rotter's theory, the extent to which a person believes that reinforcements are controlled by his or her own behavior (internal locus) or by other people or outside forces (external locus).

logotherapy Frankl's theory that suggests people have realized freedom but have not necessarily taken responsibility for their freedom.

love In Fromm's theory, productive relationship with others and the self, entailing care, responsibility, respect, and knowledge.

macro theory Theory that seeks to be global and that emphasizes comprehension of the whole person.

Mahayana Sanskrit for "great vehicle," one of the two major divisions of Buddhism, concerned with the liberation of all sentient beings.

manas Sanskrit for "mind," the seventh of the Eight Consciousnesses, where the illusion of the ego arises.

mandala A concentrically arranged figure often found as a symbol in the East that denotes wholeness and unity. In Jung's theory, a symbol for the emerging self.

manifest dream In Freud's theory, the dream as it is remembered the next morning.

manovijnana Sanskrit for "mental consciousness," the sixth of the Eight Consciousnesses and the basis for the five sensory consciousnesses.

marketing orientation In Fromm's theory, a character type in which the person experiences him- or herself as a commodity in the marketplace.

masculine protest In Adler's early theory, the compensation for one's inferiorities.

masochism A disorder in which a person obtains pleasure by receiving pain.

mechanisms of escape In Fromm's theory, common ways of trying to cope with freedom that do not resolve the underlying problem but merely mask it.

melancholic One of Hippocrates' temperaments, referring to an individual characterized by depression.

mergers In Orlofsky's theory, individuals who commit themselves to a relationship at the price of their own independence.

metacommunication In Lazarus's theory, the fact that people not only communicate but also think and communicate about their communications.

metamotivation Maslow's term for growth tendencies within the organism.

metapsychological A term used by Freud to indicate the fullest possible description of psychic processes.

micro theory Theory that has resulted from specific research focused on limited aspects of human behavior.

mindfulness A discipline of noting thoughts and feelings without becoming enmeshed in them.

minimum goal level In Rotter's theory, the lowest level of potential reinforcement that is perceived as satisfactory in a particular situation.

mirror neurons Neurons that are activated when an animal observes or performs an action.

mirrored In Kohut's theory, the need for children to have their talk and their accomplishments acknowledged, accepted, and praised.

mistaken style of life In Adler's theory, a style of life that belies one's actual capabilities and strengths.

modality profile In Lazarus's therapy, a specific list of problems and proposed treatments across the client's BASIC-ID.

moral anxiety In Freud's theory, fear of the retribution of one's own conscience.

moral disengagement In Bandura's theory, practices that permit one to separate one's self from ethical behavior.

Morita therapy A system of psychotherapy developed in Japan early in the twentieth century by Shoma Morita, combining elements of Zen Buddhism and psychoanalysis.

motivation Maslow's term for the reduction of tension by satisfying deficit states or lacks.

moving against One of Horney's three primary modes of relating to other people, in which one seeks to protect him- or herself by revenge or controlling others.

moving away One of Horney's three primary ways of relating to other people, in which one isolates him- or herself and keeps apart.

moving toward One of Horney's three primary modes of relating to other people, in which one accepts his or her own helplessness and becomes compliant in order to depend on others.

multimodal therapy Lazarus's method of therapy.

musturbatory belief system In Ellis's theory, escalating probalistic statements into absolutes.

mutuality A way of relating and sharing in which all participants are fully participating.

myths In May's theory, narrative patterns that give significance to our existence.

Naikan therapy In Japanese culture, a form of introspective therapy emphasizing the development of responsibility and obligation.

narcissism A form of self-encapsulation in which an individual experiences as real only that which exists within him- or herself.

necrophilous character In Fromm's theory, a character orientation in which an individual is attracted to that which is dead and decaying and seeks to destroy living things.

need In Murray's theory, a force in the brain that organizes perception, understanding, and behavior in such a way as to change an unsatisfying situation and increase satisfaction. In Rotter's theory, a behavior that leads to a reinforcement.

need potential In Rotter's theory, the likelihood that a set of behaviors directed toward the same goal will be used in a given situation.

need value In Rotter's theory, the importance placed on a goal.

negative identity In Erikson's theory, an identity at odds with the dominant values of one's culture.

negative reinforcement Unpleasant or aversive stimuli that can be changed or avoided by certain behavior.

NEO-PI The Neuroticism Extraversion Openness Personality Inventory developed by Costa and McCrae.

NEO-PI-R The Neuroticism Extraversion Openness Personality Inventory, Revised, developed by McCrae and Costa.

neopsychoanalytic theories Psychoanalytic theories that revise or modify Freud's original theories.

neurotic anxiety In Freud's theory, the fear that one's inner impulses cannot be controlled.

neurotic needs or trends In Horney's theory, exaggerated defense strategies that permit an individual to cope with the world.

Nigrescence In the theory of Cross and others, the development of ethnic identity in African Americans.

nirvana Sanskrit for a mental state where craving and suffering have been completely extinguished.

nomothetic In Allport's theory, an approach to studying personality that considers large groups of individuals in order to infer general variables or universal principles.

nondirective Rogers's term for therapies whose course is primarily determined by the patient.

normal curve of distribution A bell-shaped curve representing many events in nature in which most events cluster around the mean.

nuclear self In Kohut's theory, a well-developed self that ideally emerges in the second year.

object In Freud's theory, any target through which an infant seeks to satisfy the aim of a drive. In object relations theory, the aim of relational needs in human development.

object relations The intrapsychic experience of early relationships with others.

objective data Data acquired through extrospection, the act of looking outward on the world as object.

objectivism The philosophical view that valid knowledge arises gradually in the course of experience through observation and experimentation.

objectivity The quality of recognizing or expressing reality without distortion by personal feeling. In test construction, construction of a test in such a way that it can be given and scored in a way that avoids the scorer's subjective bias.

observational learning In Bandura's theory, learning that occurs through observation without any direct reinforcement.

Oedipus complex In Freud's theory, an unconscious psychological conflict in which the child loves the parent of the opposite sex.

open system A concept of personality that conceives of it as having a dynamic potential for growth, reconstitution, and change through extensive transactions within itself and the environment.

operant behavior In Skinner's theory, a response that acts on the environment and is emitted without a stimulus necessarily being present.

operant conditioning In Skinner's theory, the process by which an operant response becomes associated with a reinforcement through learning.

operational definition A definition that specifies those behaviors that are included in the concept.

oral stage Freud's psychosexual stage in which the major source of pleasure and potential conflict is the mouth.

organismic valuing process In Rogers's theory, a subconscious natural phenomenon that guides an individual toward productive growth experiences.

outer space In Erikson's theory, tendency on the part of boys to emphasize qualities of highness or lowness in space.

overcompensation In Adler's theory, an exaggerated effort to cover up a weakness that entails a denial rather than an acceptance of the real situation.

overt behavior Behavior that can be observed by an external observer.

paradigm A pattern or model.

paradox Two opposites that seem to negate each other but cannot exist without each other. In May's theory, two opposing things that are posited against and seem to negate each other yet cannot exist without each other. In Lazarus's therapy, the use of contradictions.

parataxic experience In Sullivan's theory, a cognitive process in which one perceives causal relations but not on the basis of reality or logic.

paraworld A world of quantified, logical, and mathematical imaginary constructs used by the scientist to draw conclusions about the everyday world.

parenting style Variations in parenting due to differences in behaviors expressing warmth and control.

participant observation In Sullivan's theory, a concept that refers to the fact that an observer of an interpersonal relationship is also a participant in it.

peak experience In Maslow's theory, an intensified experience in which there is a loss of self or transcendence of self.

penis envy In Freud's theory, the concept that women view themselves as castrated males and envy the penis.

performance phase In Dollard and Miller's therapy, a phase in which the patient acquires new, more adaptive responses and habits.

perseverative functional autonomy In Allport's theory, acts or behaviors that are repeated even though they may have lost their original function.

persona In Jung's theory, an archetype referring to one's social role and understanding of it.

personal construct In Kelly's theory, a hypothesis an individual forms in order to predict and control events, which makes the world meaningful and which is tested by later experience.

personal construct theory George Kelly's theory of personality.

personal dispositions In Allport's theory, traits that are unique to an individual.

personal unconscious In Jung's theory, experiences of an individual's life that have been repressed or temporarily forgotten.

personality In social speech, one's public image. In Fromm's theory, the totality of an individual's psychic qualities. In Cattell's theory, that which permits prediction of what a person will do in a given situation. In Sullivan's theory, the characteristic ways in which an individual deals with other people.

person-centered psychotherapy The most recent name for Rogers's method of psychotherapy.

personification In Sullivan's theory, a group of feelings, attitude, and thoughts that have arisen out of one's interpersonal experiences.

personology Murray's term for his study of individual persons.

phallic stage One of Freud's psychosexual stages, in which pleasurable and conflicting feelings are associated with the genital organs.

phenomenal field In Rogers's theory, the total sum of experiences an organism has.

phenomenology The study of phenomena or appearances.

phenotype An individual's observable appearance and behavior.

philosophical assumption An underlying view of the world that influences a person's thinking.

philosophy The systematic love and pursuit of wisdom.

phlegmatic One of Hippocrates' temperaments, referring to an individual who is slow, solid, and apathetic.

pleasure principle In Freud's theory, the seeking of tension reduction followed by the id.

polymorphous perverse A phrase used by Freud to emphasize the point that children deviate in many ways from what is thought to be normal reproductive sexual activity.

positive psychology A branch of psychology that seeks to study and understand the complex positive behavior of people in order to emphasize the systematic building and amplifying of human strengths and virtues.

positive regard In Rogers's theory, being loved and accepted for who one is.

positive reinforcement Anything that serves to increase the frequency of a response.

positive self-regard In Rogers's theory, viewing the self favorably and with acceptance.

predictive power A criterion for evaluating rival hypotheses: the range or scope of the hypothesis.

preemptive construct In Kelly's theory, a construct that limits its elements to one range only.

press In Murray's theory, a force coming from the environment that helps or hinders an individual in reaching goals.

primary drive A drive associated with a physiological process that is necessary for the organism's survival.

primary modes of relating In Horney's theory, three major types of interpersonal coping strategies.

primary process In Freud's theory, a psychological activity of the id characterized by immediate wish fulfillment and the disregard of realistic concerns.

primary reinforcer A reinforcer that is inherently rewarding as it satisfies a primary drive.

proactive Referring to theories of personality that view the human being as acting on his or her own initiative rather than simply reacting.

probing response In Rogers's theory, a response that seeks further information.

proceeding In Murray's theory, a short, significant behavior pattern that has a clear beginning and ending.

productive orientation In Fromm's theory, the character type that represents the ideal of humanistic development.

projection In Freud's theory, a defense mechanism that refers to the unconscious attribution of an impulse, attitude, or behavior to someone else or some element in the environment.

projective techniques Personality tests in which an ambiguous stimulus is presented to the subject who is expected to project aspects of his or her personality into the response.

propositional construct In Kelly's theory, a construct that leaves its elements open to other constructions.

propriate functional autonomy In Allport's theory, acquired interests, values, attitudes, intentions, and life-style that are directed from the proprium and are genuinely free of earlier motivations.

propriate functions In Allport's theory, the functions of the proprium.

propriate striving In Allport's theory, a propriate function that entails projection of long-term purposes and goals and development of a plan to attain them.

proprium In Allport's theory, the central experiences of self-awareness that a person has as he or she grows and moves forward.

prototaxic experience In Sullivan's theory, a cognitive process in which the infant does not distinguish between the self and the external world.

psyche From the Greek term meaning "breath" or "principle of life," often translated as "soul" or "self." In Freud's theory, the id, ego, and superego. In Jung's theory, the total personality encompassing all psychological processes: thoughts, feelings, sensations, wishes, and so on.

psychoanalysis A method of therapy developed by Freud that concentrates on cultivating a transference relationship and analyzing resistances to the therapeutic process.

psychohistory The combined use of psychoanalysis and history to study individuals and groups.

psychological behaviorism Staats's theory of personality, which translates personality concepts into behavioral language.

psychological situation The psychological context within which an organism responds.

psychology The scientific study of behavior and mental processes.

psychometrics The quantitative measurement of psychological characteristics through statistical techniques.

psychophysical Entailing components of both the mind and the body.

psychosexual stages In Freud's theory, developmental stages through which all people pass as they move from infancy to adulthood.

psychosis An abnormal personality disturbance characterized by loss or distortion of reality testing and the inability to distinguish between reality and fantasy.

psychosocial stages A series of developmental stages proposed by Erikson to emphasize the social dimension of personality.

psychotherapy Treatment of emotional disorders by psychological means.

psychoticism One of Eysenck's personality dimensions, involving the loss or distortion of reality and the inability to distinguish between reality and fantasy.

punishment An undesirable consequence that follows a behavior and is designed to stop or change it.

Q-sort technique A card-sorting technique employed by Rogers for studying the self-concept.

radical behaviorism A label that has been given to B. F. Skinner's point of view.

random assignment In an experiment, ensuring that every subject has an equal chance of being assigned to any of the treatment groups.

ratio reinforcement A schedule of reinforcement in which the organism is reinforced after a number of appropriate responses.

rational emotive behavior therapy Ellis's method of psychotherapy.

rationalism The philosophical view that the mind can, in and of its own accord, formulate ideas and determine their truth.

rationalization In Freud's theory, a defense mechanism that entails dealing with an emotion or impulse analytically and intellectually, thereby not involving the emotions.

reaction formation In Freud's theory, a defense mechanism in which an impulse is expressed by its opposite.

reactive Referring to theories of personality that view the human beings as primarily responding to external stimuli.

real self In Horney's theory, that which a person actually is.

reality anxiety In Freud's theory, the fear of a real danger in the external world.

reality principle In Freud's theory, the way in which the ego satisfies the impulses of the id in an appropriate manner in the external world.

reassuring response In Rogers's theory, a response that attempts to soothe feelings.

receptive orientation In Fromm's theory, a character type in which the individual reacts to the world passively.

reciprocal inhibition In behavior therapy, introducing a competitive response that will interfere with the original maladaptive response.

reconstructive (or intensive) psychotherapy Therapeutic methods that seek to remove defenses and reorganize the basic personality structure.

reflective response In Rogers's theory, a response that seeks to capture the underlying feeling expressed.

reflexes Inborn automatic responses.

regression In Freud's theory, a defense mechanism that entails reverting to earlier forms of behavior.

reinforcement The process of increasing or decreasing the likelihood of a particular response.

reinforcement value In Rotter's theory, a variable that indicates the importance or preference of a particular reinforcement for an individual.

reinforcer Any event that increases or decreases the likelihood of a particular response.

relatedness In Fromm's theory, the basic need to relate to and love other people.

relational-cultural theory A perspective for understanding personality developed by scholars working out of the Stone Center at Wellesley College.

relationship-differentiation The process of cultivating increasing levels of complexity and maturity within the framework of human relationships.

relevance One of the criteria for evaluating philosophical statements, the quality of having some bearing or being pertinent to one's view of reality.

reliability The quality of consistently yielding the same results over time.

Rep Test Role Construct Repertory Test: a device developed by Kelly to reveal personal constructs.

repression In Freud's theory, the key defense mechanism, which entails blocking a wish or desire from expression so that it cannot be experienced consciously or directly expressed in behavior. In Dollard and Miller's theory, a learned process of avoiding certain thoughts and thereby losing verbal control.

reproduction of mothering In Chodorow's theory, a cyclical process in which women as mothers produce daughters with mothering capacities and the desire to mother.

resignation solution One of Horney's three basic orientations, representing the desire to be free of others.

respondent behavior In Skinner's theory, reflexes or automatic responses elicited by a stimulus.

response A behavior that results from a stimulus. In Dollard and Miller's theory, one's reaction to a cue or stimulus.

reticular activating system   The part of the brain that controls levels of arousal.

Rinzai   One of the two major schools of Zen Buddhism in Japan, stressing the use of koans and zazen to reach enlightenment.

role   In social psychology, a set of behavioral expectations set forth by a particular society and fulfilled by its members. In Kelly's theory, a process or behavior that a person engages in based on his or her understanding of the behavior and constructs of other people.

role confusion   In Erikson's theory, an inability to conceive of oneself as a productive member in one's society.

role-playing   A therapeutic technique in Kelly and Beck's therapy, in which clients are asked to rehearse situations that will later happen in real life.

rootedness   In Fromm's theory, the basic need to feel that one belongs in the world.

ruling type   In Adler's theory, aggressive, dominating people who have little social interest or cultural perception.

sadism   A disorder in which a person obtains pleasure by inflicting pain.

safeguarding tendencies   In Adler's theory, compensatory mechanisms that ward off feelings of insecurity.

Saijojo Zen   Zen practiced for its own sake, with no expectations and no thought of gain.

sanguine   One of Hippocrates' temperaments, referring to a personality marked by sturdiness, high color, and cheerfulness.

sanzen   Individual consultations between a Zen Buddhist monk and his master.

satiation   Engaging in a behavior until one tires of it.

satori   Japanese for "enlightenment," the goal of Zen practice.

schedule of reinforcement   A program for increasing or decreasing the likelihood of a particular response.

schemas   In Beck's theory, cognitive structures that consist of an individual's fundamental core beliefs and assumptions about how the world operates.

science   A system or method of acquiring knowledge based on specific principles of observation and reasoning.

scientific construct   An imaginary or hypothetical construct used to explain what is observed in science.

scientific (or empirical) generalization   An inductive conclusion based on a number of different instances of observation.

scientific method   A method of inquiry that consists of five steps: recognizing a problem, developing a hypothesis, making a prediction, testing the hypothesis, and drawing a conclusion.

scientific statement   A statement about the world based on observations arising from a currently held paradigm.

scientism   Exclusive reliance on a narrow conception of science.

secondary dispositions   In Allport's theory, specific, focused tendencies of an individual that tend to be situational in character.

secondary drive   A drive that is learned or acquired on the basis of a primary drive.

secondary processes   In Freud's theory, higher intellectual functions that enable the ego to establish suitable courses of action and test them for their effectiveness.

secondary reinforcer   A reinforcer that is originally neutral but that acquires reward value on the basis of association with a primary reinforcer.

security operation   In Sullivan's theory, an interpersonal device that a person uses to minimize anxiety and enhance security.

self   In Jung's theory, a central archetype representing the striving for unity of all parts of the personality. In Rogers's theory, the psychological processes that govern a person's behavior.

self-actualization   In the theories of Rogers and Maslow, a dynamic within the organism leading it to actualize, fulfill, and enhance its inherent potentialities.

self-analysis   In Horney's theory, a systematic effort at self-understanding conducted without the aid of a professional.

self-as-rational coper   In Allport's theory, a propriate function that entails the perception of oneself as an active problem-solving agent.

self-concept   In Rogers's theory, a portion of the phenomenal field that has become differentiated and is composed of perceptions and values of "I" or "me."

self-construct   In Kelly's theory, perception of similarities in one's behavior based on role relationships with other people.

self-effacing solution   One of Horney's three basic orientations toward life, which represents an appeal to be loved by others.

self-efficacy   In Bandura's theory, a person's perception of his or her effectiveness.

self-esteem   In Allport's theory, a propriate function that entails feelings of pride as one develops the ability to do things.

self-expansive solution   One of Horney's three basic orientations toward life, which represents a striving for mastery.

self-extension   In Allport's theory, a propriate function that entails a sense of possession.

self-identity   In Allport's theory, a propriate function that entails an awareness of inner sameness and continuity.

self-image   In Allport's theory, a propriate function that entails a sense of the expectations of others and its comparison with one's own behavior.

self-love   In Fromm's theory, love of self that is a prerequisite for love of others.

self-orientation A new character type, informed by Fromm's theory, that is highly narcissistic.

self-realization In Jung's theory, a drive within the self to realize, fulfill, and enhance one's maximum human potentialities.

self-regulation In Bandura's theory, the influencing of one's own behavior.

self-sentiment In Cattell's theory, an environmental-mold dynamic source trait composing a person's self-image.

self-system In Bandura's theory, cognitive structures that underlie the perception, evaluation, and regulation of behavior. In Sullivan's theory, a dynamism made up of security operations that defend the self against anxiety.

self-theory Theory and school of psychology developed by Heinz Kohut.

sensation One of Jung's functions, referring to sense perception of the world.

sense of identity In Fromm's theory, the need to be aware of oneself as an individual.

sentiment In Cattell's theory, an environmental-mold dynamic source trait.

separation-individuation A sequence of stages posited by Mahler through which the ego passes in the process of becoming an individual.

shadow In Jung's theory, an archetype that encompasses one's animalistic and unsocial side.

shaping In Skinner's theory, a process by which an organism's behavior is gradually molded until it approximates the desired behavior.

shikantaza Japanese for "just sitting," the form of zazen practice stressed particularly in the Soto Zen tradition.

shinkeishitsu A Japanese label for a group of neuroses overlapping with the anxiety disorders in the DSM-IV classification.

Shojo Zen Zen practiced for personal enlightenment or for relief from suffering.

simplicity A criterion for evaluating rival hypotheses: the quality of being simple and avoiding complicated explanations.

skandha Sanskrit for "aggregate" or "heap." The five skandhas are form, feelings, perceptions, impulses, and consciousness.

slips In Freud's theory, bungled acts, such as a slip of the tongue, a slip of the pen, or a memory lapse.

social interest In Adler's theory, an urge in human nature to adapt oneself to the conditions of one's environment and society.

social learning theories Theories that attempt to explain personality in terms of learned behavior within a social context.

social psychoanalytic theories Psychoanalytic theories that emphasize the role of social forces in shaping personality.

socially useful type In Adler's theory, people who have a great deal of social interest and activity.

sociotropic dimension In Beck's theory, a personality dimension characterized by dependence on interpersonal relationships and needs for closeness and nurturance.

somatotonia In Sheldon's theory, a component of temperament characterized by a predominance of muscular activity and vigorous bodily assertiveness.

somatotype Sheldon's term for the expression of body type through three numbers that indicate the degree of each physical component.

Soto One of the two major schools of Zen Buddhism in Japan, stressing the practice of zazen as shikantaza and the identity of practice and enlightenment.

source traits In Cattell's theory, underlying variables that determine surface manifestations.

species-specific behavior Complex automatic behaviors that occur in all members of a species.

specific responses In Eysenck's theory, behaviors that we can actually observe, such as someone answering a phone.

specification equation An equation by which Cattell suggests we may eventually be able to predict human behavior.

spirituality A search for meaning or for a power beyond the self rather than an adherence to particular tenets as in a formal religion.

splitting In object relations therapy, separating an object image into opposites.

spontaneous recovery Following extinction, the return of a learned behavior.

standardization Pretesting of a large and representative sample in order to determine test norms.

statement An utterance that makes an assertion or a denial.

statistics The application of mathematical principles to the description and analysis of measurements.

stereotype Prejudgment that we make about people on the basis of their membership in certain groups.

stimulus An agent that rouses or excites a response.

structural profile In Lazarus's therapy, a quantitative assessment of the relative involvement of each of the elements of the BASIC-ID in a client.

structuralism Early school of psychology that suggested that psychology study conscious experience.

style of life In Adler's theory, the specific ways in which an individual seeks to attain the goal of superiority.

subception In Rogers's theory, a discriminative evaluative response of the organism that precedes conscious perception.

subjective data Data acquired through introspection, the act of looking inward on the self as subject.

subjectivism A philosophical view that constructs of knowledge are creations of the self.

sublimation In Freud's theory, a defense mechanism that refers to translating a wish, the direct expression of which would be socially unacceptable, into socially acceptable behavior.

subsidiation In Cattell's theory, the principle that certain traits are secondary to other traits.

successive approximations In Dollard and Miller's therapy, the interpretations of the therapist that provide increasingly more accurate labels for the patient's responses.

superego In Freud's theory, a function of the personality that represents introjected and internalized values, ideals, and moral standards.

superiority complex In Adler's theory, a neurotic pattern in which an individual exaggerates his or her importance.

supportive psychotherapy Therapeutic measures that seek to strengthen adaptive instincts and defenses.

surface traits In Cattell's theory, clusters of overt behavior responses that appear to go together.

sutra Sanskrit for a sermon or discourse, usually of the Buddha.

symbiotic relationship In Fromm's theory, a relationship in which one or the other of two persons loses or never attains his or her independence.

symbol An element in a dream that stands for something else.

synchronicity A phenomenon in which events are related to one another through simultaneity and meaning.

syntality In Cattell's theory, the behavior of a group as a whole or its "group personality."

syntaxic experience In Sullivan's theory, the highest level of cognitive activity, entailing the use of symbols and relying on consensual validation.

systematic desensitization In behavior therapy, conditioning a patient to stop responding to a stimulus in an undesired manner and to substitute a new response.

Tao A Chinese term for "Way" or "Path"; the absolute and ineffable nature of ultimate reality.

Taoism A Chinese philosophy and way of life based on the teachings of Lao-tse (ca. 4th century B.C.), stressing harmony with the Tao.

T-data In Cattell's theory, objective tests.

technical eclecticism In Lazarus's therapy, deriving treatment methods from many sources without necessarily agreeing with the theories that generated them.

telos A purpose or goal.

temperament traits In Cattell's theory, traits that determine how a person behaves in order to obtain his or her goal.

terror management theory A theory suggesting that the awareness and fear of death creates an ever-present prospect of terror and efforts to manage it.

Thanatos In Freud's theory, the death impulse or drive, the source of aggression, the ultimate resolution of all of life's tension in death.

Thematic Apperception Test (TAT) A projective test consisting of ambiguous pictures to which a subject is asked to respond.

theory A set of abstract concepts made about a group of facts or events to explain them.

therapy The practical application of psychology in ways that will assist individuals.

Theravada Pali for "the teaching of the Elders," the form of Buddhism dominant in Sri Lanka, Burma, Thailand, Laos, and Cambodia. Sometimes referred to as the Hinayana.

thinking One of Jung's functions, referring to giving meaning and understanding to the world.

thresholds In Lazarus's theory, tolerance levels for pain, frustration, or stress.

time-out Psychological intervention that eliminates undesired behavior by removing the individual from the situation in which the undesired behavior is occurring.

token economy A community based on Skinnerian principles in which individuals are rewarded for appropriate behavior with tokens that can be exchanged for various privileges.

tracking In Lazarus's therapy, paying careful attention to the "firing order" of the different modalities.

trait Continuous dimension that an individual can be seen to possess to a certain degree. In Allport's theory, a determining tendency to respond that represents the ultimate reality of psychological organization. In Cattell's theory, an imaginary construct or inference from overt behavior that helps to explain it.

trait theories Theories that conceive of personality as being composed primarily of traits.

transcendence In Jung's theory of self-realization, a process of integrating the diverse systems of the self toward the goal of wholeness and identification with all humanity. In Fromm's theory, the basic human need to rise above the accidental and passive creatureliness of animal existence and become an active creator.

transference In Freudian psychoanalysis, a process in which the patient projects onto the analyst emotional attitudes felt as a child toward important persons.

transference-focused psychotherapy Kernberg's method of treatment which emphasizes current behavior and focuses on the patient's distortions of reality, such as a distorted view of the therapist.

transpersonal psychology A branch of psychology that studies the transcendent or spiritual dimensions of persons.

triadic reciprocal causation In Bandura's theory, the regulation of behavior by an interplay of behavioral, cognitive, and environmental factors.

Tripitaka Sanskrit for the "Three Baskets" or collections of Buddhist scriptures.

trust versus mistrust Erikson's psychosocial stage, corresponding to Freud's oral stage, in which infants face the task of trusting the world.

typology Division of human beings into distinct, separate categories.

tyranny of the should In Horney's theory, creating false needs instead of meeting genuine ones.

unawareness In Sullivan's theory, an empirically based observation that a person may be unconscious or unaware of some of his or her motives and behaviors.

unconditional positive regard In Rogers's theory, positive regard that is not contingent on any specific behaviors.

unconditioned response A reflex or automatic response to a stimulus.

unconditioned stimulus A stimulus that normally elicits a particular reflex or automatic response.

unconscious process In Freud's theory, processes of which a person is unaware because they have been repressed or never permitted to become conscious. In Dollard and Miller's theory, drives or cues of which we are unaware because they are unlabeled or repressed.

usefulness In scientific theorizing, the ability of a hypothesis to generate predictions about experiences that we might observe. In Adler's theory, the ability of a goal to foster productive living and enhance one's life.

validating evidence Observable consequences that follow an experiment designed to test a hypothesis and are used to support a construct or theory.

validity The quality of measuring what a construct is supposed to measure.

variable A characteristic that can be measured or controlled.

variable reinforcement A schedule of reinforcement in which the time period or number of responses prior to reinforcement varies.

verifiability Capable of being tested by a method that ultimately relies on empirical observation.

vijnana Sanskrit for "consciousness."

virtues In Erikson's theory, ego strengths that develop out of each psychosocial stage.

visceral brain The limbic system and the hypothalamus.

Walden II Skinner's name for his utopian comunity.

wish fulfillment In Freud's theory, a primary-process activity that seeks to reduce tension by forming an image of the object that would satisfy needs.

wishes In Freud's theory, desires that may be rendered unconscious if they go against a person's ego-ideal.

withdrawal-destructiveness relationship In Fromm's theory, a relationship characterized by distance, apathy, or aggression.

womb envy In Horney's theory, the concept that men and boys experience jealousy over women's ability to bear and nurse children.

yang Chinese Taoist term for the positive, masculine, active, external aspect of the complementary yin and yang polarity.

yin Chinese Taoist term for the negative, feminine, passive, internal aspect of the complementary yin and yang polarity.

zazen Japanese for "sitting meditation," the most important and indispensable aspect of Zen practice. The typical length of a period of *zazen* in Japan is 40 minutes.

Zen Japanese rendering of the Chinese *ch'an*, meaning absorption or meditation. It can refer to a school of Buddhism or to the ineffable experience of oneness with reality.

References

Abraham, A., Windmann, S., Daum, I., & Gunturkin, O. (2005). Conceptual expansion and creative imagery as a function of psychoticism. *Consciousness and Cognition, 14*(3), 520–534.

Abrams, D. M. (1999). Six decades of the Bellak Scoring System among others. In L. Geiser & M. I. Stein (1999), *Evocative images: The TAT and the art of projection* (pp. 143–159). Washington, DC: American Psychological Association.

Abzug, R. H. (1996). Rollo May as friend to man. *Journal of Humanistic Psychology, 36,* 17–22.

Adams, J., & Gorton, D. (2004). Southern trauma: Revisiting caste and class in the Mississippi Delta. *American Anthropologist, 106*(2), 334–345.

Adler, A. (1917). *Study of organ inferiority and its psychical compensation.* New York: Nervous and Mental Diseases Publishing Co.

Adler, A. (1927). *The practice and theory of individual psychology.* New York: Harcourt, Brace, & World.

Adler, A. (1929a). *The science of living.* New York: Greenberg.

Adler, A. (1929b). *Problems of neurosis.* London: Kegan Paul.

Adler, A. (1930). Individual psychology. In C. Murchison (Ed.), *Psychologies of 1930.* Worcester, MA: Clark University Press.

Adler, A. (1931). *What life should mean to you.* Boston: Little, Brown.

Adler, A. (1936). The neurotic's picture of the world. *International Journal of Individual Psychology, 2,* 3–10.

Adler, A. (1939). *Social interest.* New York: Putnam.

Adler, A. (1954). *Understanding human nature.* New York: Fawcett.

Adler, A. (1964). *Superiority and social interest: A collection of later writings* (H. L. & R. R. Ansbacher, Eds.). Evanston, IL: Northwestern University Press.

Adler, J. (2006, March 27). Freud in our midst. *Newsweek,* pp. 43–49.

Adorno, T. W., Frenkel-Brunswick, E., Levinson, D., & Sanford, N. (1950). *The authoritarian personality.* New York: Harper.

Agarwal, R., & Misra, G. (1986, January). Locus of control and attribution for achievement outcomes, *Psychological Studies, 31*(1), 15–20.

Ainsworth, M. D. S., Blehar, M. C., Walters, E., & Wall, S. (1978). *Patterns of attachment: A psychological study of the strange situation.* Hillsdale, NJ: Erlbaum.

Akhtar, S. (1994). Object constancy and adult psychopathology. *International Journal of Psycho-Analysis, 75,* 441–455.

Alexander, F. (1950). *Psychosomatic medicine: Its principles and applications.* New York: Norton.

Alford, B. A., & Beck, A. T. (1997). *The integrative power of cognitive therapy.* New York: Guilford Press.

Allport, G. W. (1937). *Personality: A psychological interpretation.* New York: Holt.

Allport, G. W. (1950). *The individual and his religion.* New York: Macmillan.

Allport, G. W. (1954). *The nature of prejudice.* Boston: Beacon Press.

Allport, G. W. (1955). *Becoming: Basic considerations for a psychology of personality.* New Haven, CT: Yale University Press.

Allport, G. W. (1960). The open system in personality theory. *Journal of Abnormal and Social Psychology, 60,* 301–310.

Allport, G. W. (1961). *Pattern and growth in personality.* New York: Holt, Rinehart and Winston.

Allport, G. W. (1965). *Letters from Jenny.* New York: Harcourt, Brace & World.

Allport, G. W. (1968). *The person in psychology: Selected essays.* Boston: Beacon Press.

Allport, G. W., & Odbert, H. S. (1936). Trait-names: A psycho-lexical study. *Psychological Monographs, 47,* 1–211.

Altemeyer, B. (1989). *Enemies of freedom.* San Francisco: Jossey-Bass.

Altus, D. E., & Morris, E. K. (2004). B. F. Skinner's utopian vision. *Contemporary Justice Review, 7*(3), 267–286.

American Academy of Pediatrics. (2001). Policy statement. *Pediatrics, 107*(2), 423–426.

American Psychiatric Association. (1994). *Diagnostic and Statistical Manual of Mental Disorders.* Washington, DC: Author.

Anderson, C. A., & Bushman, B. J. (2002, June/July). Media violence and the American public revisited. *American Psychologist,* 448–450.

Anderson, C. A., & Bushman, B. J. (2003). Effects of violent video games on aggressive behavior. *Psychological Science, 12,* 19–41.

Anderson, M. (1991). *Thinking about women: Sociological perspectives on sex and gender* (3rd ed.). New York: Macmillan.

Anderson, M. C., Ochsner, K., Kuhl, B., Cooper, J., Robertson, E., Gabrieli, S. W., et al. (2004). Neural systems underlying the suppression of unwanted memories. *Science, 303,* 232–235.

Anderson, R., & Kirkland, J. (1990). Constructs in context. *International Journal of Personal Construct Psychology, 3*(1), 21–29.

Ang, R. & Goh, D. (2006). Authoritarian parenting style in Asian societies. *Contemporary Family Therapy, 28*(1), 131–151.

Ansbacher, H. L. (1990). Alfred Adler's influence on the three leading co-founders of humanistic psychology. *Journal of Humanistic Psychology, 30*(4), 45–53.

Archer, S. L. (1989). Gender differences in identity development: Issues of process, domain, and timing. *Journal of Adolescence, 12,* 117–138.

Aries, E., & Moorehead, K. (1989). The importance of ethnicity in the development of identity of Black adolescents. *Psychological Reports, 65*(1), 75–82.

Arnett, J. J. (2000). Emerging adulthood. *American Psychologist, 55,* 469–480.

Aron, L. (1996). From hypnotic suggestion to free association: Freud as a psychotherapist, circa 1892–1893. *Contemporary Psychoanalysis, 32,* 99–114.

Aspy, D. N. (2004). Beyond both traditional scientist/humanists and humanist/scientists. *Journal of Humanistic Counseling, Education and Development, 43*(1), 72–82.

Atkinson, R. (1990). Life stories and personal mythmaking. *Humanistic Psychologist, 18*(2), 199–207.

Austin, J. H. (1998). *Zen and the brain: Toward an understanding of meditation and consciousness.* Cambridge, MA: MIT Press.

Austin, J. H. (2006). *Zen-brain reflections.* Cambridge, MA: MIT Press.

Averett, S., Argys, L. M., & Rees, D. I. (2006). *Birth order and risky adolescent behavior.* Washington, DC: National Institute of Health.

Bacciagaluppi, M. (1996). Guilt according to Erich Fromm. *Contemporary Psychoanalysis, 32,* 455–462.

Badcock, C. (1992). *Essential Freud* (2nd ed.). Oxford, England: Blackwell.

Bagby, L. J. (1995). The question of Jung and racism reconsidered. *Psychohistory Review, 23,* 283–298.

Baird, C. V. (2004, May 2). If we're happy, we don't know it. Newark (NJ) *Star-Ledger,* sec. 2, p. 8.

Bakan, D. (1966). *The duality of human existence: Isolation and communion in Western man.* Boston: Beacon Press.

Bakan, D. (1969). *On method: Toward a reconstruction of psychological investigation.* San Francisco: Jossey-Bass.

Baker, L. A., Bezdjian, S., & Raine, A. (2006). Behavioral genetics: The science of antisocial behavior. *Law and Contemporary Problems, 69*(1/2) 7–47.

Balbus, I. D. (2004). The psychodynamics of racial reparations. *Psychoanalysis, Culture, and Society, 9,* 159–185.

Baldwin, J. A. (1985). *African (Black) personality: From an Africentric framework.* Chicago: Third World Press.

Balter, L., & Spencer, J. H. (1991). Observation and theory in psychoanalysis: The self psychology of Heinz Kohut. *Psychoanalytic Quarterly, 60*(3), 361–395.

Bandler, R., & Grinder, J. (1976). *The structure of magic: A book about communication and change* (Vol. 2). Palo Alto, CA: Science and Behavior Books.

Bandura, A. (1969). *Principles of behavior modification.* New York: Holt, Rinehart and Winston.

Bandura, A. (1973). *Aggression: A social learning analysis.* Englewood Cliffs, NJ: Prentice-Hall.

Bandura, A. (1974). A behavior theory and the models of man. *American Psychologist, 29,* 859–869.

Bandura, A. (1977). *Social learning theory.* Englewood Cliffs, NJ: Prentice-Hall.

Bandura, A. (1978). The self system in reciprocal determinism. *American Psychologist, 33,* 344–358.

Bandura, A. (1986a). *Social foundations of thought and action: A social cognitive theory.* Englewood Cliffs, NJ: Prentice-Hall.

Bandura, A. (1986b). The explanatory and predictive scope of self-efficacy theory. *Journal of Social and Clinical Psychology, 4*(3), 359–373.

Bandura, A. (1989). Human agency in social cognitive theory. *American Psychologist, 44*(9), 1175–1184.

Bandura, A. (1990). Some reflections on reflections. *Psychological Inquiry, 1,* 101–105.

Bandura, A. (1991a). The changing icons in personality psychology. In J. Cantor (Ed.), *Psychology at Iowa: Centennial Essays.* Hillsdale, NJ: Erlbaum.

Bandura, A. (1991b). Self-efficacy. In R. Schwarzer & R. Wicklund (Eds.), *Anxiety and self-focused attention.* New York: Harwood Academic.

Bandura, A. (1991c). Social cognitive theory of moral thought and action. In W. Kurtines & J. Gewirtz (Eds.), *Handbook of moral behavior and development* (pp. 45–103). Hillsdale, NJ: Erlbaum.

Bandura, A. (1991d). Social cognitive theory of self-regulation. *Organizational Behavior and Human Decision Processes, 50*(2), 248–287.

Bandura, A. (1992). Social cognitive theory. In R. Vasta (Ed.), *Six theories of child development: Revised formulations and current issues* (pp. 1–60). London: Jessica Kingsley.

Bandura, A. (Ed.). (1995). *Self-efficacy in changing societies.* New York: Cambridge University Press.

Bandura, A. (1996). Ontological and epistemological terrains revisited. *Journal of Behavior Therapy and Experimental Psychiatry, 27,* 323–345.

Bandura, A. (1997a). Health promotion from the perspective of social cognitive theory. *Psychology and Health,* 1–27.

Bandura, A. (1997b). *Self-efficacy: The exercise of control.* New York: Freeman.

Bandura, A. (1999a). Social cognitive theory of personality. In L. Pervin & O. P. John (Eds.), *Handbook of personality* (2nd ed.). New York: Guilford Press.

Bandura, A. (1999b). Moral disengagement in the perpetration of inhumanities. *Personality and Social Psychology Review, 3*(3), 193–209.

Bandura, A. (2000). The changing face of psychology at the dawning of a globalization era. *Canadian Psychology, 42*(1), 14–24.

Bandura, A. (2001). Social cognitive theory: An agentic perspective. *Annual Review of Psychology, 52,* 1–26.

Bandura, A. (2002). Growing primacy of human agency in adaption and change in the electronic era. *European Psychologist, 7*(1), 2–16.

Bandura, A. (2004a). Swimming against the mainstream. *Behavior Research and Therapy, 42,* 613–630.

Bandura, A. (2004b). Health promotion by social cognitive means. *Health Education and Behavior, 31*(2), 143–164.

Bandura, A. (2004c). Selective exercise of moral agency. In T. A. Thorkildsen, & H. J. Walberg (Eds.), *Nurturing morality* (pp. 37–51). Boston: Kluwer Academic.

Bandura, A. (2006a). Toward a psychology of human agency. *Perspective on Psychological Science, 1*(2), 164–180.

Bandura, A. (2006b). Going global with social cognitive theory. In S. I. Donaldson, D. E. Berger, & K. Pezdek (Eds.), *Applied psychology* (pp. 53–79) Mahwah, NJ: Erlbaum.

Bandura, A., Adams, N. E., Hardy, A. B., & Howells, G. N. (1980). Tests of the generality of self-efficacy theory. *Cognitive Therapy and Research, 4,* 39–66.

Bandura, A., Barbaranelli, C., Caprara, G. V., & Pastorelli, C. (1996). Mechanisms of moral disengagement in the exercise of moral agency. *Journal of Personality and Social Psychology, 71,* 364–374.

Bandura, A., Ross, D., & Ross, S. A. (1961). Transmission of aggression through imitation of aggressive models. *Journal of Abnormal and Social Psychology, 63,* 575–582.

Bandura, A., & Walters, R. (1963). *Social learning and personality development.* New York: Holt, Rinehart and Winston.

Bankart, C. (1997). *Talking cures: A history of Western and Eastern psychotherapies.* Pacific Grove, CA: Brooks/Cole.

Banks, A. (2001). *Post-traumatic stress disorder: Relationships and brain chemistry.* Wellesley, MA: Stone Center Publications.

Banks, A. (2004, June 12). *More than words can say.* Lecture presentation for the Jean Baker Miller Summer Training Institute, Wellesley, MA.

Banks, W., Ward, W., McQuater, G., & DeBritto, A. (1991). Are blacks external: On the status of locus of control in black populations. In J. Reginald (Ed.), *Black psychology* (pp. 181–192). Berkeley, CA: Cobb & Henry.

Bannister, D., & Fransella, F. (1966). A grid test of schizophrenic thought disorder. *British Journal of Social and Clinical Psychology, 5,* 95–102.

Bannister, D., & Mair, J. M. M. (1968). *The evaluation of personal constructs.* New York: Academic Press.

Bannister, D., & Salmon, P. (1966). Schizophrenic thought disorder: Specific or diffuse? *British Journal of Medical Psychology, 39,* 215–219.

Barash, D. P. (2005). B. F. Skinner, revisited. *Chronicle of Higher Education, 51*(30), B10–B11.

Barber, B. K. (1996). Parental psychological control. *Child Development, 67*(6), 3296–3319.

Baron-Cohen, S. (2003). *The essential difference: The truth about the male and female brain.* New York: Basic Books.

Barone, D. F., Herson, M., & Van Hasselt, V. B. (1998). *Advanced personality.* New York: Plenum Press.

Barrett, P., & Eysenck, S. (1994). The assessment of personality factors across 25 countries. *Personality and Individual Differences, 5,* 615–632.

Barrick, M. R., & Mount, M. K. (1991). The Big Five personality dimensions and job performance: A meta-analysis. *Personnel Psychology, 44,* 1–26.

Bartholomew, K., & Horowitz, L. M. (1991). Attachment styles among young adults. *Journal of Personality and Social Psychology, 61*(2), 226–244.

Bartholow, B., & Anderson, C. A. (2002). Effects of violent video games on aggressive behavior. *Journal of Experimental Social Psychology, 38,* 283–290.

Barton, S. (1994). Chaos, self-organization, and psychology. *American Psychologist, 49,* 5–14.

Basch, M. F. (1995). Kohut's contribution. *Psychoanalytic Dialogues, 5,* 367–373.

Baumrind, D. (1971). Current patterns of parental authority. *Developmental Psychology Monograph, 4*(1), part 2.

Baumrind, D. (1972). Socialization and instrumental competence in young children. In W. W. Hartup (Ed.), *The young child: Reviews of research* (Vol. 2, pp. 202–224). Washington, DC: National Association for the Education of Young Children.

Baumrind, D. (1991). The influence of parenting style on adolescent competence and substance use. *Journal of Early Adolescence, 11*(1), 56–95.

Beck, A. (1991). *Biographical sketch.* Unpublished manuscript.

Beck, A. (2005a). Cognitive therapy found to cut attempted suicide risk in half. *Mental Health Weekly, 15*(31), 5, 8–9.

Beck, A. (2005b). *Reflections on my public dialogue with the Dalai Lama, Goteburg, June 13, 2005.* Retrieved from www.beckinstitute.org

Beck, A., & Freeman, A. (1990). *Cognitive therapy of personality disorders.* New York: Guilford Press.

Beck, A. T. (1967). *Depression: Clinical, experimental, and theoretical aspects.* New York: Hoeber. (Republished as *Depression: Causes and treatment.* Philadelphia: University of Pennsylvania Press, 1972.)

Beck, A. T. (1972). *Depression: Causes and treatments.* Philadelphia: University of Pennsylvania Press.

Beck, A. T. (1999). *Prisoners of hate.* New York: Perennial.

Beck, A. T., & Clark, D. A. (1997). An information processing model of anxiety. *Behaviour Research and Therapy, 35*(1), 49–58.

Beck, A. T., & Emory, G. (1979). *Cognitive therapy of anxiety and phobic disorders.* Philadelphia: Center for Cognitive Therapy.

Beck, A. T., & Emory, G. (1985). *Anxiety disorders and phobias: A cognitive perspective.* New York: Basic Books.

Beck, A. T., Epstein, N., & Harrison, R. (1983). Cognitions, attitudes, and personality dimensions in depression. *British Journal of Cognitive Psychotherapy, 1*(1), 1–16.

Beck, A. T., & Hollon, S. (1993). Controversies in cognitive therapy: A dialogue with Aaron T. Beck and Steve Hollon. *Journal of Cognitive Psychotherapy, 7,* 79–93.

Beck, A. T., & Rector, N. A. (2000). Cognitive therapy of schizophrenia: A new therapy for the new millennium. *American Journal of Psychotherapy, 54*(3), 291–300.

Beck, A. T., Rush, A. J., Shaw, B. F., & Emory, G. (1979). *Cognitive therapy of depression.* New York: Guilford Press.

Becker, P. (1998). Beyond the big five. *Personality and Individual Differences, 52,* 511–530.

Beckwith, J., & Alper, J. S. (2002). Genetics of human personality: Social and ethical implications. In J. Benjamin, R. Ebstein, & R. H. Belmaker (Eds.), *Molecular genetics of human personality* (pp. 315–331). Washington, DC: American Psychiatric Publishing.

Beer, C. (2003). The cognitive neuroscience of consciousness. *Quarterly Review of Biology, 78,* 123–125.

Benjamen, L. S. (1996). *Interpersonal diagnosis and treatment of personality disorders* (2nd ed.). New York: Guilford Press.

Berg, M. B., Janoff-Bulman, R., & Cotter, J. (2001). Perceiving value in obligations and goals. *Personality and Social Psychology Bulletin, 27,* 982–995.

Bergman, S. J., & Surrey, J. L. (1997). The woman-man relationship: Impasses and possibilities. In J. V. Jordan (Ed.), *Women's growth in diversity* (pp. 260–287). New York: Guilford Press.

Berk, M. S., & Andersen, S. M. (2000). The impact of past relationships on interpersonal behavior: Behavioral confirmation in the socio-cognitive process of transference. *Journal of Personality and Social Pyschology, 79,* 546–562.

Berkowitz, L. (1962). *Aggression: A social psychological analysis.* New York: McGraw-Hill.

Berkowitz, L., & Powers, P. (1979). Effects of timing and justification of witnessed aggression on observers' punitiveness. *Journal of Research in Personality, 13,* 71–80.

Bernadez, T. (1988). *Women and anger—Cultural prohibitions and the feminist ideal.* Work in Progress Series. Stone Center for Developmental Studies, Wellesley College, Wellesley, MA.

Bernal, M. E., Knight, G. P., Garza, C. A., Ocampo, K. A., et al. (1990). The development of ethnic identity in Mexican-American children. *Hispanic Journal of Behavioral Sciences, 12*(1), 3–24.

Bernard, M. E. (1986). *Staying alive in an irrational world: The psychology of Albert Ellis.* Melbourne, Australia: Carlton & Macmillan.

Bernstein, A. (2001). Beyond countertransference: The love that cures. *Modern Psychoanalysis, 26*(2), 249–256.

Bernstein, D. (1991). The female oedipal complex. In P. Hartocollis & I. D. Graham (Eds.), *The personal myth in psychoanalytic theory.* Madison, CT: International Universities Press.

Bertalanffy, L. von. (1974). General systems theory and psychiatry. In S. Arieti (Ed.), *American handbook of psychiatry* (Vol. 1, pp. 1095–1117). New York: Basic Books.

Bertenthal, B. I. (2002). Challenges and opportunities in the psychological sciences. *American Psychologist, 57*(3), 215–218.

Berzonsky, M. D., & Adams, G. R. (1999). Reevaluating the identity status paradigm. *Developmental Review, 19*, 557–590.

Bettelheim, B. (1977). *The uses of enchantment.* New York: Knopf.

Bettelheim, B. (1982). *Freud and man's soul.* New York: Knopf.

Bezjak, J., & Lee, W. (1990). Relationship of self-efficacy and locus of control constructs in predicting college students' physical fitness behaviors. *Perceptual and Motor Skills, 71*(2), 499–508.

Bishop, F. M. (2000). Helping clients manage addictions with REBT. *Journal of Rational-Emotive and Cognitive-Behavior Therapy, 18*(3), 127–151.

Bitter, J. R. (1991). Conscious motivations: An enhancement to Dreikurs' goals of children's misbehavior. *Individual Psychology: Journal of Adlerian Theory, Research and Practice, 47*(2), 210–221.

Blackman, D. (1991). B. F. Skinner and G. H. Mead: On biological science and social science. *Journal of the Experimental Analysis of Behavior, 55*(2), 251–265.

Bloch, S. (2004). A pioneer in psychotherapy research: Aaron Beck. *Australian and New Zealand Journal of Psychiatry, 38*(11/12), 885–867.

Block, J. (1995). A contrarian view of the five-factor approach to personality description. *Psychological Bulletin, 117*, 187–215.

Bobrow, J. (2000). Reverie in Zen and psychoanalysis: Harvesting the ordinary. *Journal of Transpersonal Psychology, 32*(2), 165–175.

Bohart, A. C., & Byock, G. (2005). Experiencing Carl Rogers from the client's point of view. *Humanistic Psychologist, 33*(3), 187–211.

Bohman, M., Cloninger, C., Sigardson, S., & van Korring, A. (1982). Predisposition to petty criminalities in Swedish adoptees: Genetics of environmental heterogeneity. *Archives of General Psychiatry, 39*, 1233–1241.

Boneau, C. A. (1992). Observations on psychology's past and future. *American Psychologist, 47*(12), 1586–1596.

Boone, C., DeBrabander, B., Carree, M., de Jong, G., van Olffen, W., & van Witteloostuijn, A. (2002). Locus of control and learning to cooperate in a prisoner's dilemma game. *Personality and Individual Differences, 32*, 929–946.

Bornstein, R. F. (2005). Reconnecting psychoanalysis to mainstream psychology. *Psychoanalytic Psychology, 22*(3), 323–340.

Bouchard, T. J., Jr. (1994). Genes, environment, and personality. *Science, 264*, 1700–1701.

Bouchard, T. J., Lykken, D. T., McGue, M., Segal, N., & Tellegen, A. (1990). Sources of human psychological differences: The Minnesota study of twins reared apart. *Science, 250*, 223–228.

Bouchard, T. J., Jr., & Propping, P. (Eds.). (1993). *Twins as a tool of behavioral genetics.* New York: Wiley.

Bowlby, J. (1969). *Attachment and loss.* Vol. 1: *Attachment* (2nd ed.). New York: Basic Books.

Bowlby, J. (1977). The making and breaking of affectional bonds. *British Journal of Psychiatry, 130*, 201–210.

Bowlby, J. (1988). *A secure base: Parent-child attachment and healthy human development.* New York: Basic Books.

Bozarth, J. D. (1990). The evolution of Carl Rogers as a therapist. Special Issue: Fiftieth anniversary of the person-centered approach. *Person-Centered Review, 5*(4), 387–393.

Brazier, D. (1995). *Zen therapy: Transcending the sorrows of the human mind.* New York: Wiley.

Breger, L. (2000). *Freud: Darkness in the midst of vision.* New York: Wiley.

Breger, L., Hunter, I., & Lane, R. W. (1971). The effect of stress on dreams. *Psychological Issues, 7* (3, Monograph 27), 1–213).

Bringmann, M. W. (1992). Computer-based methods for the analysis and interpretation of personal construct systems. In R. A. Neimeyer & G. J. Neimeyer (Eds.), *Advances in personal construct psychology* (Vol. 2, pp. 57–90). Greenwich, CT: JAI Press.

Brooke, R. W. (1991). Psychic complexity and human existence: A phenomenological approach. *Journal of Analytical Psychology, 36*, 505–518.

Brown, J. S. (1948). Gradients of approach and avoidance responses and their relation to motivation. *Journal of Comparative and Physiological Psychology, 41*, 450–465.

Brumann, H. (1996). Metapsychology and professional politics. The Freud-Klein controversy. *Luzifer-Amor: Zeitschrift zur Geschichte der Psychoanalyse, 9*, 49–112.

Brunell, L. J., & Young, W. T. (Eds.). (1982). *Multimodal handbook for a mental hospital.* New York: Springer.

Bruner, J. S. (1965). A cognitive theory of personality. *Contemporary Psychology, 1*, 355–358.

Brunner, J. (2002). Freud's (de)construction of the conflictual mind. *Thesis Eleven, 71*, 24–40.

Brunner, J. (1994). Looking into the hearts of the workers: Or how Erich Fromm turned critical theory into empirical research. *Political Psychology, 15*, 631–654.

Bryant, B. L. (1987, March). Birth order as a factor in the development of vocational preferences. *Individual Psychology: Journal of Adlerian Theory, Research and Practice, 43*(1), 36–41.

Bubenzer, D., Zimpfer, D., & Mahrle, C. (1990). Standardized individual appraisal in agency and private practice: A survey. *Journal of Mental Health Counseling, 12*, 51–66.

Buchanan, R. D. (2002). On not "giving psychology away": The Minnesota Multiphasic Personality Inventory and public controversy over testing in the 1960s. *History of Psychology, 5*, 284–309.

Bucher, M. (2004, October 10). C. G. Jung—prophet of the self. *Swiss News*, pp. 39–42.

Buckley, W. (1967). *Modern systems research for the behavioral scientist.* Chicago: Aldine.

Bugental, J. F. T. (1996a). Rollo May (1909–1994): Obituary. *American Psychologist, 51*, 418–419.

Bugental, J. F. T. (1996b). Aristophanes, William James, Rollo May, and our dog Dickens. *Humanistic Psychologist, 24*, 221–230.

Bugental, J. F. T. (2000). Outcomes of an existential-humanistic psychotherapy: A tribute to Rollo May. *Humanistic Psychologist, 28*(1–3), 251–259.

Bullock, W. A., & Gilliland, K. (1993). Eysenck's arousal theory of introversion-extraversion: A converging measures investigation. *Journal of Personality and Social Psychology, 64*, 113–123.

Burger, J. M., & Cosby, M. (1999). Do women prefer dominant men? The case of the missing control condition. *Journal of Research in Personality, 33*, 358–368.

Burkitt, I. (1991). *Social selves: Theories of the social formation of personality.* Newbury Park, CA: Sage.

Burlingham, M. J. (1990). The relationship of Anna Freud and Dorothy Burlingham. *Journal of the American Academy of Psychoanalysis, 19*(4), 612–619.

Burns, C. P. E. (2006, Spring). A Jungian perspective on religious violence and personal responsibility. *Cross Currents, 56*(1), 16–29.

Buss, A. (1991). The EAS theory of temperament. In J. Stelau & A. Angleitner (Eds.), *Exploration in temperament: International perspectives on theory and measurement* (p. 43). New York: Plenum Press.

Buss, A. H., & Plomin, R. A. (1984). *Temperament: Early developing personality traits.* Hillsdale, NJ: Erlbaum.

Buss, D. (1990). Biological foundations of personality. *Journal of Personality, 58,* 1–345.

Buss, D. (1991). Evolutionary personality psychology. *Annual Review of Psychology, 42.*

Buss, D. M. (1984). Evolutionary biology and personality psychology: Toward a conception of human nature and individual differences. *American Psychologist, 39,* 1135–1147.

Buss, D. M. (1995). Evolutionary psychology: A new paradigm for psychological science. *Psychological Inquiry, 6,* 1–30.

Buss, D. M. (2004). *Evolutionary psychology: The new science of the mind* (2nd ed.). Boston: Allyn & Bacon.

Buss, D. M. (2005). *The murderer next door: Why the mind is designed to kill.* New York: Penguin.

Buswell, R. (2007). *Zen in practice.* Princton, NJ: Princeton University Press.

Butt, T. (1995). Ordinal relationships between constructs. *Journal of Constructivist Psychology, 8,* 227–236.

Cacioppo, J. T., & Bernston, G. G. (2005). *Social neuroscience.* New York: Psychology Press.

Cain, D. J. (1990). Celebration, reflection, and renewal: 50 years of client-centered therapy and beyond. Special Issue: Fiftieth anniversary of the person-centered approach. *Person-Centered Review, 5*(4), 357–363.

Cambray, J. (2006). Towards the feeling of emergence. *Journal of Analytical Psychology, 15*(1), 1–20.

Campbell, J. (1949). *The hero with a thousand faces.* New York: Pantheon.

Campbell, J. B., & Hawley, C. W. (1982). Study habits and Eysenck's theory of extraversion-introversion. *Journal of Research in Personality, 16,* 139–146.

Canli, T. (Ed.). (2006). *Biology of personality and individual differences.* New York: Guilford Press.

Caper, R. (2000). *Immaterial facts: Freud's discovery of psychic reality and Klein's development of his work.* London: Routledge.

Caporael, L. R. (2001). Evolutionary psychology: Toward a unifying theory and a hybrid science. *Annual Review of Psychology, 52,* 607–628.

Cappas, N. M., Andres-Hyman, R., & Davidson, L. (2005). What psychotherapists can begin to learn from neuroscience. *Psychotherapy: Theory, Research, Practice, Training, 42*(3), 374–383.

Capps, W. H. (1996). Erikson's contribution toward understanding religion. *Psychoanalysis and Contemporary Thought, 19,* 225–236.

Carlson, J., & Sperry, L. (Eds.). (2000). *Brief therapy with individuals and couples.* Phoenix, AZ: Zeig Tucker.

Carlson, J. G. (1985). Recent assessments of the Myers-Briggs Type Indicator. *Journal of Personality Assessment, 49,* 356–365.

Carlyn, M. (1977). An assessment of the Myers-Briggs Type Indicator. *Journal of Personality Assessment, 41,* 461–473.

Carskadon, T. G. (1979). Clinical and counseling aspects of the Myers-Briggs Type Indicator: A research review. *Research on Psychological Types, 1,* 2–31.

Cartwright, D. S. (1979). *Theories and models of personality.* Dubuque, IA: W. C. Brown Co.

Carver, C. S. (1996). Emergent integration in contemporary personality psychology. *Journal of Research in Personality, 30,* 319–334.

Caspi, A. (2000). The child is father of the man: Personality continuities from childhood to adulthood. *Journal of Personality and Social Psychology, 78,* 158–172.

Cassidy, J., & Shaver, P. R. (Eds.). (1999). *Handbook of attachment: Theory, research and clinical application.* New York: Guilford Press.

Cattell, R. B. (1943). The description of personality: Basic traits resolved into clusters. *Journal of Abnormal and Social Psychology, 38,* 476–506.

Cattell, R. B. (1948). Concepts and methods in the measurement of group syntality. *Psychological Review, 55,* 48–63.

Cattell, R. B. (1950). *Personality: A systematic, theoretical and factual study.* New York: McGraw-Hill.

Cattell, R. B. (1960). The multiple abstract variance analysis equations and solutions for nature-nurture research on continuous variables. *Psychological Review, 67,* 353–372.

Cattell, R. B. (1965). *The scientific analysis of personality.* Chicago: Aldine.

Cattell, R. B. (Ed.). (1966). *Handbook of multivariate experimental psychology.* Chicago: Rand McNally.

Cattell, R. B. (1972). *A new morality from science: Beyondism.* New York: Pergamon.

Cattell, R. B. (1990). Advances in Cattellian personality theory. In L. A. Pervin (Ed.), *Handbook of personality: Theory and research* (pp. 101–110). New York: Guilford Press.

Cavell, M. (1991). The subject of mind. *International Journal of Psycho-Analysis, 72*(1), 141–154.

Cervone, D. C., Shadel, W. G., & Jencius, S. (2001). Social-cognitive theory of personality assessment. *Personality and Social Psychology Review, 5*(1), 33–51.

Chadwick, D. (1999). *Crooked cucumber: The life and Zen teachings of Shunryu Suzuki.* New York: Broadway Books.

Chadwick, D. (Ed.). (2001). *To shine one corner of the world: Moments with Shunryu Suzuki: Stories of a Zen master told by his students.* New York: Broadway Books.

Chambers, W. V., & Epting, F. R. (1985, December). Personality and personal construct: Logical consistency. *Psychological Reports, 57*(3), 1120.

Chambers, W. V., & Graves, P. (1985, December). A technique for eliciting personal construct change. *Psychological Reports, 57*(3), 1041–1042.

Chambers, W. V., & Stonerock, B. (1985, December). Truth and logical consistency of personal constructs. *Psychological Reports, 57*(3), 1178.

Chandler, C. K. (1995). Guest editorial: Contemporary Adlerian reflections on homosexuality and bisexuality. *Individual Psychology: Journal of Adlerian Theory, Research and Practice, 51,* 82–89.

Chang, R., & Page, R. C. (1991). Characteristics of the self-actualized person: Visions from the East and West. *Counseling and Values, 36*(1), 2–10.

Chernin, J., & Holdren, J. M. (1995). Toward an understanding of homosexuality: Origins, status, and relationship to individual psychology. *Individual Psychology: Journal of Adlerian Theory, Research and Practice, 51,* 90–101.

Cheshire, N., & Thoma, H. (1991). Metaphor, neologism, and "open texture": Implications for translating Freud's scientific thought. *International Review of Psycho-Analysis, 18*(3), 429–455.

Chessick, R. (2000). Psychoanalysis at the millennium. *American Journal of Psychotherapy, 54*(3), 277–290.

Chodorow, N. (1985). Gender, relation, and difference in psychoanalytic perspective. In H. Eisenstein & A. Jardine (Eds.), *The future of difference.* New Brunswick, NJ: Rutgers University Press.

Chodorow, N. J. (1978). *The reproduction of mothering.* Berkeley: University of California Press.

Chodorow, N. J. (1989). *Feminism and psychoanalytic theory.* New Haven, CT: Yale University Press.

Chodorow, N. J. (1991). Freud on women. In J. Neu (Ed.), *The Cambridge companion to Freud.* New York: Cambridge University Press.

Chodorow, N. J. (1994). *Femininities, masculinities, sexualities: Freud and beyond.* Lexington: University of Kentucky Press.

Chodorow, N. J. (1995). Gender as a personal and cultural construction. *Signs: Journal of Women in Culture and Society, 20,* 516–544.

Chodorow, N. J. (1996a). Nancy J. Chodorow talks to Anthony Elliot. *Free Associations, 6,* 161–173.

Chodorow, N. J. (1996b). Reflections on the authority of the past in psychoanalytic thinking. *Psychoanalytic Quarterly, 65,* 32–51.

Chodorow, N. J. (1999a). Preface to the second edition. In N. J. Chodorow, *The Reproduction of Mothering* (2nd ed.). Berkeley: University of California Press.

Chodorow, N. J. (1999b). *The power of feeling: Personal meaning in psychoanalysis, gender, and culture.* New Haven, CT: Yale University Press.

Chodorow, N. J. (2000a). The sexual sociology of adult life. In R. Satow (Ed.), *Gender and social life* (pp. 9–25). Boston: Allyn & Bacon.

Chodorow, N. J. (2000b, Winter). The future of mothering. *Radcliffe Quarterly,* 3–6.

Chodorow, N. J. (2002). Gender as a personal and cultural construction. In M. Dimen & V. Goldner (Eds.), *Gender in psychoanalytic space* (pp. 237–261). New York: Other Press.

Chodorow, N. J. (2004). Gender on the modern-postmodern and classical-relational divide. *Journal of the American Psychoanalytic Association, 53*(4), 1097–1118.

Chomsky, N. (1959). Review of Skinner's *Verbal behavior. Language, 35,* 26–58, 234, 246–249.

Christopher, M. S. (2003). Albert Ellis and the Buddha: Rational soul mates? *Mental Health, Religion and Culture, 6*(3), 283–293.

Clark, D. A., & Beck, A. T. (1999). *Scientific foundations of cognitive theory and therapy of depression.* New York: Wiley.

Clark, L. A., Vorhies, L., & McEwen, J. (2002). Personality disorder symptomatology from the Five-Factor Model perspective. In P. T. Costa, Jr. & T. A. Widiger (Eds.), *Personality disorders and the Five-Factor Model of personality* (pp. 125–148). Washington, DC: American Psychological Association.

Clark, N. (2005). Have we forgot the art of loving? *New Statesman, 134*(4727), 34–36.

Clarke, J. J. (1992). *In search of Jung: Historical and philosophical enquiries.* London: Routledge.

Clarkin, J. F., Levy, K. N., & Schiavi, J. M. (2005). Transference focused psychotherapy. *Clinical Neuroscience Research, 4*(5/6), 379–386.

Cleary, T. (1998). *Teachings of Zen.* Boston: Shambhala.

Clements, J., Ettling, D., Jenett, D., & Shields, L. (1998). *Organic inquiry: If research were sacred* (Institute of Transpersonal Psychology, Palo Alto, CA). Retrieved January 31, 2004, from http://www.Serpintina.com

Cloninger, S. (2008). *Theories of personality.* Upper Saddle River, NJ: Prentice Hall.

Coan, R. W. (1991). Self-actualization and the quest for the ideal human. Special Issue: Handbook of self-actualization. *Journal of Social Behavior and Personality, 6*(5), 127–136.

Coelho, M. C. (1993). *The universe story.* Unpublished manuscript.

Coelho, M. C. (2002). *Awakening universe, emerging personhood.* Lima, OH: Wyndham Hall Press.

Coles, R. (1970). *Erik H. Erikson: The growth of his work.* Boston: Little, Brown.

Coles, R. (1974). Karen Horney's flight from orthodoxy. In J. Strouse (Ed.), *Women and analysis.* New York: Grossman.

Comstock, G., & Strasburger, V. (1990). Deceptive appearances: Television violence and aggressive behavior. *Journal of Adolescent Health Care, 11*(1), 31–44.

Connolly, A. (2003). Psychoanalytic theory in times of terror. *Journal of Analytical Psychology, 48*(4), 407–432.

Coolidge, F. L., Moor, C. J., Yamazaki, T. G., Stewart, S. E., & Segal, D. L. (2001). On the relationship between Karen Horney's tripartite neurotic type theory and personality disorder features. *Personality and Individual Differences, 30,* 1387–1400.

Coolidge, F. L., Seagl, D. L. Benight, C. C., & Danielian, J. (2004). The predictive power of Horney's psychoanalytic approach: An empirical study. *American Journal of Psychoanalysis, 64*(4), 363–374.

Coons, E. E. (2002). Neal Elgar Miller (1909–2002). *American Psychologist, 57,* 784–786.

Cooper, A. B., & Guynn, R. W. (2006). Transcriptions of fragments of lectures in 1948 by Harry Stack Sullivan. *Psychiatry, 69*(2), 101–106.

Cooper, J., & Mackie, D. (1986). Video games and aggression in children. *Journal of Applied Social Psychology, 16*(8), 726–744.

Cooper, S. H. (1989). Recent contributions to the theory of defense mechanisms: A comparative view. *Journal of the American Psychoanalytic Association, 37,* 865–891.

Corcoran, D. W. J. (1964). The relation between introversion and salivation. *American Journal of Psychology, 77,* 298–300.

Corcoran, K. (1991). Efficacy, "skills," reinforcement, and choice behavior. *American Psychologist, 46*(2), 155–157.

Cormack, E. (2005). Meaning making: The future of integrative therapy. *Counselling and Psychotherapy Journal, 16*(5), 19–22.

Corsini, R. J., & Wedding, D. (Eds.). (2005). *Current psychotherapies* (7th ed.). Belmont, CA: Brooks/Cole.

Cosimides, L., & Tooby, J. (1997). *Evolutionary psychology: A primer.* Santa Barbara, CA: Online Center for Evolutionary Psychology, University of California.

Costa, P. T., Jr., & McCrae, R. R. (1985). *The NEO Personality Inventory manual.* Odessa, FL: Psychological Assessment Resources.

Costa, P. T., Jr., & McCrae, R. R. (1992a). *Revised NEO Personality Inventory: NEO PI and NEO Five-Factor Inventory*

(NEO FFI) professional manual. Odessa, FL: Psychological Assessment Resources.

Costa, P. T., Jr., & McCrae, R. R. (1992b). Trait psychology comes of age. In T. B. Sonderegger (Ed.), *Nebraska Symposium on Motivation: Psychological and aging* (pp. 169–204). Lincoln: University of Nebraska Press.

Costa, P. T., Jr., & McCrae, R. R. (1997). Stability and change in personality assessment: The revised NEO Personality Inventory in the year 2000. *Journal of Personality Assessment, 68,* 86–94.

Costa, P. T., Jr., & McCrae, R. R. (1998). Six approaches to the explication of facet-level traits: Examples from conscientiousness. *European Journal of Personality, 12,* 117–134.

Costa, P. T., Jr., & Widiger, T. A. (2002). *Personality disorders and the Five-Factor Model of personality.* Washington, DC: American Psychological Association.

Coupey, R. P. (2006). *Zen: Simply sitting—a Zen monk's commentary on the Fukanzazengi (Universal guide on the correct practice of zazen) by Master Dogen (1200–1253).* Prescott, AZ: Hohm Press.

Coy, D. R., & Kovacs-Long, J. (2005). Maslow and Miller: An exploration of gender and affiliation in the journey to competence. *Journal of Counseling and Development, 83*(2), 138–146.

Cozzarelli, C., Karafa, J. A., Collins, N. L., & Tagler, M. J. (2003). Stability and change in adult attachment styles. *Journal of Social and Clinical Psychology, 21*(2), 315–346.

Crabbe, J. C. (2002). Genetic contributions to addiction. *Annual Review of Psychology, 53,* 435–462.

Cramer, P. (2000). Defense mechanisms in psychology today: Further processes for adaption. *American Psychologist, 55,* 158–172.

Crews, F. (1996). The verdict on Freud. *Psychological Science, 7,* 63–68.

Crews, F. C. (Ed.). (1998). *Unauthorized Freud: Doubters confront a legend.* New York: Viking.

Crockett, W. H. (1982). The organization of construct systems: The organization corollary. In J. C. Mancuso & R. Adams-Webber (Eds.), *The construing person.* New York: Praeger.

Cross, W. (1971). The Negro-to-Black conversion experience. *Black World, 20*(9), 13–27.

Cross, W. E., Jr. (1991). *Shades of black: Diversity in African-American identity.* Philadelphia: Temple University Press.

Crowson, H. M., Debacker, T. K., & Thoma, S. J. (2005). Does authoritarianism predict post-9/11 attitudes? *Personality and Individual Differences, 39*(7), 1273–1283.

Csikszentmihalyi, M. (1985). *Beyond boredom and anxiety: The experience of play in work and games.* San Francisco: Jossey-Bass.

Csikszentmihalyi, M. (1990). *Flow: The psychology of optimal experience.* New York: HarperCollins.

Csikszentmihalyi, M. (1993). *The evolving self: A psychology for the third millennium.* New York: HarperCollins.

Csikszentmihalyi, M. (2003). *Good business: Flow, leadership and the making of meaning.* New York: Viking.

Cyranowski, J. M., & Anderson, B. L. (2000). Evidence of self-schematic cognitive processing of women with different sexual self-views. *Journal of Social and Clinical Psychology, 19,* 519–543.

Cyranowski, J. M., & Bookwala, J. (2003). Adult attachment profiles. *Journal of Social and Clinical Psychology, 21*(2), 191–217.

Damasio, A. R. (2001). Fundametnal feelings. *Nature, 413,* 781.

D'Amico, A., & Cardaci, M. (2003). Relations among perceived self-efficacy, self-esteem, and school achievement. *Psychological Reports, 92*(3), 745–755.

Darling, D. (1996). *Zen physics.* New York: HarperCollins.

Darwin, C. (1859). *On the origin of species by natural selection.* London: Murray.

Das, A. K. (1989). Beyond self-actualization. *International Journal for the Advancement of Counseling, 12,* 13–27.

Davidson, L. (1987, Fall). What is the appropriate source for psychological explanation? *Humanistic Psychologist, 15*(3), 150–166.

Davidson, L., Shahar, G., Lawless, M. S., Sells, D., & Tondora, J. (2006). Play, pleasure, and other positive life events. *Psychiatry, 69*(2), 151–163.

Davidson, R. J. (1992). Emotion and affective style: Hemispheric substrates. *Psychological Science, 3,* 39–43.

Davidson, R. J., Jackson, D. C., & Kalin, N. H. (2000). Emotion, plasticity, content, and regulation. *Psychological Bulletin, 126,* 890–909.

Davis, N. H. (1991). Dispensing and prescribing cautions for medical care during recovery from alcohol and drug addictions. *Journal of Pharmacy Practice, 4*(6), 362–368.

Davis, P. J. (1987, September). Repression and the inaccessibility of affective memories. *Journal of Personality and Social Psychology, 53*(3), 585–593.

Davison, G. C., & Lazarus, A. A. (1994). Clinical innovation and evaluation: Integrating practice with inquiry. *Clinical Psychology: Science and Practice, 1,* 157–168.

Dearborn, G. (2001). How to organize what needs to be done. *Constructive Living Quarterly, 8*(3), 1, 8–9, 14–15.

de Brabander, B., & Boone, C. (1990). Sex differences in perceived locus of control. *Journal of Social Psychology, 130*(2), 271–272.

de Courcy-Hinds, M. (1993, October 19). Not like the movie: A dare leads to death. *New York Times,* p. C1.

de La Valle Poussin, Louis. (1989–1990). *Abhidharmakosabasyam.* 4 vols. Berkeley, CA: Asian Humanities Press.

de Mann, A., Leduc, C., & Labreche-Gauthier, L. (1992). Parental control in child rearing and multidimensional locus of control. *Psychological Reports, 70*(1), 320–322.

DeCamp, M., & Sugarman, J. (2004). Ethics in behavioral genetic research. *Accountability in Research, 11,* 27–47.

DeCarvalho, R. J. (1989). Contributions to the history of psychology: LXII. Carl Rogers' naturalistic system of ethics. *Psychological Reports, 65*(3, Pt. 2), 1155–1162.

DeCarvalho, R. J. (1990). Contributions to the history of psychology: LXIX. Gordon Allport on the problem of method in psychology. *Psychological Reports, 67*(1), 267–275.

DeCarvalho, R. J. (1991). *The founders of humanistic psychology.* New York: Praeger.

DeCarvalho, R. J. (1992). The humanistic ethics of Rollo May. *Journal of Humanistic Psychology, 32,* 7–18.

DeCarvalho, R. J. (1996). Rollo R. May (1909–1994): A biographical sketch. *Journal of Humanistic Psychology, 36,* 8–16.

Deci, E. L., & Ryan, R. M. (1991). A motivational approach to self: Integration in personality. In R. Dienstbier (Ed.), *Nebraska Symposium on Motivation: Vol. 38. Perspectives on motivation* (pp. 237–288). Lincoln: University of Nebraska Press.

Deci, R. L., & Ryan, R. M. (2002). The "what" and "why" of goal pursuits: Human needs and the self-determination of behavior. *Psychological Inquiry, 11,* 227–268.

Deci, E. L., Ryan, R. M. (Eds.). (2004). *Handbook of self-determination research.* Rochester, NY: University of Rochester Press.

DeMartino, R. J. (1991). Karen Horney, Daisetz T. Suzuki, and Zen Buddhism. *American Journal of Psychoanalysis, 51*(3), 267–283.

Demont, W. C., & Wolper, E. A. (1958). The relationship of eye movements, body motility, and external stimuli to dream content. *Journal of Experimental Psychology, 55,* 543–553.

Depue, R. A., Luciana, M., Arbisi, P., Collins, P., & Leon, A. (1994). Dopamine and the structure of personality. *Journal of Personality and Social Psychology, 67,* 485–498.

DeRobertis, E. M. (2006). Deriving a humanistic theory of child development from the works of Carl R. Rogers and Karen Horney. *Humanistic Psychologist, 34*(2), 177–199.

Dershimaru, T. (1999, December). Dogen's seven principles. *Zen Bulletin de l'Association Zen Internationale,* no. 80, pp. 51–53.

di Pellegrino, G., Fadiga, L., Gallese, V., & Rizzolatti, G. (1992) Understanding motor events: A neurophysiological study. *Experimental Brain Research, 91,* 176–180.

Diamond, J. (2004, February–March). Epigenetics: Genetic studies gain a new level of complexity. *Who, What, Where: The Magazine,* pp. 37–40.

Diamond, L. M. (2001). Contributions of psychophysiology to research on adult attachment. *Personality and Social Psychology Review, 5*(4), 276–295.

Diener, E., Oishi, S., & Lucas, R. (2003). Personality, culture, and subjective well-being. *Annual Review of Psychology, 54,* 403–425.

DiGiuseppe, R. (1998). Rational emotive behavior therapy. In H. T. Prout & D. T. Brown (Eds.), *Counseling and psychotherapy with children and adolescents* (pp. 270–301). New York: Wiley.

Digman, J. M. (1990). Personality structure: Emergence of the five-factor model. *Annual Review of Psychology, 41,* 417–440.

Digman, J. M., & Inouye, J. (1986). Further specification of the five robust factors of personality. *Journal of Personality and Social Psychology, 50,* 116–123.

Dinkmeyer, D. (1989). Adlerian psychology. *A Journal of Human Behavior, 26*(1).

Dinkmeyer, D., & McKay, G. (1976). *Systematic training for effective parenting.* Circle Pines, MN: American Guidance Service.

Dinsmoor, J. A. (2004). The etymology of basic concepts in the experimental analysis of behavior. *Journal of the Experimental Analysis of Behavior, 82*(3), 311–316.

DiTommaso, E., Brannen-McNulty, C., Ross, L., & Burgess, M. (2003). Attachment styles, social skills and loneliness in young adults. *Personality and Individual Differences, 35*(2), 303–313.

Dixon, P. N., & Strano, D. A. (1989). The measurement of inferiority: A review and directions for scale development. *Individual Psychology, 45.* Austin: University of Texas Press.

Doherty, W. J., & Baldwin, C. (1985, April). Shifts and stability in locus of control during the 1970s: Divergence of the sexes. *Journal of Personality and Social Psychology, 48*(4), 1048–1053.

Dollard, J. (1937). *Caste and class in a southern town.* New Haven, CT: Yale University Press.

Dollard, J., Doob, L. W., Miller, N. E., Mowrer, O. H., & Sears, R. R. (1939). *Frustration and aggression.* New Haven, CT: Yale University Press.

Dollard, J., & Miller, N. (1941). *Social learning and imitation.* New Haven, CT: Yale University Press.

Dollard, J., & Miller, N. (1950). *Personality and psychotherapy: An analysis in terms of learning, thinking, and culture.* New York: McGraw-Hill.

Dolliver, R. H. (1995). Carl Rogers's personality theory and psychotherapy as a reflection of his life and personality. *Journal of Humanistic Psychology, 35,* 111–128.

Domhoff, G. W. (2001). A neurocognitive theory of dreams. *Dreaming, 11,* 13–33.

Donahue, E. M. (1994). Do children use the Big Five, too? Content and structural form in personality description. *Journal of Personality, 62,* 45–66.

Donaldson, G. (1996). Between practice and theory: Melanie Klein, Anna Freud and the development of child analysis. *Journal of the History of the Behavioral Sciences, 32,* 160–176.

Dooley, C., & Fedele, N. (1999). *Mothers and sons: Raising relational boys.* Work in Progress Series. Stone Center for Developmental Studies, Wellesley College, Wellesley, MA.

Dornbusch, S., Gross, R., Duncan, P., & Ritter, P. (1987). Stanford studies of adolescence using the national health examination survey. In R. Lerner & T. Fuch (Eds.), *Biological-psychosocial interactions in early adolescence* (pp. 189–206). Hillsdale, NJ: Erlbaum.

Douglas, C. (1993). *Translate this darkness: The life of Christiana Morgan.* New York: Simon & Schuster.

Douvan, E. (1997). Erik Erikson: Critical times, critical theory. *Child Psychiatry and Human Development, 28*(1), 15–21.

Dreikurs, R., & Soltz, V. (1964). *Children: The challenge.* New York: Hawthorne.

Drwal, R. L., & Wiechnik, R. (1984). The effect of locus of control and self-esteem on attributions and expectancies after success and failure. *Polish Psychological Bulletin, 15*(4), 257–266.

Dryden, W. (1991). *A dialogue with Arnold Lazarus: "It depends."* Philadelphia: Open University Press.

Dryden, W., & Golden, W. (Eds.). (1986). *Cognitive behavioral approaches to psychotherapy.* London: Harper & Row.

Ducat, S. (1985). Science and psychoanalysis: The implications of recent findings in psychopathology research and neurophysiology for the Freudian theory of the mind. *International Journal of Biosocial Research, 7*(2), 94–107.

Dudley, R. (2000). Evolutionary origins of human alcoholism in primate frugivory. *Quarterly Review of Biology, 75*(1), 3–15.

Dudley, R. (2002). Fermenting fruit and the historical ecology of ethanol ingestion: Is alcoholism in modern humans an evolutionary hangover? *Addiction, 97,* 381–388.

Duhs, L., & Gunton, R. (1988). TV violence and childhood aggression: A curmudgeon's guide. *Australian Psychologist, 23*(2), 183–195.

Durbin, P. G. (2005). Introduction to Alfred Adler. *Subconsciously Speaking, 19–20*(6), 16.

Durbin, P. G. (2006). Alfred Adler's four basic life styles. *Subconsciously Speaking, 21*(2), 12.

Durkheim, E. (1897). *Suicide.* London: Routledge.

Dyer, R. (1983). *Her father's daughter: The work of Anna Freud.* New York: Jason Aronson.

Eagle, M. N. (1984). *Recent developments in psychoanalysis: A critical evaluation.* New York: McGraw-Hill.

Eckhardt, M. H. (1991). Feminine psychology revisited: A historical perspective. *American Journal of Psychoanalysis, 51*(3), 235–243.

Eckhardt, M. H. (2005). Karen Horney: A portrait. *American Journal of Psychoanalysis, 65*(2), 95–101.

Edelson, M. (1986, October). The convergence of psychoanalysis and neuroscience: Illusion and reality. *Contemporary Psychoanalysis, 22*(4), 479–519.

Edmonson, B. (2006, October). Powers of concentration. *AARP Bulletin,* 22–23.

Edmundson, M. (2006, April 30). Freud and the fundamentalist urge. *New York Times Magazine,* p. 15.

Ehrenreich, J. H. (1997). Personality theory: A case of intellectual and social isolation. *Journal of Personality, 131,* 33–44.

Eisenberger, N., & Lieberman, M. (2005). Why it hurts to be left out: The neurocognitive overlap between physical and social pain. In K. D. Williams, J. P. Forgas, & W. von Hippel (Eds.), *The social outcast: Ostracism, social exclusion, rejection and bullying* (pp. 109–128). New York: Psychology Press.

Eisenman, R. (1992). Birth order, development, and personality. *Acta Paedopsychiatrica: International Journal of Child and Adolescent Psychiatry, 55,* 25–27.

Eisner, D. (2000). *The death of psychotherapy.* Westport, CT: Praeger.

Eissler, K. R. (2001). *Freud and the seduction theory: A brief love affair.* Madison, CT: International Universities Press.

Elkis-Abuhoff, D. L. (2003). The impact of coping strategies, negative life events and health locus of control for persons living with the pain of osteoarthritis. *Dissertation Abstracts, 63* (8-B), 3910.

Ellenberger, H. F. (1970). *The discovery of the unconscious.* New York: Basic Books.

Elliot, B. A. (1992). Birth order and health: Major issues. *Social Science and Medicine, 35*(4), 443–452.

Elliott, R. Greenberg, L., & Lietaer, G. (2003). Research on experiential and person-centered therapies. In M. Lambert, A. Bergin, & S. Garfield (Eds.), *Handbook of psychotherapy and behavior change* (5th ed., pp. 493–539). New York, Wiley.

Ellis, A. (1955). New approaches to psychotherapy techniques. *Journal of Clinical Psychology Monograph Supplement.* Brandon, VT.

Ellis, A. (1958). Rational psychotherapy. *Journal of General Psychology, 59,* 35–49.

Ellis, A. (1962). *Reason and emotion in psychotherapy.* New York: Lyle & Stuart.

Ellis, A. (1969). A weekend of rational encounter. *Rational Living, 4*(2), 1–8.

Ellis, A. (1973). *Humanistic psychotherapy.* New York: Julian Press.

Ellis, A. (1976). The biological basis of human irrationality. *Journal of Individual Psychology, 32,* 145–168.

Ellis, A. (1978). Toward a theory of personality. In R. J. Corsini (Ed.), *Readings in current personality theories.* Itasca, IL: Peacock.

Ellis, A. (1985a). *Overcoming resistance: Rational-emotive therapy with difficult clients.* New York: Springer.

Ellis, A. (1985b). Expanding the ABC's of rational emotive therapy. In M. Mahoney & A. Freemany (Eds.), *Cognition and psychotherapy* (pp. 313–323). New York: Plenum Press.

Ellis, A. (1985c). Two forms of humanistic psychology: Rational-emotive therapy vs. transpersonal psychology. *Free Inquiry, 15*(4), 14–21.

Ellis, A. (1987a). How rational-emotive therapy (RET) helps to actualize the human potential. *New Jersey Journal of Professional Counseling, 50,* 2.

Ellis, A. (1987b). A sadly neglected cognitive element in depression. *Cognitive Therapy and Research, 11,* 121–146.

Ellis, A. (1988). *How to stubbornly refuse to make yourself miserable about anything—yes anything.* Secaucus, NJ: Lyle & Stuart.

Ellis, A. (1991a). My life in clinical psychology. In C. E. Walker (Ed.), *The history of clinical psychology in autobiography* (Vol. 1, pp. 1–37). Pacific Grove, CA: Brooks/Cole.

Ellis, A. (1991b). Using RET effectively: Reflections and interview. In M. E. Bernard (Ed.), *Using rational-emotive therapy effectively* (pp. 1–33). New York: Plenum Press.

Ellis, A. (1994a). My response to "Don't throw the therapeutic baby out with the holy water": Helpful and hurtful elements of religion. *Journal of Psychology and Christianity, 13,* 323–326.

Ellis A. (1994b). Post-traumatic stress disorder (PTSD): A rational emotive behavior theory. *Journal of Rational-Emotive and Cognitive Behavior Therapy, 12,* 3–25.

Ellis, A. (1994c). *Reason and emotion in psychotherapy* (Revised and updated ed.). New York: Birch Lane Press.

Ellis, A. (1995). Psychotherapy is alarmingly encumbered with disposable myths. *Psychotherapy, 32,* 495–499.

Ellis, A. (1996). Responses to criticsms of rational emotive behavior therapy. *Journal of Rational-Emotive and Cognitive Behavior Therapy, 14,* 97–121.

Ellis, A. (1997). Using rational emotive behavior therapy techniques to cope with disability. *Professional Psychology: Research and Practice, 28,* 17–22.

Ellis, A. (1998a). How rational emotive behavior therapy belongs in the constructivist camp. In M. F. Hoyt (Ed.), *The handbook of constructive therapies.* (pp. 83–89). San Francisco: Jossey-Bass.

Ellis, A. (1998b). Optimal aging: Get over getting older. Chicago: Open Court.

Ellis, A. (2000). Spiritual goals and spirited values in psychotherapy. *Journal of Individual Psychology, 56*(3), 277–284.

Ellis, A. (2002). An interview with Albert Ellis about REBT (M. F. Shaughnessy & V. Mahan, Interviewers). *North American Journal of Psychology, 4*(3), 355–366.

Ellis, A. (2003). Similarities and differences between rational emotive behavior therapy and cognitive therapy. *Journal of Cognitive Psychotherapy, 17*(3), 225–240.

Ellis, A. (2004). Post-September 11th perspectives on religion, spirituality, and philosophy. *Journal of Counseling and Development, 82*(4), 439–443.

Ellis, A. (2006). Why I (really) became a therapist. *Journal of Clinical Psychology, 61*(8), 945–948.

Ellis, A., & Becker, I. (1982). *A guide to personal happiness.* North Hollywood, CA: Wilshire.

Ellis, A., & Bernard, M. E. (Eds.). (1983). *Rational-emotive approaches to the problems of childhood.* New York: Plenum Press.

Ellis, A., & Bernard, M. E. (Eds.). (1985). *Clinical applications of rational-emotive therapy.* New York: Plenum Press.

Ellis, A., & Dryden, W. (1997). *The practice of rational emotive therapy.* New York: Springer.

Ellis, A., & Harper, R. A. (1975). *A new guide to rational living.* North Hollywood, CA: Wilshire.

Emmons, R. A. (1999). Religion in the psychology of personality. *Journal of Personality, 67*(6), 873–888.

Epstein, M. (1995). *Thoughts without a thinker: Psychotherapy from a Buddhist perspective.* New York: Basic Books.

Epstein, M. (1999). *Going to pieces without falling apart: A Buddhist perspective on wholeness.* New York: Random House.

Epstein, R. (1985). The transformation of consciousness into wisdom: The path of the bodhisattva according to the Ch'eng Wei-shih Lun. *Vajra Bodhi Sea, 15*(176) 22–23; (177) 15–17; (178) 14–15.

Epstein, R. P. (2006). The molecular genetic architecture of human personality. *Molecular Psychiatry, 11*(5), 427–445.

Epstein, S. (1996). Recommendations for the future development of personality psychology. *Journal of Research in Personality, 30,* 435–446.

Epting, F. R., & Leitner, L. M. (1992). Humanistic psychology and personal construct theory. Special Issue: The humanistic movement in psychology: History, celebration, and prospectus. *Humanistic Psychologist, 20*(2–3), 243–259.

Epting, F. R., & Paris, M. E. (2006). A constructive understanding of the person: George Kelly and humanistic psychology. *Humanistic Psychologist, 34*(1), 21–37.

Erdelyi, M. H. (2001). Defense processes can be conscious or unconscious. *American Psychologist, 56*(9), 761–763.

Erikson, E. H. (1958). *Young man Luther.* New York: Norton.

Erikson, E. H. (1963). *Childhood and society* (2nd ed.). New York: Norton.

Erikson, E. H. (1964). *Insight and responsibility.* New York: Norton.

Erikson, E. H. (1968). *Identity, youth and crisis.* New York: Norton.

Erikson, E. H. (1969). *Gandhi's truth.* New York: Norton.

Erikson, E. H. (1974). *Dimensions of a new identity.* New York: Norton.

Erikson, E. H. (1975). *Life history and the historical moment.* New York: Norton.

Erikson, E. H. (1982, 1997). *The life cycle completed: A review.* New York: Norton.

Erikson, E. H. (1997). *The life cycle completed* (Extended version with new chapters on the ninth stage of development by Joan M. Erikson). New York: Norton.

Erikson, E. H., with Erikson, J., & Kivnick, H. (1986, 1994). *Vital involvement in old age.* New York: Norton.

Erlenmeyer-Kimling, L., & Jarvik, L. F. (1963). Genetics and intelligence: A review. *Science, 142,* 1477–1479.

Espin, O., & Gawelek, M. (1992). Women's diversity: Ethnicity, race, class, and gender in theories of feminist psychology. In L. Brown & M. Ballou (Eds.), *Personality and psychopathology: Feminist reappraisals.* New York: Guilford Press.

Esterson, A. (1998). Jeffrey Masson and Freud's seduction theory: A new fable based on old myths. *History of the Human Sciences, 11*(1), 1–21.

Etkin, A., Klemenhagen, K. C., Dudman J. T., Rogan, M. T., Hen, R., Kandel, E. R., & Hirsch, J. (2004). Individual differences in trait anxiety predict the response of the basolateral amygdale to unconsciously processed fearful faces. *Neuron, 44,* 1043–1055.

Evans, R. I. (1967). *Dialogue with Erik Erikson.* New York: Harper & Row.

Evans, R. J. (1976). *The making of psychology: Discussions with creative contributors.* New York: Knopf.

Evans, T. D., & Meredith, D. W. (1991). How far can you go and still be Adlerian? Special Issue: "On beyond Adler." *Individual Psychology: Journal of Adlerian Theory, Research and Practice, 47*(4), 541–547.

Eysenck, H. J. (1947). *Dimensions of personality.* London: Routledge & Kegan Paul.

Eysenck, H. J. (1952). The effects of psychotherapy: An evaluation. *Journal of Consulting Psychology, 16,* 319–324.

Eysenck, H. J. (1956). The inheritance of extraversion-introversion. *Acta Psychologica, 12,* 95–110.

Eysenck, H. J. (1957). *The dynamics of anxiety and hysteria.* London: Routledge & Kegan Paul.

Eysenck, H. J. (Ed.). (1961). *Handbook of abnormal psychology: An experimental approach.* New York: Basic Books.

Eysenck, H. J. (1964). Involuntary rest pauses in tapping as a function of drive and personality. *Perceptual and Motor Skills, 18,* 172–174.

Eysenck, H. J. (1965). *Fact and fiction in psychology.* Baltimore: Penguin.

Eysenck, H. J. (1967). *The biological basis of personality.* Springfield, IL: Charles C. Thomas.

Eysenck, H. J. (1970). *The structure of human personality* (3rd ed.). New York: Methuen.

Eysenck, H. J. (1970–1971). *Readings in extraversion-introversion.* London: Staples.

Eysenck, H. J. (1972). *Psychology is about people.* New York: Library Press.

Eysenck, H. J. (1975). *The inequality of man.* San Diego: EdITS.

Eysenck, H. J. (1976). The learning theory model of neurosis—a new approach. *Behavior Research and Therapy, 14,* 251–267.

Eysenck, H. J. (Ed.). (1981). *A model for personality.* New York: Springer-Verlag.

Eysenck, H. J. (1982). *Personality, genetics, and behavior: Selected papers.* New York: Praeger.

Eysenck, H. J. (1985). Revolution in the theory and measurement of intelligence. *Evaluación Psicológica 1*(1–2), 99–158.

Eysenck, H. J. (1989, December). Health's character. *Psychology Today,* pp. 28–32, 34–35.

Eysenck, H. J. (1990a). Biological dimensions of personality. In L. A. Pervin (Ed.), *Handbook of personality: Theory and research* (pp. 244–276). New York: Guilford Press.

Eysenck, H. J. (1990b). Genetic and environmental contributions to individual differences: The 3 major dimensions of personality. *Journal of Personality, 58,* 245–261.

Eysenck, H. J. (1991). Dimensions of personality: The biosocial approach to personality. In J. Strelau & A. Angleitner (Eds.), *Exploration in temperament: International perspectives on theory and measurement* (p. 365). New York: Plenum Press.

Eysenck, H. J. (1992). Four ways five factors are *not* basic. *Personality and Individual Differences, 13,* 667–673.

Eysenck, H. J. (1993). The relationship between IQ and personality. In G. L. Van Heck (Ed.), *Personality psychology in Europe* (Vol. 4, pp. 159–181). Tilbur, Netherlands: Tilbourg University Press.

Eysenck, H. J. (1994a). The outcome problem in psychotherapy: What have we learned? *Behavior Research and Therapy, 32,* 477–495.

Eysenck, H. J. (1994b). Personality and intelligence: Psychometric and experimental approaches. In R. J. Sternberg (Ed.), *Personality and intelligence* (pp. 3–31). New York: Cambridge University Press.

Eysenck, H. J. (1994c). Personality and temperament. In D. Tantam & M. Birchwood (Eds.), *Psychology and the social science* (pp. 187–202). Gaskell, United Kingdom: Royal College of Psychiatrists.

Eysenck, H. J. (1995). Mental health and physical disease: A new paradigm. *Journal of Mental Health, 4,* 221–225.

Eysenck, H. J. (1996). Personality and the experimental study of education. *European Journal of Personality, 10,* 427–439.

Eysenck, H. J. (1997). Personality and experimental psychology: The unification of psychology and the possibility of a paradigm. *Journal of Personality and Social Psychology, 73*(6), 1224–1237.

Eysenck, H. J. (2000). Personality as a risk factor in cancer and coronary heart disease. In D. T. Kenny and J. G. Carlson (Eds.), *Stress and health: Research and clinical applications* (pp. 291–318). Amsterdam: Harwood Academic.

Eysenck, H. J., & Eysenck, M. W. (1985). *Personality and individual differences.* London: Plenum Press.

Eysenck, H. J., & Eysenck, S. B. G. (1976). *Psychoticism as a dimension of personality.* New York: Crane, Russak.

Eysenck, H. J., & Rachman, S. (1965). *The causes and cures of neurosis.* San Diego, CA: Knapp.

Eysenck, H. J., & Wilson, G. (1991). *The Eysenck Personality Profiler.* Guildford, England: Psi Press.

Eysenck, S. B. J., Eysenck, H. J., & Barrett, P. (1985). A revised version of the psychoticism scale. *Personality and Individual Differences, 6,* 21–29.

Fancher, R. E. (2000). Snapshots of Freud in America, 1899–1999. *American Psychologist, 55,* 1025–1058.

Fanon, F. (1967). *Black skin, white masks.* New York: Grove Press.

Farmer, J. J. (1993, July 29). Vince Foster's reasons may never be known. *Star-Ledger.*

Farran, D., Haskins, R., & Galligher, J. (1980). Poverty and mental retardation: A search for explanations. *New Directions for Exceptional Children, 1,* 47–66.

Fava, G., & Ruini, C. (2003). Development and characteristics of a well-being-enhancing psychotherapeutic strategy. *Journal of Behavior Therapy and Experimental Psychology, 34,* 45–63.

Faveret, B. M. S. (2002). Psychoanalysis and biology: An epistemological re-discussion. *International Forum of Psychoanalysis, 11,* 202–209.

Fay, A. (1976). Clinical notes on paradoxical therapy. In A. A. Lazarus, *Multimodal behavior therapy.* New York: Springer.

Fay, A. (1978). *Making things better by making them worse.* New York: Hawthorne.

Feinberg, T. (2002). *Altered egos.* New York: Oxford University Press.

Feiring, C. (1984). Behavioral styles in infancy and adulthood. *American Journal of Psychoanalysis, 44,* 197–208.

Feixas, G. (1989). Personal construct psychology in Spain: A promising perspective. *International Journal of Personal Construct Psychology, 2*(4), 433–442.

Feldmann, T. B., & Johnson, P. W. (1995). Cult membership as a source of self-cohesion: Forensic implications. *Bulletin of the American Academy of Psychiatry and the Law, 23,* 239–248.

Feshbach, S. (1984, September). The "personality" of personality theory and research. *Personality and Social Psychology Bulletin, 10*(3), 446–456.

Fickling, W. (1991, Fall/Winter). Zen as therapy. *The Ten Directions,* pp. 38–40.

Fiebert, M. S. (1997). In and out of Freud's shadow: A chronology of Adler's relationship with Freud. *Individual Psychology: Journal of Adlerian Theory, Research and Practice, 53,* 241–269.

Fingarette, H. (1963). *The self in transformation: Psychoanalysis, philosophy, and the life of the spirit.* New York: Basic Books.

Finn, M. (2000, Spring). Buddhism and psychotherapy enter the new millennium. *Mountain Record, 18*(3), 111–112.

Fisher, S., & Greenberg, R. P. (1977). *Scientific credibility of Freud's theories and therapy.* New York: Basic Books.

Fisher, S., & Greenberg, R. P. (1985). *The scientific credibility of Freud's theories and therapy.* New York: Columbia University Press.

Fisher, S., & Greenberg, R. P. (1995). *Freud scientifically reappraised: Testing theories and therapy.* New York: Wiley.

Flax, J. (1994). Final analysis? Psychoanalysis in the postmodern West. *Annual of Psychoanalysis, 22,* 1–20.

Fletcher, J. K. (1996). *Relational theory in the workplace.* Work in Progress Series. Stone Center for Developmental Studies, Wellesley College, Wellesley, MA.

Fletcher, J. K., Jordan, J. V., & Miller, J. B. (2000). Women and the workplace: Applications of a psychodynamic theory. *American Journal of Psychoanalysis, 60*(3), 243–261.

Foa, E. B. (1990). Continuous exposure and complete response prevention of obsessive compulsive neuroses. *Behavior Therapy, 32,* 821–829.

Ford, J. G. (1991). Inherent potentialities of actualization: An initial exploration. *Journal of Humanistic Psychology, 31*(3), 65–88.

Ford, K. M., & Adams-Webber, J. R. (1991). The structure of personal construct systems and the logic of confirmation, *International Journal of Personal Construct Psychology, 4*(1), 15–41.

Fordham, F. (1953). *An introduction to Jung's psychology.* Baltimore: Penguin.

Fordham, S., & Ogbu, J. U. (1986). Black students' school success: Coping with the "burden of 'acting white.'" *Urban Review, 18,* 176–206.

Forisha-Kovach, B. (1983). *The experience of adolescence: Development in context.* Glenview, IL: Scott, Foresman.

Fox, D. (2006). Cognitive behavioural therapy. *Update, 72*(1), 26–28.

Frank, C. M. (1956). Conditioning and personality: A study of normal and neurotic subjects. *Journal of Abnormal and Social Psychology, 52,* 143–150.

Frankl, V. E. (1960). Paradoxical intention: A logo-therapeutic technique. *American Journal of Psychotherapy, 14,* 520–535.

Frankl, V. E. (1978). *The unheard cry for meaning.* New York: Simon & Schuster.

Frankl, V. E. (1997). *Man's search for ultimate meaning.* New York: Simon & Schuster.

Franks, C. M. (1976). Foreword. In A. A. Lazarus, *Multimodal behavior therapy.* New York: Springer.

Franks, C. M. (1997). Foreword. In A. A. Lazarus, *Brief but comprehensive Psychotherapy: The multimodal way* (p. xii). New York: Springer.

Fransella, F. (Ed.). (2003). *International handbook of personal construct psychology.* New York: Wiley.

Freeman, M. (1992). Self as narrative: The place of life history in studying the life span. In T. Brinthaupt & R. Lipka (Eds.), *The self: Definitional and methodological issues.* Albany: State University of New York Press.

Freud, A. (1946). *The ego and the mechanisms of defense.* New York: International Universities Press.

Freud, A. (1958). Adolescence. In *The Writings of Anna Freud.* New York: International Universities Press.

Freud, A. (1965–). *The Writings of Anna Freud.* New York: International Universities Press.

Freud, S. (1953–). *The complete psychological works: Standard edition* (24 vols.). J. Strachey (Ed.). London: Hogarth

Press. (Hereafter referred to as *SE* with year of original publication.)

Freud, S. (1895). Studies in hysteria. *SE* (Vol. 2).

Freud, S. (1900). The interpretation of dreams. *SE* (Vols. 4 & 5).

Freud, S. (1901). The psychopathology of everyday life. *SE* (Vol. 6).

Freud, S. (1905). Three essays on sexuality. *SE* (Vol. 7).

Freud, S. (1910). Five lectures on psychoanalysis. *SE* (Vol. 11).

Freud, S. (1917). Introductory lectures on psychoanalysis. *SE* (Vols. 15 & 16).

Freud, S. (1923). The ego and the id. *SE* (Vol. 19).

Freud, S. (1926). The question of lay analysis. *SE* (Vol. 20).

Freud, S. (1933). New introductory lectures on psychoanalysis. *SE* (Vol. 22).

Freud, S. (1937). Analysis terminable and interminable. *SE* (Vol. 23).

Freud, S. (1940). An outline of psychoanalysis. *SE* (Vol. 23).

Frey, L. L., Beesley, D., & Newman, J. L. (2005). The Relational Health Indices. *Measurement and Evaluation in Counseling and Development, 38*(3), 153–163.

Friedman, H., & MacDonald, D. A. (2003). Introduction to special issue on transpersonal psychology. *Humanist Psychologist, 31,* 2–5.

Frixione, E. (2003). Sigmund Freud's contribution to the history of the neuronal cytoskeleton. *Journal of the History of the Neurosciences, 12*(1), 12–25.

Fromm, E. (1941). *Escape from freedom.* New York: Rinehart.

Fromm, E. (1947). *Man for himself.* New York: Rinehart.

Fromm, E. (1955). *The sane society.* New York: Rinehart.

Fromm, E. (1956). *The art of loving.* New York: Harper & Row.

Fromm, E. (1964). *The heart of man.* New York: Harper & Row.

Fromm, E. (1973). *The anatomy of human destructiveness.* New York: Rinehart.

Fromm, E. (1976). *To have or to be.* New York: Harper & Row.

Fromm, E., & Maccoby, M. (1970). *Social character in a Mexican village.* Englewood Cliffs, NJ: Prentice-Hall.

Fuld, P. J. (1991, Fall/Winter). Zen and the work of a psychotherapist. *The Ten Directions,* pp. 40–41.

Fullerton, C. S., Ursano, R. J., Harry, P., & Slusarcick, A. (1989). Birth order, psychological well-being, and social supports in young adults. *Journal of Nervous and Mental Disease, 177*(9), 556–559.

Funder, D., & Sneed, C. (1993). Behavioral manifestations of personality: An ecological approach to judgmental accuracy. *Journal of Personality and Social Psychology, 64,* 479–490.

Funder, D. C. (2001). Personality. *Annual Review of Psychology, 52,* 197–221.

Funder, D. C. (2004). *The personality puzzle* (3rd ed.). New York: Norton.

Furnham, A. (1990). Can people accurately estimate their own personality test scores? *European Journal of Personality, 4*(4), 319–327.

Gaillard, C. (1995). The presbyopic vision of C. G. Jung. *Cahiers Jungiens de Psychanalyse, 82,* 105–118.

Galin, D. (1974). Implications for psychiatry of left and right cerebral specialization. *Archives of General Psychiatry, 31,* 572–583.

Gallard, M. (1995). Jung and Nazi Germany: The facts, the context. *Cahiers Jungiens de Psychanalyse, 82,* 69–76.

Gallo, L. C., Smith, T. W., & Ruiz, J. M. (2003). An interpersonal analysis of attachment style. *Journal of Personality, 71*(2), 141–182.

Gardner, H. (1992). Scientific psychology: Should we bury it or praise it? *New Ideas in Psychology, 10*(2), 179–190.

Gardner, W. L., & Martinko, M. J. (1996). Using the Myers-Briggs Type Indicator to study managers: A literature review and research agenda. *Journal of Management, 22,* 45–83.

Garfield, S. (1992). Response. In W. Dryden & C. Feltham (Eds.), *Psychotherapy and its discontents* (pp. 124–137). Buckingham, England: Open University Press.

Garofalo, D. (1996). The clinical application of Karen Horney's theory to group psychoanalysis. *American Journal of Psychoanalysis, 56,* 193–202.

Garrison, D. (1981). Karen Horney and feminism. *Signs: Journal of Women in Culture and Society, 6,* 4.

Gauchet, M. (2002). Redefining the unconscious. *Thesis Eleven, 71,* 4–24.

Gazzaniga, M. S. (2005). *The ethical brain.* New York: Dana Press.

Geiser, L., & Stein, M. I. (1999). *Evocative images: The TAT and the art of projection.* Washington, DC: American Psychological Association.

Geisler, C. (1985). Repression: A psychoanalytic perspective revisited. *Psychoanalysis and Contemporary Thought, 8*(2), 253–298.

Geller, L. (1982). The failure of self-actualization theory. *Journal of Humanistic Psychology, 22,* 56–73.

Geller, L. (1984, Spring). Another look at self-actualization. *Journal of Humanistic Psychology, 24*(2), 93–106.

Gergen, K. (1992, November/December). The decline and fall of personality. *Psychology Today,* pp. 59–60.

Gilbert, D. (2006). *Stumbling on happiness.* New York: Knopf.

Gilligan, C. (1977). In a different voice: Women's conception of self and morality. *Harvard Educational Review, 47,* 481–517.

Gilligan, C. (1982). *In a different voice.* Cambridge, MA: Harvard University Press.

Gilligan, C. (1990). Joining the resistance: Psychology, politics, girls and women. *Michigan Quarterly Review, 29,* 501–536.

Ginsberg, C. (1984, Spring). Toward a somatic understanding of self: A reply to Leonard Geller. *Journal of Humanistic Psychology, 24*(2), 66–92.

Giorgi, A. (1987, Spring). The crisis of humanistic psychology. *Humanistic Psychologist, 15*(1), 5–20.

Glasser, W. (1998). *Choice theory: A new psychology of personal freedom.* New York: HarperCollins.

Glasser, W. (2000). *Counseling with choice theory: The new reality therapy.* New York: HarperCollins.

Glucksberg, S., & King, I. (1967, October 27). Motivated forgetting mediated by implicit verbal chaining: A laboratory analog of repression. *Science,* pp. 517–519.

Glymour, C. (1991). Freud's androids. *The Cambridge companion to Freud.* New York: Cambridge University Press.

Goldberg, A. (2003). Images in psychiatry: Heinz Kohut, 1913–1981. *American Journal of Psychiatry, 160*(4), 690.

Goldberg, L. R. (1981). Language and individual differences: The search for universals in personality lexicons. In L. Wheeler (Ed.), *Review of personality and social psychology* (Vol. 2, pp. 141–165). Beverly Hills, CA: Sage.

Goldberg, L. R. (1990). An alternative "description of personality": The big-five factor structure. *Journal of Personality and Social Psychology, 59,* 1216–1229.

Goldberg, L. R. (1993). The structure of phenotypic personality traits. *American Psychologist, 48,* 26–34.

Goldman, D., & Mazzanti, C. (2002). From phenotype to gene and back. In J. Benjamin, R. Ebstein, & R. H. Belmaker

(Eds.), *Molecular genetics of human personality* (pp. 273–290). Washington, DC: American Psychiatric Publishing.

Goldrick, M. (Ed.). (1996). *Ethnicity and family therapy.* New York: Guilford Press.

Goldrick, M. (Ed.). (1998). *Re-visioning family therapy.* New York: Guilford Press.

Goldstein, J., Freud, A., & Solnit, A. J. (1973). *Beyond the best interests of the child.* New York: Free Press.

Goldstein, J., Freud, A., & Solnit, A. J. (1979). *Before the best interests of the child.* New York: Free Press.

Goleman, D. (1987, February 6). Carl R. Rogers, 85, leader in psychotherapy, dies. *New York Times,* p. D16.

Goleman, D. (1992). New light on how stress erodes health. *New York Times,* p. C1.

Goleman, D. (1993a, May 4). Some patients arouse hatred, therapists find. *New York Times,* p. C1.

Goleman, D. (1993b, April 6). Studying the secrets of childhood memory. *New York Times,* p. C1.

Goleman, D. (1994, January 11). Childhood depression may herald adult ills. *New York Times,* p. C1.

Goleman, D. (1994, March 22). The "wrong" sex: A new definition of childhood pain. *New York Times.*

Goleman, D. (1996, January 24). Critics say managed-care savings are eroding mental care. *New York Times,* p. C9.

Goleman, D. (2006). *Social intelligence.* New York: Bantam.

Goleman, D. (1981). Buddhist and Western psychology: Some commonalities and differences. *Journal of Transpersonal Psychology, 13,* 125–136.

Goode, E. (2000, January 11). A therapy modified for patient and times. *New York Times.*

Gould, S. J. (1996). *The mismeasure of man.* New York: Norton.

Gray, J. A. (1985). Issues in the neuropsychology of anxiety. In H. Tuma & J. D. Masser (Eds.), *Anxiety and the anxiety disorders* (pp. 5–26). Hillsdale, NJ: Erlbaum.

Gray, J. A. (1987). Perspectives on anxiety and impulsivity: A commentary. *Journal of Research in Personality, 21,* 493–509.

Green, C. D. (1992). Of immortal mythological beasts: Optionism in psychology. *Theory and Psychology, 2*(3), 291–320.

Green, L. R., Richardson, D. S., Lago, T., & Schatten-Jones, E. C. (2001). Network correlates of social and emotional loneliness in young and older adults. *Personality and Social Psychology Bulletin, 27,* 281–288.

Green, R. G. (1981). Behavioral and physiological reactions to observed violence. *Journal of Personality and Social Psychology, 40,* 43–63.

Greenberg, G. (1995). If a self is a narrative: Social construction in the clinic. *Journal of Narrative and Life History, 5,* 269–283.

Greenberg, J. (1981, August 11). A psychiatrist who wouldn't take no for an answer. *New York Times,* pp. C1–C2.

Greenberg, R. P., & Fisher, S. (1995). *Freud scientifically reappraised.* New York: Wiley.

Greisers, C., Greenberg, R., & Harrison, R. H. (1972). The adaptive function of sleep: The differential effects of sleep and dreaming on recall. *Journal of Abnormal Psychology, 80,* 280–286.

Grotstein, J. S. (1991). An American view of the British psychoanalytic experience: Psychoanalysis in counterpoint: The contributions of the British Object Relations School. *Melanie Klein and Object Relations, 9*(2), 34–62.

Grotstein, J. S. (1997). "Internal objects" or "chimerical monsters"?: The demonic "third forms" of the internal world. *Journal of Analytical Psychology, 42,* 47–80.

Grünbaum, A. (1984). *The foundations of psychoanalysis: A philosophical critique.* Berkeley: University of California Press.

Grünbaum, A. (1993). *Validation in the clinical theory of psychoanalysis.* New York: International Universities Press.

Grünbaum, A. (2006). Is Sigmund Freud's psychoanalytic edifice relevant to the 21st century? *Psychoanalytic Psychology, 23*(2), 257–284.

Guilford, J. P. (1967). *The nature of human intelligence.* New York: McGraw-Hill.

Gupta, M. D. (1987, January). Role of age and birth order in Machiavellianism. *Psychological Studies, 32*(1), 47–50.

Guteri, F. (2002, November 11). What Freud got right: His theories, long discredited, are finding support from neurologists using modern brain imaging. *Newsweek,* p. 50.

Guttman, M. G. (2001). *The enigma of Anna O.: A biography of Bertha Pappenheim.* New York: Moyel Bell.

Hagen, S. (1995). *How the world can be the way it is: An inquiry for the new millennium into science, philosophy, and perception.* Wheaton, IL: Theosophical Publishing.

Hagen, S. (1997). *Buddhism plain and simple.* Rutland, VT: Tuttle.

Hagen, S. (2003). *Buddhism is not what you think.* San Francisco: Harper.

Haitch, R. H. (1995). How Tillich and Kohut both find courage in faith. *Pastoral Psychology, 44,* 83–97.

Hall, C. S., & Lindzey, G. (1978). *Theories of personality* (3rd ed.). New York: Wiley.

Hall, C. S., Lindzey, G., & Campbell, J. B. (1998). *Theories of personality* (4th ed.). New York: Wiley.

Hall, C. S., & Van de Castle, R. (1965). An empirical investigation of the castration complex in dreams. *Journal of Personality, 33,* 20–29.

Hall, G. C., & Barongan, C. (2002). *Multicultural psychology.* Upper Saddle River, NJ: Prentice-Hall.

Hall, M. (1968, July). A conversation with Abraham H. Maslow, *Psychology Today,* pp. 34–37; 54–57.

Hall, M. (1983, June). A conversation with Erik Erikson. *Psychology Today, 17*(6).

Hamacheck, D. (1990). Evaluating self-concept and ego status in Erikson's last three psychosocial stages. *Journal of Counseling and Development, 68*(6), 677–683.

Hamer, D. (2005). *The God gene: How faith is hardwired into our genes.* New York: Anchor.

Hamilton, W. D. (1964). The genetical evolution of social behavior. *Journal of Theoritical Biology, 7,* 1–52.

Hammer, J. (1970). Preference for gender of child as a function of sex of adult respondents. *Journal of Individual Psychology, 33,* 20–20.

Hamon, S. A. (1987, Summer). Some contributions of Horneyan theory of enhancement of the Type A behavior construct. *American Journal of Psychoanalysis, 47*(2), 105–115.

Hanh, N. (1999). *The heart of the Buddha's teaching: Transforming suffering into peace, joy, and liberation.* New York: Broadway Books.

Hanh, N. (2005a). *Being peace* (2nd ed.). Berkeley, CA: Parallax Press.

Hanh, N. (2005b). *Calming the fearful mind: A Zen response to terrorism.* Berkeley, CA: Parallax Press.

Hanh, N. (2007). *The Art of Power.* New York: Harper Collins.

Hanh, T. N. (1974). *Zen keys.* Garden City, NY: Anchor/Doubleday.

Hanh, T. N. (1975). *The miracle of mindfulness! A manual on meditation.* Boston: Beacon Press.

Hanh, T. N. (1985). *A guide to walking meditation.* Nyack, NY: Fellowship.

Hanh, T. N. (1988). *The heart of understanding.* Berkeley, CA: Parallax Press.

Hanh, T. N. (1991). *Peace is every step: The path of mindfulness in everyday life.* New York: Bantam.

Hanh, T. N. (1992). *Touching peace.* Berkeley, CA: Parallax Press.

Hanh, T. N. (1993). *The blooming of a lotus: Guided meditation exercises for healing and transformation.* Boston: Beacon Press.

Hanh, T. N. (2003). *Opening the heart of the cosmos: Insights on the Lotus Sutra.* Berkeley, CA: Parallax Press.

Hanley, S. J., & Abell, S. C. (2002). Maslow and relatedness: Creating an interpersonal model of self-actualization. *Journal of Humanistic Psychology, 42*(4), 37–57.

Harari, C. (1989). Humanistic and transpersonal psychology: Values in psychotherapy. *Psychotherapy in Private Practice, 7*(4), 49–56.

Harkness, A. R., & McNulty, J. L. (2002). Implications of personality individual differences science for clinical work on personality disorders. In P. T. Costa, Jr. & T. A. Widiger (Eds.), *Personality disorders and the Five-Factor Model of personality* (pp. 391–404). Washington, DC: American Psychological Association.

Harlow, H. F. (1958). The nature of love. *American Psychologist, 13,* 673–685.

Harrington, D. M., Block, J. H., & Block, J. (1987, April). Testing aspects of Carl Rogers's theory of creative environments: Child-rearing antecedents of creative potential in young adolescents. *Journal of Personality and Social Psychology, 52*(4), 851–856.

Harris, K. A., & Morrow, J. B. (1992). Differential effects of birth order and gender on perceptions of responsibility and dominance. *Individual Psychology: Journal of Adlerian Theory, Research and Practice, 48*(1), 109–118.

Harris, T. (1969). *I'm OK—You're OK.* New York: Harper & Row.

Harrison, W., Lewis, G., & Straka, T. (1984, September). Locus of control, choice, and satisfaction with an assigned task. *Journal of Research in Personality, 18*(3), 342–351.

Hartling, L. M. (2003a). *Prevention through connection: A collaborative approach to women's abuse.* Work in Progress Series. Stone Center for Developmental Studies, Wellesley College, Wellesley, MA.

Hartling, L. M. (2003b). *Strengthening resilience in a risky world.* Work in Progress Series. Stone Center for Developmental Studies, Wellesley College, Wellesley, MA.

Hartling, L., & Sparks, E. (2003). *Relational-cultural practice: Working in a nonrelational world.* Work in Progress Series. Stone Center for Developmental Studies, Wellesley College, Wellesley, MA.

Hartmann, H. (1958). *Ego psychology and the problem of adaptation.* New York: International Universities Press.

Hartmann, H. (1964). *Essays in ego psychology: Selected problems in psychanalytic theory.* New York: International Universities Press.

Harzem, P. (1987, Fall). On the virtues of being a psychologist. *Behavior Analyst, 10*(2), 175–181.

Hayes, S., & Hayes, L. (1988). Inadequacies not just obstacles. *Counseling Psychology Quarterly, 1*(2–3), 291–294.

Hayes, S. C., Barnes-Holmes, D., & Roche, B. (2001). *Relational frame theory: A post-Skinnerian account of human language and cognitive.* New York: Kluwer Academic/Plenum Press.

Hayes, S. C., Masuda, A., Bissett, R., Luoma, J., & Guerrero, L. F. (2004). DBT, FAP, and ACT. How empirically oriented are the new behavior therapy techniques? *Behavior Therapy, 35,* 35–54.

Hayes, S. C., & Smith, S. (2005). *Get out of your mind and into your life: The new acceptance and commitment therapy.* New York: New Harbinger.

Hayes, S. C., Strosahl, K. D., & Wilson, K. G. (1999). *Acceptance and commitment therapy: An experiential approach to behavior change.* New York: Guilford Press.

Hayes, S. H. (2001). *Relational frame theory.* New York: Kluwer Academic.

Hayes, T. L. (1996). Personality correlates of performance: Does disability make a difference? *Human Performance, 9,* 121–140.

Hazan, C., & Shaver, P. (1987). Romantic love conceptualized as an attachment process. *Journal of Personality and Social Psychology, 52,* 511–524.

Heine, S. J. (2001). Self as cultural product: An examination of East Asian and North American selves. *Journal of Personality, 69*(6), 881–906.

Helms, J. E. (1990). *Black and white racial identity theory, research, and practice.* Westport, CT: Praeger.

Henwood, K. L., & Pidgeon, N. F. (1992). Qualitative research and psychological theorizing. *British Journal of Psychology, 83*(1), 97–111.

Hermans, J. J., Kempen, H. J., & Van Loon, R. J. (1992). The dialogical self: Beyond individualism and rationalism. *American Psychologist, 47*(1), 23–33.

Hermsen, E. (1996). Person-centered psychology and Taoism: The reception of Lao-tzu by Carl R. Rogers. *International Journal for the Psychology of Religion, 6,* 107–125.

Herrera, N. C., Zajonc, R. B., Wieczorkowska, G., & Cichomski, B. (2003). Beliefs about birth order and their reflection in reality. *Journal of Personality and Social Psychology, 85*(1), 142–150.

Herron, W. G. (1995). Development of the ethnic unconscious. *Psychoanalytic Psychology, 12,* 521–532.

Heston, L. L. (1966). Psychiatric disorders in foster home reared children of schizophrenic mothers. *British Journal of Psychiatry, 112,* 819–825.

Hibbard, S. (1993). Behavior, adaption, and intentionality. *Journal of Mind and Behavior, 14,* 373–384.

Hinds, M. (1993, October 19). Not like the movie: A dare leads to death. *New York Times,* p. C1.

Hirai, T. (1989). *Zen meditation and psychotherapy.* Tokyo: Japan Publications.

Hirsch, P. (2005). Apostle of freedom: Alfred Adler. *History of Education, 35*(5) 473–481.

Hjelle, L. A. (1991). Relationship of social interest to internal-external control and self-actualization in young women. Special Issue: Social interest. *Individual Psychology: Journal of Adlerian Theory, Research and Practice, 47*(1), 101–105.

Hobfoll, S. E., Schroder, K. R., Wells, M., & Malek, M. (2002). Communal versus individualistic sense of mastery in facing life's challenges. *Journal of Social and Clinical Psychology, 21*(4), 362–399.

Hoffman, E. (1988). *The right to be human: A biography of Abraham Maslow.* Los Angeles: Tarcher.

Hoffman, E. (1994a). *The drive for self: Alfred Adler and the founding of individual psychology.* Reading, MA: Addison-Wesley.

Hoffman, E. (1994b, November 20). Karen Horney. *New York Times Book Review*, p. 20.

Hogan, R. (1982). A socioanalytic theory of personality. In M. Page (Ed.), *Nebraska Symposium on Motivation*. Lincoln: University of Nebraska Press.

Hogan, R., & Hogan, J. (1995). *Hogan Personality Inventory manual* (2nd ed.). Tulsa, OK: Hogan Assessment Systems.

Hogan, R., Hogan, J., & Roberts, B. W. (1996). Personality measurement and employment decisions: Questions and answers. *American Psychologist, 5*, 469–477.

Hogan, R. J. (1976). *Personality theory: The personological tradition*. Englewood Cliffs, NJ: Prentice-Hall.

Holland, J. L. (1996). Exploring careers with a typology: What we have learned and some new directions. *American Psychologist, 51*, 397–406.

Honey, P., & Mumford, A. (1992). *The manual of learning styles*. Maidenhead, England: Peter Honey and Alan Mumford (Publishers).

Hoover, I. (1980). *The Zen experience*. New York: New American Library.

Horley, J. (1991). Values and beliefs as personal constructs. *International Journal of Personal Construct Psychology, 4*(1), 1–14.

Horney, K. (1937). *The neurotic personality of our time*. New York: Norton.

Horney, K. (1939). *New ways in psychoanalysis*. New York: Norton.

Horney, K. (1942). *Self-analysis*. New York: Norton.

Horney, K. (1945). *Our inner conflicts*. New York: Norton.

Horney, K. (1950). *Neurosis and human growth*. New York: Norton.

Horney, K. (1967). *Feminine psychology*. New York: Norton.

Howard, G. (1991). Culture tales: A narrative approach to thinking, cross-cultural psychology, and psychotherapy. *American Psychologist, 46*(3), 187–197.

Howard, R., & McKillen, M. (1990). Extraversion and performance in the perceptual maze test. *Personality and Individual Differences, 11*, 391–396.

Hull, C. L. (1943). *Principles of behavior*. New York: Appleton-Century-Crofts.

Huopainen, H. (2002). Freud's view of hysteria in light of modern trauma research. *Scandinavian Psychoanalytic Review, 25*(2), 92–108.

Hyman, R. (1999). *Creating psychotherapy*. New York: Norton.

Iaccino, J. F. (1994). *Psychological reflections on cinematic terror: Jungian archetypes in horror films*. London: Praeger.

Ingram, D. H., & Lerner, J. A. (1992). Horney theory: An object relations theory. *American Journal of Psychoanalysis, 52*(1), 37–44.

Ishiyama, F. I., Munson, P. A., & Chabassol, D. J. (1990). Birth order and fear of success among midadolescents. *Psychological Reports, 66*(1), 17–18.

Jackson, C., & Lawty-Jones, M. (1996). Explaining the overlap between personality and learning style. *Personality and Individual Differences, 20*, 293–300.

Jackson, D. J. (1991). Contributions to the history of psychology: LXXXI. The friendship of Anna Freud and Dorothy Burlingham. *Psychological Reports, 68*(3, Pt. 2), 1176–1178.

Jacobson, L. (1996). The Grünbaum debate: Introduction. *Psychoanalytic Dialogues, 6*, 497–502.

Jacobson, N. S. (1987). Psychotherapists in clinical practice: Cog-

nitive and behavioral perspectives. New York: Guilford Press.

Jager, B. (1989). Language and human science: The vocabularies of academic psychology and psychoanalysis. *Humanistic Psychologist, 17*(2), 112–130.

Jang, K. L., Livesley, W. J., Angleitner, A., Riemann, R., & Vernon, P. A. (2002). Genetic and environmental influences on the covariance of facets defining the domains of the five-factor model of personality. *Personality and Individual Differences, 33*, 83–101.

Jankowicz, A. D. (1987, May). Whatever became of George Kelly? Applications and implications. *American Psychologist, 42*(5), 481–487.

Jenkins, Y. M. (2000). The Stone Center theoretical approach revisited: Applications for African American women. In L. C. Jackson & B. Greene (Eds.), *Psychotherapy with African American women* (pp. 62–81). New York: Guilford Press.

Jennings, G. H. (1999). *Passages beyond the gate: A Jungian approach to understanding the nature of American psychology at the dawn of the new millennium*. New York: Ginn Press.

Jensen, A. R. (1969). How much can we boost IQ and scholastic achievement? *Harvard Educational Review, 39*, 1–123.

John, O. P. (1990). The "Big Five" factor taxonomy: Dimensions of personality in the natural language and in questionnaires. In L. A. Pervin (Ed.), *Handbook of personality: Theory and research* (pp. 66–100). New York: Guilford Press.

John, O. P., & Robins, R. W. (1993). Gordon Allport: Father and critic of the Five-Factor Model. In K. H. Craik, R. Hogan, & R. N. Wolfe (Eds.), *Fifty years of personality psychology* (pp. 215–236). New York: Plenum Press.

Johnson, R. A. (1991). *Understanding the dark side of the psyche*. San Francisco, CA: Harper San Francisco.

Jones, E. (1953–1957). *The life and work of Sigmund Freud* (3 vols.). New York: Basic Books.

Jones, R. A. (2000). On the empirical proof of archetypes. *Journal of Analytical Psychology, 45*, 599–605.

Jones, R. L. (Ed.). (2001). *Black psychology* (4th ed.). Hampton, VA: Cobb & Henry.

Jordan, J. J., & Hartling, L. M. (2002). The development of relational cultural theory. In M. Ballou & L. J. Brown (Eds.), *Rethinking mental health and disorder*. New York: Guilford Press.

Jordan, J. V. (1990). *Courage in connection: Conflict, compassion, creativity*. Work in Progress Series. Stone Center for Development Studies, Wellesley College, Wellesley, MA.

Jordan, J. V. (1991). Women and empathy: Implications for psychological development and psychotherapy. In J. V. Jordan et al. (Eds.), *Women's growth in connection: Writings from the Stone Center* (pp. 27–50). New York: Guilford Press.

Jordan, J. V. (1994). *A relational perspective on self esteem*. Work in Progress Series. Stone Center for Development Studies, Wellesley College, Wellesley, MA.

Jordan, J. V. (Ed.). (1997a). *Women's growth in diversity*. New York: Guilford Press.

Jordan, J. V. (1997b). Clarity in connection: Empathic knowing, desire, and sexuality. In J. V. Jordan (Ed.), *Women's growth in diversity* (pp. 50–73). New York: Guilford Press.

Jordan, J. V. (1997c). Relational development: Therapeutic implications of empathy and shame. In J. V. Jordan (Ed.), *Women's growth in diversity*. New York: Guilford Press.

Jordan, J. V. (2003a). *Learning at the margin: New models of strength*. Work in Progress Series. Stone Center for Developmental Studies, Wellesley College, Wellesley, MA.

Jordan, J. V. (2003b). *Valuing vulnerability: New definitions of courage*. Work in Progress Series. Stone Center for Developmental Studies, Wellesley College, Wellesley, MA.

Jordan, J. V. (2005). *Commitment to connection in a culture of fear*. Work in Progress Series. Stone Center for Developmental Studies, Wellesley College, Wellesley, MA.

Jordan, J. V., Kaplan, A. G., Miller, J. B., Stiver, I. P., & Surrey, J. L. (Eds.). (1991). *Women's growth in connection: Writings from the Stone Center*. New York: Guilford Press.

Jordan, J. V., Walker, M., & Hartling, L. M. (2004). *The Complexity of connection*. New York: Guilford Press.

Joseph, S. (2004). Client-centered therapy, post-traumatic stress disorder and post-traumatic growth. *Psychology and Psychotherapy, 77*(1), 101–119.

Josephs, R., Markus, R., & Tafarodi, R. (1992). Gender and self-esteem. *Journal of Personality and Social Psychology, 63*, 391.

Juda, D. P. (1991). Freud versus Freud: Healing the divided field of victimization. *Psychoanalysis and Psychotherapy, 9*(1), 3–17.

Judge, T. A., Erez, A., Bono, J. E., & Thoresen, C. J. (2002). Are measures of self-esteem, neuroticism, locus of control, and generalized self-efficacy indicators of a common core construct? *Journal of Personality and Social Psychology, 83*(3), 693–710.

Jung, C. G. (1953). *Collected works*. H. Read, M. Fordham, & G. Adler (Eds.). Princeton: Princeton University Press. (Hereafter referred to as *CW* with year of original publication.)

Jung, C. G. (1916). Symbols of transformation. *CW* (Vol. 5).

Jung, C. G. (1933). *Psychological types*. New York: Harcourt, Brace.

Jung, C. G. (1934). A review of complex theory. *CW* (Vol. 8).

Jung, C. G. (1936). The archetypes and the collective unconscious. *CW* (Vol. 9).

Jung, C. G. (1938). Psychology and religion. *CW* (Vol. 11).

Jung, C. G. (1939). The integration of the personality. *CW* (Vol. 17).

Jung, C. G. (1948). On psychic energy. *CW* (Vol. 8).

Jung, C. G. (1951). Two essays on analytical psychology. *CW* (Vol. 7).

Jung, C. G. (1954). Psychological aspects of the mother archetype. *CW* (Vol. 9).

Jung, C. G. (1955). Mandalas. *CW* (Vol. 9).

Jung, C. G. (1958). Answer to Job. *CW* (Vol. 11).

Jung, C. G. (1960). Synchronicity: An acausal connecting principle. *CW* (Vol. 8).

Jung, C. G. (1961). *Memories, dreams, and reflections*. New York: Random House.

Jung, C. G. (1964). *Man and his symbols*. New York: Doubleday.

Jung, C. G. (1976). The symbolic life. *CW* (Vol. 18).

Kaasinen, V., Maguire, R. P., Kurki, T., Bruck, A. Rinne, J. O. (2005). Mapping brain structure and personality in late adulthood. *NeuroImage, 24*(2), 315–322.

Kabat-Zinn, J. (1990). *Full catastrophe living: Using the wisdom of your body and mind to face stress, pain, and illness*. New York: Delacorte.

Kaczor, L. M., Ryckman, R. M., Thornton, B., & Kuelnel, R. H. (1991). Observer hyper-competitiveness and victim precipitation of rape. *Journal of Social Psychology, 131*, 131–134.

Kafka, J. S. (2006). The trouble with Sullivan's "malevolent transformation." *Psychiatry, 69*(2), 113–114.

Kagan, J. (1972). Motives and development. *Journal of Personality and Social Psychology, 22*, 51–56.

Kagan, J. (1991). The theoretical utility of constructs for self. Special Issue: The development of self: The first three years. *Developmental Review, 11*(3), 244–250.

Kagan, J. (1994). *Galen's prophecy: Temperament in human nature*. New York: Basic Books.

Kahn, E., & Rachman, A. W. (2000). Carl Rogers and Heinz Kohut. *Psychoanalytic Psychology, 17*, 294–312.

Kalb, C. (2006, March 27). The therapist as scientist. *Newsweek*, pp. 50–51.

Kalekin-Fishman, D. (1993). The two faces of hostility: The implications of personal construct theory for understanding alienation. *International Journal of Personal Construct Psychology, 6*(1), 27–40.

Kalupahana, D. J., & Kalupahana, I. (1982). *The way of Siddhartha: A life of the Buddha*. Boulder, CO: Shambhala.

Kandel, E. (2006, March 27). Biology of the mind: A Nobel Prize winner on psychiatry, Freud and the future of neuroscience [Interview by Claudia Kalb]. *Newsweek*, p. 47.

Kant, I. (1798). *Anthropology from a pragmatic point of view*. (V. L. Dowdel, Trans.). Carbondale: Southern Illinois University Press. Translation published in 1978.

Kantrowitz, R. E., & Ballou, M. A. (1992). A feminist critique of cognitive-behavioral therapy. In L. S. Brown & M. Ballou (Eds.), *Personality and psychopathology: Feminist reappraisals* (pp. 70–87). New York: Guilford Press.

Kaplan, R. D. (1994, February 20). There is no "Middle East." *New York Times Magazine*, p. 14.

Katagiri, D. (1988). *Returning to silence: Zen practice in daily life*. Boston: Shambhala.

Katagiri, D. (1998). *You have to say something* (Steve Hagen, Ed.). Boston: Shambhala.

Katagiri, D. (1999). Katagiri Dainin lectures on Kuge: Flowers in the sky. *Zen Quarterly, 11* (2–3), 13–19.

Katagiri, D. (2007). *Each moment is the universe: Zen and the way of being time*. Boston: Shambhala.

Katzko, M. W. (2003). Unity versus multiplicity: A conceptual analysis of the term "self" and its use in personality theories. *Journal of Personality, 71*(1), 84–114.

Keenan, J., & Gallup, G. G. (2004). *The face in the mirror*. New York: Ecco.

Keirsey, D., & Bates, M. (1984). *Please understand me: Character and temperament types*. Del Mar, CA: Prometheus Nemesis.

Kelly, G. A. (1955). *The psychology of personal constructs* (2 vols.). New York: Norton.

Kelly, G. A. (1958). Man's construction of his alternatives. In G. Lindzey (Ed.), *Assessment of human motives*. New York: Rinehart & Winston.

Kelly, G. A. (1970). A brief introduction to personal construct theory. In D. Bannister (Ed.), *Perspectives in personality construct theory*. New York: Academic Press.

Kelly, W. L. (1991). *Psychology of the unconscious*. Buffalo, NY: Prometheus Books.

Kernberg, O. F. (1975). *Borderline conditions and pathological narcissism*. New York: Jason Aronson.

Kernberg, O. F. (1990). Sexual excitement and rage: Building blocks of the drives. *Sigmund Freud House Bulletin, 15*(1), 3–38.

Kernberg, O. F. (1992). *Aggression in personality disorders and perversions*. New Haven, CT: Yale University Press.

Kernberg, O. F. (1994). The present state of psychoanalysis. *Psyche: Zeitschrift f, r Psychoanalyse und ihre Anwendungen, 48*, 483–508.

Kernberg, O. F. (1995a). Omnipotence in the transference and in the countertransference. *Scandinavian Psychoanalytic Review, 18*, 2–21.

Kernberg, O. F. (1995b). Technical approach to eating disorders in patients with borderline personality organization. *Annual of Psychoanalysis, 23*, 33–48.

Kernberg, O. F. (1996a). Hatred as the core affect of aggression. *Zeitschrift f, r Psychosomatische Medizin und Psychoanalyse, 42*, 281–305.

Kernberg, O. F. (1996b). The analyst's authority in the psychoanalytic situation. *Psychoanalytic Quarterly, 65*, 137–157.

Kernberg, O. F. (1996c). Thirty methods to destroy the creativity of psychoanalytic candidates. *International Journal of Psycho-Analysis, 77*, 1031–1040.

Kernberg, O. F. (2000). Psychoanalytic perspectives on the religious experience. *American Journal of Psychotherapy, 54*(4), 452–457.

Kernberg, O. F. (2003). Some reflections on confidentiality in clinical practice. In C. Levin & A. Furlong (Eds.), *Confidentiality: Ethical perspectives and clinical dilemmas* (pp. 79–83). Hillsdale, NJ: Analytic Press.

Kernberg, O. F. (2004). *Aggressivity, narcissism, and self-destructiveness in the psychotherapy of severe personality disorders.* New York: Libra.

Kernberg, O. F. (2006). Discussion of Dr. Glen Gabbard's paper "A neurobiological perspective on mentalizing and internal objects relations in traumatized borderline patients." *International Congress Series, 1286*, 197–200.

Kernberg, O. F., Selzer, M. A., Koenigsberg, H. W., Carr, A. C., & Appelbaum, A. H. (1989). *Psychodynamic psychotherapy of borderline patients.* New York: Basic Books.

Kidwell, J. (1982). The neglected birthorder: Middleborns. *Journal of Marriage and the Family, 44*, 225–235.

Kiel, J. M. (1999). Reshaping Maslow's hierarchy of needs to reflect today's educational and managerial philosophies. *Journal of Instructional Psychology, 26*(3), 167–168.

Kihlstrom, J. F. (1999). The psychological unconscious. In L. A. Pervin & O. P. John (Eds.), *Handbook of personality: Theory and research* (pp. 671–685). New York: Guilford Press.

Kimura, D. (1979). The asymmetry of the human brain. *Scientific American, 2128*, 70–78.

Kinkead, G. (1994, April 10). Spock, Brazelton, and now Penelope Leach. *New York Times Magazine*, p. 32.

Kiracofe, N. M., & Kiracofe, H. N. (1990). Child-perceived parental favoritism and birth order. *Individual Psychology: Journal of Adlerian Theory, Research and Practice, 46*(1), 74–81.

Kirby, S. (2004). Dimension and meanings of anxiety. *Existential Analysis, 15*(1), 73–86.

Kirschenbaum, H. (2004). Carl Rogers's life and work. *Journal of Counseling and Development, 82*(1), 116–125.

Kirschenbaum, H., & Jourdan, A. (2005). The current status of Carl Rogers and the person-centered approach. *Psychotherapy: Theory, Research, Practice, Training, 42*(1), 37–51.

Kitayama, S., & Markus, H. R. (1992, May). *Construal of self as cultural frame: Implications for internationalizing psychology.* Paper presented to symposium on Internationalization and Higher Education, Ann Arbor, MI.

Klatzky, R. L. (1980). *Human memory: Structures and processes* (2nd ed.). San Francisco: Freeman.

Klein, M. (1932). *The psychoanalysis of children.* London: Hogarth.

Klein, M. (1975). *The writings of Melanie Klein* (Vol. 3). London: Hogarth.

Klein, S. (1984, March). Birth order and introversion-extraversion. *Journal of Research in Personality, 18*(1), 110–113.

Kline, P. (1972). *Fact and fantasy in Freudian theory.* London: Methuen.

Kline, P. (1987, September). The experiential study of the psychoanalytic unconscious. *Personality and Social Psychology Bulletin, 13*(3), 363–378.

Kluger, J. (2006, July 10). The new science of siblings. *Time*, pp. 47–55.

Koch, E. (1991). Nature-nurture issues in Freud's writings: The complemental series. *International Review of Psycho-Analysis, 18*, 473–487.

Kohut, H. (1971). *The analysis of the self.* New York: International Universities Press.

Kohut, H. (1977a). *The restoration of the self.* New York: International Universities Press.

Kohut, H. (1977b). Preface. In *Psychodynamics of drug dependence* (NIDA Research Monograph No. 12, pp. vii–ix). Washington, DC: U.S. Government Printing Office.

Kohut, H. (1978). The psychoanalyst in the community of scholars. In P. Ornstein (Ed.), *The search for the self: Selected writings of Heinz Kohut* (Vol. 2, pp. 685–724). New York: International Universities Press.

Kohut, H. (1984). How does analysis cure? In A. Goldberg and P. Stepansky (Eds.), *Contributions to the psychology of the self.* Chicago: University of Chicago Press.

Kolata, G. (1994, March 8). In ancient times, flowers and fennel for family planning. *New York Times*, p. C1.

Kolb, D. (1984). *Experiential learning,* Englewood Cliffs, NJ: Prentice-Hall.

Kole, W. J. (2006, May 3). Analyze this: Freud would be 150. *Star Ledger*, p. 1.

Kosko, B. (1993). *Fuzzy thinking: The new science of fuzzy logic.* New York: Hyperion.

Kotulak, R. (2005, October 27). Genetic map points way to root of disease. *Star-Ledger*, p. 5.

Kramer, P. D. (2006) *Freud: Inventor of the modern mind.* New York: HarperCollins.

Krantrowitz, R. E., & Ballou, M. (1992). A feminist critique of cognitive-behavioral therapy. In L. S. Brown & M. Ballou (Eds.), *Personality and psychopathology* (pp. 70–87). New York: Guilford Press.

Krech, G. (2000). The art of self-reflection. *Constructive Living Quarterly, 7*(4), 1–2.

Krimerman, L. (2001). Participatory action research. *Philosophy of the Social Sciences, 31*(1), 60–82.

Kruger, D. (1986, December). Phenomenology and the fundamentals of psychology. *South African Journal of Psychology, 16*(4), 109–116.

Krystal, H. (1990). An information processing view of object-relations. *Psychoanalytic Inquiry, 10*(2), 221–251.

Kuhn, T. S. (1970). *The structure of scientific revolutions.* Chicago: University of Chicago Press.

Kurtz, E., & Ketchum, K. (1992). *The spirituality of imperfection.* New York: Bantam Books.

Kwee, M. G. T. (1981). Towards the clinical art and science of multimodal psychotherapy. *Current Psychological Reviews, 1*, 55–68.

Kwong, J. (2003). *No beginning, no end: The intimate heart of Zen.* Nevada City: Harmony Books.

Lachmann, F. M., & Beebe, B. (1995). Self psychology: Later, the same day. *Psychoanalytic Dialogues, 5,* 415–419.

Lambert, M. (1988). Beyond psychology as the science of behavior. *Counselling Psychology Quarterly, 1*(2–3), 313–315.

Lamielle, J. T. (1981). Toward an idiothetic psychology of personality. *American Psychologist, 36,* 276–289.

Lamielle, J. T., & Trierweiler, S. J. (1986, June). Interactive measurement, idiothetic inquiry, and the challenge to conventional nomotheticism. *Journal of Personality, 54*(2), 460–469.

Lanchester, J. (2006, February 27). Pursuing happiness. *The New Yorker,* 78f.

Land, D. (2003). *Brain images reveal effects of antidepressants.* Retrieved October 14, 2003, from http://www.news.wisc.edu/view.html?get=8239

Landfield, A. W. (1988). Personal science and the concept of validation. *International Journal of Personal Construct Psychology, 1*(3), 237–249.

Landman, J. T., & Dawes, R. M. (1982). Psychotherapy outcomes. *American Psychologist, 37*(5), 504–516.

Landrine, H., & Klonoff, E. (1992). Culture and health-related schemas: A review and proposal for interdisciplinary integration. *Health Psychology, 11,* 267–276.

Lang, K. L., & Livesley, W. J. (1996). Heritability of the big five personality dimensions and their facets: A twin study. *Journal of Personality, 64,* 577–597.

Lawton, H. W. (1990). The field of psychohistory. *Journal of Psychohistory, 17*(4), 353–364.

Layard, R. (2005). *Happiness: Lessons from a new science.* New York: Penguin.

Lazarus, A. A. (1956). A psychological approach to alcoholism. *South African Medical Journal, 30,* 707–710.

Lazarus, A. A. (1958). New methods in psychotherapy: A case study. *South African Medical Journal, 32,* 660–664.

Lazarus, A. A. (1966). Broad spectrum behavior therapy and the treatment of agoraphobia. *Behavior Research and Therapy, 4,* 95–97.

Lazarus, A. A. (1971). *Behavior therapy and beyond.* New York: McGraw-Hill.

Lazarus, A. A. (1973). Multimodal behavior therapy: Treating the BASIC-ID. *Journal of Nervous and Mental Disorders, 156,* 404–411.

Lazarus, A. A. (1976). *Multimodal behavior therapy.* New York: Springer.

Lazarus, A. A. (1978). *In the mind's eye: The power of imagery for personal enrichment.* New York: Rawson.

Lazarus, A. A. (1982). Personal enrichment through imagery. New York: BMA Audio Cassettes.

Lazarus, A. A. (1985). *Casebook of multimodal therapy.* New York: Guilford Press.

Lazarus, A. A. (1989). *The practice of multimodal therapy.* Baltimore: Johns Hopkins University Press.

Lazarus, A. A. (1993). Theory, subjectivity and bias: Can there be a future? *Psychotherapy, 30,* 674–677.

Lazarus, A. A. (1994). How certain boundaries and ethics diminish therapeutic effectiveness. *Ethics and Behavior, 4,* 255–261.

Lazarus, A. A. (1995). Different types of eclecticism and integration: Let's be aware of the dangers. *Journal of Psychotherapy Integration, 5,* 27–39.

Lazarus, A. A. (1996a). Fixed rules versus idiosyncratic needs. *Ethics and Behavior, 6,* 80–81.

Lazarus, A. A. (1996b). Some reflections after 40 years of trying to be an effective psythotherapist. *Psychotherapy, 33,* 142–145.

Lazarus, A. A. (1996c). The utility and futility of combining treatments in psychotherapy. *Clinical Psychology: Science and Practice, 3,* 59–68.

Lazarus, A. A. (1997). *Brief but comprehensive psychotherapy: The multimodal way.* New York: Springer.

Lazarus, A. A. (2000). Multimodal replenishment. *Professional Psychology Research and Practice, 31*(1), 93–94.

Lazarus, A. A. (2001). Multimodal therapy in clinical practice. In N. J. Smelse & P. B. Baltes (Eds.), *Encyclopedia of the social and behavioral sciences* (Vol. 15, pp. 10193–10197). Oxford, England: Elsevier Press.

Lazarus, A. A. (2002). An interview with Arnold Lazarus (M. F. Shaughnessy, Interviewer). *North American Journal of Psychology, 4*(2), 171–182.

Lazarus, A. A. (2004). Multimodal therapy. In W. E. Craighead & C. B. Nemeroff (Eds.), *The concise Corsini encyclopedia of psychiatry and behavioral science* (pp. 589–590). Hoboken, NJ: Wiley.

Lazarus, A. A. (2008). Technical eclecticism and multimodal therapy. In J. Lebow (Ed.), *Twenty-first century psychotherapists.* New York: Wiley.

Lazarus, A. A., & Zur, O. (2002). *Dual relationships and psychotherapy.* New York: Springer.

Lear, J. (2005). *Freud* (The Routledge Philosophers). New York: Routledge.

LeDoux, J. (1996). *The emotional brain.* New York: Simon & Schuster.

LeDoux, J. (2002). *Synaptic self.* New York: Viking.

Lefcourt, H. (1976). *Locus of control: Current trends in theory and research.* Hillsdale, NJ: Erlbaum.

Lefcourt, H. (1992). Durability and impact of the locus of control construct. *Psychological Bulletin, 112*(3), 411–414.

Lefcourt, H. M., Martin, R. A., & Saleh, W. E. (1984, August). Locus of control and social support: Interactive moderators of stress. *Journal of Personality and Social Psychology, 47*(2), 378–389.

Leith, G. (1974). Individual differences in learning: Interaction of personality and teaching methods. In *Personality and Academic Process* (pp. 14–25). London: Association of Educational Psychologists.

Leman, K. (2004). *The birth order book: Why you are the way you are.* New York: Revell.

Lent, R. W., & Lopez, F. G. (2002). Cognitive ties that bind. *Journal of Social and Clinical Psychology, 21*(3), 256–286.

Leone, G. (1995). Zen meditation: A psychoanalytic conceptualization. *Journal of Transpersonal Psychology, 27,* 87–94.

Lerman, H. (1992). The limits of phenomenology: A feminist critique of the humanistic personality theories. In L. S. Brown & M. Ballou (Eds.), *Personality and psychopathology.* New York: Guilford Press.

Lester, D. (1992). Cooperative/competitive strategies and locus of control. *Psychological Reports, 71*(2), 594.

Lester, D., Eleftheriou, L., & Peterson, C. A. (1992). Birth order and psychological health: A sex difference. *Personality and Individual Differences, 13,* 379–380.

Levinson, D. J., Darrow, C. N., Klein, E. B., Linson, M. H., & McKee, B. (1978). *The seasons of a man's life.* New York: Knopf.

Levinson, D. J., & Levinson, J. D. (1996). *The seasons of a woman's life.* New York: Ballantine Books.

Levitz-Jones, E. M., & Orlofsky, J. L. (1985). Separationindividualization and intimacy capacity in college women. *Journal of Personality and Social Psychology, 49*, 156–169.

Lewin, K. (1936). *Principles of topological psychology.* New York: McGraw-Hill.

Lewis, A. (1991). Developing social feeling in the young child through his play life. *Individual Psychology: Journal of Adlerian Theory, Research and Practice, 47*(1), 72–75.

Lewis, H. B. (1988, Winter). Freudian theory and new information in modern psychology. *Psychoanalytic Psychology, 5*(1), 7–22.

Lewis, J. L. (1995). Two paradigmatic approaches to borderline patients with a history of trauma. *Journal of Psychotherapy Practice and Research, 5*, 1–19.

Liang, B., Tracy, A., Taylor, C., Williams, L., Jordan, J. V., & Miller, J. B. (2002). The Relational Health Indices: A study of women's relationships. *Psychology of Women Quarterly, 26*, 25–35.

Lickliter, R., & Honeycutt, H. (2003). Developmental dynamics: Toward a biologically plausible evolutionary psychology. *Psychological Bulletin, 129*(6), 819–835.

Liebert, R. M., & Baron, R. A. (1973). Some immediate effects of televised violence on children's behavior. *Developmental Psychology, 6*, 20–41.

Lietaer, G. (2002). Sixty years of client-centered/experiential psychotherapy and counseling: Bibliographical survey of books. *Journal of Humanistic Psychology, 42*(2), 97–131.

Likierman, M. (1990). "Translation in transition": Some issues surrounding the Strachey translation of Freud's works. *International Review of Psycho-Analysis, 17*, 115–120.

Likierman, M. (1995). The debate between Anna Freud and Melanie Klein: An historical survey. *Journal of Child Psychotherapy, .*

Lindorff, D. (1995). Psyche, matter and synchronicity: A collaboration between C. G. Jung and Wolfgang Pauli. *Journal of Analytical Psychology, 40*, 571–586.

Livesley, W. J. (2001). Commentary on reconceptualizing personality disorder categories using trait dimensions. *Journal of Personality, 69*(2).

Livesley, W. J., Schroeder, M. L., Jackson, D. N., & Jang, K. L. (1994). Categorical distinctions in the study of personality disorder: Implications for classification. *Journal of Abnormal Psychology, 103*(1), 6–17.

Loehlin, J. C. (1992). *Genes and environment in personality development.* Newbury Park, CA: Sage.

Loevinger, J. (1996). In defense of the individuality of personality theories. *Psychological Inquiry, 7*, 344–346.

Loewenberg, P. (2001). Freud as a cultural subversive. *Annual of Psychoanalysis, 29*, 117–131.

Loftus, E. (1993). The reality of repressed memories. *American Psychologist, 48*, 518–537.

Lombardi, D. N., & Elcock, L. E. (1997). Freud versus Adler on dreams. *American Psychologist, 52*, 572–573.

Long, K. R. (2001, December 23). DNA auditing begs questions: Is there a pink slip in your genes? *Newark (NJ) Star-Ledger,* p. 1.

Loomis, M. E. (1991). *Dancing the wheel of psychological types.* Wilmette, IL: Chiron.

Loori, J. D. (1988). *Mountain record of Zen talks.* Boston: Shambhala.

Loori, J. D. (Ed.). (2004). *The art of just sitting: Essential writings on the Zen practice of shikantaza.* Boston: Wisdom.

Lopez, S. J., & Snyder, R. (2003). *Positive psychological assessment: A handbook of models and measures.* Washington, DC: American Psychological Association.

Lothane, Z. (2001). A response to Grünbaum's "A century of psychoanalysis critical retrospect and prospect" (and other texts): Requiem or reveille? *International Forum of Psychoanalysis, 10*(2), 113–133.

Lovaas, O. T., et al. (1966). Acquisition of imitative speech in schizophrenic children. *Science, 151*, 705–707.

Loy, D. (1992). Avoiding the void: The lack of self in psychotherapy and Buddhism. *The Journal of Transpersonal Psychology, 24*, 151–180.

Lykken, D. (1999). *Happiness: What studies of twins shows us about nature, nurture, and the happiness set point.* New York: Golden Books.

Maccoby, E. E., & Martin, J. A. (1983). Socialization in the context of the family: Parent-child interaction. In E. M. Hetherington (Ed.), *Handbook of child psychology: Socialization, personality, and social development* (Vol. 4, pp. 1–102). New York: Wiley.

Maccoby, M. (1976). *The gamesman.* New York: Simon & Schuster.

Maccoby, M. (1981). *The leader.* New York: Simon & Schuster.

MacDougall, C. (2002). Rogers's person-centered approach: Consideration for use in multicultural counseling. *Journal of Humanistic Psychology, 42*, 48–65.

MacIntyre, A. (1958). *The unconscious: A conceptual analysis.* London: Routledge & Kegan Paul.

MacIntyre, A. (1984). *After virtue* (2nd ed.). Notre Dame, IN: University of Notre Dame Press.

MacKenzie, K. R. (1996). Group psychotherapy: Managed care's reluctant bride. *Behavioral Health Management, 16*, 18–24.

Macmillan, M. (1991). *Freud evaluated: The completed arc* (Advances in Psychology 75). Amsterdam: North-Holland.

Macmillan, M. (1997). *Freud evaluated: The complete ARC.* Cambridge, MA: MIT Press.

Macy, J. (1991). *Mutual causality in Buddhism and general systems theory.* Albany: State University of New York Press.

Maezumi, T. (2001, Winter). The essence of Zen: Do it over and over and over. *Mountain Record, 19*(2), 76–78.

Magid, B. (Ed.). (1993). *Freud's case studies.* Hillsdale, NJ: Analytic Press.

Magid, B. (2005). *Ordinary mind: Exploring the common ground of Zen and psychotherapy* (2nd ed.). Somerville, MA: Wisdom.

Magnavita, J. J. (1999). *Relational therapy for personality disorders.* New York: Wiley.

Magnusson, D., & Törestad, B. (1993). A holistic view of personality: A model revisited. *Annual Review of Psychology, 44*, 427–452.

Maguire, J. (2003). *Waking up: A week inside a Zen monastery.* Woodstock, VT: Skylight Paths.

Mahers, B. A. (1991). Deception rational man and other rocks on the road to a personality psychology of real people. In P. E. Meehl (Ed.), *Matters of public interest: Vol. 2. Personality and psychopathology.* Minneapolis: University of Minnesota Press.

Mahler, B. (Ed.). (1969). *Clinical psychology and personality: The selected papers of George Kelly.* New York: Wiley.

Mahler, M. (1975). *The psychological birth of the human infant.* New York: Basic Books.

Maiello, S. (1996). Epistemological contribution of the Horney theory to group psychoanalysis. *American Journal of Psychoanalysis, 56*, 187–192.

Mair, M. (1988). Psychology as storytelling. *International Journal of Personal Construct Psychology, 1*(2), 125–137.

Maloney, A. (1999). Preference ratings of images representing archetypal themes: An empirical study of the concept of archetypes. *Journal of Analytical Psychology, 44,* 101–116.

Mancillas, A. (2006). Challenging the stereotypes about only children: A review of the literature and implications for practice. *Journal of Counseling and Development, 84*(3), 268–276.

Mancuso, J. C. (1996). Constructionism, personal construct psychology and narrative psychology. *Theory and Psychology, 6,* 47–70.

Mansfield, V., & Spiegelman, J. M. (1991). The opposites in quantum physics and Jungian psychology: I. Theoretical foundations. *Journal of Analytical Psychology, 36*(3), 267–287.

Marcia, J. E. (1966). Development and validation of ego-identity status. *Journal of Personality and Social Psychology, 49,* 156–169.

Marcia, J. E. (1980). Identity in adolescence. In J. Adelson (Ed.), *Handbook of adolescent psychology.* New York: Wiley.

Margolis, D. P. (1989). Freud and his mother. *Modern Psychoanalysis, 14,* 37–56.

Marin, P. (1975). The new narcissism. *Harper's* (October), 45–56.

Markova, I. (1992). On solos, duets, quartets, and quintets: A response to Gardner. *New Ideas in Psychology, 10*(2), 215–221.

Markstrom-Adams, C. (1992). A consideration of intervening factors in adolescent identity formation. In G. R. Adams, T. P. Gullotta, & R. Montemayor (Eds.), *Adolescent identity formation. Advances in adolescent development* (Vol. 4, pp. 173–192). Newbury Park, CA: Sage.

Markus, H. R., & Kitayama, S. (1991). Culture and the self: Implications for cognition, emotion, and motivation. *Psychological Review, 98,* 224–253.

Maruna, S. (1997). Going straight. In A. Lieblich & R. Josselson (Eds.), *The narrative study of lives* (Vol. 5, pp. 59–93). Thousand Oaks, CA: Sage.

Masling, J. M., Rabie, L., & Blondheim, S. H. (1967). Obesity, level of aspiration, and Rorschach and TAT measures of oral dependence. *Journal of Consulting Psychology, 31,* 233–239.

Maslow, A. (1970). *Motivation and personality* (2nd ed.). New York: Harper & Row.

Masse, G. (1994). From complex to spirit: Jung and the spiritual dimension. *Cahiers Jungiens de Psychoanalyse, 80,* 81–94.

Masson, J. M. (1983). *The assault on the truth: Freud's suppression of the seduction theory.* New York: Farrar, Straus, & Giroux.

Matthews, G., & Gilliland, K. (2001). Personality, biology, and cognitive science. *Personality and Individual Differences, 30,* 353–362.

Mattmiller, B. (1998). UW research bringing emotions into focus. *Wisconsin Week, 13,* 16.

Mattmiller, B. (2000). Brain study sheds light on impulsive violence. Retrieved October 14, 2003, from http://www.news.wisc.edu/view.html?id=5121

May, R. (1953). *Man's search for himself.* New York: Norton.

May, R. (1967). *Psychology and the human dilemma.* New York: Van Nostrand Reinhold.

May, R. (1969). *Love and will.* New York: Norton.

May, R. (1972). *Power and innocence.* New York: Norton.

May, R. (1975). *The courage to create.* New York: Norton.

May, R. (1977). *The meaning of anxiety.* New York: Norton.

May, R. (1981). *Freedom and destiny.* New York: Norton.

May, R. (1983). *The discovery of being.* New York: Norton.

May, R. (1991). *The cry for myth.* New York: Norton.

May, R., Angel, E., & Ellenberger, H. F. (Eds.). (1958). *Existence: A new dimension in psychiatry and psychology.* New York: Basic Books.

Mayer, E. L. (1996). Erik H. Erikson on bodies, gender, and development. *Psychoanalysis and Contemporary Thought, 19,* 237–257.

Mayer, E. L. (1998). Erik Erikson on bodies, gender, and development. In R. S. Wallenstein & L. Goldberger (Eds.), *Ideas and identities: The life and work of Erik Erikson* (pp. 79–98). Madison, CT: International Universities Press.

McAdams, D. P. (1992a). Unity and purpose in human lives: The emergence of identity as a life story. In R. A. Zucker, A. I. Rabin, J. Aronoff, & S. J. Frank (Eds.), *Personality structure in the life course: Essays on personology in the Murray tradition* (pp. 323–375). New York: Springer.

McAdams, D. P. (1992b). The five-factor model in personality: A critical appraisal. *Journal of Personality, 60,* 329–361.

McAdams, D. P. (1993). *The stories we live by: Personal myths and the making of the self.* New York: William Morrow.

McAdams, D. P. (1994). A psychology of the stranger. *Psychological Inquiry, 5,* 145–148.

McAdams, D. P. (1995). What do we know when we know a person? *Journal of Personality, 63,* 366–396.

McAdams, D. P. (1996a). Personality, modernity, and the storied self: A contemporary framework for studying persons. *Psychological Inquiry, 4,* 295–321.

McAdams, D. P. (1996b). Alternative futures for the study of human individuality. *Journal of Research in Personality, 30,* 374–388.

McAdams, D. P. (1997). Three voices of Erik Erikson. *Contemporary Psychology, 42,* 575–578.

McAdams, D. P. (2001a). *The person: An integrated introduction to personality psychology.* New York: Harcourt.

McAdams, D. P. (2001b). The psychology of life stories. *Review of General Psychology, 5*(2), 100–122.

McAdams, D. P. (2001c). Generativity in midlife. In M. Lachman (Ed.), *Handbook of midlife development* (pp. 395–445). New York: Wiley.

McAdams, D. P. (2006). *The redemptive self: Stories Americans live by.* New York: Oxford University Press.

McAdams, D. P., & de St. Aubin, E. (1992). A theory of generativity and its assessment through self-report, behavioral acts, and narrative themes in autobiography. *Journal of Personality and Social Psychology, 62,* 1003–1015.

McAdams, D. P., & de St. Aubin, E. (Eds.) (1998). *Generativity and adult development.* Washington, DC: American Psychological Association.

McAdams, D. P., Diamond, A., de St. Aubin, E., & Mansfield, E. (1997). Stories of commitment: The psychosocial construction of generative lives. *Journal of Personality and Social Psychology, 72,* 678–694.

McAdams, D. P., & Ochberg, R. C. (Eds.). (1988, March). Special Issue: Psychobiography and life narratives. *Journal of Personality, 56*(1).

McAdams, D. P., & Pals, J. L. (2006). A new big five: Fundamental principles for an integrative science of personality. *American Psychologist 61*(3): 204–271, p. 212.

McCabe, R., & Priebe, S. (2004). The therapeutic relationship in the treatment of severe mental illness. *International Journal of Social Psychology, 50,* 115–128.

McCartney, K. (Rapporteur). (1993). Group report: What can twin studies contribute to the understanding of personality? In T. J. Bouchard Jr. & P. Propping (Eds.), *Twins as a tool of behavioral genetics.* New York: Wiley.

McClelland, D. C. (1961). *The achieving society.* New York: Free Press.

McClelland, D. C. (1996). Does the field of psychology have a future? *Journal of Research in Personality, 30,* 429–434.

McClelland, D. C., Atkinson, J. W., Clark, R. A., & Lowell, E. L. (1953). *The achievement motive.* New York: Appleton-Century-Crofts.

McCrae, R. R. (1992). The Five-Factor Model: Issues and applications. *Journal of Personality, 60*(2).

McCrae, R. R. (1993–1994). Openness of experience as a basic dimension of personality. *Imagination, Cognition and Personality, 13,* 39–55.

McCrae, R. R. (1996). Integrating the levels of personality. *Psychological Inquiry, 7,* 353–356.

McCrae, R. R., & Allik, J. (Eds.). (2002). *The five-factor model of personality across cultures.* New York: Kluwer Academic.

McCrae, R. R., & Costa, P. T. (1989). Validation of the five-factor model of personality across instruments and observers. *Journal of Personality and Social Psychology, 52,* 81–90.

McCrae, R. R., & Costa, P. T. (1990). *Personality in adulthood.* New York: Guilford Press.

McCrae, R. R., & Costa, P. T., Jr. (1985). Updating Norman's adequate taxonomy: Intelligence and personality dimensions in natural language and in questionnaires. *Journal of Personality and Social Psychology, 49,* 710–721.

McCrae, R. R., & Costa, P. T., Jr. (1987). Validation of the five-factor model of personality across instruments and observers. *Journal of Personality and Social Psychology, 52,* 81–90.

McCrae, R. R., & Costa, P. T., Jr. (1997). Personality trait structure as a human universal. *American Psychologist, 52,* 509–516.

McCrae, R. R., & Costa, P. T., Jr. (1999). A five-factor theory of personality. In L. A. Pervin & O. P. John (Eds.), *Handbook of personality* (2nd ed., pp. 139–153). New York: Guilford Press.

McCrae, R. R., & Costa, P. T., Jr. (2003). *Personality in adulthood: A Five-Factor perspective* (2nd ed.). New York: Guilford Press.

McCrae, R. R., Costa, P. T., Jr., del Pilar, G. H., Rolland, J. P., & Parker, W. D. (1998). Cross-cultural assessment of the Five-Factor Model: The revised NEO Personality Inventory. *Journal of Cross-Cultural Psychology, 29,* 171–188.

McCrae, R. R., Costa, P. T., Jr., Lima, M. P., Simoes, A., Ostendork, F., Angleitner, A., et al. (1999). Age differences in personality across the adult lifespan: Parallels in five cultures. *Developmental Psychology, 35,* 466–477.

McCrae, R. R., & Terracciano, A. (2005a). Universal features of personality traits from the observer's perspective. *Journal of Personality and Social Psychology, 88*(33), 547–561.

McCrae, R. R., & Terracciano, A. (2005b). Personality profiles of cultures. *Journal of Personality and Social Psychology, 89*(3), 407–425.

McKay, J., Pyke, S. W., & Goranson, R. (1984, November–December). Whatever happened to "inner-space": A failure to replicate. *International Journal of Women's Studies, 7*(5), 387–396.

McLaughlin, R. J., & Eysenck, J. J. (1967). Extraversion, neuroticism, and paired-associate learning. *Journal of Experimental Research in Personality, 2,* 128–132.

Meares, R. (1996). The psychology of self: An update. *Australian and New Zealand Journal of Psychiatry, 30,* 312–316.

Meichenbaum, D., & Deffenbacher, J. L. (1988). Stress inoculation training. *The Counseling Psychologist, 16,* 69–90.

Meissner, W. W. (2000). *Freud and psychoanalysis.* Notre Dame, IN: University of Notre Dame Press.

Mencher, J. (1997). Intimacy in lesbian relationships: A critical reexamination of fusion. In J. V. Jordan (Ed.), *Women's growth in diversity* (pp. 311–330). New York: Guilford Press.

Mendoza-Denton, R., Ayduk, O., Mischel, W., Shoda, Y., & Testa, A. (2001). Person X situation interactionism in self-encoding (I am . . . When . . .). *Journal of Personality and Social Psychology, 70,* 856–867.

Menec, V. H., & Chipperfield, J. G. (1997). Remaining active in later life. *Journal of Aging and Health, 9*(1), 105–125.

Mervielde, I., & Asendorpf, J. B. (2000). Variable-centred and person-centred approaches to childhood personality. In S. E. Hampson (Ed.), *Advances in personality psychology.* Philadelphia: Psychology Press, Taylor & Francis Group.

Metzger, R. (1996). The Buddhist six-worlds model of consciousness and reality. *Journal of Transpersonal Psychology, 28,* 155–166.

Miccolis, G. (1996). Sociocultural influences in the theory of Karen Horney. *American Journal of Psychoanalysis, 56,* 141–147.

Michalski, R. L., & Shackelford, T. K. (2002). An attempted replication of the relationships between birth order and personality. *Journal of Research in Personality, 36,* 182–188.

Mickelson, K. D., Kessler, R. C., & Shaver, P. R. (1997). Adult attachment in a nationally representative sample. *Journal of Personality and Social Psychology, 73,* 1092–1106.

Mikulincer, M., Shaver, P. R., Gillath, O., & Nitzberg, R. A. (2005). Attachment, caregiving, and altruism. *Journal of Personality and Social Psychology, 89*(5), 817–839.

Millán, S., & Gojman, S. (2000). The legacy of Fromm in Mexico. *International Forum of Psychoanalysis, 9,* 207–215.

Miller, C. (1991). Self-actualization and the consciousness revolution. Special Issue: Handbook of self-actualization. *Journal of Social Behavior and Personality, 6*(5), 109–126.

Miller, J. (1976). *Toward a new psychology of women.* Boston: Beacon Press.

Miller, J., Fletcher, K., & Kabat-Zinn, J. (1995). Three-year follow-up and clinical implications of a mindfulness meditation-based stress reduction intervention in the treatment of anxiety disorders. *General Hospital Psychiatry, 17,* 192–200.

Miller, J. B. (1984). *The development of women's sense of self.* Work in Progress Series. Stone Center for Developmental Studies, Wellesley College, Wellesley, MA.

Miller, J. B. (1986). *What do we mean by relationships?* Work in Progress Series, no. 22. Stone Center for Developmental Studies, Wellesley College, Wellesley, MA.

Miller, J. B. (1991). The development of women's sense of self. In J. V. Jordan, A. G. Kaplan, J. B. Miller, I. P. Stiver, & J. L. Surrey (Eds.), *Women's growth in connection: Writings from the Stone Center* (pp. 11–26). New York: Guilford Press.

Miller, J. B. (2003). *Telling the truth about power.* Work in Progress Series. Stone Center for Developmental Studies, Wellesley College, Wellesley, MA.

Miller, J. B. (2006). Forced choices, false choices. *Research and Action Report, 27*(2). (Wellesley Centers for Women)

Miller, J. B., Jordan, J., Stiver, I. P., Walker, M., Surrey, J., & Eldridge, N. S. (1999). *Therapists' authenticity.* Work in Progress Series. Stone Center for Developmental Studies, Wellesley College, Wellesley, MA.

Miller, J. B., & Stiver, I. P. (1997). *The healing connection: How women form relationships in therapy and in life.* Boston: Beacon Press.

Miller, J. B., & Surrey, J. L. (1997). Revisioning women's anger: The personal and the global. In J. V. Jordan (Ed.), *Women's growth in diversity* (pp. 199–216). New York: Guilford Press.

Miller, J. D., & Lyman, D. R. (2003). Psychopathy and the Five-Factor Model of personality. *Journal of Personality Assessment, 81*(2), 168–178.

Miller, N. E. (1944). Experimental studies of conflict. In J. M. Hunt (Ed.), *Personality and the behavior disorders* (pp. 431–465). New York: Ronald Press.

Miller, N. E. (1951). Comments on theoretical models: Illustrated by the development of a theory of conflict behavior. *Journal of Personality, 20,* 82–100.

Miller, N. E. (1959). Liberalization of basic S-R concepts: Extensions to conflict behavior, motivation, and social learning. In S. Koch (Ed.), *Psychology: A study of a science* (Vol. 2). New York: McGraw-Hill.

Miller, N. E. (1982). Obituary of John Dollard (1900–1980). *American Psychologist, 37,* 587–588.

Miller, N. J. (1991, Fall/Winter). To study the self. *The Ten Directions,* pp. 35–37.

Miller, P., Potts, R., Fung, H., & Hoogstra, L. (1990). Narrative practices and the social construction of self in childhood. *American Psychologist, 17*(2) 292–311.

Miller, R. L., & Mulligan, R. D. (2002). Terror management: The effects of mortality salience and locus of control on risk-taking behaviors. *Personality and Individual Differences, 33,* 1202–1214.

Milliones, J. (1980). The Pittsburgh project: Construction of a Black consciousness measure. *Psychotherapy: Theory, Research, and Practice, 17*(2), 175–182.

Millon, T. (2000a). *Personality disorders in modern life.* New York: Wiley.

Millon, T. (2000b). Reflections on the future of DSM axis II. *Journal of Personality Disorders, 14*(1), 30–41.

Millon, T. (2003). It's time to rework the blueprints: Building a science for clinical psychology. *American Psychologist, 58*(11), 949–970.

Minami, M., & McCabe, A. (1991). Haiku as a discourse regulation device: A stanza analysis of Japanese children's personal narratives. *Language in Society, 20*(4), 577–599.

Mindell, A. (2000). *The quantum mind.* Portland, OR: Lao Tse Press.

Miranda, A. O., Goodman, E. D., & Kern, R. M. (1996). Similarities between social interest and contemporary definitions of corporate leadership. *Individual Psychology: Journal of Adlerian Theory, Research and Practice,* 261–269.

Mischel, W. (1968). *Personality and assessment.* New York: Wiley.

Mischel, W. (1973). Toward a cognitive social learning reconception of personality. *Psychological Review, 80,* 252–283.

Mischel, W. (1983). Alternatives in the pursuit of the predictability and consistency of persons: Stable data that yield unstable interpretations. *Journal of Personality, 51,* 578–604.

Mischel, W. (2004). Toward an integrative science of the person. *Annual Review of Psychology, 55,* 1–22.

Mischel, W., & Shoda, Y. (1995). A cognitive-affective system theory of personality: Reconceptualizing situations, dispositions, dynamics, and invariance in personality structure. *Psychological Review, 102,* 246–268.

Mitchell, J. (1974). *Psychoanalysis and feminism: Freud, Reich, Laing and women.* New York: Vintage.

Mitchell, J. (1991). "Deconstructing difference: Gender, splitting and transitional space": Commentary. *Psychoanalytic Dialogues, 1*(3), 353–357.

Mogenson, G. (1990). The resurrection of the dead: A Jungian approach to the mourning process. *Journal of Analytical Psychology, 35*(3), 317–333.

Mollon, P. (2002) *Releasing the self: The healing legacy of Heinz Kohut.* London: Whurr.

Monaghan, P. (1999, December 10). A leading gender theorist explains how feelings shape who we are. *The Chronicle of Higher Education,* pp. A21–22.

Monte, C. F. (1999). *Beneath the mask.* New York: Harcourt Brace.

Moore, J. (1992). On private events and theoretical terms. *Journal of Mind and Behavior, 13*(4), 329–345.

Moraglia, G. (1994). C. G. Jung and the psychology of adult development. *Journal of Analytical Psychology, 39,* 55–75.

Morita, M. (1998). *Morita therapy and the true nature of anxiety-based disorders (Shinkeishitsu).* (Akihisa Kondo, Trans.). Albany: State University of New York Press.

Morreale, Don (Ed.). (1998). *The complete guide to Buddhist America.* Boston: Shambhala.

Morris, E. K., Lazo, J. F., & Smith, N. G. (2004). Whether, when, and why Skinner published on biological participation and behavior. *The Behavior Analyst, 27,* 153–169.

Morse, S. J. (2006). Addiction, genetics, and criminal responsibility. *Law and Contemporary Problems, 6*(2), 165–208.

Morvay, Z. (1999). Horney, Zen, and the Real Self. *American Journal of Psychoanalysis, 59*(1), 25–35.

Mosig, Y. D. (1988). Karate-do and the actualization of enlightenment. *Udumbara: Journal of Zen Practice, 4*(2)/5(1), 45–50.

Mosig, Y. D. (1989). Wisdom and compassion: What the Buddha taught. *Theoretical and Philosophical Psychology, 9*(2), 27–36.

Mosig, Y. D. (1990). Zen meditation and the art of kobudo. *U.S.K.A. Forum, 1*(1), 2–3.

Mosig, Y. D. (1991). A guide to Zen practice. *U.S.K.A. Forum, 2*(1), 2–3.

Mosig, Y. D. (2006). Conceptions of the self in Western and Eastern psychology. *Journal of Theoretical and Philosophical Psychology, 26*(1/2), 39–50.

Mozdzierz, G. J., & Krauss, H. H. (1996). The embeddedness of Alfred Adler in modern psychology. *Individual Psychology, 52*(3), 224–236.

Mruk, C. J. (1989). Phenomenological psychology and the computer revolution: Friend, foe, or opportunity? *Journal of Phenomenological Psychology, 20*(1), 20–39.

Mruk, C. J., & Hartzell, J. (2006). *Zen and psychotherapy: Integrating traditional and non-traditional approaches* (2nd ed.). New York: Springer.

Mueller, E., & Tingley, E. (1990). The Bears' Picnic: Children's representations of themselves and their families. *New Directions for Child Development, 48,* 47–65.

Murk, D., & Addleman, J. (1992). Relations among moral reasoning, locus of control, and demographic variables among college students. *Psychological Reports, 70*(2), 467–476.

Murphy, M., & Donovan, S. (1988). *The physical and psychological effects of meditation.* San Rafael, CA: Esalen Institute.

Murray, H. A. (1938). *Explorations in personality.* New York: Oxford University Press.

Murray, J. B. (1990). Review of research on the Myers-Briggs Type Indicator. *Perceptual and Motor Skills, 70,* 1187–1202.

Myers, I. B., & McCaulley, M. H. (1985). *A guide to the development and use of the Myers-Briggs Type Indicator.* Palo Alto, CA: Consulting Psychologists Press.

Myyra, J. (1992). The great mother. In K. Bjorkqvist & P. Niemela (Eds.), *Of mice and women: Aspects of female aggression* (pp. 263–271). San Diego, CA: Academic Press.

Naidu, R. (1991). Etic principles in psychology: An evaluation of the myth in support of indigenous psychologies. *Indian Journal of Current Psychological Research, 5*(2), 93–100.

Narayan, C. (1990). Birth order and narcissism. *Psychological Reports, 67*(3, Pt. 2), 1184–1186.

Nelson-Jones, R. (2001). *Theory and practice of counseling and therapy.* New York: Continuum.

Neubauer, P., & Neubauer, A. (1990). *Nature's thumbprint: The new genetics of personality.* Reading, MA: Addison-Wesley.

Neufeldt, A. (1989). Applying psychology: Some real world possibilities for scientists and practitioners. *Canadian Psychology, 30*(4), 681–691.

Nichols, M. P., & Schwartz, R. C. (1998). *Family therapy: Concepts and methods* (4th ed.). Boston: Allyn & Bacon.

Nicholson, I. A. (2001). "Giving up maleness": Abraham Maslow, masculinity, and the boundaries of psychology. *History of Psychology, 4*(1), 79–91.

Nicholson, I. A. M. (2000). "A coherent datum of perception." *Journal of the History of the Behavioral Sciences, 36*(4), 463–470.

Nielsen, S. L., & Ellis, A. (1994). A discussion with Albert Ellis: Reason, emotion and religion. *Journal of Psychology and Christianity,* 13, 327–341.

Noble, B. P. (1993, February 21). Infant bonding and guilty mothers. *New York Times,* p. 25.

Noel, D. C. (1991). Traveling with Jung toward an archetypal ecology. *Quadrant, 24*(1), 83–91.

Norcross, J. (2002). *Psychotherapy: Relations that work.* London: Oxford University Press.

Norcross, J. C. (1986). Handbook of eclectic psychotherapy. New York: Brunner/Mazel.

Norcross, J. C., & Goldfried, M. R. (Eds.). (2005). *Handbook of psychotherapy integration.* New York: Oxford University Press.

Norman, W. T. (1963). Toward an adequate taxonomy of personality attributes. *Journal of Abnormal and Social Psychology, 66,* 574–583.

Nutt, A. E. (2005, December 18). The militant mind. *Sunday Star Ledger,* sec. 1, pp. 1, 18–19.

Nybourg, H. (Ed.). (1997). *The scientific study of human nature: Tribute to Hans J. Eysenck at eighty.* New York: Pergamon.

Oatley, K. (1992). Not psychologists but psychology: A response to Gardner. *New Ideas in Psychology, 10*(2), 207–214.

O'Connor, B. P., & Dyce, J. A. (2002). Tests of general and specific models of personality disorder configuration. In P. T. Costa Jr. & T. A. Widiger (Eds.), *Personality disorders and the Five-Factor Model of personality* (pp. 223–248). Washington, DC: American Psychological Association.

O'Donohue, W., Fisher, J. E., & Hayes, S. C. (Eds.). (2003). *Cognitive behavior therapy.* Hoboken, NJ: Wiley.

O'Hara, M. (1992). Relational humanism: A psychology for a pluralistic world. *Humanistic Psychologist, 20*(2–3), 439–446.

O'Hara, M. (1995). Carl Rogers: Scientist and mystic: *Journal of Humanistic Psychology, 35,* 40–53.

O'Keefe, E. J., & Castaldo, C. (1981). Multimodal management: A systematic and holistic approach for the 80's. *Proceedings of the Marist College Symposium on Local Government Productivity.* Poughkeepsie, NY.

Okumura, S. (Ed.). (1985). *Shikantaza.* Kyoto, Japan: Kyoto Soto-Zen Center.

Okumura, S. (1997, May 1). Untitled. *Sanshin Zen Community Newsletter, 2,* 1.

Okumura, S. (2000, Summer). To study the self. *Mountain Record, 18*(4), 57–65.

Orlofsky, J. L. (1976). Intimacy status: Relationship of interpersonal perception. *Journal of Youth and Adolescence, 5,* 73–88.

Ornstein, A. (1993). Little Hans. In B. Magid (Ed.), *Freud's case studies.* Hillsdale, NJ: Analytic Press.

Ornstein, R. (1997). *The right mind: Making sense of hemispheres.* New York: Harcourt Brace.

Ornstein, R. E. (1977). *The psychology of consciousness.* New York: Harcourt Brace Jovanovich.

Ortmeyer, D. H. (1998). Revisiting Erich Fromm. *International Forum of Psychoanalysis, 7*(1), 25–33.

Overholser, J. C. (2003). Rational-emotive behavior therapy: An interview with Albert Ellis. *Journal of Contemporary Psychotherapy, 33*(3), 187–204.

Ozer, D. J. (1999). Four principles for personality assessment. In L. A. Pervin & O. P. John (Eds.), *Handbook of personality: Theory and research* (pp. 671–686). New York: Guilford Press.

Packer, M. (1992). Toward a postmodern psychology of moral action and moral development. In W. Kurtines, M. Azmitia, & J. Gewirtz (Eds.), *The role of values in psychology and human development* (pp. 30–59). New York: Wiley.

Padesky, C. A., & Beck, A. T. (2003). Science and philosophy: Comparison of cognitive therapy and rational emotive behavior therapy. *Journal of Cognitive Psychotherapy, 17*(3), 211–224.

Page, R. C., & Berkow, D. N. (1991). Concepts of the self: Western and Eastern perspectives. *Journal of Multicultural Counseling and Development, 19,* 83–93.

Panksepp, J., & Panksepp, J. B. (2000). The seven sins of evolutionary psychology. *Evolution and Cognition, 6*(2), 108–131.

Papini, D. R., Micka, J. C., & Barnett, J. K. (1989). Perceptions of intrapsychic and extrapsychic functioning as basis of adolescent ego identity statuses. *Journal of Adolescent Research, 4*(4), 462–482.

Parens, E., Chapman, A. R., & Press, N. (Eds.). (2006). *Wrestling with behavioral genetics.* Baltimore: Johns Hopkins University Press.

Parham, T. A., & Helms, J. E. (1985). Attitudes of racial identity and self-esteem of Black students. *Journal of College Student Personnel, 26*(2), 194–203.

Paris, B. J. (1994). *Karen Horney: A psychoanalyst's search for self-understanding.* New Haven, CT: Yale University Press.

Paris, B. J. (1996). Introduction to Karen Horney. *American Journal of Psychoanalysis, 56,* 135–140.

Parker, M. J., Guarino, A. J., & Smith, R. W. (2002). Self-efficacy in a sample of education majors and teachers. *Psychological Reports, 91*(3), 935–940.

Patrick, E. (2005). An alternative to rats and pigeons. *Counselling and Psychotherapy Journal, 16*(5), 19–22.

Patterson, S. J., Sochting, I., & Marcia, J. E. (1992). The inner space and beyond: Women and identity. In G. R. Adams,

T. P. Gullotta, & R. Montemayor (Eds.), *Adolescent identity formation: Advances in adolescent development* (Vol. 4, pp. 9–24). Newbury Park, CA: Sage.

Paul, R. A. (1989). Psychoanalytic anthropology. *Annual Review of Anthropology, 18,* 177–202.

Paul, R. A. (1992). Bettelheim's contribution to anthropology. *Educating the emotions: Bruno Bettelheim and psychoanalytic development.* New York: Plenum Press.

Paunonen, S. V. (2003). Big Five Factors of personality and replicated predictions of behavior. *Journal of Personality and Social Psychology, 84*(2), 411–424.

Paunonen, S. V., & Jackson, D. N. (2000). What is beyond the big five? Plenty! *Journal of Personality, 68*(5), 821–835.

Pavlov, I. P. (1927). *Conditional reflexes.* London: Routledge & Kegan Paul.

Pawelski, J. O. (2004). *The promise of positive psychology for the assessment of character outcomes.* Retrieved April 1, 2007, from www.collegevalues.org/proceedings

Pelham, B. W. (1993). The idiographic nature of human personality: Examples of the idiographic self-concept. *Journal of Personality and Social Psychology, 64*(4), 665–677.

Perrez, M. (1991). The difference between everyday knowledge, ideology, and scientific knowledge. *New Ideas in Psychology, 9,* 227–231.

Pervin, L. A. (1994). A critical analysis of current trait theory. *Psychological Inquiry, 5,* 103–113.

Pervin, L. A. (1996). Personality: A view of the future based on a look at the past. *Journal of Research in Personality, 30,* 309–318.

Pervin, L. A., & John, O. P. (1997). *Personality theory and research* (7th ed.). New York: Wiley.

Pervin, L. A., & John, O. P. (Eds.). (1999). *Handbook of personality: Theory and research* (2nd ed.). New York: Guilford Press.

Pervin, L. A. (2003). *The science of personality* (2nd ed.). New York: Oxford University Press.

Peterson, C., & Seligman, M. E. (2003). *Values in Action (VIA) Classification of Strengths Manual.* Retrieved from www.positivepsychology.org/taxonomy.htm

Pettigrew, T. (1999). Gordon Willard Allport: A tribute. *Journal of Social Issues, 55*(3), 415–427.

Phinney, J. S. (1992). The multigroup ethnic identity measure. *Journal of Adolescent Research, 7*(2), 156–176.

Pietikainen, P. (1998). Archetypes as symbolic forms. *Journal of Analytical Psychology, 43,* 325–343.

Pine, F. (1994). The era of separation-individuation. *Psychoanalytic Inquiry, 14,* 4–24.

Pine, F. (2004). Mahler's concepts of "symbiosis and separation-individuation: Revisted, reevaluated, refined. *Journal of the American Psychoanalytic Association, 52*(20), 511–533.

Pinquart, M., & Sorenson, S. (2001). Influences on loneliness in older adults: A meta-analysis. *Basic and Applied Social Psychology, 23,* 245–266.

Pittenger, D. J. (2005). Cautionary comments regarding the Myers-Briggs Type Indicator. *Consulting Psychology Journal: Practice and Research, 57*(3), 210–225.

Piyadassi, T. (1974). *The Buddha's ancient path.* Kandy, Sri Lanka: Buddhist Publication Society.

Place, U. (1988). What went wrong? *Counselling Psychology Quarterly, 1*(2–3), 307–309.

Plomin, R., Chipuer, H. M., & Loehlin, J. C. (1990). Behavioral genetics and personality. In L. A. Pervin (Ed.), *Handbook of personality: Theory and research* (pp. 225–243). New York: Guilford Press.

Pollack, A. (2006, September 12). The wide, wild world of genetic testing, *New York Times,* p. G4.

Portman, T. A., & Garrett, M. T. (2005). Beloved women: Nurturing the sacred fire of leadership from an American Indian perspective. *Journal of Counseling and Development, 83*(3), 284–291.

Potrikus, A. S. (2003, September 21). World wide, girls have surged ahead of boys academically, report says. *Newark (NJ) Star-Ledger,* sec. 1, p. 7.

Potter, J., & Wetherell, M. (1992). On the literary solution: A response to Gardner. *New Ideas in Psychology, 10*(2), 223–227.

Powell, L. (1992). The cognitive underpinnings of coronary-prone behaviors. *Cognitive Therapy and Research, 16*(2), 123–142.

Power, M. (1988). Seven sins of behaviourism. *Counselling Psychology Quarterly, 1*(2–3), 279–286.

Power, M. (2000). Freud and the unconscious. *The Psychologist, 13*(12), 612–614.

Power, T., & Chapleski, M. (1986). Childrearing and impulse control in toddlers: A naturalistic investigation. *Developmental Psychology, 22,* 271–275.

Privette, G. (1986, April). From peak performance and peak experience to failure and misery. *Journal of Social Behavior and Personality, 1*(2), 233–243.

Prosky, P. S., & Keith, D. V. (2003). *Family therapy as an alternative to medication.* New York: Brunner-Routledge.

Prouty-Lyness, A. M. (Ed.). (2003). *Feminist perspectives in medical family therapy.* New York: Haworth Press.

Puhakka, K. (1998). Dissolving the self: Rinzai Zen training at an American monastery. *Journal of Transpersonal Psychology, 30*(2), 135–160.

Puhakka, K. (1999). Ken Wilber: Mapping the evolution of consciousness. In D. Moss (Ed.), *Humanistic and transpersonal psychology.* Westport, CT: Greenwood Press.

Puhan, B. N., & Sahoo, F. M. (1991, October). Indigenization of psychological studies: Research agenda. *Indian Journal of Current Psychological Research, 6*(2), 101–107.

Pyszczynski, T., Solomon, S., & Greenberg, J. (2003). *In the wake of 9/11: The psychology of terror.* Washington, DC: American Psychological Association.

Quinn, S. (1994). Awakened to life: Sources of independence in the girlhood of Karen Horney. In M. Berger (Ed.), *New concepts of feminine psychology.* New York: Brunner/Mazel.

Rafaeli-Mor, E., & Steinberg, J. (2002). Self-complexity and well-being: A review and research synthesis. *Personality and Social Psychology Review, 6*(1), 31–58.

Rahula, W. (1974). *What the Buddha taught.* New York: Grove Press.

Ramachandran, V. S. (2000, May 29). Mirror neurons and imitation learning as the driving force behind "the great leap forward" in human evolution. *Edge.*

Rapaport, D. (1953). A critique of Dollard and Miller's *Personality and psychotherapy. American Journal of Orthopsychiatry, 23,* 204–208.

Raskin, J. D. (1995). On ethics in personal construct theory. *Humanistic Psychologist, 23,* 97–114.

Raskin, J. D. (2001, April). The modern, the postmodern, and George Kelly's personal construct psychology. *American Psychologist,* p. 368.

Rattner, J. (1983). Alfred Adler. New York: Ungar.

Reichlin, R. E., & Niederehe, G. (1980). Early memories: A comprehensive bibliography. *Journal of Individual Psychology, 36*(2), 209–218.

Restak, R. (2003). *The naked brain.* New York: Holtzbrinck.

Retief, A. (1986, September). The need for theory development in psychology: Some care studies. *South African Journal of Psychology, 16*(3), 71–78.

Retief, A. (1989). The debate about the relevance of South African psychology: A metatheoretical imperative. *South African Journal of Psychology, 19*(2), 75–83.

Revkin, A. C. (2007, October 4). A new measure of well-being from a happy little country. *New York Times,* p. 5.

Reynolds, D. (1995). *A handbook for constructive living.* New York: William Morrow.

Reynolds, D. K. (1976). *Morita psychotherapy.* Berkeley: University of California Press.

Reynolds, D. K. (1980). *The quiet therapies: Japanese pathways to personal growth.* Honolulu: University of Hawaii Press.

Rhee, S. H., & Waldman, I. D. (2002). Genetic and environmental influences on antisocial behavior: A meta-analysis of twin and adoption studies. *Psychological Bulletin, 128*(3), 490–529.

Rhymer, B. (1988). *Morita-Psychotherapie und Zen-Buddhismus.* Zurich, Switzerland: Volkerkundemuseum der Universitat Zurich.

Richards, A. D. (1990). The future of psychoanalysis: The past, present, and future of psychoanalytic theory. *Psychoanalytic Quarterly, 59,* 347–369.

Ricoeur, P. (1970). *Freud and philosophy.* New Haven, CT: Yale University Press.

Ridley, M. (2003, June 2). What makes you who you are? *Time,* pp. 55–63.

Riemann, R. (1990). The bipolarity of personal constructs. *International Journal of Personal Construct Psychology, 3*(2), 149–165.

Rizzetto, D. E. (2006). *Waking up to what you do: A Zen practice for meeting every situation with intelligence and compassion* (2nd ed.). Boston: Shambhala.

Rizzolatti, G., & Craighero, L. (2004). The mirror-neuron system. *Annual Review of Neuroscience, 27,* 169–192.

Robb, C. (2006). *This changes everything: The relational revolution in psychology.* New York: Farrar, Straus and Giroux.

Roberts, B. W., & Del Vecchio, W. F. (2000). The rank-order consistency of personality traits from childhood to old age: A quantitative review of longitudinal studies. *Psychological Bulletin, 126,* 3–25.

Roberts, T. K., Jackson, L. J., & Phelps, R. (1980). Lazarus' multimodal therapy model applied to an institutional setting. *Professional Psychology, 11,* 150–156.

Robertson, R., & Combs, A. (Eds.). (1995). *Chaos theory in psychology and the life sciences.* Mahwah, NJ: Erlbaum.

Robinson, F. G. (1992). *Love's story told: A life of Henry A. Murray.* Cambridge, MA: Harvard University Press.

Robinson, P. (1993). *Freud and his critics.* Berkeley: University of California Press.

Rodgers, J. L., Cleveland, H. H., van den Oord, E., & Rowe, D. C. (2000). Resolving the debate over birth order, family size, and intelligence. *American Psychologist, 55,* 599–612.

Rogers, C. R. (1951). *Client-centered therapy: Its current practice, implications, and theory.* Boston: Houghton Mifflin.

Rogers, C. R. (1959). A theory of therapy, personality, and interpersonal relationships as developed in the client-centered framework. In S. Koch (Ed.), *Psychology: A study of a science* (Vol. 3). New York: McGraw-Hill.

Rogers, C. R. (1961). *On becoming a person.* Boston: Houghton Mifflin.

Rogers, C. R. (1963). The concept of a fully functioning person. *Psychotherapy: Theory, Research, and Practice, 1*(1), 17–26.

Rogers, C. R. (1964). Toward a modern approach to values: The valuing process in the mature person. *Journal of Abnormal and Social Psychology, 68,* 160–167.

Rogers, C. R. (1965). Intellectualizing psychotherapy. *Contemporary Psychology, 1,* 355–358.

Rogers, C. R. (1980). *A way of being.* Boston: Houghton Mifflin.

Rogers, C. R., & Dymond, R. S. (Eds.). (1954). *Psychotherapy and personality change.* Chicago: University of Chicago Press.

Rogers, C. R., & Roethlisberger, F. J. (1952, July–August). Barriers and gateways to communication. *Harvard Business Review,* pp. 28–35.

Rokeach, M. (1960). *The open and closed mind.* New York: Basic Books.

Romaniello, J. (1992). Beyond archetypes: A feminist perspective on Jungian theory. In L. S. Brown & Mary Ballou (Eds.), *Personality and psychopathology: Feminist reappraisals.* New York: Guilford Press.

Rorer, L. F., & Widiger, T. A. (1983). Personality structure and assessment. *Annual Review of Psychology, 34,* 401–430.

Rose, H., & Rose, S. (Eds.). (2000). *Alas poor Darwin: Arguments against evolutionary psychology.* New York: Jonathan Cape.

Rose, S. (2005). *The 21st century brain.* New York: Jonathan Cape.

Rosolack, T., & Hampson, S. (1991). A new typology of health behaviours for personality-health predictions: The case of locus of control. *European Journal of Personality, 5*(2), 151–168.

Roth, M. (1998). *Freud: Conflict and culture.* New York: Knopf.

Rothbaum, F., Weisz, J., Pott, M., Miyake, K., & Morelli, G. (2000). Attachment and culture. *American Psychologist, 55,* 1093–1104.

Rotter, J. B. (1954). *Social learning and clinical psychology.* Englewood Cliffs, NJ: Prentice-Hall.

Rotter, J. B. (1966). Generalized expectancies for internal versus external control of reinforcement. *Psychological Monographs, 80* (whole no. 609).

Rotter, J. B. (1980). Interpersonal trust, trustworthiness, and gullibility. *American Psychologist, 35*(1), 1–7.

Rotter, J. B. (1982). *The development and application of social learning theory: Selected papers.* New York: Praeger.

Rotter, J. B., Chance, J. E., & Phares, E. J. (1972). *Applications of a social learning theory of personality.* New York: Holt, Rinehart and Winston.

Rotter, J. B., & Hochreich, D. J. (1975). *Personality.* Glenview, IL: Scott, Foresman.

Rottschaefer, W. (1991). Some philosophical implications of Bandura's social cognitive theory of human agency. *American Psychologist, 46*(2), 153–155.

Rousselle, R. (1990). On the nature of psychohistorical evidence. *Journal of Psychohistory, 17*(4), 425–434.

Rowan, J. (1998). Maslow amended. *Journal of Humanistic Psychology, 38*(1), 81–93.

Rowan, J. (1999). Ascent and descent in Maslow's theory. *Journal of Humanistic Psychology, 39*(3), 125–131.

Ruggiero, K. M., & Kelman, H. C. (1999). Introduction to a symposium on prejudice and intergroup relations. *Journal of Social Issues, 55*(3), 405–414.

Runco, M. A., & Bahleda, M. D. (1987, March). Birth-order and divergent thinking. *Journal of Genetic Psychology, 148*(1), 119–125.

Russell, G. (1992). Response of the macho male to viewing a combatant sport. *Journal of Social Behavior and Personality, 7*(4), 631–638.

Ryan, R. M., & Deci, E. L. (2001). On happiness and human potential: A review of research on hedonic and eudaimonic well-being. *Annual Review of Psychology, 52,* 141–166.

Ryan, R. M., & Deci, E. L. (2006). Self-regulation and the problem of human autonomy. *Journal of Personality, 74,* 1557–1586.

Rychlak, J. (1968). *A philosophy of science for personality theory.* Boston: Houghton Mifflin.

Rychlak, J. F. (1973). *Introduction to personality and psychotherapy.* Boston: Houghton Mifflin.

Rychlak, J. F. (1981). Logical learning theory: Propositions, corollaries, and research evidence. *Journal of Personality and Social Psychology, 40*(4), 731–749.

Rychlak, J. F. (1986, December). Logical learning theory: A teleological alternative in the field of personality. *Journal of Personality, 54*(4), 734–762.

Rychlak, J. F. (1990). George Kelly and the concept of construction. *International Journal of Personal Construct Psychology, 3*(1), 7–19.

Ryckman, R. M., et al. (1985, September). Physical self-efficacy and actualization. *Journal of Research in Personality, 19*(3), 288–298.

Ryckman, R. M., & Malikiosi, M. X. (1975). Relationship between locus of control and chronological age. *Psychological Reports, 36,* 655–658.

Ryckman, R. M., Hammer, M., Kaczor, L. M., & Gold, A. (1990). Construction of a hypercompetitive attitude scale. *Journal of Personality Assessment, 55,* 630–639.

Saeeduzzafar, R., & Sharma, R. (1991). A study of independence-proneness among Hindu and Muslim youths in relation to locus of control. *Journal of Personality and Clinical Studies, 7*(2), 199–202.

Saggino, A. (2000). The big three or the big five? *Personality and Individual Differences, 28,* 879–886.

Saggino, A., Cooper, C., & Kline, P. (2001). A confirmatory analysis of the Myers-Briggs Type Indicator. *Personality and Individual Differences, 30,* 3–9.

Saltzman, K. M., & Holahan, C. J. (2002). Social support, self-efficacy, and depressive symptoms. *Journal of Social and Clinical Psychology, 21*(3), 309–322.

Sampson, E. E. (1991). The democraticization of psychology. *Theory and Psychology, 1*(3), 275–298.

Samuels, A. (1992). National psychology, national socialism, and analytical psychology: Reflections on Jung and anti-Semitism: II. *Journal of Analytical Psychology, 37*(2), 127–147.

Sanchez, L. M., & Turner, S. M. (2003). Practicing psychology in the era of managed care. *American Psychologist, 58*(2), 116–129.

Sanders-Thompson, V. L. (1991). African American race consciousness and racial identification. *Western Journal of Black Studies, 15*(3), 154–158.

Sanders-Thompson, V. L. (1995). The multidimensional structure of racial identification. *Journal of Research in Personality, 29*(2), 208–222.

Sanville, J. B. (2003). Contemporary psychoanalytic voices in North America. In J. B. Sanville & E. B. Ruderman (Eds.), *Therapies with women in transition* (pp. 27–57). Madison, CT: International Universities Press.

Sarason, S. (1989). The lack of an overarching conception in psychology. *Journal of Mind and Behavior, 10*(3), 263–279.

Sarbin, T. (Ed.). (1986). *Narrative psychology: The storied nature of human conduct.* New York: Praeger.

Sass, L. (1982, August 22). The borderline personality. *New York Times Magazine.*

Saucier, G., & Goldberg, L. R. (1996). The language of personality. In J. S. Wiggins (Ed.), *The Five-Factor Model of personality: Theoretical perspectives* (pp. 21–50). New York: Guilford Press.

Saucier, G., & Goldberg, L. R. (1998). What is beyond the Big Five? *Journal of Personality, 66,* 495–524.

Saucier, G., Hampson, S. E., & Goldberg, L. R. (2000). Cross-language studies of lexical personality factors. In S. E. Hampson (Ed.), *Advances in personality psychology.* Philadelphia: Psychology Press, Taylor & Francis Group.

Saudino, K. J., & Plomin, R. (1996). Personality and behavioral genetics: Where have we been and where are we going? *Journal of Research in Personality, 30,* 335–347.

Saunders, P., & Skar, P. (2001). Archetypes, complexes, and self-organization. *Journal of Analytic Psychology, 46,* 305–323.

Saunders, S. (2001). Fromm's marketing character and Rokeach values. *Social Behavior and Personality, 29*(2), 191–196.

Saunders, S. & Munro, D. (2000). The construction and validation of a consumer orientation questionnaire (SCOI) designed to measure Fromm's "marketing character" in Australia. *Social Behavior and Personality, 28,* 219–240.

Saunders, S., & Munro, D. (2001). An exploratory look at Fromm's marketing character and individualism/collectivism. *Social Behavior and Personality, 29*(2), 153–158.

Schafer, R. (1995). In the wake of Heinz Hartmann. *International Journal of Psycho-Analysis, 72,* 223–235.

Schaller, M. (2002). Any theory can be useful theory, even if it gets on our nerves. *Personality and Social Psychology Review, 6*(3), 199–203.

Scherl, C. R., & Haley, J. (2000). Computer monitor supervision. *American Journal of Family Therapy, 28,* 275–282.

Schimek, J. G. (1987). Fact and fantasy in the seduction theory: A historical review. *Journal of the American Psychoanalytic Association, 35*(4), 937–965.

Schmitt, D. P. (2003). Are men universally more dismissing than women? *Personal Relationships, 10*(3), 307–331.

Schneider, K. J. (1999). Rollo May: Liberator and realist. In D. Moss (Ed.), *Humanistic and transpersonal psychology.* Westport, CT: Greenwood Press.

Schneider, K. J. (2005). Biology and awe: Psychology's critical juncture. *Humanistic Psychologist, 33*(2), 167–173.

Schneider, K. J., & May, R. (1995). *The psychology of existence: An integrative, clinical perspective.* New York: McGraw-Hill.

Schore, A. (1994). *Affect regulation and the origin of the self: The neurobiology of emotional development.* Hillsdale, NJ: Erlbaum.

Schroeder, M. L., Wormworth, J. A., & Livesley, W. J. (2002). Dimensions of personality disorder and the Five-Factor Model of personality. In P. T. Costa Jr. & T. A. Widiger (Eds.), *Personality disorders and the Five-Factor Model of personality* (pp. 149–160). Washington, DC: American Psychological Association.

Schulz, C. G. (2006). Applying Sullivan's theory of anxiety versus fear. *Psychiatry, 69*(2), 110–112.

Schultz, D. (1990). *Theories of personality* (4th ed.). Pacific Grove, CA: Brooks/Cole.

Schwartz, J. (1996). Physics, philosophy, psychoanalysis, and ideology: On engaging with Adolf Grünbaum. *Psychoanalytic Dialogues, 6,* 503–513.

Sears, R. R. (1943). Survey of objective studies of psychoanalytic concepts. *Social Science Research Council Bulletin, 51.*

Segal, Z. V., Williams, M. G., & Tinsdale, J. D. (2002). *Mindfulness-based cognitive therapy for depression: A new approach.* New York: Guilford Press.

Seligman, M. E. (2002). *Authentic happiness.* New York: Free Press.

Seligman, M. E., & Csikszentmihalyi, M. (2000). Positive psychology: An introduction. *American Psychologist, 55*(1), 5–14.

Seligman, M. E., Stein, T. A., Park, N., & Peterson, C. (2005). Positive psychology progress. *American Psychologist, 60*(5), 410–421.

Sellers, R. M., Smith, M. A., Shelton, N. J., Rowley, S. A. J., & Chavous, T. M. (1998). Multidimensional model of racial identity. *Personality and Social Psychology Review, 2*(1), 18–39.

Shea, C. (1997, April 4). No less violence on TV, study says. *Chronicle of Higher Education.*

Shell, W. E., Hargrove, L., & Falbo, T. (1986, September). Birth order and achievement motivation configurations in women and men. *Individual Psychology: Journal of Adlerian Theory, Research and Practice, 42*(3), 428–438.

Sheng-yen, M. (1987). *The advantages one may derive from Zen meditation.* Elmhurst, NY: Dharma Drum.

Sheng-yen, M. (2000). *Setting in motion the Dharma wheel: Talks on the Four Noble Truths of Buddhism.* Elmhurst, NY: Dharma Drum.

Sherman, N. (1995). The moral perspective and the psychoanalytic quest. *Journal of the American Academy of Psychoanalysis, 23,* 223–241.

Sherry, J. (2001). The effects of violent video games on aggression. *Human Communication Research, 27,* 409–431.

Shevrin, H. (1995a). Is psychoanalysis one science, two sciences, or no science at all?A discourse among friendly antagonists. *Journal of the American Psychoanalytic Association, 43,* 963–986.

Shevrin, H. (1995b). Is psychoanalysis one science, two sciences, or no science at all? Commentary reply. *Journal of the American Psychoanalytic Association, 43,* 1035–1049.

Shiyong, X., Danling, P., Zhen, J., Hongyan, L., & Jie, Y. (2005). Personality and neurochemicals in the brain. *Chinese Science Bulletin, 50*(20), 2318–2322.

Shlain, L. (1991). *Art and physics: Parallel visions in space, time and light.* New York: Morrow.

Shoda, Y., & Mischel, W. (1996). Toward a unified, intra-individual dynamic conception of personality. *Journal of Research in Personality, 30,* 414–428.

Shoda, Y., Tiernan, S., & Mischel, W. (2002). Personality as a dynamical system. *Personality and Social Psychology Review, 6*(4), 316–325.

Shorey, H. S., & Snyder, C. R. (2006). The role of attachment styles in psychopathology and psychotherapy outcomes. *Review of General Psychology, 10*(1), 1–20.

Shur, M. (1972). *Freud: Living and dying.* New York: International Universities Press.

Shurcliff, J. (1968). Judged humor, arousal, and the relief theory. *Journal of Personality and Social Psychology, 8,* 360–363.

Shweder, R. A., & Bourne, E. J. (1984). Does the concept of person vary cross-culturally? In R. A. Shweder & R. Levin (Eds.), *Culture theory: Essays on mind, self, and emotion* (pp. 158–199). New York: Cambridge University Press.

Sidman, M. (1960). *Tactics of scientific research.* New York: Basic Books.

Sidman, M. (1994). *Equivalence relations and behavior: A research story.* Boston: Authors Cooperative.

Siegel, D. (1999). *The developing mind: How relationships and the brain interact to shape who we are.* New York: Guilford Press.

Silberman, I., Higgens, E. T., & Dweck, C. S. (2005). Religion and world change: Violence and terrorism versus peace. *Journal of Social Issues, 61*(4), 761–784.

Silva, C. O. (2006). *Psychotherapy and religion in Japan: The Japanese introspection practice of naikan.* New York: Routledge.

Silverman, L. H. (1976). Psychoanalytic theory: The reports of my death are greatly exaggerated. *American Psychologist, 31,* 621–637.

Silvern, S. B., & Williamson, P. A. (1987, October–December). The effects of video game play on young children's aggression, fantasy, and prosocial behavior. *Journal of Applied Developmental Psychology, 8*(4), 453–462.

Silverstein, L. B., & Goodrich, T. J. (2003). *Feminist family therapy: Empowerment in social context.* Washington, DC: American Psychological Association.

Simpson, J. A., & Rholes, W. S. (1998). *Attachment theory and close relationships.* New York: Guilford Press.

Simpson, J. A., & Rholes, W. S., Tran, S., Wilson, C. L., & Campbell, L. (2003). Adult attachment, the transition to parenthood and depressive symptoms. *Journal of Personality and Social Psychology, 84*(6), 1172–1187.

Singer, J. (1991). Closeness and androgyny. In H. A. Wilmer (Ed.), *Closeness in personal and professional relationships.* Boston: Shambhala.

Singer, J. A. (1997). *Message in a bottle: Stories of men and addiction.* New York: Free Press.

Singh, K. (1990). Tough-mindedness in relation to birth order, family size, and sex. *Individual Psychology: Journal of Adlerian Theory, Research and Practice, 46*(1), 82–87.

Singh, R. P. (1984, January). Experimental verification of locus of control as related to conformity behavior. *Psychological Studies, 29*(1), 64–67.

Skhiri, T., & Gaha, L. (1994). Evolution of ideas on the psychogenesis of depression. *Psychologie Medicale, 26,* 511–514.

Skinner, B. F. (1938). *The behavior of organisms.* New York: Appleton-Century-Crofts.

Skinner, B. F. (1948). *Walden II.* New York: Macmillan.

Skinner, B. F. (1953). *Science and human behavior.* New York: Macmillan.

Skinner, B. F. (1969). *Contingencies of reinforcement: A theoretical analysis.* New York: Appleton-Century-Crofts.

Skinner, B. F. (1971). *Beyond freedom and dignity.* New York: Knopf.

Skinner, B. F. (1972, November). Will success spoil B. F. Skinner? (Interview). *Psychology Today, 6,* 66–72, 130.

Skinner, B. F. (1974). *About behaviorism.* New York: Random House.

Skinner, B. F. (1981). *Why are we not acting to save the world?* Paper prepared for the annual meeting of the American Psychological Association.

Skinner, B. F. (1983a, Spring). Can the experimental analysis of behavior rescue psychology? *Behavior Analyst, 6*(1), 9–17.

Skinner, B. F. (1983b, September). Origins of a behaviorist. *Psychology Today, 17*(7).

Skinner, B. F. (1984, December). Selection by consequences. *Behavior and Brain Sciences, 7*(4), 477–510.

Skinner, B. F. (1985). *The shaping of a behaviorist.* New York: New York University Press.

Skinner, B. F. (1986, January). The evolution of verbal behavior. *Journal of the Experimental Analysis of Behavior, 45*(1), 115–122.

Skinner, B. F. (1987, August). Whatever happened to psychology as the science of behavior? *American Psychologist, 42*(8), 780–786.

Skinner, B. F. (1989). The origins of cognitive thought. *American Psychologist, 44,*13–18.

Sliker, G. (1992). *Multiple mind: Healing the split in psyche and world.* Boston: Shambhala.

Small, F. E. (1989). The psychology of women: A psychoanalytic review. *Canadian Journal of Psychiatry, 34*(9), 872–878.

Smelser, N. J. (1996). Erik Erikson as social scientist. *Psychoanalysis and Contemporary Thought, 19,* 207–224.

Smith, C. (2000). Sigmund Freud: The ambition theory. *The Psychologist, 13*(10), 508–509.

Smith, D. (1982). Trends in counseling and psychotherapy. *American Psychologist, 37*(7), 802–809.

Smith, G. L. (1998). The present state and future of symbolic-experiential family therapy. *Contemporary Family Therapy, 20*(2), 147–161.

Smith, L. S. (2003). Freud and Adler on agency and determinism in the shaping of the personality. *Journal of Individual Psychology, 59*(3), 263–280.

Smith, M. B. (1990). Humanistic psychology. *Journal of Humanistic Psychology, 30*(4), 6–21.

Smith, M., & Glass, J. (1977, September). Meta-analysis of psychotherapy outcome studies. *American Psychologist,* 752–760.

Soffer, J. (1993). Jean Piaget and George Kelly: Toward a stronger constructivism. *International Journal of Personal Construct Psychology, 6*(1), 59–77.

Solnit, A. J. (1994). Heinz Hartmann—Psychoanalysis and health values unfolding. *Psychoanalytic Study of the Child, 49,* 36–45.

Sonnek, S. M. (1999). Perception and parenting style: The influence of culture. *Dissertation Abstracts International, 60,* 3021.

Spiegel, R. (1994). Reflections on our heritage from Erich Fromm. *Contemporary Psychoanalysis, 30,* 419–424.

Spitz, R. A. (1945). Hospitalization: An inquiry into the genesis of psychiatric conditions in early childhood. In A. Freud (Ed.), *The psychoanalytic study of the child* (Vol. 1, pp. 53–74). New Haven, CT: Yale University Press.

Spranger, E. (1928). *Types of men.* New York: Stechert.

Staats, A. W. (1971). *Child learning, intelligence, and personality.* New York: Harper.

Staats, A. W. (1996). *Behavior and personality: Psychological behaviorism.* New York: Springer.

Staddon, J. E., & Cerutti, D. T. (2003). Operant conditioning. *Annual Review of Psychology, 54,* 115–144.

Stasio, M. J., & Capron, E. W. (1998). Social interest as a distinct personality construct. *Journal of Individual Psychology, 54*(1), 10–23.

Steelman, L. C. (1985). A tale of two variables: A review of the intellectual consequences of sibship size and birth order. *Review of Educational Research, 55,* 353–386.

Steelman, L. C. (1986). The tale retold: A response to Zajonc. *Review of Educational Research, 56,* 373–377.

Stein, D. J. (1997). *Cognitive science and the unconscious.* Washington, DC: American Psychiatric Press.

Stelmack, R. M. (1990). Biological basis of extraversion: Psychophysiological evidence. *Journal of Personality, 58,* 291–311.

Sternberg, R. (1992). Too young to die—Let's not bury psychology alive: A response to Gardner. *New Ideas in Psychology, 10*(2), 195–205.

Stevens, A. (1994). *Jung. Past masters.* Oxford, England: Oxford University Press.

Stewart, A. E., & Barry, J. R. (1991). Origins of George Kelly's constuctivism in the work of Korzybski and Moreno. *International Journal of Personal Construct Psychology, 4*(2), 121–136.

Stiver, I. P. (1991a). Beyond the Oedipus complex: Mothers and daughters. In J. V. Jordan et al. (Eds.), *Women's growth in connection: Writings from the Stone Center.* New York: Guilford Press.

Stiver, I. P. (1991b). The meanings of "dependency" in female-male relationships. In J. V. Jordan et al. (Eds.), *Women's growth in connection: Writings from the Stone Center.* New York: Guilford Press.

Stiver, I. P., Rosen, W. B., Surrey, J., & Miller, J. B. (2001). *Creative moments in relational cultural therapy.* Work in Progress Series. Stone Center for Developmental Studies, Wellesley College, Wellesley MA.

Stolorow, R. D. (1995). An intersubjective view of self psychology. *Psychoanalytic Dialogues, 5,* 393–399.

Storm, L. (1999). Synchronicity, causality, and acausality. *Journal of Parapsychology, 63*(3), 247–269.

Straussner, S. L., & Spiegel, B. R. (1996). An analysis of 12-step programs for substance abusers from a developmental perspective. *Clinical Social Work Journal, 24,* 299–309.

Strickland, B. R. (1978). I-E expectations and health-related behaviors. *Journal of Consulting and Clinical Psychology, 46,* 1192–1211.

Strickland, B. R. (1979). I-E expectations and cardiovascular functioning. In L. C. Perlmuller & R. A. Monty (Eds.), *Choice and perceived control.* Hillsdale, NJ: Erlbaum.

Stricklin-Parker, E., & Schneider, B. A. (2005). Ann. *Clinical Case Studies, 4,*(4), 315–328.

Suchecki, J. (1989). Can scientific method be perceived as mythical text? *Polish Psychological Bulletin, 20*(2), 83–93.

Sullivan, H. S. (1953). *The interpersonal theory of psychiatry.* New York: Norton.

Sullivan, H. S. (1954). *The psychiatric interview.* New York: Norton.

Sullivan, H. S. (1964). *The fusion of psychiatry and social science.* New York: Norton.

Sullivan, H. S. (1972). *Personal psychopathology.* New York: Norton.

Sulloway, F. J. (1996). *Born to rebel: Birth order, family dynamics, and creative lives.* New York: Pantheon.

Sulloway, F. J. (2007). Birth order and intelligence. *Science, 316:* 5821, June 22, 1711–1712.

Sumerlin, J. R., & Bundrick, C. M. (1996). Brief Index of Self-Actualization: A measure of Maslow's model. *Journal of Social Behavior and Personality, 11,* 153–172.

Surrey, J. L. (1990). *Empathy revisited.* Work in Progress Series, no. 40. Stone Center for Developmental Studies, Wellesley College, Wellesley, MA.

Surrey, J. L. (1991). The self-in-relation: A theory of women's development. In J. V. Jordan et al. (Eds.), *Women's growth in connection: Writings from the Stone Center.* New York: Guilford Press.

Sutton, S. K., & Davidson, R. J. (1997). Prefrontal brain asymmetry: A biological substrate of the behavioral approach and behavioral inhibition systems. *Psychological Science, 8,* 204–210.

Suzuki, S. (2003). *Not always so: Practicing the true spirit of Zen*. New York: Quill.

Swann, W. B., Stein-Seroussi, A., & Giesler, R. B. (1992). Why people self-verify. *Journal of Personality and Social Psychology, 62*, 392–401. Austin: University of Texas.

Swenson, C. R. (1994). Freud's "Anna O.": Social work's Bertha Pappenheim. *Clinical Social Work Journal, 22*, 149–163.

Swick-Perry, H. (1982). *Psychiatrist of America: The life of Harry Stack Sullivan*. Cambridge, MA: Belknap Press.

Symonds, A. (1991). Gender issues and Horney theory. *American Journal of Psychoanalysis, 51*(3).

Szehidewicz, A. (1999, July–September). Die Analyse der Menschlichen. Persoenlichkeit. *Tenshin* (Verteljahresheft der Ersten Berliner Zen-Gemeinschaft), *15*(3), 16–22.

Szehidewicz, A. (2000, July–September). Das Entstehen in Abhaengigkeit. *Tenshin* (Verteljahresheft der Ersten Berliner Zen-Gemeinschaft), *16*(3), 13–17.

Tabin, J. K. (2006). What Freud called "the psychology for neurologists" and the many questions it raised. *Psychoanalytic Psychology, 23*(2), 383–407.

Tacey, D. (1997). Jung in the academy: Devotions and resistance. *Journal of Analytical Psychology, 42*, 269-283.

Tamres, L. K. (2002). Sex differences in coping behavior: A meta-analytic review. *Personality and Social Psychology Review 6*(1), 2–30.

Tart, C. T. (Ed.). (1975). *Transpersonal psychologies*. New York: Harper & Row.

Tatum, B. D. (1997). Racial identity development and relational theory: The case of black women in white communities. In J. V. Jordan (Ed.), *Women's growth in diversity*. New York: Guilford Press.

Taylor, E. (2000). What is man, psychologist, that thou art so unmindful of him? *Journal of Humanistic Psychology, 40*(3), 29–42.

Taylor, S. E., Klein, L. C., Lewis, B. P., Gruenewalk, T. L., Gurung, R. A., & Updegraff, J. A. (2000). Female responses to stress: Tend and befriend, not fight or flight. *Psychological Review, 107*(3), 41–42.

Tena, C. (1993). Impact of the theories of Carl Rogers and Teilhard de Chardin in Mexico. In G. M. Gonzalez, I. Alvarado, & A. S. Segrera (Eds.), *Challenges of cultural and racial diversity to counseling, 2*, 105.

Terracciano, A., et al. (2005). National character does not reflect mean personality trait levels in 49 cultures. *Science, 310*, 96–100.

Tett, R. P., Jackson, D. N., & Rothstein, M. (1991). Personality measures as predictors of job performance: A meta-analytic review. *Personnel Psychology, 44*, 703–742.

Thomas, C. S. (1971). *Boys no more*. Beverly Hills, CA: Glencoe Press.

Thomas, M. H., Horton, R. W., Lippencott, E. C., & Drabman, R. S. (1977). Desensitization to portrayals of real-life aggression as a function of exposure to television violence. *Journal of Personality and Social Psychology, 35*, 450–458.

Thompson, B., & Borrello, G. (1986). Construct validity of the Myers-Briggs Type Indicator. *Educational and Psychological Measurement, 46*, 745–752.

Thompson, M. G. (1996). The rule of neutrality. *Psychoanalysis and Contemporary Thought, 19*, 57–84.

Thompson, S., & Spacapan, S. (1991). Perceptions of control in vulnerable populations. *Journal of Social Issues, 47*(4).

Thorndike, E. L. (1913). *Educational psychology*. New York: Teachers College.

Thorne, B. (1990). Carl Rogers and the doctrine of original sin. Special Issue: Fiftieth anniversary of the person-centered approach. *Person-Centered Review, 5*(4), 394–405.

Thrasher, P. (1991). A Jungian view of postmodernism: A response to "Psychology and postmodernity." *Humanistic Psychologist, 19*(2), 242–245.

Thurstone, L. L. (1934). The vectors of mind. *Psychological Review, 41*, 1–32.

Thurstone, L. L. (1948). Psychological implications of factor analysis. *American Psychologist, 3*, 402–408.

Tisdale, S. (2006). *Women of the way: Discovering 2,500 years of Buddhist wisdom*. San Francisco: HarperSanFrancisco.

Tobacyk, J. J., & Downs, A. (1986, October). Personal construct threat and irrational beliefs as cognitive predictors of increases in musical performance anxiety. *Journal of Personality and Social Psychology, 51*(4), 779–782.

Tokar, D. M., & Subich, L. M. (1997). Relative contributions of congruence and personality dimensions to job satisfaction. *Journal of Vocational Behavior, 50*, 482–491.

Tori, C., & Bilmes, M. (2002). Multiculturalism and psychoanalytic psychology: The validation of a defense mechanism measure in an Asian population. *Psychoanalytic Psychology, 19*, 701–721.

Torrey, E. F. (1992). *Freudian fraud: The malignant effect of Freud's theory on American thought and culture*. New York: HarperCollins.

Triandis, H. C., & Suh, E. M. (2002). Cultural influences on personality. *Annual Review of Psychology, 53*, 133–160.

Tribich, D., & Messer, S. (1974). Psychoanalytic character type and states of authority as determiners of suggestibility. *Journal of Consulting and Clinical Psychology, 42*, 842–848.

Triet, R. (2000, December). Dogen's eight aspects of the awaking of the great man. *Zen Bulletin de l'Association Zen Internationale*, no. 82, p. 50.

Trivers, R. L. (1971). The evolution of reciprocal altruism. *Quarterly Review of Biology, 46*, 35–57.

Trivers, R. L. (1985). *Social evolution*. New York: Benjamin/Cummings.

Tupes, E. C., & Christal, R. E. (1961). *Recurrent personality factors based on trait ratings* (Tech. Rep. No. ASDTR61–97). Lackland Air Force Base, TX: U.S. Air Force. Republished in *Journal of Personality* (1992), *60*, 223–251.

Turner, C. (1997). *Clinical applications of the Stone Center theoretical approach to minority women*. Work in Progress Series, no. 28. Stone Center for Developmental Studies, Wellesley College, Wellesley, MA.

Turner, L. W., & Berkowitz, L. (1972). Identification with film aggression. *Journal of Personality and Social Psychology, 21*, 256–264.

Uchiyama, K. (2004). *Opening the hand of thought: Foundations of Zen Buddhist practice*. Boston: Wisdom.

Ugwu-Oju, D. (1993, November 14). Hers: Pursuit of happiness. *New York Times Magazine*.

Urbanowski, F., & Miller, J. (1996). Trauma, psychotherapy, and meditation. *Journal of Transpersonal Psychology, 28*, 31–48.

Vaillant, G. E. (1992a). *Ego mechanisms of defense: A guide for clinicians and researchers*. Washington, DC: American Psychiatric Press.

Vaillant, G. E. (1992b). The historical origins and future potential of Sigmund Freud's concept of the mechanisms of defense. *International Review of Psycho-Analysis, 19*(1), 35–50.

Valentine, E. (1988). Teleological explanations and their relation to causal explanations in psychology. *Philosophical Psychology, 1*(1), 61–68.

Vallacher, R. R., Read, S. J., & Nowak, A. (2002). The dynamical perspective in personality and social psychology. *Personality and Social Psychology Review, 6*(4), 264–273.

Vande Kempe, H. (1995). Religion in college textbooks: Allport's historic 1948 report. *International Journal for the Psychology of Religion, 5,* 199–211.

Van den Daele, L. (1987, Summer). Research in Horney's psychoanalytic theory. *American Journal of Psychoanalysis, 47*(2), 99–104.

Van Eenwyk, J. R. (1991). Archetypes: The strange attractors of the psyche. *Journal of Analytical Psychology, 36,* 1–25.

Van Hiel, A., Mervielde, I., & Fruyt, F. (2006). Stagnation and generativity: Structure, validity, and different relationships with adaptive and maladaptive personality. *Journal of Personality, 74*(2), 543–574.

Van Kalmthout, M. A. (1995). The religious dimension of Rogers's work. *Journal of Humanistic Psychology, 35,* 23–39.

van Krogten, I. (1992). *Proustian love.* Amsterdam: Swets & Zeitlinger.

Varela, F. (Ed.). (1997). *Sleeping, dreaming, and dying: An exploration of consciousness with the Dalai Lama.* Somerville, MA: Wisdom.

Vaughn, C. M., & Pfenninger, D. T. (1994). Kelly and the concept of developmental stages. *Journal of Constructivist Psychology, 7,* 177–190.

Vessey, V. A., & Lee, J. E. (2000). Violent video games affecting our children. *Pediatric Nursing, 26,* 607–613.

Viner, R. (1996). Melanie Klein and Anna Freud: The discourse of the early dispute. *Journal of the History of the Behavioral Sciences, 32,* 4–15.

Visher, S. (1986, May). The relationship of locus of control and contraception use in the adolescent population. *Journal of Adolescent Health Care, 7*(3), 183–186.

Vitz, P. (1990). The use of stories in moral development: New psychological reasons for an old education method. *American Psychologist, 45*(6), 709–720.

Volkow, N. (2007, January 1). Addiction. *Newsweek,* pp. 78–80.

W., Bill (1988). *The language of the heart: Bill W's Grapevine writings.* New York: AA Grapevine.

Walker, A., & Parmar, P. (1993). *Warrior marks: Female genital mutilation and the sexual blinding of women.* New York: Harcourt Brace.

Walker, B. M. (1990). Construing George Kelly's construing of the person-in-relation. *International Journal of Personal Construct Psychology, 3*(1), 41–50.

Walker, B. M. (1992). Values and Kelly's theory: Becoming a good scientist. Special Issue: Papers from the Eighth International Congress on Personal Construct Psychology. *International Journal of Personal Construct Psychology, 5*(3), 259–269.

Walker, M. (1999). *Race, self, and society: Relational challenges in a culture of disconnection.* Work in Progress Series. Stone Center for Developmental Studies, Wellesley College, Wellesley, MA.

Walker, M. (2001). *When racism gets personal: Toward relational healing.* Work in Progress Series. Stone Center for Developmental Studies, Wellesley College, Wellesley, MA.

Walker, M. (2002). *How therapy helps when the culture hurts.* Work in Progress Series. Stone Center for Developmental Studies, Wellesley College, Wellesley, MA.

Walker, M. (2003). *Power and effectiveness: Envisioning an alternative paradigm.* Work in Progress Series. Stone Center for Developmental Studies, Wellesley College, Wellesley, MA.

Walker, M., & Miller, J. B. (2001). *Racial images and relational possibilities.* Work in Progress Series. Stone Center for Developmental Studies, Wellesley College, Wellesley, MA.

Walker, M., & Rosen, W. (2004). *How connections heal.* New York: Guilford Press.

Wallach, M. A., & Wallach, L. (1983). *Psychology: Sanction for selfishness.* San Francisco: Freeman.

Wallerstein, R. S. (1998). Erik H. Erikson, 1902–1994: Setting the context. In R. S. Wallerstein & L. Goldberger (Eds.), *Ideas and identities: The life and work of Erik Erikson* (pp. 1–26). Madison, CT: International Universities Press.

Wallwork, E. (1991). *Psychoanalysis and ethics.* New Haven, CT: Yale University Press.

Walsh, R. (1995). Asian psychotherapies. In J. Corsini & D. Wedding (Eds.), *Current psychotherapies* (pp. 387–398). Itasca, IL: Peacock.

Warner, S. L. (1991). Freud and the mighty warrior. *Journal of the American Academy of Psychoanalysis, 19*(2), 282–293.

Warren, W. G. (1990). Is personal construct psychology a cognitive psychology? *International Journal of Personal Construct Psychology, 3*(4), 393–414.

Warren, W. G. (1992). Personal construct theory and mental health. Special Issue: Papers from the Eighth International Congress of Personal Construct Psychology. *International Journal of Personal Construct Psychology, 5*(3), 223–237.

Wastell, C. A. (1996). Feminist developmental theory: Implications for counseling. *Journal of Counseling and Development, 74,* 575–581.

Waterman, A. S. (1982). Identity development from adolescence to adulthood: An extension of theory and a review of research. *Developmental Psychology, 18,* 341–358.

Watkins, C. E., Campbell, V. L., Nieberding, R., & Hallmark, R. (1995). Contemporary practice of psychological assessment by clinical psychologists. *Professional Psychology: Research and Practice, 26*(1), 54–60.

Watson, J. B., & Raynor, R. (1925). *Behaviorism: Psychology and physiology.* New York: People's Institute.

Watson, P. J., Little, T., & Biderman, M. D. (1992). Narcissism and parenting styles. *Psychoanalytic Psychology, 9*(2), 231–244.

Watts, A. W. (1961). *Psychotherapy east and west.* New York: Ballantine.

Watzlawick, P., Weakland, J., & Fisch, R. (1974). *Change: Principles of problem formation and problem resolution.* New York: Norton.

Weegmann, M. (2003). *The Psychodynamics of addiction.* London: Whurr.

Weinberger, J., & Westen, D. (2001). Science and psychodynamics: From arguments about Freud to data. *Psychological Inquiry, 12*(3), 129–166.

Weingberg, L. (1991). Infant development and the sense of self: Stern vs. Mahler. *Clinical Social Work Journal, 19*(1), 9–22.

Weinraub, W. (1993, December 28). Despite Clinton, Hollywood is still trading in violence. *The New York Times,* A1.

Weiss-Rosmarin, T. (1990). Adler's psychology and the Jewish tradition. *Individual Psychology: Journal of Adlerian Theory, Research and Practice, 46,* 108–118.

Wessler, R. L. (1986). Conceptualizing cognitions in the

cognitive-behavioral therapies. In W. Dryden & W. Golden (Eds.), *Cognitive-behavioral approaches to psychotherapy* (pp. 1–30). London: Harper & Row.

West, C. K. (2005). The map of relational-cultural theory. *Women and Therapy, 28*(3/4), 93–110.

Westen, D. (1998). The scientific legacy of Sigmund Freud: Toward a psychodynamically informed psychological science. *Psychological Bulletin, 124,* 333–371.

Westen, D., Novotny, C. M., & Thompson-Brenner, H. (2004). The empirical status of empirically supported psychotherapies. *Psychological Bulletin, 130*(4), 631–663.

Westkott, M. (1996). Summaries of Karen Horney's major works. *American Journal of Psychoanalysis, 56*(2), 213–225.

Westkott, M. (1998). Horney, Zen, and the Real Self. *American Journal of Psychoanalysis, 58*(3), 287–301.

White, R. W. (1992). Exploring personality the long way: The study of lives. In R. A. Zucker, A. I. Rabin, J. Aronoff, & S. J. Frank (Eds.), *Personality structure in the life course: Essays on personology in the Murray tradition* (pp. 3–21). New York: Springer.

Whiteside, S. P., & Lynam, D. R. (2001). The five factor model and impulsivity: Using a structural model of personality to understand impulsivity. *Personality and Individual Differences, 30,* 669–689.

Widiger, T. A. (1993). The DSM-III-R categorical personality disorder diagnoses: A critique and an alternative. *Psychological Inquiry, 4,* 75–90.

Widiger, T. A., & Costa, P. T., Jr. (1994). Personality and personality disorders. *Journal of Abnormal Psychology, 103*(1), 778–791.

Widiger, T. A., Costa, P. T., Jr., & McCrae, R. R. (2002). A proposal for Axis II: Diagnosing personality disorders using the Five-Factor Model. In P. T. Costa Jr. & T. A. Widiger (Eds.), *Personality disorders and the Five-Factor Model of personality.* Washington, DC: American Psychological Association.

Widiger, T. A., & Frances, A. J. (2002). Toward a dimensional model for the personality disorders. In P. T. Costa Jr. & T. A. Widiger (Eds.), *Personality disorders and the Five-Factor Model of personality* (pp. 23–44). Washington, DC: American Psychological Association.

Widiger, T. A., & Trull, T. J. (1997). Assessment of the five-factor model of personality. *Journal of Personality Assessment, 68,* 228–250.

Widiger, T. A., Trull, T. J., Clarkin, J. F., Sanderson, C., & Costa P. J., Jr. (2002). A description of the DSM-IV personality disorders with the Five-Factor Model of personality. In P. T. Costa Jr. & T. A. Widiger (Eds.), *Personality disorders and the Five-Factor Model of personality* (pp. 89–101). Washington, DC: American Psychological Association.

Wiener, D. J., & Pels-Roulier, L. (2005, Summer). Action methods in marriage and family therapy: A review. *Journal of Group Psychotherapy, Psychodrama, and Sociometry, 58*(2), 86–102.

Wiggins, J. S. (1984, April–July). Cattell's system from the perspective of mainstream personality theory. *Multivariate Behavioral Research, 19*(2–3), 176–190.

Wilber, K. (1977). *The spectrum of consciousness.* Wheaton, IL: Quest.

Wilber, K. (1995). *Sex, ecology, spirituality: The spirit of evolution.* Boston: Shambhala.

Wilber, K., Engler, J., & Brown, D. P. (1986). *Transformation of consciousness: Conventional and contemplative perspective on development.* Boston: Shambhala.

Wilde, L. (2004). *Erich Fromm and the quest for solidarity.* New York: Palgrave Macmillan.

Wilson, A. (1996). The irrelevance of infant observations for psychoanalysis: Commentary. *Journal of the American Psychoanalytic Association, 44,* 452–464.

Wilson, E. O. (1999). *Consilience: The unity of knowledge.* New York: Knopf.

Winn, M. (2002). *The Plug-in drug: Television, computers and family life.* New York: Penguin Putnam.

Winnicott, D. W. (1993). C. G. Jung's memories, dreams, reflections. *Cahiers Jungiens de Psychoanalyse, 78,* 83–92.

Winson, J. (2002). The meaning of dreams. *Scientific American, 12*(1), 54–62.

Winter, D. G. (1993). Gordon Allport and "Letters from Jenny." In K. H. Craik, R. Hogan, & R. N. Wolfe (Eds.), *Fifty years of personality psychology* (pp. 147–163). New York: Plenum Press.

Wolberg, A. (1989). Pilgrim's progress through the psychoanalytic maze. *Psychoanalysis and Psychotherapy, 7*(1), 18–26.

Wolpe, J. (1958). *Psychotherapy by reciprocal inhibition.* Stanford, CA: Stanford University Press.

Wolpe, J. (1973). *The practice of behavior* (2nd ed.). New York: Pergamon.

Wood, R. E., & Bandura, A. (1989). Impact of conceptions of ability on self-regulatory mechanisms and complex decision making. *Journal of Personality and Social Psychology, 56,* 407–415.

Woodall, K., & Matthews, K. (1993). Changes in and stability of hostile characteristics: Results from a 4-year longitudinal study of children. *Journal of Personality and Social Psychology, 64,* 491–499.

Woodward, W. (1992). On opening the psychology of personality to philosophy and literature in our time: A response to Gardner. *New Ideas in Psychology, 10*(2), 191–194.

Woody, R. H. (1971). *Psychobehavioral counseling and therapy: Integrating behavioral and insight techniques.* New York: Appleton-Century Crofts.

Workman, L. (2004). Evolutionary psychology: Concepts and criticisms. *Psychology Review, 10*(4), 2–5.

Wright, J. C., & Mischel, W. (1988). Conditional hedges and the intuitive psychology of traits. *Journal of Personality and Social Psychology, 55,* 454–469.

Wrightsman, L. S. (1993). Allport's personal documents: Then and now. In K. H. Craik, R. Hogan, & R. N. Wolfe (Eds.), *Fifty years of personality psychology* (pp. 165–175). New York: Plenum Press.

Yalom, I. D. (1995). *The theory and practice of group psychotherapy.* New York: Basic Books.

Yalom, I. D. (2002). *The gift of therapy.* New York: HarperCollins.

Yang, K., & Bond, M. H. (1990). Exploring implicit personality theories with indigenous or imported constructs: The Chinese case. *Journal of Personality and Social Psychology, 58,* 1087–1095.

Young, S. (2005, July 22). Obesity brains. *Brain Research,* pp. 1–2.

Young, T. W., & Shorr, D. N. (1986, November). Factors affecting locus of control in school children. *Genetic, Social and General Psychology Monographs, 112*(4), 405–417.

Young-Bruehl, E. (2004). Anna Freud and Dorothy Burlingham at Hempstead. *Annual of Psychoanalysis, 32,* 185–197.

Young-Eisendrath, P., & Muramoto, S. (Eds.). (2003). *Awakening and insight: Zen Buddhism and psychotherapy.* London: Brunner-Routledge.

Yunt, J. D. (2001). Jung's contribution to an ecological psychology. *Journal of Humanistic Psychology, 41*(2), 96–121.

Zajonc, R. (2003, November). *Demonization and collective violence.* Paper presented at the conference on A New Look at Race.

Zajonc, R. B. (1986). Family factors and intellectual test performance: A reply to Steelman. *Review of Educational Research, 56,* 365–371.

Zajonc, R. B. (2001). The family dynamics of intellectual development. *American Psychologist, 56,* 490–496.

Zajonc, R. B., & Markus, G. B. (1975). Birth order and intellectual development. *Psychological Review, 82,* 74–88.

Zajonc, R. B., & Mullally, P. R. (1997). Birth order: Reconciling conflicting effects. *American Psychologist, 52,* 685–699.

Zayas, V., Shoda, Y., & Ayduk, O. N. (2002). Personality in context: An interpersonal systems perspective. *Journal of Personality, 70*(6), 851–901.

Zeig, J. K. (Ed.). (1982). *Eriksonian approaches to hypnosis and psychotherapy.* New York: Brunner/Mazel.

Zhang, L. (2001). Thinking styles and personality types revisited. *Personality and Individual Differences, 31,* 883–894.

Zhang, Y. (2006). *Zen and psychotherapy.* Victoria, BC: Trafford.

Ziegler, D. J. (2000). Basic assumptions concerning human nature underlying REBT personality theory. *Journal of Rational-Emotive and Cognitive-Behavior Therapy, 18*(2), 67–85.

Zimmerman, B. J., & Schunk, D. H. (2003). Bandura: The scholar and his contributions to educational psychology. In B. J. Zimmerman (Ed.), *Educational psychology: A century of contributions* (pp. 431–457). Mahwah, NJ: Erlbaum.

Zlate, M. (1989). The place and role of the self in the pattern of personality: Controversial questions. *Revue Roumainē des Sciences Sociales—Serie de Psychologie, 33*(1), 3–15.

Zohar, D., & Marshall, I. (1990). *The quantum self: Human nature and consciousness defined by the new physics.* New York: William Morrow.

INDEX

Learning Cen
C Coastcasn

Photo credits

p. 3 top left: © Mary Evans Picture Library; p. 3 top middle: © Stock Montage; p. 3 top right: © Bettmann/Corbis; p. 3 bottom right: © Stock Montage; p. 3 middle: © Bettmann/Corbis; p. 3 bottom left: © Bettmann/Corbis; p. 3 bottom far left: © Stock Montage; p. 7 top left: © Duomo/Corbis; p. 7 top right: © Patrice Crocker/fotosbolivia/The Image Works; p. 7 bottom right: © Bill Hickey/Getty Images; p. 7 bottom left: © Joe Sohm/The Image Works; p. 30: © Mary Evans Picture Library; p. 32: © Mary Evans Picture Library; p. 37: © Gianni Dagli Orti/Corbis; p. 41: © Elizabeth Crews; p. 50: © cocorophotos/Bloomimage/Corbis; p. 70: © Dimitri Kessel/Time Life Pictures/Getty Images; p. 75: © Scott Cunningham/Jupiter Images; p. 79: © New Line/courtesy Everett Collection; p. 94: © Topham/The Image Works; p. 97: © Mug Shots/Corbis; p. 100: © Karen Moskowitz/Getty Images; p. 107: © Bettmann/Corbis; p. 110: © Michael Weisbrot and Family; p. 111: © Mina Chapman/Corbis; p. 117: © Bruce Ayres/Getty Images; p. 123: © Bettmann/Corbis; p. 129: © Jeff Greenber/The Image Works; p. 129: © Jim Cambon; p. 132: © Charles Thatcher; p. 135: © Renee Burri/Magnum Photos; p. 136: © David Woolley/Getty Images; p. 140: © LWA/Sharie Kennedy/Blend Images/Jupiter Images; p. 150: © Getty Images; p. 152: © Archives of the History of American Psychology—The University of Akron; p. 157: © Michael Prince/Corbis; p. 159: © Tom Grill/Corbis; p. 167: Courtesy of Dan McAdams; p. 176 top left: © Melanie Klein Trust, courtesy Harvard College Library; p. 176 top middle: © Margaret Mahler Papers, Manuscripts & Archives, Yale University Library; p. 176 top right: Courtesy of Thomas Kohut; p. 176 bottom left: Courtesy of Otto Kernberg; p. 176 bottom right: Courtesy of Tom Sandberg; p. 179: © Barbara Engler; p. 186: © Wellesley Center for Women; p. 189: © Barry Austin/Digital Vision/Getty Images; p. 192: © Pascal Broze/Getty Images; p. 196: © Evan Richman/Boston Globe Photo; p. 207: Courtesy of John Dollard; p. 207: © Rockefeller University Public Information; p. 217: © Topham/The Image Works; p. 221: © R.P.G./Corbis/Sygma; p. 223: © PictureNet/Corbis; p. 235: Courtesy of Albert Bandura; p. 238: © M. Siluk/The Image Works; p. 243: © Dream Pictures/Ostrow/Getty Images; p. 253: Courtesy of Julian Rotter; p. 253: Courtesy of Walter Mischel; p. 264: © Stock Montage; p. 266: © JP Laffont/Corbis/Sygma; p. 274: © AP Photo/Wide World; p. 278: © Jerry Howard/Positive Images; p. 280: Reprinted by permission of the publishers from Henry A. Murray, Thematic Apperception Test, Plate 12F, Cambridge, Mass.: Harvard University Press, Copyright © 1943 by the President and Fellows of Harvard College, © 1971 by Henry A. Murray; p. 287: © Stock Montage; p. 300: © In The Light Studio, courtesy of Barbara Engler; p. 293: Courtesy of Paul Costa; p. 293: Courtesy of Robert McCrae; p. 306: Courtesy of David Buss; p. 302: © UpperCut Images/Alamy; p. 314: © Mark Gerson/Camera Press, Ltd.; p. 329: © Science Source/Photo Researchers; p. 350: © Bettmann/Corbis; p. 355: © Robert Isaacs/Photo Researchers; p. 359: © Bettmann/Corbis; p. 361: © Nicole Hill/Rubberball/Jupiter Images; p. 361: © Ingolf Hatz/Zefa/Corbis; p. 361: © Blend Images/Getty Images; p. 365: © Digital Vision/Getty Images; p. 370: © Getty Images; p. 382: © Getty Images; p. 383: © AFP/Getty Images; p. 388: © Getty Images; p. 391: © Tom Grill/Corbis; p. 408: © The Ohio State University Photo Archives; p. 420: © Kelly Redinger/Design Pics/Corbis; p. 428: Courtesy of the Albert Institute for Rational Emotive Behavior Therapy; p. 436: © Leif Skoogfors/Woodfin Camp; p. 443: © Rutgers/Alan Goldsmith, courtesy Dr. Arnold A. Lazarus; p. 450: © Jon Bradley/Getty Images; p. 458: © Richard Bend; p. 466: Photo by Rick L. Simonson; model: Anne M. Cummings; p. 470: © The New Yorker Collection 1980 Gahan Wilson from cartoonbank.com. All Rights Reserved; p. 473: © B.S.P.I./Corbis; p. 491: The Fuller Projection Map design is a trademark of the Buckminster Fuller Institute © 1938, 1867, 1992. All rights reserved; p. 491: © NASA.